Handbook of Research on Network-Enabled IoT Applications for Smart City Services

K. Hemant Kumar Reddy
VIT AP University, India

Diptendu Sinha Roy
National Institute of Technology, Meghalaya, India

Tapas Kumar Mishra
SRM University, India

Mir Wajahat Hussain
Alliance University, India

IGI Global
PUBLISHER of TIMELY KNOWLEDGE

A volume in the Advances in Electronic Government, Digital Divide, and Regional Development (AEGDDRD) Book Series

Published in the United States of America by
IGI Global
Information Science Reference (an imprint of IGI Global)
701 E. Chocolate Avenue
Hershey PA, USA 17033
Tel: 717-533-8845
Fax: 717-533-8661
E-mail: cust@igi-global.com
Web site: http://www.igi-global.com

Library of Congress Cataloging-in-Publication Data

Names: Reddy, K. Hemant Kumar, 1977- editor.
Title: Handbook of research on network-enabled IoT applications for smart city services / edited by K. Hemant Kumar Reddy, Diptendu Sinha Roy, Tapas Kumar Mishra, and Mir Wajahat Hussain.
Description: Hershey, PA : Information Science Reference, [2023] | Includes bibliographical references and index. | Summary: "The rapid growth of IoT and its applications in smart cities pose significant challenges for academic scholars. The increasing number of interconnected devices and the massive amounts of data they generate strain traditional networks, leading to inefficiencies and security vulnerabilities. Additionally, the centralized control plane in Software Defined Networks (SDN) presents a single point of failure, hindering network performance, while IoT devices themselves are susceptible to attacks, compromising user data and privacy. To address these pressing issues, Network-Enabled IoT Applications for Smart City Services offers a compelling solution"-- Provided by publisher.
Identifiers: LCCN 2023031163 (print) | LCCN 2023031164 (ebook) | ISBN 9798369307441 (h/c) | ISBN 9798369307458 (ebook)
Subjects: LCSH: Smart cities--Handbooks, manuals, etc. | Internet of things--Handbooks, manuals, etc. | Software-defined networking (Computer network technology)--Handbooks, manuals, etc.
Classification: LCC TD159.4 .H3653 2023 (print) | LCC TD159.4 (ebook) | DDC 307.1/416--dc23/eng/20230918
LC record available at https://lccn.loc.gov/2023031163
LC ebook record available at https://lccn.loc.gov/2023031164

This book is published in the IGI Global book series Advances in Electronic Government, Digital Divide, and Regional Development (AEGDDRD) (ISSN: 2326-9103; eISSN: 2326-9111)

British Cataloguing in Publication Data
A Cataloguing in Publication record for this book is available from the British Library.

List of Contributors

Table of Contents

Detailed Table of Contents

All over the world, smart city projects and related initiatives have reached new technological heights thanks to the enormous organization of the internet of things (IoT). One of the newest methods for integrating ICT solutions and sensors is the internet of things. Numerous smart city projects have been implemented during this time—roughly as a proof-of-concept, nevertheless a rising number as everlasting, production-level dispositions, enhancing the metropolis's operations and citizens' eminence of life cycle. The IoT by means of the empowering expertise for the smart city is the motivation of this chapter. The chapter scrutinizes the recent state of IoT- empowered smart cities by examining pertinent experiences and metropolitan initiatives those have incorporated IoT hooked on their amenities and the ways in which these initiatives have had an impact. The most important skills that have been industrialized besides how they are serving the Smart City life have been represented in this chapter.

The current advent of new technological advancements like the internet of things, artificial intelligence, and big data have not only ventured in applications management like regular transactional systems but also large applications like managing cities. The main objective of a "smart city" is the improvement in the living conditions of the people of all strata in the city. The city ideally should provide technological, innovative, and sustainable solutions by utilizing the resources. The smart city concept is providing a higher quality of life (QoL) for all its citizens. The areas which are mainly covered in the purview of smart city are governance, efficient mobility and public transport facility, healthcare facility, affordable housing for all citizens, digitization, and robust IT connectivity; along with focus on good sanitization, sufficient water supply, solid waste management, and electricity supply. In this chapter, the authors investigate the possibility and feasibility of the concept of digital twin in the applications of smart city.

Artificial intelligence has recently gained great importance in healthcare and has played an important role in the making the lives of patients, doctors, radiologists, clinical laboratories, emergency medical services, etc., better. Remote health monitoring is possible in less time and low cost for rural areas where doctors are not available all the time. Assistance is provided to the medical professionals when required in the time of emergency through deep learning algorithms which is beneficial. The anomalies in the medical images can be easily detected and predicted with the help of AI, which were impossible to detect by the human eye, thus adding extra value for the healthcare sector. The lack of specialized medical professionals and increasing number of patients with lifestyle diseases necessitate the digitization for the mundane tasks of healthcare. Explainable AI is important in healthcare sector, where the consequences of incorrect AI predictions or decisions can be severe.

The 'smart city' notion places a lot of emphasis on using information and communication technologies to boost connectedness and quality of life and effectiveness of various local authorities (ICT). Smart city services stimulate the practice of cloud- and IoT-based services that have included actual web applications that make use of sensors, smart phones, and RFIDs. Cloud platforms besides the IoT persist the two ICT models that are currently dealing the greatest influence on the Industrial IoT as well. Both concepts significantly influence the way it has developed and put into practice applications and smart city solutions. The first phase of this study highlights key features of IoT and Cloud along with smart city applications. Further in the second phase the research investigates the confluence of cloud platforms with IoT to build up the smart city besides various challenges associated in smart city implementation. Lastly, the research focuses on the smart cities' requirement for cloud-based IoT applications and provides the future direction in adaptability of smart city.

Recent years have seen a significant increase in the use of artificial intelligence (AI) and machine learning (ML) concepts across a variety of academic domains. AI's major objective is to build intelligent systems and give machines human intelligence. Artificial intelligence is a tool for creating systems, making judgements, solving problems, learning, and linguistic intelligence, as well as for imitating human conduct. Electrical and computer engineers are at the forefront of intellectual creativity as they participate in the planning, creation, evaluation, and production processes for newer generations of gadgets and technology. Even if these professionals want to grow, their objectives might conflict with the consequences of artificial intelligence, which are continually expanding. The practice of Artificial Intelligence (AI) and Machine Learning (ML) applications in industrial industries that have a significant influence on sustainability and the environment, such as renewable energy, smart grids, the catalyzed industry, and power storage and distribution The main popular approaches are artificial neural networks and Machine learning. Demand for energy is skyrocketing at a higher pace than production in the industry between 2004 and 2017, implying a decline in energy efficiency (EE). Under the premise of steady future output, an explicit energy efficiency enhancement target of 26% from 2017 and 2050 is set.

With the idea of shifting towards a smart future there is a lot of research being done in the area of internet of things (IoT) and wireless communication, especially 5G network technology. These technologies are instrumenting society towards a world of high connectivity, through secure evolutionary telecommunication methodologies. In this chapter we understand the role of 5G networks in enhancing IoT devices and discuss their security aspects. Integration of IoT and software defined network termed as SDIoT enables automatic traffic rerouting, device reconfiguration, and bandwidth allocation seamlessly. Smart cities utilize the SDIoT integrated with 5G to gather real-time data, better understand how demand patterns are changing, and respond with quicker and more affordable solutions. The authors try to understand the existing research scenario in 5G networks and IoT, and what areas are being taken into consideration for improvement in the coming future.

Traffic in the 5G network is growing exponentially and is predictable to grow in the future. Providing a high quality of service with ever-increasing traffic volumes is challenging in 5G networks. Software defined networking (SDN) along with emerging cloud technologies plays a significant responsibility in enhancing the performance of 5G networks. The 5G SDN paradigm is designed to support real-time and latency-sensitive applications. This chapter aims to summarize the existing technologies, benefits, and challenges of the 5G network. Also, a novel multivariate traffic analysis framework using time series analysis is proposed to enhance traffic management and its performance. Evaluation is performed on open traffic flow datasets and the analysis results show that the proposed framework performs better despite the inherent uncertainty in terms of classification and forecast accuracy.

With the increment in population, the problems of big cities regarding highly congested traffic are gaining more and more attention, with a goal of making them efficient and environmentally friendly. Most contain rich information and complex techniques that oppose ongoing optimization procedures. As security threats continue to grow, Vehicles are subject to various service attacks that can compromise security. To address these concerns, the US and European Intelligent Transportation System (ITS) standards select elliptic curve cryptography (ECC) algorithms for safe vehicle interactions. They introduced a two-layer taxonomy to Evolutionary computation for intelligent check transportation in smart cities is studied. This chapter will analyze the security architecture of the ETSI ITS standard. The results show that the existing security solution is better than the achieved level/quality of service (quality of service) and vehicular application performance regarding rising inter-arrival packet delay, packet and crypto loss, and reduced security awareness in security applications.

The internet of things (IoT) is still in its early stages, but it has sparked interest in a wide range of industries, including healthcare, logistics tracking, smart cities, and transportation. However, it is also vulnerable to a variety of serious network infiltration concerns. This chapter contributes to attack detection and alert system for IoT networks. This system provides alert and detection of cyber-attacks at the router level by configuring Rpi as a wireless router for IoT network. For the detection method, the authors used an anomaly-based approach that learns the packets in the network using deep learning. IoTID20 dataset is used for training the deep learning model. This model detects four kinds of attack: DoS, MITM, port scan, and scan. When the attack is detected, the user is alerted via e-mail and SMS.

Smart city incorporates multiple living methods for the sustainability of resources. As the number of interconnected devices is expanding day by day, we need to secure the transmission of data. Blockchain is seen as a way to eliminate tampering and reduce the risks of malware threats with IoT devices and data. In smart cities, blockchain-based IoT applications can be used for a wide variety of services in a secure and decentralized way. This chapter introduces blockchain technology and how it secures the data and then explores the integration of blockchain technology in smart city services like healthcare, transportation, supply chain management, smart grid, and banking.

After the COVID-19 pandemic, the healthcare sector has faced many challenges as telehealth increased and the need for a secure and efficient healthcare record system became essential. Nowadays, the healthcare sector suffers from many problems, such as security, trust, availability of data, and drug traceability. Blockchain technology is a recent technology that has proven its efficiency in many sectors, such as finance, banking, bitcoin, and healthcare sectors. This chapter describes blockchain integration in the healthcare sector to cover these problems. The authors will start by introducing blockchain technology. After that, they will present the healthcare sector challenges. Then, they focus on advantages of blockchain usage to resolve existing problems in the healthcare sector, especially in the electronic health record and drug traceability.

Sensor deployment in smart city scenarios introduce multiple challenges such as node capacity management, node management, and communication latency. As the size of the sensor network increases, there must be novel or multiple strategies to improve efficiency of the network. The goal of this chapter is to explore and highlight research strategies in this area. There has been work in this area, but there are multiple emerging challenges in this area due to explosion in number of sensor nodes and the functionalities embedded in these nodes in smart city and healthcare applications. Node co-operation or node collaboration is a method to localize large-scale sensor networks. This method has been explored in cellular networks to improve spectrum utilization. There is much interest and scope in node co-operation/node collaboration in sensor networks as collaboration can be exploited to control the topology, minimize communication overhead, and conserve energy at the node.

On account of continuous increase in concerns about environmental deterioration and electrical usage, sustainable energy sources are being commonly used to generate power and offer several benefits like clean energy and reduced price. To meet the fast growth in power stipulation, major renewable sources must be attained. Though renewables present a long-term solution as an alternative to fossil fuels, they are associated with uncertainty in generating power. In this chapter, to overcome the above problem, a combination of energy bases will be able to be implemented called as HRES. Due to the relatively low environmental effects, HRES have become a major choice for rural electrification. In this work, an endeavor has been made to present the outline of role of HRES. This chapter will also dispense about the power control strategies, energy assessment of a hybrid system, and battery energy storage devices in electrical networks.

The more technology advances, the extra benefits to the public and devices that connect to the internet have increased as well, commonly known as internet of things (IoT). The battery lifespan of these devices rises with technical concerns where an alternative to traditional energy attainment is needed. As the way forward, wireless sensor networks (WSNs) and IoT are tested to be used as novel energy alternatives through energy harvesting (EH). This study identifies the availability of energy by location. Similarly, it focuses on the sensor node's architecture with EH capabilities expanding to the classification of five EH techniques. It evaluates the EH developments in search of minimal resource utilization associated with WSNs. Its extensive distribution of interconnected devices is connected via the internet and other related high-tech innovations. Finally, it discusses the feasibility of energy storage and its potential for WSNs, paving the way for future trends and motivations.

related applications, in addition to challenges and future directions for using artificial intelligence to provide smart city services.

Preface

AN OVERVIEW OF THE SUBJECT MATTER

The Internet of Things (IoT) has made it possible to provide cutting-edge services for the development of various essential applications, including smart cities and smart homes. The Internet of Things (IoT) enables the linking of disparate objects to create a network with processing, sensing, and communication capabilities without the need for manual human interaction. It is projected that a big number of devices will be connected to the Internet and produce a lot of data due to the IoT's numerous applications. The traditional networks may not be able to handle the amount of data created by these devices, thus they need to be protected from security threats. Due to vendor lock-in, traditional networks are rigid, making it difficult to handle the high frequency data streams coming from IoT devices. Due to the removal of the control plane from the data plane, which makes the adoption of any more recent policy deployment promising, Software Defined Networks (SDN) has been touted as the next generation networking paradigm. By guaranteeing end-to-end bandwidth and lowering latency while using the centralization of SDN controller, the enormous amount of data created by IoT devices can be handled effectively. SDN's centralized controller may be open to various attacks, which would reduce network performance. Additionally, IoT devices are susceptible to numerous assaults that could harm user data and privacy among other things, necessitating the provision of a comprehensive solution. Due to its capability of preserving privacy and being extremely secure, blockchain can be a viable solution for IoT applications. Blockchain is a term used to describe a decentralized, tamper-proof, and transactional database that offers a safe way to store and process data across a sizable number of network participants. Higher availability and reliability are challenging because the controller in SDN is a single point of failure and a device failure in IoT might hamper entire network performance. A potential method of managing the data effectively and securely could be provided by the integration of Blockchain into SDN and IoT devices.

A DESCRIPTION OF WHERE THE TOPIC FITS IN THE WORLD TODAY

The idea of "Network-Enabled IoT Applications for Smart City Services" has grown significantly relevant and well-known in today's world of quick advancement. Cities have the difficulty of effectively managing resources and raising the standard of living for their citizens as urban populations continue to increase. A possible approach to overcoming these difficulties and transforming cities into smart, interconnected urban settings is provided by network-enabled Internet of Things (IoT) applications. IoT refers to a wide network of interconnected devices that are equipped with connection, software, and sensors. These gadgets have the ability to gather and exchange data, allowing them to interact with their environment and offer insightful information. IoT technology serves as the basis for a number of applications that improve urban living in a variety of fields when used with smart city services.

IoT solutions that are network-enabled allow for easy integration and communication between various urban systems and services. Smart transportation systems, for instance, can use IoT sensors built into cars, roads, and other infrastructure to track traffic patterns, plan better routes, and ease congestion. IoT-enabled waste management systems can optimize collection routes, monitor garbage levels in bins, and encourage effective waste disposal. IoT applications can dramatically increase public safety by monitoring key infrastructure, detecting and responding to criminal activity, and enhancing emergency response systems. IoT technology can be used by smart energy management systems to track energy usage, improve distribution, and encourage sustainability. It can also improve residents' quality of life in a number of ways. Real-time information about available parking spaces can be provided via smart parking systems, which will ease traffic and frustration. Smart lighting systems can change the amount of light output based on the surrounding environment, conserving energy and improving safety. To maintain a better living environment, environmental monitoring devices can evaluate elements like noise levels and air quality.

The seamless integration of devices, networks, and data platforms is essential for the success of network-enabled IoT applications. The huge volume of IoT devices and quick, reliable data transmission are made possible by advanced connectivity infrastructure, such 5G networks and SDN. However, while implementing network-enabled IoT applications in smart cities, it is crucial to address issues with data security, privacy, and ethical considerations. To protect citizen data and ensure openness in data collection and use, safeguards and regulations must be in place.

A DESCRIPTION OF THE TARGET AUDIENCE

The target audience is represented by industry experts, UG and PG students, researchers and academicians and entrepreneurs.

A DESCRIPTION OF THE IMPORTANCE OF EACH CHAPTER

1. Smart Cities Powered by IoT: Perspective and Change

In the wave of changes being made in the lifestyle of the generation and the fastest growing requirements have invented the many equipment. Thus, the human being needs all the facilities should be available in its fingerprint. One such example is services rendered in the advance cities which is called as smart cities because of the ease of fulfilment of demands. The technological developments made this possible specially services by the internet connectivity among the daily used devices which is called as internet of things (IOT). As change is the only constant in the nature, human beings interest changes in every couple of years and it will continue. Thus, it is very much important to identify and monitor the advanced services provided in the smart cities by the help of IoT devices. Further, it is important to identify the changes may be required in the upcoming years so that the current generation can focus on those perspectives. Thus, the current chapter will be useful to the audience to note the power of IoT and possible changes required to develop the next generation smart city.

2. Digital Twin-Enabled Solutions for Smart City Applications

The recent technology introduced in the smart city model is quite interesting. But it is alarming when we think about its vulnerability and maintenance. Let us take an example of intelligent water supply of a city that monitors the use of water in a particular region and its necessity. The job of the authority is to supply water to each region of the city according to its requirements. It can be possible by having the previous experience which is available in the form of information stored in a database. Machine learning algorithms can be used to predict the requirement of water. Several sensors are supposed to be deployed in the path of the water pipes which will monitor the supply of the water and can identify if any leakage is there. In this case, the system has to depend on the input provided by the sensors and the proper prediction of the machine learning algorithm backed system. The system may collapse if some sensors behave abnormally, and the total water supply may be disrupted. Thus, there is a need of monitoring system of the infrastructure and the technology used in the system which will work as an interface between the physical system and service model. The digital twin is a solution model which can monitor the system and can generate alarm in case of any failure in the system. This chapter deals makes aware about the digital twin system and its various applications which will be beneficial to the readers to develop a sustainable system which can provide the technology enabled service to the smart city management.

3. Issues, Current Challenges, and Research Directions in Designing a Smart, Explainable AI-Based Healthcare System

The important component of a smart city management system is advanced transportation system and health care system apart from its fundamental services available like sanitation, water supply, power supply. Currently, many IoT based healthcare systems have been designed which helps to predict the abnormality or any kind of happenings. But, it is very important to decide what actions can be taken to avoid the bad happenings. Normally, the decisions are taken manually by the officers deployed in the service. Sometimes, lack of intellectual experience may lead to failure of the system. Thus, there is a need of the technological adviser which can provide a suggestion that would be logical justification. Thus, the chapter highlights the current challenges of the smart city services. The chapter has a descriptive analysis about the current challenges of healthcare systems and how explainable AI can be used to improve the service. The chapter will provide sufficient information about the current trend, issues, challenges in solving problems and the stand of explainable artificial intelligence.

4. Adaptability of IoT and Cloud for Enabling the Smart City: Applications and Challenges

Now a days, almost every individual in urban areas access internet through its gadget. Considering the density of the of internet connections in a highly populated city, we can imagine the amount of data transmission occurs in every second. Although, there are high performance devices are established, still the amount of data is quite high. Further, to retrieve data from the large database is an emerging issue. Furthermore, to get the query result for a particular problem raised by any individual, it is highly essential to get the query be resolved at the earliest. Thus, it is very important to understand the use of IoT devices and their magnitude have forced us to think about the storage and maintenance of the data efficiently. The data should be stored in such a way that the query result should come fast and only the important and relevant information should participate in resolving any query. The cloud makes this possible by providing the important service and data as per the requirement of the individuals. Hence, it is very important to study the pros and cons of the IoT and cloud in the services rendered in smart cities. The current chapter describes the various aspects of the IoT and cloud which will be really helpful to design the next generation infrastructure.

5. Smart City Ecosystem: An Exploration of Requirements, Architecture, Applications, Security, and Emerging Motivations

The current generation is looking for the fastest and quality service form all the domains including healthcare, transportation, daily life services and many more. Even, sometimes the people want the services before they ask for. As the demand and choice of the generation is highly dynamic, the system has to be designed in such a way that it will meet the needs of time. The current chapter provides a systematic review of the smart city ecosystem. The chapter explores requirements, architecture being used with their pros and cons along with future scope. They have discussed the available technologies in some developed nations' notable smart cities such as London, New York, Singapore, Busan, Amsterdam, and Sunshine Coast Regions, highlighting their unique features as a case studies. Thus, the chapter will provide a significant amount of information to deal with the technologies deployed for smart city services. Further, it highlights some important drawbacks of the existing systems that will motivate the current generation service providers to redesign the models and innovate some new technologies which will be a gift for the next generation that includes the integration of blockchains, security considerations, collaborative filtering, and infrastructure upgrades in smart city applications.

6. Interaction Between IoT-Enabled Services in Smart Cities

Smart cities are becoming a reality with the help of IoT enabled services. These services allow for communication between different devices and systems in order to provide better services to citizens. The interaction between these services can be either peer-to-peer or centralized, depending on the type of service being used. The use of IoT enabled services in smart cities is growing rapidly, providing citizens with improved safety, convenience, and efficiency. With the communication between these services becoming more efficient, it is possible to create a more connected environment that will benefit everyone living in the city. The connectivity between various IOT enabled services is the main topic of this study. Here, peer level interaction and the utilization of a centralized server are two strategies utilized. The duty of a central server is to register all IoT-enabled services and promptly provide any necessary data to the appropriate services. When necessary, peer level services communicate with one another. The merits and disadvantages of each of these strategies are also examined in this study.

7. A Role of Artificial Intelligence and Machine Learning Algorithms for Energy Efficiency Applications

Artificial Intelligence (AI) and Machine Learning (ML) algorithms are playing an increasingly important role in energy efficiency. AI and ML can be used to develop smart energy systems that can reduce global emissions while improving energy efficiency. These algorithms can be used to analyze data from various sources, such as weather forecasts, electricity demand, and other factors that affect the use of energy. They can then provide insights into how best to optimize energy consumption for maximum efficiency. AI and ML also enable the development of predictive models that allow us to anticipate future needs in order to better manage our resources. In addition, these technologies are being used to create smarter grids that allow us to better monitor and control our electricity usage. The catalyzed industry, and power storage and distribution Artificial neural networks and machine learning are the two most widely used techniques. Between 2004 and 2017, the industry's demand for energy increased faster than production, which suggests a drop in energy efficiency (EE). An explicit energy efficiency enhancement target of 26% between 2017 and 2050 is set under the assumption of constant future output.

8. 5G-Enabled Secure IoT Applications in Smart Cities Using Software-Defined Networks

With the advent of 5G networks, the Internet of Things (IoT) is set to revolutionize smart cities. 5G networks enable faster and secure communication between IoT devices, making them more efficient and reliable. This will help in improving security and safety in smart cities by providing real-time monitoring of activities. Furthermore, Software Defined Networks (SDN) can be used to manage and control these IoT devices effectively. This will help in creating secure applications that are tailored to meet the specific needs of a city or region. In conclusion, 5G enabled secure IoT applications through SDN can provide an effective means for managing smart cities. This chapter explains how 5G networks improve IoT devices and covers some of their security concerns. The Software Defined Internet of Things, or SDIoT, allows for smooth bandwidth allocation, automatic traffic rerouting, and device reconfiguration. To collect real-time data, analyse how demand patterns are evolving, and provide speedier and more inexpensive solutions, smart cities use the SDIoT combined with 5G. We make an effort to comprehend the current research environment for 5G networks and IoT, as well as the sectors that are being taken into account for advancement in the near future.

9. Traffic Management of SDN/NFV-Based Smart 5G Networks Using Time Series Analysis

The advent of 5G networks requires a new approach to network management and traffic control. Software Defined Networking (SDN) and Network Function Virtualization (NFV) are two technologies that enable the dynamic control of network resources. However, managing traffic in these networks is still a challenge due to their complexity. Time Series Analysis and Multivariate Analysis can be used to analyze the flows in SDN/NFV based 5G networks, providing insights into the performance of the network and allowing for more efficient traffic management. By leveraging Flow Analyzer tools, operators can gain visibility into their 5G networks and make informed decisions about how best to manage traffic. The goal of this chapter is to provide an overview of the 5G network's current technologies, advantages, and difficulties. To improve traffic management and its effectiveness, a unique multivariate traffic analysis paradigm based on time series analysis is also suggested. The suggested framework performs better despite the inherent uncertainty in terms of categorization and forecast accuracy, according to study of open traffic flow statistics.

10. Intelligent Infrastructure of Route Scheduling for Smart Transportation System in Smart Cities

With the rise of smart cities, intelligent transportation systems have become an important factor in urban planning. Intelligent infrastructure of route scheduling for smart transportation system in smart cities is a key component of this system. This includes the use of Elliptic Curve Cryptography to ensure secure data transmission between vehicles and the server, as well as quality-of-service measures to ensure smooth operation of the system. Smart vehicles are also used to optimize routes and reduce traffic congestion in cities. All these components are essential for ensuring a reliable and efficient transportation system in smart cities. The security architecture of the European Telecommunication Standards Institute-Intelligent Transportation System (ETSI-ITS) standard will be examined in this chapter. The results demonstrate that, in terms of increasing inter-arrival packet latency, packet and crypto loss, and decreased security awareness in security applications, the current security solution performs better than the level/quality of service (QoS) attained and vehicular application performance.

11. An Alert and Detection System for Cyber-Attacks on IoT Devices

As more and more devices become connected to the Internet of Things, it is becoming increasingly important to ensure that they are secure from cyber-attacks. With the advancement of deep learning algorithms, an alert and detection system for cyber-attacks on IoT devices can be developed. This system can help protect smart cities from malicious actors who may try to exploit vulnerable networks or devices. The system would use deep learning algorithms to detect suspicious activity in real-time and alert administrators so that they can take action quickly. The attack detection and alert system for IoT networks is improved by this article. By setting up the Raspberry Pi as a wireless router for an Internet of Things network, this method enables alarm and detection of cyber attacks at the router level. We employed an anomaly-based methodology for the detection method, which applies deep learning to learn the network packets. The deep learning model is trained using the IoTID20 dataset, and it can recognise four different types of attacks, including DoS, MITM, port scans, and scans, among others. Email and SMS notifications are sent to the user when the attack is discovered.

12. Blockchain-Enabled Secured Smart City Services

Smart cities are the future of urban living. With the help of IoT and Blockchain technology, smart cities can offer citizens a secure and private way to access services. Blockchain technology enables citizens to have full control over their data while providing them with a secure platform for transactions and communication. This will help in creating an efficient and transparent system for city services like healthcare, education, energy management, transportation, etc. Blockchain-enabled smart city services are also more secure than traditional methods as they provide enhanced security features such as encryption and digital signatures. This chapter explains blockchain technology and how it protects data before examining how it might be used to improve services provided by smart cities like banking, healthcare, transportation, and supply chain management.

13. Blockchain in the Healthcare Sector

Blockchain technology is revolutionizing the healthcare sector by providing a secure and transparent platform for storing and sharing data. With the help of blockchain, healthcare organizations can ensure that patient data is secure, traceable and readily available. It also helps in establishing trust between different stakeholders in the healthcare industry. Blockchain can be used to improve drug traceability, enhance data security, streamline Electronic Health Record (EHR) systems and improve data transparency. Additionally, it can be used to make sure that all relevant stakeholders have access to real-time data which helps them make informed decisions quickly. In short, blockchain technology has immense potential to revolutionize the healthcare sector by making it more secure, efficient and transparent. To address these issues, this chapter explores blockchain integration in the healthcare industry. First, blockchain technology is discussed. The problems facing the healthcare industry will then be discussed. The benefits of using blockchain to address current issues in the healthcare sector, particularly with the electronic health record and drug traceability, are then the main focus.

14. Co-operation in Wireless Sensor Networks for Smart Cities

The concept of Smart Cities is becoming increasingly popular in the modern world. In order to make this concept a reality, Wireless Sensor Networks (WSNs) and Mobile Ad hoc Networks (MANETs) are being used to connect different devices and enable them to communicate with each other. To ensure that these networks are reliable and efficient, node collaboration and cooperation plays an important role. Node collaboration involves nodes working together to share resources and information for a common goal. Node cooperation, on the other hand, requires nodes to cooperate with each other by exchanging data or messages in order to achieve their goals. With the help of these two techniques, WSNs can be used for various applications such as monitoring traffic conditions in smart cities or providing real-time health monitoring services. This chapter clarifies and emphasizes the idea of WSN node cooperation in this chapter. The intention is to appropriately emphasise node cooperation and its importance, particularly in IoT installations for smart cities. This should make technology implementers aware of how to make their deployments more effective and open up new research vistas, particularly for smart city situations.

15. A Review on the Impact of Hybrid Renewable Energy Systems for Sustainability and Energy Management

Hybrid renewable energy systems (HRES) are becoming increasingly popular as a sustainable and cost-effective way to generate electricity. These systems combine photovoltaic (PV) systems, wind energy systems, and energy storage devices to maximize the efficiency of the system. They also use power converters and control strategies to ensure that the system operates at peak efficiency. This review will cover the impact of hybrid renewable energy systems on sustainability and energy management, with a focus on their potential for reducing emissions, improving reliability, and providing cost savings. HRES have emerged as a top option for rural electrification due to their very minimal environmental effects. An effort has been made to outline the role of HRES in this study and solve numerous problem. Additionally, this chapter will discuss power control tactics, a hybrid system's energy evaluation, and battery energy storage systems in electrical networks.

16. IoT-Based Energy Harvesting and Future Research Trends in Wireless Sensor Networks

Energy Harvesting (EH) is a key technology for powering Internet of Things (IoT) devices and Wireless Sensor Networks (WSN). It involves the collection of energy from ambient sources such as light, heat, and vibration, which can then be used to power IoT devices. As more IoT devices are deployed in various environments, it is becoming increasingly important to understand the energy supply chain. This requires research into new technologies and trends in energy harvesting as well as the development of innovative solutions for energy storage. This study categorises the locations where energy is available. Like this, it emphasises the architecture of the sensor node while expanding EH capabilities to the classification of five EH approaches and evaluates the EH advances in pursuit of the least amount of resource use related to WSNs. The internet and other related high-tech advances connect its wide dispersion of interconnected gadgets. To set the stage for upcoming trends and reasons, it concludes by discussing the viability of energy storage and its potential for WSNs.

17. Future Indian Smart Cities' Renewable Energy Scenarios

India is one of the most rapidly developing countries in the world. With the government's initiatives to create smart cities, India is now looking to make its cities more sustainable and efficient by using renewable energy sources. This will not only reduce carbon emissions but also ensure that development is done in a responsible way. The future of India's smart cities lies in renewable energy sources such as solar, wind, and hydroelectricity. These distributed energy sources can be used to power homes and businesses as well as provide electricity for public services like transportation systems. Government initiatives such as tax incentives for installing solar panels are helping to promote the use of renewable energy in urban areas. With these measures, India is well on its way towards creating a greener future for its citizens and setting an example for other countries when it comes to sustainable development. The remainder of this chapter discusses the many choices for switching power generation from conventional fossil fuel-powered sources to renewable energy and deals with the issue of sustainable development. As more renewable energy is used, the existing grid will receive more clean energy like solar energy, wind energy, and photovoltaic systems. The net metering programme has additional advantage.

18. Smart Cities: Operational Concepts for an Elusive Framework

Smart Cities are becoming a reality as Information and Communication Technologies (ICTs) continue to proliferate. With the Internet of Things (IoT) connecting physical objects to the digital world, cities are now able to leverage data generated from connected devices to create more efficient and sustainable operations. Without ignoring the significance of efficiency and innovation in a holistic system, the influence of ITC to improve SC management was also taken into consideration. The findings support the composite nature of SC, the requirement for increased SC uniformity, measuring scales, and connectedness between SC management and its residents, all of which are necessary for a higher sustainable quality of life.

19. Artificial Intelligence and Machine Learning Approaches in Smart City Services

In today's world, Artificial Intelligence (AI) and Machine Learning (ML) are playing an increasingly important role in the development of Smart City services. AI and ML have the potential to help cities become more efficient, safe, and sustainable by providing automated solutions to various problems. Deep learning (DL) algorithms can be used to analyse large amounts of data from different sources such as sensors, cameras, and other Information and Communication Technology (ICT) devices. This data can then be used to create intelligent systems that can help cities improve their services. AI and ML are also being used to develop predictive models that can help cities anticipate future needs or events based on past trends. With the help of AI and ML technologies, Smart City services will become smarter than ever before. Along with the DL strategy, this chapter describes the roles that AI and ML play in smart cities.

The Internet of Things (IoT) has made it possible to provide cutting-edge services for the development of various essential applications, including smart cities and smart homes. The Internet of Things (IoT) enables the linking of disparate objects to create a network with processing, sensing, and communication capabilities without the need for manual human interaction. It is projected that a big number of devices will be connected to the Internet and produce a lot of data due to the IoT's numerous applications. The traditional networks may not be able to handle the amount of data created by these devices, thus they need to be protected from security threats.

Due to vendor lock-in, traditional networks are rigid, making it difficult to handle the high frequency data streams coming from IoT devices. Due to the removal of the control plane from the data plane, which makes the adoption of any more recent policy deployment promising, Software Defined Networks (SDN) has been touted as the next generation networking paradigm. By guaranteeing end-to-end bandwidth and lowering latency while using the centralization of SDN controller, the enormous amount of data created by IoT devices can be handled effectively.

SDN's centralized controller may be open to various attacks, which would reduce network performance. Additionally, IoT devices are susceptible to numerous assaults that could harm user data and privacy among other things, necessitating the provision of a comprehensive solution. Due to its capability of preserving privacy and being extremely secure, blockchain can be a viable solution for IoT applications. Blockchain is a term used to describe a decentralised, tamper-proof, and transactional database that offers a safe way to store and process data across a sizable number of network participants. Higher availability and reliability are challenging because the controller in SDN is a single point of failure and a device failure in IoT might hamper entire network performance. A potential method of managing the data effectively and securely could be provided by the integration of Blockchain into SDN and IoT devices.

CONCLUSION

This edited book is a unique collection of emerging technologies and its integration, which depicts the major challenges of smart cities with respect to network IoT, SDN, and Blockchain. It also addresses the integration of these emerging technologies to address the issues of smart cities. It highlights the adaptability of IoT and cloud computing for enabling the smart city applications, role of artificial intelligence and machine learning in reducing the energy consumption of cloud and IoT resources in provisioning the customer service requests in real time basis, traffic management issues of SDN/NFS in 5G enabled smart city particularly in health care systems and it also deals with infrastructure routing for scheduling of smart transportation system in smart city with the help of artificial intelligent. At the end, it depicts the future renewable energy scenarios of Indian smart cities with proposing smart and intelligent solutions. In conclusion, the idea of IoT applications for smart city services that are network-enabled is very significant in the modern world. IoT technology offers a potent tool to establish a linked urban ecosystem that enhances several elements of urban life, including transportation, energy, waste management, public safety, and overall citizen well-being, as cities try to become more sustainable, effective, and livable.

Hemant Kumar Reddy
VIT-AP University, India

Diptendu Sinha Roy
National Institute of Technology, Meghalaya, India

Tapas Mishra
SRM University, India

Mir Wajahat Hussain
Alliance University, India

Acknowledgment

Writing a book is a journey that involves the contributions and support of numerous individuals and organizations. We would like to express our heartfelt gratitude to all those who have been instrumental in making this book a reality. We are indebted to the team at IGI Global. The expertise of the IGI team, attention to detail, and constructive criticism has been instrumental in refining this book and bringing out its best.

We would like to extend our gratitude to the researchers, scholars, and experts in the field whose groundbreaking work and insights have laid the foundation for this book. Your contributions have been a constant source of inspiration, and we are honoured to build upon your achievements.

We are grateful to the reviewers who have generously shared their time and knowledge for improving this book. Your expertise and willingness to contribute have added depth and authenticity to the content. Lastly, we would like to express our appreciation to the readers of this book. Your curiosity, engagement, and interest in the subject matter motivated us to continue exploring and sharing knowledge. Thank you all for being a part of this journey and for helping us bring this book to life.

With deep appreciation,

Hemant Kumar Reddy
VIT-AP University, India

Diptendu Sinha Roy
National Institute of Technology, Meghalaya, India

Tapas Mishra
SRM University, India

Mir Wajahat Hussain
Alliance University, India

Chapter 1
Smart Cities Powered by IoT:
Perspective and Change

Sudipta Sahana
https://orcid.org/0000-0002-9694-6399
Institute of Engineering and Management Kolkata, India & University of Engineering and Management, Kolkata, India

Buddhadeb Pradhan
Institute of Engineering and Management Kolkata, India & University of Engineering and Management, Kolkata, India

ABSTRACT

All over the world, smart city projects and related initiatives have reached new technological heights thanks to the enormous organization of the internet of things (IoT). One of the newest methods for integrating ICT solutions and sensors is the internet of things. Numerous smart city projects have been implemented during this time—roughly as a proof-of-concept, nevertheless a rising number as everlasting, production-level dispositions, enhancing the metropolis's operations and citizens' eminence of life cycle. The IoT by means of the empowering expertise for the smart city is the motivation of this chapter. The chapter scrutinizes the recent state of IoT- empowered smart cities by examining pertinent experiences and metropolitan initiatives those have incorporated IoT hooked on their amenities and the ways in which these initiatives have had an impact. The most important skills that have been industrialized besides how they are serving the Smart City life have been represented in this chapter.

INTRODUCTION

The rising turn of events and spread of Internet of things (IoT) and Internet of everything (IoE) advances address a significant empowering agent in the ongoing savvy urban areas scene, driving the shrewd city worldview to the huge information scale. In fact, a specialized Ericson report projected that 29 billion nodes would be associated by 2022, as shown in Ejaz and Anpalagan (2019). According to a report that Statista Exploration released in 2019, and as per the estimation, by 2025 the overall quantity of linked IoT gadgets will reach approximately 75 billion by Fizza et al. (2021), resulting in a prospective IoT financial

DOI: 10.4018/979-8-3693-0744-1.ch001

effect that could extent 11 trillion USD annually by 2025 Bauer et al. (2021). Therefore, these statistics are enlightening that IoT would be on the top of the greatest worth troublesome advancements, opening new wildernesses, conceivable outcomes, and difficulties in the creation of brilliant administrations and applications. The significance of IoT is increasingly more firmly associated with the advancement of shrewd urban communities, for which IoT addresses one of the vital drivers for more astute advancement and maintainable turn of events. Savvy urban communities are mind-boggling socio-specialized foundations, made out of human entertainers (various partners and clients, like residents, city administrators, managerial organizations, public and privately owned businesses, and so on) and computerized gadgets (e.g.: city sensors and actuators took advantage of in numerous spaces, for example, portability and transportation, climate, energy, medical care, administration, industry 4.0 and so on; brilliant home and shrewd structures gadgets; and individual gadgets, for example, cell phones). This intricacy is replicated in the huge assortment of diverse methodologies, settings, application spaces & mechanical arrangements that have been proposed in the writing for the acknowledgment and the executives of brilliant urban areas. The principal objective of executing and coordinating IoT arrangements is to permit shrewd urban communities to progress further, giving new capacities and highlights while altogether lessening human intercession by Janani et al. (2021). Moreover, it is likewise essential to zero in on the social difficulties tended to and the cultural advantages accomplished by the reception of these advancements, for example evaluating how they can add to the Feasible Improvement Objectives (SDGs) created by Joined Countries inside the setting of the 2030 Plan according to UN-GGMI Report (2017). A portion of the super-specialized difficulties for present-day IoT-empowered savvy urban communities are addressed by the prerequisites of supporting a large number of various information suppliers, managing a wide range of conventions and information designs, as well as supporting the sharing of parts and ensuring versatility and interoperability. For information ingestion, it is essential to avoid performing additional responses, stockpiling and investigation, subsequently bringing down employable expenses and upgrading the city's maintainability. In the accompanying, a refreshed and far reaching (albeit not thorough) outline is given about research writing on shrewd city areas, arrangements, and systems, as well as information on significant IoT advancements and applications coordinated in smart metropolis components. The rest of the chapter is organized as follows: Section 2 deep dives into the architecture of the IoT. Applications of IoT in the context of smart city is discussed is section 3. The vulnerability of the smart city is further elaborated in section 4. The chapter is concluded in the section 5 which presents the future work.

ARCHITECTURE OF IOT

There are various stages in the engineering of IoT yet they can change as per the circumstances, however, for the most part, there are these four stages in the design of IoT –

Networked Devices

These are the actual gadgets that incorporate sensors, actuators, and transducers. These are the genuine gadgets that gather and send the information for handling. They are fit for getting continuous information and they can change over the actual amounts into electrical signs which can be sent through an organization.

Data Aggregation

It is a vital stage as it incorporates changing over the crude information gathered by sensors into significant information which can be utilized to make moves. It additionally incorporates Information Procurement Frameworks and Web Passages. It changes over the Simple signs given by sensors into advanced signals.

Final Analysis

This is a phase that incorporates edge IT investigation and the handling of information to make it more effective and completely equipped for execution. It likewise incorporates overseeing and finding every one of the gadgets accurately

Cloud Analysis

The last information is gotten here and dissected intently and definitively in Data Centres. They interact and clean the information to make it liberated from any sort of mistakes and missing qualities. After this stage, information is fit to be sent back and executed to perform tasks.

Now let us see the basic architecture of IoT which is shown in Figure 1 and it comprises of four phases as displayed in the graph given underneath –

Figure 1. IoT architecture

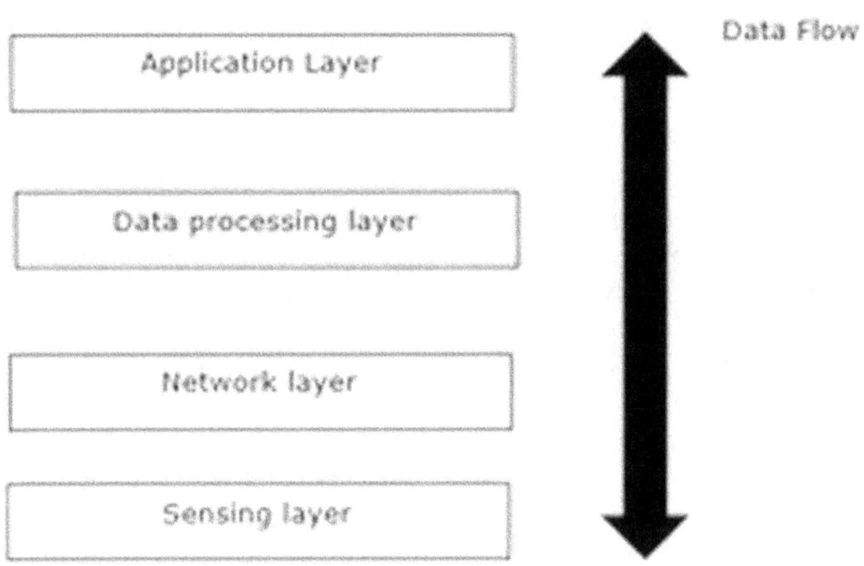

Sensing Layer – The principal phase of IoT incorporates sensors, gadgets, actuators and so on which gather information from the actual climate, process it and afterward send it over to the organization.

Network Layer – The second phase of the IoT comprises of Organization Entryways and Information Obtaining Frameworks. DAS changes over the simple information (gathered from Sensors) into Advanced Information. It likewise performs malware discovery and information on the board.

Data Processing Layer – The third phase of IoT is the main stage. Here, information is pre-handled on its assortment and isolated as needs be. After this, it is shipped off Server farms. Here Edge IT comes into utilization.

Application Layer – The fourth phase of IoT comprises Cloud/Server farms where information is overseen and utilized by applications like horticulture, safeguard, medical care, and so forth.

SMART CITY APPLICATION

For the vast majority of individuals perusing this article, odds are good that you live in a city. In point of fact, cities and urban areas are home to more than 55% of the world's population, and this proportion may rise to 70% in the not-too-distant future as more people move to cities in search of employment. But this means that cities need better infrastructure and planning if they want to be energy efficient and good for the environment and offer a good quality of life (Hussain et al., 2020). To put it another way, cities need to become smarter! The Internet of Things, sensors that collect data, and machine learning that applies the insights gleaned from the data make this possible (Hussain et al, 2023), (Pradhan et al, 2022). The Internet of Things (IoT) can be used in a variety of ways to improve city efficiency, including traffic management, pollution control, waste management, smart buildings, disaster planning, and more. Therefore, let's investigate how civic planning and cutting-edge technology can produce smarter, more cost-effective cities.

Smart Administration

The incorporation of ICT into city administration is managed by Smart Administration, which demonstrates how to further develop the dynamic interaction and accelerate regulatory and managerial systems through a more intelligent cooperation among various partners and social entertainers, including public organizations, city officials, privately owned businesses and residents. This can be effectively achieved by giving creative city administrations, devoted channels and organization incorporation for residents. For example, residents can be participated in taking part with city administration exercises &policy making procedures by means of ICT-based gadgets & virtual entertainment as evidence of the adaptable, broadly supported worldview, as per which residents can go about as "clients as sensors" with their cell phones and cell phones, taking part as people and in bunches in the procurement cycle of information of interest for savvy networks.

Things about Smart Administration: The most crucial aspect of smart governance is e-governance and public participation in decision-making. The following are the instruments used to achieve them:

The practice of Information and Communication Technology: This means that data is collected, processed, shared, and retrieved using digital equipment like computers, the Internet, and telecommunications. Improved information transmission through telecommunication channels like cable, radio, telephones, and satellite systems. Utilization of Geographical Information System (GIS) for movement and transport, video conferencing, and texting in banking, medical care, energy, and security administrations.

E-Consultation: The primary characteristic of smart governance is people participation. Between the government and the people, there needs to be a good way to talk to each other. They must be given the authority to express their ideas and opinions about government programs, schemes, and other topics. Their feedback ought to be sent directly to leaders, counsellors, city managers, or the head of the locality.

E-Data: Public information and data on government expenditures, investments, and funds must be easily accessible online. Data must be freely and openly shared, with the exception of vital information regarding citizens' safety and security. As a result, the government will be more accountable and citizens will be more involved in its operation.

Models of Smart Governance

Government to Citizen (G2C) Model: This refers to a system of software (classically web& mobile based) that facilitates connections within open organizations and residents, for example, policy management online interfaces and additionally portable applications and virtual entertainment channels utilized for correspondence and collaboration between neighbouring states and residents. In addition, according to various legislative guidelines, IoT advancements i.e. RFID & biometric sensors are progressively being incorporated into electronic identity cards & movable electronic gadgets for identification, signature &electronic verification. These highlights are ordinarily expected to get to administrations that are given by open organizations and counsel residents' very own information connected with public administrations, and so forth, subsequently improving on a ton of the correspondence and communication between legislative specialists and residents;

Government to Business (G2B) Model: This model respects the communications between open organizations and organizations. In this model, e-obtainment arrangements are taken on, i.e., computerized devices, through which neighborhood states distribute tenders, contests, projects, offices aimed at the buy/offer of products, and supplementary overall administrations for and from privately owned businesses. IoT advances are generally taken on in G2B exercises, working with and improving the connection between neighboring states and organizations that offer public and confidential types of assistance to residents. For example, transportation organizations use area-based sensors (normally taking advantage of GPS innovation) and administrations, imparting them to nearby organizations and permitting the simpler and more productive metropolitan making arrangements for portability and transportation by Badii et al. (2018). Furthermore, it incorporates comparative viewpoints engaged with numerous different spaces that offer public and principal types of assistance, like waste administration, water, energy, and so forth. To this end, the utilization of distributed computing is by and large embraced to store and divide information and results between the various partners (city administrators, organizations, and residents).

Government to Government (G2G) Model

The direct interactions between government organizations, departments, and agencies are the focus of the model. In order to create a system that is more user-friendly and all-encompassing, the objective is to integrate all governance channels. More openness, accountability, and streamlined administration will result from this.

A paperless, digital service model will emerge through the use of ICT. Corruption in public offices and unnecessary clutter will be reduced as a result. Officials and citizens will establish proper two-way communication, particularly at the municipal and regional levels, enhancing accountability and efficiency in government operations.

Product arrangements that aim to further develop interchanges between the various policy implementation elements and gatherings are connected to G2G (Government-to-government), thereby accelerating all cycles that require the association of these entertainers. This implies that distributed computing and web/variable-based administrations are utilized in conjunction with IoT advancements for the collection, storage, and sharing of information. A report from the European Joint Research Center (JRC) also found that legislatures could benefit from combining various information sources (such as IoT and the web) with reasonable analytical methods (such as simulated intelligence-based methods) to recognize and plan specific managerial strategies more easily Barcevicius et al. (2019).

Government to Employee (G2E) Model

The objective of this model is to provide online software and tools for employees, the government, and businesses to communicate with one another. Each worker's social security number, bank account number, and other personal information should be stored in a separate account. Numerous worker-related undertakings, for example, finance, clinical remuneration, opportune assets, annuity plans, bank credits can be completed on the web.

Infrastructures and Smart Living

The smart residing space incorporates all parts connected with creating more brilliant city frameworks (e.g., savvy homes, savvy structures, and so forth) also the administration and improvement of public administrations, for example, social exercises, the travel industry and schooling, which are engaged with upgrading the overall personal satisfaction of residents:

Smart Structures: IoT permits the quickly developing execution of numerous sorts of offices for brilliant structures, for example, cooling the executives, water waste, security frameworks for overseeing verified admittance to structures, video reconnaissance and human action checking Shi et al. (2020), alarms for occasions, for example, fires and gas spills, instruments for observing the underlying uprightness of structures Lombardi et al. (2021), and so on. A wide range of IoT advances are engaged with the living and frameworks space, contingent upon the particular use case or situation. Concerning smart structures, A high-constancy portrayal of structures and spatial properties as a collection of virtual resources, i.e., a computerized twin of the structure, is produced when IoT and Building Data Demonstrating (BIM) devices are combined Tang et al. (2019);

Smart Homes: A smart home framework can be something that makes our life very simple. Beginning from energy the executives where the power controls framework in the air conditioner machines where we utilize the indoor regulator, this is figured out how to chop down the power utilization that is occurring. An entryway the board framework, security the executives framework, water the executives framework are the piece of this too. In any case, these are fundamental things that hang out in the smart home framework. The constraint of IoT in smart home application stops where our creative mind stops. Anything that we wish to computerize or need to make our life more straightforward can be a piece of smart home, a smartphone framework too.

Presently, a smart home normally will be a base of a smart city. The smart city is a development of a smart home. Here, it isn't simply the sensors of a solitary home that is associated, here its relationship or an organization or an association between different associations, different spaces as well as various fragments of that city overall. In the smart city, the existence of each and every ward turns out to be more agreeable and in order truly help to foster that city to more noteworthy reaches out accordingly. Presently, the vital variable for a smart city is government support too, and in the event that the states will make this stride, we truly want to believe that we would see a smart city totally expand on the Web of Things.

Smart homes urban communities coordinate with the whole urban areas by making and controlling an organization.

Smart indoor regulators: Smart homes incorporate indoor regulators that are fit for detecting and controlling the temperature. This controls the stream.

Area-based smart gadgets: Smart gadgets can follow your area and quickly send messages to different gadgets to work. For instance, your smart indoor regulators can follow your area from a smart vehicle and switch on the ACs before you show up

Voice-empowered gadgets: These gadgets can decipher human voices and convert these into text that is deciphered by the machines. Machines then play out the fundamental errand. Models incorporate alexa and siri.

Smart security frameworks: Security frameworks that are made utilizing IOT use highlights like facial acknowledgment, iris scanners and other security modes.

Facial acknowledgment: This is one of the most moving purposes of the IoT. facial acknowledgment models track the highlights of the face, for example, the indeed, noses, jawline and lips to anticipate the result of the individual. In light of the exactness the machine is additionally prepared or sent for advancement.

Movement location: Like facial detainment yet here the sensors record the developments or changes on the environmental elements. These conduct changes are then shipped off the model for additional investigation.

Biometric access control: Biometrics have turned into the foundation of any association's security frameworks. They are not difficult to oversee and bother free. The representatives and the staff individuals basically record their thumb or iris impacts on appearance and the machine denotes their attendances. This model saves time and cost.

Smart Living Administrations: IoT devices are widely used in a variety of fields and activities that help educated residents improve their overall level of personal satisfaction. Social activities like savvy the travel industry are using mobile applications, GIS-empowered and area-based administrations, multimedia system, virtual reality &augmented reality, and web-based entertainment to manage and provide partners in the travel industry with a better experience. By following the behaviors and streams of customers, these applications can improve supportability, objective seriousness, and the traveler experience. With the inclusion of ICT and IoT components, education is experiencing a growing decentralization process. This makes it possible to develop new educational administrations that can improve collaboration in real-world and remote learning activities.

Transportation and Smart Mobility

Smart transportation and smart city traffic executives are altering the way that urban communities approach versatility and crisis reaction while lessening clog on city roads. How? With sensors, high-level correspondence advancements, computerization, and fast organization.

The workmanship and study of moving starting with one spot then onto the next is an intrinsic piece of our lives — today as well as over the entire course of time. From chariots and ponies to carriages, vehicles, steam trains and shuttle — being moving is a piece of being human.

Civilization has made considerable progress from riding ponies and camels to get from one spot to another. With the rise of astute transportation frameworks and the Internet of Things (IoT), the world is entering the following phase of development — smart transportation. Assuming the term sounds ambiguous or triggers mental pictures of independent cars with the capability to fly and hamster-like, high-velocity tubes, sit back and relax.

This article will spread out what precisely smart transportation is, the way it works, and a considerable lot of the advantages it carries alongside a few genuine models being used today. What's more, we'll likewise cover the various sorts of keen transportation frameworks being sent today.

Transportation demand management (TDM) is a critical part of the development of smart city techniques and smart portability all over the planet. The job of innovation is supposed to increment as ICTs keep on being coordinated in urban communities in clever ways. With the ascent of the sharing economy, new modes, and an assortment of application-based portability administrations, individuals have more options for getting around than at any other time. The test for organizers and enormous businesses is to advance productivity and assist workers with getting a handle on and utilizing these new decisions in protected, maintainable ways.

While smart mobility frequently depends on innovation, it is basic to create and execute insightful projects and strategies to help it.

In view of those factors, we should investigate a couple of arising ideas around smart mobility& smart transportation.

The advantages of smart innovation & the benefits they bring to transportation inside a smart city are various. Smart Transportation is

More Secure: By consolidating AI with IoT and 5G, independent transportation frameworks (both in vehicles and in fixed foundation like convergences) have demonstrated to decrease the "human variable" in mishaps. PCs don't get occupied or exhausted or close to home.

Well Managed: Information assortment is a significant key to mindful public administration of foundation. Smart transportation not just gives nitty gritty information focuses to each part of the transportation framework, yet permits chairmen to more readily screen activities, track upkeep needs, and recognize key causes of issues that should be fixed.

More Effective: With better administration comes more proficient use. Quality information can assist with pinpointing regions where productivity can be gotten to the next level. Perhaps a slight change in train timetables would accommodate better fill rates, or, maybe transport courses would better serve the local area in the event that stops were designated in an unexpected way.

Cost-Effective: In light of the fact that smart transportation utilizes the assets accessible, it can reduce down expenses thanks to precaution upkeep, lower energy utilization, and less assets utilized towards mishaps. Cost reserve funds can likewise be acquired by riders when economical public travel is adequately effective to rival private vehicle proprietorship.

Provides Rapid Insights: City traffic the executives' communities (TMCs) can get quick permeability and notices for pain points or extensive issues influencing clog on city roads, public well-being and crisis reaction frameworks, to make a move or impart all the more successfully with different organizations and crisis responders.

Smart Budget

Smart Budget is built on the advanced use of ICT to connect native and universal marketplaces, providing e-commerce & e-business amenities to improve delivery and throughput Kezai et al. (2020). This area also encompasses the idea of a distributing budget, wherein individuals' otherwise private businesses offer facilities by utilizing their individual belongings and trusty marketplaces. Peer-to-peer labour facilities, wherein citizens &shareholders offer their assistance and work for precise jobs, are another option Kumar (2017). Predictive models & recommendation systems intended for e-commerce & trade shopping have both been improved using AI and machine learning techniques Bellini et al. (2021). The payment & transaction procedures have been prepared stress-free by the use of wireless sensor technologies& NFC. Cash and bank cards are being replaced by smartphones and mobile phones in daily transactions and information access in Shenzen.

Smart Industry and Production

Smart industry & industry 4.0 characterize one change cycle wherein IoT advances, digital actual frameworks (CPS), M2M correspondence frameworks and cloud-based assembling Liu et al. (2018) permit a creative and less human-subordinate useful climate. As to mechanization of products supply chains, they can be handily followed from the assembling system to definite dispersion utilizing sensor advances, like RFID and NFC. Ongoing data can be gathered and dissected for shipment following, as well with respect to the evaluation of the quality and ease of use of items Sethi and Sarangi (2017). The shrewd business and creation space remembers every fields where ICT prompts the computerization of the useful work process, accordingly likewise incorporates brilliant horticulture and cultivating, which tends to the test of supportable food creation. Shrewd horticulture frameworks frequently utilize IoT gadgets to further develop water system effectiveness Lopes et al. (2020) and artificial intelligence arrangements are frequently sent in IoT devices towards farming that is towards crop observing, infection detection & facts driven harvest supply chain managing. For example, smart industry 4.0 has been utilized by Dublin Air terminal to substitute the baggage-handling methods in 2nd Terminal as per the Six Real World Examples of Digital Transformation report (2022).

Smart Power

Smart Power systems aim to reduce energy consumption by intelligently integrating and efficiently disseminating decentralized renewable and sustainable energy sources. For improved controlling of energy production & distribution, smart grids make use of ICT and Internet of Things (IoT) technologies, for instance prediction models made as of composed consumption data & frequently guaranteeing the self-restoration of the power grid supply by Shirazi, and Jadid (2019). Power distribution is made easier by smart grids that adjust for usage and availability. Now a days it is feasible to automatically change to unconventional energy sources, forecast future power demand, & estimate power availability and price in this manner.

For alternative energy harvesting, new direction of smart energy Internet of Things gadgets, such as electrostatic energy harvesters (EEH) &triboelectric nanogenerators(TENG), have been developed by Liu et al. (2021). In the context of smart energy, a variety of Internet of Things (IoT) sensors are involved, including LDRs(light dependent resistors), sensors for determining light beam luminosity, as well as the amount of sun radiation & energy used.

The advancement of smart energy administration has been done through scheduling the consumption of electricity in both residential and commercial locations by the country like Nice, France etc. By supplying and storing distributed electricity, a smart solar community in urban areas of Nice created the smart grid Silva et al. (2018). An intelligent lights system wherein each smart light device is geolocated within the town and driven by photometer sensors that observe the intensity of the beam emitted by the lamps and verify whether the bulbs are operating correctly is one of several intelligent energy management initiatives implemented by Padova city Zanella et al. (2014). A smart neighborhood project has been implemented in Atlanta to lower the Home Energy Rating System (HERS) score. Home appliances are managed by energy optimization platforms, which, when available, switch to solar energy and batteries. In Helsinki, smart grids aid in a 15% reduction in energy consumption Okai et al. (2018). Utilizing renewable energy technologies, the Masdar City development targeted to be one of the UAE's supreme eco-friendly & efficient systems. A solar powered array& rooftop solar panels capable of producing over 10 MW have been planned by the city. Together with technologies for harvesting wind energy, this can provide energy for approximately 40,000 people and this is mentioned by Sankaran, and Chopra (2020).

Smart Environment

Natural information gathering, observing and examination aimed at contamination decrease, water quality & supply observing, & climate & environmental events for executives are all part of the smart environment. As a result, monitoring air quality is an essential component for the subsequent stages of air poisons (for example CO2, NOx, N2O, PM2.5, O3, PM10, & so on), which address a challenging problem for human health affected by transport, climate change, & modern outflows. Smart waste the board is furthermore known for this zone because it takes different effects on the weather. Brilliant waste canisters equipped with sensors and equipped to provide ongoing investigation of the limit that is currently available are used to control waste production methods.

When evaluating the quantity and quality of smart water, detecting devices typically quantity parameters that is pH, turbidity, conductivity, total broken down solids, and so on. For the purpose of examining the water utilization rate, electromagnetic and ultrasonic sensors are used to calculate the strain. The utilization of WSNs for water sum and quality checking systems has opened up one more period of insightful water noticing structures, giving a further evolved setting care and near consistent participation.

Tech Savvy climate apps & services characteristically rely on outside & synthetic sensing devices to measure actual amounts that communicate ecological boundaries and conditions like temperature, stickiness, pressure, and a variety of poisons. Ozone depleting substance (GHG) discharges and land use are applications of brilliant detecting and representation advancements (satellites, LiDAR). Additionally, GIS data and area-based administrations are utilized.

The Coordinated Waste Administration Office (IWMF) in Singapore is in charge of managing solid waste. It uses innovative IoT technology to take into account increased process efficiency and decreased emissions of greenhouse gases. The Green City Watch is a geospatial man-made intelligence stage in Amsterdam that uses computer-based intelligence calculations and satellite images to screen urban green structures on an ongoing basis. Sunlight-based controlled waste containers have been introduced in Stockholm. These containers perform waste bundling and report after they are completely charged. The smart city of Busan in South Korea uses smart water the board structures throughout the metropolitan water cycle.

Smart Healthcare

In this current period of the Coronavirus pandemic, IoT advancements and omnipresent figuring have been extensively executed to flexible medical care for out-of-the-way observation, telemedicine & telenursing, opposing medication responses, local medical services, and so on. Wearable or embedded devices (such as cardiovascular devices, airflow observation, blood glucometers, and so on) which are connected to the cloud using WSN advancements can be applied for monitoring remotely. wireless body area networks (WBANs) or Body sensor networks have developed as a result. These organizations coordinate a variety of heterogeneous information sources to safeguard patients' biometric & physiological facts towards IoT medical care submissions. The recognizable proof and checking of patients in emergency clinics and the savvy the board of clinical instruments supporting dynamic cycles in clinics are two examples of the kinds of assistance that brilliant clinics rely on IoT advancements to provide for patients & clinical staff .High Level Seven (HL7), PACS-DICOM in biomedical picture handling, and others are examples of obvious guidelines that are mandated by these application fields and the requirements that are associated with them. Artificial intelligence (AI) predictions and the estimation of biometric boundaries or side effects from sight and sound (using portable recordings or voice messages, through profound learning-and discourse acknowledgment based techniques) have recently been proposed as examples of creative applications.

The Health Hub stage, which includes executive health records and clinical information about patients and residents, has been supported by Singapore. The New Karolinska Solna Clinic in Stockholm utilized client-centered services for patients, guests, and clinical staff by coordinating savvy energy and BIM advancements. The emergency clinic in Hefei, China, is one of the earliest smart clinics in China. It provides tech savvy structure administrations and practical energy to the board in addition to monitoring all of the patients through IoT and the associated medical care. During the Coronavirus pandemic, the Helsinki College Medical Clinic used a constant finding framework (RTLS) to collect &distribute anonymized area information about on-location developments for area monitoring. Additionally, cloud administrations are made available to enable medical professionals and caregivers to communicate remotely with Coronavirus patients.

VULNERABLE COMPLICATIONS FOR IOT-EMPOWERED SMART CITIES

As populace expansion and metropolitan focus speed up, different issues, for example, traffic jamming, energy and asset depletion, and so on are showing up everywhere, and nations are attempting to take care of these issues by utilizing IoT-empowered brilliant city. In light of our experience and examination in the past areas, obviously brilliant city advancements can be a promising arrangement. In any case, obviously brilliant city advancements are unfinished nevertheless have numerous issues that should be survived. For instance, interoperability issues because of the shortfall of worldwide guidelines, various understandings of savvy urban communities, and openness of individual data are central point that block the supportability of brilliant urban communities. Previously, the creators of this paper have amassed many encounters on brilliant urban areas through the improvement of savvy city administrations and stages in light of worldwide IoT norms. In view of these encounters and the examination led in this paper, different difficulties to be overwhelmed by brilliant urban communities are inferred.

As a prerequisite towards the success of IoT-enabled Smart Cities, we offer a point of view on the challenges which is presently being addressed in the following paragraphs.

Sort Out of Application Silos

Most current smart city projects was industrialized in silos, frequently with robust combination between applications &fundamental data resources, especially sensing devices. Because of this, it is difficult to share and reuse information because each application must be overtly unified with each available information source & every transformation in technology, such as the underlying sensing equipment or inter-communication network, necessitates a technology adaptation.

However, a true value of Internet of Things will only be comprehended when additional info turns out to be accessible & can be pooled between applications &implementation domains. Deploying a real Internet of Things infrastructure for an application is often difficult enough, although the same is unrealistic to set up the similar or a comparable setup for each subsequent application. Collaborations can be created when infrastructure is shared, and sometimes infrastructure deployment is only possible when infrastructure is shared. It is necessary to decouple applications and information sources in order to accomplish this.

This can be accomplished technically by utilizing an Internet of Things podium& the contract on least interactiveness mechanisms, such as the OASC (Open Agile Smart Cities) city network's definition. Administrative and organizational aspects are at least as crucial as the technical aspects in overcoming application silos. Applications are frequently considered to be "possessed" by metropolitan subdivisions or administrations, who have paid for the infrastructure and wish to maintain control. Additionally, financial plan is frequently allocated in a rigid manner, creating distribution challenging. As a result, attaining a global understanding, establishing high-level goals, such as those for the entire city, & working to achieve these goals crossways administrative units—recurrently disabling individual rivalries—are crucial.

Go Forward in the Direction of Flexible IoT Frameworks

At the moment, every smart city looks different in terms of the infrastructure that is in place, the applications that are available, and frequently also the IoT platforms that are used. This hinders the expansion of a smart city market &makes it challenging to re-claim whatever thing established for one city in another. Furthermore, developing individualized platforms for each city is not financially feasible.

Many merchants have begun offering Inter of Things infrastructures for smart cities, characteristically based on whatever has been established for a pilot city, as described above. As a result, these platforms are frequently unsuitable for other metropolises, and metropolises are also concerned about merchant lockin, or being tied to a single vendor for all future infrastructure and application enhancements because everything must be tailored to the vendor's platform. Modular infrastructures based on standards, such as oneM2M, and OMA Lightweight M2M, NGSI-LD should be the direction of travel.

The interfaces and information modeling that OASC defines as the minimum interoperability mechanisms must be agreed upon. Furthermore, common open-source components, such as those offered by FIWARE, can be used as a foundation to cut costs. Complementing these are proprietary vendor components. However, vendor lock-in is prevented by using standards at the interface level.

Conception of Business Opportunities

Digital revolution is introducing novel openings in addition to the escalation of the metropolitan amenities which have usually been presented to its inhabitants (movement, lights, water supply, waste supervision, etc.), whereas the smart city notion is characteristically supervised by city administrators to implement sustainability and efficiency. The smart city must be endorsed like a state in which fresh commercial models are developed based on sharing of information& services. Cities, for instance, are evolving into the sharing economy's playground. The speedy, geographical position-based interchange of facilities& products between citizens, between businesses, and between B2C is made easier by the attentiveness of financial movements & the widespread availability of expertise in cities.

Applying information as the new key upright for dealing in the afresh generated digital markets, innovative commercial notions like the Commons Collaborative Economy will be able to:

(1) Favor shared relations - rather than the customarily various leveled order and legally binding connections.
(2) Settle new worth appropriation and administration among the local area of friends where benefit isn't its primary/extraordinary main thrust.
(3) Utilize a public infrastructure that is sensitive to privacy, resulting in the (usually) exposed supply of corporate capitals that favor right of entry, reproducibility, &imitativeness.

In any case, distribution of data isn't trifling, particularly on the off chance that it isn't anticipated in existing agreements. Subsequently, it is vital to make mindfulness and consider this angle while setting up agreements, particularly while rethinking exercises. The adaptation of data ought to become conceivable, nonetheless, there is in many cases a disparity between the assumption and genuine worth of data. Adaptation must be connected with genuine worth, e.g., likewise as it is the situation for publicizing on the web, where the utilization is estimated and financial worth is straightforwardly connected with it.

Work Towards IoT Platforms and Applications for Multiple Players and Organizations

Cities are not solitary islets; rather, they frequently border other cities and are a part of districts, counties, regions, and nations. It is essential for many applications to continue working within city limits. Because citizens may live in one city, work in another, and spend their leisure time in a third, it is unacceptable for them to require different applications or to rework their applications when they cross a city boundary. For instance, there ought to be a single application that, regardless of where they are at the moment, can assist them in finding a parking spot by taking into account traffic.

This necessitates the interoperability of IoT platforms, which can be accomplished by federating IoT platforms, making information available to this federation in part. For instance, united IoT stage structures are expressly upheld in the NGSI-LD determination. Since there are multiple players involved and the federated system needs to function across organizations, it is necessary to clarify responsibilities and allocate budgets, so technically, such a setup is possible. However, administrative and organizational issues still need to be resolved.

Information and application marketplaces can be established using federated IoT platform infrastructures that make information sharing possible. Applications can be offered for sale by businesses, and while basic data may be available for free, premium data may be available for a fee.

Attain Transparency and Recognition

While the smart metropolitan networks perspective has been, for quite a while, shaped by bargains pitches of greater development merchants and system integrators, for this vision of self-practicality and occupant's very own fulfilment improvement to transform into a reality, it is essential to leave early "smart city 1.0" models like Masdar or Songdo (with development or advancing driven approach as opposed to keeping an eye on useful and occupant prerequisites) as well as to grow the pool of organizations maintained by not simply taking the perspective of the city subject matter experts, yet what's more license watching out for the specific necessities of the inhabitants.

In this sense, whether or not there are basic social differentiations all over the planet, it means quite a bit to set up parts to voice the occupant's viewpoint in the continuous conversation about IoT instrumentation. For splendid city organizations to have the choice to truly affect occupants, and be a lot of seen by all of the accomplices and performers drew in with metropolitan networks' confounding natural frameworks, inhabitants ought to be empowered with the assets to have a central impact in the creation and plan of such organizations.

The co-creation thought addresses the participatory progression of usages and organizations helpfully between a couple of accomplices. For this present circumstance to be engaged, stages supporting splendid metropolitan networks need to give a combination of normal instruments and enabling impacts that grant the specific and improvement of creative applications. Additionally, it means quite a bit to counter the perspective on loss of safety to develop the stage to be dealt with by anyway numerous city assets as could be anticipated in light of the current situation, and the information that they make.

Another vital piece of the co-creation thought is its capacity to attract heterogeneous accomplices in aiding clever city potential. Subsequently, shrewd city stages need to give engaging specialists connected with the rousing powers and remunerations of participating eventually practicality of the whole stage and sharp city organic framework. In this sense, it is at this point critical to encourage a security-by-plan approach extending the straightforwardness of all the IoT asset organization stream moving from the progressing perspective of discrete bound together trusted in experts to a perspective of liquid and decentralized trust of the association overall. This moving responses the providers' prerequisites and to the buyers' solicitations. The first since they are reluctant to share a datasets due to weakness of how and for what purposes the data is used. The last since they require comfort of the data's quality.

Reconciliation on Future Organizations and Novel Figuring Ideal Models

By means of additional Smart metropolitan organizations are completed, the amount of contraptions related with & chipped away at the association is rising emphatically. Likewise, through the presentation of 5th Generation organization innovation, different administrations like brilliant urban communities, savvy industrial facilities, and shrewd vehicles are being created. Such different IoT administrations should uphold necessities, for example, high data transfer capacity and super low dormancy.

Distributed computing strategies offered by customary support suppliers, however, must go through a focal IoT stage to handle different information produced by the gadgets. This has prompted a fast expansion in the backhaul information traffic, unavoidably dialing back administration speeds. To deal with this issue, expansive investigation is actuality driven converging in on usage of verge enrolling development to decrease networking load achieved by traffic flow upsurge & to help the organizations which is IoT driven from a to some degree tiny distance, consequently, empowering the provisioning of really low inactivity organizations.

Aimed at instance, correspondence normalization associations, for example, 3GPP and ETSI, as well as IoT normalization associations, for example, oneM2M recognize the significance of edge registering normalization, helping out different foundations to foster guidelines what's more, improve similarity. The versatile-access Edge Processing Industry Particular Bunch (MEC-ISG), a gathering in ETSI, is chipping away at using multi-access in edge processing & empowering similarity through guidelines for networking segmentation given by the 3GPP center organization. Notwithstanding the virtualization of the organization, virtualization &edge registering of IoT stage highlights are being directed: Single edge hub would be capable to have a 3GPP organization, ETSI MEC edge registering, and super low inertness IoT administration stage includes powerfully to help different administrations.

Protection Guidelines on Data in Various Nations

Since a smart city accumulates &employs monstrous proportions of statistics, that undeniably harbours the possible meant for individual data breach. For instance, sensing equipment on internet of things-based devices may be used to accumulate facts as of inside the home. Sensing devices in within a smart vehicle may similarly be cast-off to see the driving penchants for the driver. Doing data mining methodology on which evidence can provoke the ID of explicit folks. Accordingly, state run administrations are areas of strength for sanctioning on the security of individual data to efficiently safeguard individual data and keep data collecting specialist co-ops from mishandling it.

For instance, Europe established GDPR to control individual data assurance and use. GDPR conscientiously characterizes the privileges and commitments of individual data holders and processors, accordingly reinforcing the obligations of organizations that gather and oversee information. As this regulation applies to all frameworks taking care of information, information based shrewd urban areas should normally consent to it.

Stipulations of the GDPR underwrite consent Badii et al. (2020), precise to be dismissed, pseudonymization, amid others. These assertions ought to be reproduced as system essentials &embedded into stage features, consequently such circumstances can be used inside a splendid urban city stage. Doing so can enable different smart town organizations to deal with individual material in a method predictable through GDPR. For instance, assent the board as characterized by GDPR expects that individual data should be handled in view of the assent of the information proprietor. Nonetheless, existing savvy city information stages don't give an element that processes information proprietor assent. For this, the entrance approval element of the current stages ought to be extended to carry out the capability of deliberately getting client assent and arranging such information inside tech savvy metropolitan framework.

CONCLUSION

By means of should be visible starting the models portrayed, plenty of canny metropolitan services & administrations seemed created. A considerable lot of them are at a proof-of-idea level, yet all the same more also, additional have proactively accepted the pilot stage & have formed interested in creation level arrangements. This indicates that the base arrangement of innovation empowering agents being now accessible also, is being conveyed in urban areas & coordinated with certifiable public administrations.

Nonetheless, frequently this type of administrations is being created & conveyed in implementation silos, restricting a worth of data that remain gathered as re-use and it is challenging to portion of this data. The utilization of IoT stages empowers such information openness and trade, yet the utilization of exclusive stages that have been grown separately and in a confined way by enormous organizations brings about additional limitations as arrangements can't be imitated across urban communities depending on an alternate restrictive stage. As applications can't be re-utilized, they must be worked without any preparation or be adjusted to an alternate stage, making improvements costly.

As we have depicted, there are critical advances on the specialized side that make savvy urban communities possible. In any case, there are a few mechanical difficulties to survive, chiefly connected with ensuring the vital versatility on information and organizations to help mission critical administrations (e.g., crisis reaction, basic foundations continuous checking and the board, and so on.). Reconciliation of novel registering standards like mist processing furthermore, 5G and past organizations in IoT situations divulges a promising way to address such application situation. Be that as it may, the greatest difficulties might be on managerial & hierarchical verges. A tech savvy city arrangements frequently call for participation amid various offices or even various associations. This might expect spending plans to be corrected, as there is the requirement for introductory ventures. These might be fundamentally counterbalanced by investment funds at a future point, however not really somewhere the underlying ventures was made.

In addition, mechanical as well as public organizations impulsion can't, all alone, untap the complete worth of tech-savvy metropolitan worldview. Doubtlessly, it can start the progress &resolve the origins for every one of the partners & entertainers engaged with metropolitan conditions (e.g., residents, organizations, associations, guests, and so on) to turn out to be effectively taken part in the brilliant city, not just as shoppers of administrations or information that others give, yet in addition as makers of significant data that would present new administrations, in this way adding to an idealistic series with unpredictable advantages. In any case, intended for this visualization to transform into a authenticity, its essential to manage hardships of data safety & self-power thus data creators are sure that the data produced by them is applied for those, & simply the explanations behind that it was distributed, & they are furthermore reasonably and modestly made up for the value where their information has delivered.

At long last, there is much of the time protection from change, particularly in the event that it doesn't carry prompt advantages to the people who need to adjust. Constructing the metropolitan smart will prompt alters in the manner the metropolitan works. In the event that new bits of knowledge are acquired, moves might need to be made subsequently. These must be ready and it requires purchase in from every one of the gatherings in question. In any case, shrewd urban areas over the long haul will give huge advantages as their activity turns out to be more effective and the personal satisfaction of their residents gets to the next level. Consequently, it is advantageous to deal with conquering the impediments, on the specialized as well as the managerial and hierarchical side.

REFERENCES

Badii, C., Bellini, P., Difino, A., & Nesi, P. (2018). Sii-mobility: An IoT/IoE architecture to enhance smart city mobility and transportation services. *Sensors (Basel), 19*(1), 1. doi:10.339019010001 PMID:30577434

Badii, C., Bellini, P., Difino, A., & Nesi, P. (2020). *Smart City IoT Platform Respecting GDPR Privacy and Security Aspects*. IEEE.

Barcevicius, E.; Cibaite, G.; Codagnone, G.; Gineikyte, V.; Klimaviciute, L.; Liva, G.; Matulevic, L.; Misuraca, G.; Vanini, I. (2019). *Exploring Digital Government transformation in the EU*. Publications Office of the European Union: Luxembourg.

Bauer, M., Sanchez, L., & Song, J. S. (2021). IoT-enabled smart cities: Evolution and outlook. *Sensors (Basel), 21*(13), 4511. doi:10.339021134511 PMID:34209436

Ejaz, W., & Anpalagan, A. (2019). *Internet of Things for Smart Cities: Technologies, Big Data, and Security*. Springer. doi:10.1007/978-3-319-95037-2

Fizza, K., Banerjee, A., Mitra, K., Jayaraman, P. P., Ranjan, R., Patel, P., & Georgakopoulos, D. (2021). QoE in IoT: A vision, survey and future directions. *Discov. Internet Things, 1*(1), 4. doi:10.100743926-021-00006-7

Hussain, M. W., Pradhan, B., Gao, X. Z., Reddy, K. H. K., & Roy, D. S. (2020). Clonal selection algorithm for energy minimization in software defined networks. *Applied Soft Computing, 96*, 106617. doi:10.1016/j.asoc.2020.106617

Hussain, M. W., & Roy, D. S. (2023). Performance Optimization Strategies for Big Data Applications in Distributed Framework. In: Dash, S.R., Das, H., Li, KC., Tello, E.V. (eds) Intelligent Technologies: Concepts, Applications, and Future Directions. Springer, Singapore. doi:10.1007/978-981-99-1482-1_10

Janani, R. P., Renuka, K., Aruna, A., & Lakshmi Narayanan, K. (2021). IoT in smart cities: A contemporary survey. *Global Transitions Proceedings, 2*(2), 187–193. doi:10.1016/j.gltp.2021.08.069

Kezai, P. K., Fischer, S., & Lados, M. (2020). Smart economy and startup enterprises in the Visegrád Countries—A comparative analysis based on the Crunchbase Database. *Smart Cities, 3*(4), 70. doi:10.3390martcities3040070

Kumar, T. M. V. (2017). *Smart Economy in Smart Cities: International Collaborative Research*. Springer

Liu, L., Guo, X., & Lee, C. (2021). Promoting smart cities into the 5G era with multi-field Internet of Things (IoT) applications powered with advanced mechanical energy harvesters. *Nano Energy, 88*, 106304. doi:10.1016/j.nanoen.2021.106304

Liu, Y. Y., Hung, M. H., Lin, Y. C., Chen, C. C., Gao, W. L., & Cheng, F. T. (2018). A Cloud-based pluggable manufacturing service scheme for smart factory. In *Proceedings of the 14th IEEE International Conference on Automation Science and Engineering (CASE)*. IEEE. 10.1109/COASE.2018.8560401

Lombardi, M., Pascale, F., & Santaniello, D. (2021). Internet of Things: A general overview between architectures, protocols and applications. *Information (Basel), 12*(2), 87. doi:10.3390/info12020087

Lopes, S. F., Pereira, R. M., Lopes, S. O., Coutinho, M., Malheiro, A., & Fonte, V. (2020). Yet a smarter irrigation system. *Lect. Notes Inst. Comput. Sci. Soc. Inform. Telecommun. Eng. LNICST*, *323*, 337–346.

Okai, E., Feng, X., & Sant, P. (2018). Smart cities survey. In *Proceedings of the IEEE 20th International Conference on High Performance Computing and Communications and IEEE 16th International Conference on Smart City*. IEEE.

Pradhan, B., Hussain, M. W., Srivastava, G., Debbarma, M. K., Barik, R. K., & Lin, J. C. W. (2022). A neuro-evolutionary approach for software defined wireless network traffic classification. *IET Communications*, cmu2.12548. doi:10.1049/cmu2.12548

Sankaran, V., & Chopra, A. (2020). Creating global sustainable smart cities (a case study of Masdar City). *Journal of Physics: Conference Series*, *1706*(1), 012141. doi:10.1088/1742-6596/1706/1/012141

Sethi, P., & Sarangi, S. R. (2017). Internet of Things: Architectures, protocols, and applications. *Journal of Electrical and Computer Engineering*, *2017*, 9324035. doi:10.1155/2017/9324035

Shi, Q., Zhang, Z., He, T., Sun, Z., Wang, B., Feng, Y., Shan, X., Salam, B., & Lee, C. (2020). Deep learning enabled smart mats as a scalable floor monitoring system. *Nature Communications*, *11*(1), 4609. doi:10.103841467-020-18471-z PMID:32929087

Shirazi, E., & Jadid, S. (2019). Autonomous self-healing in smart distribution grids using multi agent systems. *IEEE Transactions on Industrial Informatics*, *15*(12), 6291–6301. doi:10.1109/TII.2018.2889741

Silva, B. N., Khan, M., & Han, K. (2018). Towards sustainable smart cities: A review of trends, architectures, components, and open challenges in smart cities. *Sustainable Cities and Society*, *38*, 697–713. doi:10.1016/j.scs.2018.01.053

Smart Industry. (2022). *Six Real World Examples of Digital Transformation*. Smart Identity. https://www.smartindustry.com/blog/smart-industry-connect/six-real-world-examples-of-digital-transformation/ (accessed on 17 January 2022).

Tang, S., Shelden, D. R., Eastman, C. M., Pishdad-Bozorghi, P., & Gao, X. (2019). A review of building information modeling (BIM) and the internet of things (IoT) devices integration: Present status and future trends. *Automation in Construction*, *10*, 127–139. doi:10.1016/j.autcon.2019.01.020

Zanella, A., Bui, N., Castellani, A., Vangelista, N., & Zorzi, M. (2014). Internet of Things for smart cities. *IEEE Internet of Things Journal*, *1*(1), 22–32. doi:10.1109/JIOT.2014.2306328

Chapter 2
Digital Twin-Enabled Solutions for Smart City Applications

Samaya Venkatesh Pillai
Symbiosis Institute of Digital and Telecom Management, India

Pradnya Purandare
Symbiosis Centre for Information Technology, Symbiosis International University (Deemed), India

Rajashree Jain
Symbiosis Institute of Computer Studies and Research, Symbiosis International University (Deemed), India

ABSTRACT

The current advent of new technological advancements like the internet of things, artificial intelligence, and big data have not only ventured in applications management like regular transactional systems but also large applications like managing cities. The main objective of a "smart city" is the improvement in the living conditions of the people of all strata in the city. The city ideally should provide technological, innovative, and sustainable solutions by utilizing the resources. The smart city concept is providing a higher quality of life (QoL) for all its citizens. The areas which are mainly covered in the purview of smart city are governance, efficient mobility and public transport facility, healthcare facility, affordable housing for all citizens, digitization, and robust IT connectivity; along with focus on good sanitization, sufficient water supply, solid waste management, and electricity supply. In this chapter, the authors investigate the possibility and feasibility of the concept of digital twin in the applications of smart city.

INTRODUCTION

An urban place is an experimental, application ground for emerging technologies Internet of Things, Artificial Intelligence, Big Data expanded beyond traditional transactional systems management to find uses in urban management applications. A smart city provides innovative and sustainable technological solutions by using available resources.

DOI: 10.4018/979-8-3693-0744-1.ch002

Smart city focusses on governance, efficient mobility, public transport facility, healthcare facility, affordable housing for all citizens, digitization and robust IT connectivity with focus on good sanitization, sufficient water supply, solid waste management, electricity supply etc.

A Digital Twin is an interface of the virtual and physical system. It can help to manage the complex system of smart city. It can simulate, predict and provide numerous insights for short term and long-term management of a smart city. In this article, the authors investigate the use of digital twin in smart city. The chapter defines "digital twins", smart city and the need of digital twin. In the flow of the chapter, the authors discuss the implementation of digital twin in the applications of Smart city, the tools used during this implementation. And finally, there is an attempt to point out some open issues for future research.

More than 65 percent of the population these days reside in urban spaces and it is expected that every 7 out of 10 would live in cities by 2050. Considering the increase in the exodus of people coming to cities, city resources need to be managed efficiently and effectively. Catering to these ever-exploding needs of cities, cities are becoming smart cities. The term "smart city" originates back in the 1990s (Van Bastelaer, B. 1998). It is an urban place, which makes the best use of current upcoming-technology, information and raw data to improve upon a number of factors. The factors can be access to resources, efficient management of resources like water, electricity, shelter, education, healthcare etc. It is therefore of interest to all stakeholders like Citizens communities, industries and governments.

The success of implementation of technology solutions in a smart city development relies on understanding of city dynamics, spatially as well as temporally. The ability to understand this dynamism is very essential to understand the interdependence considering the smart city as a connected place and a system of systems. Considering the dynamism in the systems, smart digital twin concept can be used for observing cities' infrastructure, technology and human interface. A digital twin, enabled with virtualization and connectivity, for a city becomes smarter to propose preventive, prescriptive and predictive insights into the city's development and growth. (Papyshev, Gleb & Yarime, Masaru. (2021))

As more and more cities are featuring in the list of smart cities, Gartner Top Strategic Technology Trends 2023 suggests digital twins in combination with web3 and spatial computing under metaverse may become responsible for increasing the revenue of a number of organizations. (2023 Gartner Top Strategic Technology Trends: Detailed Guide (eBook), n.d.-b)

The present chapter explores the concept of digital twin in a networked world connected with sensors and intelligent hardware and software. The study area chosen is a smart city. The application areas within the smart city are water management, asset and civil infrastructure management.

The chapter is organized in five sections. Section II brings details about a Digital Twin and various parameters that involve defining the term. Section III lists down applications of Digital Twin in a smart City. Section IV describes the two case studies in the smart city as mentioned above. Section V provides concluding remarks along with open research areas for future.

DIGITAL TWINS

This section aims at one of the study objectives of "Network enabled Internet of Things(IOT) based applications facilitated by a Digital Twin (DT)". Hence the aim of this section is to explore how and where Digital Twin and its applications are facilitated by network based IOT. It also discusses IoT, data analytics, and digital twin applications, problems, links, and supporting technologies. (Fuller, A., et. al. 2020).

A number of definitions for the term DT are available in the literature. Some of them are given in the following section. The differences in defining the term DT shows diverse perspectives about its usage in the industry. Basically DT is an integration of data amongst physical and virtual machines. Figure 1 describes a digital twin mirroring a physical object through tis life cycle. The virtual model alias the digital twin can provide capabilities of learning for future while providing simulations at run time.

Figure 1. Digital twin components

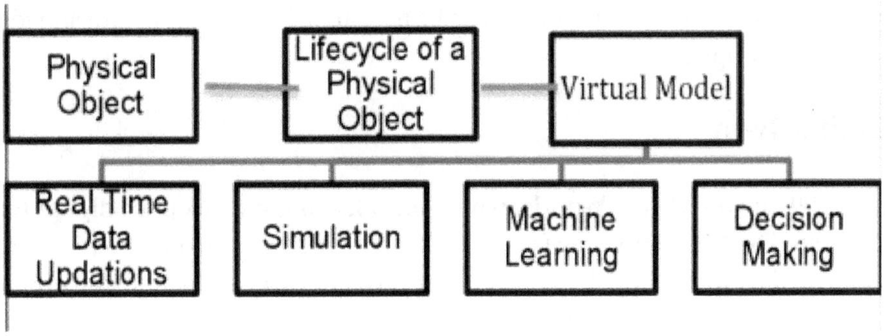

IBM defines Digital Twin as a virtual model of a physical object. The design is an accurate model of the physical object. The model spans over the entire life cycle of the physical object. It mirrors its life-cycle. The real time data helps it to get updates. Simulation, machine learning and reasoning helps a DT in managing the physical object and execute decision making related to the physical object." (IBM, 2023)

According to Gartner, DT is a digital representation of system, which exists in the real world. In other words, a digital object or a model that is a replica of a particular physical thing, process, organization, person, or other abstraction is identified and termed as its DT. Garner report also mentions that data from various digital twins can be used for a combined representation. For example, processes of power plant or a city and its associated processes can be combined in viewed in composition. (Gartner, January 2023.)

According to Amazon, it's a digital replica created to faithfully represent the real thing. (Amazon, January 2023)

In another definition by digital twin consortium, a DT is considered as a virtual representation of people, places, and things. A DT needs to be mapped and configured for a certain level of accuracy and range of frequencies of their respective physical objects. DTs support improve business by a holistic understanding of the real system. Therefore ideal for decision-making and efficient execution. Digital twins portray the past, present, and simulate predicted futures using historical and current data. They are deployed in a number of systems. DTs are driven by the outcome, guided based on domain knowledge, based on data, have found number of use cases. (Digitaltwinconsortium, January 2023)

The research study's authors present the results of a study that looked at the most recent definitions of DT, considered the essential qualities a DT should possess, studied the fields where DT applications are currently being developed, and studied the key qualities a DT should have. The study's design implications are then discussed, concentrating on DT lifespan and socio-technical design elements. (Barricelli et al., 2019)

A digital twin consists of three elements:

- The actual- real physical system – in real time environment,
- The virtual system – in digital or virtual environment, and
- The data that connects or bridges these two systems.

Examples include a digital twin of an airplane that can be used to monitor its performance and identify potential issues. Another example can be a digital twin of a bridge, power plant or historical buildings that can be used to monitor their performance and identify potential issues related to wear and tear of the structure. A digital twin of a vehicle-car can be used to monitor its performance and identify potential issues and a digital twin of an individual-person can be used to monitor their health and identify potential issues are a few more examples.

History of Digital Twin

David Gelernter's 1991 novel Mirror Worlds, which introduced the concept of digital twin technology, was the first to do so. Dr. Michael Grieves, University of Michigan Professor pioneered digital twin concept in software and using it to apply the concept of digital twins to manufacturing for the first time in 2002 (IBM 2023), (Wikipedia 2023), (Global 2023).

Professor Grieves spoke about the concept of DT during his one the session at University of Michigan in the year 2003. It was in the eyar 2010, John Vickers from NASA coined the term DT. He addressed the problems like sustaining the health of spacecraft- utilizing the idea of digital twins. (Rathore, M. M. U. et al., 2021)

In fact, it is more precise to mention that it was NASA, which the first most organizations to use digital twin as technique in space investigation tasks. Spacecraft was specifically imitated, simulated for the earthbound version during nineteen sixty, the NASA personnel serving on flight crews used for these digital replicas or digital twins for study and simulation purposes (Cantena, 2023).

Application Areas for Digital Twins

Over the past 20 years, DT has been propelled forward by ongoing advancements in technologies including artificial intelligence (AI), big data, machine learning (ML), cloud computing, high dimensional data coding, sensor technologies, and the internet of things (IoT) (Pradhan et al, 2022); (Hussain, et al, 2021). As a result, various DTs have been developed and are currently in use across a variety of sectors, including manufacturing, systems engineering, the aerospace industry, robotics, healthcare, and medicine. (Barricelli et al., 2019).

There have been a number of applications of Digital Twins with IOT. Application of Digital Twin with IOT has been found in a research paper based on thorough review especially in the domains of manufacturing, healthcare and smart cities (Fuller, A., et. al. 2020).

Industry 4.0 can be enabled with IOT and other technologies. Digital Twin is a forerunner of Industry 4.0. IOT allows an increase in the data usage in manufacturing, healthcare, and smart city environment applications supported by Digital Twin. IOT based data can support predictive maintenance and fault detection, business process health monitoring, in manufacturing and smart city applications (Bilberg A., et. al. 2019).

One of the issues of smooth data integration among IoT devices in a network can be managed well by Digital Twin via creating network enabled connected physical and virtual twins.

IoT devices are cheaper in cost as well as easy to implement which allows better connectivity and usage of IoT devices that can be used in Digital Twin (Joordens, M., et. al 2018), (Liu, Y., et al 2019).

This increase in connectivity of network enabled IoT devices will increase the Usage of Digital Twin in healthcare applications too (Gahlot, S., et. al. 2019).

Harvesting of IoT based data through role based user interface to yield data insights o users with data analytics by developing a smooth environment for Digital Twin.This is an example of a Digital Twin with AI technology IoT enabled platform called "ThinkWrox" (Chen, X., et. al. 2018).

IBM's Watson IoT platform features are real time data collections, cloud-based services, edge computing, analytics, blockchain usage etc. from unlimited IoT devices. These all IoT features help in Digital Twin.

Digital twin technology creates new opportunities for the economical and successful development of sustainable electric vehicle technologies, from conception to operation. But in order to make these vehicles popular, it is essential to have the supporting architecture. This supporting-architecture optimizes the vehicle's sustainability. Digital Twin technique is a virtual mapping technique that stems from this new architecture and is capable of investigating the lifespan of multisystem bodies in a digital environment inquiry. The research of digital twin technologies has recently become important worldwide. Thus, fresh individual studies on the use of digital twins to various smart vehicle features have surfaced in academic and industry studies, leading to the advancement of digital twin technology over time. (Bhatti et al., 2021)

The use of DIGITAL TWIN applications is becoming more prevalent across a variety of industries, and when it is combined with enabling emergent technologies it becomes lethal. Technologies like big data, ML, advanced modeling, advanced simulation, AR,VR, XR and few of the innovative progressive communication mediums, to help give better understandings about the operation of its real identical kind which the designer or operator can use to take appropriate action. The main benefit of DIGITAL TWINs in several fields is the insight that results in data-driven decision making.

Core services in a Smart City will have increased data collected from IoT sensors and emergent technologies like AI algorithms too. More Smart Cities developments will have well connected communities. Hence this requires usage of Digital Twin drastically (Mohammadi, N.,et.a. 2017), (Sivalingam, K., et. al 2018), (Pargmann, H., et. al. 2018)

All Smart city services and IT Infrastructure will have sensors, and these sensors as well as data requires to be monitored by IoT devices continuously for security as well as performing core processes. IoT devices will do future proofing of infrastructure and services based on Digital Twins. IOT enables networking and Digital twins for a smart city will be covered in more details in Section III.

Challenges With Digital Twins

Digital Twin challenges include infrastructure, usefulness and insights of data, privacy, security, trust, standardized modeling, domain modeling etc.

1) IT infrastructure
2) Quality of Data
3) Privacy and Security
4) Trust (Fuller et al., 2020)

Data, privacy, security, trust issues with respect to Digital twin and IoT are always discussed upon for various reasons such as quality of data, data privacy and security, compliance related parameters.

Digital Twin and network enabled IoT shares some common challenges such as huge amounts of data collection, data flow control, effective usage of this data, to be able to create meaningful data insights. More issues arise when the data is defined as Big data and unstructured data also pose challenges (Ashu et al., 2021). Cyber risk of attacks on IoT devices and data is a concern for Digital Twin.

Infrastructure requirements considering the short shelf life of both hardware and software products and services always poses a challenge to keep it up to date. One more challenge is to upgrade old systems in the network as per latest IoT devices by ensuring no damage to the data.(Botín-Sanabria,2022)

Other challenges with network enabled IoT devices are connectivity, expectations of performance.

SinceDT technology is still in its infancy, overcoming significant obstacles that face a contemporary DT application, like charges, data intricacy, upkeep, unavailability of compliances templates checklists governance rules, complications with cyber security and networking communications, will be necessary for it to realize its full potential.

Functioning of Digital Twins

Products' behavior in the actual world and the development process can be predicted, observed, diagnosed, and regulated using a DT. Objective of the product digital twin is its ability to trigger, configure and record, observe, analyze, predict, and coordinate the behavior of physical processes or objects in the real world. World. The tasks performed by the digital twin can be classified as follows:

a) Simulation
b) Monitoring and diagnosis
c) Prediction
d) Control

Characteristics of Digital Twin

Any physical entity such as process, object or an individual can have one or more "digital twins" that are (physical and/or virtual) machines. These are computer-based models used to mimic the real world counterpart. Through a special key, each DT is connected to its physical twin, identifying the physical twin and enabling the establishment of an objective relationship between the DT and its twin.

A Cyber-Physical System, often known as a set of physical elements (such as machines, products, equipment, or people), can include a DT. This system interacts with a virtual Mirror image in cyberspace over a communication network. Thus, every physical object /thing having a cyber-counterpart, functions as its digital twin also reflected as DT.

The major characteristics of digital twins are as discussed below.

DT enables seamless communication between the physical and its virtual counterpart. This has become possible with the help of developments in the areas of IOT and ICT. It also enables connectivity between organizations, products and customers. (Jiang, Zongmin.et. al, 2021).

To ensure a seamless connection, networking communication devices must be used to connect both the physical and digital twins. This connection is the medium through which the continuous data exchange occurs. Either the connectivity enables the digital twin to directly communicate to it physical counterpart or indirectly through the cloud-based systems.(Hu, W.,2021)

The DT continuously collects dynamic environment data—which describes the status of the surrounding environment and varies over time as it moves through its lifecycle—and dynamic physical twin data thanks to the seamless connection. Additionally, it continuously transmits predictions and recommendations for system upkeep and function optimization to its physical counterpart, the pertinent experts, and other nearby DTs. Three primary categories of communication processes exist. Designing communication procedures primarily involves three categories: 1) between the actual twin and its digital counterpart. 2) Between the DT and other DTS in its local vicinity or area.3) through usable and accessible interfaces, between the DT and subject specialists who engage with and use the DT.

With the help of a DT any type of information can now be stored in digital format making it homogeneity.

A virtual system in the digital format enables de coupling of its physical source. (Tilson et. al., 2010).

Modularization, Reprogrammable and digital trace are also major characteristics of a DT.

Types of Digital Twin

Component Twin: For certain parts of a system, like a sensor or actuator, component twins are made. They can be viewed as digital reproductions of particular parts or systems within of a bigger system. Digital twins come in several forms, but component twins are the most basic. They can be applied to model the component's behavior and test how changes to the component would impact the rest of the system.

Asset twins or Product twins: Asset twins are virtual copies of real-world objects, such machines or vehicles. Asset twins can be used to keep track of an asset's location and state, as well as to forecast when maintenance will be necessary. Component twins are used to create asset twins, which are then utilized to observe component twin behavior.

System Twins or Unit Twins: Complex systems, including power grids or transportation networks, are observed by system twins. Asset twins make up the majority of system twins, which are utilized to observe asset twin behavior.

Process Twins: Digital reproductions of business processes, such as the process of producing a product, are called process twins. Twins of the process can be used to streamline it and spot bottlenecks or other problems. They act out processes like the flow of people or things through an establishment.

Section III highlights how network enabled IoT devices can be helpful majorly for Digital Twin applications in a smart city (Porter, Michael.et. al, 2015)

DIGITAL TWINS IN A SMART CITY

The concept of smart city may vary from place to place and country to country. It basically depends on the willingness of city development authorities to strategize on the change and reforms. Smart cities are those that implement scalable solutions that use information and communications technology (ICT) to improve efficiencies, cut costs, and improve quality of life, according to businesses like Cisco.". (Falconer and Mitchell, 2019).

Digital twin technology constituting the IoT devices, configured network can be used very efficiently in smart cities for the purpose of security and tracking. The security and tracking can be of civil structures like school buildings, heritage buildings, important structures like defense structures, airports, hospitals, banks, places of worship, etc.

According to the British Standards Institute (BSI) "a smart city is a combination of digital and human systems existing in an orchestrated environment for the effective delivery of continual, successful, comprehensive forthcoming for residents" (BSI, 2014). Smart cities are termed "smart", since they use capabilities of techniques, informed data for city management. They offer solutions to the city's challenges and improve its infrastructure and services. Some of these services can be access to possessions like aquatic, power, transportation, government services, etc. This can also be used for redeveloping or developing unplanned and poorly planned areas. Areas in the cities like the slums, monitoring heritage buildings and structures. The core objective is to prepare a secured city with lesser issues, adversities. For example, security of womenfolk, kids needs can be safeguarded, with highly decreased illegal activities like audiovisual surveillance

Networking based applications are supported by IoT connected to multiple devices. These devices gather information from connected environment, send that information to the IOT device server, server processes it. It used communication technologies. Smart building, city, AI, tracking, remote sensing, emergency healthcare are few places where IOT can be used effectively. IoT network helps in routing effectively. Paper has proposed cryptography based cost-effective model. It enhances data security. It also determines monetary value of IoT Network records. (Sonam, Johari R,2023)

The goal is to determine how and for which applications, partial or complete processes, functions of the smart city, and digital twins can be useful due to technological advancements in IoT devices, data analytics and insights, and artificial intelligence to represent the applications of the smart city using virtual and physical forms.

Gartner (2023), in a report shares that users can save on the cost, support improvements in the production especially in the areas of carbon emissions. A number of new and innovative ways can help DTs to optimize on a number of business operations such as operations, finance, and decision-making for emissions reduction in large, complex building projects and assets. (Gartner, January 2023).

Digital twins are built on a two-way mapping interaction between the physical and digital worlds. Bidirectional mapping transfers data in both directions, as opposed to unidirectional mapping, which exclusively transfers data from real items to digital objects. In accordance with (Kritzinger, et al.,2018) and (Zheng et al., 2019), the latter is also known as a "digital shadow since"a change in state of the physical object leads to a change in the digital object, but not vice versa". Although, unlike digital shadows, digital twins have a property that enables virtual things to have an impact on physical entities without the need for human participation. (Enders and Hoßbach, 2019). (Deren, L. et. al,2021).

This particular concept is very innovative and also creepy, that any changes in the virtual objects may affect the real world objects, but as of now it is still an idea, the practical part of this looks to be distant and difficult to put in practice.

If an online 3D model is made available to the public of a city, they can view the improvements in the city planning & policy. Before putting these judgements into action, this makes public disclosure and transparency easier. An additional virtual feedback loop where citizens can participate and provide feedback on recommended changes to the city is made possible by this open and transparent architecture. Additionally, residents can engage with components to flag and report issues in their neighborhood. When 3D data is required, such as for planning flood evacuation, the digital twin also enables further experimentation.(Gary,White et.al.2021)

In support to the main research study (Gary White et al., 2021) the researchers have exhibited, an open and public DT can provide the feedback for Dublin's Docklands. It was used for planning the city's skyline, green spaces and urban planning. It will facilitate citizens to not only access these areas but interactively provide their feedback.

Similar kind of experiment was carried out by the leader of "physi" by collecting feedback from citizens in designing the Dunakapu Square in Gyor from an environment aka climate perception. The model could help in design, costing, impact on the neighbour environment. Also the maintenance and design world-heritage site of Vienna, was also tried and tested with people feedback.(Nora Rado, 2021)

There are cities, globally using the digital twin technology like the city of Helsinki discussed by authors (Ruohomäki et al., 2018), the city of Zurich, discussed by authors (Schrotter and Hürzeler, 2020), and the city of Vienna discussed by authors (Lehner and Dorffner,2020). These cities and their digital twins are clustered conceptually under one umbrella of Digital Twin concept (Vander Valk et al., 2020). In all these cities, the digital application is implied for different services. The cities need to be sensitive and respond to internal and external factors as well.

The agenda of the United Nations for 2030 for sustainable development has many goals which revolves around creating safe, resilient, sustainable cities. China has also started to implement digital twins in cities like Xiong. It uses 3D modeling techniques in improving urban public-services supporting government policies. (Digital Twin Cities: Framework and Global Practices, 2022). The authors have discussed a 4+ 5 framework. The 4 stands for elements like infra, data sources, capacity, target domains. And the 5 elements stand for the supporting elements like strategy, the main stakeholders, finance, standards, and cybersecurity techniques.

The Boston's urban planners use ArcGIS Urban to include several pieces of data, such as building footprint, height, and location, explore various scenarios, and achieve their goals—in this example, reducing the amount of shadows thrown on the park.(Soward, E., & Li, J. (2021). (Triantafilou, J. T.,2021).

A dashboard is created by New York City for its Vision Zero programme, displays crucial metrics for pedestrian safety using data from sources and IoT devices like traffic sensors, intelligent cameras, and pedestrian traffic tracking integrated into a geospatial context. Using predictive analytics and real-time traffic collision monitoring, this data assists public safety agencies in managing traffic flow and enhancing pedestrian safety.

As a result of businesses moving out of the downtown area, the City of Oshkosh, Wisconsin, created a plan called Imagine Oshkosh to boost business and create investment opportunities. Oshkosh used ArcGIS tools like Business Analyst and CityEngine to create, assess, and present the Imagine Oshkosh strategy.

The University of Zulia was instrumental in creating a digital twin of Maracaibo, Venezuela's second-largest city, using ArcGIS Urban and associated products like CityEngine. The digital twin combines a wide range of indicators and factors, including data on particular buildings and developments, zoning and restrictions, transportation patterns, and energy usage. This comprehensive, place-based perspective aids in assessing the effects of various scenarios and the degree to which plans comply with stated policy goals.

Singapore, the "smartest city in the world 2019," has been working on creating its "Virtual Singapore" model, a digital twin that not only maps the unique infrastructure of this modern city-state but also includes crucial data for future development. As the simulation is used by the municipal council to determine where to remove architectural barriers, it is said to have aided individuals with decreased mobility. However, it can also give advice to city planners on a variety of topics, such as how to create a pneumatic garbage collecting system or how to deploy solar panels effectively.

The digital twin, a 3D FBX model that contains the first three layers of topography, buildings, and infrastructure, was created using the Unity3D Software (Unity). It allowed crowd simulations with various agent-kind. It included adult and elderly users, road walker's mobilization related models being formed using Unity. To create perfect simulations, the smart city data was used from the Dublinked7 website. The city's multidisciplinary modeling is made possible by the twining of the model with actual public data through an open portal. (Gary White. et. al, 2021).

The present chapter focuses on the use of DT in a smart city for smart water management.

SMART CITY: DIGITAL TWIN EXAMPLES

Application of Digital Twin for Smart City: Water Management Applications

Water is the most needed resource for human beings. Water management is a basic requirement for cities. Water is a natural resource and due to urbanization and industrialization providing quality water for its citizens is a mandate for most of the Governments.

Figure 2. Digital twin in smart city for smart water management

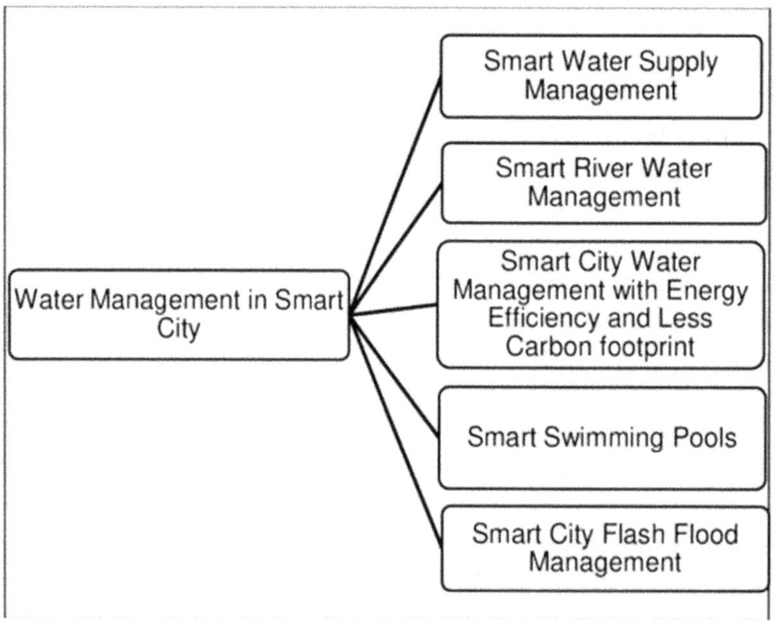

Smart Water Supply Management

The Indian Government initiative of Smart Cities is based on smart infrastructure solutions and services. Smart water management is one of the basic needs which needs to be addressed. These water management uses multiple machinery and techniques. Techniques used in these water systems perform supervision through sensor applied mechanisms. The actual real data acquisition related to water supply, usage of water, maintenance of the distribution system, managing the entire system requires IoT sensors, and a well-connected network. This data managing, analysis allows for leakage management, water distribution management, repairs and maintenance etc.

In their paper (Mankad U., Arolkar H, 2022) the authors have proposed the design, proposal, standardization of the system needs to be introduced. Its applications lack a systematic framework of real-world design, implementation of water meter systems. Authors proposed framework, tested and implemented prototype. This paper aimed to reduce smart water meter application development work to some extent. Framework is based on open-source technology. It introduced features like the device-installation and maintenance, the statistics of water utilization, digital invoice pay, and dispersed data broadcast architecture. The challenges of smart metering still needs to penetrate to optimum level.

Here if the digital twin technology is implied, it will be the enabler or the trigger to real-time data capturing, maintenance, tracking of the system. With the tracking of the system it can help to efficiently manage the distribution of water, the loss due to leakage etc.

Due to high levels of urbanisation, climate change, rising and shifting consumer demands, and depleted water supplies, urban water delivery systems are complex. Aim should be towards sustainable water supply for fulfilling the increasing consumer demand. For operations intelligent systems help.

Water systems are looking forward to being digitized and sustainable. Water 4.0 is introduced. It will help water systems, methods, processes and operations to be sustainable. The authors (Mankad U., Arolkar H, 2022) have discussed important features of water 4.0. They discuss also how water 4.0 applications can improvise water supply system operations. Sustainable operation of municipal water service is essential, and still there are its challenges and still opportunities in future.

Smart River Water Management

The collection, storage, and recycling of rainfall as well as the upkeep and repair of rivers and treatment facilities might all be made more effective. SCUBIC – An AI-based software platform to monitor utility water networks is an IoT System. It supports in improving the functionality of water utilities – A digital twin can help to keep track of, maintenance, and safety of the treatment plants.

AI and IOT has catered to numerous applications in telecom, network, computing, and embedded systems. AI and IOT together improvise application productivity with reducing consumption, provision of real time information. Industry 4.0 application in smart city is discussed. Water consumption operations for monitoring, tracking models are proposed with an OCR, AI based algorithm, YoLo 4 proposed as a machine learning model. The aim was to achieve desired results in optimum time. The algorithm accuracy is ninety-eight percent. (Adedeji K.B.,2022)

Smart City Water Management With Energy Efficiency and Less Carbon Footprint

(Ktari, J. et. A, 2022) in their paper proposed for sustainable development, a water delivery system's digital transformation is considered. In this case, a real-time continuous measurement that corresponds to network state is obtained using an IoT-based smart water network management (SWNM) application. In order to make the best decisions possible, the data must be continuously gathered, analysed, and wirelessly supplied to a remote centre. The Digital Twin programme can help with this in an efficient manner.

Smart cities have a variety of applications like logistics, fleet management etc. IOT can connect a variety of devices for these system operations. Smart city applications require huge energy consumption, high cost, high battery life when IOT applications are used for it. IOT device capacity is a challenge. It proposed an algorithm to extend IOT devices battery life called 'LoRa end-nodes'. It has been successfully verified on water quality monitoring systems with IOT implementation. It saved sixty two percent of battery energy. It also carries out carbon footprint analysis and saved eight point six kilograms of annual carbon emission per node. The IOT implementation here can be with a digital twin, which help to efficiently manage energy as well as quality of water quality monitoring systems. (Philip M.S. et. Al, 2022)

Smart Swimming Pools

IOT is becoming more popular in a number of industries, including the creation of intelligent environments, remote control, and smart city monitoring. It aims to reduce manual, human efforts for it. Quality of swimming pool is monitored and controlled by IOT enabled boat. It is lower in cost, uses wireless sensor, actuators. IOT based boat uses aluminum, mechanical, electric parts and is lightweight. It reduces manpower utilization at the swimming pool. The IOT boat with net cleans water of swimming pool of leaves and wastes. It is controlled remotely as an IOT enabled device. Fresh water misuse in routine is a challenge. Water quality records are required to be maintained, and alert to user when water can have risk.

The aim was to provide water sustainability, water saving and cost effectiveness to user. User can login remotely from Android mobile having this IOT based application. It has features to manage swimming pool parameters in real time, quick data analysis, parameter-based threshold risk alert indication to user. These IOT devices are controlled in automated or in manual way. This smart boat can be doing the work of an assistant security guard at swimming pools, which has been verified, tested and is successfully implemented. (Asiri, 2022)

In the coming years, Fresh water management is going to be a challenging area. Facilities like swimming pools need to be managed and the digital twins can help to manage this in terms of water quality, safety, control etc.

Smart City Flash Flood Management

Ever increasing urban demographics, climatic changes, increasing urban area locations impact urban water and its management cycle. It causes water deficiencies as well as flood situations due to urbanization. Smart city development is hampered by severe climatic disasters, often urban flash floods. Flood management strategies should be integrated and sustainable for smart city development and performance. Urban flash floods impact socially, cost wise, infrastructure wise to people's life and governance of smart cities. Random, unplanned urban areas cause flash floods, runoffs to be real time managed. Poor drainage systems, lack of real time marinating technologies is an issue to be solve in smart cities.

Authors (Yereseme A.K,2022) have examined the foundation for planning for smart cities, digital automations, remote-sensing programmes, and real-time technology. Different urban flood management techniques are discussed.

Water being a sensitive and is an important requirement of a smart city. Better drainage systems, real time monitoring systems are challenges to be overcome with smart water systems. Flash floods, which have been observed happening recurring need to be addressed. The core reasons to resolve them and manage with the help of systemic drainage systems, planned and monitored development of urban areas with the help of digital twins can to some extent resolve the issue.

Application of Digital Twins in Smart City: Facility Management and Structural Health Monitoring

In the Digital twin implementation in smart cities, the concepts of GIS and GPS have been widely used. GIS allows the use of geographic information systems and GPS is the global positioning system along with BIM, which is the Building Information Modelling. These two technologies can represent the buildings, people, vehicles and help in building a digital environment of the same. (Jincheng, S. 2022)

The Wired brand labs of IBM showcases a number of facility management strategies using digital twins. The buildings and other civil infrastructure stood tall all these past years without communication or to the external world. With Internet of Things (IOT) enabled tracking system and with a sensor network the pulse of the such assets can be monitored for its efficacy including a number of measurements like power utilization of particular floor in building, are there any leaking in the water system leading to wastage, how is the elevator system functioning, how many square foot floor areas is under use or guiding the service personnel to the right geolocation of an air conditioner and whom to send the bill post services etc., can be efficiently managed by implying a digital twin of the building itself. (IBM, 2022)

Buildings and civil structures should have their structural health monitored (Jinecheng, 2022). The fragility and damage brought on by deterioration, corrosion, etc. present significant measuring issues. A digital twin and the data it produces can be utilised to offer current status and forecast the building's health. Researchers have discussed their usage of a digital twin to monitor the structural health of bridges (Ye, Cong et al., 2019). Based on real-time data obtained from sensors in the building information management system, they have examined the strength of the bridges under consideration. (BIM) and, the underlying physics on the structural strength of the bridges. Using digital twins, the real-time data that was obtained during the procedure enabled bridge health monitoring. For the example study, they employed two monitored railroad overpasses in Staffordshire, UK. The heterogeneous nature of data sources and integrating the collaborative models for simulation needs to be addressed. Authors in (Jiang et.al., 2021) have clearly distinguished between a digital Twin and BIM and Cyber-Physical System. (Francisco,et. al.,2020).

Important feature of intelligent security system is to re-identify individual across cameras. In tracking and security systems, person should be re identified. Cameras need to track multiple targets. An individual should be identified uniquely by multiple cameras. From the image sets, best matching image should be re-identified for any individual with accuracy. Smart bank, smart factory, smart city construction can be supported with security systems with re-identification. With AI deep learning helps in re-identification in security systems with unmatched results. Generalization, temporal information, occluded objects are still not impactful in re identification. Research is ongoing on these challenges. This research study reviews pros and cons of the deep learning technique application for re-identification. The flow of the paper includes introducing re-identification, its applications, datasets and assessment indicators, deep learning basic techniques for re identification. Local features, generative adversarial networks, video data, and re-ranking are parameters for re-identification parameters categorized with deep learning. Its comparison is conducted. (Li Q.,et.al, 2022)In spite of multiple proposed networks to cater re identification systems, are used yet lot of challenges exist still to be solved. These networks have higher representation capabilities, increased accuracy of individual re identification. Current issues and future opportunities need to be explored, analyzed, and discussed.

Visualizations, real-time auto monitoring of smart cities with IOT is evident with Industry 4.0. For smart city monitoring filtering algorithms can be helpful. Visual monitoring, impactful monitoring with cognitive aspects is complex practically. Monitoring techniques are not aligned to human cognitive system, hence re monitoring is not strong. The authors have studied the innovative ways a human mind or brain operates with the video surveillance of smart cities. A concept called long term memory associated with some high reliability object is conceptualized. Likewise, a short term memory associated with some low reliability object. This concept is used alternatively during the monitoring. It is combined with stored target appearance attributes. It does not misuse original model in memory due to external changes in occlusion, motion, clutter etc. The algorithm is fast, tracks the objects in complex scenarios. (Wang S. et. Al, 2022)Smart city monitor with industry 4.0 based IOT filtering applications are used with surveillance environments. Its complexity and limited resource constraints are the challenges and these issues should be solved.

IOT is successfully employed in applications for smart cities such as the smart factory, smart health monitoring, and smart tracking. Security and Privacy challenges of IOT is major hurdle in its acceptance. User access authorization in network services with paired network devices smart phone, laptop etc. has most security issues

This research study, proposes continual behavioural authentication system of IoT devices to optimize IOT devices battery power and other computational resources. By taking into account the constraints of IoT devices, such as battery life and other processing resources, this research introduces a magnificent continuous behavioural authentication system to handle this difficulty. In order to identify dishonest user behaviour, the suggested authentication model uses machine learning-based techniques to analyse application usage patterns. The correlation coefficient is additionally utilised for feature ranking. (Kumar et. al, 2022)

Three different machine learning techniques, including a multi-layer perceptron, radial basis function-based SVM-SMO, and support vector machine (SVM) with sequential minimal optimization (SMO), use the ranking features (MLP). A real-world application usage dataset was used for the experimental research to show how well the suggested continuous behavioural authentication mechanism worked. need of a secured authorization system to monitor device The digital twins can be incorporated in the health monitoring, safety, remote tracking of the civil structures like hospitals, old civil structures like bridges, schools where in any kind of accidents can prove fatal in terms of life loss, asset loss and monetary loss.

The cases discussed above are all the typical, regular cases related to digital twin applications.

DISCUSSIONS AND CONCLUSION

Digital twins have a virtually limitless number of uses and benefits. Digital twins can improve our understanding of how infrastructure will perform in a number of conditions, such as when facing a natural disaster, by simulating the interactions between various components. The smart city development with digital twins can benefit multifolds as some of the solutions, simulations and predictions used from DTs can enhance their efficiency in city operations. These can very well be utilized in planning future solutions for cities which are environmentally, economically and socially sustainable.

Advancement of DTs call for inter and mutli-disciplinary research and collaboration efforts as we see a number use cases of DTs for example from trees, roads, water to asset management, building management to traffic management to health care, manufacturing and various other domains. DTs therefore help in improved project visualization and urban planning.

It can assemble knowledge to enhance city infrastructure. Increasing cooperation among a wide range of city stakeholders will provide value for cities and inhabitants. Build resilient infrastructure by anticipating, responding to, and recovering from severe shocks. Get the public involved and establish a feedback loop. Encourage the use of open data efforts so that others can create, develop, and offer services using reliable data on city and infrastructure.

Further advancements in DTs will be made possible by data processing and analysis techniques and technologies. Future research should focus on, among other things, superior latest cloud based IT services capabilities of enhanced microprocessors, big data analytics, machine learning, artificial intelligence processing, analysis of IoT data, 5G communication, interdependent operations combination for simulation, modeling, analysis, visualization software, simulation, modeling techniques to reduce computational complexity.

The threats posed to the physical systems because of its virtual counterpart i.e. a DT, in terms of information and cybersecurity threats needs to be still worked upon. We need intelligent data driven solutions to prevent attacks. A number of standards are coming up so that stricter compliance to these by DTs in our user case will make them robust, reliable and efficient. (Suhail, S.,2022)

REFERENCES

Adedeji, K.B., Ponnle, A.A., Abu-Mahfouz, A.M., & Kurien, A.M. (2022). Towards Digitalization of Water Supply Systems for Sustainable Smart City Development—Water 4.0. *Applied Sciences (Switzerland), 12*(18).

Amazon. (n.d.). *What is Digital Technology?* Amazon. https://aws.amazon.com/what-is/digital-twin/

Ashu, A., Hussain, M. W., Sinha Roy, D., & Reddy, H. K. (2021). Intelligent data compression policy for Hadoop performance optimization. In *Proceedings of the 11th International Conference on Soft Computing and Pattern Recognition (SoCPaR 2019)* (pp. 80-89). Springer International Publishing. 10.1007/978-3-030-49345-5_9

Asiri, S. A. (2022). Smart solutions for monitoring, control, and safety of swimming pools using a savvy boat. *Measurement and Control*, *55*(Jul), 603–615. doi:10.1177/00202940221113593

Barricelli, B. R., Casiraghi, E., & Fogli, D. (2019). A survey on digital twin: Definitions, characteristics, applications, and design implications. In I. E. E. E. Access (Ed.), *Institute of Electrical and Electronics Engineers Inc* (Vol. 7). doi:10.1109/ACCESS.2019.2953499

Bhatti, G., Mohan, H., & Raja Singh, R. (2021). Towards the future of smart electric vehicles: Digital twin technology. In *Renewable and Sustainable Energy Reviews* (Vol. 141). Elsevier Ltd. doi:10.1016/j.rser.2021.110801

Bilberg, A., & Malik, A. A. (2019). Digital twin driven human–robot collaborative assembly. *CIRP Annals*, *68*(1), 499–502. doi:10.1016/j.cirp.2019.04.011

Botín-Sanabria, D. M., Mihaita, S., Peimbert-García, R. E., Ramírez-Moreno, M. A., Ramírez-Mendoza, R. A., & Lozoya-Santos, J. de J. (2022). Digital Twin Technology Challenges and Applications: A Comprehensive Review. In Remote Sensing, 14(6). MDPI. doi:10.3390/rs14061335

British Standards Institute. (2014). *Smart city framework – Guide to establishing strategies for smart cities and communities*. BSI.

Chen, X., Kang, E., Shiraishi, S., Preciado, V. M., & Jiang, Z. (2018). Digital behavioral twins for safe connected cars. In *Proceedings of the 21st ACM/IEEE Int. Conf. Model Driven Eng. Lang. Syst. Models* (pp. 144–153). IEEE. 10.1145/3239372.3239401

Deren, L., Wenbo, Y., & Zhenfeng, S. (2021). Smart city based on digital twins. *Computational Urban Science, 1*(1), 1–11. doi:10.100743762-021-00005-y

Enders, M. R., & Hoßbach, N. (2019). *Dimensions of digital twin applications-a literature review.*

Falconer, G., & Mitchell, S. (2012). *Smart City Framework A Systematic Process for Enabling Smart Connected Communities.* CISCO. https://www.cisco.com/web/about/ac79/docs/ps/motm/Smart-City-Framework.pdf

Francisco, A., Mohammadi, N., & Taylor, J. (2020). Smart city digital twin–enabled energy management: Toward real-time urban building energy benchmarking. *Journal of Management in Engineering, 36*(2).

Fuller, A., Zhong, F., Day, C., & Barlow, C. (2020). IDigital twin: Enabling technologies, challenges and open Research. *IEEE Access, 8*, 108952–108971

Gahlot, S., Reddy, S. R. N., & Kumar, D. (2019, April). Review of smart health monitoring approaches with survey analysis and proposed framework. *IEEE Internet of Things Journal, 6*(2), 2116–2127. doi:10.1109/JIOT.2018.2872389

Gartner Top Strategic Technology Trends. (2023). *Detailed Guide (eBook).* Gartner. https://www.gartner.com/en/information-technology/insights/top-technology-trends

Hu, W., Zhang, T., Deng, X., Liu, Z., & Tan, J. (2021). Digital twin: A state-of-the-art review of its enabling technologies, applications and challenges. *Journal of Intelligent Manufacturing and Special Equipment, 2*(1), 1-34.

Hussain, M. W. (2021). A counter based approach for reducer placement with augmented Hadoop rackawareness. *Turkish Journal of Electrical Engineering and Computer Sciences, 29*(1), 437–453. doi:10.3906/elk-2001-106

Jiang, F., Ma, L., Broyd, T., & Chen, K. (2021). Digital twin and its implementations in the civil engineering sector. *Automation in Construction, 130*, 103838. doi:10.1016/j.autcon.2021.103838

Jiang, Z., Guo, Y., & Wang, Z. (2021). Digital twin to improve the virtual-real integration of industrial IoT. *Journal of Industrial Information Integration, 22*, 100196. doi:10.1016/j.jii.2020.100196

Jincheng, S. (2022). Research on Digital Twin for Building Structure Health Monitoring. In *Business Intelligence and Information Technology: Proceedings of the International Conference on Business Intelligence and Information Technology BIIT 2021* (pp. 754-760). Springer International Publishing 10.1007/978-3-030-92632-8_71

Joordens, M., & Jamshidi, M. (2018). On the development of robot fish swarms in virtual reality with digital twins. In Proc. *13th Annu. Conf. Syst. Syst. Eng. (SoSE)* (pp. 411–416). IEEE. 10.1109/SYSOSE.2018.8428748

Kritzinger, W., Karner, M., Traar, G., Henjes, J., & Sihn, W. (2018). Digital Twin in manufacturing: A categorical literature review and classification. *IFAC-PapersOnLine*, *51*(11), 1016–1022. doi:10.1016/j.ifacol.2018.08.474

Ktari, J., Frikha, T., Hamdi, M., Elmannai, H., & Hmam, H. (2022). Lightweight AI framework for industry 4.0 case study: Water meter recognition. *Big Data and Cognitive Computing*, *6*(3), 72. doi:10.3390/bdcc6030072

Kumar, V., & Ray, S. (2022). *Continuous Behavioral Authentication System for IoT Enabled Applications*. Lecture Notes in Networks and Systems. doi:10.1007/978-981-19-3182-6_5

Lehner, H., & Dorffner, L. (2020). *Towards a digital twin city as Geodata Hub*. Digital geo Twin Vienna.

Li, Q., Hu, W.-Y., Li, J.-Y., Liu, Y., & Li, M.-X. (2022). A survey of person re-identification based on deep learning. Chinese Journal of Engineering, 8(3), 920-932.

Liu, Y., Zhang, L., Yang, Y., Zhou, L., Ren, L., Wang, F., & Deen, M. J. (2019). A novel cloud-based framework for the elderly healthcare services using digital twin. *IEEE Access : Practical Innovations, Open Solutions*, *7*, 49088–49101. doi:10.1109/ACCESS.2019.2909828

Mankad, U., & Arolkar, H. (2022). Smart Water Metering Implementation. *Lecture Notes in Networks and Systems, 6th International Conference on Smart Trends in Computing and Communications, SmartCom*, (*Vol 396*, pp. 721-731). IEEE.

Mohammadi, N., & Taylor, J. E. (2017). Smart city digital twins. In *Proc. IEEE Symp. Ser. Computational Intelligence (SSCI),* (pp. 1–5). IEEE. 10.1109/SSCI.2017.8285439

Papyshev, G., & Yarime, M. (2021). Exploring city digital twins as policy tools: A task-based approach to generating synthetic data on urban mobility. *Data & Policy*, *3*, e16. doi:10.1017/dap.2021.17

Pargmann, H., Euhausen, D., & Faber, R. (2018). Intelligent big data processing for wind farm monitoring and analysis based on cloud-technologies and digital twins: A quantitative approach. In *Proc. IEEE 3rd Int. Conf. Cloud Comput. Big Data Anal. (ICCCBDA)* (pp. 233–237). IEEE. 10.1109/ICCCBDA.2018.8386518

Philip, M. S., & Singh, P. (2022). An energy efficient algorithm for sustainable monitoring of water quality in smart cities. *Sustainable Computing: Informatics and Systems*, *35*, 721–731. doi:10.1016/j.suscom.2022.100768

Porter, M., & Heppelman, J. (2015, October). How smart, connected products are transforming companies. *Harvard Business Review*, *93*, 96–114.

Pradhan, B., Hussain, M. W., Srivastava, G., Debbarma, M. K., Barik, R. K., & Lin, J. C. W. (2022). A neuro-evolutionary approach for software defined wireless network traffic classification. *IET Communications*, cmu2.12548. doi:10.1049/cmu2.12548

Radó, N., Girasek, E., Békási, S., & Győrffy, Z. (2022). Digital Technology Access and Health-Related Internet Use Among People Experiencing Homelessness in Hungary: Quantitative Survey. *Journal of Medical Internet Research*, *24*(10), e38729. doi:10.2196/38729 PMID:36260379

Rathore, M. M. U., Shah, S. A., Shukla, D., Bentafat, E., & Bakiras, S. (2021, February). The role of AI, machine learning, and big data in digital twinning: A systematic literature review, challenges, and opportunities. *IEEE Access : Practical Innovations, Open Solutions*, *99*, 1–1. doi:10.1109/ACCESS.2021.3060863

Ruohomäki, T., Airaksinen, E., Huuska, P., Kesäniemi, O., Martikka, M., & Suomisto, J. (2018, September). Smart city platform enabling digital twin. In *2018 International Conference on Intelligent Systems (IS)* (pp. 155-161). IEEE 10.1109/IS.2018.8710517

Schrotter, G., & Hürzeler, C. (2020). The digital twin of the city of Zurich for urban planning. PFG–Journal of Photogrammetry. *Remote Sensing and Geoinformation Science*, *88*(1), 99–112.

Sivalingam, K., Sepulveda, M., Spring, M., & Davies, P. (2018). A review and methodology development for remaining useful life prediction of offshore fixed and floating wind turbine power converter with digital twin technol- ogy perspective. *In Proceedings of the 2nd Int. Conf. Green Energy Appl. (ICGEA)* (pp. 197–204). IEEE. 10.1109/ICGEA.2018.8356292

Sonam, J. R., & Johari, R. (2023). Crypto-Economic Model for Data Security in IoT Network. *Lecture Notes in Networks and Systems*, *492*, 427–434. doi:10.1007/978-981-19-3679-1_34

Soward, E., & Li, J. (2021). ArcGIS Urban: An application for plan assessment. *Computational Urban Science*, *1*(1), 1–10. doi:10.100743762-021-00016-9

Suhail, S., Zeadally, S., Jurdak, R., Hussain, R., Matulevičius, R., & Svetinovic, D. (2022). *Security attacks and solutions for digital twins*. arXiv preprint arXiv:2202.12501

Tilson, D., Lyytinen, K., & Sørensen, C. (2010). Digital Infrastructures: The Missing IS Research Agenda (PDF). *Information Systems Research, 21* (4), 748–759. . JSTOR 23015642 doi:10.1287/isre.1100.0318

Triantafilou, J. T. (2021, August 27). The role of digital twins in smart cities. https://resources.esri.ca/news-and-updates/the-role-digital-twins-in-smart-cities. https://resources.esri.ca/news-and-updates/the-role-digital-twins-in-smart-cities

Van Bastelaer, B. (1998). *Digital cities and transferability of results*. In European digital cities: 4th conference: changing patterns of urban life, Salzburg, Austria. https://www.info.fundp.ac.be/~cita/publications/4thEDC.pdf

Vander Valk, H., Haße, H., Möller, F., Arbter, M., Henning, J. L., & Otto, B. (2020, August). A Taxonomy of Digital Twins. In AMCIS.

Wang, S., Liu, X., Liu, S., Muhammad, K., Heidari, A. A., Ser, J. D., & De Albuquerque, V. H. C. (2022). Human Short Long-Term Cognitive Memory Mechanism for Visual Monitoring in IoT-Assisted Smart Cities. *IEEE Internet of Things Journal*, *9*(10), 7128–7139. doi:10.1109/JIOT.2021.3077600

White, G., Zink, A., Codecá, L., & Clarke, S. (2021). A digital twin smart city for citizen feedback. *Cities (London, England)*, *110*, 103064. doi:10.1016/j.cities.2020.103064

Ye, C., Butler, L., Calka, B., Iangurazov, M., Lu, Q., Gregory, A., Girolami, M., & Middleton, C. (2019). *A Digital Twin of Bridges for Structural Health Monitoring*. Conference: Proceedings of the 12th International Workshop on Structural Health Monitoring 2019, Stanford, California, USA.10.12783hm2019/32287

Yereseme, A. K., Surendra, H. J., & Kuntoji, G. (2022). Sustainable integrated urban flood management strategies for planning of smart cities: A review. *Sustainable Water Resources Management*, *8*(3), 603–615. doi:10.100740899-022-00666-5

Zheng, Y., Yang, S., & Cheng, H. (2019). An application framework of digital twin and its case study. *Journal of Ambient Intelligence and Humanized Computing*, *10*(3), 1141–1153. doi:10.100712652-018-0911-3

Chapter 3
Issues, Current Challenges, and Research Directions in Designing a Smart, Explainable AI-Based Healthcare Systems

B. S. Rajeshwari
B.M.S. College of Engineering, India

M. Namratha
B.M.S. College of Engineering, India

Jyothi S. Nayak
B.M.S. College of Engineering, India

ABSTRACT

Artificial intelligence has recently gained great importance in healthcare and has played an important role in the making the lives of patients, doctors, radiologists, clinical laboratories, emergency medical services, etc., better. Remote health monitoring is possible in less time and low cost for rural areas where doctors are not available all the time. Assistance is provided to the medical professionals when required in the time of emergency through deep learning algorithms which is beneficial. The anomalies in the medical images can be easily detected and predicted with the help of AI, which were impossible to detect by the human eye, thus adding extra value for the healthcare sector. The lack of specialized medical professionals and increasing number of patients with lifestyle diseases necessitate the digitization for the mundane tasks of healthcare. Explainable AI is important in healthcare sector, where the consequences of incorrect AI predictions or decisions can be severe.

DOI: 10.4018/979-8-3693-0744-1.ch003

INTRODUCTION

The usage of AI applications has been increasing in recent years especially in the healthcare domain. Every year, 100,000 hospitalized patients suffer unnecessary harm and as a result 400,000 of them die. Given this, one of the most exciting medical uses of AI has the potential to improve the diagnosing procedure (Shuo Tian, Wenbo Yang, Jehane Michael Le Grange, Peng Wang, Wei Huang, Zhewei Ye,2019). The electronic medical record database contains a vast quantity of patient data, including diagnoses, prescriptions, and lab results. The patient dataset is analyzed using AI algorithms. AI in the healthcare sector uses machine learning algorithms and other cognitive disciplines to evaluate medical data and take action with the intention of foreseeing a specific outcome. It is providing a way to the doctors, nurses, radiologists, clinical laboratories, researchers, pharmacists, and many other healthcare professionals to make their decisions and to assist in diagnosing, treatment planning and health management. AI approaches are increasingly used for molecular biological testing, medical picture recognition, medical text recognition, and semantic recognition in addition to data analysis. When evaluating patients, the medical staff can also utilize the research's findings as a guide.

AI-driven systems in the medical profession build predictive models, identify groups of high-risk patients, aid doctors in their diagnosis, and understand patterns from vast amounts of health-related data. Unfortunately, human biases may be present in actual historical data used in the learning process, which could result in unfair or incorrect choices. The lack of transparency in algorithms' behavior and the inability to explain the reasoning behind decisions may limit social acceptance and trust in their use in a variety of delicate circumstances, which continues to draw criticism. This is why Explainable AI (XAI) is a hot topic in technology. One of the most hotly contested issues in the use of AI in healthcare is explain ability (F. Doshi-Velez and B. Kim, 2017).

The XAI intends to offer a collection of machine learning methods that:

- Generate more explicable models while keeping a high level of prediction accuracy.
- Provide users the accuracy which they can rely on and also be able to comprehend the result obtained.

The healthcare sector has been transformed into a smart healthcare system by using AI approaches across almost all industries. A couple of cases of the innovations utilized in healthcare nowadays incorporate automated surgery, computerized picture conclusion, extortion of location, clinical trial cooperation, drug improvement, precise cancer determination, early discovery of deadly blood infections, adjust treatment, administration of therapeutic records, and dose mistake decrease.

The Support Vector Machine (SVM) algorithm has demonstrated to be very successful in tackling classification issues in many biological disciplines, particularly in bioinformatics. In contrast to logistic regression, which conforms data to a logistic curve to predict whether or not a binary event will occur, SVM makes distinctions between two classes once the input data have been processed into a high-dimensional space. The data-driven and model-free nature of the SVM technique may provide it considerable discriminative potential for classification, particularly when working with small sample sizes and a large number of variables (high-dimensionality space). The application of this technology has helped recent developments in automated disease categorization and illness detection methods.

SVM-based techniques can be employed for discerning between individuals with diabetes or prediabetes who have not yet received a diagnosis and those who do. Only straightforward clinical measurements without the need for laboratory tests were employed as the variables to create the SVM models. But a number of dangers and difficulties are posed by AI systems, including the possibility of patient injuries due to its systemic flaws, data privacy and security, biases and inequalities in algorithms, exponential growth of healthcare data, lack of quality medical data and more.

The coronavirus illness 2019 (COVID-19) is brought on by SARS-CoV-2 virus. The bulk of the cities and countries around the world experienced rapid spread. Direct contact with droplets of breath from infected individuals is the primary method of SARS-CoV-2 transmission. Both moderate upper respiratory tract infection symptoms and highly serious sepsis and shock may be brought on by the illness. In susceptible groups, especially in the elderly with concomitant conditions, it may result in severe and fatal consequences. The sparse healthcare resources in the system are severely strained by the rising incidence of COVID-19 and associated high deaths. Effective tools are needed to increase medical effectiveness in hospitals and hasten COVID-19 diagnosis, treatment, and surveillance. Studies now underway suggest artificial intelligence is capable of growing up more successfully than other technologies, analyzing data more quickly, and even outperforming people in some healthcare-related jobs making it a viable field. AI's advantages can be seen in its high object identification sensitivity and specificity, quick reporting, and consistency of results. By making new inferences from the massive amounts of data generated by the experiences of many patients, Medical technologies based on artificial intelligence and machine learning (AI/ML) are intended to raise the standard of care, boost diagnostic precision, decrease possible mistakes, and forecast result. The most crucial steps to stop the COVID-19 pandemic's spread are early diagnosis, precise prognosis, increased surveillance, and efficient therapies. The considerable strain the pandemic has imposed on the meagre medical resources would be lessened as a result. Numerous reviews in this area have also been published. Few studies, most of which solely address issues like diagnosis or treatment, have attempted to systematically evaluate the use of AI for COVID-19 in line with PRISMA. As a result, the outcomes of these studies are uneven.(M.M. Ahsan, K.D. Gupta, M.M. Islam, S. Sen, M.L. Rahman, M.S. Hossain, 2020 & R.M. Wehbe et al., 2020)

NLP is supported with huge applications in healthcare system. Rapid text analysis is made possible by NLP technologies, which generate and compress natural language. Doctors are bale to understand the medical records in a more accurate fashion by analyzing the results of XAI. NLP in healthcare such as coding of medical data and monitoring has been explained using XAI (Loh, Hui Wen, Chui Ping Ooi, Silvia Seoni, Prabal Datta Barua, Filippo Molinari, U. Rajendra Acharya, 2022). In order to maintain a thorough medical history of the patients, medical coding is often done manually. These manual medical coding processes are laborious technically and prone to mistakes made by humans. But this is achievable because to XAI's explainability.

Online psychological therapies are another area of use. This XAI in NLP aids individuals with mental illnesses who are housebound because of the COVID-19 epidemic or for other personal reasons. A network model was created to analyse patient text and recognise phrases exhibiting signs of mental illness, thereby aiding in the diagnosis of a sizable patient population (U. Ahmed, G. Srivastava, U. Yun, J.C.W. Lin, 2022)

XAI may be very useful in identifying certain disease patterns in biosignals and pictures. Undoubtedly, the XAI model aids in the categorization of breast cancer and the detection of certain disease patterns in ultrasound pictures.

Additionally, XAI aids in the analysis of images, data extraction from them, and skin cancer diagnosis. In their discussion of the XAI approaches currently being developed for application in dermatological and dermatopathological support systems were evaluated and the efforts being made to ascertain the methods' applicability in clinical settings (Hauser, Katja, Alexander Kurz, Sarah Haggenmüller, Roman C. Maron, Christof von Kalle, Jochen S. Utikal, Friedegund Meier, 2022)

In section 1 of this chapter, the architecture of AI based healthcare systems is presented. The advantages and limitations of an AI based healthcare system are explained in section 2 of the chapter. The section 3 of the chapter covers the effect of AI based health care systems and some of the applications of AI in the healthcare system. Section 4 elaborates issues, recent advancements in artificial intelligence-based health services, current challenges and research direction towards designing an optimized AI based healthcare systems. This gives an intuition for researchers, health professionals as well as designers in analyzing and designing smart AI based health care systems which is very much necessary in today's digital era. Finally section 5 concludes the chapter with the future directions.

Architecture of XAI in Health Care System

The concept of a XAI and AI-based healthcare system is depicted in Figure 1. AI aids researchers, emergency medical services, radiologists, nurses, patients, and physicians.

AI models often arrives at a result using machine learning algorithms, but the architects of the AI systems do not fully understand how the algorithm actually reached that result, difficult to understand and trust for the doctors and other healthcare professionals. XAI, on the other hand develops methodology or process to confirm on the results obtained by machine learning and the whole process can be tracked and also explained. XAI will produce more explainable models. These models will be combined with the system to interface and the results of the algorithm are reasoned and useful results are collected which enables doctors, nurses, radiologists, clinical laboratories, researchers, pharmacists, and many other healthcare professionals to make their decisions and to assist in diagnosing, treatment planning and health management.

Figure 1. Architecture of XAI in health care system

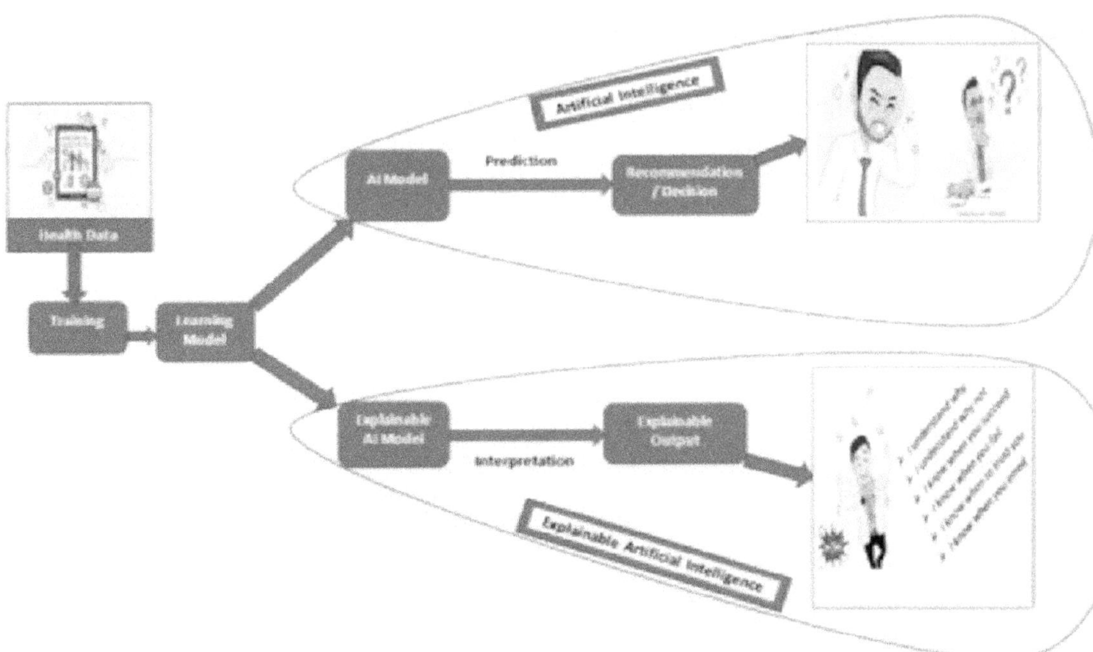

Principles of Explainable AI

The four principles for Explainable AI are as below:

1. AI systems should provide explanations with supporting evidences.
2. Explanations should be meaningful enabling doctors, nurses, radiologists, clinical laboratories, researchers, pharmacists, and many other healthcare professionals to make their decisions and to assist in diagnosing and treatment planning. The system must provide several explanations on the basis of the available user groups.
3. Explanations should be clear and accurate in describing the AI system's process which helps healthcare professionals in taking correct decisions.
4. AI systems should operate within its knowledge limits that they were designed for to ensure a reasonable outcome.

In section 1 of this chapter, the architecture of AI based healthcare systems is presented. The advantages and limitations of an AI based healthcare system are explained in section 2 of the chapter. The section 3 of the chapter covers the effect of AI based health care systems and some of the applications of AI in the healthcare system. Finally, section 4 elaborates issues, recent advancements in artificial intelligence based health services, current challenges and research direction towards designing an optimized AI based healthcare systems. This gives an intuition for researchers, health professionals as well as designers in analyzing and designing smart explainable AI based health care systems which is very much necessary in today's digital era.

PROS AND CONS OF EXPLAINABLE ARTIFICIAL INTELLIGENCE IN HEALTHCARE SYSTEM

Advantages of XAI Based Healthcare System

XAI has the ability to play significant roles in the healthcare system, despite the fact that the field is still relatively new (W. Nicholson Price II, 2019). Figure 2 illustrates numerous advantages in the healthcare system.

Figure 2. Benefits of XAI in health care system

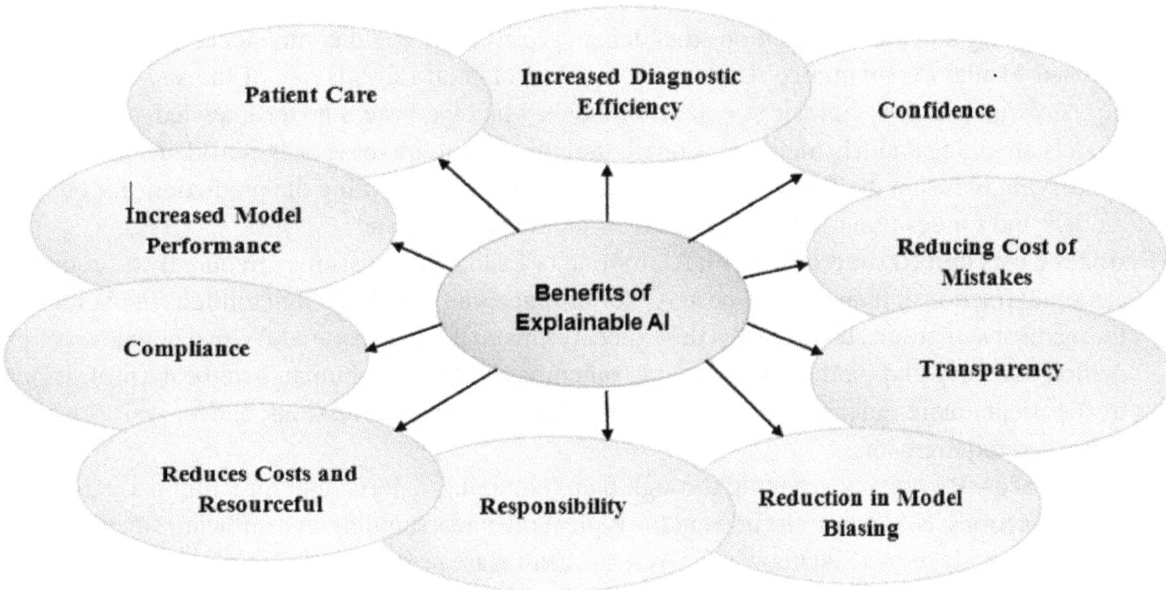

- **Increased Diagnostic Efficiency** -Improved diagnostic performance of XAI in healthcare is one advantage (Nenad Tomašev et al., 2019). In the medical profession, AI-driven systems build predictive models and learn patterns, but during the learning process, there may be human biases that could result in unfair or incorrect conclusions. By revealing the underlying workings of these opaque models, XAI satisfies the evolving requirements of AI engineering. Performance can be significantly enhanced with oversight.
- **Transparency**: The use of AI-driven systems in the medical field may be constrained in many critical situations due to the lack of transparency in the behavior of algorithms and the inability to explain the reasons behind the decision-making process. XAI explains the predictions made by machine learning models, and it also helps us comprehend and evaluate these predictions.
- **Reducing Cost of Mistakes –** When estimates are off, some industries that require quick decisions, like healthcare, are severely impacted. Monitoring the outcomes lessens the impact of incorrect findings and identifies the underlying cause, strengthening the underlying model.
- **Reduction in Model biasing** -There is strong bias evidence for AI models. For instance, racial and gender bias in autonomous vehicles, Apple Cards, and Amazon Rekognition. When making decisions, a XAI system lessens the impact of such biased predictions.
- **Responsibility** - The effectiveness of the system as a whole can be increased by allowing a person who might be in charge of those mistakes. Predictions made by AI models almost always have some degree of error.
- **Confidence** -For more effective use, some vital systems, including medical diagnosis, require a high level of coding confidence from the user. XAI's support in giving the predictions along with its explanation gains the system's confidence.

- **Compliance** - Companies are under increasing pressure from regulatory bodies to adapt and use XAI in order to quickly comply with the law. Explainable AI in healthcare can help to build confidence in an industry and the organizations that demands governance and compliance.
- **Increased Model Performance** -Understanding the potential flaws is one of the keys to maximizing performance. It is simpler to enhance models when we have a better knowledge of what the models are doing and why they occasionally fail. In order to increase user confidence, XAI aids in identifying biases in the data and model defects. It aids in confirming the predictions for bettering models and for developing fresh perspectives on the issue at hand.
- **Reduces Costs and Resourceful** -With AI, routine tasks like diagnosis may frequently be completed at a small fraction of their original cost. AI, for instance, can search through millions of photographs for medical symptoms. It eliminates the expensive manual labor required. With a high level of prediction accuracy and more understandable outcomes, XAI helps human healthcare professionals treat patients more quickly and efficiently, resulting in fewer admissions, longer wait times, and fewer bed requirements.
- **Patient Care -** By quickly scanning through data, obtaining reports, and directing patients for additional actions, XAI can assist prevent the typical misunderstanding in healthcare situations. XAI uses a vast body of medical knowledge to assist healthcare professionals in providing patients with impartial and ethical care.

Limitations in AI Based Healthcare System

- In explainable AI, sometimes some things are impossible to explain or difficulty in understanding the explanations as they get more complex.
- XAI gives justification to the decisions developed by the model without interpreting the model directly which leads to wrong diagnosis and disparate treatment.
- Explainable AI occasionally leaves out key details about how a model generates a forecast. It does not describe the decision-making process; it only discusses the effect on model projections. Workers are then forced to choose between an accurate, uninterpretable model and an inaccurate, interpretable model.
- Evaluating the trade-offs between “truly explainable and transparent AI” is another important aspect of an explainable AI. Intellectual property would no longer serve as a competitive advantage if an AI platform’s whole internal workings were made open to the public.
- Also, recent research has found many limitations in the gradient-based method.

The Process of XAI

The steps followed during the XAI process are as follows:

(a) Because it is believed that XAI will be useful for system enhancements in the future. As a result, the following are the first stages needed for the XAI process:

Pre-processing: This phase describes data cleansing, imputation and feature analysis. Data imputation is the use of replacement values to fill in the gaps left by missing data, whereas data cleaning is the management of inaccurate or not compelte datasets. In the instance of SHapley Additive exPlanations (SHAP), a game theoretic method for improved prediction outcomes, the top dominant characteristics are identified. (Marzyeh Ghassemi, Luke Oakden-Rayner, Andrew L Beam, 2021)

(b) Methodology: The model is especially created for the development and adjustment of machine learning or deep learning. There are several machine learning techniques, such as naive bayes, linear regression, decision trees, support vector machines (SVM), etc., while neural networks are utilised to simulate human brains by offering a number of algorithms for identifying correlations within the dataset (D. Wang, Q. Yang, A. Abdul and B. Y. Lim, 2019 & A. Holzinger, C. Biemann, C. S. Pattichis and D. B. Kell, 2017). Similar ideas are covered by interpretable deep learning, but it examines data processing at each layer, assisting the designer in managing data flow and internal mathematical operations. Additionally, the layers may be built up by choosing the activation functions, max pooling, fully linked classification, and feature learning via convolution, among other options.

(c) Explanation: To understand the significance and actions done by the algorithm, this phase explicitly explains each choice. The explanation gives thorough justification for every choice made throughout the model, including preprocessing, prediction method, classification, evaluation, and conclusion. The explanations that make up XAI's core content help the end user, industry experts, or clients accept the deployed system more readily.

(d) Re-evaluation: Feedback to differentiate the human results from the obtained system results is incorporated. At the end, user engages with the system by giving the appropriate input on each choice and set of parameters, which can then be evaluated successfully by re-configuration in a subsequent version. As a result, the user friendly feature is and can boost the future iteration of the training data and weights augmentation.

APPLICATIONS OF AI BASED HEALTHCARE SYSTEM

- ❖ **Bed Side Sensors:** By utilizing XAI approaches to explain how an AI system came to a particular conclusion, it is possible to increase openness of how AI systems function and trust in them. This results in increased transparency of healthcare equipment.
- ❖ **X-Ray machines:** Result tracing is more efficient since the explanations generated by XAI techniques can be utilized to track the factors that affected the AI system to forecast an occurrence.
- ❖ **Managing Medical Records and Other Data:** Data management is where artificial intelligence and digital automation are most frequently used, because gathering and analyzing data is the first stage in providing healthcare (such as medical records and other historical data). Robots gather, archive, convert, and track data to offer quicker, more trustworthy access.
- ❖ **Doing Repetitive Jobs:** Robots can perform regular tasks like data input, X-rays, CT scans, and test analysis more rapidly and accurately. The radiology and cardiology departments must analyze a lot of data, which can be challenging and time-consuming. Future radiologists and cardiologists should concentrate on cases that require human supervision and are the most challenging.

- **Treatment Design:** Systems with artificial intelligence have been developed to evaluate data, including clinical judgment, outside research, and notes and reports from a patient's file, to assist in selecting the best, most individualized treatment plan.
- **Digital Consultation:** UK apps like Babylon employ artificial intelligence to offer medical consultations based on user medical histories and standard medical procedures. Users submit their symptoms through the app, which uses speech recognition to compare them against a database of diseases. Then, after taking into account the user's medical background, Babylon provides a suggested course of action.
- **Virtual Nurses:** The firm Sense.ly created Molly, a virtual nurse in order to help people, monitor patients' conditions and follow up on treatments in between doctor appointments. With a focus on chronic conditions, the initiative supports patients using machine learning. Boston Children's Hospital created an app for Amazon Alexa in 2016 that provides parents of sick children with fundamental health information and guidance. The app responds to queries regarding prescription drugs and whether certain symptoms necessitate seeing a doctor.
- **Medication Management:** The National Institutes of Health created the AiCure app to monitor a patient's medication use. Together, AI and the webcam on a smartphone can help patients manage their condition by automatically confirming that they are taking their meds. The people with serious medical conditions, people who routinely disobey medical advice, and participants in clinical research are the most regular users.
- **Drug Creation:** Drug development for clinical trials can take over ten years and cost billions of dollars. If this procedure could be accelerated and made more widely available, the world might change. An artificial intelligence (AI) system was employed to look for current pharmaceuticals that could be altered to treat the illness during the most recent Ebola virus outbreak. Despite the fact that studies of this kind often take months or years, the algorithm discovered two drugs that potentially reduce Ebola infectivity in just one day.
- **Precision Medicine:** In order to find mutations and connections to disease, genetics and genomics analyze DNA data. A person's genetic makeup can be used to anticipate potential health problems, and AI-powered body scans can also identify cancer and vascular diseases at the early stages (A. Holzinger, C. Biemann, C. S. Pattichis and D. B. Kell, 2017).
- **Health Monitoring:** Heart rate and activity levels can be tracked with wearable health monitors from FitBit, Apple, Garmin, and other manufacturers. The user can be encouraged to exercise more by providing this information to doctors (and AI systems) so they can learn more about patient requirements and behaviors (Noseworthy PA, et al., 2019 & Bonner C, Bell K, Jansen J, Glasziou P, Irwig L, Doust J, et al., 2018)
- **Healthcare System Analysis:** Medical bills in the Netherlands are almost entirely computerized. The data is combed through by a Dutch company using AI to identify ineffective processes, bad medical judgements, and potentially preventable patient hospitalisations.
- **Patient Readmission**: Patient readmission prediction process uses Deep Learning Techniques such as Long Short Term Memory (LSTM) since they can capture complex patterns in healthcare system. To overcome the challenge of interpretation of the deep learning techniques, researchers have developed a variety of explainers that can provide explanations for the predictions made by deep learning models. Few commonly used explainers for patient readmission prediction include LIME, SHAP, DICE, and ANCHORS.

CURRENT CHALLENGES, POSSIBLE SOLUTIONS, AND RESEARCH DIRECTIONS TOWARDS AI BASED HEALTHCARE SYSTEM

This section discusses current obstacles to developing intelligent AI-based healthcare systems, including the risk of patient injuries caused by AI system flaws, data accessibility, integrations, security concerns, privacy concerns, biases and inequalities in algorithms, exponential growth of healthcare data, a lack of high-quality medical data, and more. It elaborates on the problems and potential remedies for handling the dangers of AI-based healthcare. Also noted and presented are research directions for the aforementioned problems. This provides knowledge that researchers, designers, and other experts can use to design intelligent AI-based healthcare system.

Artificial Intelligence is a very popular technology to analyze the numerous picture modalities utilized in healthcare. The capacity to analyze has been further improved by deep learning, which automatically created features from the image data. Deep learning models typically target a single disease and require discrete instantiation and retraining for additional diseases. As a result, each setting has a profusion of specialized models. The task-specific models may not extrapolate or interpolate in the task context, thus not possible to adapt these models to new diseases with domain change. The models need a huge quantity of data to train, but there isn't much of it available in the healthcare industry, and gathering that data is also a labor-intensive process. There is a critical need for universal, moldable, AI-based models for smart health care that can function for all types of medical issues. These models should be too general to be useful for any ailment. Future trends in the AI-based healthcare system may include cost-effective neuroimaging, particularly for stroke patients.

Patient-specific clinical aids: In order to solve a Precision Health problem, patient-specific prostheses like implants, surgical aids, etc. may need to be tested before being made available to patients. Surgical aids will be designed and turned into dependable, high-quality products through a phased approach that includes designing, prototyping, and validation. Using artificial intelligence-based architecture, the entire process may be visualized and modeled.

The earlier healthcare age faced difficulties in combating communicable diseases. Non-communicable diseases (NCDs), which is also known as chronic diseases, have recently taken the lead, and have a protracted duration and a slow pace of progression.

The high cost of medical care and persistent chronic illnesses have greatly increased society's financial burden. The prevention and treatment of chronic diseases are still urgently needed in every country today, but especially in low- and middle-income nations. The rehabilitation center's use of the AI-based smart healthcare system for monitoring, remedial action, and assistive living is significant.

The expense of therapy is the major issue for cancer sufferers. Drug and infusion expenses make up the majority of treatment costs. The cost resulting from hospital in-patient fees makes up the majority of the expense. By shifting patients to lower-cost care locations, such as from a crowded metropolis to a second-tier town for the same drug's infusion or to undergo radiotherapy, this is promoting distributed cancer care. To provide cost-effective yet high-quality care, these issues require technological advancement and process adaptation. Moving chemotherapy infusions from in- and out-patient settings, doctor's offices, and hospitals to private homes has been a significant cost-cutting measure. Home infusion and shifting care are an emerging trend that is advantageous to everyone. Home infusion can be performed in community clinics, hospitals, and primary care institutions in impoverished countries. In order to transmit knowledge to primary care facilities, the proposal searches for approaches to create forecasting models for oncology patients' home infusions and monitoring. Create a digital twin to predict risk, identify cancer patients who might benefit from home infusions, and determine what actions should be taken to remotely monitor them following treatment (Noseworthy PA, t al., 2019).

Device may produce patient-specific summaries. Chronic disease patients frequently go through protracted multimodal treatments that involve numerous rounds of diagnosis, treatment, and monitoring interactions with various healthcare professionals. Each of these interactions leads in clinical reports and notes, which together form a historical account of the disease's course, its treatments, and its outcomes. However, as the patient trip lengthens, so does the cognitive load placed on the clinician, who must review the patient's history before making treatment recommendations. Doctors around the world have noted that a significant obstacle to patient treatment is a lack of time for reading patient reports. Therefore, computer aid is absolutely necessary to enable clinicians to manage the patient journey effectively. One method of offering computer assistance is to utilize AI/NLP techniques to provide a succinct summary of each clinical report so that the doctor can decide whether or not to pay attention to a particular report right away. By employing AL/NLP algorithms to generate succinct summaries of clinical reports, you can give oncologists, cardiologists, and endocrinologists AI assistance to help them traverse the patient's clinical reports effectively.

The use of AI in the healthcare industry demands a lot of precise results, endorsement by medical experts, and a lot of stakeholders. Despite being widely employed in other fields, deep learning models are still in their infancy in the healthcare industry due to the black box problem. The "black box" problem refers to deep learning algorithms' inability to explain how they arrive at their conclusions.

When developing AI-based smart healthcare, some of the challenges that we look at include the risks of patient injuries due to AI system errors, data availability, data integration, data annotation, security issues, privacy issues, biases and inequities in algorithms, the exponential growth of healthcare data, the lack of high-quality medical data, and other issues.

While AI may offer certain benefits, there are also a lot of drawbacks as well:

Accidents and mistakes. The most apparent risk is that occasionally malfunctioning artificial intelligence (AI) systems could put patients in danger or cause other problems for the healthcare system. The patient can suffer if an AI system selects one patient over another for a hospital room based on incorrect predictions of who will benefit the most, misses a malignancy during a radiological test, or gives the wrong prescription. The bulk of injuries are brought on by medical errors in the current healthcare system, even in the absence of artificial intelligence. Errors made by machines and people can differ in at least two ways. Machine and human errors can differ in at least two ways. First, different responses from patients and doctors may be elicited when injuries are caused by software as opposed to human error. A single AI system's defect might hurt thousands of patients instead of just the few people affected by a single provider's error if AI technologies are widely adopted.

A few examples of sources used to train AI systems are electronic health records, pharmaceutical records, insurance claims records, and consumer-generated data like activity tracker or purchase history. These sources provide the necessary quantities of data. Various platforms typically use scattered data. Even without the aforementioned diversity, patients frequently move insurance plans and providers, which results in data being spread across numerous systems and formats. Due to this fragmentation, data collection becomes more expensive, the dataset is less comprehensive, and there is a greater chance that the data will be erroneous. It also restricts the types of companies that can create efficient health-care AI.

Privacy concerns. There are more threats to privacy. Developers collect this information from a lot of patients since they need big datasets (Ashu et al., 2021; Hussain et al., 2021). Several legal disputes regarding the exchange. Some consumers may worry that their privacy would be violated by this data collecting, which has raised privacy issues in response to the data interchange between big health institutions and AI businesses (Nenad Tomašev et al., 2019). Due to AI's capacity to anticipate patient-specific information that has never been given to the algorithm, privacy may be violated in yet another way. Actually, this is a usual goal for AI in the healthcare industry. For instance, even if a person has never stated having Parkinson's disease, an AI system may recognize them by the movement of a computer mouse. (or were ignorant). Particularly if the AI system's judgment was made public and disclosed to third parties like banks or life insurance firms, patients would regard this as an invasion of their privacy (D. Wang, Q. Yang, A. Abdul and B. Y. Lim, 2019 & A. Holzinger, C. Biemann, C. S. Pattichis and D. B. Kell, 2017).

Prejudice and injustice. AI in healthcare has issues with bias and equity. Since AI systems learn from the data, they use to train themselves, they can include biases in the data. For instance, the resulting AI systems will know less about and treat patients from populations who do not frequently attend academic medical centers-less well-if the vast majority of the data used to develop AI systems is obtained in academic medical institutions. When encounter notes are transcribed by a source who belongs to a racial or gender group that is underrepresented in training data, similar to the preceding scenario, AI systems for speech recognition may perform poorly (M. T. Ribeiro and C. Guestrin, 2016).

Training of AI systems on accurate, representative data doesn't guarantee an unbiased output as the built-in biases and disparities in the healthcare system may still lead to problems (S. M. Lundberg and S.-I. Lee, 2017). Even though the recommendation to prescribe lesser doses of analgesics to African-American patients is driven by systemic bias rather than biological reality, an AI system that learns from health-system records may someday learn to do so. In contrast to biological truth, white patients are prescribed pain medicine more frequently than African-American patients (S. M. Lundberg and S.-I. Lee, 2017), a practice that is founded on systematic bias. By providing fewer resources to patients who are seen by healthcare systems to be less attractive or profitable for a variety of reasons, resource-allocation AI systems may lead to inequality.

Repositioning professionally. Change in the medical industry is one of the longer-term concerns. Some medical careers, notably radiology, are anticipated to experience major change given that a large portion of their labor can now be automated. Some academicians are concerned that as AI grows more prevalent, human capacity and knowledge may deteriorate. As a result, medical staff could be unable to spot and fix AI system errors and enhance medical knowledge (D. Wang, Q. Yang, A. Abdul and B. Y. Lim, 2019).

The erroneous idea of Nirvana. There must be one more threat included. AI has the potential to greatly advance medical technology. According to the nirvana fallacy, issues arise when people make decisions and evaluate new options in comparison to perfection rather than the current circumstance. Healthcare AI is in danger and facing challenges. The current approach, however, also has some serious drawbacks. Inaction runs the risk of sustaining the status quo due to AI's limitations.

There are many approaches, that might address potential health care AI issues:

Data generation and availability. A number of concerns are raised by the challenging task of gathering high-quality data while protecting patient privacy. The government's provision of the infrastructure required for data collection, such as standards for electronic health records and direct funding of projects for high-quality data collection in health systems lacking the required resources, is crucial for a certain set of viable solutions. A different strategy is to make direct investments in the creation of superior datasets. Both the US-based All of Us project and the UK-based BioBank project make an effort to compile thorough health care data on a sizable population. Maintaining patient confidence and engagement for these vast databases will definitely require setting up appropriate privacy protections.

Excellent guidance. Controlling the quality of AI systems will make it possible to reduce the danger of patient harm. Several commercially accessible medical care The Food and Drug Administration is responsible for monitoring AI products (FDA). The group has previously approved the distribution of a number of devices and is currently discussing new rules for the use of AI in the healthcare industry (A. Holzinger, C. Biemann, C. S. Pattichis and D. B. Kell, 2017).

Participation and training of the providers. The introduction of AI will likely impact how healthcare employees are employed. One benefit is that doctors and other healthcare providers will have more time to speak with patients one-on-one and provide better, more individualized treatment (Noseworthy PA, et al., 2019). Service providers would have to deal with an abundance of confusing predictions and suggestions from rival algorithms in a less perfect future.

Explainable Artificial Intelligence (XAI) is booming much in medicine. But there are some weakness in designing a XAI based Healthcare Systems. Occasionally the input information and models are too intricate, composite, and multidimensional to be well explained by a straightforward correlation between the two. Examples include models created to assess audio, visual, and textual data. In these situations, the emphasis has been on analyzing the model's decision-making process to determine how much each component of the picture contributed to a particular choice. Despite being well-liked by the healthcare system, they are seen as problematic in the larger explainability literature. The weakness was in dealing with uncertainties in the real world. Day by day applications in the field of healthcare system became increasingly successful, but at the same time becoming increasingly opaque.

The threat associated with Explainable Artificial Intelligence's development is another. Professionals frequently have profound understanding of the nature of society issues and the best course of action to address them. If the experts are replaced with the new Explainable Artificial Intelligence, their tacit knowledge would be gone. The Explainable Artificial Intelligence approaches may not always work well for the issues they were not intended to address. XAI might not always be the best option for automating decision-making. Prior to implementing any remedies, it is usually best to assess the problem and make an appropriate choice (Marzyeh Ghassemi, Luke Oakden-Rayner, Andrew L Beam, 2021). However, the tremendous amount of data being processed means it's not without its pitfalls, particularly when it comes to decision making for complex tasks.

Sometimes the nature of explanations provided through XAI may overlook important information which leads to wrong decision making by the professionals in the healthcare system (Petch, Jeremy, Shuang Di, and Walter Nelson, 2022).

CONCLUSION

The chapter will assist designers, professionals, and researchers in creating intelligent health-care systems that are optimized. The chapter goes into detail on the design of an AI-based healthcare system. Applications, benefits, and drawbacks of an AI-based healthcare system are examined. Researchers, designers, and professionals can gain insight into the current research difficulties, potential solutions, and direction towards developing an AI-based smart healthcare system from the information provided.

FUTURE DIRECTION

This chapter discusses the role of XAI research currently in healthcare, architecture of XAI in pros and cons, issues, challenges and XAI in some healthcare applications. As said, the XAI models that are now being developed may recognize patient inconsistencies and provide an explanation for them. The ability to extract critical clinical data for effective patient data recording could greatly streamline hospital workflow, allowing nurses or other healthcare professionals to concentrate more on other crucial tasks while handing off all the routine tasks to AI models. Future systems that enable real-time monitoring of irregularities in certain physiological signals like ECGs, might be created using XAI models. Similar to how wearable technology allows for continuous monitoring of a user's health, XAI can identify abnormal trends in biosignals. As a result, it is useful to assess individuals who had a heart attack or stroke. There presently is little XAI research on critical text detection in clinical notes and 1D biosignal abnormality explanations. Researchers could draw attention on these two areas and promote healthcare system to a larger extent. Additionally, researchers could focus on how XAI may affect dermatologists' practises related to the identification of skin cancer. It lacks a methodical and thorough assessment of its applicability in this case.

A comprehensive cloud system that supports both hospital and ambulatory applications is being developed via more research. Researchers might endeavor to advance community healthcare and the Internet of Health Things' (IoHT) sustainability in hospital and outpatient settings.

REFERENCES

Ahmed, U., Srivastava, G., Yun, U., & Lin, J. C. W. (2022). EANDC: An explainable attention network based deep adaptive clustering model for mental health treatment. *Future Generation Computer Systems*, *130*, 106–113. doi:10.1016/j.future.2021.12.008

Ahsan, M.M. Gupta, K.D. Islam, M.M. Sen, S. Rahman, M.L. & Hossain, M. S. (2020). *Study of Different Deep Learning Approach With Explainable AI for Screening Patients With Covid-19 Symptoms: Using CT Scan and Chest X-ray Image Dataset*". arXiv.

Amann, J., Blasimme, A., Vayena, E., Frey, D., & Madai, V. I. (2020). Explainability for artificial intelligence in healthcare: A multidisciplinary perspective. *BMC Medical Informatics and Decision Making*, *20*(1), 310. doi:10.118612911-020-01332-6 PMID:33256715

Ashu, A., Hussain, M. W., Sinha Roy, D., & Reddy, H. K. (2021). Intelligent data compression policy for Hadoop performance optimization. In *Proceedings of the 11th International Conference on Soft Computing and Pattern Recognition (SoCPaR 2019) 11 (pp. 80-89).* Springer International Publishing. 10.1007/978-3-030-49345-5_9

Bonner, C., Bell, K., Jansen, J., Glasziou, P., Irwig, L., Doust, J., & McCaffery, K. (2018). Should heart age calculators be used alongside absolute cardiovascular disease risk assessment? *BMC Cardiovascular Disorders*, *18*(1), 18–19. doi:10.118612872-018-0760-1 PMID:29409444

Doshi-Velez, F., & Kim, B. (2017). *Towards A Rigorous Science of Interpretable Machine Learning.* Ml.

Gerlings, J., Jensen, M. S., & Shollo, A. (2022). Explainable AI, But Explainable to Whom? An Exploratory Case Study of xAI in Healthcare. In C. P. Lim, Y. W. Chen, A. Vaidya, C. Mahorkar, & L. C. Jain (Eds.), *Handbook of Artificial Intelligence in Healthcare. Intelligent Systems Reference Library* (Vol. 212). Springer. doi:10.1007/978-3-030-83620-7_7

Ghassemi, M., Oakden-Rayner, L., & Beam, A. L. (2021). The false hope of current approaches to explainable artificial intelligence in health care. *The Lancet. Digital Health, 3*(11), E745–E750. doi:10.1016/S2589-7500(21)00208-9 PMID:34711379

Hauser, K., Kurz, A., Haggenmüller, S., Maron, R. C., von Kalle, C., Utikal, J. S., Meier, F., Hobelsberger, S., Gellrich, F. F., Sergon, M., Hauschild, A., French, L. E., Heinzerling, L., Schlager, J. G., Ghoreschi, K., Schlaak, M., Hilke, F. J., Poch, G., Kutzner, H., & Brinker, T. J. (2022). Explainable artificial intelligence in skin cancer recognition: A systematic review. *European Journal of Cancer, 167*, 54–69. doi:10.1016/j.ejca.2022.02.025 PMID:35390650

Holzinger, A., Biemann, C., Pattichis, C. S., & Kell, D. B. (2017). *What do we need to build explainable AI systems for the medical domain?* M1.

Hussain, M. W. (2021). A counter based approach for reducer placement with augmented Hadoop rackawareness. *Turkish Journal of Electrical Engineering and Computer Sciences, 29*(1), 437–453. doi:10.3906/elk-2001-106

Khedkar, S., Subramanian, V., Shinde, G., & Gandhi, P. (2019) "*Explainable AI in Healthcare*", SSRN Electronic Journal. doi:10.2139/ssrn.3367686

Lakkaraju, H., Bach, S. H., & Leskovec, J. (2016). *Interpretable decision sets: A joint framework for description and prediction.* Proceedings of the ACM SIGKDD International Conference on Knowledge Discovery and Data Mining, (pp. 1675-1684). ACM. 10.1145/2939672.2939874

Loh, H. W., Ooi, C. P., Seoni, S., Barua, P. D., Molinari, F., & Acharya, U. R. (2022). Application of explainable artificial intelligence for healthcare: A systematic review of the last decade (2011–2022). *Computer Methods and Programs in Biomedicine, 226*, 107161. doi:10.1016/j.cmpb.2022.107161 PMID:36228495

Lundberg, S. M., & Lee, S.-I. (2017). A unified approach to interpreting model predictions. *Advances in Neural Information Processing Systems*, 4765–4774.

Morley, J., Machado, C. C. V., Burr, C., Cowls, J., Joshi, I., Taddeo, M., & Floridi, L. (2020). The ethics of AI in health care: A mapping review. *Social Science & Medicine, 260.*

Nicholson Price, W. II. (2019). *Artificial intelligence in the medical system: four roles for potential transformation.* Yale Journal of Health Poly L. & Ethics.

Noseworthy, P. A., Kaufman, E. S., Chen, L. Y., Chung, M. K., Elkind Mitchell, S. V., & Joglar, J. A. (2019). Subclinical and device-detected atrial fibrillation: pondering the knowledge gap: a scientific statement from the American Heart Association. *Circulation, 2019*(140), e944–e963. doi:10.1161/CIR.0000000000000740 PMID:31694402

Srinivasu, P., Sandhya, N., Jhaveri, R., & Raut, R. (2022). From Blackbox to Explainable AI in Healthcare: Existing Tools and Case Studies. Mobile Information Systems.

Petch, J., Di, S., & Nelson, W. (2022). Opening the black box: The promise and limitations of explainable machine learning in cardiology. *The Canadian Journal of Cardiology*, *38*(2), 204–213. doi:10.1016/j.cjca.2021.09.004 PMID:34534619

Rajpurkar, P., Chen, E., Banerjee, O., & Topol, E. J. (2022). AI in health and medicine. *Nature Medicine*, *28*(1), 31–38. doi:10.103841591-021-01614-0 PMID:35058619

Reddy, S., Allan, S., Coghlan, S., & Cooper, P. (2020, March). A governance model for the application of AI in health care. *Journal of the American Medical Informatics Association : JAMIA*, *27*(3), 491–497. doi:10.1093/jamia/ocz192 PMID:31682262

Ribeiro, M. T., & Guestrin, C. (2016). *Why Should I Trust You?* Explaining the Predictions of Any Classifier. doi:10.1145/2939672.2939778

Rong, G., Mendez, A., Assi, E., Zhao, B., & Sawan, M. (2020). Artificial Intelligence in Healthcare: Review and Prediction Case Studies. *Engineering, 6*(3), 291-301.

Saraswat, D., Bhattacharya, P., Verma, A., Prasad, V. K., Tanwar, S., Sharma, G., Bokoro, P. N., & Sharma, R. (2022). Explainable AI for Healthcare 5.0: Opportunities and Challenges. *IEEE Access : Practical Innovations, Open Solutions*, *10*, 84486–84517. doi:10.1109/ACCESS.2022.3197671

Tian, S., Yang, W., Le Grange, J. M., Wang, P., Huang, W., & Ye, Z. (2019). Smart healthcare: Making medical care more intelligent. *Global Health Journal (Amsterdam, Netherlands)*, *3*(3), 62–65. doi:10.1016/j.glohj.2019.07.001

Tomašev, N., Glorot, X., Rae, J. W., Zielinski, M., Askham, H., Saraiva, A., Mottram, A., Meyer, C., Ravuri, S., Protsyuk, I., Connell, A., Hughes, C. O., Karthikesalingam, A., Cornebise, J., Montgomery, H., Rees, G., Laing, C., Baker, C. R., Peterson, K., & Mohamed, S. (2019). A clinically applicable approach to continuous prediction of future acute kidney injury. *Nature*, *572*(7767), 116–119. doi:10.103841586-019-1390-1 PMID:31367026

Wang, D., Yang, Q., Abdul, A., & Lim, B. Y. (2019). Designing Theory-Driven User-Centric Explainable AI. *Proceedings of the 2019 CHI Conference on Human Factors in Computing Systems - CHI '19,* (pp. 1-15). ACM. 10.1145/3290605.3300831

Wehbe, R. M. (2020). Deep COVID-XR: An artificial intelligence algorithm to detect COVID-19 on chest radiographs trained and tested on a large US clinical dataset. *Radiology*, 203511. PMID:33231531

Chapter 4
Adaptability of IoT and Cloud for Enabling the Smart City:
Applications and Challenges

Archana Sharma
IIMT College of Engineering, Greater Noida, India

Prateek Jain
Amity University, Noida, India

ABSTRACT

The 'smart city' notion places a lot of emphasis on using information and communication technologies to boost connectedness and quality of life and effectiveness of various local authorities (ICT). Smart city services stimulate the practice of cloud- and IoT-based services that have included actual web applications that make use of sensors, smart phones, and RFIDs. Cloud platforms besides the IoT persist the two ICT models that are currently dealing the greatest influence on the Industrial IoT as well. Both concepts significantly influence the way it has developed and put into practice applications and smart city solutions. The first phase of this study highlights key features of IoT and Cloud along with smart city applications. Further in the second phase the research investigates the confluence of cloud platforms with IoT to build up the smart city besides various challenges associated in smart city implementation. Lastly, the research focuses on the smart cities' requirement for cloud-based IoT applications and provides the future direction in adaptability of smart city.

INTRODUCTION

Smart city aims in improving the niche of services provided to citizens while lowering operating expenses for the utilization of government money by the public sector more efficiently. Cities are required to collect information about their surroundings, infrastructure, events, and residents to serve smart services. Its primary facilitators and drivers are the IoT & Cloud computing. An IoT is a collective global IT platform that connects networked objects and unified networks & is a critical concept in the developing

DOI: 10.4018/979-8-3693-0744-1.ch004

internet. Virtualization comes in two flavors: ones that involve and don't involve people. It gets rather taxing managing such an excess of data. As a result, IoT applications are widely employed in diversified industries which includes education, healthcare, agriculture, and smart cities. It uses various approaches to collect cloud and sensor data, which is then cleaned, processed, and analyzed. Smart cities tend to use many digital and physical devices for data collection. A city's performance is enhanced because of the data these sensors gather, and the information received from such devices is successfully used to manage resources, assets, and revenues, among other things.

Cloud-based IoT apps may enable smart cities by processing and analyzing data from users, devices, and various sources for the management and monitoring of water supply systems, energy utilities, waste management, criminal detection, security systems, competency, digital libraries, healthcare facilities, environmental monitoring, traffic services, and other opportunities. IoT thus enables the development of fully novel smart city facilities besides the transformation of current city services into smart services. This is made possible through Big Data, IoT & Cloud for various enhancements. By providing public cloud services, service providers enable third parties to apprise the IoT environment and integrate IoT data into IoT-enabled electrical devices.

Fundamental Layers in Smart Cities Operations

- Technological Layer: Numerous connected devices and sensors that are utilized to offer many services.
- Dedicated Requests: Information systems utilized by people and experts for enhancing its operations.
- Usage of Application: The installation and its usage by authorized users within the city.

The subsequent development of internet-based computing is cloud computation. As soon as intelligent devices leave the cloud computing environment, the IoT has the potential to increase throughput, performance, and efficiency. Smart cities are metropolitan places that systematically strive to attain environmental sustainability, urban system authority, better public health, knowledge development, and network-driven advancement. Besides communication technology, smart cities also observe for themselves the direction of records. ICT resources can be transferred across a network because of cloud computing, the upcoming stage of internet-based computing. Some advantages of cloud infrastructure for IoT include increased payload, productivity, and performance, the ways in which electronic packaging can be created, sold, and distributed thanks to cloud computing. Considering this, IoT and cloud are now very close to new internet technologies that are compatible with IoT systems. Today's connected, diversified devices number in the billions, and they generate a tone of data. They consist of various items, including as sensors, actuators, vehicles, telephones, smart gadgets, and home and office equipment.

Problems that arise in a dynamic, shared environment primarily emphasizes the IoT & it refers to a broad category that includes a vast range of adaptable and unusual devices with limited storage, power, and performance capabilities. IoT system development is impeded by these constraints, which include complex issues like compatibility, efficiency, full functionality, and availability. The cloud provides shared resources, which stand out for their accessibility, affordability, and aesthetic appeal. These resources include networks, storage, computers, and software. This platform may utilize cloud-based resources and services for data collection, transport, processing, and storage. It may also use cloud resources and services to collect, transmit, search for, examine, and store data generated by complex situations. The various sectors like commercial & public one's have also helped in embracing the IoT by means of urgent delivery, public transportation, public safety, and city lighting.

With the expansion of IoT, cities are connecting more frequently, which enables them to increase the dependability and taking into account how well the infrastructure works, besides that the emergency services' responsiveness. With the usage of smart infrastructure like smart parking, smart transportation, and smart health, the IoT has raised the standard of living for their residents. It has become a common fixture in many households rather than just being used to make cities smarter.

The first section of the chapter highlights the key features of IoT, Cloud and Big Data as well as their relationship. The research highlights the various smart city applications and focus towards the problems associated with Smart City implementation. The second section of the chapter suggests the smart city implementation using Cloud Based IoT. An IoT can get the benefits from improved cloud infrastructure payload, performance, and efficiency. Section 3 highlights about the problems faced in the smart city implementation. Section 4 about the suggestions in the smart city context. Lastly, the research proposes the future direction of smart implementation with emerging technologies and conclusion in section 5 and 6.

LITERATURE REVIEW

IoT

It is a growing network with sensors and computer devices connected together with embedded technology for gathering and exchanging data. The IoT includes plenty of intelligent devices that have been given unique personalities (Moustafa, 2021). The ability for physical smart objects to gather and exchange data is enabled by a vast network of these objects, including gadgets, sensors, transporters, and buildings connected to software, electronics, hardware, and networks. For the operation of an IoT network the management of unique identities is crucial (Whitmore et al, 2015). IoT networks must offer coupling links among their distinct identities because they are task-oriented. Due to IoT- enabled devices, connected smart items may be recognized from one another and remotely managed by the current system, which results in improved accuracy, increased productivity, and favorable financial outcomes. The embedded software makes every object distinct and recognizable (Malik, V., & Singh, S. 2019). The adoption of mobile based devices and international services grew significantly in the earlier decade due to the enormous advancements in remote communication technologies.

The opportunity of connecting the real world as well as the cybernet world has, however, grown, and cyber-physical systems has been increased. (Conti et al., 2012). The phenomenon of "cyber-physical systems" users in an era of embedded ICT in which computation and network interaction coexist with physical processes. These systems manage and control their dynamic forces in order to be effective, reliable, adaptable, and more secure (Zaman et al., 2015; Barro-Torres et al., 2012). Digital environment possesses the information that simulates physical processes is transferred, produced, and used, for instance, data gathered by various sensors. However, by using input feedback loops such as actuators, this information may also affect the physical processes (Jameer et al., 2018).

Characteristics of the IoT

Figure 1 highlights the various characteristics of IoT.

Figure 1. IoT key characteristics

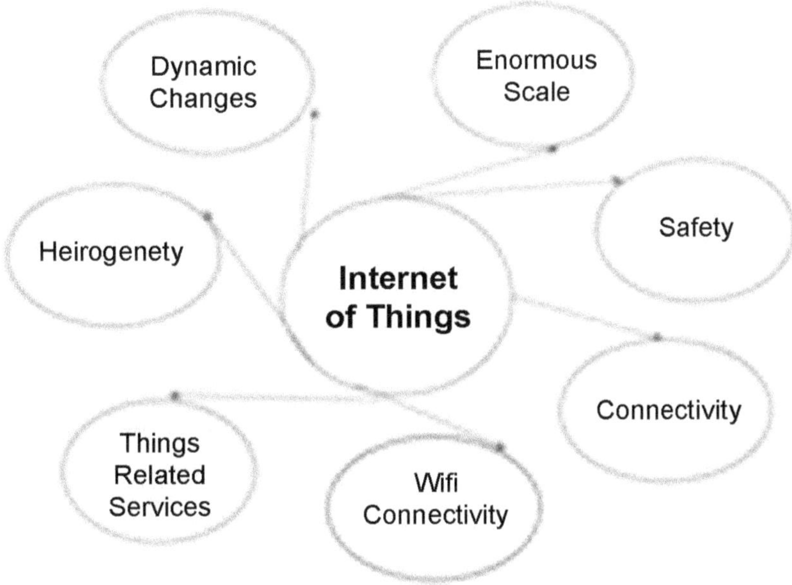

Massive scale: Compared to the various internet-connected IoT nodes currently in use, the count of IoT nodes that will require management and connection will be many orders of magnitude higher. It will be necessary to manage the information produced and analyze it for application-related objectives. The key factors are content management and content semantics.

Security: Customers should not overlook security due to IoT advantages. As IoT senders and receivers, they should prepare for security. Both the security of client information and indeed the security of their health are protected by all this.

Dynamic changes: The status of a device can vary depending on things like sleep and awareness, connectivity and disconnection, & IoT node information like speed and position. Additionally, the IoT node count is subject to dynamic fluctuation.

Connectivity: IoT may be used more widely and with more devices. Interoperability on the network, which offers the similar capabilities for accessing and producing content, facilitates access.

Things-related services: IoT can offer many things-related services within the limitations of things. Both global & data world procedures will be involved for providing services connected to things within the limits of things itself.

IoT Architecture

It constitutes many different parts, including actuators, protocols, sensors, cloud services, etc. It often includes dissimilar layers that permit administrators to observe, monitor, and keep up the system in a consistent manner. It necessitates a strategy for organizational integration, like any system design plan besides systems already in place at your business.

5 Levels in the architecture of IoT

- Things
- Sensors
- Internet Gateways
- Edge IT
- Cloud Plarform

These are shown in below figure 2:

Figure 2. IoT architecture's five levels

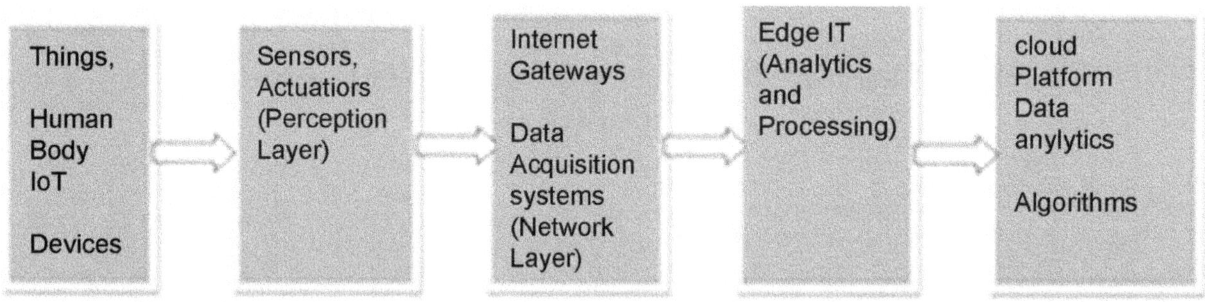

IoT connectivity technologies

There are presently several IoT based applications & commonly used IoT networking protocols. Choosing the connectivity technology according to the suitability of applications is crucial.

Important Considerations While Selecting Connectivity With IoT

IoT connectivity parameters include power consumption, range, dependability, bandwidth, cost, and scaling qualities. Certain decisions require a certain environment, such as one with less electromagnetic interference, and are utterly useless in other settings, such as the underground or the open air. When selecting the best response to an IoT situation, keep the following things in mind:

Area Coverage: An access card's range might be a few inches, while an agricultural drone's range might be a few miles.

Battery Usage: The majority of IoT-based devices are not constantly plugged in or near a charging station. Some, like field-installed soil sensors, are dispersed over a large region and require a robust, almost indestructible battery alternate for the data segments transmission without battery replacement.

Bandwidth: It implies the data transmission between modules in the sensor besides the cloud storage. Its connecting means range from those that offer very high bandwidth, like WiFi, to those that only allow minimal data can be sent periodically, like every few hours.

Cost: several variables, including the data volume.

Conditions: As was mentioned at the outset, some connectivity solutions operate without issue in the presence of obstructions, noise, interference.

The IoT components facilitate the smooth interconnection of IoT devices for delivering services that are smarter, safer, and better. The IoT's components are made up of 70% software and 30% hardware. Relevant hardware devices are shown in the below table 1 (Sehrawat & Gill, 2019).

Table 1. IoT hardware and its application

Sl. No	Sensor	Description	Applications
1	Temperature Sensor Ex: Thermocouples, Resistor temperature detectors, thermistors etc.	This device is generally used to measure heat energy by detecting an environment temperature change in some particular form and converting it for user or device.	A/C control, refrigerators, agriculture, health sector and manufacturing processes.
2	Proximity sensor Ex: Capacitive sensor, photoelectric sensors, ultrasonic sensors	It can determine whether an object is nearby and its characteristics by detecting its presence or absence. Additionally, object's properties can be translated into machine- or It makes use of comprehensible formats for end users.	The retail industry, parking availability in stadiums, mall or airports.
3	Pressure sensor Ex: Pirani gauge	a pressure sensor that transforms pressure readings into electrical signals.	Manufacturing, Water/ Heating system maintenance.
4	Water Quality Sensor Ex: Organic carbon sensors.	This sensor measures water quality and iron monitoring in distribution systems of water.	Waste water management
5	Chemical sensor Ex: Nano rod sensor	To detect chemical changes in air or liquid, chemical sensors are used.	Controlling processes, detecting incendiary devices, and identifying radioactive materials
6	Gas sensor Ex: carbon monoxide sensor, gas detector, hygrometer, air pollution sensor	The utilization od Gas sensors may be to detect changes in quality of air with presence of various gasses similar to chemical sensors.	Manufacturing & agriculture

Cloud Basics

Large mainframe computers were first used by businesses in the 1950s, but purchasing a computer for every user was prohibitively expensive leading to a creation of a method known as time sharing in 1960's to utilize the central mainframe's expensive processing time more effectively. Cloud computing has developed and expanded into a broad range of services and tools intended to meet virtually any imaginable corporate need.

Computing services — including servers of computer resources, such as storage, processing capabilities, databases, network, analytics, machine learning, and software, by utilizing the internet. No need to purchase and maintain on-premise physical IT infrastructure by companies because they may outsource these resources and get the computing assets whenever they're needed by them. Economy of scale is offered, as well as flexible resources and quicker innovation. The modernization of data and IT is a direct result of many businesses' cloud migrations.

In this computing, one has access to a pool of shared computer resources (servers, storage, programmes, and so forth). Resource scaling can be increased or decreased for the optimum resource usage. It is managed by the CSP and is operated as a virtual computing environment with a deployment architecture that varies as per the data volume you wish to store and who has access to the infrastructure. Since the software does not need to be installed locally on the PC, cloud computing gives platform independence. Consequently, Cloud Computing is enabling the mobility and collaboration of our business applications. It uses the TCP/IP protocol for data maintenance as well as applications(Manogaran, 2018, Humayun, 2020).. An application is virtual which contains all the applications & components which are required with a good operating system(Sharma & Roy., 2010).

Cloud Services and Cloud Distribution Models

It describes the particular sort of cloud computing environment based on the Cloud access, scale, and control. It also specifies the connections between users and infrastructure. It has various models as mentioned below:

Public cloud: It is an internet-based cloud infrastructure service that is made open for general public or important business sectors. It is built on the cloud architecture, where a CSP who is the owner makes availability of resources like apps and storage in either free or paid manner. The public cloud can be less secure due to its accessibility.

Private cloud: It's an infrastructure that is maintained internally or by another organization, hosted inside or outside, and is only used by one business. In a one-on-one situation, a single user is present (customer). No one else is allowed to use the equipment.

Hybrid cloud: It is a mixture of private & public cloud that are still separate but linked together, providing the advantages of various deployment types. It provides the best services by incorporating various types of models together and also gives the user an option to choose according to their requirements.

Big Data

It is used for data collection that is large and is still increasing exponentially. Some examples of BGD include the American stock exchange market with generation of more than one Terabyte of data per day, Facebook where 500 plus TB data is ingested into the database every day (Bosch, 2022; Burhanuddin et al, 2017; Byk et al, 2021). Figure 3 express the Various V's which include volume, value, velocity, variety, veracity, variability, vulnerability, volatility, validity, and visualization (Hussain et al, 2021; Ashu et al, 2021).

Figure 3. Big data's 10 V

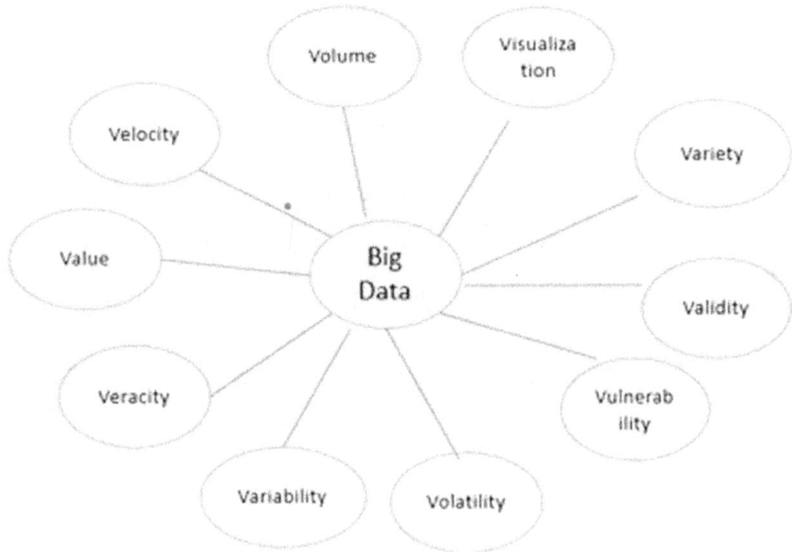

The above 10Vs must all be satisfied to make the data considered as BGD, thus merely having enormous quantities of data is not enough(Zaragoza, 2018;Conti 2012; Manogaran, 2017; Bosch,2022). Organizations can benefitted from processing it in plenty of ways, such as by using external intelligence in decision-making, enhancing customer service, identifying and reducing risks early, and improving operational efficiency (Amazon, 2021& Yassine, 2019).

Relationship Among IoT, Cloud, and Big Data

These approaches usually deal simultaneously. IoT serves as a data provider as IoT technologies gather enormous amounts of data from numerous networked IoT devices, Cloud offers storage and administration for this data, and BGD entails treating this data to extract meaningful information. IoT and CC are mutually supportive of one another as huge data has been produced by IoT, and the latter facilitates transfer of that data and move throughout the internet (Whitmore, 2015; Khan & Kiani, 2012; Dey, 2017; Chen, 2017). BGD systems receive data from IoT sensors for analysis and report preparation, which is yet another way that BGD and IoT cooperate. A relationship between CC and BGD is inherently present(Jagadeeswari 2018; Hossain & Muhammad, 2017; Ahmad, 2017; Manogaran, 2017; Rath 2020; Elhoseny, 2018). Therefore, the merging of these three approaches can bring improvement in various real-life applications if they are aligned in the best way. The combining of these technologies can increase ROI for the business sector, smarter healthcare industry & can also help in the rise of self-service analytics, (Khan, 2012; Li, 2015; Liu, 2018). The same study is shown in the table 2 below.

Table 2. Comparative study of IoT, cloud platform, and big data

Points	IoT	Cloud Platform	Big Data
Meaning	Pervasive: Interconnecting real- world entities	Universal: Virtual resources available everywhere	Support to control the Massive Data
Computing capabilities	Limited	Virtually unlimited	Unlimited
Working mode	Network	Distributed computing	Internet usage for providing cloud-built services
Benefits	Automation of daily tasks and round the clock monitoring, total transparency	Lesser Maintenance, Backup mechanism & a centralization based platform.	vigorous and profitable parallelism
Challenges	Accessibility, safety		Data diversity, data maintenance, and resource management

Smart City

A smart city leverages ICT to improve operating efficiency, exchange information and deliver better government services and social well-being. A smart city's major goal is to apply smart technologies and data analysis to enhance citizen quality of life, optimize city operations, and foster economic growth. In this, numerous areas of daily life, operations, and management are automated and streamlined by efficient and typically intelligent computing technologies. The sensors are a smart city system's core component. To monitor and record city parameters, various sensors, capacities, and functionalities are used.

Smart City's Fields

Smart Governance

Through a more intelligent collaboration between various stakeholders and social actors, such as public administrations, city officers, private companies, and citizens, the unification of ICT into city good governance is discussed for improving the decision-making process and has ten bureaucratic & administrative processes(Demirel, 2021).

Smart Living

Smart living is constructed on linking common household appliances, such refrigerators, thermostats, and HVAC systems, to a centralized cloud computing system. Technology is accessible and operated through a web-based app by data made available through IoT devices & the same can be sensed through the big data.

Smart Mobility and Transportation

It means the idea of moving away from earlier transportation systems and toward Mobility-as-a-Service (MaaS), which involves connecting citizens, public administration etc., entities like vehicles, personal devices, city sensors, etc.), and various technologies such as smart IoT infrastructure (Syed et al, 2022

).The IoT and ITs (Kezai et al, 2020) enable the delivery of intelligent applications to manage things including individual and public traffic flows, dynamic traffic routing, smart parking, vehicle sharing and sustainable mobility, linked driving, etc. Smart traffic solutions typically use predictive models to provide the early warnings, prevent incidents, and manage traffic congestion in real-time.

Smart Economy

Its foundation is the creative ICT-based linking of local and international markets, enabling electronic commerce and business services to boost output and delivery (Gill et al, 2018). This domain also encompasses the sharing economy, in which private businesses or people provide services by utilizing their own resources & peer-to-peer marketplaces (Kumar, 2018).

Smart Industry and Production

Industry 4.0, a transformation process, which includes various technologies like IoT, cyber-physical systems (CPS), and cloud-based manufacturing (Tariq & Asim, 2019) help in enabling an innovation on individuals' productive environment (Oztemel & Gursev, 2020). The field of smart industries and manufacturing, thereby tackling the food security issue, covers all industries and production procedures where ICT tends to automation. In the interest of enhancing irrigation efficiency, IoT is usually applied in smart agriculture systems (Oztemel & Gursev, 2020) and AI based solutions are frequently used with IoT to improve crop monitoring, disease diagnosis, and data-driven crop supply management (Paiva et al, 2021).

Smart Healthcare

Using technologies like wearable sensor networks, BAN, and IoT, smart healthcare connects individuals, resources, and organizations in this industry to access information dynamically. It produces universally individualized medical services and aids in the advancement of telemedicine. Smart healthcare is frequently utilized to support medical diagnosis and treatment, health management, illness prevention, risk handling, and providing the patient's results via an automated ledger and communication services (Xie et al, 2019; Khan et al, 2014). The health sector can get the benefits in the below form:

- Assist medical professionals with disease differential diagnosis.
- Pre-primary care information and remote monitoring for reducing the life risk.
- Prediction model to check up diseases by evaluating patient's electronic health records.

PROBLEMS ASSOCIATED WITH SMART CITY IMPLEMENTATION

Smart cities tend to make city-related decisions easier for its residents by the relevant information to be provided at the appropriate time and location. By allowing communication between people and objects including between items, IoT-based solutions establish the foundation for the certification of services.

Mobility: IoT devices roam freely inside the network, causing their IP addresses to change as per their location.

Reliability: The IoT applications demand extremely dependable data, which must be gathered quickly and communicated to users to make informed decisions. This is typically necessary for emergency reactions. By picking the right routing and protocols of the application layer, IoT applications' dependability can be increased with the appropriate perception layer hardware.

Scalability: Because there are more devices linked to the same network, scalability presents a barrier for various IoT applications. The network now has a few extra hardware pieces and services. Therefore, IoT designs should support scalable operations and services.

Management: Managing all the devices is considered as the IoT's biggest concerns along with failure tracking, performance, and configurations of those devices. The makers of such devices oversee fault management, configuration, performance, device accounting, and all other aspects.

Availability: It mentions the facility of necessary hardware besides software to service subscribers and in any location. Software availability is the service offered to guarantee that systems are operational and accessible. Hardware availability states to the service that ensures hardware availability.

Heterogeneity within IoT is described as a platform that permits communication between various devices. The platform's ability to support different devices from diverse suppliers is another asset. The IoT employs a diversity of protocols, including MQTT, COAP and Modbus.

Vulnerable to Hacks

RFID will be used to enable the majority of connections with objects, and this technology is hacker-prone. The development of smart cities will progress more rapidly if such an IoT ecosystem that really is resistant to hacking is permitted.

Lack of Compatibility and Interconnection Among IoT Devices

Impossibility of IoT devices from different manufacturers to communicate with one another and exchange data.

Poorly Designed IoT Devices

The utilization of network resources and the overall operation of a smart city may be greatly affected by poor design and implemented systems.

Economic Viability

With a great deal of detecting and actuating components for use in IoT applications, cost and payback time are important aspects.

Updation and Insufficient Analysis of Data Collection

An IoT device's need for updated hardware and software is important for detecting privacy, and the identification of abnormalities (anomalous data) and traffic patterns.

Ethical and Societal Issues

Major ethical and societal concerns raised by the proliferation of IoT also include misuse of data for hidden agendas, the release of private data, a lack of fairness, and social injustice.

Costing Issues

Networks of sensors, screens, cameras, tech devices, the smart grid, and a secured information-sharing infrastructure should be created, but there may not always be an equitable amount of the benefits.

Technological Problems

Device quality varies, and IoT is still developing. In order to get any benefits, it is also essential to use contemporary technologies like cloud computing, machine learning, data analysis methods, and intelligent sensors.

Standardization and Network Flexibility Issues

IoT systems and data collection do not adhere to consistent standards, which restricts network flexibility. It could be extremely challenging to swap out old equipment and add new equipment. IoT devices technical standards should be established and standardized by the government.

Stakeholder Engagement and Collaboration Issues

Since diverse commercial and governmental players have different interests, the majority of smart city initiatives lack collaboration, cooperation, and coordination.

SUGGESTIONS

The next phase of internet-based computer expansion is cloud computing which permits the use of information technology expertise on a service basis. IoT has the prospective for enhancing the productivity, throughput, and efficiency when smart devices leave the cloud environment. In order to attain environmental sustainability, urban system authority, enhanced health, knowledge development, and network-driven advancement, smart cities are residential regions that systematically endeavor to notice for themselves the new locations of records and various techniques of communication (Sharma & Roy, 2010; Sharma et al, 2018; Suciu et al, 2013). The next stage in evolution of internet-based computing is cloud computing, which enables the distribution of ICT resources over a network. An IoT can get the benefits from improved cloud infrastructure payload, performance, and efficiency. The rise of cloud-based computing has assisted in its growth and expansion thereby additionally give support for the packing of industrial electronic business. Hence, these technologies are very close to emerging internet technologies that work with IoT systems.

Smart Cities' Requirement for Cloud-Based IoT Applications

Due to many aspects, cities have shifted to IoT and communication technology.

- IoT systems allow sensors to gather data to control appliance consumption, potentially saving money.
- Cost is a big factor in deciding whether to go offline or online because deploying and maintaining IoT apps is easier to do. Additionally, costs are dropping, and communications' robustness and power output enable novel situations that weren't before achievable;
- Another factor is efficiency (Ge et al, 2018). For the utmost solutions, cloud providers must physically visit the website to inspect and implement communications equipment;
- Through various analyses, wireless communication enables monitoring and IoT transmission management. Administrators can do this to enable firmware updates, apply security fixes to all finished plans, and receive automatic alerts in case of a problem;
- In operational circumstances, when intelligent street lighting in addition to tracking devices are maintained, decreased assistance is typically to blame.

Smart Cities Applications by Using Cloud-Based IoT

BT Suite From Bosch

Bosch unveiled the first cloud-based toolset for IoT developers in 2015 that aided in the evolution of cutting-edge items and cutting-edge business models. IoT is a key approach for enhancing procedures, enhancing performance, and fostering continuous improvement. Businesses make a use of IoT for a better understanding of customer needs, improve aircraft operations, and instantly offer distinctive qualities (Bosch, 2022).

ABB Robotics

Protecting and using linked sensors for robots is one that the IIoT has taken on with the most visibility. Offering cutting-edge technologies to a variety of industries, which includes telecommunications manufacturing, and transportation, It is a world leader in AI based robots, automation & cloud solutions (ABB, 2023).

Airbus

A company that offers IoT solutions globally is Airbus. Airbus deploys its IoT technology and connectivity network using Astrocast nanosatellites for global connectivity. It consists of a communication link inside its centralized design mechanism. It depends on a solid infrastructure that can support many users that are using the similar sensors and radio signals (Airbus, 2023).

Amazon Stockroom

The online-only supermarket is not typically thought of as an IIoT business, but the company has brought up some innovations w.r.t their inventories and its planning. Amazon examines the boundaries between automation and human connection, and the company's discussion of the usage of delivery drones drew significant attention (Burhanuddin et al., 2017).

Boeing: Using IoT to Improve Manufacturing Efficiency

William Boeing, a pioneer in aviation, famously said that "no one behaves to dismiss any innovative concept with the assertion, it can't be done." The international airline formed by Boeing is unquestionably consistent with that ethos. In repurposing its corporate enterprise, the organization has gone a long way. They have integrated IoT-built services for driving their factory operations and other chains. Smart technologies, including gadgets to communicate with devices controlled by networks, may be incorporated into the atmosphere of the flight cabin and allow passengers to interact with the aircraft in new ways (Mathur & Nishchal, 2010).

IIoT, a Caterpillar Pioneer

Caterpillar is increasing output by utilizing the IoT. The business has created various software tools including data analysis, and APIs to help the issue and its clients handle, analyze, and store information. Notably, the company and Zuora have established a new partnership to offer customers cloud-based management and analysis tools for subscription facilities (Marr, 2017).

Fanuc: In Favor of Reducing Factory Downtime

The robotics company is dedicated to reducing unscheduled downtime in industrial facilities.By utilizing sensors together with cloud analytics, they are able to predict when a robotic equipment or system may fail. With more than 240 service centers spread over 107 countries, it provides continuous product servicing to users, exhibiting its dedication to the "Service First" philosophy (Alam, 2021).

Hitachi: Long-Standing IIoT Practice

Hitachi, a Japanese company, integrates its business processes and software through various institutions. The H.X Family Models from them are a revolutionary industrial controller that is prepared for the IoT. This controller may execute computer network connections and software platforms created for data processing and features, like motion control and sequence control, without impairing control operations (Alam, 2021).

Agriculture's Future with John Deere

The various issues that farming encounters is the changing climate. Three significant technological advancements that will influence the future are automation to autonomy, electrification and AI (Boeing, 2017).

Komatsu

The manufacturer of heavy machinery in Japan has a large supply of cutting-edge IIoT components. It spent the time associated with its Japanese production plants in 2011. All of Komatsu's robots are in connection with the company's major production facilities and network, giving management real-time access to information on all operations worldwide. It's a revolution in mining (Xu, et al, 2019).

Kuka: Robotic

Their IoT mechanism connects to numerous businesses. Robotics and manufacturing IIoT are produced by Kuka. Their training philosophy continuously emphasizes value addition (Alam, 2021).

Maersk

International Air Freight Transportation: Although Maersk is well known for its services in industrialized cargo shipping, it is growing beyond that. By integrating solutions, it is evolving into a full-service logistics provider for the supply chain. Customers will always be focused to the location of their products, and other conditions may be altered to guarantee that food and medications travel from other locations for doing it perfectly. Because of the growth and versatility of the platform, it has faith in Azure's IoT capabilities (Alam, 2021).

Magna Steyr: Intelligent Automobile Manufacturing

Magna Steyr, an Austrian automaker, is an expert in the smart industry sector. Utilizing cutting-edge technology, its 161,000 employees work on car parts and components while automatically ordering cashback. Additionally, Magna is working with "smart packaging" and ways to enhance it using IoT (Alam, 2021).

BlueScope

According to Andrew Spence, they can enhance existing systems and create whole new alternatives thanks to smart, connected gadgets.Process factors include acid content, pressure, temperature, fluxes, continuing, tier, and continuing. For instance, according to Spence, it is now easy to assess changes to the operational process and the collection of data that can be applied to models to support more sophisticated and accurate control systems (Suciu et al., 2013).

Real Time Innovations

Real-Time Innovations is the leading provider of software frameworks for autonomous systems which is the paradigm that is most frequently utilized to develop intelligent, decentralized systems globally. Its setting is distinctive in that it instantly disseminates information and connects AI methods to actual device networking to create autonomous systems (Alam, 2021).

Shell

In a Rigzone, Shell was recognised as the top employer for oil and gasoline in 2016. According to executive director for technology at shell, Yuri Sebregts, “Right now, this will assist us in scaling concepts we’ve been going to create” and “The new possibilities in dealing with data over the last several years have unlocked huge promise in all sections of what we do in the firm.” Shell is also collaborating with various experts to improve horizontal drilling through AI in addition to machine learning. The oil besides gas industry has experienced significant cost savings by transitioning from conventional drilling wells to long, horizontal drilling, reduced its environmental impact, and found new oil as well as gas resources grounded (Alam, 2021).

Black & Decker Stanley

It offers software and pioneering solutions for the builders, explorers, and creators who shape and reshape the world through their labor of love and creative imagination. It teams to create practical, applicable products and solutions that improve the standard of life and give people access to smart & healthy occupations (Alam 2021).

FUTURE DIRECTIONS

AI-Powered IOT With Big Data Analytics

IoT big data analysis is a procedure that continuously gathers, mixes, and evaluates a variety of heterogeneous data gathered by sensors in order to address the problems the city is facing. ICT is essential for developing as well as keeping up smart cities there by leading to the emerging demand of various technologies. In recent years, a variety of machine learning issues have benefited greatly from the use of ANN based models (Nalluri et al, 2017). Due to its remarkable spatiotemporal feature learning capabilities, it has been extensively made available for the use in IoT based big data prediction learning, pattern recognition, anomaly detection, and categorization. In a world where artificial intelligence permeates every aspect of life, the usage of big data is encouraged to improve societal, economic, transformational, and ecological well-being. The smart cities’ “intelligence” is supported by artificial intelligence, IoT & Big data analytics, which have emerged as essential disruptive technologies.

Smart Cities Need Smart Security

Today, certain towns all around the world are embracing cutting-edge technology and becoming into “smart cities.” Modern technologies improve people’s quality of life. However, using any technology brings up fresh problems and difficulties. A single careless act by a person or group can endanger the entire city in a “smart city.” The smart city’s behavior is impacted by cyber-security issues (such as information leakage and harmful cyber-attacks). Cyber security must therefore be used in an advanced manner for adapting to the enthusiastic adoption of global smart city technology.

CONCLUSION

Due to advances in sensor technology and falling costs, the smart city as an application of the IoT along with the cloud ecosystem is expanding quickly. Smart systems are therefore needed in such cities to handle emergency circumstances. Accessing, analyzing, and managing precise data made possible by cloud-based enabling technologies which could help professionals, businesses, and individuals make better decisions to improve the standard of living for people. Residents in smart cities utilize mobile devices to communicate with connected autos and smart homes. The physical infrastructure and facilities of a city can interact with technology and data to improve the productivity and cut expenses. This study highlighted cloud founded IoT applications along with its impact in smart cities. It has also highlighted smart city applications based on cloud and other IoT technologies. Future study can uncover the smart city applications like AI-Powered, IoT & Big data analytics, Smart Security etc.

REFERENCES

Ahmad, M., Zaman, N., & Al-Amin, M. (2017). An experimental research in health informatics for enhancing ovarian cancer identification in ovarian imaging analysis using fuzzy histogram equalization. *Journal of Medical Imaging and Health Informatics*, *7*(6), 1385–1390. doi:10.1166/jmihi.2017.2218

Airbus (2023). Available online: https://www.airbus.com/

Alam, T. (2021). Cloud-based IoT applications and their roles in smart cities. *Smart Cities*, *4*(3), 1196–1219. doi:10.3390martcities4030064

Ashu, A., Hussain, M. W., Sinha Roy, D., & Reddy, H. K. (2021). Intelligent data compression policy for Hadoop performance optimization. In *Proceedings of the 11th International Conference on Soft Computing and Pattern Recognition (SoCPaR 2019)* (pp. 80-89). Springer International Publishing. 10.1007/978-3-030-49345-5_9

Barro-Torres, S., Fernández-Caramés, T. M., Pérez-Iglesias, H. J., & Escudero, C. J. (2012). Real-time personal protective equipment monitoring system. *Computer Communications*, *36*(1), 42–50. doi:10.1016/j.comcom.2012.01.005

Bellini, P., Nesi, P., & Pantaleo, G. (2022). IoT-enabled smart cities: A review of concepts, frameworks and key technologies. *Applied Sciences (Basel, Switzerland)*, *12*(3), 1607. doi:10.3390/app12031607

Burhanuddin, M. A., Mohammed, A. A. J., Ismail, R., & Basiron, H. (2017). Internet of things architecture: Current challenges and future direction of research. *International Journal of Applied Engineering Research: IJAER*, *12*(21), 11055–11061.

Byk, C., Abareshi, A., Paz, A., Ruiz, R. A., Battarra, R., Rogers, C. D., & Lizarraga, C. (2021). *Smart Mobility Adoption: A Review of the Literature.* University of Birmingham.

Chen, M., Ma, Y., Li, Y., Wu, D., Zhang, Y., & Youn, C. H. (2017). Wearable 2.0: Enabling human-cloud integration in next generation healthcare systems. *IEEE Communications Magazine*, *55*(1), 54–61. doi:10.1109/MCOM.2017.1600410CM

Conti, M., Das, S. K., Bisdikian, C., Kumar, M., Ni, L. M., Passarella, A., Roussos, G., Tröster, G., Tsudik, G., & Zambonelli, F. (2012). Looking ahead in pervasive computing: Challenges and opportunities in the era of cyber–physical convergence. *Pervasive and Mobile Computing*, *8*(1), 2–21. doi:10.1016/j.pmcj.2011.10.001

Demirel, D. (2021). *How the smart governance model shapes cities? Cases from Europe*. J. Enterprising Communities.

Dey, N., Ashour, A. S., & Bhatt, C. (2017). Internet of things driven connected healthcare. In *Internet of things and big data technologies for next generation healthcare* (pp. 3–12). Springer. doi:10.1007/978-3-319-49736-5_1

Elhoseny, M., Ramírez-González, G., Abu-Elnasr, O. M., Shawkat, S. A., Arunkumar, N., & Farouk, A. (2018). Secure medical data transmission model for IoT-based healthcare systems. *IEEE Access : Practical Innovations, Open Solutions*, *2018*(6), 20596–20608. doi:10.1109/ACCESS.2018.2817615

Ge, M., Bangui, H., & Buhnova, B. (2018). Big data for internet of things: A survey. *Future Generation Computer Systems*, *87*, 601–614. doi:10.1016/j.future.2018.04.053

Gill, S. S., Arya, R. C., Wander, G. S., & Buyya, R. (2018). Fog-based smart healthcare as a big data and cloud service for heart patients using IoT. In *International Conference on Intelligent Data Communication Technologies and Internet of Things* (pp. 1376-1383). Springer, Cham.

Hossain, M. S., & Muhammad, G. (2017). Emotion-aware connected healthcare big data towards 5G. *IEEE Internet of Things Journal*, *5*(4), 2399–2406. doi:10.1109/JIOT.2017.2772959

Humayun, M. (2020). Role of emerging IoT big data and cloud computing for real time application. *International Journal of Advanced Computer Science and Applications*, *11*(4). doi:10.14569/IJACSA.2020.0110466

Hussain, M. W. (2021). A counter based approach for reducer placement with augmented Hadoop rackawareness. *Turkish Journal of Electrical Engineering and Computer Sciences*, *29*(1), 437–453. doi:10.3906/elk-2001-106

Jagadeeswari, V., Subramaniyaswamy, V., Logesh, R., & Vijayakumar, V. (2018). A study on medical Internet of Things and Big Data in personalized healthcare system. *Health Information Science and Systems*, *6*(1), 1–20. doi:10.100713755-018-0049-x PMID:30279984

Jameer, B., Malathi, M., Balaganes, S., & Maheshwari, R. (2018). Patient Tracking Using IoT and Big Data. In *Proceedings of First International Conference on Smart System, Innovations and Computing* (pp. 613-621). Springer, Singapore. 10.1007/978-981-10-5828-8_59

Kézai, P. K., Fischer, S., & Lados, M. (2020). Smart economy and startup enterprises in the Visegrád Countries—A comparative analysis based on the Crunchbase Database. *Smart Cities*, *3*(4), 1477–1494. doi:10.3390martcities3040070

Khan, R., Khan, S. U., Zaheer, R., & Khan, S. (2012). Future internet: the internet of things architecture, possible applications and key challenges. In *2012 10th international conference on frontiers of information technology*(pp. 257-260). IEEE. 10.1109/FIT.2012.53

Khan, Z., & Kiani, S. L. (2012). A cloud-based architecture for citizen services in smart cities. In *2012 IEEE Fifth international conference on utility and cloud computing* (pp. 315-320). IEEE. 10.1109/UCC.2012.43

Khan, Z., Pervez, Z., & Ghafoor, A. (2014). Towards cloud based smart cities data security and privacy management. In *2014 IEEE/ACM 7th International Conference on Utility and Cloud Computing* (pp. 806-811). IEEE. 10.1109/UCC.2014.131

Kumar, T. V. (Ed.). (2018). *Smart Economy in Smart Cities: International Collaborative Research: Ottawa, St. Louis, Stuttgart, Bologna, Cape Town, Nairobi, Dakar, Lagos, New Delhi, Varanasi, Vijayawada*. Springer Singapore.

Li, S., Xu, L. D., & Zhao, S. (2015). The internet of things: A survey. *Information Systems Frontiers, 17*(2), 243–259. doi:10.100710796-014-9492-7

Liu, Y. Y., Hung, M. H., Lin, Y. C., Chen, C. C., Gao, W. L., & Cheng, F. T. (2018). A Cloud-based pluggable manufacturing service scheme for smart factory. In *2018 IEEE 14th International Conference on Automation Science and Engineering (CASE)* (pp. 1040-1045). IEEE. 10.1109/COASE.2018.8560401

Malik, V., & Singh, S. (2019). Cloud, big data & IoT: risk management. In *2019 International Conference on Machine Learning, Big Data, Cloud and Parallel Computing (COMITCon)* (pp. 258-262). IEEE.

Manogaran, G., Lopez, D., Thota, C., Abbas, K. M., Pyne, S., & Sundarasekar, R. (2017). Big data analytics in healthcare Internet of Things. In *Innovative healthcare systems for the 21st century* (pp. 263–284). Springer. doi:10.1007/978-3-319-55774-8_10

Manogaran, G., Thota, C., Lopez, D., & Sundarasekar, R. (2017). Big data security intelligence for healthcare industry 4.0. In *Cybersecurity for industry 4.0* (pp. 103–126). Springer. doi:10.1007/978-3-319-50660-9_5

Manogaran, G., Varatharajan, R., Lopez, D., Kumar, P. M., Sundarasekar, R., & Thota, C. (2018). A new architecture of Internet of Things and big data ecosystem for secured smart healthcare monitoring and alerting system. *Future Generation Computer Systems, 82*, 375–387. doi:10.1016/j.future.2017.10.045

Marr, B. (2017). *IoT and big data at Caterpillar: How predictive maintenance saves millions of dollars.*

Mathur, P., & Nishchal, N. (2010). Cloud computing: New challenge to the entire computer industry. In *2010 First International Conference On Parallel, Distributed and Grid Computing (PDGC 2010)* (pp. 223-228). IEEE. 10.1109/PDGC.2010.5679897

Moustafa, N. (2021). A Systemic IoT–Fog–Cloud Architecture for Big-Data Analytics and Cyber Security Systems: A Review of Fog Computing. *Secure Edge Computing*, 41-50.

Nalluri, M. R., & Roy, D. S. (2017). Hybrid disease diagnosis using multiobjective optimization with evolutionary parameter optimization. *Journal of Healthcare Engineering*. doi:10.1155/2017/5907264 PMID:29065626

Oztemel, E., & Gursev, S. (2020). Literature review of Industry 4.0 and related technologies. *Journal of Intelligent Manufacturing, 31*(1), 127–182. doi:10.100710845-018-1433-8

Paiva, S., Ahad, M. A., Tripathi, G., Feroz, N., & Casalino, G. (2021). Enabling technologies for urban smart mobility: Recent trends, opportunities and challenges. *Sensors (Basel)*, *21*(6), 2143. doi:10.339021062143 PMID:33803903

Pradhan, B., Hussain, M. W., Srivastava, G., Debbarma, M. K., Barik, R. K., & Lin, J. C. W. (2022). A neuro-evolutionary approach for software defined wireless network traffic classification. *IET Communications*, cmu2.12548. doi:10.1049/cmu2.12548

Rath, M. (2020). Big data and iot-allied challenges associated with healthcare applications in smart and automated systems. In data analytics in medicine: Concepts, methodologies, tools, and applications (pp. 1401-1414). IGI Global. doi:10.4018/978-1-7998-1204-3.ch070

Sehrawat, D., & Gill, N. S. (2019, April). Smart sensors: Analysis of different types of IoT sensors. In *2019 3rd International Conference on Trends in Electronics and Informatics (ICOEI)* (pp. 523-528). IEEE.

Sharma, A., & Roy, S. (2010). Cloud computing 21st Century Paradigm for Internet. *Proceeding of national seminar on Advancement in Cloud Computing & Green IT Technology*. Springer.

Sharma, S., Chen, K., & Sheth, A. (2018). Toward practical privacy-preserving analytics for IoT and cloud-based healthcare systems. *IEEE Internet Computing*, *22*(2), 42–51. doi:10.1109/MIC.2018.112102519

Suciu, G., Vulpe, A., Halunga, S., Fratu, O., Todoran, G., & Suciu, V. (2013, May). Smart cities built on resilient cloud computing and secure internet of things. In *2013 19th international conference on control systems and computer science* (pp. 513-518). IEEE. 10.1109/CSCS.2013.58

Syed, A. S., Sierra-Sosa, D., Kumar, A., & Elmaghraby, A. (2022). Making Cities Smarter—Optimization Problems for the IoT Enabled Smart City Development: A Mapping of Applications, Objectives, Constraints. *Sensors (Basel)*, *22*(12), 4380. doi:10.339022124380 PMID:35746161

Tariq, N., Asim, M., Al-Obeidat, F., Zubair Farooqi, M., Baker, T., Hammoudeh, M., & Ghafir, I. (2019). The security of big data in fog-enabled IoT applications including blockchain: A survey. *Sensors (Basel)*, *19*(8), 1788. doi:10.339019081788 PMID:31013993

Whitmore, A., Agarwal, A., & Da Xu, L. (2015). The Internet of Things—A survey of topics and trends. *Information Systems Frontiers*, *17*(2), 261–274. doi:10.100710796-014-9489-2

Xie, Y., Gao, G., & Chen, X. A. (2019). Outlining the design space of explainable intelligent systems for medical diagnosis. *arXiv preprint arXiv:1902.06019*.

Xu, X., Liu, Q., Luo, Y., Peng, K., Zhang, X., Meng, S., & Qi, L. (2019). A computation offloading method over big data for IoT-enabled cloud-edge computing. *Future Generation Computer Systems*, *95*, 522–533. doi:10.1016/j.future.2018.12.055

Yassine, A., Singh, S., Hossain, M. S., & Muhammad, G. (2019). IoT big data analytics for smart homes with fog and cloud computing. *Future Generation Computer Systems*, *91*, 563–573. doi:10.1016/j.future.2018.08.040

Zaman, N., Seliaman, M. E., Hassan, M. F., & Márquez, F. P. G. (Eds.). (2015). *Handbook of research on trends and future directions in big data and web intelligence*. Information Science. doi:10.4018/978-1-4666-8505-5

Zaragoza, M. G., Kim, H. K., & Lee, R. Y. (2017, May). Big data and IoT for u-healthcare security. In *International Conference on Computer and Information Science* (pp. 1-11). Springer, Cham.

Chapter 5
Smart City Ecosystem:
An Exploration of Requirements, Architecture, Applications, Security, and Emerging Motivations

Wasswa Shafik
https://orcid.org/0000-0002-9320-3186
School of Digital Science, Universiti Brunei Darussalam, Bandar Seri Begawan, Brunei & Dig Connectivity Research Laboratory, Kampala, Uganda

Kassim Kalinaki
https://orcid.org/0000-0001-8630-9110
Islamic University in Uganda, Uganda

ABSTRACT

This chapter explores the growing use of technology in various aspects of people's lives and focuses on smart cities. First, it provides a comprehensive survey that examines the need for smart cities, their architectural elements, and the characteristics and purposes of different architectural layers. The chapter also offers an overview of notable smart cities such as London, New York, Singapore, Busan, Amsterdam, and Sunshine Coast Regions, highlighting their unique features. Next, privacy and security concerns associated with smart cities are addressed, emphasizing the importance of privacy issues and suggesting potential solutions. The chapter discusses future research directions, including the integration of blockchains, security considerations, collaborative filtering, and infrastructure upgrades in smart city applications. The analysis of privacy and security concerns is organized into three subsections: smart city security traits, leveraging issues, and privacy challenges and solutions. Finally, the chapter concludes by presenting future research trends in this field.

DOI: 10.4018/979-8-3693-0744-1.ch005

INTRODUCTION

The concept of a "smart city" strives to create environmental sustainability by integrating advanced information and communication technologies (ICT) while promoting efficient use of resources. Sustainable development and the creation of smart cities have gained widespread acceptance as urbanization trends. The most cutting-edge innovative information and technology integration has made it possible to create a model smart city (Yang et al., 2021). Intelligent living environments, abundant connectivity, easy access to goods and services, smart decision-making via high-tech government, and optimum resource management are all merits that the public in smart cities can use. More applications of smart cities are presented together with the identification of prominent smart city examples worldwide.

Residents of smart cities will have convenient and continuous access to resource sharing, allowing them to efficiently manage their daily lives using collective secure digital intelligence (Elrawy et al., 2018). Availing an acceptable life experience for inhabitants is part of the smart city concept, encompassing intelligent transportation, decentralized economics, and government. To appreciate these smart developments in existing smart cities, there is a need to pay attention to the application and its associated related impact on both the public and the technology industry. The prediction is that the number will increase to 70% regardless of the current covid-19 pandemic (Nam & Pardo, 2011).

A self-sufficient community known as a smart city prioritizes its residents' quality of life above everything else. A smart city requires sustainability, comprising a comfortable social life and a greener way of living. The smart city ecosystem is preserved by ecological effluence reduction and effective waste management like recycling and smart grids. Decentralized and fully transparent government and economy are essential. In addition, several security assaults might jeopardize the infrastructure and applications of smart cities (Shafik, 2023). Numerous businesses, for instance, banks, insurance firms, hospitals, and others, may suffer from data loss and experience a severe technological catastrophe.

A detailed analysis of various applications and potential research areas for smart cities highlights the need for increased security and safety measures. They pointed out that while monitoring everything online in a smart city can enhance security, it may also raise privacy concerns (Gharaibeh et al., 2017). Components and applications overview of smart city infrastructure to better understand its architecture (Sookhak et al., 2019). Thoroughly examined security concerns, protocols, intrusion problems, and responses based on the Internet of Things (IoT) in smart cities. The authors also presented a comprehensive analysis of fault detection systems, providing a thorough overview.

A thorough summary of the architecture, use, and future trends of smart cities and broad and thorough representations of the architecture, uses, and characteristics of many smart cities across the world has been presented in the recent literature (Du et al., 2019; Silva et al., 2018). An accurate review of recent research on smart city challenges, including a comparison of these studies, was presented (Sánchez-Corcuera et al., 2019). The authors provide an overview of designs, applications, examples of smart cities, and upcoming research paths. An explanation of the state of the smart city around the ecosphere illustrating the contemporary problems associated with smart cities' privacy and their cutting-edge remedies was depicted (Curzon et al., 2019).

To give the researcher a clear knowledge of the smart city motivations and outstanding research questions, (Chen et al. 2019) gave an exhaustive assessment of the recently expanding study field of AI in smart city applications. Lau et al. (2019) provided an exhaustive analysis of AI-based approaches for addressing numerous smart city difficulties. Laufs et al. (2020) discussed security and architectural problems. One of the most recent works on smart city surveys explored smart cities, reviewed the research on smart city surveys and valid summaries on the applications, components, and smart city future (Kirimtat et al., 2020).

After an exhaustive search, a sizable research gap has been identified grounded on the related works studied above. Thus, this research mainly tackles applications, security requirements, privacy, smart city worldwide, and future research trends is necessary. Also emphasizes and depicts data related to this idea, development, and potential future smart city research areas. This chapter can be an essential resource for future research directions and background information for learners, scientists, and researchers. This work serves as a succinct introduction to the advent of smart cities and the necessity for urbanization.

Key Contributions of the Chapter

This chapter contributes the following:

- A detailed description and examination of the need for smart cities and various architectural elements.
- The architectural layers of a smart city and their characteristics and purposes are presented in a tabular manner.
- Present an overview of the top recognized smart cities (namely, London, New York, Singapore, Busan, Amsterdam, and Sunshine Coast Regions) and their distinctive traits.
- Privacy and security concerns together with the attributes leveraged are highlighted, and privacy issues and possible solutions are demonstrated.
- Avails future research motivations for smart city applications, some identified ones entailing blockchain integration, security considerations, collaborative filtering, and infrastructure upgrades.

Chapter Organization

The remainder of this chapter is arranged as details. Section 2 portrays the contextual smart city in three ways: the need for smart cities, requirements, application, data management, transmission, and sensing layers. Section 3 portrays the application of a smart city entailing the most considered smart entities like smart transportation, healthcare, power and energy management system, network connectivity infrastructures, and homes. In Section 4, international standard smart cities examples are presented. Section 5 discusses smart city privacy and security concerns categorized into three subsections: security traits, privacy concerns and leveraging issues with solutions. Finally, section 6 exhaustively presents future trends like smart cities blockchain, cost management, sustainable energy management, data storage, processing, and security, among others, and the conclusion is presented within Section 7.

SMART CITY ENVIRONMENT

The population is growing at an exponential rate, making urbanization more challenging. This calls for properly managing sectors such as education, transportation, energy, and healthcare. Better administrative decision-making and implementation involve transparency, reliability, optimization, and monitoring (Nam & Pardo, 2011). A smart city's significance and its elements, pillars, prerequisites, and architecture are highlighted.

Smart City Necessities

Since these cities utilize cutting-edge technology and data-driven solutions to enhance the quality of life for their residents and promote sustainable development, the following are some of notable contributions.

Connectivity

A connected society and a community approach to learning will foster innovation and, in the end, make people smarter. Smart cities live with connectivity. The smart city offers wired and wireless connections (Laufs et al. 2020). The unified connectivity of a smart city facilitates data transmission and offers residents of the city real-time application.

Sustainability

Sustainable health systems and smart buildings are a framework for justifiable energy utilization, and encouraging a greener routine are all smart city goals. Building a smart city requires addressing climate change, social challenges, waste and pollution control, and proper use of nature. The mental and physical well-being of people is frequently diminishing due to technological innovation.

Decentralization

Decentralizing government, healthcare, education, finance, and other functions is a significant aim of creating the smart city so that individuals can receive services without limitations at any time and in any location. Furthermore, transparency and immutability of individual records kept using blockchain technologies will stop fraudulent actions. In some countries, digital identity is already in use and can be applied for individual and corporate authentication motives (Jun et al., 2021).

Security

Modern technology, including smart city infrastructure, enhances the protection of physical structures. blockchain technology's pseudo-anonymity secures smart city's large data transfer. As a result of eliminating third parties and fostering trustless transactions, Blockchain reduces fraud. However, various smart city infrastructures are vulnerable to cyberattacks. Smart cities leverage several sensor networks and IoT devices to create context-aware applications. Because of their architecture and construction, sensor networks are vulnerable to cyberattacks (Ghandour et al., 2018).

Devices may become unavailable, data loss may occur, people in smart cities may experience privacy breaches, and malicious software may be introduced to feed false information and thereby infect the infrastructure of Smart cities because of attacks on the infrastructure. Giving people false information can seriously lower their standard of living and inflict catastrophic environmental damage (Jun et al., 2021). Because of this, intelligent cities deploy advanced security countermeasures to protect against attacks at any time. The city's residents may suffer severe harm in case the personal information of the people is exposed because of any kind of software or hardware malfunction.

Smart City Requirements

Recent urbanization of cities demonstrates secure connectivity and environmental friendliness. As discussed below, many areas can be considered to create an innocuous and protected smart city.

Quality of Life and Sustainable Environment

Every form of technology offers a good setting for leading a healthy life. Government functions as a service. Effective governance can improve quality of life. Decisions and administrative processes should be visible to the public and automated. Citizens will experience standard benefits because of harmonious coherence across various smart city infrastructure components. Sustainable and environmentally friendly cities are essential (Elrawy et al. 2018). Climate change is accelerated by rapid urbanization, an increase in industry, and declining amounts of greenery (Xie et al., 2019). Therefore, it is imperative to create the possibility of leading a greener lifestyle. Effective waste management that reduces pollutants and biodegradable materials is essential for a cleaner, greener environment.

Privacy and Security Component

IoT devices like sensors are heavily used in modern urbanization, there are applied in several infrastructures. For better strategic management, data gathered from various devices is analyzed. Data analysis may greatly enhance administrative decisions and practices. However, the entire system may be in danger if any of the infrastructures suffer a security compromise. Social security needs necessitate constant monitoring of residents in smart cities (Shokoor et al., 2019). Any privacy violation endangers individuals and society since smart cities depend on gathering and processing sensitive information on inhabitants' personal, locational, and personal characteristics.

Patients' physical and personal information, including location, heart rate, and other health-related information, is collected through wearable technology and health monitoring equipment. The information is private in both situations and should not be accessible to the public. People who have their privacy violated may be subject to serious attacks (Haque et al., 2021). A smart city has enough privacy and security safeguards for everyone's digital identification and footprint (Eckhoff & Wagner, 2018).

Intelligent Services

These services contain a system for managing patient records, a smart appointment system, data storage, and data sharing across linked institutions. People who require medical attention may be able to access remote healthcare services. It is possible to analyze healthcare data to find diseases and prescribe treatments. Financial services, such as banking and insurance, are essential for citizens (Arora, 2018). Critical services should be available from the city administration whenever someone needs them. The online banking industry is expanding; heraldry services can be used to provide citizens with cutting-edge services.

Smart Infrastructure

A city's infrastructure can be developed if it is to grow. Infrastructure upgrades in smart cities include smart buildings. The smart building uses energy effectively while protecting the environment. Solar power can be used in structures. Such an infrastructure uses a variety of sensors and IoT technologies for improved performance. Intelligent transportation systems are a component of the infrastructure development for smart cities. The importance of Global Positioning Systems (GPS) and various autonomous ad hoc network infrastructures for smart infrastructure cannot be overstated (Maier, 2016).

Smart Human Resources

Effective and competent human capital makes up smart human availability. The most imperative components of any sort of society are its human resource base. People practice their knowledge, education, intelligence, and creativity to grow as individuals. Sustainable social infrastructures also have a significant impact on social learning. Critical thinking is an essential skill for a citizen to progress both personally and socially. It is necessary to monitor and have authoritative control over citizen data properly. The seamless use of all services by citizens will be made possible through digital identity.

Smart City Architecture

Despite the deployment of a few smart city features, the components and implementation are still inadequate. Since every choice in a city is made only after a thorough study of the data gathered from diverse infrastructures, the data is crucial to its success. There are four tiers based on the suggested works and methodologies; the following are explanations of the architectural layers of a smart city.

Application Layer

Through this layer, citizens of smart cities gain access to several advantages. As a result, this layer is crucial for providing services to the user. First, a choice is provided using data from the preceding layer that has been analyzed. People are more interested in the outcome than in the underlying working theory or algorithms that serve as the smart city brain. These amenities will impact individuals' personal and professional lives (Syed et al., 2021). With load balancing, a smart grid, and reliable electricity supply, effective citywide distribution methods, automatic electricity utilization, data bill generation, and other features are all guaranteed.

Data Management Layer

The management and processing of data are tasks performed by this layer. Different infrastructure generates data. Large amounts of data are produced daily by citizens as well. The fundamental data characteristics that are guaranteed are integrity, confidentiality, availability, and authenticity. Data from diverse sources can also be processed later, including cleaning, editing, and merging. The issue of data processing and storage is brought up by the enormous amount of data (Syed et al. 2021). In addition, infrastructure and services will develop over time. Therefore, data storage needs to be scalable as well.

Thus, data centers can be constructed for the backup and storage of data. Table 1 summarizes the several infrastructure layers of smart cities and their unique characteristics.

Table 1. Smart city features corresponding to the identified layer (4G, Fourth generation; LTE, long-term evolution; WiMaX, Worldwide Interoperability for Microwave Access; BLE, Bluetooth Low Energy, WiFi, Wireless Fidelity)

smart city Traits	Smart City Layers			
	Application	Data management	Transmission	Sensing
Technology	Home automation, Healthcare Monitoring, Smart Grid, Application Development	Decision-making algorithms, Data Processing, Analysis technologies	Wide Range Communication, WiFi, 4G/LTE, WiMaX	Humidity sensors, RFID, BLE, Temperature Sensors
Connected layers	Data Management	Application, Transmission	Sensing, Data Management,	Transmission, Physical world
Devices	Tracking devices, Smart devices, Smart distribution	Data processing equipment, Storage Devices	Transmission Devices	Various sensors
Functions	Data visualization = visual data + better user experience/interaction	Protecting, Integrity, Authenticity, Data processing, Confidentiality, Availability, Data Analysis and Management.	Remote maintenance, Data Transmission, Fault detection, and Communication among connected devices	Interaction with surrounding, Collecting data

Transmission Layer

An interconnected network of devices gathers data in the preceding layer. Data can be transferred to the destination after collection. Additionally, the devices that are connected communicate with one another. Device-to-device communication helps in remote maintenance, decision-making, and fault detection. The transmission layer includes the communication methods utilized for data processing (send/receive). Long-range communication occurs between standard smart devices like mobile phones and various wired and wireless smart equipment. Cellular networks' most recent addition is 4G/LTE (Silva et al. 2018). In addition, wireless local area networks like WiFi are common and often utilized. The device varieties and specifications for the sensing layer have expanded along with the demand for communication.

Sensing Layer

Practical data analysis is a critical component in most decision-making processes. Therefore, gathering accurate data is an essential duty. However, gathering data from diverse infrastructures is a complicated operation. The infrastructure for smart cities is made up of a variety of components, including sensor networks, IoT devices, and more. Sensors gather information from several kinds of devices. Healthcare, medicine, intelligent transportation, and other industries all heavily rely on IoT-enabled devices and applications (Chen et al., 2019). Sensors, particularly IoT devices utilized in various appliances, are important sources for data collecting. Infrared, Radio-frequency identification (RFID), temperature, humidity sensors, Bluetooth, cameras, and other types of sensors are used to collect data.

APPLICATIONS OF SMART CITY

When there is a traffic jam, IoT sensors send a warning notification to the closest traffic control facility for possible fast root navigation. Within this section, some applications of Smart cities are presented.

Intelligent Transportation System

The traffic control system, which is automated and efficient in some places, is a major problem for smart cities. A cloud-assisted IoT intelligent transportation system was recommended as a resolution to the problems of traffic management (Zantalis et al., 2020). An integrated IoT sensor camera is mounted at each intersection's traffic signal to track the movement of vehicles. An algorithm that detects traffic direction and regulates the signal lights is performed using the data from numerous signal corners.

Some developed models to aid this smart transportation system include, for instance, IoT information and communications technology integration in transportation framework design, secure smart transportation, privacy-protecting system, and drivers' location tracking (Lin et al., 2019), traffic control and crowd management (Boukerche & Coutinho 2019), machine learning (ML) application for transportation effectiveness (Yan et al., 2020), vehicular technology topology implementation (Kelley et al., 2019), Traffic pattern prediction (Shukla et al., 2016), cruise control (Khazaei et al., 2016), and fog centered architectures (Giang et al., 2016; Reddy et al., 2022).

Smart Home

Disability, activity restriction, and participation restriction all have strong correlations. Technology has advanced significantly recently and will likely continue to do so. Intelligent home and communication methods provide new ways to get around some limits and limitations affecting persons with disabilities. This scoping review's objective was to investigate how smart home and wireless technologies affected the results for those with complex needs and impairments (Ali et al., 2020). Consequently, people with disabilities and complex needs appear to benefit from technology regarding independence, involvement, and quality of life.

Notwithstanding, ethical issues were brought up due to the population's susceptibility, including possible threats from social interaction and privacy issues with monitoring technologies. Other models include deep learning disease detection, hypothetical and research tasks (Tripathi et al., 2020), healthcare resource distribution (Abou-Nassar et al., 2020), efficiency analysis (Tanwar et al., 2020), smart healthcare traffic network (Ismail et al., 2019), data integrity (Ahad et al., 2019), AI established disease recognitions (Oueida et al., 2018; Mahmoud et al., 2018), Blockchain oriented method (Zhang et al., 2018), Edge computing-based method (Chen et al., 2018), tracking using global positioning system (Chui et al., 2017).

Smart Connectivity Infrastructure

Integration of AI technologies and Blockchain is changing the design of the network of smart cities to create sustainable ecosystems. The technological advances have produced both opportunities and problems for us as we work to construct smart cities (Duda et al., 2022). The safety problems and difficulties that distress the use of blockchains in creating maintainable and intelligent communities are key. A thorough discussion of many important topics for combining AI with blockchain knowledge aids in developing smart societies.

Intelligent Energy And Power Management Systems

The study analyzes the application of probabilistic ML in fundamental energy technologies, the integration of thermal, electric, and large-scale renewable energy resources and fuel grid is greatly aided by ML approaches (Ahmad et al., 2022). It is covered how to use several tools for effective management, operation, and control of energy systems. The most significant recent ML advancements, their difficulties, and cutting-edge next research prospects are briefly reviewed. Some other models include privacy for stakeholders (Gai et al., 2019), energy management and consumption (Abate et al., 2019; Hussain et al., 2020), Effective and intelligent energy supervision (Kim and Lim., 2018), big data for intelligent grid administration (Marinakis et al., 2018), energy markets (Mengelkamp et al., 2018), energy storage management (Olabi et al., 2017), Cloud service integrations (Rivera and RodriguezMartinez, 2016), big data analytics (Zhou et al., 2016; Ashu et al., 2020), vehicle integrations and (Tan et al., 2016).

SMART CITY EXAMPLES

Smart city adoption globally has been slow due to much-unresolved security and other challenges. Despite those challenges, several cities worldwide have adopted smart cities due to technological advancement. Such cities include London, Paris, New York, Reykjavik, Amsterdam, Singapore, Tokyo, Dubai, Busan, Santander, and Stockholm (Ismagilova et al., 2020). A summary of top cities that have implemented smart methods in daily operation and their characteristics with some initiative automated meter reading (AMR) is demonstrated within Table 2

Table 2. Selected smart cities corresponding to their initiatives

Smart city	Initiatives	References
London	Street lamp posts, London data store, electric vehicle charge points, self-driving Heathrow pods, Air quality sensors and public Wi-Fi, smart surveillance	(Willems et al., 2017)
New York	Air quality monitoring, AMR, Solar powered trash bins, Energy efficient smart lighting, Web-based crime prediction system. Etc.	(Angelidou, 2017)
Singapore	Smart National IDs, Core Operations Development and eXchange(CODEX), E-Payments, Smart Urban Mobility, Moments of Life, Smart Nation Sensor Platform	(Chang & Das, 2020)
Busan	Smart streetlights, Smart crosswalks, Smart parking, Building energy management, socially disadvantaged individuals service, Smart store management system, Lost child prevention system	(Bauer et al., 2021)
Amsterdam	Open Data, MyNeighbour App (MijnBuur), Wyzer App, Social Glass, Plastic free rivers, IoT Living Lab,	(Amsterdam Smart City, n.d.; Bauer et al., 2021)
Sunshine Coast Region	Waste bin sensors, Networked LED Street lighting, Sunshine Coast Council App, Networked flood sensors, Smart Street, Pedestrian and cyclist counters, Networked irrigation system	(Sunshine Smart City, n.d.)
Santander	Parks and gardens irrigation, Environmental Monitoring, Outdoor Parking Management, Participatory sensing and Guidance, Traffic Intensity Monitoring, Waste management	(Galache et al., 2012)
Paris	Halle Pajol solar power station, IoT-enabled park benches, and E-bike renting schemes, among others.	(Kylili & Fokaides, 2015)
Tokyo	Tokyo Rinkai disaster, Smart Grids, Prevention Park, Energy Management, Smart homes, buildings, and factories	(Bauer et al., 2021)

Smart City Security Attributes

This section discusses the security attributes of such solutions that every smart city should have to guarantee security for users and connected IoT devices.

Secure, Mutual Authentication

Through various network communication protocols, different IoT devices can communicate with each other across the different layers of the smart city. Providing a secure communication link between those devices hinges on non-repudiation, integrity, confidentiality features, and implemented network security (Khadidos et al., 2022). The mutual and secure substantiation attribute of smart cities ensures that data transmission occurs between the IoT device and smart city service after the proof of their identities is established. By undergoing a rigorous validation process, IoT devices connected to the smart city network can ensure their validity and prevent potential security breaches from fraudulent devices.

Security Life Cycle Management

The IoT device life cycle generally consists of three phases, namely, device provisioning, firmware or software update, and decommissioning, OEMs can ensure the security life cycle management attribute for smart city devices and mitigate the fallout from any security compromises (El-Jaouhari, 2022)Furthermore, measures such as secure device shutdown guarantee that decommissioned IoT devices will not be re-purposed to connect to a smart city amenity without approval from the security executive for cyber free threat (Kalinaki et al., 2023).

Secure Boot and Firmware Integrity

To ensure the security of a smart city, a cryptographic code signing method is used for the modus operandi of the secure boot and firmware integrity attribute. This method ensures that an IoT device can only execute code generated by its OEM or a verified and trusted party, thereby preventing malicious attacks by denying code execution from programs that contain unsigned malware such as viruses, worms, and malware. In addition, this attribute restricts hackers from replacing the original firmware with compromised versions of instruction sets (Singh et al., 2020). For smart city devices, the secure boot attribute preserves the authenticity and integrity of program packages by preventing the execution of unsigned code (Nath & Nath, 2022).

Updating and Patching

Due to the constantly evolving nature of cyber-attacks on the increasing number of IoT devices in a smart city, service providers and OEMs occasionally update software packages inherent within their supplied IoT devices. Such updates ensure the devices' proper functioning and enhance inbuilt security features that protect them against new and sophisticated attacks from multiple attack vectors (Obaidat, 2022). Moreover, updating and patching provide a means through which security vulnerabilities can be identified and resolved by different security architects and enterprises.

Security Analysis, Response, and Monitoring

The security attribute of a smart city involves an automated capability for its communications network to collect, record, and monitor data transmission between multiple interconnected IoT devices and their connectivity traffic. Additionally, this attribute requires the analysis and processing of the collected data to identify possible security and privacy breaches and evaluate the severity of any detected threats or attacks. Following established security policies, any identified threats or privacy breaches can be resolved by disabling and quarantining the compromised devices or disconnecting and removing them entirely. Given the vulnerability of numerous heterogeneous IoT devices in a smart city, this attribute is crucial for mitigating the potential fallout from any security breaches.

Privacy and Security Concerns

The heterogeneous nature of IoT devices in a smart city makes them vulnerable to various security threats and privacy breaches. These concerns include cyber-attacks, threats to device and connectivity security, issues related to data collection and transmission security, physical attacks on smart city infrastructure, and cloud-related security issues. These and many other security concerns have been a significant obstacle to the widespread adoption of smart city services. This section provides a detailed description of these security and privacy issues.

Cyberattacks

Different IoT devices have unique inbuilt security measures from their OEMs. This renders them vulnerable to attacks as hackers can take advantage of the weakly implemented security measures in the devices and disrupt the entire smart city network. Several studies have documented different cyber-attacks on smart city services (Ismagilova et al., 2020). These cyber-attacks (both passive and active) can lead to security and privacy breaches leading to data loss, service disruption, and degradation of the user experience of smart city dwellers.

Such violations can undermine the fundamental security goals (confidentiality, integrity, and availability) preserved by imaginative city security architects, service providers, and OEMs to safeguard end-users, data, and IoT devices. The table below briefly summarizes the cyberattacks on the smart city network with their corresponding impacts on the security goals affected. In addition to the above attacks, the following attacks have been reported and include malware attacks, ransomware attacks, social engineering, brute force attacks, hardware trojan, and eavesdropping attacks, detailed in Table 4 (Al-Turjman et al., 2022; Yaqoob et al., 2017).

Table 4. Summarized selected attacks and their targeted implications

Attack	Impact	References
Man in the Middle attack	Confidentiality, Integrity	(Ismagilova et al., 2020)
Denial of Service (DoS) and Distributed DoS (DDoS)	All	(Khalifa et al., 2022)
Eavesdropping attack	Confidentiality, Non-repudiation, Privacy	(Thilakarathne & Madhuka Priyashan, 2022)
Replay attack	Confidentiality, Integrity	(Yaacoub et al., 2020)
Botnet attack	Availability, Confidentiality	(Al-Turjman et al., 2022)
Jamming attack	Availability	(Reynvoet et al., 2022)
Flooding attack	Availability	(Shafiq et al., 2020)
Packet Analysis attacks	Integrity, Confidentiality, Non-repudiation, Privacy	(Koshy et al., 2022)

Device Power, Storage, and Connectivity Security Issues

IoT devices are heavily impacted by their low power and storage capabilities in the service layer of the smart city architecture. Such challenges greatly limit their processing powers which are mitigated using third-party applications and services located in the cloud. However, these third-party cloud solutions areusceptible to security attacks such as adversarial attacks, cyber kill chain-based attacks, backdoor attacks, trojan attacks, and data manipulation attacks (Qayyum et al., 2020; Rao & Deebak, 2022). Using third-party methods may result in enterprises having no control over their data, which may lead to potential risks of data leakage by the service provider. Hence, secure communication channels that deploy lightweight end-to-end encryption schemes between the IoT devices, applications, and third-party cloud storage providers must be provided to ensure the necessary authentication, authorization, identification, and device management (Rao & Deebak, 2022).

Physical Attack on the Smart City Infrastructure

In addition to data protection through the prevention of security and privacy breaches in the virtual space, the physical security of the smart city infrastructure is equally important in all smart city services. All IoT devices, wired and wireless communications, sensors, powerlines, base stations, substation facilities, and others in an urban setting can be stolen and vandalized by intruders in case they have access to them (Yang et al., 2022) Such physical disruptions and vandalism to smart city infrastructure can lead to outages, data leakage, degradation of user experience, and serious financial losses to enterprises due to the fact they are stationed in outdoor settings. Therefore, physical security solutions (see discussed in the next section) can be instituted to ensure smart cities' smooth and uninterruptible functioning.

Cloud-Related Security Issues

The introduction of cloud computing in smart cities is mainly to tackle resource constraints such as storage, hosting, and processing for IoT devices. However, being a shared multi-tenancy and multiuser environment that accommodates various enterprises and service providers with different cloud service needs, there exist loopholes that lead to security and privacy breaches. Such breaches include malicious code injection, unauthorized data access, data sniffing using a man-in-the-middle attack, and DDoS attacks, among others, which have the potential to destroy the quality of life (QoL) of smart city users (Alam et al., 2022). Therefore, solutions capable of mitigating cloud-based security issues can be put in place to ensure the smooth operation of smart cities.

PRIVACY AND SECURITY SOLUTIONS FOR SMART CITIES

In this section, we summarize some of the different commonly deployed security and privacy solutions for IoT-based smart cities. Their detailed modes of operation have been fully explained in their corresponding references. Cyber-attacks on the smart city infrastructure can be mitigated by deploying cyber-safe utilities such as demilitarized zones (Dhungana et al., 2015), intrusion detection and prevention systems (Singh et al., 2020), honeypots (Dalamagkas et al., 2019) and firewalls (Haar & Buchmann, 2019). Such utilities can protect against potential cyber-attacks targeting different smart city services. Furthermore, blockchain-based cloud architecture for secret sharing was proposed by (Cha et al., 2021) for smart cities to solve the challenges of managing and accessing storage devices provided by cloud-based service providers. Their framework improves the integrity and security of different end-user information through a secret sharing algorithm. Their proposed approach depicts enhanced privacy and security via security analysis and demonstrates faster transaction speed and data storage efficiency compared to existing research.

Authors (Gheisari et al., 2021) proposed an ontology-based framework for preserving privacy in smart cities. Firstly, their proposed model enables seamless, secure interactions between heterogeneous IoT devices from various OEMs. Moreover, it identifies abnormal patterns of interactions while addressing the quality of the services provided through its semantic reasoning rules. Finally, by constantly changing the privacy behaviors of connected IoT devices, the framework's third module addresses privacy challenges through the privacy rules manager. Compared to other frameworks, its effectiveness was proved through extensive testing on synthetic smart city datasets while providing affordability and robustness against data leakage.

The use of biometrics has broadly been used for end-user authentication in IoT-based Smart cities. These human-dependent methods can automatically recognize individuals based on their biodata, such as fingerprints, facial appearance, handwritten signatures, and voice. Brainwave-based and mutual authentication protocols have been the most widely deployed in smart cities to authenticate users and secure their private information due to their high accuracy and efficiency (Al-Turjman et al., 2022).

Authors (Alzubi et al., 2022) proposed a dynamic software-defined network-based privacy-preserving framework for IoT-based smart cities using the trust technique. Its software-defined network (SDN) controller operates under the nodes' mutual trust and depends on the confidence level to choose packet routes from the IoT device to the cloud domain. By identifying a device that lacks trust in its neighbor, it can reroute the packet on a different path.

To enhance the security of data storage, transmission, and processing in a multi-tenancy and multi-access smart city infrastructure, lightweight encryption schemes (referred to as tiny cryptography) can be utilized for resource-constrained IoT devices, as suggested by Noura et al. (2019). In their research, they proposed an economical, efficient, and resilient lightweight stream cipher scheme (referred to as Lsmart city), demonstrating a high level of security for IoT devices with limited resources.

To mitigate physical threats and attacks posed by intruders on the smart city infrastructure (Yang et al., 2022), we provided four countermeasur, including circuit and system design, installing additional sensors, biometry, and analysis tools and theft tracking devices. The circuit design involves embedding a chip theft detection technique installing additional sensors, such as cameras, motion sensors, and RFID can help detect and physical theft and vandalism. Schemes such as biometry and behavior analysis apply acquired data originating from embedded sensors to authenticate different users and evaluate the operation state of equipment. Finally, tracking mechanisms for stolen devices can be deployed using GPS and location-based services for outdoor equipment. For indoor equipment, Bluetooth tracking, ZigBee, RFID, and infrared are the most used tracking options with limited distances of up to 10 meters.

FUTURE RESEARCH DIRECTION

Within this section, some sampled future research directions are presented below:

Data Storage and Processing

Real-time data accessibility can lead to digital culture and literacy, improving future urban societies, online consultation platforms, and public involvement (Nagarajan et al., 2022). The future of cities will be shaped by collective and civic intelligence (Chaves et al., 2022), crowdsourcing, the emergence of wireless internet and mobile applications, the impact of neogeography, simulations, and three-dimensional virtual surroundings that replicate and evaluate complex social phenomena and cities, as well as the impact of these technologies (Skaržauskienė et al., 2022). Data-driven Smart cities are areas where business intensive should be done at the academic and industrial levels and advance the quality of life, safety, environmental preservation, and the design of the smart city future.

Emergency Services

To properly analyze smart city public engagement from an emergency perspective, the authors (Zhu et al., 202) depicted that for quality services, a continuous experience between the issues affecting health service quality and citizen engagement using the current technology must be availed. Cities have significantly impacted a nation's economic and social growth. They are actual locations where people reside, work, conduct business, and get services. Nations should consider factors like effectiveness and sustainable development as an early presentation of the United Nations (Moyle et al., 2022), quality of life, and prudent resource management while considering this scenario. Technology and communications are crucial for achieving sustainable development goals where cities will effectively manage vital infrastructure and provide integrated public services (Blasi et al., 2022). Emergency services should be a key component of the definition of smart cities because they assist people in dire circumstances and communicate risks.

Collaborative Filtering

These artificial intelligence-based systems filter massive data content or responses to an individual depending on the search history. There are sometimes referred to as recommender systems as defined by the authors. The sparsity of the data can be impacted using the proposed model, for example, the Naive Bayesian classifier (Zhang et al., 2022), the three-way Naive Bayesian collaborative filtering recommendation approach demonstrated a minimum risk decision process. Furthermore, the authors (Wang et al., 2022) still suggested intelligent security sensors as an ideal to play a vital collaborative ability in human source administration.

A considerable number of Smart cities have encountered, for instance, water shortages, traffic congestion, waste management, energy inadequacy, and low public participation in city governance due to the traditional filtering approaches that are used. This makes it complex to identify such loopholes in operation; it is vital to categorize the most life-threatening and urgent concerns that smart city solutions must address in developing, operating, and maintaining as suggested (Khadidos et al., 2022), smart security frameworks based on collaborative reciprocated authentication models.

Smart Cities Security

As the public gets into the operation of smart operations in their daily life because of these technological advancements like smart farming, transportation, e-government, digital citizenships, buildings, and healthcare, among others, security and privacy breaches are more likely to increase due to the public. The majority want to take advantage of smart city initiatives and experience greater levels of safety, lower crime rates, and generally better quality of life (Hussain et al., 2022). Many individuals doubt smart city projects because of the security issues they face. IoT gadgets have security issues, and the concerns about the proliferation of IoT sensors and the tighter coupling of infrastructure silos in cities are logical (Singh et al., 2022). On the other hand, technology industries are developing security solutions based on blockchain technology, big data analytics, and encryption technologies to combat more complex cyber-attacks.

Blockchain

Initially meant for decentralized financial transactions among different parties, Blockchain has seen wider applications in several domains such as agriculture, healthcare, power grids, home, supply chain, and governance, among many others. The robustness of blockchain technology, as evidenced by its ability for immutability, anonymity, and confidentiality, has shown large potential in solving many smart city security problems highlighted in the previous sections (Bracco et al., 2022; Rejeb et al., 2021) Blockchain-as-a-service (Baas) is another trend that integrates IoT-enabled smart city devices in blockchain-enabled Cyber-physical systems like smart power grids, smart homes, smart healthcare, etc. Baas promises greater security for smart city services and users as it allows management, access, and monitoring of blockchain applications with minimal security requirements (Li et al., 2022).

Sustainable Energy Management

As one of the components of smart cities, the main purpose of smart power grids is to meet the increasing energy demand as more cities adopt smart city features. This is geared towards ensuring that there's enough supply ability to minimize energy loss and enhance power grid reliability, sustainability, cost-effectiveness, and operational efficiency. The application of renewable energy resources (RES) such as solar and wind is one such initiative that is becoming popular in emerging smart cities (Majeed et al., 2021)In addition, bckchain application in smart grids also promises to ensure computerized decentralized power transmission and distribution along with real-time operational surveillance of the power grid (Musleh et al., 2019).

Cost Management

As smart cities evolve, the operational costs of upgrading existing infrastructure with smart city technologies to improve the quality of life for city dwellers are becoming too high. To ensure sustainable progression towards smart city status measures such as public-private partnerships geared towards funding smart cities will have to be instituted. Another means of managing operational costs is using the alliance approach, which involves the creative financing model based entirely on coalitions, procuring products & services, androviding supervision to achieve smart city promises (*Smart Cities Funding and Financing Strategies | Deloitte*, n.d.).

CONCLUSION

This chapter presents architectural smart city levels, applications, requirements, security concerns, and emergent trends in detail. With technological advancements, developing a smart city has become possible with added benefits to the public. It has been identified that security, collaborative filtering, emergency services, sustainable energy management, and Blockchain will be highly needed to operate smart cities. These include enhanced connectivity, intelligent decision-making, and enhanced resource supervision. Furthermore, various security concerns have emerged due to the increasing acceptance of smart cities. These include data security, authentication, and unauthorized access. It further also explored the various applications of this technology.

REFERENCES

Abate, F., Carratù, M., Liguori, C., & Paciello, V. (2019). A low cost smart power meter for IoT. *Measurement, 136*, 59–66. doi:10.1016/j.measurement.2018.12.069

Abou-Nassar, E. M., Iliyasu, A. M., El-Kafrawy, P. M., Song, O., Bashir, A. K., & El-Latif, A. A. (2020). DITrust chain: Towards Blockchain-based trust models for sustainable healthcare IoT systems. *IEEE Access : Practical Innovations, Open Solutions, 8*, 111223–111238. doi:10.1109/ACCESS.2020.2999468

Ahad, A., Tahir, M., & Yau, K. A. (2019). 5G-based smart healthcare network: Architecture, taxonomy, challenges, and future research directions. *IEEE Access : Practical Innovations, Open Solutions, 7*, 100747–100762. doi:10.1109/ACCESS.2019.2930628

Ahmad, T., Madonski, R., Zhang, D., Huang, C., & Mujeeb, A. (2022). Data-driven probabilistic machine learning in sustainable smart energy/smart energy systems: Key developments, challenges, and future research opportunities in the context of the smart grid paradigm. *Renewable & Sustainable Energy Reviews, 160*, 112128. doi:10.1016/j.rser.2022.112128

Al-Turjman, F., Zahmatkesh, H., & Shahroze, R. (2022). An overview of security and privacy in smart cities' IoT communications. *Transactions on Emerging Telecommunications Technologies, 33*(3), e3677. doi:10.1002/ett.3677

Alam, T., Tajammul, M., & Gupta, R. (2022). Towards the Sustainable Development of Smart Cities Through Cloud Computing. *Studies in Computational Intelligence, 1002*, 199–222. doi:10.1007/978-981-16-7498-3_13

Ali, F., El-Sappagh, S., Islam, S. R., Kwak, D., Ali, A., Imran, M., & Kwak, K. (2020). A smart healthcare monitoring system for heart disease prediction based on ensemble deep learning and feature fusion. *Information Fusion, 63*, 208–222. doi:10.1016/j.inffus.2020.06.008

Alzubi, J. A., Movassagh, A. A., Gheisari, M., Najafabadi, H. E., Abbasi, A. A., Liu, Y., Pingmei, Z., Izadpanahkakhk, M., & Najafabadi, A. H. P. (2022). A Dynamic SDN-based Privacy-Preserving Approach for Smart City Using Trust Technique. *2022 9th Iranian Joint Congress on Fuzzy and Intelligent Systems,* CFIS 2022.

Amsterdam Smart City. (n.d.). *Amsterdam Smart City.* ASC. https://amsterdamsmartcity.com/

Angelidou, M. (2017)... *The Role of Smart City Characteristics in the Plans of Fifteen Cities., 24*(4), 3–28.

Ashu, A., Hussain, M. W., Sinha Roy, D., & Reddy, H. K. (2020). Intelligent Data Compression Policy for Hadoop Performance Optimization. *Advances in Intelligent Systems and Computing*, 80–89. . doi:10.1007/978-3-030-49345-5_9

Bauer, M., Sanchez, L., & Song, J. (2021). IoT-Enabled Smart Cities: Evolution and Outlook. *Sensors, 21*(13), 4511.

Blasi, S., Ganzaroli, A., & De Noni, I. (2022). Smartening sustainable development in cities: Strengthening the theoretical linkage between smart cities and SDGs. *Sustainable Cities and Society, 80*, 103793. doi:10.1016/j.scs.2022.103793

Boukerche, A., & Coutinho, R. W. (2019). Crowd management: The overlooked component of smart transportation systems. *IEEE Communications Magazine*, *57*(4), 48–53. doi:10.1109/MCOM.2019.1800641

Bracco, S., Rosales-Asensio, E., González-Martínez, A., Rosen, M. A., & Badidi, E. (2022). Edge AI and Blockchain for Smart Sustainable Cities: Promise and Potential. *Sustainability, 14*(13), 7609. doi:10.3390/su14137609

Cha, J., Singh, S. K., Kim, T. W., & Park, J. H. (2021). Blockchain-empowered cloud architecture based on secret sharing for smart city. *Journal of Information Security and Applications*, *57*, 102686. doi:10.1016/j.jisa.2020.102686

Chang, F., & Das, D. (2020). Smart Nation Singapore: Developing Policies for a Citizen-Oriented Smart City Initiative. *Developing National Urban Policies*, 425–440.

Chaves, R., Motta, C., Correia, A., Paredes, H., Caetano, B., De Souza, J. M., & Schneider, D. (2022, May). Crowd and Urban Storytelling: Evaluating a Collective Intelligence Model to Support Discussions about the City. In 2022, *IEEE 25th International Conference on Computer Supported Cooperative Work in Design (CSCWD) (pp. 1473-1479), Hangzhou, China.* IEEE.

Chen, Q., Wang, W., Wu, F., De, S., Wang, R., Zhang, B., & Huang, X. (2019). A survey of an emerging area: Deep learning for smart city data. *IEEE Transactions on Emerging Topics in Computational Intelligence*, *3*(5), 392–410. doi:10.1109/TETCI.2019.2907718

Chen, Q., Wang, W., Wu, F., De, S., Wang, R., Zhang, B., & Huang, X. (2019). A survey of an emerging area: Deep learning for smart city data. *IEEE Transactions on Emerging Topics in Computational Intelligence*, *3*(5), 392–410. doi:10.1109/TETCI.2019.2907718

Chui, K., Alhalabi, W., Pang, S., Pablos, P., Liu, R., & Zhao, M. (2017). Disease diagnosis in smart healthcare: Innovation technologies and applications. *Sustainability (Basel)*, *9*(12), 2309. doi:10.3390u9122309

Curzon, J., Almehmadi, A., & El-Khatib, K. (2019). A survey of privacy enhancing technologies for smart cities. *Pervasive and Mobile Computing*, *55*, 76–95. doi:10.1016/j.pmcj.2019.03.001

Dalamagkas, C., Sarigiannidis, P., Ioannidis, D., Iturbe, E., Nikolis, O., Ramos, F., Rios, E., Sarigiannidis, A., & Tzovaras, D. (2019). A Survey On Honeypots, Honeynets And Their Applications On Smart Grid. *2019 IEEE Conference on Network Softwarization (NetSoft),* (pp. 93–100). IEEE. 10.1109/NETSOFT.2019.8806693

Dhungana, D., Engelbrecht, G., Parreira, J. X., Schuster, A., & Valerio, D. (2015). Aspern smart ICT: Data analytics and privacy challenges in a smart city. *2015 IEEE 2nd World Forum on Internet of Things (WF-IoT)*, (pp. 447–452). IEEE.

Du, R., Santi, P., Xiao, M., Vasilakos, A. V., & Fischione, C. (2019). Sensable city: A Survey on the deployment and management of smart city monitoring. *IEEE Communications Surveys and Tutorials*, *21*(2), 1533–1560. doi:10.1109/COMST.2018.2881008

Duda. O., Kunanets. N., Matsiuk. O & Pasichnyk. V. (2022). Cloud-based IT Infrastructure for "Smart City" Projects. *InDependable IoT for Human and Industry,* 389-409 River Publishers.

el Jaouhari, S. (2022). Toward a Secure Firmware OTA Update for constrained IoT devices. *2022 IEEE International Smart Cities Conference (ISC2),* (pp. 1–6). IEEE. 10.1109/ISC255366.2022.9922087

Elrawy, M. F., Awad, A. I., & Hamed, H. F. (2018). Intrusion detection systems for IoT-based smart environments: A survey. *Journal of Cloud Computing (Heidelberg, Germany)*, *7*(1), 1–20. doi:10.118613677-018-0123-6

Gai, K., Wu, Y., Zhu, L., Qiu, M., & Shen, M. (2019). Privacy-preserving energy trading using consortium Blockchain in smart grid. *IEEE Transactions on Industrial Informatics*, *15*(6), 3548–3558. doi:10.1109/TII.2019.2893433

Gai, K., Wu, Y., Zhu, L., Xu, L., & Zhang, Y. (2019). Permissioned blockchain and edge computing empowered privacy-preserving smart grid networks. *IEEE Internet of Things Journal*, *6*(5), 7992–8004. doi:10.1109/JIOT.2019.2904303

Galache, J. A., Santana, J. R., Gutiérrez, V., Sánchez, L., Sotres, P., & Muñoz, L. (2012). Towards experimentation service duality within a Smart City scenario. *2012 9th Annual Conference on Wireless On-Demand Network Systems and Services, WONS* 2012, 175–181.

Gharaibeh, A., Salahuddin, M. A., Hussini, S. J., Khreishah, A., Khalil, I., Guizani, M., & Al-Fuqaha, A. (2017). Smart cities: A survey on data management, security, and enabling technologies. *IEEE Communications Surveys and Tutorials*, *19*(4), 2456–2501. doi:10.1109/COMST.2017.2736886

Gheisari, M., Najafabadi, H. E., Alzubi, J. A., Gao, J., Wang, G., Abbasi, A. A., & Castiglione, A. (2021). OBPP: An ontology-based framework for privacy-preserving in IoT-based smart cities. *Future Generation Computer Systems*, *123*, 1–13. doi:10.1016/j.future.2021.01.028

Giang, N. K., Leung, V. C., & Lea, R. (2016). On developing smart transportation applications in the fog computing paradigm. *Proceedings of the 6th ACM Symposium on Development and Analysis of Intelligent Vehicular Networks and Applications - DIVANet '16*. ACM. 10.1145/2989275.2989286

Haar, C., & Buchmann, E. (2019). *Fane: A Firewall Appliance for The Smart Home,* 449–458. Annals of Computer Science and Information Systems.

Hussain, M. W., Pradhan, B., Gao, X. Z., Reddy, K. H. K., & Roy, D. S. (2020). Clonal selection algorithm for energy minimization in software defined networks. *Applied Soft Computing*, *96*, 106617. doi:10.1016/j.asoc.2020.106617

Hussain, S., Mahmood, K., Khan, M. K., Chen, C. M., Alzahrani, B. A., & Chaudhry, S. A. (2022). Designing secure and lightweight user access to drones for smart city surveillance. *Computer Standards & Interfaces*, *80*, 103566. doi:10.1016/j.csi.2021.103566

Ismagilova, E., Hughes, L., Rana, N. P., & Dwivedi, Y. K. (2020). Security, Privacy and Risks Within Smart Cities: Literature Review and Development of a Smart City Interaction Framework. *Information Systems Frontiers, 24*(2), 393–414.

Ismail, L., Materwala, H., & Zeadally, S. (2019). Lightweight Blockchain for healthcare. *IEEE Access : Practical Innovations, Open Solutions*, *7*, 149935–149951. doi:10.1109/ACCESS.2019.2947613

Jamwal, R., Jarman, H. K., Roseingrave, E., Douglas, J., & Winkler, D. (2022). Smart home and communication technology for people with disabilities: A scoping review. *Disability and Rehabilitation. Assistive Technology*, *17*(6), 624–644. doi:10.1080/17483107.2020.1818138 PMID:32924660

Kalinaki, K., Thilakarathne, N. N., Mubarak, H. R., Malik, O. A., & Abdullatif, M. (2023). Cybersafe Capabilities and Utilities for Smart Cities. In *Cybersecurity for Smart Cities* (pp. 71–86). Springer. doi:10.1007/978-3-031-24946-4_6

Kelley, S. B., Lane, B. W., Stanley, B. W., Kane, K., Nielsen, E., & Strachan, S. (2019). Smart transportation for all? A typology of recent U.S. smart transportation projects in midsized cities. *Annals of the American Association of Geographers*, *110*(2), 547–558. doi:10.1080/24694452.2019.1643702

Khadidos, A. O., Shitharth, S., Manoharan, H., Yafoz, A., Khadidos, A. O., & Alyoubi, K. H. (2022). An Intelligent Security Framework Based on Collaborative Mutual Authentication Model for Smart City Networks. *IEEE Access : Practical Innovations, Open Solutions*, *10*, 85289–85304. doi:10.1109/ACCESS.2022.3197672

Khadidos, A. O., Shitharth, S., Manoharan, H., Yafoz, A., Khadidos, A. O., & Alyoubi, K. H. (2022). An intelligent security framework based on collaborative mutual authentication model for smart city networks. *IEEE Access : Practical Innovations, Open Solutions*, *10*, 85289–85304. doi:10.1109/ACCESS.2022.3197672

Khalifa, O. O., & Japar, D. F. bin, Rahman, F. D. A., & Nasir, H. (2022). Authentication of IoT in Smart City Applications. *2022 IEEE 8th International Conference on Smart Instrumentation, Measurement and Applications (ICSIMA),* (pp. 58–63). IEEE.

Khazaei. H., Zareian. S. Veleda. R & Litoiu. M. (2016). Sipresk: A big data analytic platform for smart transportation. *Smart City 360 Lecture Notes of the Institute for Computer Sciences, Social Informatics and Telecommunications Engineering,* 419–430.

Kim, S., & Lim, H. (2018). Reinforcement learning based energy management algorithm for smart energy buildings. *Energies*, *11*(8), 2010. doi:10.3390/en11082010

Kirimtat, A., Krejcar, O., Kertesz, A., & Tasgetiren, M. F. (2020). Future trends and current state of smart city concepts: A survey. *IEEE Access : Practical Innovations, Open Solutions*, *8*, 86448–86467. doi:10.1109/ACCESS.2020.2992441

Koshy, A. S., Fatima, N., Agarwal, P., & Rodrigues, J. J. P. C. (2022). Security and Privacy Threats in IoT-Enabled Smart Cities. *Internet of Things,* 277–300.

Kylili, A., & Fokaides, P. A. (2015). European smart cities: The role of zero energy buildings. *Sustainable Cities and Society*, *15*, 86–95. doi:10.1016/j.scs.2014.12.003

Lau, B. P. L., Marakkalage, S. H., Zhou, Y., Hassan, N. U., Yuen, C., Zhang, M., & Tan, U. X. (2019). A survey of data fusion in smart city applications. *Information Fusion*, *52*, 357–374. doi:10.1016/j.inffus.2019.05.004

Laufs, J., Borrion, H., & Bradford, B. (2020). Security and smart city: A systematic review. *Sustainable Cities and Society*, *55*, 102023. doi:10.1016/j.scs.2020.102023

Li, D., Deng, L., Cai, Z., & Souri, A. (2022). Blockchain as service model in the Internet of Things management: Systematic review. *Transactions on Emerging Telecommunications Technologies*, *33*(4), e4139. doi:10.1002/ett.4139

Lin, J., Niu, J., Li, H., & Atiquzzaman, M. (2019). A secure and efficient location-based service scheme for smart transportation. *Future Generation Computer Systems*, *92*, 694–704. doi:10.1016/j.future.2017.11.030

Mahmoud, M. M., Rodrigues, J. J., Ahmed, S. H., Shah, S. C., Al-Muhtadi, J. F., Korotaev, V. V., & De Albuquerque, V. H. C. (2018). Enabling technologies on the cloud of things for smart healthcare. *IEEE Access : Practical Innovations, Open Solutions*, *6*, 31950–31967. doi:10.1109/ACCESS.2018.2845399

Majeed, U., Khan, L. U., Yaqoob, I., Kazmi, S. M. A., Salah, K., & Hong, C. S. (2021). Blockchain for IoT-based smart cities: Recent advances, requirements, and future challenges. *Journal of Network and Computer Applications*, *181*, 103007. doi:10.1016/j.jnca.2021.103007

Marinakis, V., Doukas, H., Tsapelas, J., Mouzakitis, S., Sicilia, A., Madrazo, L., & Sgouridis, S. (2018). From big data to smart energy services: An application for intelligent energy management. *Future Generation Computer Systems*, *110*, 572–586. doi:10.1016/j.future.2018.04.062

Mengelkamp, E., Notheisen, B., Beer, C., Dauer, D., & Weinhardt, C. (2018). A blockchain-based smart grid: Towards sustainable local energy markets. *Computer Science -. Research for Development*, *33*, 207–214.

Moyle, B. D., Weaver, D. B., Gössling, S., McLennan, C. L., & Hadinejad, A. (2022). Are water-centric themes in sustainable tourism research congruent with the UN Sustainable Development Goals? *Journal of Sustainable Tourism*, *30*(8), 1821–1836. doi:10.1080/09669582.2021.1993233

Musleh, A. S., Yao, G., & Muyeen, S. M. (2019). Blockchain Applications in Smart Grid-Review and Frameworks. *IEEE Access : Practical Innovations, Open Solutions*, *7*, 86746–86757. doi:10.1109/ACCESS.2019.2920682

Nagarajan, S. M., Deverajan, G. G., Chatterjee, P., Alnumay, W., & Muthukumaran, V. (2022). Integration of IoT based routing process for food supply chain management in sustainable smart cities. *Sustainable Cities and Society*, *76*, 103448. doi:10.1016/j.scs.2021.103448

Nam, T., & Pardo, T. A. (2011). Conceptualizing a smart city with dimensions of technology, people, and institutions. *Proceedings of the 12th Annual International Digital Government Research Conference on Digital Government Innovation in Challenging Times,* (pp. 282-291). ACM. 10.1145/2037556.2037602

Nath, N. R., & v Nath, H. (2022). Critical analysis of layered and systematic approaches for understanding IoT security threats and challenges. *Computers & Electrical Engineering*, *100*, 107997. doi:10.1016/j.compeleceng.2022.107997

Noura, H., Couturier, R., Pham, C., & Chehab, A. (2019). Lightweight Stream Cipher Scheme for Resource-Constrained IoT Devices. *International Conference on Wireless and Mobile Computing, Networking and Communications*. IEEE. 10.1109/WiMOB.2019.8923144

Obaidat, M. A. (2022). Threats and vulnerabilities of wireless sensor networks in smart cities. *The Rise of Smart Cities: Advanced Structural Sensing and Monitoring Systems,* 463–491.

Olabi, A. G. (2017). *Renewable energy and energy storage systems.* Elsevier. doi:10.1016/j.energy.2017.07.054

Oueida, S., Aloqaily, M., & Ionescu, S. (2018). A smart healthcare reward model for resource allocation in smart city. *Multimedia Tools and Applications, 78*(17), 24573–24594. doi:10.100711042-018-6647-4

Qayyum, A., Ijaz, A., Usama, M., Iqbal, W., Qadir, J., Elkhatib, Y., & Al-Fuqaha, A. (2020). Securing Machine Learning in the Cloud: A Systematic Review of Cloud Machine Learning Security. *Frontiers in Big Data, 3*, 43. doi:10.3389/fdata.2020.587139 PMID:33693420

Rao, P. M., & Deebak, B. D. (2022). Security and privacy issues in smart cities/industries: Technologies, applications, and challenges. *Journal of Ambient Intelligence and Humanized Computing, 2022*, 1–37. doi:10.100712652-022-03707-1

Reddy, K. H. K., Luhach, A. K., Kumar, V. V., Pratihar, S., Kumar, D., & Roy, D. S. (2022). Towards energy efficient Smart city services: A software defined resource management scheme for data centers. *Sustainable Computing: Informatics and Systems, 35*, 100776. doi:10.1016/j.suscom.2022.100776

Rejeb, A., Karim, S, Simske, J., Keogh, J. G., Rejeb, K., Simske, S. J., & Org, J. (2021). Blockchain technology in the smart city: a bibliometric review. *Quality & Quantity, 56*(5), 2875–2906. doi:10.1007/s11135-021-01251-2

Reynvoet, M., Gheibi, O., Quin, F., & Weyns, D. (2022). Detecting and Mitigating Jamming Attacks in IoT Networks Using Self-Adaptation. *2022 IEEE International Conference on Autonomic Computing and Self-Organizing Systems Companion (ACSOS-C),* (pp. 7–12). IEEE. 10.1109/ACSOSC56246.2022.00019

Rivera, W., & Rodriguez-Martinez, M. (2016). *Towards cloud services in smart power grid. 2016 IEEE innovative smart grid technologies - Asia.* ISGT-Asia.

Shafik, W. (2023). Cyber Security Perspectives in Public Spaces: Drone Case Study. In *Handbook of Research on Cybersecurity Risk in Contemporary Business Systems* (pp. 79–97). IGI Global. doi:10.4018/978-1-6684-7207-1.ch004

Shafiq, M., Tian, Z., Bashir, A. K., Du, X., & Guizani, M. (2020). IoT malicious traffic identification using wrapper-based feature selection mechanisms. *Computers & Security, 94*, 101863. doi:10.1016/j.cose.2020.101863

Shukla, S., Balachandran, K., & Sumitha, V. S. (2016). A framework for smart transportation using big data. *International Conference on ICT in Business Industry & Government (ICTBIG)*, Indore, India.

Silva, B. N., Khan, M., & Han, K. (2018). Towards sustainable smart Cities: A review of trends, architectures, components, and open challenges in smart cities. *Sustainable Cities and Society, 38*, 697–713. doi:10.1016/j.scs.2018.01.053

Singh, D., Pati, B., Panigrahi, C. R., & Swagatika, S. (2020). *Security Issues in IoT and their Countermeasures in Smart City Applications.* doi:10.1007/978-981-15-1483-8_26

Singh, J., Sajid, M., Gupta, S. K., & Haidri, R. A. (2022). Artificial Intelligence and Blockchain Technologies for Smart City. *Intelligent Green Technologies for Sustainable Smart Cities,* 317-330.

Skaržauskienė, A. (2022). Monitoring collective intelligence in Lithuania's online community. *In Proceedings of the 55th Hawaii International Conference on System Sciences* (pp. 357-365). University of Hawai'i at Manoa. 10.24251/HICSS.2022.043

Deloitte. (n.d.). *Smart Cities Funding and Financing Strategies*. Deloitte. https://www.deloitte.com/global/en/Industries/government-public/perspectives/smart-cities-funding-and-financing-strategies.html

Sookhak, M., Tang, H., He, Y., & Yu, F. R. (2019). Security and privacy of smart cities: Survey research issues and challenges. *IEEE Communications Surveys and Tutorials*, *21*(2), 1718–1743. doi:10.1109/COMST.2018.2867288

Sunshine Smart City. (n.d.). *Smart Cities*. Sunshine Coast. https://www.sunshinecoast.qld.gov.au/smartcities

Syed, A. S., Sierra-Sosa, D., Kumar, A., & Elmaghraby, A. (2021). IoT in smart cities: A survey of technologies, practices, and challenges. *Smart Cities*, *4*(2), 429–475. doi:10.3390martcities4020024

Tan, H., & Chung, I. (2020). Secure authentication and key management of Blockchain in vanets. *IEEE Access : Practical Innovations, Open Solutions*, *8*, 2482–2498. doi:10.1109/ACCESS.2019.2962387

Tanwar, S., Parekh, K., & Evans, R. (2020). Blockchain-based electronic healthcare record system for healthcare 4.0 applications. *Journal of Information Security and Applications*, *50*, 102407. doi:10.1016/j.jisa.2019.102407

Thilakarathne, N. N., & Madhuka Priyashan, W. D. (2022). *An Overview of Security and Privacy in Smart Cities*. doi:10.1007/978-3-030-82715-1_2

Tripathi, G., Ahad, M. A., & Paiva, S. (2020). S2HS- A Blockchain based approach for smart healthcare systems. *Health Care*, *8*(1), 100391. PMID:31753750

Wang, S., Cao, H., Wang, D., & Li, A. (2022). Security of Intelligent Sensors and Their Collaborative Roles in Human Resource Management in the Development of Smart Cities. *Wireless Communications and Mobile Computing*, *2022*, 2022. doi:10.1155/2022/6285777

Wang, S., Cao, H., Wang, D., & Li, A. (2022). Security of intelligent sensors and their collaborative roles in human resource management in the development of smart cities. *Wireless Communications and Mobile Computing*, *2022*, 2022. doi:10.1155/2022/6285777

Willems, J., van den Bergh, J., & Viaene, S. (2017). Smart city projects and citizen participation: the case of London. *Public Sector Management in a Globalized World,* 249–266.

Yaacoub, J.-P. A., Noura, M., Noura, H. N., Salman, O., Yaacoub, E., Couturier, R., & Chehab, A. (2020). Securing Internet of medical things systems: Limitations, issues, and recommendations. *Future Generation Computer Systems*, *105*, 581–606. doi:10.1016/j.future.2019.12.028

Yan, J., Liu, J., & Tseng, F. (2020). An evaluation system based on the self-organizing system framework of smart cities: A case study of smart transportation systems in China. *Technological Forecasting and Social Change*, *153*, 119371. doi:10.1016/j.techfore.2018.07.009

Yang, X., Shu, L., Liu, Y., Hancke, G. P., Ferrag, M. A., & Huang, K. (2022). Physical security and safety of IoT equipment: A survey of recent advances and opportunities. *IEEE Transactions on Industrial Informatics*, *18*(7), 4319–4330. doi:10.1109/TII.2022.3141408

Yang, Z., Jianjun, L., Faqiri, H., Shafik, W., Talal Abdulrahman, A., Yusuf, M., & Sharawy, A. M. (2021). Green internet of things and big data applications in smart city development. *Complexity*, *2021*, 1–15. doi:10.1155/2021/4922697

Yaqoob, I., Ahmed, E., Hashem, I. A. T., Ahmed, A. I. A., Gani, A., Imran, M., & Guizani, M. (2017). Internet of Things Architecture: Recent Advances, Taxonomy, Requirements, and Open Challenges. *IEEE Wireless Communications*, *24*(3), 10–16. doi:10.1109/MWC.2017.1600421

Zantalis, F., Koulouras, G., Karabetsos, S., & Kandris, D. (2019). A review of machine learning and IoT in smart transportation. *Future Internet*, *11*(4), 94. doi:10.3390/fi11040094

Zhang, C., Duan, X., Liu, F., Li, X., & Liu, S. (2022). Three-way naive Bayesian collaborative filtering recommendation model for smart city. *Sustainable Cities and Society*, *76*, 103373. doi:10.1016/j.scs.2021.103373

Zhang, H., Babar, M., Tariq, M. U., Jan, M. A., Menon, V. G., & Li, X. (2020). SafeCity: Toward safe and secured data management design for IoT-enabled Smart City planning. *IEEE Access : Practical Innovations, Open Solutions*, *8*, 145256–145267. doi:10.1109/ACCESS.2020.3014622

Zhou, K., Fu, C., & Yang, S. (2016). Big data driven smart energy management: From big data to big insights. *Renewable & Sustainable Energy Reviews*, *56*, 215–225. doi:10.1016/j.rser.2015.11.050

Zhu, W., Yan, R., & Song, Y. (2022). Analysing the impact of smart city service quality on citizen engagement in a public emergency. *Cities (London, England)*, *120*, 103439. doi:10.1016/j.cities.2021.103439 PMID:34539020

Chapter 6
Interaction Between IoT-Enabled Services in Smart Cities

Sumathi Pawar
Nitte Mahalinga Adyanthaya Memorial Institute of Technology, India

Manjula Gururaj Rao H.
Nitte Mahalinga Adyanthaya Memorial Institute of Technology, India

Niranjan N. Chiplunkar
Nitte Mahalinga Adyanthaya Memorial Institute of Technology, India

ABSTRACT

Smart cities are IOT enabled applications which provide services from controlling streetlight according to weather conditions, smart parking vehicles according to free parking slots, up to traffic management according to train arrival time. They also concern access to education, health, cultural and sports services. If all the applications are based on interaction between each other according to the requirement, then it will be great success in achieving robust smart city services. Many services factors such as availability, quality, affordability, and continuity can be increased by enabling communication between the services. This research is focused on communication between different IOT enabled services. Two techniques used here are centralized level interaction and peer level interaction. The task of centralized level interaction is registering all IOT enabled services and sending required information to the respective services in time. Peer level services speak to each other whenever required. This research also analyses advantages and drawbacks of both of these techniques.

INTRODUCTION

Smart parking, transport, power and water supply, telecommunication services, public transport and many other services including access to a high-speed internet connection, free Wi-Fi, 4G/5G coverage and many more are part of smart cities. People uses smart city applications such as smart homes, connected cars through smartphones. Sustainability can be improved by pairing systems of infrastructure of smart cities and also cost can be reduced. With the help of smart city communities' energy distribution

DOI: 10.4018/979-8-3693-0744-1.ch006

can be optimized, traffic congestion can be reduced and air quality can be improved. If the services of the smart city speak each other there will be numerous benefits.

Advantages of communication between services are given here.

- The usage of connected lights of the traffic receive data through sensors and corrects the light to real time traffic thus reducing the congestion of the road.
- Drivers directed to nearest parking slots through connected car services.
- Waste management companies automatically get information to pick-up wastes according to pre-planned timings.
- Smart city services and government services can be accessed through mobile phones of citizens by their digital credentials and ID cards.

In olden days distributed systems were using message queues to handle communication between different parts of system. Huge amounts of data were transferred for massive amounts of activities to the cloud server (Ashu et al, 2021). The model used by traditional system were asynchronous processing architectures which was working in only single direction.

Smart cities' Internet of things requires different kind of messaging styles and messaging between the services required to follow appropriate protocols and existing network architecture to speed-up the services. To integrate the different components of application stack, messaging models need to be more complex.

One way messaging and 2-way messaging are 2 kinds of messaging models used by IOT-enabled services to interact between server or cloud services. One-way model was asynchronous and to overcome this 2-ways model was used. Sending messages between IOT services to cloud and cloud to IOT services requires 2-way messaging model.

Message brokers/Queue: This allows the queues support from one-to-many connected clients which supports massive huge amounts of big data scenarios () . Identifying, authenticating and addressing of IOT devices are done through message brokers. Among many platform-as-a-service providers such as Azure IoT Hub, Microsoft Azure cloud, IOT message broker service support huge events or telemetry from numerous IOT components. Due to message brokers, the burden of installing up and maintaining virtual machines in the cloud are reduced and it is required to focus on only maintain and building IOT solutions (Renuka et al, 2018).

Benefits of IOT message brokers compared to traditional brokers are

- Device authentication for device management
- Tracking messages from connected IOT devices
- Uniquely addressing IOT devices to support "Cloud-to-Device" messaging model

The proposed system is focussed on 2 kinds of communication between services and messaging models with their architecture. That is centralized message-based system and peer to peer to level messaging system.

The organization of this research paper is as follows; section 2 discusses literature survey, section 3 explains methodology, section 4 focusses on the centralized communication system, section 5 discusses about implementation, section 6 on results, section 7 describes analysis, and finally section 8 mentions about conclusion and future work.

LITERATURE REVIEW

Advantages of P2P based middleware compared to centralized system is made it to use P2P middleware system as proposed by (Genaud et al, 2007) and (W. T. Teacy et.al, 2012). The important task of the P2P MPI is fault-tolerance, scalability, ease of maintenance and resource discovery. When there are large number of IOT services, one of the goal of P2P middleware is scheduling the jobs of IOT services. The performance of middleware is measured by throughput of the system(H. Rajab and T. Cinkelr, 2018) and (J. Wang et. al, 2016).

The performance of the peer-to-peer based networks depend on workflows, knowledge of the scheduler and also depends upon whether parallel jobs or independent tasks. The set of resources need to be co-allocated to start job immediately. The optimal scheduling is very important to increase the speed of IOT services because every IOT device needs required resources. The network locality, available bandwidth, load balance and availability of resources are factors influence the speedy communication between IOT services. But in a peer-to-peer communication this information is not known much and therefore in a distributed systems it is challenging to achieve highest throughput. Because individual peers not knowing all information of other IOT services state, distance etc factors, it is very much required to suitably design P2P network.

IOT messaging architecture is classified as One-way messaging model and 2-way messaging model.

One-Way Messaging Model

Providing of asynchronous communication among the components of IOT services were done through 1-way messaging model and it was used by disconnected systems. There was only sending communication messages from cloud to IOT devices through message brokers and no interaction form IOT services to back. Limited ability of managing large amount of connected IOT services and security issues, made it use of 2 way messaging model.

Figure 1. One- way messaging model

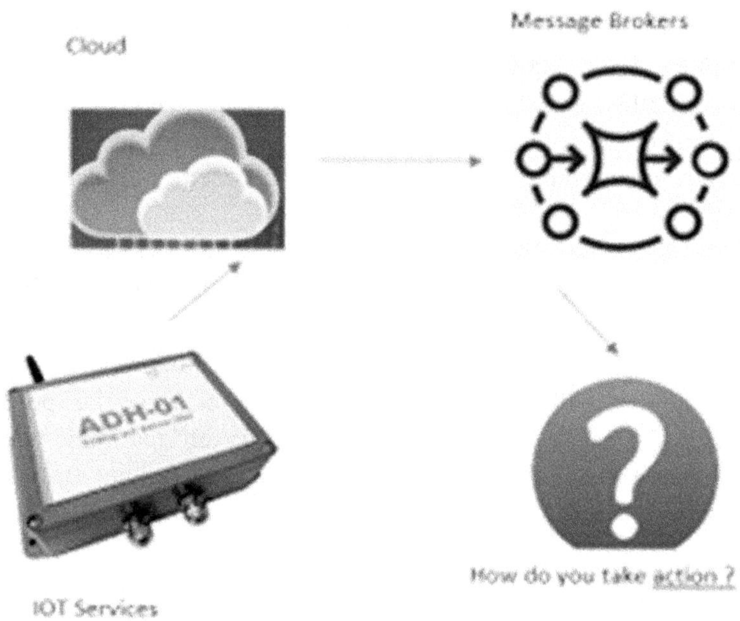

Two-Way Messaging Model

Device-to-cloud messaging and Cloud-to-Device messaging are 2 kinds of communication provided by 2-way messaging model.

Figure 2. Two-way messaging model

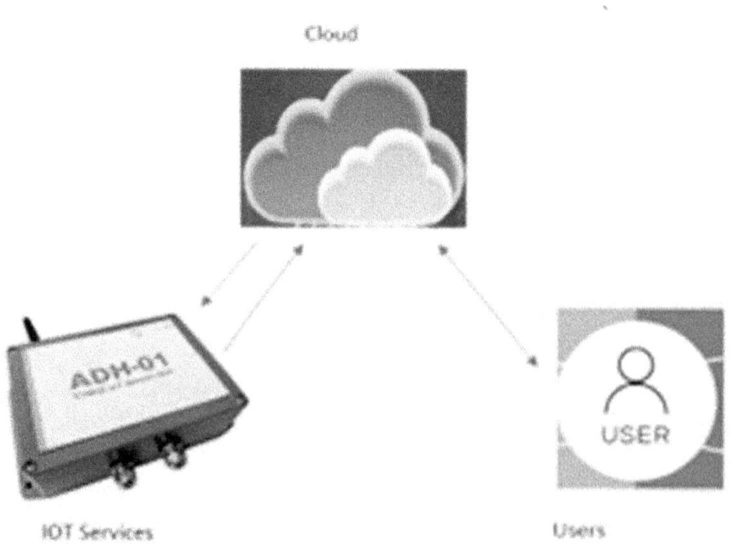

Device-To-Cloud Messaging

Here sensors' data are transferred from device to cloud. Each device data is gathered and massive amount of Big-data are transferred to cloud. The event telemetry and sensor's data are 2 kinds of data sent from IOT-enabled services to cloud. The messages of events are sent from sensor's to cloud through queue or message brokers which is consumed by processing components of real-time or batch processing. The function of message broker is to gather message from sensors and convert them into message stream which is sent to cloud.

Cloud-to-Device Messaging

Sending messages from cloud services to IOT devices is bit different compared to big data messages (Hussain et al., 2021) of other distributed systems. The control messages sent by cloud to other IOT devices and integration of cloud-based components with IOT enabled services through other types messages also done via this messaging model.

The properties of 2-way messaging model are

- Communication of control messages from Cloud to IOT services for device configurations
- Changing the behaviour of IOT devices also accomplished through messages from cloud
- Updates of firmware also done through cloud messages to IOT services
- User feed back sent from cloud to IOT devices through this communication model.
- Most of the message brokers does not support communication from message brokers to IOT enabled devices.

Types of Peer-to-Peer Architecture

- Query Flooding
- Centralized Directory
- Exploiting Heterogeneity
- Centralized Directory: There is huge central server which resembles client-server architecture and provides directory service. Here IP address of each peer will be informed by each peers. Server send token query in regular interval to check whether peers are alive or not. Data base is maintained by middle layer to know which service is present at which IP address.
- Query flooding: In this distributed system, there is a overlay network where there is path exists between one each peer, which results in graph-like structure. The nodes connected to overlay network gets request from client and if nodes don't have requested file, then this query will be passed to their neighbors. When client gets required service then this query flood stops. "Gnutella" is oldest example for peer to peer network.
- Exploiting Heterogeneity: This makes use of distributed system and there is centralized server for request processing. There is supernodes or group leaders which have huge network connectivity and higher bandwidth. Peers connected to these supernodes share their IP address and services. Thus after getting information about peers' availability, file sharing begins.

P2P Messaging API

JXTA(Bilal Siddiqui, 2012) was an early P3(Power Plan Project) built P2P overlay network which presented client server oriented API and message-passing APIs. Because there was no control on the selection of peers by middleware system, another project ProActive(Denis Caromel et. al, 2007) was added as infrastructure to make it ease the resource discovery. To dynamically acquire a peer in the P2P infrastructure, the discovery service is used. This is a ProActive system, which allowed a manager to dynamically choose peers at the beginning of the program execution. But this infrastructure does not have knowledge about the infrastructure and network topology, network locality is does not taken into account as proposed by(Niels Drost et al, 2006) and (Z. Su et al, 2015). The overlay network of P2P aware about peer locality. The algorithm of Bamboo project(Vignesh Venkateshan, 2022) used by Vignesh, found close resources with the help of a simple DNS name affinity. A local group is formed by sharing hosts in a common domain name. According to the work of Zorilla which proposed flood scheduling that is originated at a peer and broadcasted to all the neighbours according to depth of given radius. Until suitable number of peers, or until enough peers accepted the job, the flooding steps are performed successively. Finding suitable parameters for flooding is challenging task here.

METHODOLOGY

P2P communication adresses directly without VPN. Sim card of each IOT device gets a static IP and can communicate each other through this IP addresses in the LAN. Instead of going through cloud server, IOT devices communicate each other directly. Here one of the IOT device act as router and direct IP access of all the devices will be done from the server. No need of Virtual Private Network and even though it is not secure as VPN, this network is secure compared to general IOT devices' communication.

Figure 3. Overview of the proposed system

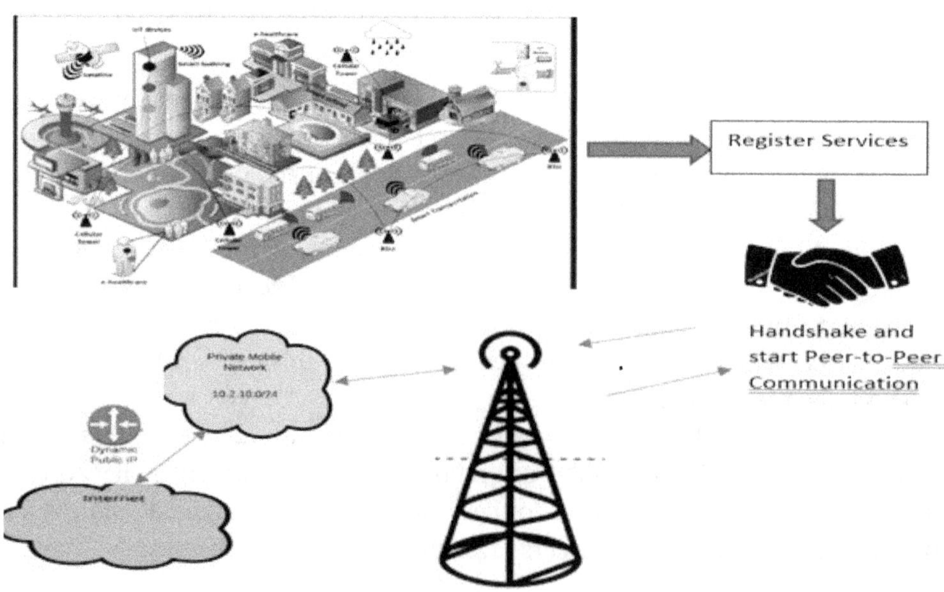

Registering IOT Service

Registering Services: This process is nothing but avertising the existence of the IOT device to its peers. This advertisement is done throgh a small XML message. Every IOT service need to register its presence through registration process. The steps are given here.

- Send connection establishment request message with Registration service.
- After establishing the connection, a request is sent for registering the service.
- Registration service validates this request and sends security token
- Then IOT service creates IOT object and sends registration information to registration service with registration request.
- Registration service sends authentication message based on security token
- Then registration service forwards registration information to IOT service
- Then IOT service will be connected to peer network
- IOT service will send confirmation message to registration service.

The registration service act as a super node. The registration information of the IOT device have IOT service details such as type of service, IOT service name, IOT service port information and static IP of IOT service.

The registration service keeps track of all peer registrations, through its service ports and "last seen" time stamp. The list of peers tracked by supernode and a peer network is constructed by broadcasting this information to all services of peer networks.

HandShake Service

Ping message is a test message of P2P network to check for availability of IOT services. Sending ping message to required nodes of P2P is initiated by handshake service through middle-ware. Middle-ware service need to prepare task list and lookup method of handshake service gets port addresses of required services from service registry and initiates handshake process. Once handshake service receives the live information, the peer-to-peer communication started through a middle-ware.

Middleware Layer

When a user request is submitted then a service table is created by a middle layer according to available services information of service registration list. The network topology is constructed by middle-ware and sent to required peer-to-peer IOT services. Construction of network topology is a challenging task because middle-ware should know what are the required services for a user request. There will be a set of tasks need to be performed for a user request and this task list is need to be constructed. For example, for a smart home system as soon as temperature reaches a threshold value, air condition needs to switched on. For this purpose, the set of tasks are temperature sensing service, a controlling service which checks for a threshold value and instructs air condition to swich on and an air condition service. The sequence of service task for a given request is need to be stored in the middle layer and according to this sequence peer-to-peer topology is constructed. After checking availability through handshake service and trust vector of required service, the network is constructed by the middleware. Middleware checks for availability of the service by sending alive message to its peers. Thus, middleware maintains a big database to hold IP address of different registered live services.

Peer-to-Peer Communication

Peer service sends reservation message to its subordinate and reserves required service as proposed by (Heba Kurdi et al, 2018) and (Zanella et. al, 2014). Distributed Eigen trust algorithm is used by all the peers for trusting and limiting the flow of data in traffic. As shown in the given figure 4, checking trust worthiness of each service during interaction is important to decide whether that service is included for interaction or not whenever required. The infrastructure management table is used by middle-ware to avoid deadlock. According to the task list of middle-ware layer, peer IOT service is executed for performing the required task.

Figure 4. P2P Communication model

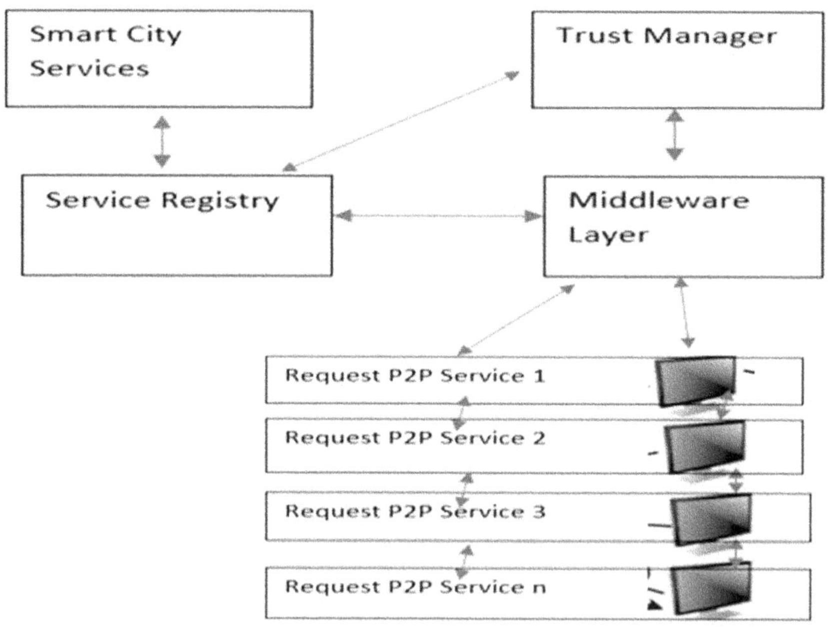

Trust Manager

This process uses Distributed Eigen trust(Sepandar et. al, 2015) algorithm for checking trust-worthy of services. A global trust vector computed by this algorithm to minimize the overhead of the computation. Local trust vector and global trust vectors are stored by each node of the peer network. Pre-trusted peers will have highest trust value. In P2P networks, peers have very limited interaction with other peers and very less number of message passing between peers and therefore limited number of local trust values reported by each peer.

Eigen Trust Algorithm

```
Pi: Let 'Pi' is peers' set that downloaded files from peer 'i'
Qi: Let 'Qi' is peers' set that downloaded files from peer 'i'
Each peer named 'i' do
{
Request all peers j€Pi for tj(0)=pj
Repeat
       Compute ti(k+1)=(1-a)(c1it1(k) +c2it2(k) + ....+Cnitn(k))+api
       Send cijti(k+1) to all peers j€Qi
       Compute  δ = | ti(k+1) - ti(k) |
                Wait for all peers j€Pi to return cjitj(k+1)
Until δ<€
}
```

Here 'c' is normalized local trust value and in distributed systems, each peers rate with each other after transaction. When 'P' and 'Q' download files from peer 'I', then rating of transaction as positive or '1' when transaction is successful i.e. tr(P,i)=1. When 'Q' transaction is successful then tr(Q,i)=1. When transaction is not successful then tr(P,i)=-1 and tr(Q,i)=-1. The average of ratings of 'n' transactions will be calculated using Eigen value process and sent to all peers and this rating is taken as trust value for further transactions.

CENTRALIZED COMMUNICATION SYSTEM

Here service registry information is passed to a centralized system which maintains the task list and act as co-ordinator of the entire system. The problem of this system is if centralized system fails, then entire system will get disconnected. There is robust co-ordination, highest efficiency and great speed between the task execution of centralized system, but very smaller number of nodes can be connected between server and network. (Rodriguez, 2018)Some of the key capabilities of the centralized system are service management, Event notification, event processing, device discovery, event notification and system integration.

Figure 5 shows centralized model of service communication. Services share information through centralized server and data of each system will be stored in central repository. Even though this system has huge capability, there are several drawbacks which are discussed in the analysis section. Task list of required services for a given request is maintained by central server and controlling, coordinating the services is job of centralized server.

Figure 5. Centralized communication of IOT services

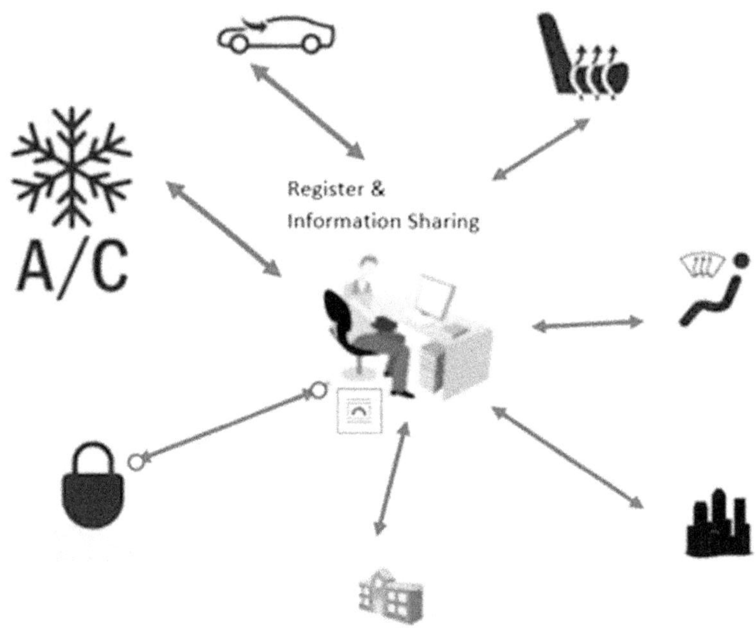

IMPLEMENTATION

The usage of P2P-MPI from library of JAVA used "run everywhere" feature which made it easy to implement P2P networking model. The MPI(Huaiqing et. al, 2009) has no defacto standard as with popular implementations of OpenMPI(Huaiqing et. al, 2009) and MPICH(Ferrer et. al, 2012) because no bindings proposed for Java. MPJ/Ibis (Mark Baker, 2006) and MPJ Express(Mark Baker, 2006) were an efficient communications supported over TCP or myrinet devices. The portability layer (IPL)(Bouras et al, 2018) of Ibis multilayer system, presented a network communication features through an object-oriented interface. The above layer of this model supported different programming models. But this does not support fault-tolerence and resources available are discovered by the system.

MPI_Scatter, MPI-Gather, MPI_Allgather and MPI_Bcast are APIs used to deploy P2P-MPI system. The proposed system is tested for several processes as IOT services and function of each API is briefly discussed here.

```
int MPIAPI MPI_Allgather(
  _In_  void          *sendbuf,
  _In_  int           sendcount,
  _In_  MPI_Datatype sendtype,
  _Out_ void          *recvbuf,
        int           recvcount,
        MPI_Datatype recvtype,
        MPI_Comm      comm
);
```

Following data structures are used by the MPI_Allgather() service.

"sendbuf " Points to data that need to be sent to all services in the group. "Sendtype" and "sendcount" shows data type of each element and count of elements that sent from each process. The comm shows an intra-communicator where value stored is "MPI_IN_PLACE" to an in-place option. "recvbuf " is pointer to the buffer where received data from the process or service is stored. "recvCount" and "recvType" shows count of elements and data type of received elements. Comm is communicator handle.

Thus MPI_Allgather service sends data through sendbuf[] and receives data through recvbuf[], count shows number of characters sent, datatype of sending and receiving data are indicated by "sendtype" and "recvtype" data structures.

MPI_Bcast and MPI_Scatter Sends data to all the processes through communicator from a specified root. MPI_Scatter sends small pieces of data and MPI_Bcast sends chunks of an array to different processes.

- MPI_Gather is another function which sends data to only to root using function MPI_Gather (sendbuf,sendcount,sendtype,recvbuf,recvcount, recvtype,root,comm) for root = 0, ..., n-1.

RESULTS

System is simulated with computer node's processes instead of real smart city services by assuming each process as a service. The speed of responding to ping message in peer-to-peer network is compared to centralized system.

Figure 6. Performance of P2P system

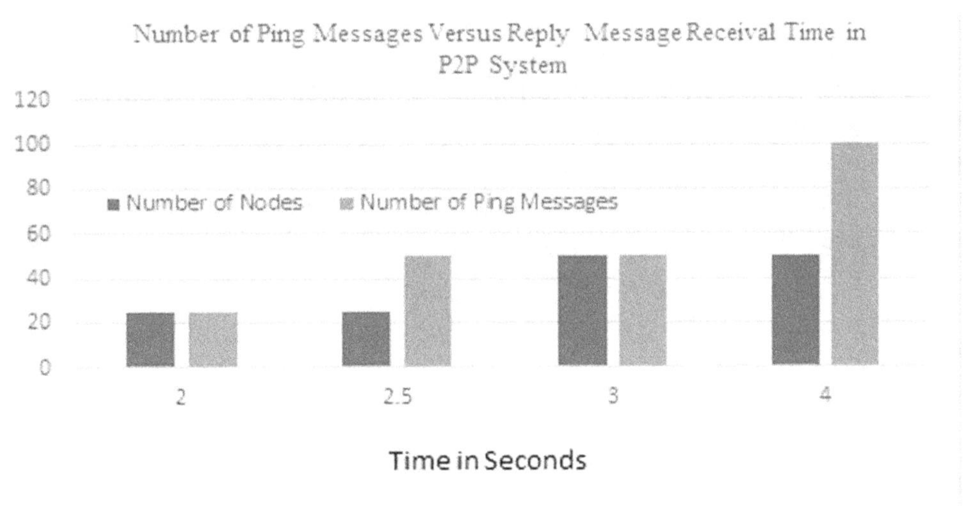

It is found in P2P system from result of figure 6 that, when 25 ping messages are transferred from 25 nodes it is taken 2 second to reply, for 25 nodes(doubling of messages) i.e. 50 messages, system has taken 2.5 seconds to reply, from 50 nodes and 50 messages, it has taken 3 seconds for reply, for 50 nodes and 100 messages, the P2P network has taken 4 seconds to reply.

Figure 7. Performance of centralized system

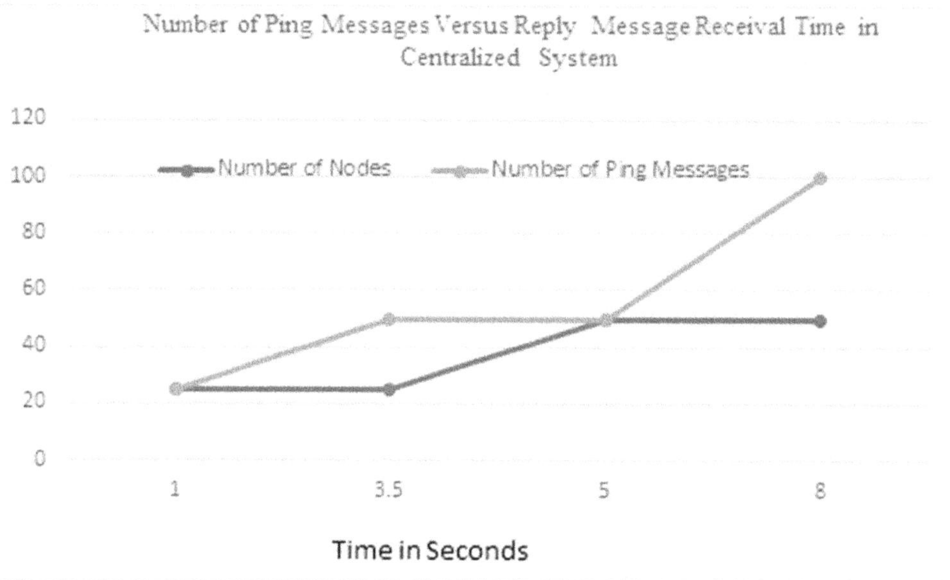

For same set of nodes and messages in same machine configuration, centralized system has taken more time than P2P system due to congestion of network and many other factors which is discussed in the analysis section.

It is found from the result that speed of execution of ping message from centralized system is faster when there is a smaller number of nodes. Performance is improved in distributed system compared to centralized system as number of nodes increases. Also, as the number of nodes increases, server bandwidth will be bottle neck and managing the nodes also time consuming in centralized system compared to distributed system. Therefore, it is more tedious for centralized system to manage the required resources compared to distributed system which is explained clearly in analysis section.

ANALYSIS

While comparing distributed system to centralized system it is found that, distributed system is more stable and applicable for huge applications as given in table 1.

Table 1. Analysis between centralized and P2P system

Performance Factors	Centralized System	P2P System
Scale	Unable to support huge scale of IOT services. Therefore scaling limitations need to be addressed in centralized system.	Cisco is reported that 50 billion IOT services will be connected by 2022. For huge applications distributed systems are applicable.
Cost	To serve multiple services at same time huge resources required parallelly which increases the cost of entire system. Cost of deployment of centralized server also increased due to storage of large data(piyushji et al, 2016)	In P2P systems, the resources are consumed after completion of execution of its tasks from its subordinate peers, therefore no demand of same resources parallelly or simultaneously.
Privacy	Data is vulnerable because all the data is stored in one place and there will be security risk. There can be damage to this data and privacy maintaining is another issue in the centralized system.	As data is stored in their own node in P2P network, there is no much data privacy risk because private data is stored in its own peers.
Security	Centralized server and IOT devices are vulnerable to security attacks and will be easy target for DOS and DDOS attacks.	In P2P network there is no such risk because all data is not stored in centralized server.
Single point of failure	Single point of failure is another drawback of the system because if server gets fails then entire system corrupted. Redundant switches can be connected to avoid this.	There is no single point of failure in P2P network due to interconnectivity between different nodes and even one node fails another node can achieve given task.
Diversity and Access	Diverse systems cannot be accessed through centralized system because lack of flexibility in diverse needs(Bilal Siddiqui, 2018)	In P2P network, as different nodes can support heterogeneous services, flexibility of connecting diverse system increases.
Inflexibility	Centralized server is associated with delays produced due to peak-load concerns and due to tight schedule.	In P2P network, as load is shared by different nodes, there will be rare cases of tight schedule due to peak loads.

Since centralized system manages all processes with a central server system, this kind of system scale well for small networks. Large business system cannot deploy this due to hard transportation (Garcerá et al,2017) of data to different locations. Also due to massive increase of IOT devices it is suitable to use P2P networks for efficient communication between IOT services.

CONCLUSION AND FUTURE WORK

Even though large number of nodes deployed by P2P networks, setting up 600 peers will not overflow by requests because most of information cached by peers locally. IOT services are heterogeneous in nature and ensuring access of these devices should be a basic need. Implementation of distributed P2P network for smart cities services communication is more benefitted than centralized system while comparing scale, privacy, cost, diversity and security. Centralized systems can be used for small set of services, while P2P network are applicable to large set of services. This system uses network topology which is designed through middleware for a particular request. As a future work it is decided to design sequence of task list of required functions dynamically according to QoS(Quality of Services) parameters to provide robust outcome.

Conflict of interest: There is no conflict of interest.

REFERENCES

Aggarwal, S., Kumar, N., Tanwar, S., & Alazab, M. (2021). A Survey on Energy Trading in the Smart Grid: Taxonomy, Research Challenges and Solutions. *IEEE Access : Practical Innovations, Open Solutions, 9*, 116231–116253. doi:10.1109/ACCESS.2021.3104354

Ashu, A., Hussain, M. W., Sinha Roy, D., & Reddy, H. K. (2021). Intelligent data compression policy for Hadoop performance optimization. In *Proceedings of the 11th International Conference on Soft Computing and Pattern Recognition (SoCPaR 2019) 11* (pp. 80-89). Springer International Publishing. 10.1007/978-3-030-49345-5_9

Baker, M., Carpenter, B., & Shafi, A. (2006). MPJ Express: Towards thread safe Java HPC, *IEEE International Conference on Cluster Computing*, (pp. 1-10). IEEE. 10.1109/CLUSTR.2006.311890

Bouras, C., Kapoulas, V., Kokkinos, V., Leonardos, D., Pipilas, C., & Papachristos, N. (2018). Extension to Middleware for IoT Devices, with Applications in Smart Cities. In Cloud Infrastructures, Services, and IoT Systems for Smart Cities. Springer, Cham. doi:10.1007/978-3-319-67636-4_13

Caromel, D., di Costanzo, A., & Mathieu, C. (2007, May). Peer-to-peer for computational grids: Mixing clusters and desktop machines. *Parallel Computing, 33*(4-5), 275–288. doi:10.1016/j.parco.2007.02.011

Drost, N., van Nieuwpoort, R. V., & Bal, H. (2006). Simple locality-aware co-allocation in peer-to-peer supercomputing. In *Sixth IEEE International Symposium on Cluster Computing and the Grid Workshops (CCGRID'06)*, (pp. 14–21). IEEE.

Ferrer, A. J., Hernández, F., Tordsson, J., Elmroth, E., Ali-Eldin, A., Zsigri, C., Sirvent, R., Guitart, J., Badia, R. M., Djemame, K., Ziegler, W., Dimitrakos, T., Nair, S. K., Kousiouris, G., Konstanteli, K., Varvarigou, T., Hudzia, B., Kipp, A., Wesner, S., & Sheridan, C. (2012). OPTIMIS: A holistic approach to cloud service provisioning. *Future Generation Computer Systems, 28*(1), 66–77. doi:10.1016/j.future.2011.05.022

Filali, F. Z., & Yagoubi, B. (2015). Global trust: A trust model for cloud service selection. *International Journal of Computer Network and Information Security, 7*(5), 41–50. doi:10.5815/ijcnis.2015.05.06

Garcerá, G. (2017). A Novel Locality Algorithm and Peer-to-Peer Communication Infrastructure for Optimizing Network Performance in Smart Microgrids. *Special Issue Control and Communication in Distributed Generation Systems, 10*(9).

Genaud, S., & Rattanapoka, C. (2007). P2P-MPI: A Peer-to-Peer Framework for Robust Execution of Message Passing Parallel Programs on Grids. *Journal of Grid Computing, 5*(1), 27–42. doi:10.100710723-006-9056-2

Genaud, S., & Rattanapoka, C. (2009). *A Peer-to-Peer Framework for Message Passing Parallel Programs*. 10.1145/775152.775242

Fatos, X. Parallel Programming, Models and Applications in Grid and P2P Systems, (pp.118–147). IOS Press.

Sepandar, D. Kamvar, Schlosser, M., & Garcia-Molina, H. (2003). *The EigenTrust Algorithm for Reputation Management in P2P Networks.* Proceedings of the 12th international conference on World Wide Web, (pp. 640–651). Stanford University. doi:10.1145/775152.775242

Gropp, W., Lusk, E., & Skjellum, A. (1999). Using MPI, Portable Parallel Programming with the Message-Passing Interface. Scientific and Engineering Computation Series. MIT Press, 2nd edition edition.

Huaiqing, L., Xuezhi, W., & Haitao, L. (August 2009). Hierarchical fuzzy trust management for peer-to-peer network. In *Proceedings of the 2009 Second ISECS International Colloquium on Computing, Communication, Control, and Management, CCCM 2009*, China.

Hussain, M. W. (2021). A counter based approach for reducer placement with augmented Hadoop rackawareness. *Turkish Journal of Electrical Engineering and Computer Sciences*, *29*(1), 437–453. doi:10.3906/elk-2001-106

Heba Kurdi, H., Alshayban, B., Altoaimy, L., & Alsalamah, S. (2018). *TrustyFeer: A Subjective Logic Trust Model for Smart City Peer-to-Peer Federated Clouds.* Wireless Communications and Mobile Computing. https://doi.org/. doi:10.1155/2018/1073216

Piyushji. (2022). Peer to Peer P2P communications for IoT. IOT. https://iot.onesimcard.com/Peer-to-Peer-communications-for-IoT

Piyushji(2022).Communication Models in IoT (Internet of Things - GeeksforGeeks, https://www.geeksforgeeks.org/communication-models-in-iot-internet-of-things, Retrieved on 20/10/2022

Rajab, H., & Cinkelr, T. (2018). IoT based Smart Cities. *2018 International Symposium on Networks, Computers and Communications (ISNCC)*, (pp. 1-4). IEEE. 10.1109/ISNCC.2018.8530997

Rao, M. G., Pawar, S. H. P., & Reddy, H. K. (2023). Minimize the Energy Consumption for Communication Protocol in IoT. In R. Gatti, C. Singh, S. P., & S. Bhat (Eds.), Energy Systems Design for Low-Power Computing (pp. 214-234). IGI Global. doi:10.4018/978-1-6684-4974-5.ch011

Renuka, K., Das, S. N., & Reddy, K. H. (2018). An Efficient Context Management Approach for IoT. *IUP Journal of Information Technology, 14*(2).

Rodriguez, J. (2022). *Building an IOT Platform: Centralized vs. Decentralized Models.* LinkedIn. https://www.linkedin.com/pulse/building-iot-platform-centralized-vs-decentralized-models-rodriguez

Siddiqui, B. (June 2018). *JXTA-A Messaging System for Wireless Java.* Developer.com. https://www.developer.com/mobile/java-mobile/jxta-a-messaging-system-for-wireless-java/

Snir, M., Otto, S. W., Walker, D. W., Dongarra, J., & Huss-Lederman, S. (1995). *MPI: The Complete Reference*. MIT Press.

Su, Z., Liu, L., Li, M., Fan, X., & Zhou, Y. (2015). Reliable and resilient trust management in distributed service provision networks [TWEB]. *ACM Transactions on the Web*, *9*(3), 14. doi:10.1145/2754934

Teacy, W. T., Luck, M., Rogers, A., & Jennings, N. R. (2012). An efficient and versatile approach to trust and reputation using hierarchical Bayesian modelling. *Artificial Intelligence*, *193*, 149–185. doi:10.1016/j.artint.2012.09.001

Venkatesan, V. (2022). *Bamboo by Vignesh Venkatesan.* ArchDaily. https://my.archdaily.com/us/@vignesh-venkatesan-1/folders/bamboo,

Wang, J., & Liu, J. (2016). The comparison of distributed P2P trust models based on quantitative parameters in the file downloading scenarios. *Journal of Electrical and Computer Engineering, 2016*, 4361719. doi:10.1155/2016/4361719

Zanella, N. Bui, A. Castellani, L. Vangelista, & Zorzi, M. (2014). Internet of Things for Smart Cities. IEEE Internet of Things Journal, 1(1), 22-32. doi:10.1109/JIOT.2014.2306328

Chapter 7
A Role of Artificial Intelligence and Machine Learning Algorithms for Energy Efficiency Applications

M. Senbagavalli
https://orcid.org/0000-0003-3806-8257
Alliance University, India

Shekarappa G. Swetha
Alliance University, India

R. Rajagopal
Alliance University, India

ABSTRACT

Recent years have seen a significant increase in the use of artificial intelligence (AI) and machine learning (ML) concepts across a variety of academic domains. AI's major objective is to build intelligent systems and give machines human intelligence. Artificial intelligence is a tool for creating systems, making judgements, solving problems, learning, and linguistic intelligence, as well as for imitating human conduct. Electrical and computer engineers are at the forefront of intellectual creativity as they participate in the planning, creation, evaluation, and production processes for newer generations of gadgets and technology. Even if these professionals want to grow, their objectives might conflict with the consequences of artificial intelligence, which are continually expanding. The practice of Artificial Intelligence (AI) and Machine Learning (ML) applications in industrial industries that have a significant influence on sustainability and the environment, such as renewable energy, smart grids, the catalyzed industry, and power storage and distribution The main popular approaches are artificial neural networks and Machine learning. Demand for energy is skyrocketing at a higher pace than production in the industry between 2004 and 2017, implying a decline in energy efficiency (EE). Under the premise of steady future output, an explicit energy efficiency enhancement target of 26% from 2017 and 2050 is set.

DOI: 10.4018/979-8-3693-0744-1.ch007

INTRODUCTION

The main techniques of AI are automation and robotics, Natural Language Processing, machine vision and machine learning. Some examples of Artificial Intelligence algorithms are classification, clustering, regression, and ensemble learning algorithms. Applications of Artificial Intelligence (AI) incorporates Healthcare, the auto industry, robotics, agriculture, e-commerce, education, data security, and social media, among other industries. The energy sector is facing challenges from heightened competition, productivity, a lack of statistics necessary for effective management, and altering supply and demand trends. Artificial intelligence is incorporated into renewable energy technology such as resource prediction, energy efficiency, and energy affordability.

(ONU World Population Prospects, 2019) by the end of this era, there will be more than 10.9 billion people on the planet, up from 7.7 billion in 2019 and 9.7 billion in 2050. Consumption for water, energy, and natural resources will rise in tandem with a spike in people on the planet, overtaxing biological systems and causing nature to gradually deteriorate because of increased energy use. This will have a broad impact on the built landscape. As a means of reducing greenhouse gas emissions, limiting global warming, and reducing the carbon footprint, ecological and efficient energy use is becoming more and more prevalent. The attempts of several administrations, businesses, and stakeholders demonstrate the widespread concern for effective energy management and energy efficiency as a means of reducing climate change and promoting environmental preservation. India's Nationally Determined Contributions (NDCs) were centred on Zero Effect, Zero Defect (ZED) manufacturing to improve energy and resource efficiency, to decrease pollution and handle waste, and to utilise renewable energy sources against the backdrop of the global efforts. The Indian government has reduced subsidies and raised taxes on fossil fuels by about 26% as a step towards the ZED aim, converting the carbon subsidy regime into a carbon taxation system. This section's main goal is to shed light on the direction that actual research into energy recommender systems is taking as well as the problems that are driving significant R&D in the near and distant future. The increasing success of machine learning (ML) approaches in handling routine categorization or prediction tasks has significantly increased the number of applications that use ML models, often implementing them as "black boxes" that are challenging for end users to comprehend. The shift of existing modern AI applications to modern explainable AI models is thought to depend on an ML model's capacity to "explain itself and its actions" to the consumers.

A component of artificial intelligence called machine learning uses many data kinds to complete tasks. A machine learning algorithm first gains knowledge from user data before solving prediction problems on its own. Machine learning approaches can be divided into three basic categories: supervised, unsupervised, and reinforcement learning. techniques use different mechanism to solves problem make use of machine learning. Applications of Machine learning includes self- driving cars, email spam and malware filtering, traffic prediction, image, and speech recognition etc (Pradhan B. et al, 2022).

Machine learning and natural linguistic interpretation have made an impact on practically every business and field of academic experiments, including engineering. Artificial intelligence (AI) is used by specialists in machine learning and electrical engineering to develop and improve technologies as well as provide the most recent data for AI to analyse. While the existing environment is conducive for the advancement of energy efficient techniques, the industry still lacks information, expertise, and experience in how to put these principles into practice. The efficient AI algorithms for various energy efficient applications includes Deep learning and Artificial Neural Networks.

As state-of-the-art literature, this study aimed to review, analyse, investigate, and project the various models incorporating artificial intelligence, machine learning, and certain leading indicators important in economic projection about renewable energy. Using machine learning algorithms, obtaining the pertinent research publications on the topic of energy efficiency. Analize areas and significant opportunities by capturing research interest in this field. Explaining how these technologies are used to get useful information about energy efficiency issues. Assessing the ideal client to respond for the traits and demands, appealing price, organizing, and monitoring amenities, rewarding demand response participants, and supporting them evenly and financially are all AI ways that can be used to tackle various issues. The presented approach review study shows the potential to enhance energy efficiency and the usage of renewable energy resources by implementing AI and ML.

Two of the most important drivers of the global energy shift are global warming and air pollutants. Regional environmental pollution is a big problem in countries like China and India. However, in Europe, the negative health effects of air pollution, which are mostly linked to power supply and consumption, are gaining traction. The increasing proclivity of organisations toward globalisation has several environmental implications. The influence on the ecology has now become a global problem. Even though several levels of research provide contradictory results, numerous studies have found that globalisation has had a detrimental influence on the ecology and has worsened ecological harm. This research study targets to examine the multicollinearity of globalisation and environmental contamination.

This book chapter explains the importance of Artificial Intelligence (AI) and Machine Learning (ML) concepts in energy optimization and the focus of this book chapter is to review and give an overall idea on some Artificial Intelligence (AI) and Machine Learning (ML) based intelligent algorithms which is implemented for energy efficiency and identifying the exposed challenges and leanings in the current research. The sections below are contained in this book chapter. Section I focused on AI and ML ideas in Introduction, Section II focused on the AI, Section III focused role of AI and ML optimization algorithms in energy efficiency, Section IV focused on different sectors of energy efficiency using AI and ML optimization, Section V on latest trends, future scopes and challenges, Section VI on Key Challenges of AI and ML in Energy sector and at last Section VII focused on conclusion and future work.

ARTIFICIAL INTELLIGENCE (AI)

It is a large phrase that refers to the use of technology to accomplish the tasks that bear a resemblance to human intellectual function. It is described as a machine's ability to simulate intelligent human behaviour. Theory and development of computer systems accomplished of working responsibilities generally requiring human intellect, such as speech recognition, visual perception, language translation and decision-making, according to the Artificial Intelligence definition. Building an AI system requires a laborious process of mirroring our traits and skills in a machine and then utilising its processing power to outperform our skills.

Types of Artificial Intelligence

Different Artificial Intelligence objects are built for a variety of purposes. AI can be classified based upon on the functionalities.

- Artificial Narrow Intelligence(ANI)
- Artificial Super Intelligence (ASI)
- Artificial General Intelligence (AGI)

Artificial Narrow Intelligence (ANI)

This is the highly conventional type of AI on the market right now. A specific problem can be addressed by this Artificial Intelligence systems and these can perform a single task exceptionally effectively. They only have a few capabilities, including suggesting produced goods to an online shopper or predicting the weather. Currently, only this kind of artificial intelligence is accessible.

Artificial Super Intelligence (ASI)

Even if we are moving into science fiction territory, ASI is seen as the logical progression from Artificial General Intelligence. In every regard, an artificial superintelligence system would be superior to humans. This would entail making decisions and sensible decisions, as well as producing greater art and growing emotional connections.

Artificial General Intelligence (AGI)

The concept of artificial general intelligence (AGI) is still in its infancy. It is described as AI with a mortal-position of cognitive function throughout a range of disciplines, including image and language processing, among others. An AGI system would need to consist of thousands of Artificial Narrow Intelligence systems working together and interacting with one another in order to mimic human reasoning. In addition to the aforementioned categories, there are also Strong and Weak AIs.

Types of AI Algorithms

Regression Algorithms

Regression is mostly used to build models that can predict one variable from the values of other known variables. The system factors for a function that will be appropriate to a set of detected data and useful for future predictions are established using regression analysis. A fundamental statistical method that has been applied in machine learning is regression. It is helpful in many circumstances when numerical estimations are required, including corporate strategy, financial forecasting, marketing, and trend research.

Decision-Tree Algorithms

These algorithms are used for extracting information from groups of samples. In this Algorithm, each node in a tree signifies input characteristics, branches signify attribute values and leaves signifies individual decisions. With the knowledge of algorithm, each node of the tree is managed recursively. The child node properties can be reduced by states of preceding nodes.

Association Rule Learning Algorithms

One of the most well-known data mining approaches is association discovery, which includes examining a set of properties from a database for recurrent dependencies. Associative rules and parameters are the end result of this strategy. When the goal is to construct cause and effect correlations between occurrences recorded in the examined database, mining approaches based on extracting associative rules are used. The outcomes of this methodology could be quite beneficial for assessing shopping carts or developing offers for specific client groups.

Instance-Based Algorithms

It is a kind of algorithm that contrasts examples of training data stored in memory with new issue cases rather than actually training. The objective is to find the most similar matches. Instead of creating a target function for the entire collection, instance-based algorithms evaluate each new case separately using just training examples. When the target function is complex but can be reduced to a more basic generalisation, they work brilliantly.

Clustering Algorithms

A method for classifying things into groups that are similar in nature is clustering. The basis for grouping in the majority of algorithms is the similarity between components provided by the similarity function. The identification of homogenous groups that can be submitted to statistical, economic, or data mining analysis is accomplished using clustering techniques. Grouping, for instance, can be used to divide clients into smaller groups.

Ensemble Algorithms

The outcomes of many smaller, separately trained machine learning algorithms used in ensemble techniques are combined into a single performance. The right models must be chosen for this technique, and their integration must be done in the correct way. When applied correctly, this group of methods can be highly powerful.

Artificial Neural Network Algorithms

These are models based on the framework of biological neural network systems. They're frequently employed in regression and classification problems. The field of artificial neural networks is exceedingly complex, with numerous versions and solutions for specific challenges.

Deep Learning Algorithms

Deep learning is a brand-new way of thinking about neural networks. Stronger designs with a hierarchical system structure made of numerous nonlinear layers are used in these methods. These algorithms are particularly useful for jobs like object recognition and machine translation. Researchers also use other techniques, such as regularization, that is used to initiate extra details to solve a problem and enhance the quality of the software, or the Bayesian theorem, which is used to estimate the possibility of an event based solely on preceding information of circumstances that could be connected to the event. The method employed is mostly determined by the problem's kind and complexity. Some models are effective for certain situations but ineffective for others. Therefore, scientists are always developing new approaches and combining old ones to create new equipment and systems. Because artificial intelligence and machine learning is such a big and intricate field, there is no one-size-fits-all solution.

Strong and Weak Artificial Intelligence

Artificial Intelligence is further divided into two classifications based on extensive research: Strong Artificial Intelligence and Weak Artificial Intelligence. Here are a few key distinctions between them. The first difference is that strong AI applications have incredible human-level intelligence, whereas weak AI applications are good at specific tasks. The second difference is purely related to scope, the strong AI is a wider application with a larger extent, whereas weak AI is a narrow product with a smaller scope. The final distinction is that strong AI processes data through clustering and association, whereas weak AI processes data through supervised and unsupervised learning. Finally, Advanced Robotics is an example of strong AI, while Siri and Alexa are examples of weak AI. In practice, AI is a catch-all word that incorporates a wide range of technologies and operations, some of which are detailed here.

Machine Learning (ML)

The area of computer science that uses techniques to handle and learn from massive amounts of data is that field. In contrast to conventional rules-based programming, machine learning (ML) models learn from incoming data to make predictions or identify significant patterns without requiring open coding. There are different types of machine learning algorithms there and algorithms are varied with respect to size which is based on effectiveness. Types of different Learning Algorithms are listed here.

- ***Supervised Machine Learning:*** Supervised model is trained with labelled input information that compares to a certain production.
- ***Unsupervised Machine Learning:*** The input data is not labelled, and the production is not specified in unsupervised Machine Learning. Instead, enormous amounts of raw data are input into the models, and the procedures are meant to find any fundamental relevant patterns. The procedures may group comparable data, but they do the same without any expectation of outcome.
    - ***Reinforcement Learning:*** In this Learning, through trial and error, the model learns dynamically to obtain the desired result. The prototype algorithm is rewarded if it performs well and produces the desired result. It is, on the other hand, penalised if it does not deliver the intended output. As a result, the prototype learns to operate in a specific approach that maximises the gain reward over time.
    - ***Deep Learning:*** This Learning approach is purely based upon the artificial neural network; it uses multiple layers of learning to interpret vast volumes of unlabelled or unstructured data in a way like how the neural networks works in brain. These prototypes are often employed when the fundamental data is huge in volume, comes from a variety of resources and can be in a variety of formats (e.g., text, voice, and video).

- *Natural Language Processing (NLP):* It is a subset of artificial intelligence that enables robots to read out or recognise text and voice, extract information from a problem, and maybe transform that information into a desired output format, such text or voice.
- *Computer Vision (CV):* It is also suggested to as machine vision. It is a discipline of computer science that aims to enable workstations to perceive, recognise, and analyse images in the similar manner that humans do, and then again deliver suitable output." ML models are frequently used by CV applications to translate what it "sees" and generate determinations or expectations.
- *Robotics Process Automation (RPA):* Robotic process automation, or RPA, is the use of pre-programmed software devices that communicate with other applications to carry out repetitive manual tasks with increased accuracy, efficiency, and speed. RPA (Robotic Process Automation) systems are frequently used for high-volume, repetitive tasks involving structured data, such as account resolution, account payable processing, and check accumulation. RPA focuses on process automation in a way that is more comparable to a rules-based system than AI, according to some market participants. Others, though, consider it to be a more basic form of artificial intelligence, especially when combined with other innovations like machine learning. Each ML task often requires a different set of steps, depending on the data at hand and the objectives selected.

ROLE OF AI AND ML OPTIMIZATION ALGORITHMS IN ENERGY EFFICIENCY

Around 70% of the electricity generated is used to power companies and houses, with 60% of that being squandered. That is billions of money paid out on energy production that we haven't used. To prevent this from taking place, we must initially comprehend where and how the waste occurs. This is where artificial intelligence enters the picture. Max-impact integrates AI applications into energy saving strategies to assist metropolises, business, and commercial businesses with energy forecasting, energy supervision, renewable energy storage, and future sustainable development.

Artificial intelligence is used to track, gather, control, assess, and manage energy use in buildings and enterprises. It continuously analyses energy handling, lowering it during peak hours, spotting and signalling problems, and anticipating equipment malfunctions. It is important for monitoring and understanding data generated by the energy sectors in order to reduce energy use since it can compress and analyse vast volumes of data. Depending on the company or industry, bottlenecks might occur at various stages of the process. By using data to inform decision-making, Max-impact may aggressively evaluate such processes and, using predictive analysis, identify concerns before they become problems. AI systems can use numbers, text, images, and videos to generate these predictions. This increases the utility of AI but also calls for the employment of a skilled problem solver to tailor each AI response to each circumstance.

Figure 1. Role of AI and ML in energy efficiency

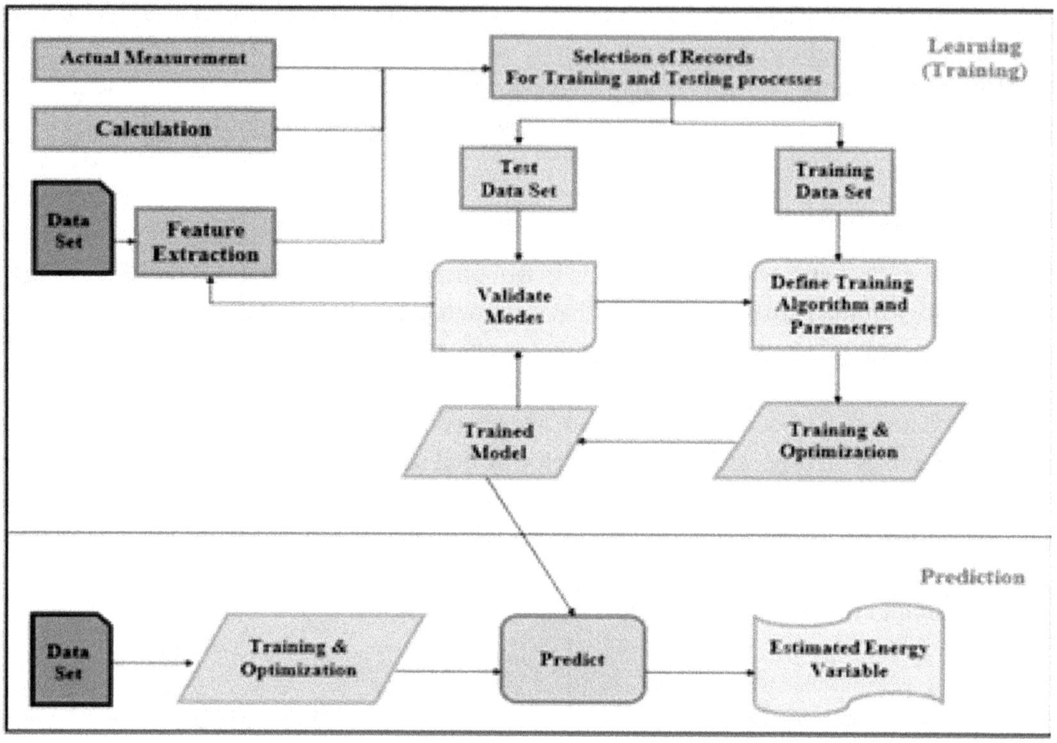

Figure 1 depicts the overall process of AI and machine learning in energy efficiency, which may be used to a variety of industries for energy optimization. The first and most significant stage is to collect a data set, as a dataset is a critical resource for finding answers to any problem. Once it's ready, the feature extraction process begins, with the identification of precise Artificial Intelligence (AI) and Machine Learning (ML) techniques and parameters being critical for proving the best answer. Finally, the above stages, which are depicted in this figure, can be used to predict the estimated energy variable.

Common Steps of AI Algorithm for Smart Energy Systems

1. The public sector's Big Information gathering level is based on the data from the energy management information system (EMIS) databases and the IoT Smart Building network.
2. Preparing input for prediction models utilising the methodologies is done at the data pre-processing stage using R or Python programming.
3. Machine learning forecasting level is to estimate energy efficiency by using various learning methods.
4. Level of data interpretation and visualisation is the next step. In this, the results of machine learning techniques are presented clearly to the users using dynamic charts and tables, which are integrated by several R and Python libraries.
5. At this level, users make the decisions about power generation and investments in rebuilding efforts, among other things. A rule-based decision tree in the software can back up these findings.

Literature Review on AI and ML Optimization Algorithms in Energy Efficiency

(Zili Yang et al., 2021) This research provides an AI-based arrangement model that achieves dynamic energy utilisation efficiency optimisation through the knowledge and assessment of various current stimulation policies. In this paper, they proposed model which is managed with superior performance in the profitable goal collaboration and hydrate recovery by changing the portions of the optimization control policy function as substantiated by the optimization results. The model raised the energy product injection rate by 4.5 times grounded on methodical assessment of the energy utilisation effectiveness of colourful thermal stimulation programs. The AI reproduction learning findings also revealed that hydrate recovery at the reactor scale had a range effect, and later the energy efficiency that could be achieved in a great level. The proven correlation linking each thermal stimulus policy and its evolving energy usage efficiency is also established using model learning.

(Ghezlane Halhoul Merabeta et al., 2021) This paper conducts a wide-ranging and in-depth systematic reassess of AI-based building control techniques by evaluating the outputs of these methods and their implementations in the re-examined works, as well as examining their capabilities to improve energy efficiency while preserving thermal comfort. This gives researchers in the area a complete observation of the challenges of on condition that thermal comfort to consumers inside the buildings in an energy-efficient manner, and the corresponding catalogue information to aid researchers and specialists for handling in the field such a dispute. Identification and recognition patterns, optimization, and predictive control are among the twenty AI techniques urbanized for comfort control and energy consumption. The application of AI technology in control of the building, which is based on the findings of this study, it is a potential spot of research that is still uncompleted, that is the performance of Artificial Intelligence based control is not yet totally adequate. It is partly owing to the piece of evidence that these algorithms typically require a substantial amount of high-class real-world data, which is scarce in the construction or, extra specifically, the energy sectors. According to the current analysis, from the year 1993 to 2020, the use of Artificial Intelligence approaches and individualised comfort models resulted in average energy investments of 21.81 to 44.36 percent and comfort improvements of 21.67 to 85.77 percent. Finally, this article analyses the obstacles to using AI to get better energy efficiency and comfort, as well as the major future possibilities in AI based building control systems for energy administration and human comfort.

(Aparna Kumaria et al., 2020) AI-based techniques provide a variety of services, including energy load prediction, customer classification, load control, and analysis, all of which require the BC to provide data immutability and a trust mechanism for secure energy management. As a result, this article examines several existing AI-based techniques, as well as the benefits and limitations of combining BC technology and AI in an ECM system.

(Kypros Milidonis et al., 2021) Artificial intelligence technique is becoming gradually more important in designing part of energy system. Several AI ideas are already extensively used throughout the energy business in activities like production predicting, energy conservation monitoring, power storage, and total energy system design. This paper examines the application of critical AI techniques to assessment, optimisation, operations, and safeguarding of Solar Tower systems, which are amongst the high common forms of Solar Thermal systems. Initial, key AI approaches is for a short time introduced, with examples of how they might be applied to solar systems. Following that, a thorough examination of how the AI methods is applied to main part in solar tower systems is presented. The re-examinations are organised in the region of several subsystems that make up a solar tower system.

(Muhammad Uzair Mehmooda et al., 2019) They discuss how AI may be used to propose and operate energy efficient business constructions and residential residences in this study. The present research emphasises that AI, when combined with Big Data (Hussain M. W. et al, 2021), can dramatically improve the energy optimization and cost effectiveness of buildings that are designed to offer residents with a pleasant indoor living situation. The findings in this research show that AI is increasingly playing an essential responsibility in design and operation of energy-efficient buildings with a suitable indoor living environment in the future. Fast datamining and optimal skewing of climate data from various resources, such as satellite data and individual weather stations, more comprehensible interfaces to suit dissimilar user's favourites and functioning conditions and prototypes, and applications of AI and Big Data to smart homes and buildings with highly adaptable building mechanisms are some of the not compulsory research guidelines in this area.

(Yassine Himeur et al., 2021) The CVX(Convex)modelling framework for convex optimization was used to create a multi-objective optimization problem in MATLAB software. The tested network's topology consists of 4, 6, and 10 patients moving in four zones at a minimum speed of 2 m/s and a maximum speed of 6 m/s using the STEPS mobility model. The simulation was carried out using a single Computer Aided Engineering (CAE) model as an example, demonstrating the effectiveness of employing the CAE model as an adaptive compression strategy in reducing the transmission energy of huge medical data. (Miguel Angel Bermeo et al.,2021) In the multi-objective optimization problem, they employed simulation parameters. Finally, the use of recommender systems in the building energy sector is a very promising subject because it not only recommends energy-saving acts but can also be expanded to assist consumers in purchasing products.

(Abeer Al-Marridi et al., 2020) In m-Health applications, AI-based algorithms on edge devices to optimise energy efficiency, The usual method of communication between the patient and the doctor is no longer appropriate. As a result, academics believe that the widespread use of mobile phones around the world, together with speedy improvement of knowledge domains such as smartphones, communication barriers, sensors, and much more, will help to alleviate the health-care shortfall. (Al-Marridi AZ., et al.,2019) The advancement of smart-phone gadgets provides researchers with new options to include them into the therapeutic process. (Lee J, 2011). As a result, smart-Health (s-Health) was classified as a subset of m-Health. Because practically all smart gadgets have a built-in sensor for biosensing tracking, there is no need to integrate separate sensors with patients. Furthermore, as mobile cellular network coverage expands fast, smart gadgets will be used to solve the connectivity problem.

(DiogoA.C.Narciso and F.G.Martins, 2020) This research investigates the potential utility of manufacturing data using methods of Machine Learning to achieve energy efficiency targets. This project recognises and examines the scientific contributions that have been published to date. There is a totality of nearly 42 published papers in this topic that make innovative ideas and address a variety of energy efficiency concerns. The amount of published works in this topic is quickly increasing, according to a descriptive analysis. Most of the contributions deal with issues in the petrochemical industry, specifically ethylene production. The proposed framework can be used as a suggestion guideline for the industrialized and process sectors for selecting appropriate Machine Learning techniques to achieve energy efficiency goals using industrial data.

(Won Shina et al., 2021), (Kasaeian A et al., 2020) Predictive maintenance was the focus of this study since it's a very important constituent for the booming operation of renewable energy systems and extending predictive maintenance to adequately regular and intermittent inspections is expected. They examined a typical bearing failure detection scenario in which endoscopic pictures were collected for inspection. They considered the merits and drawbacks of human-only and AI-only procedures, as well as the advantages of AI-assistance. According to the findings, AI-assisted generalist and specialised groups can improve all variables, including specificity, sensitivity, and time efficiency. Inspectors benefited from AI-assisted inspections even when AI-only performance was inferior to individual performance. (T.S. Ibrahim et al., 2020) The special effects of perception were also examined, with promising grades. Future research could include regular operating tests as well as unlimited experiments in renewable energy domains outer surface of wind farm operation. For the treatment of high-organic-content sludge, the AI system is an excellent solution in terms of energy efficiency.

(Cheng Chen et al., 2021), (Haupt SE et al.,2020) Artificial Intelligence was created using physics-based methods (AI-PBM). The structure provided by State of Kuwait for the Green Energy Park is explained by AI-PBM. Wind turbines, photovoltaic panels, and solar-focused renewables with luggage compartment capacity make up the park. The methodologies, how they are coupled with every AI approach, and the quantitative significance to the forecasting system are all briefly explained in AI-PBM. Each component of operational AI provides value to the device.

(Prince and Ananda Shankar Hati, 2021) In this paper, they assessed the effectiveness of three alternative methods for forecasting daily electricity usage in a local industrial sector (the studied case). At first, as a probabilistic system, an alternative of the Multiple Model Particle Filter is suggested. Then, two distinct ANNs(Artificial Neural networks), one with one hidden layer and the other with 2 hidden layers, are calculated and experienced. Lastly, we show how a built Artificial Neural Network based design may modify its structure in response to chronological fluctuations supplied by a dataset containing the used electricity for the same observed region between the year 2011 and 2015 that is 1825 days. The prospective of AI-based methods will be highlighted by summarising a harmonize heuristic learning that uses an evolutionary algorithm to recommend an optimum solution outage routine for original creators supplying the support higher in order to perform scheduled maintenance that may be needed from periodically or to rest several of the units if the anticipated utilisation for a given time period doesn't really require the total generated power.

(KhalidHamid et al., 2021) Experiments on different masses of Problems that could occur are maintained at a constant air velocity in order to determine different evaluation characteristics such as the heat pump's conversion efficiency, evaporation of water, humidity extraction efficiency, and specific humidity mining efficiency in this paper. Study was designed to compare loads, achieve a higher level of highest efficiency and heat transfer characteristics. The rate of evaporation elimination is determined by the moisture permeability, which improves as the drying air temperature and speed rise. In addition to that, a machine and deep learning model using the most powerful dryer inlet conditions like air temperature, and airflow rate as input features, load, and time to approximate dryer opening conditions and weight diminution for measurement of drying kinetics of the measured material was developed. It's a straightforward and reliable way to estimate freshening performance of diverse resources with a closed loop heat pump drier because of its excellent accuracy.

(KiJeonNam et al., 2021) To pick up environmental operations of wastewater treatment plants, most favourable active solutions have been widely used. Membrane bioreactor (MBR) plants, on the other hand, have been subjected to insufficient optimization systems, ensuing in high energy expenditure suitable to unknown influent and difficult natural and substantial interactions connected with membrane fouling. They employ simulation software to build up a dual-objective optimisation method that is based on the cuckoo search approach. A multimodal gated recurrent unit provided the most precise predictions of increasing fluctuations in everyday prominent amongst competing products. And operational advice was based on the projected influent data. Using an incorporated biological and physical model, the optimization system looked for predictive operating techniques, such as ventilation intensities and permeation-cleaning periods. The indicated aeration intensities for cleaning air on top of membrane surfaces were applied after systemic absorption duration was optimised. A pilot MBR plant outfitted with the recommended optimization method enhanced energy consumption by 4% and decreased fouling by 39% when comparing to a conventionally run system. At a full-scale MBR system, dual-objective tuning increased energy efficiency by 12percent and reduced fouling by 26%, demonstrating viability and consistency.

(C.Solaimuthu et al., 2015) This study was conducted with the energy consumption of pumps connected to diesel engines for irrigation and locomotive tractors in developing countries in mind. According to the findings, Mahua biodiesel provides comparable performance and lower emissions, making it a viable alternative fuel for diesel locomotives and irrigation pumps that do not require engine modification.

(G.RaviK and R.Kashwan, 2015) In this paper, they have mentioned Energy-Aware Span Routing Protocol (EASRP) is a new algorithm that applied energy discounting technique such as the Adaptive Fidelity Energy Conservation Algorithm (AFECA). The use of a hardware track known as the Remote Activated Switch (RAS) to make active in sleeping nodes significantly reduces energy consumption (Hussain M. W., et al, 2020) and this energy-saving technique is well time-honoured in reactive protocols. Still, when employing EASRP in a mixture protocol, particularly a proactive protocol, there are several concerns to consider. When compared to Energy-Aware Zone Routing Protocol (EAZRP) and (Zone Routing Protocol) ZRP, simulation findings for the EASRP procedure reveal a 12.2 percent and 17.45 percent increase in energy efficiency, respectively.

(Vinith KumarLakshmanan et al., 2021) The use of an Eco-Driving Optimal Controller to apply cooperation to a detachment of electric vehicles is discussed in this study (EDOC). It is offered a hypothetical examination of sequence stability with and with no cooperation. The simulation findings reveal that a subdivision with cooperative EDOC outperforms a platoon without collaboration in the form of energy efficiency and twine firmness.

(Miguel AngelBermeo et al., 2021) Adjustment and monitoring of machinery's energy use leads to a more efficient and sustainable industry. As a result, and in accordance with a digital twin strategy, this study proposes and describes an online data determined energy modelling system with balanced abilities. This method can be used to create reliable energy management systems that improve industrial machinery's energy efficiency. Without employing phenomenological principles, the dynamic behaviour of their energy consumption can be represented in this way. Traditional techniques, on the other hand, rarely analyse such dynamic behaviour or employ an intensive modelling process. The suggested method comprises an adaptive mechanism that considers natural machinery degradation. This approach relies on an idea go with the flow detector, which identifies when the machine's current utilization is not accurately characterized by this corresponding model assessment and make to fit the model to accommodate for these new behaviours. (Zhou. R et al., 2020), (aidya S and Nandi C, 2020) The idea drift detector has a wide range of applications in terms of lowering preservation costs, monitoring the contact and progression of anomalous behaviours, and determining which fundamentals vary. An industrial testbed has been used to validate the suggested methodology. The testbed was used to conduct experimentation with 3 simulated concept flows. Finally, they have concluded that the proposed adaptive technique has highest fit rate of the energy prediction or estimation and correctly detected these changes in energy use than the non-adaptive technique. (Senbagavalli M and G Tholkappia Arasu, 2016), (M Senbagavalli et al., 2022), (MS Valli and GT Arasu, 2016) and (Anitha M and Senbagavalli M 2023) used various advanced machine learning and deep learning algorithms for improving efficiency of the proposed model.

SECTORS OF ENERGY EFFICIENCY USING AI AND ML OPTIMIZATION

Here, we have emphasized some of the industries that are interested in learning more about how artificial intelligence and Machine Learning is used in Energy Efficiency.

Industrial Sector

The industrial sector may now employ artificial intelligence to minimize energy expenses by optimizing, monitoring, and controlling energy consumption. Many industrial firms and sites use a lot of energy, and more than 60% of them haven't investigated how they may save energy. Through quantitative and progressive energy management methods aided by artificial intelligence and data mining, energy usage may be controlled and managed. We process data using data mining and artificial intelligence to figure out where energy waste comes from and how it might be eliminated. The AI then uses this data to regulate and control energy use while also collecting other data. It focuses on reducing waste through process innovations and supply chain efficiency in order to meet competitive pressures and lower costs.

Step 1: Max-impact uses data mining to identify energy-saving potential, process bottlenecks, and process variability issues in process and utility systems.

Step 2: Max-impact reduces energy usage by identifying the ideal operational set point and equipment using algorithms.

Step 3: The system will autonomously regulate and control energy usage to maximize efficiency by integrating artificial intelligence and combining it with data found by data mining.

In industrial production facilities, artificial intelligence reduces energy wastage by:

- Self-managing power grids — AI applications are built to handle numerous energy sources efficiently, including solar, wind, and fossil fuels, allowing the Energy Forecast to be used to energy management.
- Increasing plant yields by determining the best process set points
- Reducing energy usage for heating and cooling applications
- Reducing breakdowns - AI forecasts any potential failures of vital energy infrastructure using a combination of analytics, sensors, and operational data.
- Improving Combined Heat and Power (CHP) plant unit energy efficiency
- Predicting energy consumption and matching renewable energy production to it. This minimizes plant emissions while also reducing reliance on fuel. In places where manufacturers are solely reliant on fuel, AI can assist in optimizing fuel utilization and judiciously managing consumption.
- Optimizing performance and sequencing, as well as identifying maintenance concerns, to reduce compressed air, nitrogen, and water plant utility costs.
- In today's competitive business environment, organizations all over the world are looking for ways to save money on energy and other operational costs. In most businesses, energy accounts for a

significant amount of operational costs and is a critical resource in the manufacturing process. Due to a combination of environmental and geopolitical challenges, energy costs have been continuously rising over the last 20 years, forcing industrial players to look for ways to become more energy efficient.

- Investing in energy efficiency can also have other advantages, such as lowering your company's overall carbon impact and increasing your capacity to accomplish carbon-related goals. Industries have discovered that replacing old inefficient systems with more efficient and reliable ones has a direct impact on product quality, improved working conditions, and energy cost savings of up to 60%. Energy audits and services assist industrial establishments in determining where, why, and how they may reduce energy consumption and waste. At the same time, delivering crucial information on energy consumption to management. Max-impact's energy efficiency and renewable energy experts are highly qualified in their fields and work with a variety of significant worldwide enterprises, as well as governments, municipalities, and international development organizations. They can provide first-class advice by participating in cutting-edge energy research initiatives targeted at solving actual difficulties, which can result in significant energy savings of between 15% and 45 percent.

Municipalities

Municipalities and the public sector can use artificial intelligence to help them handle a variety of problems and transform into smart cities. Municipalities have a variety of energy-consuming assets, ranging from street and traffic lighting to heating and cooling office buildings, as well as powering shipyards, airports, schools and churches, residences and hospitals, factories, and retail stores. Artificial intelligence will not only give real-time energy consumption statistics, but it will also be able to use that data to change energy supply based on demand. It, for instance, considers the weather.An AI system can use a combination of renewable energy sources to meet its energy needs, only using fossil-fuel-generated energy when essential. Depending on the difficulty, sector, location, and size, Max-impact assists governments in selecting the best AI-controlled energy solutions.

Commercial Sector

The way energy is managed in commercial buildings will be revolutionized by artificial intelligence. Whether you're dealing with a hospital, a stadium, a retail mall, an office building, a school, or a hotel, artificial intelligence can help you save money on energy and manage your usage more effectively over time.Artificial intelligence (AI) is used to develop intelligent, or smart, profit-making buildings that find out and optimize their energy convention on their own. These apps have a wisdom curve that allows them to incessantlyprogress complex operations by organizing and analyzing massive volumes of data about your energy use habits. The AI solutions become people facility's automatic energy management system.In order to achieve energy conservation, certain AI programs monitor and control a whole building's energy activity. These are some of them:

- Air quality and Vibration
- Early problem detection and Variable air volume systems
- Heating, ventilation and air conditioning (HVAC)

- Temperature sensors and Humidity
- Gas and water supply systems

Examples of AI Applications in Commercial Sectors:

- ***Google reduced their energy bill by with percentage of 40***

Google uses a significant quantity of electricity. They are estimated to have used 4,402,836 MWh of electricity in 2014, which is about like the annual usage of 366,903 US houses. Google has decreased its energy expenditure by hundreds of millions of dollars thanks to DeepMind AI.

- ***AI helps different universities scratch their energy costs by as much as 30%.***

At six British universities, the Energy Consortium has piloted an energy efficiency AI project. An AI program will be used by different universities to discover energy waste, enhance efficiency, and save expenses.

- ***Hospital in New Delhi within six months condensed their energy usage by 35 percent***

Using an AI application, Sant Parmanand hospital in New Delhi, India was able to lower its monthly energy use by 35 percent in just six months.

LATEST TRENDS, FUTURE SCOPES, AND CHALLENGES

Uses of Artificial Intelligence in energy sectors are listed here:

Data Digitization

Since the rest of the world moves toward personalized computerized services, the energy business is falling behind. Artificial Intelligence and Machine Learning can help translate data collection process, storing and managing, permitting the energy segment to catch up with the times. Even though the industry is large and successful, it still relies heavily on physical labor. Energy firms have a lot of information to handle, and it's a lot of it. Machine Learning and Artificial Intelligencecan store the data, process the data and manage the data which is collected already with more timeand cost-efficiently. The AI data governance method can reveal fresh perceptions that have the potential to totally change the way the industry operates.

AI Forecasting

Due to global population, more and more energy needs to be maintained by modern machines. Predictive analytics is the most important job of AI and ML in the energy industry. Energy related company's needs to make progress that is predictive analysis for providing better customer service, to save energy, to cut down costs. AI and MLalgorithms are useful to bring forecasting to the subsequent level in the energy industry. In the energy sector, AI and machine learning algorithms can help take forecasting to the next level. Changes in consumer, network overloads, and potential breakdowns must all be forecasted as accurately as feasible by energy producers. In the energy sector, the cost of a mistake is extremely significant. General Electric intends to use Machine learning and artificial intelligence to enhance their business processes. Anodot is a specific example of artificial intelligence technology being successfully implemented in the solar industry.

Resource Management

Once AI forecasting is done then the Resource management is concentrated because it is the next phase in the energy business. Thanks to intelligent Intelligence forecasting procedures, energy providers would be able to more effectively deploy their resources, plan for demand ahead of time, anticipate difficulties, and conserve resources whenever possible. End-users will profit from AI-assisted energy conservation in the form of decreased effectiveness bills and tailored services, which is a major advantage of AI in sector of energy.

Failure Prediction and Prevention

AI can predict system overloads and warn operators of potential transformer breakdowns. VIA has created Trusted Analytics Chain, a blockchain-based technology that assists businesses in gathering and analyzing data in order to predict system behavior. PreNav is a start-ups that uses drones, lidar, and deep learning to assist energy companies digitize their infrastructure. This type of service can assist businesses in better visualizing their capabilities. In the energy business, PreNav came up with a great usage of AI. Their machine learning and deep learning algorithms can detect problems and dangers specific to the energy business.

Energy Storage Facilitation

The problem of storage technology efficiency is tough to tackle. As the amount of electricity to also be stored develops, more capacity and more management methods are necessary. Artificial Intelligence (AI) can assist businesses in optimizing their energy storage space. Renewable Energy (RE) is difficult to store since it is produced in a predictable, if not chaotic, manner.By combining AI-powered storage with renewable energy, the energy storage management may be considerably simplified, resulting in increased business value and reduced power losses. Consider the startup, which is called Stem, that assists businesses in improving their energy plans. 80 of the country's leading solar energy producers, assisting them with increasing project value by up to 90% by increasing storage space.

KEY CHALLENGES OF AI AND ML IN ENERGY SECTOR

Shortfall of Theoretical Background

The absence of adequate understanding about AI technology between decision-makers is one cause for the sluggish implementation of AI and ML in the energy sector. Many businesses simply be short of the technical knowledge required to grasp how AI may enhance their operations. Traditional consumers would rather remain with tried-and-true ways and technologies than take a chance on new things. Energy decision-makers are paying attention to many sectors, include education, healthcare, and transportationwith the help of AI.

Shortfall of Practical Expertise

There are many professionals that have a thorough theoretical understanding of the issue. However, finding individuals capable of developing powerful AI-powered software with real-world utility is extremely difficult. Furthermore, the energy sector is known for its conservatism. Even though energy businesses collect and process information, digitizing it with cutting-edge technology is difficult.Loss of data, inadequate customization, equipment malfunction, and unauthorized access are all potential concerns. Because the penalty of error is so significant within the energy sector, most organizations are hesitant to attempt new ways with which they are unfamiliar.

Outdated Infrastructure

The most significant impediment to power sector transformation is antiquated infrastructures. Utility firms are presently mired in a mountain of data they acquire and have no clue how to deal with it. Whereas the industry has much more information than most, it is frequently dispersed, unstructured, fragmented across multiple forms, and only saved locally. Whereas the business makes a lot of money, it also loses a lot of money due to the weaknesses of antiquated technology.

Financial Pressure

Incorporating advanced modern devices in energy subdivision may be the most excellent option, except it is not the most cost-effective. It consumes a lot of effort and resources to find a competent software provider, develop and customize technology, adjust, manage, and audit it. Before power companies can realize the rewards of adopting AI and machine learning into scheme, they must be willing to commit a sizable budget and incur the risks of replacing outmoded technologies.

CONCLUSION AND FUTURE SCOPE

This chapter begins with an opening to AI and machine learning introduction, tracked by an example of how Artificial Intelligence and machine learning may and have been used to improve energy efficiency. Also, the effects of the globalisation I the current and the future generation. Which is leading to the energy transition for the better efficiencywith the smart energy system. The second section of this chapter looks at recent articles on AI and machine learning in energy-efficient systems. In recent years, AI and machine learning have played a significant role in a variety of industries, such as industries, digitization, and forecasting, to improve energy optimization. Renewable energy is a strong financial force as well as a viable solution for sustainable development. In the context of the previous concept, the energy business is one of the primary industries where "energy digitalization" has expanded rapidly across a wide range of resource sectors. Artificial intelligence is being incorporated transversely into various industry areas, boosting data analytics capabilities. Because of the unpredictable nature of weather, suppliers may be forced to rely on conventional energy sources to congregate consumer demand. As a result, AI-driven energy forecasting tools may offer potential in giving energy suppliers the data they need to answer to and plan for changes that could negatively impact operations.

REFERENCES

Al-Marridi, A., Mohamed., A., & Erbad. A. (2020). AI-based techniques on edge devices to optimize energy efficiency in m-Health applications. *AI-based techniques on edge devices.* . doi:10.1016/B978-0-12-819045-6.00001-7

Aidya S. & Nandi C.(2020). Green Energy Generation Using Renewable Energy Technologies. In *Advances in Greener Energy Technologies* (pp. 259-276). Springer. Singapore.

Al-Marridi, A. Z., Mohamed, A., Erbad, A., Al-Ali, A., & Guizani, M. (2019). Efficient EEG mobile edge computing and optimal resource allocation for smart health applications. 15th international wireless communications & mobile computing conference (IWCMC). IEEE; June 2019. p. 1261e6.

Anitha, M., & Senbagavalli, M. (2023). Dynamic Mobile Cloud Eco System Security - A Review, *International Journal of Data Informatics and Intelligent Computing*, *2*(1), 62–69. https://doi.org/10.59461/ijdiic.v2i1.44

Bermeo-Ayerbe, M. A., Ocampo-Martinez, C., & Diaz-Rozo, J. (2022, January). CarlosOcampo., Javier-Diaz-Rozo.(2021). Data-driven energy prediction modeling for both energy efficiency and maintenance in smart manufacturing systems. *Energy*, *238*, 121691. doi:10.1016/j.energy.2021.121691

Chen, C., Hu, Y., Karuppiah, M., & Kumar, P. M. (2021, October). Artificial intelligence on economic evaluation of energy efficiency and renewable energy technologies. *Sustainable Energy Technologies and Assessments*, *47*, 101358. doi:10.1016/j.seta.2021.101358

Diogo, A. C. (2020, November). Application of machine learning tools for energy efficiency in industry: A review. *Energy Reports*, *6*, 1181–1199. doi:10.1016/j.egyr.2020.04.035

Hamid, K., Sajjad, U., Yang, K. S., Wu, S.-K., & Wang, C.-C. (2022, January). Assessment of an energy efficient closed loop heat pump dryer for high moisture contents materials: An experimental investigation and AI based modelling. *Energy*, *238*, 121819. doi:10.1016/j.energy.2021.121819

Haupt, S. E., McCandless, T. C., Dettling, S., Alessandrini, S., Lee, J. A., Linden, S., Petzke, W., Brummet, T., Nguyen, N., Kosović, B., Wiener, G., Hussain, T., & Al-Rasheedi, M. (2020). Combining artificial intelligence with physics-based methods for probabilistic renewable energy forecasting. *Energies*, *13*(8), 1979. doi:10.3390/en13081979

Himeur, Y., Alsalemi, A., Al-Kababji, A., Bensaali, F., Amira, A., Sardianos, C., Dimitrakopoulos, G., & Varlamis, I. (2021, August). A survey of recommender systems for energy efficiency in buildings: Principles, challenges and prospects. *Information Fusion*, *72*, 1–21. doi:10.1016/j.inffus.2021.02.002

Hussain, M. W. (2021). A counter based approach for reducer placement with augmented Hadoop rackawareness. *Turkish Journal of Electrical Engineering and Computer Sciences*, *29*(1), 437–453. doi:10.3906/elk-2001-106

Hussain, M. W., Pradhan, B., Gao, X. Z., Reddy, K. H. K., & Roy, D. S. (2020). Clonal selection algorithm for energy minimization in software defined networks. *Applied Soft Computing*, *96*, 106617. doi:10.1016/j.asoc.2020.106617

Ibrahim, T. S., Saleh, A. I., Elgaml, N., & Abdelsalam, M. M. (2020). A fog-based recommendation system for promoting the performance of E-learning environments. *Computers & Electrical Engineering*, *87*, 106791. doi:10.1016/j.compeleceng.2020.106791

Kasaeian A., Razmjoo A., Shirmohammadi R., Pourfayaz F., Sumper A. (2020). Deployment of a stand-alone hybrid renewable energy system in coastal areas as a reliable energy source. *Environ Prog Sustainable Energy, 39*(3). https://doi.org/. v39.310.1002/ep.13354. doi:10.1002/ep

Kumaria., A., Guptaa., R., Tanwara., S., & Kumar, N. (2020). Blockchain and AI Amalgamation for Energy Cloud Management: Challenges, Solutions, and Future Directions. *Journal of Parallel and Distributed Computing*. . doi:10.1016/j.jpdc.2020.05.004

Lee, J. (2011). Smart health: concepts and status of ubiquitous health with smartphone. In: ICTC2011. IEEE; (pp. 388e9). IEEE. doi:10.1109/ICTC.2011.6082623

Mehmood, M. U., Chun, D., Zeeshan, Han, H., Jeon, G., & Chen, K. (2019). Review of the applications of artificial intelligence and big data to buildings for energy-efficiency and a comfortable indoor living environment. *Energy and Building*, *202*, 109383. doi:10.1016/j.enbuild.2019.109383

Merabeta, G. H. (2021, July). Intelligent building control systems for thermal comfort and energy-efficiency: A systematic review of artificial intelligence-assisted techniques. *Renewable & Sustainable Energy Reviews*, *144*, 110969. doi:10.1016/j.rser.2021.110969

Milidonis, K., Blanco, M. J., Grigoriev, V., Panagiotou, C. F., Bonanos, A. M., Constantinou, M., Pye, J., & Asselineau, C.-A. (2021, August). Review of application of AI techniques to Solar Tower Systems. *Solar Energy*, *224*, 500–515. doi:10.1016/j.solener.2021.06.009

Nam, K. J., Heo, S. K., Rhee, G. H., Kim, M. J., & Yoo, C. K. (2021, May). Dual-objective optimization for energy-saving and fouling mitigation in MBR plants using AI-based influent prediction and an integrated biological-physical model. *Journal of Membrane Science*, *626*, 119208. doi:10.1016/j.memsci.2021.119208

Pradhan, B., Hussain, M. W., Srivastava, G., Debbarma, M. K., Barik, R. K., & Lin, J. C. W. (2022). A neuro-evolutionary approach for software defined wireless network traffic classification. *IET Communications*, cmu2.12548. doi:10.1049/cmu2.12548

Prince, & Hati, A. S. (2021, August). A comprehensive review of energy-efficiency of ventilation system using Artificial Intelligence. *Renewable & Sustainable Energy Reviews*, *146*, 111153. doi:10.1016/j.rser.2021.111153

Ravi, G., & Kashwan, K. R. (2015, November). A new routing protocol for energy efficient mobile applications for ad hoc networks. *Computers & Electrical Engineering*, *48*, 77–85. doi:10.1016/j.compeleceng.2015.03.023

Manju bargavi S. K. & Senbagavalli, M. (2022). Artificial Intelligence and Medical Information Modeling. In Handbook of Research on Mathematical Modeling for Smart Healthcare Systems. (pp. 1-11). IGI Global. 10.4018/978-1-6684-4580-8.ch001

Senbagavalli, M., & Tholkappia Arasu, G. (2016). Opinion Mining for Cardiovascular Disease using Decision Tree based Feature Selection. *Asian Journal of Research in Social Sciences and Humanities*, *6*(8), 891–897. doi:10.5958/2249-7315.2016.00658.4

Shina, W. (2021, April). AI-assistance for predictive maintenance of renewable energy systems. *Energy*, *221*, 119775. doi:10.1016/j.energy.2021.119775

Solaimuthu, C., Ganesan, V., Senthilkumar, D., & Ramasamy, K. K. (2015). Emission reductions studies of a biodiesel engine using EGR and SCR for agriculture operations in developing countries. *Applied Energy*, *138*, 91–98. doi:10.1016/j.apenergy.2014.04.023

Valli, M. S., & Arasu, G. T. (2016). *An Efficient Feature Selection Technique of Unsupervised Learning Approach for Analyzing Web Opinions*, 221-224. . NISCAIR-CSIR, India. https://nopr.niscpr.res.in/handle/123456789/34053

Yang, Z., Hu, S., Dongliang, Z. (2021). AI-based composition model for energy utilization efficiency optimization of gas hydrate recovery by combined method of depressurization and thermal stimulation. *Journal of Natural Gas Science and Engineering*. doi:10.1016/j.jngse

Zhou. R., Canady. S., Bao, A. Gokhale.(2020). Cost-effective hardware accelerator recommendation for edge computing, in: 3rd{USENIX}Workshop on HotTopics in Edge Computing (HotEdge 20).

Chapter 8
5G-Enabled Secure IoT Applications in Smart Cities Using Software-Defined Networks

Syed Yaser Mahmood
SRM University, India

S. Aashrit
SRM University, India

B. Venkatesh Reddy
SRM University, India

Arati Behera
SRM University, India

Tapas Kumar Mishra
https://orcid.org/0000-0002-6363-5017
SRM University, India

Kshira Sagar Sahoo
Department of Computing Science, Umeå University, Umeå, Sweden & Department of Computer Science, SRM University, Amaravati, India

ABSTRACT

With the idea of shifting towards a smart future there is a lot of research being done in the area of internet of things (IoT) and wireless communication, especially 5G network technology. These technologies are instrumenting society towards a world of high connectivity, through secure evolutionary telecommunication methodologies. In this chapter we understand the role of 5G networks in enhancing IoT devices and discuss their security aspects. Integration of IoT and software defined network termed as SDIoT enables automatic traffic rerouting, device reconfiguration, and bandwidth allocation seamlessly. Smart cities utilize the SDIoT integrated with 5G to gather real-time data, better understand how demand patterns are changing, and respond with quicker and more affordable solutions. The authors try to understand the existing research scenario in 5G networks and IoT, and what areas are being taken into consideration for improvement in the coming future.

DOI: 10.4018/979-8-3693-0744-1.ch008

INTRODUCTION

Internet of things (IOT) is collection of devices which are connected to internet where the devices are assembled with computing power and memory. The above devices also may collect information about their surroundings (Kumar et al., 2019, pp. 1-21), (Bhoi et al., 2022). Further, the devices may send data to their neighbors and/or to internet (Jain et al., 2012). In the current scenario, we already see a few IOT devices around us such as google home voice controller, which allows us to control home lights, handle other devices like TVs and mobiles to plan the day by setting up alarms or entertain ourselves with playing media etc. As IOT is such a broad technology, which has its application in various fields like manufacturing, safety, health systems, public transport and infrastructure, with the advent of technology in recent years and the huge amount of research done towards development of smart connected society it is obvious to observe the increase in number of such IOT devices in the near future (Din et al., 2017, pp. 175-182). This smart connected society comes with large volumes of data transfer, huge connectivity and a large variety of use cases of the IOT devices.

Figure 1. A sample integration of 5G, IOT and SDN

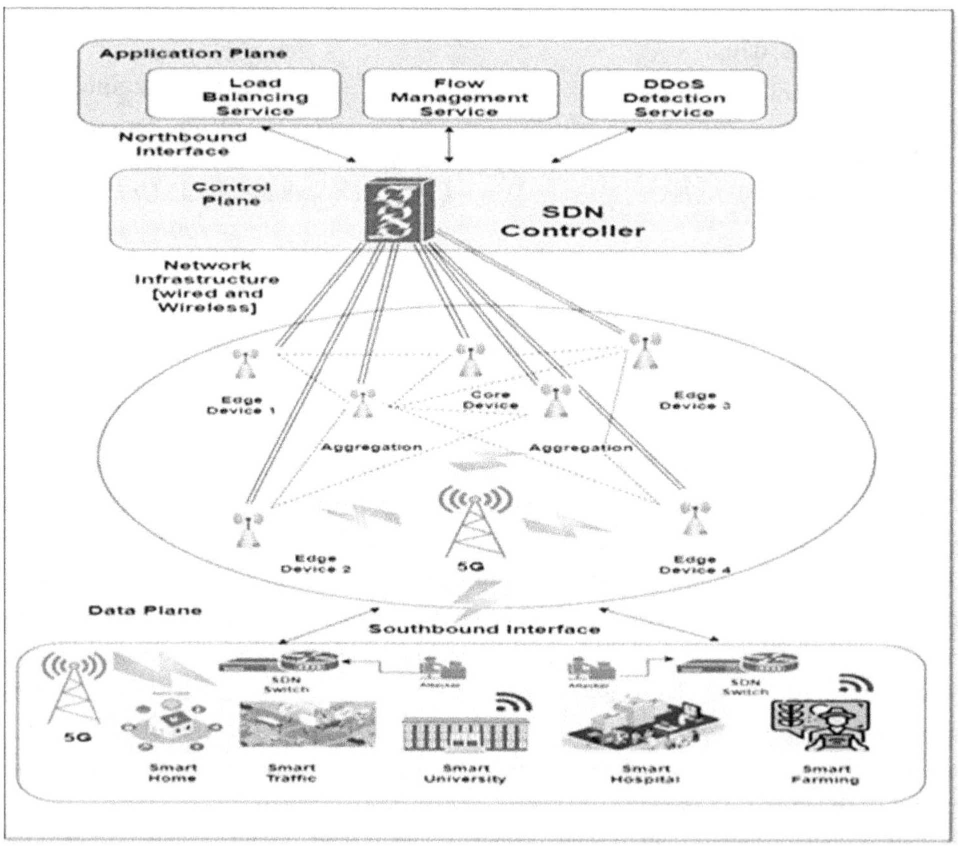

Problem Statement

The luxurious lifestyle of the peoples has created many opportunities and challenges for the generation. Recent development of the information technology and the devices made many thins possible such as smart farming, smart health care systems, smart and intelligent transportation system, etc. The large-scale use of devices and the need of information in real-time environment like smart manufacturing, smart and intelligent healthcare require fast communication along with connectivity with many devices (IOT devices). Further, there may exist many types of security threats which needs to be filtered at the arrival of the data packets at any organization server or individual computers. Thus, smart packet forwarding using artificial intelligence and machine learning is evident which is called as software defined networks (SDN). The integration of the 5G, IOT and SDN is shown in Figure 1.

FIFTH GENERATION MOBILE NETWORK (5G)

Since all these IOT devices rely on transfer of large amounts of data among a lot of interconnected devices it is required for it to have a network which is fast, energy efficient and comes with low latency rate and high throughput (data rates). This is where the fifth-generation mobile network (5G) technology plays a role as it promises to meet the demands of these smart IOT devices, which the previous network technologies could not provide (Din et al., 2017, pp. 175-182). 5G aims to improve wireless internet access when compared to existing cellular networks like 4G LTE and Mobile WiMAX. 5G is the new generation of cellular technology which is an evolution of all previous generations, and it is designed in such a way that it is compatible with the current generations so that there is a smooth transition from current network to the new network and at the same time aims at improving the efficiency of the network (Park et al. 2014). With the integration of 5G networks into the IoT devices we can see massive mobility with efficient use of energy and quick communication between devices which provides fast response. The 5G is an advanced mobile network in this new generation that not only enables innovations but edges towards a progressive change across industries like smart grids. Moreover, 5G mobile communication technology is based on a whole new architecture that is adaptable.

Table 1. Some methods that make 5G better than the existing networks

S.no	Method	Advantage
1	Millimeter Wave Communication	Increases the number of devices that can be connected to the network at one instance
2	Smart Antenna Systems	Increase in 5g network coverage
3	Cognitive Radios	Better data traffic management
4	Media Independent Handover	Easy transition from existing networks to the 5g network

Integration of IOT with 5G networks has been an active area of research. In the recent years, it also has lots of applications specially when it comes to smart cities. Massive amount of applications in a wide spectrum ranging from smart automotive industry that focuses on safety of drivers, reduced emissions from vehicles and efficient energy use to smart healthcare and infrastructure is expected when we talk about smart cities. The technological and network related demands of the smart cities can be achieved once IOT and 5G networks are integrated using the technologies such as millimeter wave communication, Software defined networks and several others which are discussed in detail further in the paper along with the potential security threats that these technologies come with. Some special techniques are adopted in 5G which are highlighted in the table 1. A brief explanation of the features of the 5G technology is presented as follows.

Millimeter Wave Communication

This method has allowed maximum possible use of mm-wave spectrum which in turn supports simultaneous mobile communication and backhaul with convergence of cellular and Wi-fi services. This has acquired significant interest as it is able to meet the requirements for 5G network (Land, Millman, 2014). This has a frequency range between 30-300 GHz. The combination of cost effective CMOS technology which can properly coordinate with the mm-wave frequency bands can strengthen wireless communication. This is done in order to carry frequency of large bandwidth with directly higher data transfer rates which enhances communication. This method improves the propagation characteristics of differing frequencies making them much more comparable and homogeneous (Yilmaz et al., 2016). As a whole we can say that the millimeter wave technology is used for better transmission speeds. Millimeter waves have high frequencies and short wavelengths, allowing for smaller antennas to receive them. Hence, fewer large-scale base stations are to be deployed, in favor of a slew of small base stations that can cover areas where huge base stations can't.

Cognitive Radios

Cognitive radio is the concept that to use idle channels by other users using some software defined techniques. Again, the potential may be executed through the mixture of the 3 parameters, spectral performance, spectrum, and spectrum reuse. The 5G networks will encompass nodes/cells with heterogeneous traits and capacities (e.g. macro cells, small cells which include Femtocells and Picocells, D2D consumer equipment's and M2M USERS etc.), with a purpose to bring about a multi-tier architecture. Due to growing complexity in community control and coordination amongst a couple of community tiers, the community nodes may have the functionality of self-employed which include interference cancellation, spectrum sharing and the electricity control. The communique performance in 5G structures may be advanced through incorporating strategies which include heterogeneous networks, interference cancellation and spectrum reuse.

Media Independent Handovers

Media independent handovers have been a hot topic in 5G. To comprehend the benefits of 5G via a media-independent HO, the following points can be considered:

- 5G will be more than just 5G base stations with their own core network. Backwards compatibility and seamless handover to 4G, 3G, and 2G will be critical, as they have been for all previous generations of cellular communications. Furthermore, handover to and from non-3GPP techniques is a requirement of 5G.

- Media-independent handover enables faster switching, lower latency, and improved Quality of Service for users during mobility events.
- Another 5G requirement is a latency of 1ms for mission critical services and 5-10ms for other services such as mobile broadband, etc.

As a result of the foregoing, it is possible to conclude that a media-independent handover will improve 5G technology performance and assist in meeting its potential and stated requirements.

In the author's research they have been trying to explore some methods that make 5G better than the existing networks. A few methods that have been discussed are Millimeter Wave Communication, Cognitive Radios, Media Independent Handovers and Smart Antenna Systems. Coming to Millimeter Wave Communication:

- it increases the spectrum bandwidth for the betterment of 5G transmission speeds. Millimeter waves produce the bandwidth of around 28 Ghz and 60 Ghz, whereas the available spectrum bandwidth for 4G is 100 MHz at the maximum carrier frequency (Land, 2020). As a whole we can say that the Millimeter wave technology is used for good or even great transmission speeds.
- As every coin has two sides, Millimeter technology has drawbacks also, one of the major drawbacks is structures and other impediments can't be penetrated by millimeter waves. Which means these waves cannot even pass through a paper.
- Millimeter waves have small wavelengths and high frequency; thus, they may be received with smaller antennas. As a result, small base stations might be developed. As a result, fewer large-scale base stations will be deployed in favor of a bevy of tiny base stations that can cover areas where giant base stations can't.

The radio access network is under increasing pressure to deliver improved coverage, capacity, and end-user throughput as end-user performance needs continue to rise.

- Because data usage is increasing at a far faster rate than revenue, mobile network operators must upgrade the RAN to cut cost per bit while meeting new end-user performance demands. The time has come for the telecommunications industry to undertake the technological leap to improved antenna systems (AAS).
- The ability to develop AAS cost-effectively and the higher performance of AAS in both uplink (UL) and downlink (DL) are the major reasons for this technology transfer. We deploy Cognitive Radio technology to meet the high mobile data load of wireless networks and effectively handle it.
- 5G intends to give increased capacity and a network speed of 10Gbps since the future of mobile broadband will be predominantly driven by ultra-high-definition video and because the things around us will always be linked. 5G equipment will also be less expensive, use less battery power, and have lower latency than 4G equipment. Many industries, including entertainment, agriculture, information technology, and manufacturing, can benefit from the 5G platform.
- Additional spectrum will be required to meet the need for more capacity, culminating in the inclusion of CR in 5G networks. CR's main goal is to make significantly more effective use of the spectrum by adapting to provide the best communication route

- There are few problems with CR like there is no complete automation, and any changes must be implemented with the help of the user, it always necessitates the use of a multi-band antenna, in comparison to typical wireless networks, cognitive radio technology presents greater opportunities for attackers.

Not only in 5G, but also in other technologies such as IEEE 802.x, media independent handovers have been a hot topic. IEEE offers a standard for facilitating media-independent handovers called 802.21. 5G will consist of more than just 5G base stations, each with its own core network. Backwards compatibility and seamless handover to 4G, 3G, and 2G, as with all prior generations of cellular communications, will be important. In addition, handover to and from non-3GPP approaches will be required in 5G. The 3GPP spec sheets TS23.501 and 23.502 also specify these needs and criticalities. When a user is experiencing mobility events, media-independent handover enables for faster switching, lower latency, and higher Quality of Service. Another criterion of 5G is a latency of less than 1 millisecond for mission-critical services and 5-10 milliseconds for other services like mobile broadband. It may be concluded that a media-independent handover will improve 5G technology performance and help it reach its full potential.

SOFTWARE DEFINED IOT (SDIOT)

The IoT network has a vast number of linked devices, making it impossible for existing IP protocols to support all of them. Another routing protocol must be added to account for the possibility that these objects will have distinct traits and attributes. While using IPv6 may be seen as a wise decision to handle such a large number of objects, it does not address the heterogeneity of the underlying objects. The capacity to control, modify, and manage network behavior dynamically using software via open interfaces as opposed to depending on closed boxes and proprietary defined interfaces is known as network programmability, or Software Designed Network (SDN). The SDN architecture makes it possible to centrally regulate data route components regardless of the network technology used to link these devices, which may come from many manufacturers. Centralized control incorporates all the intelligence and keeps track of all the data channel components and linkages from a network-wide perspective. Many efforts are being made to amalgamate SDN and IoT. The main motive of merging these technologies is effective data retrieval and achieving networks that may be configured remotely. The amount of data being transferred to-and-fro due to the various applications in the IOT field the capability of handling it must also be improved. Therefore, a flexible network architecture with high performance and stability is required to serve smart city applications. SDN's key goals are to separate the control plane from the forwarding plane, end vertical integration, and add network programming capabilities. In SDN, the control plane elements are represented by a single entity, the controller, while the data plane elements are transformed into highly effective and customizable packet forwarding devices. SDN makes it simpler to create and deploy applications than conventional networks. Big data is a crucial network application that will significantly affect how SDN is designed and run. In particular, the logically centralized controller in SDN may acquire massive data from physical to application layers with arbitrary granularity thanks to the global perspective of the network. Integration of software programmable devices with Iot devices would produce great results. The system must be able to accommodate various sensor kinds, platforms, data formats, communication standards, and hardware heterogeneity. It is also thought that any system must be built to be expandable, either vertically to provide additional storage capacity or horizontally to enable effective load balancing. That solution should also offer remote reconfiguration for the supporting devices. It should also feature fine-grained user applications to make it easy for users to access and query the data being collected. SDN enables software implementation by decoupling network control from data transmission hardware. The fundamental tenet of SDN is that data management and data transmission are distinct. The other tenet is network management is centralized through unified software and even virtualized network resources replace actual ones. Benefits like Automatic traffic rerouting, Device reconfiguration, bandwidth allocation and many others can be given by the integration of SDN and IoT technologies.

SDN in 5G Networks

Although wired enterprise networks were the primary setting for SDN's early adoption, it has recently emerged as a promising tool for other networks, including wireless sensor networks (WSNs) and next-generation wireless networking infrastructures. This is due to SDN's flexibility, programmability, speed, and cost advantages. By supplying the network virtualization capabilities required for remote and dynamic network management, SDN will be one of the biggest enablers of 5G and beyond networks. A number of IoT use cases can be supported by 5G networks thanks to their quick failover and autonomous management capabilities, which will be made possible by SDN applications. The provision of enhanced network security through global visibility and quick automatic flow rule modification is one of the main promises of and justifications for the implementation of SDN (Hussain et al., 2022). This will make it possible to identify and stop malicious activity in the network in real time. In order to interrupt network functionality, these assaults any layer of the TCP/IP model including the other layers like data plane and application plane in IOT.

Need for SDN in Smart City Communication System

SDN appeals to the idea of a smart city due to three distinct qualities in addition to its advantage in the most fundamental network operations, such as routing and end-to-end performance optimization (Tadros et al., 2020, pp. 53997-54008). A logically centralized control plane, programmability to enable in-situ configuration virtualization, and resource sharing amongst applications running on the same physical infrastructure are all requirements for efficient global view and control. But the creation of networking and security solutions that make use of SDN capabilities can open up new attack avenues for malicious users, leading to network dangers and exploitation. Examples of major assaults include Man-in-the-Middle (MITM), Link Discovery Service (LDS) exploitation, and Denial of Service (DoS). Networking infrastructures that are simple, programmable, and flexible have been shown via SDN. In fact, the SDN infrastructure layer's programmability feature allows for a flexible and affordable deployment of networks to enable smart cities.

There are still numerous technical issues that need to be resolved even though academics have been aggressive in investigating the most recent SDN technologies to ensure safe SDN-based communication systems:

1) SDN-enabled networks actually only make up a small part of the entire network architecture. We anticipate that a wide-area network will soon be a hybrid system made up of a number of linked SDN domains encircling cloud locations or data centers.

2) The wide-area network will still include numerous domains, each of which will provide end-to-end security with the potential for varying QoS needs.
3) Despite the fact that there is research on SDN security, very little has been done to address the demand for trustworthy real-time communications in smart cities.

Security is sometimes seen as an add-on in older networks since it relies so largely on manual configuration-based solutions. Therefore, administrators must configure each related network object in accordance with vendor-specific low-level instructions in order to achieve high-level security applications.

On the other hand, SDN boosts security in a networking-enabled environment thanks to its centralized management of the network system, comprehensive visibility of the network activity, and run-time manipulation of inserting/pushing forwarding rules (Hussain et al., 2020). As a result, the SDN non-distributed administration of the network enables more effective application of security regulations and a decrease in their conflicts. Additionally, security solutions like security monitoring applications might effectively query flow samples from data routes through an SDN controller (Renuka et al., 2021).

Additionally, SDN enables effective policy and application updates for security. Instead of modifying the hardware or even just upgrading its firmware, it enables the addition of security modules at the controller platform.

Automatic Traffic Rerouting

Packet is a form of transporting data for communication. Openflow protocol along with queue stat helps us ensure the suitable data is transferred,i.e the detection of packet loss. To counter this situation, the re-routing module of SDN came into play which perceives the bypass and applies to flow tables which comprises data flow and their matching with to-and-fro communication. This packet loss increases vividly because of the TCP/IP network suite Internet which contains a large amount of data traffic. As a large network is not manageable efficiently SDN uses centralized management. By using automatic traffic rerouting features, routing of data can become efficient when it comes to load balancing and loss reduction. In this feature, we assume packet drop only because of congestion. Basically, when the service rate is lower than the arrival rate for each queue, congestion arises. Rerouting finds an alternative way with the suitable topology to avoid packet loss at a minimal level. Although measuring delay is not done owing to the poor temporal realism of the mininet emulation, the average loss rate is decreased, and this may result in a drop in the average latency of each flow. The main aim being minimizing loss rate. In conclusion, automatic traffic rerouting disperses traffic over the network, resulting in a normalized loss rate. But a hindrance to its efficiency is that it is actually not reflected on real world problems as it was tested on only a small number of nodes.

$$\text{Change Rate} = \frac{\text{Maximum delay} - \text{Minimum delay}}{\text{Average delay}} \text{X } 100 \qquad (1)$$

Device Reconfiguration

IoT reconfiguration may be described as (re)programming system modules or an IoT device's full operating system at the system level. The two methods that are most often used in this field of study are full-image replacement and modular programming. Application-aware routing is made possible for the Internet of Things (IoT) thanks to SDN-based network reconfiguration. The SDN controllers present in there execute both way coordination to optimize and divide the computational power and maintain the routing patterns to IoT devices. Reconfiguring an IoT-based system at the application level is referred to as a parameter setting strategy, which attempts to enhance the deployed system's dynamic flexibility. In this study field, several current solutions have been put forth already by many researchers. The main advantage of SDN based reconfiguration technology is to provide good management, maintaining and updating activities. Practical implementation is a hurdle when creating an IoT-based system that is programmable.

$$\text{Time to Reconfigure Device} = \frac{\text{Complexity of Device} + \text{ Amount of Data to Transfer}}{\text{Efficiency of Reconfiguration Process}} \tag{2}$$

Bandwidth Allocation

With the increase in the number of IoT devices a very highly effective bandwidth allocation framework is much needed for the existing SDN architecture. It should be able to optimize bandwidth on both internal and external traffic. With a proper bandwidth allocation Quality and User experience will be at a greater level. The technologie's application is that an ISP would support thousands of IoT-enabled smart homes. Since every application needs to have a specific amount of bandwidth provided in advance, allocation of internet or network bandwidth can be a significant issue. Additionally, because this allocation does not alter dynamically, this bandwidth can be left unused when an application is not running but is still assigned to it. To address this issue, it is possible to use SDN's intelligence to make sure that network or internet capacity is dynamically assigned to applications that require it. Instead of doing this in hardware like switches and routers, SDN moves network management tasks from the network devices to an application that can be used to intelligently modify & control the network. This capability allows for the optimization of network or internet capacity so that it is dynamically distributed to the apps that use it the most.

$$\text{Bandwidth Allocation} = \frac{\text{Total Network Bandwidth X Percentage of Bandwidth Allocated}}{\text{Number of Users}} \tag{3}$$

Security Flaws and Vulnerabilities

Smart homes, autonomous vehicles, security systems, smart cities, and remote healthcare are just a few examples of IoT use cases that greatly improve the quality of our everyday lives. Future networks using software-defined networking for resource management, such as 5G and beyond, will be a crucial enabler for the pervasive IoT. Due to IoT's low computing power, short battery life, and lack of security standards, many IoT devices are unable to implement even the most basic security measures, such as encryption. This has already resulted in a significant attack surface. New use cases, protocols, and technologies increase the number of attack surfaces already present. To ensure the smooth running of these systems, it is crucial to create intrusion detection and prevention solutions for IoT networks that address both new and current risks. In order to provide prompt detection and mitigation of threats, as well as a swift reconfiguration of the networks to minimize quality deterioration and failures, it is also crucial to ensure that the established security solutions are compliant with SDN-based network topologies.

SECURITY MEASURE

There are many dangers associated with actual applications of these new integrated technologies. The older generations 4G, 3G posed serious threats which are still existent in 5G networks. With the SDN coming into play there are many other security issues which came into picture.

Security Issues

- Older Technologies:

Although 5G basically has a stronger enhanced security setup, it should be compatible with devices with older standards. The ability to communicate with devices that use the previous standards must still be supported by 5G, for this purpose they will have to use older protocols utilized by 2G–4G networks might still cause problems for newly installed 5G-based networks.

- Latest Vulnerabilities:

Although consumer adoption of 5G is still in its infancy, experts and hackers have had years to examine the technology. At least six significant security weaknesses, including holes in 5G's identification and authentication processes, have been found during that time.

- IP Attacks:

The majority of the heavy lifting for 5G is handled by the software-defined networking (SDN) layer, as opposed to earlier 2G, 3G, and 4G protocols that rely on proprietary hardware. While SDN increases the 5G network's flexibility and extensibility, it also leaves the network vulnerable to IP (Internet Protocol) assaults like DDoS. (Distributed Denial of Service).

- Man in the middle

The vulnerability of 5G to a Man-in-the-Middle assault (MiTM). In a MiTM attack, hackers impersonate the genuine mobile network operator to eavesdrop on signals delivered through the internet or cell phones, collect the information, and enter their orders. MiTM attacks are frequently carried out by attackers who pose as a legitimate network to the target device by use of a malicious fake cell tower. Verifying a network's identification tries to guarantee connectivity to a reliable network. Malicious IP addresses can be returned in response to valid DNS requests, which can be used by the attacker to launch remote malware assaults, steal passwords, and conduct MITM attacks.

- Number of connected devices

Millions of gadgets, such as household appliances, industrial automation controls, televisions, automobiles, smartphones, sensors for weather monitoring, next-generation tablets, and other diverse ranges, are anticipated to be connected to 5G, increasing the attack surface. Consumer phones and PCs won't make up the majority of user equipment on 5G networks; instead, IoT devices will. There will be around 20 billion of these gadgets by 2020. Attacks against the IoT are becoming more frequent. Malware dissemination is easily scalable, yet device security is subpar.

Possible Solutions to Security Threats

To counteract vulnerable attacks on the network, monitoring and detection mechanisms for network devices can be helpful. Specialized software can be designed to enforce network security control regulations, such as ensuring or restricting specified network accesses or taking measures to stop malicious data transmission. A potential neutralizing element is the adoption of software attestation techniques, such as autonomic trust management solutions for software components (Kreutz et al., 2013, pp. 55-60). Fault and intrusion tolerance is one of the essential components to ensure a highly robust system from a security and reliability standpoint. Utilizing intrusion detection systems with runtime root-cause analysis assistance may be able to detect irregular flows. For the purpose of ensuring confidence between the control plane and data plane devices, the usage of dynamic, automated, and ensured device association techniques may be taken into consideration. To avoid creation and deployment of malicious program on controllers, additional tools for network device monitoring and anomalous activity detection may be useful. It is possible to employ oligarchic trust models with numerous certifying authorities for trust-anchors (e.g., one for each sub-domain or controller instance). Another is using threshold cryptography to secure communication between controller replicas (where the switch needs at least n shares to receive a legitimate controller message).

DIFFERENT USE CASES OF 5G ENHANCED IOT

In this section various use cased of 5G have discussed.

Automobile

Automotive IoT focuses on integrating IoT technology into automotive systems to develop newer solutions and applications that make cars smarter and more intelligent so that drivers can travel efficiently, safely, and comfortably (Mishra et al., 2023, pp. 9000-9013). Autonomous cars rely highly on real time data from the proximity sensors and accordingly alter the speed and steering of the vehicle unlike professional licensed drivers who are accustomed to driving. This fast exchange of data through sensors can be facilitated by 5G networks. Autonomous vehicles can connect through a 5G network and communicate with each other. This communication can be between two vehicles, between vehicle and pedestrians or vehicles and the network. It creates a unified communicative vehicle in traffic management. Various applications of IoT and 5G are shown in Figure 2.

Manufacturing

On 5G networks, industrial equipment such as autonomous guided vehicles (AGVs) are employed. 5G networks' mobility management coverage and Quality of Service Assurance ensure dependable connectivity for a variety of guided vehicles, including tractors and forklifts. 5G can assist forklifts in moving more effectively and automatically on the floor (Millman, 2020). 5G and the Internet of Things will be critical in strengthening and enabling these manufacturing advancements. Manufacturers and telecom operators may employ 5G networks and Internet of Things (IoT) to build smart factories that incorporate technologies such as automation, artificial intelligence (AI), augmented reality (AR) for fine-tuning to collect information on real-time applications (Mishra et al., 2019, pp. 41-55).

Health Systems

The one industry where the use of IoT technology completely transformed treatment techniques and patient outcomes is the health care sector. Future 5G developments will be available to everyone in the nation, bringing cutting-edge technology to every home. In the healthcare industry, advancements include remote robot surgery and the provision of personalized medications based on data from wearable hospital health monitors for each individual. This technology will make it possible to get there and keep track of the other health issues.

High-quality video conversations via the 5g network enable remote doctor-patient contact. Wearable gadgets that monitor, diagnose, and treat illnesses are known as personal health systems (Land Millman, 2020). These gadgets will become more and more connected to the 5G network in order to monitor and analyze data in real time. This allows healthcare to transition from a treatment-based approach to a prevention-based one. The introduction of 5G in smart healthcare networks is thus a boon for IoT devices, since it improves network speed and expands cellular coverage, resulting in better patient care in the future.

Transport and Infrastructure

Fast mobility connectivity - 5G's signal strength allows for more mobility, allowing data to be sent through a device moving at high speeds. These can be employed in high-speed rail data transmission and autonomous drone data transfer (Mishra et al., 2023, pp. 9000-9013). Train sensors can detect unoccupied cabins and communicate the information to the station/platform, directing passengers to the empty compartments.

Thousands of IoT-based sensors can also be deployed over 5G networks across infrastructure such as large bridges. These sensors can also continuously measure the vibrations created by the automobiles and trains that pass beneath those bridges on a daily basis. Vibrations that are judged odd could be the first clue that the bridge isn't working properly. Actions may be made in response to the notification. Intelligent transport solutions to control the traffic flow, such as streetlights with cameras embedded in to monitor foot activity and divert vehicles during rush hours to prevent pedestrian accidents and ease traffic can be implemented. In this sector Mobility-as-a-service(MaaS) will be a key weapon.

It ensures that there is an integrated journey plan by minimizing the transportation industry. Government, private industries dealing with real estate or building managers all over the world can integrate IoT solutions and devices into their infrastructures in order to cut costs and enhance the quality of their buildings.

Figure 2. Various applications of IoT and 5G

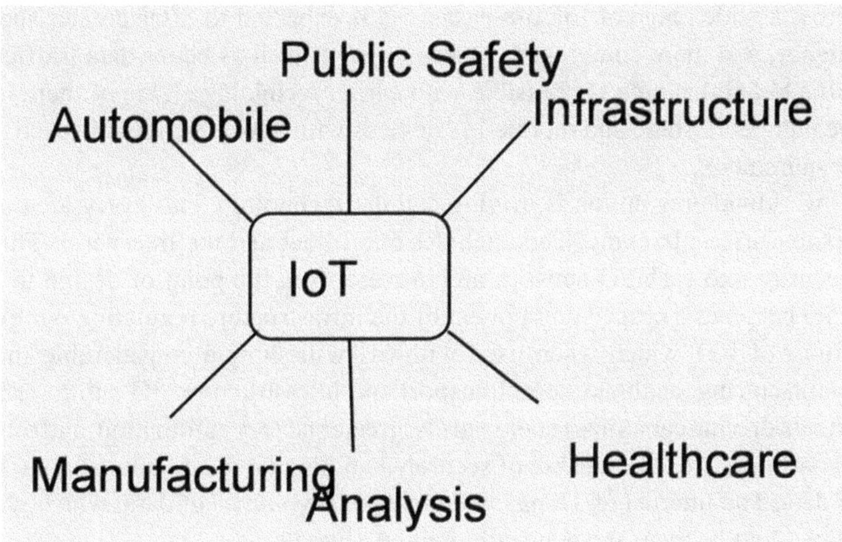

Oil Rig Production Analytics

The installation of IoT sensors in oil wells allows for production analysis on the rig. They are linked to 5G networks, which allow data to be sent and received in real time. This real-time sensor data from oil wells can be used to discover signals in the data and anticipate when the wells are not producing at their maximum capacity (Park et al. 2014). To achieve the size and speed required for future digital oilfield operations, upstream O&G players will require 5G network connectivity solutions to move enormous amounts of data in near real time with minimal latency.

Public Safety

In public safety, surveillance cameras, especially body worn cameras, broadcast real-time ultra-high resolution and 360-degree video feeds through 5g networks. These video feeds are relayed to a control room, which may monitor congested public spaces and critical infrastructure. The public-safety community will benefit greatly from the coming of 5G. 5G will enable widespread adoption of new public safety applications due to its faster speeds, increased capacity, ultra-low latencies, and advanced IoT compatibility. Remote-controlled gadgets, telemedicine in the field, increased situational awareness with drones, and video analytics to supplement mission-critical networks will be among them. Violence detection and crowd management are potential areas where we can see huge amount of 5G Iot applications.

CONCLUSION

5G will help unleash the full potential of IOT. The Interactions between IOT devices and humans will go to another level. On the way to reaching the IoT's promise, 5G will give a slew of advantages. The benefit of using a single 5G network is that it will be more efficient, cost-effective, and deliver economies of scale across a wide range of IoT use cases. 5G is expected to offer greater speeds of up to 10 Gbps, shorter latency, and more comprehensive coverage, as well as better data traffic security. There are several benefits to 5G that aren't accessible with earlier technology. One of them is 5G's potential to support a huge number of static and mobile IoT devices with a wide variety of speed, bandwidth, and service quality requirements.

A significant worldwide revolution is driving cellular technology into every area of our life, from electricity meters to car fleet tracking. This includes 5G rollout and the Internet of Things. It's crucial to incorporate security into each 5G network architecture from the point of design to installation and maintenance as 5G becomes a crucial component of the infrastructure regulating our everyday lives.

Few applications of IOT which when used with 5G will show a considerable improvement like automobiles, manufacturing, health system, transport and infrastructure. 5G's ultra-reliability and low latency might aid self-driving cars, smart energy grids, greater factory automation, and other sophisticated applications. 5G networks are also capable of securely handling large amounts of data. IoT devices will generate a lot of data. The Internet of Things will create vast volumes of data, which will require cloud computing, artificial intelligence, and edge computing to handle.

The necessity and need for safe, reliable, adaptable, and well-managed networks has been met by the development of the software-defined network. SDN is more open to attack than conventional networks, nevertheless, because of the separation of the two planes. This implies that network and control traffic's availability, consistency, authenticity, secrecy, and integrity may be severely compromised. To adapt to shifting corporate demands, server virtualization, mobility, and cloud computing are emerging as the new standard. The traditional network design is beginning to struggle to keep up with the growing needs of the network as new technologies developed. With the help of the SDN architecture, the current network may be virtualized to create platforms that are adaptable and programmable. Software-defined networking (SDN) will become the new standard for networks since networking depends more and more on it in the future. However, before the SDN can be implemented safely, a significant security risk involving the SDN controller and applications has to be addressed.

5G is embraced over the next several decades. We will benefit from smart cities that reduce waste, manage traffic data, and improve public transit and utilities. To administer treatments remotely, medical specialists will use very accurate augmented reality technology. Smart grids will improve energy production, tracking, and monitoring efficiency while also helping to protect the environment. All industries would be affected, from agriculture to retail. While at one hand we see all the applications of 5G Iot in various fields, we need to keep in mind the challenges they bring when it comes to implementation of the same.

REFERENCES

Bhoi, S. K., Panda, S. K., Jena, K. K., Sahoo, K. S., Jhanjhi, N. Z., Masud, M., & Aljahdali, S. (2022). IoT-EMS: An Internet of Things Based Environment Monitoring System in Volunteer Computing Environment. *Intelligent Automation & Soft Computing, 32*(3).

Din, S., Rathore, M. M., Ahmad, A., Paul, A., & Khan, M. (2017, October). Sdiot: Software defined internet of thing to analyze big data in smart cities. In *2017 IEEE 42nd Conference on Local Computer Networks Workshops (LCN Workshops)* (pp. 175-182). IEEE.

Hassija, V., Chamola, V., Saxena, V., Jain, D., Goyal, P., & Sikdar, B. (2019). A survey on IoT security: Application areas, security threats, and solution architectures. *IEEE Access : Practical Innovations, Open Solutions*, *7*, 82721–82743. doi:10.1109/ACCESS.2019.2924045

Hussain, M. W., Khan, M. S., Reddy, K. H. K., & Roy, D. S. (2022). Extended indirect controller-legacy switch forwarding for link discovery in hybrid multi-controller SDN. *Computer Communications*, *189*, 148–157. doi:10.1016/j.comcom.2022.03.017

Hussain, M. W., Reddy, K. H. K., Rodrigues, J. J., & Roy, D. S. (2020). An indirect controller-legacy switch forwarding scheme for link discovery in hybrid SDN. *IEEE Systems Journal*, *15*(2), 3142–3149. doi:10.1109/JSYST.2020.3011902

Jain, D., Krishna, P. V., & Saritha, V. (2012). A study on Internet of Things based applications. *arXiv preprint arXiv:1206.3891.*

Kreutz, D., Ramos, F. M., & Verissimo, P. (2013, August). Towards secure and dependable software-defined networks. In *Proceedings of the second ACM SIGCOMM workshop on Hot topics in software defined networking* (pp. 55-60). ACM. 10.1145/2491185.2491199

Kumar, S., Tiwari, P., & Zymbler, M. (2019). Internet of Things is a revolutionary approach for future technology enhancement: A review. *Journal of Big Data*, *6*(1), 1–21. doi:10.118640537-019-0268-2

Land, Millman (2020). The Future Of Telecommunications: What Is Millimeter Wave Technology? | Millman National Land Services. *Millman Land, millmanland.com.*

Minoli, D., & Occhiogrosso, B. (2019). Practical aspects for the integration of 5G networks and IoT applications in smart cities environments. *Wireless Communications and Mobile Computing*, *2019*, 2019. doi:10.1155/2019/5710834

Mishra, T. K., Sahoo, K. S., Bilal, M., Shah, S. C., & Mishra, M. K. (2023). Adaptive Congestion Control Mechanism to Enhance TCP Performance in Cooperative IoV. *IEEE Access : Practical Innovations, Open Solutions*, *11*, 9000–9013. doi:10.1109/ACCESS.2023.3239302

Mishra, T. K., & Tripathi, S. (2019). Minimizing End-to-End Delay on Real-Time Applications. *Wireless Personal Communications*, *107*(1), 41–55. doi:10.100711277-019-06239-8

Park, S. M., Ju, S., & Lee, J. (2014). Efficient routing for traffic offloading in Software-defined Network. *Procedia Computer Science*, *34*, 674–679. doi:10.1016/j.procs.2014.07.096

Renuka, K., Roy, D. S., & Reddy, K. H. K. (2021). An SDN empowered location aware routing for energy efficient next generation vehicular networks. *IET Intelligent Transport Systems*, *15*(2), 308–319. doi:10.1049/itr2.12026

Tadros, C. N., Rizk, M. R., & Mokhtar, B. M. (2020). Software defined network-based management for enhanced 5G network services. *IEEE Access : Practical Innovations, Open Solutions*, *8*, 53997–54008. doi:10.1109/ACCESS.2020.2980392

Yilmaz, T., Gokkoca, G., & Akan, O. B. (2016). Millimetre wave communication for 5G IoT applications. In *Internet of Things (IoT) in 5G Mobile Technologies* (pp. 37–53). Springer International Publishing. doi:10.1007/978-3-319-30913-2_3

Chapter 9
Traffic Management of SDN/NFV-Based Smart 5G Networks Using Time Series Analysis

Deva Priya Isravel
Karunya Institute of Technology and Sciences, India

Salaja Silas
Karunya Institute of Technology and Sciences, India

Elijah Blessing Rajsingh
Karunya Institute of Technology and Sciences, India

ABSTRACT

Traffic in the 5G network is growing exponentially and is predictable to grow in the future. Providing a high quality of service with ever-increasing traffic volumes is challenging in 5G networks. Software defined networking (SDN) along with emerging cloud technologies plays a significant responsibility in enhancing the performance of 5G networks. The 5G SDN paradigm is designed to support real-time and latency-sensitive applications. This chapter aims to summarize the existing technologies, benefits, and challenges of the 5G network. Also, a novel multivariate traffic analysis framework using time series analysis is proposed to enhance traffic management and its performance. Evaluation is performed on open traffic flow datasets and the analysis results show that the proposed framework performs better despite the inherent uncertainty in terms of classification and forecast accuracy.

INTRODUCTION

Technology has changed the way devices are connected and communicate with each other. The rapidly evolving Internet and extensively used cloud services have caused an increase in wireless data traffic (Ghafoor et al., 2022). A new network technology called 5G has the potential to provide ultra-high speeds, low latency, and high-reliable smart services. 5G technology has increased bandwidth, allowing it to seamlessly transfer data, thus improving the connectivity among devices and overall user experience

DOI: 10.4018/979-8-3693-0744-1.ch009

(El-Shorbagy, 2021), (Mendonça et al., 2022). For years, Internet service providers, cellular operators and global telecom operators have been planning to implement and use 5G technologies to have easy accessibility and feasible operations. 5G technology works faster on cellular devices than 4G and 4G LTE. 5G technology is the best option for connecting a wide range of gadgets, including drones and sensors.

There are numerous opportunities as 5G can facilitate the adoption of IoT in industries, helping them improve their productivity, streamline operations and other factors. As there is a wide range of user preferences with customers, the applications of 5G networks require services to be offered on demand in real-time. Handling emergencies and managing network traffic during peak hours is highly challenging and demanding due to the need for multiple services. High demand for services can lead to heavy traffic and restrict access to facilities owned by service providers. As 5G support multiple use cases with various integrated network applications, such as e-health, autonomous driving, the delivery of multimedia content, the Internet of Things (IoT), or machine-to-machine communication, generates a variety of needs that are difficult for a single technology to satisfy.

Therefore, the successful implementation of 5G networks depends on the architecture that can offer flexibility, automation, reconfigurability, and programmability to serve, with fine granularity, a broad and heterogeneous collection of 5G use cases. The key component to designing an efficient 5G network is to incorporate Software defined networking (SDN) (Silva et al., 2021). SDN aims to increase the flexibility and agility of networks by allowing network control to be programmed and abstraction of the underlying infrastructure for applications and network services (Hussain et al., 2021). The software defined infrastructure may boost the flexibility and responsiveness of service providers to user needs by enabling intelligent network services. A smart architecture for network programmability and the construction of different network hierarchies, in particular, will be made available by 5G SDN (Blanco et al., 2017). SDN based 5G networks support the necessary adaptability to change and adapt in response to the constantly shifting network situation.

The separation of the control plane from the data forwarding plane has been successfully implemented with Network Function Virtualization (NFV) by efficient isolation of the abstraction of capabilities from the hardware. NFV effectively extracts network activities and implements them in software. Hence NFV is a highly complementary technology to SDN. NFV enables network operations, such as routing choices, upgrades, resource allocation, etc. to be carried out in the cloud or remote servers and isolated from local devices. 5G networks have to manage dynamic traffic patterns, multi-tenancy, and heterogeneous and strict traffic needs. Network operators must manage Virtual Network Functions in 5G networks, which have different requirements and must dynamically adapt/ reconfigure in response to demand. SDN allows the network operators to handle all networking processes through reprogramming with increased flexibility and reduced deployment and operational costs.

As traffic management tasks are influenced heavily by information about the network traffic flow, there is growing interest in using time series data with multivariate analysis. Multivariate analysis analyses the traffic flow in 5G networks to optimize the performance of the network since traffic learning and prediction produce many useful results that aid in strategizing traffic management policies. The multivariate analysis enables a detailed study of the data by taking into account all potential parameters. Network operators can obtain new insights, increase efficiency, decide on policies and procedures, fix errors, and forecast future results with the aid of multivariate analysis. Multivariate analysis has the benefit of providing a more accurate forecast than univariate analysis by comparing the statistical correlations between various parameters and taking advantage of past traffic patterns by predicting the type and frequency of future traffic. The proposed technique aims to better comprehend the traffic's nature and the intensity of packet arrivals and discover the hidden traffic pattern in traffic traces of 5G networks. This chapter highlights a novel traffic forecasting framework to broaden the potential of SDN based 5G networks for varied applications. The prior knowledge of traffic flow features can be exploited to design a flow analyzer that can efficiently classify flows and provide multi-step forecasts by achieving low forecast errors. Moreover, the chapter presents a multivariate framework for handling dynamic flows in real time. The capabilities of SDN are incorporated for enhanced traffic management in 5G networks. Finally, it is demonstrated that the multivariate model is reliable due to the choice of flow features selected by the SVD of the MSSA forecast. The contribution of this chapter is as follows

- To present a systematic analysis of the existing techniques for efficient traffic management in 5G networks.
- To investigate network softwarization technologies that support quality of experience in real-life 5G networks.
- To analyze 5G application use cases to derive and classify the requirements to design traffic management of 5G networks.
- To propose and design a novel multivariate traffic analysis framework for SDN/NFV based 5G networks to handle massive traffic flows.
- To evaluate the different time series analysis techniques to monitor for significant traffic variations and provide fast and reliable analysis of 5G network traffic.
- Further, the chapter highlights the potential research challenges in 5G networks.

The rest of the chapter is structured as follows. Section 2 details the SDN/NFV technologies and SDN based 5G applications and highlights the benefits and challenges in 5G networks. Section 3 presents the related works on network softwarization technologies and traffic management techniques. Section 4 includes the system overview of the proposed multivariate traffic analysis framework and elaborates on the flow analyzer. The result analysis of the proposed framework is presented in section 5. Section 6 concludes the chapter.

SDN/NFV ENABLED 5G APPLICATIONS

The development and deployment of 5G networks have been revolutionized by advanced technologies such as cloud computing, IoT and AI/ML. The growth of smart 5G networks has been made possible through these advanced technologies. 5G is a major change in today's world and is beneficial in all industries, with smart grids, autonomous vehicles, AI-enabled smart homes and smart healthcare systems. With its high bandwidth capabilities, dependability, secure connectivity and correct trade-offs, 5G will launch a new, enormous IoT ecosystem where the network can support billions of linked devices. This high-bandwidth cellular technology is ready to have an impact as 5G is deployed globally. Several 5G-based SDN architectures have been proposed in the existing literature to support a wide variety of applications. Figure 1 depicts the most common application of SDN based 5G. The following are a few of the most prevalent application areas that have adopted the SDN/NFV for 5G networks.

5G in Agriculture

SDN/NFV-based smart 5G networks have the potential to significantly affect agricultural output since it allows for faster data transmission between sensors, machines, and people. The management of enormous volumes of data in real-time is the primary prerequisite for smart agricultural applications. Also, wireless communication systems with IoT devices for precision agriculture should have low power requirements, extended ranges, high-density connections and inexpensive costs (Y. Tang et al., 2021). 5G ecosystem facilitates by providing farmers with the information they need to make smart business decisions, increase food production and reduce the use of resources, such as water, grain, fertilizer, and pesticides to reduce runoff and soil erosion, increase operational efficiency, and improve product distribution (Van Hilten & Wolfert, 2022), (Lin, 2020). IoT sensors and devices are deployed for multiple purposes ranging from irrigation systems to soil and livestock production. Farmers can better measure things daily with the help of agricultural IoT devices. Some of the operations include sensors reporting the present and expected weather patterns, moisture, fertilization, and nutrition levels of the crops, animal analyses by observing the nutritional status and maturity of cattle, etc.

The technologies used for data communication include RFID, Bluetooth, Ultrawideband, ZigBee and Wi-Fi. To cover long distances, technologies such as 2G/3G/4G/5G, LoRa and NB-IoT. As Low Power Wide Area (LPWA) technologies such as LoRa and NB-IoT are capable to cover wide distances with fewer data transfers and low energy consumption, it is widely used in smart agriculture (Feng et al., 2019). Open field sensors with minimal power requirements, extensive coverage, and low to medium data transfers are well suited for LPWA technology. Therefore, extending 5G improves IoT systems based on SDN and NFV. The 5G-enabled edge computing improves smart farming by providing access to real-time data on weather, crops, irrigation, animals, etc. It also aids in improving the monitoring of agricultural activities, food quality control, and waste management and assists in the establishment of a fully functional autonomous farm.

Figure 1. Real-World Applications of SDN based 5G

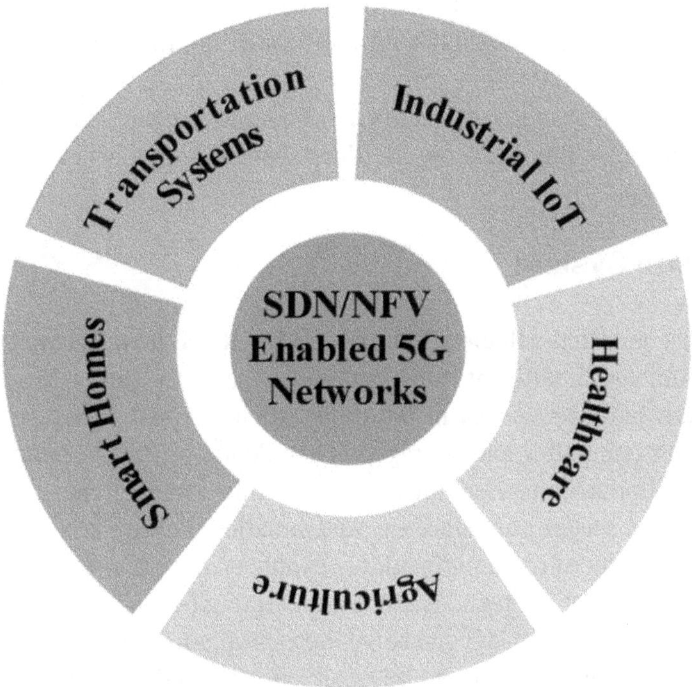

5G in Industrial IoT (IIoT)

Modern Industrial production and manufacturing systems have been driven by digital connectivity, self-automated devices and decentralized resources. IIoT is a subset of IoT that demands higher levels of safety, security, and dependable connectivity without interfering with real-time industrial activities. Due to high maintenance costs and lack of flexibility in mobility, wired connections are not widely preferred. Also, wireless technologies such as Bluetooth, RFID, IR, NFC, ZigBee, and Wi-Fi cannot satisfy the requirements of timely delivery, mobility, availability and scalability. To provide the desired flexibility, connectivity, and simple reconfigurability, Ethernet and other wired technologies must be replaced with wireless (Longo et al., 2021). Therefore, the 5G cellular system is the most appropriate technology for an Industrial network. 5G technology engineered by extremely low latency, faster speeds, and high reliability is a huge transition for Industry 4.0. To build a robust, reliable and flexible IIoT system, SDN based 5G network can obtain tremendous improvements in performance and tap into edge computing. Research focuses on the fields of IIoT designs and frameworks, communication protocols, and data management techniques

A SELFNET architecture enabled by SDN/NFV was proposed to support self-manageable 5G networks and achieve the quality of service and user experience (Neves et al., 2017a). A framework with self-optimization, self-healing and self-protection was developed. SDN has the potential for significantly improved security, simpler mobility, streamlined cross-organizational collaboration, and relatively straightforward support for existing assets and systems. To give clients access to remote resources, like computing and storage activities in the IIoT, cloud infrastructure exchanges confidential information.

For smart IIoT applications, a distributed structure will increase the speed and reliability of physical and logical data on cloud infrastructure. To increase the security, solitude, and secrecy of the current architecture, a distributed SDN-BC method with the benefit of smart IIoT was proposed (Rahman et al., 2022). It used a distributed SDN-BC approach to enhance the security, privacy, and secrecy of the provided architecture using the resource of smart IIoT. To build a secure 5G-driven network and provide security solutions, several machine learning and deep learning approaches are used in industrial IoT (Sharma et al., 2021).

5G in Transportation System

The next generation of connected vehicles is supported by 5G cellular networks. Cities with 5G connectivity will have automated, intelligent transportation systems that are safe and more efficient. This addresses the major transportation issues in big cities, such as traffic congestion, pollution, tracking parking availability, long commutes and outrageous accidents. Multiple challenges exist in vehicular applications to meet the application needs of intelligent traffic management, spatial information networks in terms of coverage, space-time reference, and situational awareness (Ji et al., 2020). Assessing 5G capabilities with the impact of roaming/handover events on the provision of timely, continuous, and seamless services in cross-border contexts, is still a challenging task (Santa et al., 2022). By enabling a fully intelligent transportation system, 5G can solve these problems. Several performance problems and difficulties in the vehicular environment can be resolved with SDN and 5G mobile communications. Demand for 5G mobile communications, cloud computing, and SDN technologies for vehicular networks has arisen with the advent of driverless cars (Din et al., 2019).

The transportation system connected with the cloud collects and analyses real-time data from linked devices, infrastructure and vehicles. From the analysis, enhanced decision-making, improved navigation, fuel efficiency maximization and time resources can be accomplished. Significant changes such as traffic information, automated driving, improved traffic flow, road safety and intelligent navigation can be achieved.

Modern automobiles have recently evolved into a sensor platform that broadcasts and receives information from their environment. Advanced safety applications focus to provide easy access to emergency vehicles, higher traffic efficiency and decreasing human error leading to reduced traffic accidents. These applications need a coordinated framework, nevertheless, with capabilities that allow extremely low latency for alert signals, increased data rates for sensor data exchange between cars and infrastructure, high mobility, high dependability, and scalability. An efficient and integrated transportation system is created with advanced transmission and sensing technology. To process and control smart transportation accurately and in real-time, advanced electronic control, and computer processing technology is essential. The traffic management center can implement automated vehicle detection, remote command and vehicle dispatch.

Smart Home

A smart home refers to a place of living with smart technology that offers residents cutting-edge amenities. To make life easier and more simple for homeowners, smart home gadgets including smart TVs, lighting systems, smart security locks and surveillance cameras, household appliances, and home medical devices are connected to the internet (Ben Azzouz & Jamai, 2019), (Isravel et al., 2020). The home area network is faced with several difficulties due to the exponential increase of divergent connected devices and the rise in home user application needs like gaming, video streaming, e-health, etc. Several studies suggested diversifying the home area network design by including techniques like network function virtualization and network slicing. The diversity of the home application makes management and control complex. Therefore, incorporating these techniques have additional advantages, such as raising the quality of service quality, network control and management.

Smart home applications are increasingly becoming complex with heterogeneous types of device connections with huge traffic volumes. Residential IoT devices demand different communication technologies for data transmission. To offer multiple services to customer premises, SDN/NFV capabilities are incorporated in the IoT gateway to manage the hardware from different vendors (Garcia Hernando et al., 2017). To handle the voluminous data generated from the IoT devices, a three-level architecture was proposed with the Hadoop ecosystem (Khan et al., 2018). The proposed architecture gathers data from the attached sensors and the load was balanced with the Hadoop ecosystem. To support a complex IoT system with self-powered sensors, and wearable devices with multifunctionality, an IoT system was proposed using 5G communication with AI technologies (Dong et al., 2021) and ensures high performances in terms of data acquisition, analysis and transmission. The architecture explores the 5G smart home with AI was able to improve the performance and sustainability of the system.

Smart Healthcare

The traditional fixed physician-focused approach to healthcare is being drastically replaced by a dynamic and distributed patient-focused approach. This quick transition in the healthcare industry is being driven by the emergence of various emerging technologies, such IoT and 5G, which efficiently and accurately deliver individualized and remote medical services. Pervasive healthcare applications are made possible by the dynamic nature of wireless communications and the mobility of IoT-connected devices via 5G networks.

It is essential to secure the IoT-5G devices and make confidential information inaccessible to snoopers and other unauthorized parties. Because existing cryptographic methods are not reliable, the attackers can compromise the authenticity of lightweight wearable and medical devices. The heterogeneous technologies that are used, their poor time efficiency and excessive computing complexity (Sodhro et al., 2022) make the systems weaker and more vulnerable. An SDN based multi-RANs architecture (Fu et al., 2017) was proposed to increase the packet transmission rate and achieve parallel utilization of RAN channels. The proposed method performed manual authentication and encrypted key transmission across RAN devices.

An SDN/NFV-enabled architecture for eHealth scenarios was proposed (Celdrán et al., 2019) to support multimedia services for remote healthcare assistance. The proposed policy-based system defines the policies to control the network and orchestrates the resources dynamically. To monitor the health-related information of patients from wireless body area networks, a novel SDWAN framework was developed (Hasan et al., 2020). The framework included a Sector-based distance (SBD) routing function to prioritize the emergency data using a classification algorithm and routes them with reduced latency and improved packet delivery ratio.

Benefits and Challenges in 5G Networks

The advent of 5G networks plays a crucial role in many applications. With 5G a huge number of heterogeneous devices can operate autonomously and intelligently with seamless connections. Wireless networks of 5G are anticipated to manage a significant amount of data generated by a variety of devices, including smartphones, autonomous vehicles, smart cities, smart buildings, and infrastructure. People increasingly rely on a variety of access points to use network-based services and applications, and their sensitive personal data is kept on servers spread across the network. As 5G provides numerous benefits, the functioning of critical future technologies related to national security and public safety, such as driverless vehicles, smart grids, and emergency systems relies on network-based processing and data management. Figure 2 summarizes the various benefits of 5G networks.

Figure 2. Benefits of 5G technology

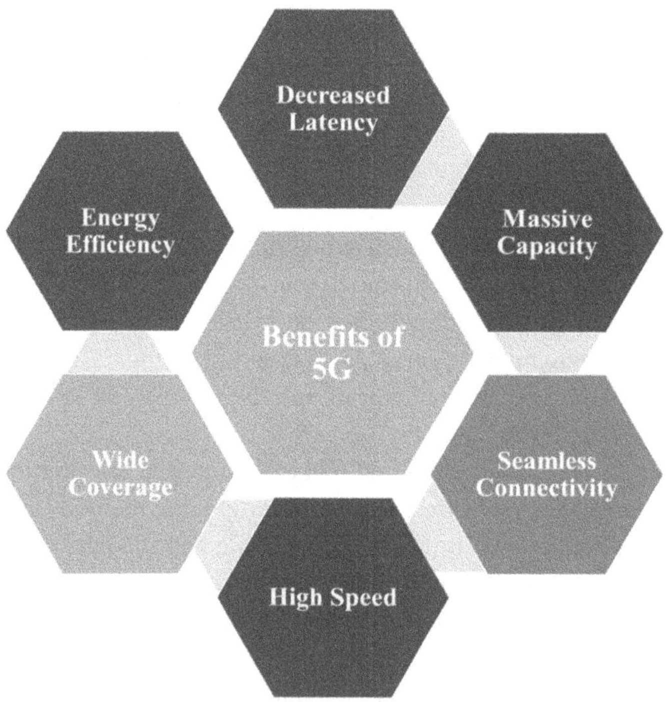

There are several challenges faced by 5G networks concerning security, reliability, latency, heterogeneity, etc (Velasquez et al., 2022). The major challenges are listed below.

- As the devices are diverse in nature, with various traffic and mobility patterns, energy needs, and computing capabilities, the management of these devices is difficult in heterogeneous situations.
- Infrastructure updates enable high speeds connectivity with low latency. But deploying high-quality 5G networks and upgrading end-user devices requires additional investment and is expensive.
- The planning of network resources and customer services have been made more difficult necessitating more distributed and AI-driven autonomous management and orchestration.

- The density of the devices in 5G has increased tremendously. The rise in device-to-device connections and mesh networks enables attackers to have a greater chance to engage in malicious behavior when there are more vulnerable devices.
- To guarantee security, technologies such as intrusion detection and blockchain are integrated into the 5G network. Despite these measures, attackers take advantage of their decentralized nature and interdependencies.
- Service isolation and automated deployment are the advantages of Network slices. However, to meet appropriate Service Level Agreement (SLA) and performance requirements, VNF and Physical Network Function (PNF) must be tailored to share among different users.

RELATED WORKS

In this section, the most relevant approaches that have focussed on (1) network softwarization technologies available for 5G networks and (2) state-of-the-art traffic management techniques are presented in detail to provide insight into how SDN based 5G networks are adopted to achieve flexibility and programmability is discussed.

Network Softwarization Technologies

First, the approaches available for 5G networks from the literature are elucidated. Technology advancements that will change the foundation of mobile communication networks underpin the 5G network (Mitra & Agrawal, 2015). By offering an entirely new network architecture, 5G will make it possible for a variety of application scenarios.

The industry anticipates that 5G will be the network where various applications and services will be automatically serviced by a highly integrated and configurable network (Neves et al., 2017b). New technologies such as Artificial Intelligence (AI), Cloud Computing, Multi-Access Edge Computing (MEC), and softwarization technologies like Software Defined Networking (SDN), Network Function Virtualization (NFV), Virtual Network Function (VNF) and Network slicing are crucial in enabling and popularising immersive solutions (Gohar & Nencioni, 2021), (Golkarifard et al., 2021). MEC is an essential architecture for applications that require decision-making and performance enhancement to be available at the edge of the network in real-time. Network latency can be decreased by processing data locally by using MEC. NFV employs virtualization technologies to implement various network functions, whereas SDN is a networking architecture that allows networks to be programmed. The SDN-based system is centrally controlled with open interfaces between each layer allow for programmability, which enhances the system's flexibility and efficiency. Flexibility in smart 5G networks can be achieved through the two complementary technologies such as softwarization and virtualization (Condoluci & Mahmoodi, 2018).

The software-based implementation of network functions, known as VNF, may include one or more virtual machines. Infrastructure for network function virtualization covers all the hardware and software elements that go into creating the setting in which VNFs are used. Networks should be able to take advantage of the combined advantages of SDN networking and network virtualization once SDN networks are virtualized. An SDN hypervisor, which isolates the underlying physical SDN network into numerous conceptually independent virtual SDN (vSDNs), is a crucial component for virtualizing SDN networks (Blenk et al., 2016) with its controller. Running and adding on-demand VNFs is possible with cloud-based environments. SDN controller can dynamically change the network topology as per the load and service requirements.

Users will just need to request the services they require in the 5G era, and the information will be sent to the location and device of their choice. Application providers that do not have physical network infrastructure can apply network slicing (Barakabitze et al., 2020). The 5G network slicing can provide radio, cloud, and networking services. Automation enables dynamic management of network slices throughout their lifecycle resource optimization for networks as well as a dynamic interaction between the management and data planes. Using SDN, which separates the data and control planes, slice customization is made possible at all layers of the abstracted network topology. Network slicing ensures performance guarantees and security.

5G networks are key in enabling multimedia services and applications with high data rates, minimal latency and high-density connectivity (Barakabitze & Walshe, 2022). To manage emerging multimedia services and to address the QoE application requirements in 5G networks, QoE-aware SDN/NFV architecture was proposed in (Barakabitze et al., 2019). The softwarized architecture was responsible for the orchestration and communication of devices across the cloud and user-mobile terminals. The architecture aimed to speed up the delivery of multimedia services with optimized and improved QoE.

Traffic Management Techniques

A surge of new applications with mobile connectivity and a consequent exponential increase in network traffic has been produced by the extensive of mobile communication networks and new types of mobile devices such as smartphones and tablets. Over the next few decades, the volume of mobile and wireless traffic is predicted to expand driven by the anticipated billions of connected devices that will be connected to the cloud (Gupta & Jha, 2015).

It is essential to manage network traffic flow while upholding a high degree of user experience given the growing variety of 5G networks, including the usage of diverse devices with dynamic traffic flow behaviors. On the other hand, managing traffic and preserving QoS performance in 5G networks is more difficult than ever due to the constantly growing data traffic in those networks. Traffic flow management becomes complex and challenging due to the dynamic nature of heterogeneous traffic flows. The explosion of global internet 5G data traffic demands more effective traffic management to address the backhaul congestion and ensure QoS for consumers.

Real-time and non-real-time traffic are the two categories of traffic kinds at the application level. These two forms of traffic differ in their flow characteristics, including packet arrival rate, service time, and other factors. There is an unregulated increase in traffic flows due to real-time and non-real-time applications operating in extremely dense 5G networks (Özçevik et al., 2017). As a result, forwarding device queues take a longer time to process and route the traffic. Additionally, in this situation, the traffic type heterogeneity rate has a considerable impact on the waiting time for each packet to transmit and significantly affects end-to-end latency. To address this latency an e2edelay framework with an optimization algorithm based on SDN was proposed.

A new SDN architecture named SoftAir was proposed for wireless 5G cellular networks (Akyildiz et al., 2015) to support increasing traffic and varying traffic patterns and to maximize the network capacity and coverage. SoftAir provided a robust SD controller that supported mobility-aware traffic engineering for balancing traffic. The adaptive controller placement and optimal path computation was performed.

The 5G networks have been greatly improved by network data analytics. This aids in supporting the high data rates, it is an important component of the 5G network. Network operators have been evaluating the network data effectively using machine learning and deep learning techniques in the 5G service-based architecture (Haider et al., 2023; Pradhan et al., 2022). To understand and analyze the behavior of traffic, a network data analytics function (NWDAF) was proposed for 5G networks (Sevgican et al., 2020). NWDAF employed any ML models and network load measurements that are essential for network quality and sustainability are predicted.

A QoS flow model that provides a QoS MAC scheduler that can categorize eXtended Reality applications traffic of 5G New Radio based on QoS indicators was proposed (Koutlia et al., 2023). Various traffic flows are classified based on QoS profiles and resources are assigned accordingly to each type of traffic. Based on the QoS indicators, the scheduler was able to classify the traffic flows.

As large-scale networks might have traffic variations that directly translate into varying traffic quantities that must be handled by various controllers in the control plane, response time is increased affecting flows of the data plane (Hussain et al., 2022). To address this, a forecast model using multi-step ARIMA was proposed to guarantee load balancing between controllers (Filali et al., 2019). Based on the load anticipated, migration is scheduled in advance. The forecast model was enabled to reduce congestion and controller response time. Since the ARIMA model analysis is based on a single parameter of the time series data, the more complex and intricate behavior cannot be understood. However, as the multivariate analysis considers more than one flow feature, the forecast is accurate with less error.

PROPOSED FRAMEWORK

System Overview

The proposed multivariate analysis for flow classification and forecasting is configured on the SDN controller. The framework of the proposed SDN based architecture for 5G networks is shown in Figure 3. The proposed architecture has two main functions. The flow analyzer module of the controller has the classifier and forecasting model for predicting future flows. The SDN based framework provides statistics on the traffic flows using multivariate analysis. The SDN controller makes routing decisions and schedules traffic upon the forecast made from the flow information. The control plane configures the infrastructure plane devices.

The controller application is run by an SDN controller that is logically centralized and has a global perspective. The control plane prepares the critical calculations of the pathways traveled by the packets and schedules the flows optimally. The source sends a flow request with the destination details and a time stamp indicating when it is transmitting and when a new flow has to be scheduled. The controller modifies the switch's flow table to route the flow based on the forecast information received from the flow analyzer. The flow analyzer aid in detecting massive flows and thereby balance the load on multiple paths that has sufficient bandwidth resources. The massive flows are long-lived flows that have a high traffic volume greater than 1Gbps/10 seconds. These flows fill the network buffers and contribute to queuing delay and latency. The forwarding device determines the size of a packet when it receives one as part of a data flow. If the packet size exceeds a threshold size, the forwarding device then identifies that the packet's data flow is an elephant flow as its size is higher. If the size is not bigger, the packet is processed and routed by the forward devices normally without requiring any additional processing (F.

Tang et al., 2019). In certain forwarding device implementations, the packet sizes connected to one or more flow entries in its flow table are examined to identify as long or short-lived flows. Some implementations treat the identified long flows differently from the normal flows.

Figure 3. SDN based architecture for 5G networks

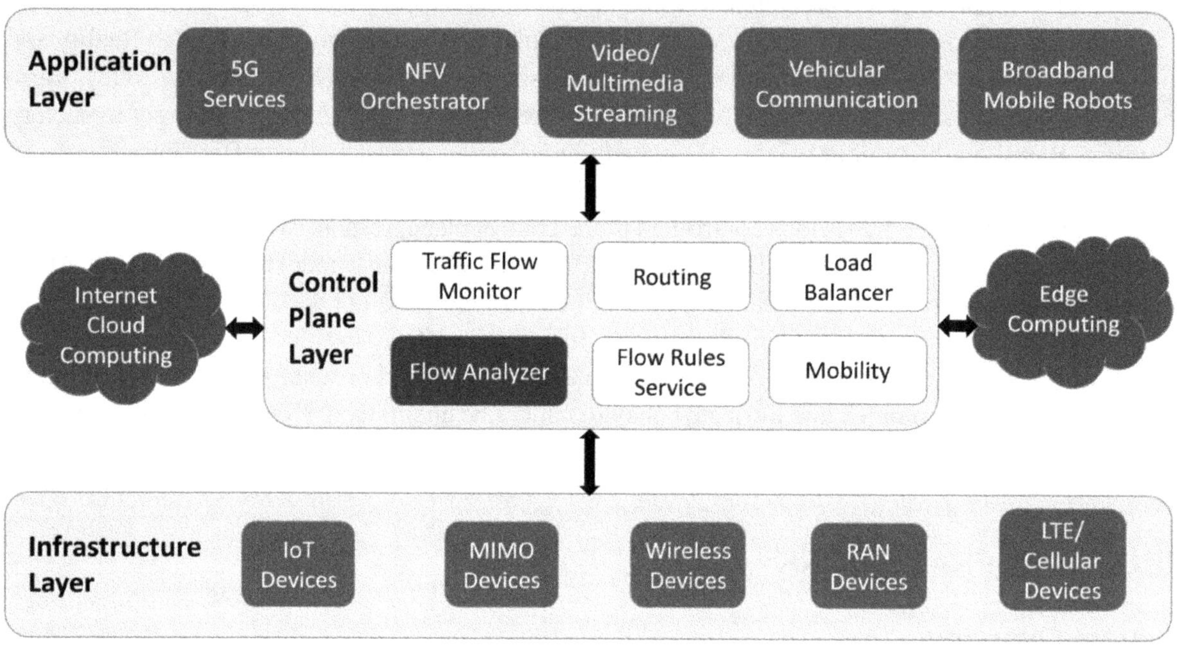

The flow-based dataset is created using the application layer payload data. Each application's payload data from the application layer includes a random selection of the flow-based learning dataset. The first N packets in the relevant flow make up a sequence of one chosen flow-based data. Path change forecasting helps enhance local node routing.

Flow Analyzer Algorithm

The two main functions of the flow analyzer are flow classification and forecasting. Multivariate network and flow features are taken as input by the analyzer module. The steps of the flow analyzer are summarized in Table 1. The multivariate classification takes multiple data attributes to understand the relationship between the variables. The feature selector and data processing in the classifier generates the training dataset. The multi-layer model learning process and parameter tuning of the models both use the generated dataset. The flow classifier uses the trained model to categorize network traffic. The performance of the classifier is measured in terms of accuracy metrics and error estimations. The categorization result is used by the SDN controller to construct the proper flow rules by following each application's QoS or scheduling policy.

To predict future flows, a Multivariate Singular Spectrum Analysis (MSSA) is used. The goal of MSSA is to break down the original series into a handful of distinct, comprehensible elements, such as a slowly changing trend, oscillatory elements, and random noise (Hassani et al., 2013), (Isravel et al., 2022). MSSA is a very helpful tool to address issues such as finding structure from time series, identifying change points and extracting seasonality components. MSSA assists in extracting complicated trends and periodicities simultaneously. In the embedding step all the original time series D = $\{ft_1, ft_2, \ldots, ft_N\}$ is mapped onto a multidimensional matrix called trajectory matrix *Y*. Assume an integer number called window length *L*, such that $K=N-L+1$ and $2<L<N/2$. The value of *L* should not exceed N/2. It is also called embedding dimensions. The trajectory matrix *Y* is computed by decomposing ft_N into lagged vectors.

$$Y = \begin{bmatrix} ft_1 & \cdots & ft_K \\ \vdots & \ddots & \vdots \\ ft_L & \cdots & ft_N \end{bmatrix}$$

The columns of the trajectory matrix is a transposed lagged vectors whose elements along the diagonal are equal. The resultant matrix has a Hankel structure. Singular Value Decomposition is computed from the trajectory matrix by computing $Y=UDV^T$, where U and V are left and right singular matrices respectively are orthogonal and *D* represents a diagonal matrix with singular eigenvalues. $Y= Em_1+Em_2+\ldots+Em_r$ are the elementary matrices of Y_i constructed from SVD such that $r=\max(i|\lambda i_>0)$ and $Em_i\sqrt{\lambda_i}U_iV_i^T$. The elementary matrices of Y_i are partitioned into $Y_1, Y_2, \ldots, Y_m$ into *m* disjoint subset with indices $\{1,\ldots,r\}$.

In the grouping stage, the matrices in each group are summed such that time series components are $Y_{I1}, Y_{I2}, \ldots, Y_{Im}$. The diagonal averaging reconstructs the time series by performing de-hankelization. The reconstructed trajectory matrix $Y' = \sum_{i=0}^{L-1} Y'_i$. From the reconstructed time series linear recurrent forecasting is evaluated. The linear combination of $L-1$ are values of reconstructed time series Y' are considered for the forecast future flows. The suitable values of the two parameters window length *L* and reconstruction component *r* are selected to achieve improved results.

Table 1. Steps of flow analyzer algorithm

Flow Analyzer Algorithm
Input:
• D = $\{ft_1, ft_2, \ldots, ft_N\}$ //N time series length
Output:
• Classified flows
• Multi-step forecast
Setups:
1. Prepare the captured flow traces for analysis by data preprocessing.
2. Identify the important flow features.
3. Choose the time series data samples to avoid processing overhead.
4. Create the training and testing sets from the time series samples.
5. Train the classifier networks with the training dataset.
6. Assess the classifier results with a 10-fold cross-validation strategy.
7. Error estimates and classification accuracy results are analyzed.
8. Classification outcome is used to make routing decisions by the SDN controller.
9. Apply MSSA forecasting
i. Use the embedding process to construct the trajectory matrix Y.
ii. Specify the window length L and define the trajectory matrix Y.
iii. Compute SVD $Y=UDV^T$ to represent the dataset matrix with a smaller dimension matrix $Y = Em_1 + Em_2 + \ldots + Em_r$.
iv. Define the separable groups of matrices $Y_{I1}, Y_{I2}, \ldots, Y_{Im}$.
v. Reconstruct the matrix using diagonal averaging $Y' = \sum_{i=0}^{L-1} Y'_i$.
vi. From the resultant matrix, the linear recurrent forecasting is measured for multistep ahead.
vii. Forecast performance and forecast errors are estimated.
10. Forecast information is used to allocate resources to future flows by the SDN controller.

The forecast data is used by the controller to load balance the traffic dynamically and find an optimal path with sufficient bandwidth for routing the traffic during network congestion. Knowing the flow forecast and its characteristics enable the controller to efficiently utilize the bandwidth.

RESULT ANALYSIS

The proposed framework for 5G traffic flow analysis is tested and validated with the data taken from the 5G trace production dataset collected from the mobile operator. The dataset contains samples from two mobility patterns namely static and driving (Raca et al., 2020). The dataset collected from static and mobile networks is analyzed to understand flow pattern behavior. The features of the dataset include context-related, channel-related, cell-related and throughput information. In each time series data, flow features are selected in the pre-processing phase and then the classification of the flows is evaluated. To enhance the forecast accuracy, the window length and grouping components are varied. As it is customary in forecasting literature to estimate the Root Mean Square Error (RMSE), Mean Absolute Error (MAE) and Mean Absolute Percentage Error (MAPE) of forecasts to compare the accuracy of the methodologies under analysis. The observations into split into training and testing sets to determine accurate RMSE values. Due to the size of the time series data, the first 200 data samples from every trace are taken to produce the findings using multiple segmentation methods. This enables the reduction of processing overhead of the validation of the proposed framework.

Classification Results

The classifiers selected by the proposed framework are Support Vector Machine, Naïve Bayes, CS Forest, Decision Tree and Random Forest (Samrat Kumar Dey, Md. Mahbubur Rahman, 2018), (Latah & Toker, 2018). The performance of the classifier is directly impacted by the number of features extracted during the training process. Furthermore, an excessive number of features may increase training complexity. Therefore, it is crucial to select the right features for training the model.

Figure 4. Classification accuracy

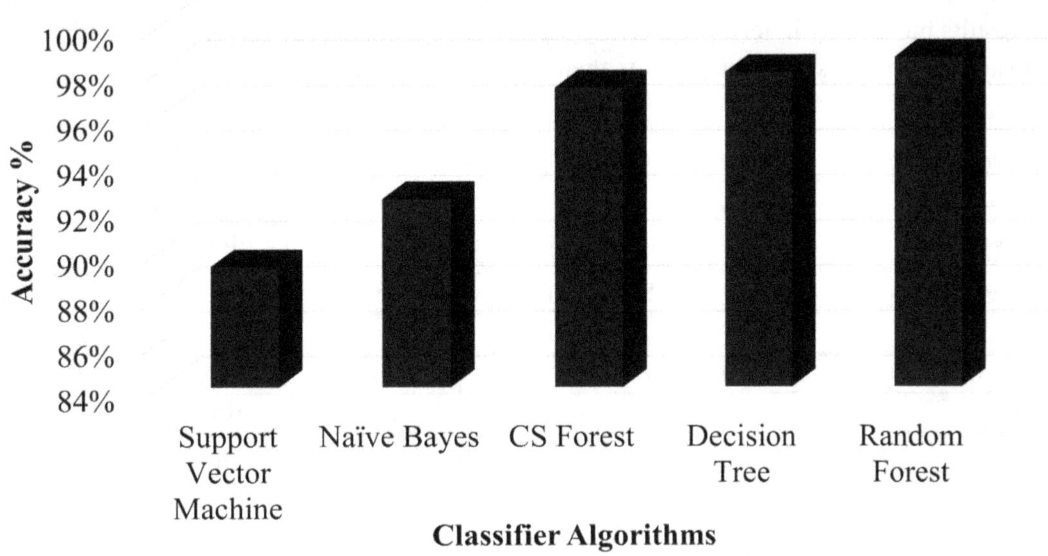

Classification accuracy was evaluated by varying the number of flow features in the training process. The classifier accuracy is shown in Figure 4. It is found that the classification accuracy was improved with 70% of the flow features. The random forest classifier obtained 98% accuracy when compared with other classical algorithms. The Errors estimation of the classifier algorithms is present in Table 2.

The accuracy of the classifier is measured in terms of True Positive (TP), False Positive (FP), Recall, Mathew Correlation Coefficient (MCC), Receiver Operating Characteristic (ROC) Area, and Precision Recall Curve (PRC) Area. The weighted average of the accuracy is summarized and presented in Table 3.

Table 2. Error estimation of the classifier models

Classifier	Mean Absolute Error	Root Mean Squared Error	Relative Absolute Error	Root Relative Squared Error
Support Vector Machine	0.2246	0.3142	80.87%	84.31%
Naïve Bayes	0.0274	0.1412	9.85%	37.89%
CS Forest	0.0274	0.0941	9.86%	25.24%
Decision Tree	0.0105	0.0813	3.78%	21.82%
Random Forest	0.1396	0.1992	50.24%	53.45%

From the experimental and statistical studies, it is found that the random forest classifier obtains high accuracy results but is slow in terms of performance. However, the Support Vector Machine algorithm is much faster yet gives less accurate results than the Random forest.

Table 3. Summary of weighted average of classification accuracy

Classifier	TP Rate	FP Rate	Recall	F-Measure	MCC	ROC Area	PRC Area
Support Vector Machine	0.893	0.021	0.893	0.893	0.872	0.975	0.855
Naïve Bayes	0.923	0.015	0.923	0.923	0.909	0.992	0.957
CS Forest	0.973	0.006	0.973	0.972	0.968	0.999	0.994
Decision Tree	0.979	0.004	0.979	0.979	0.975	0.994	0.973
Random Forest	0.986	0.003	0.986	0.986	0.983	0.991	0.998

Multivariate Forecasting Results

To further analyze the traffic flow prediction, a forecast is estimated from the time series data captured from the static and mobile 5G network. Using the MSSA forecasting method, the download bitrate speed is analyzed and future download speed is forecasted. The multivariate forecast result of download bitrate is presented in Figure 5 for the mobile 5G network. It can be understood the peak download bitrate is above 250MB. Otherwise, it is mostly around 50MB download. The upload bitrate is shown in Figure 6 for mobile 5G network. The forecast is predicted for 50 steps ahead by varying the window length L and grouping components r. The comparison of the proposed multivariate model with LSTM (Lazaris & Prasanna, 2019) is carried out to understand the forecast accuracy.

Figure 5. Download bitrate forecast of mobile 5G network

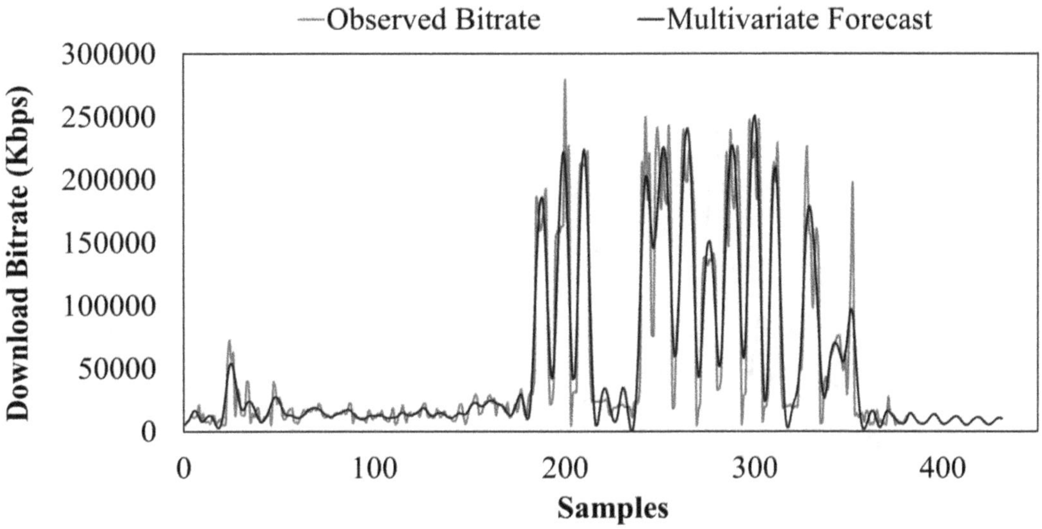

Figure 6. Upload bitrate forecast of mobile 5G network

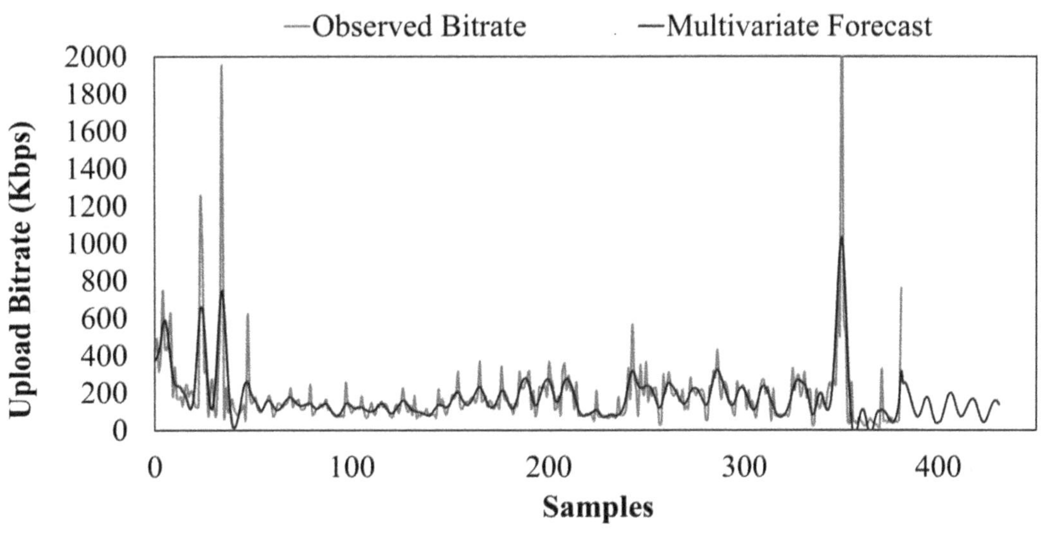

Figure 7 shows the download bitrate and Figure 8 depicts the upload bitrate forecasts of static 5G network. To estimate the multivariate forecasts, the MSSA method is used. Most of the taken samples have a download bitrate of less than 50MB of files except at a certain time duration the download bitrate is around 200MB. Also, the upload bitrate speed is around 1MB or less.

Figure 7. Download bitrate forecast of static 5G network

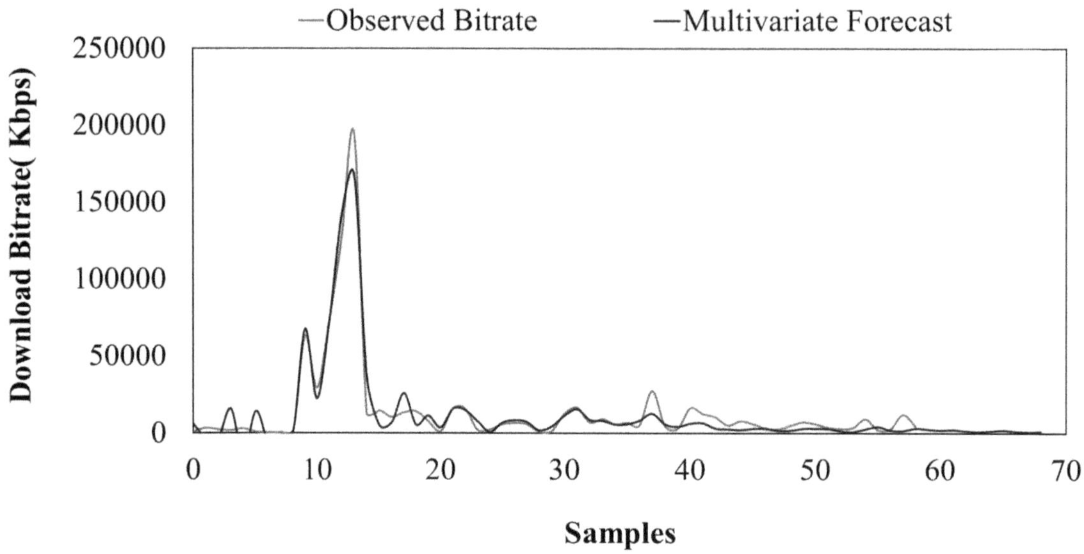

Figure 8. Upload bitrate forecast of static 5G network

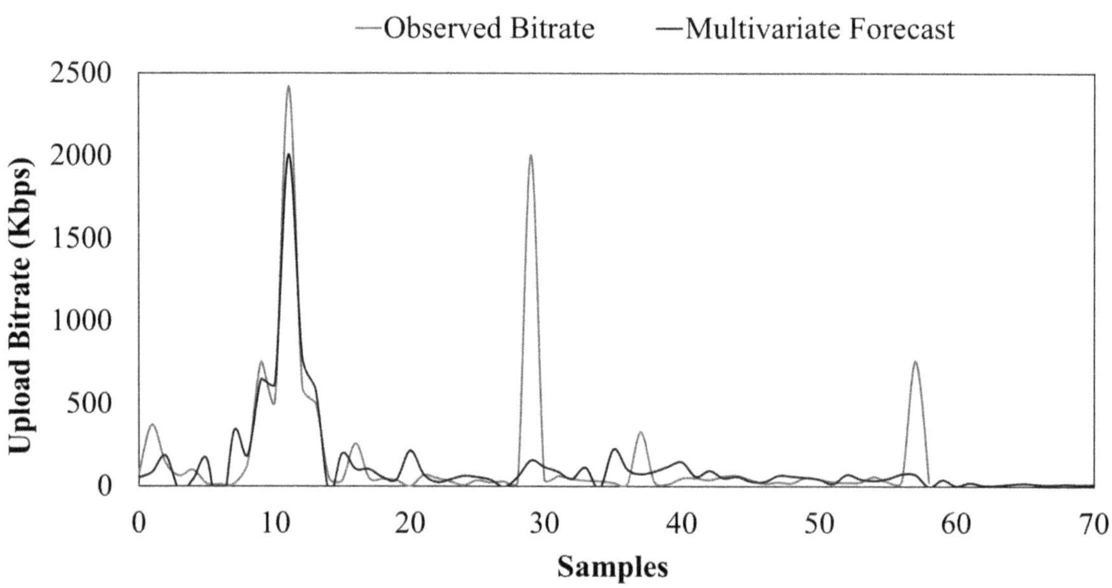

The forecast accuracy result is represented as Mean absolute percentage error (MAPE) and it is shown in Table 4. The average forecasting accuracy over all the window lengths L ranging from 10 to 50 is considered for the analysis. The MAPE obtained by varying window length L and grouping components r is presented. Table 4 shows that the MAPE is reduced with increased r and smaller L. Increasing L results in a larger matrix. As a result, the computation overhead is high. Therefore, to reduce the computation overhead smaller window length is taken. The MAPE is 13% with a window length L of 30 and r=25. Table 5 shows the comparison of the forecast errors estimation of the proposed multivariate model with the LSTM model. From the error metrics, it is evident that the proposed model obtained an error that is smaller than the LSTM model.

Table 4. Error estimation of forecast accuracy

Window length L	MAPE %				
	r=5	r=10	r=15	r=20	r=25
10	28.65	23.63	-	-	-
20	44.48	31.27	24.24	13.09	-
30	58.29	42.41	36.57	23.94	13.05
40	68.03	52.31	41.14	26.94	16.49
50	65.41	53.95	43.31	32.11	21.06

Table 5. Comparison between forecast errors

Error Metrics	Proposed Multivariate forecast	LSTM forecast
MAPE %	13.09	24.83
MAE	69.52	74.82
RMSE	84.51	97.34

CONCLUSION

Smart 5G technology has introduced several features that run on several infrastructures and adopted in many industries and businesses. Human lifestyle has altered as a result of these wireless technologies. In this chapter, an extensive overview of the SDN/NFV capabilities incorporated with 5G is presented. Several use cases and emerging applications of SDN based 5G is detailed. In addition, the benefits and challenges of 5G are highlighted. The chapter proposes a multivariate traffic analysis framework to classify and forecast flows for a 5G network. To evaluate the proposed technique, the study is conducted on a time series dataset. The findings show the classification accuracy of 98.6% is attained by a random forest classifier and the forecast error estimation of MAPE is around 13% for both static and mobile 5G data. The accuracy and error estimation proves the efficiency of the proposed multivariate analysis technique.

REFERENCES

Akyildiz, I. F., Lin, S. C., & Wang, P. (2015). Wireless software-defined networks (W-SDNs) and network function virtualization (NFV) for 5G cellular systems: An overview and qualitative evaluation. *Computer Networks*, *93*, 66–79. doi:10.1016/j.comnet.2015.10.013

Barakabitze, A. A., Ahmad, A., Mijumbi, R., & Hines, A. (2020). 5G network slicing using SDN and NFV: A survey of taxonomy, architectures and future challenges. *Computer Networks*, *167*, 106984. Advance online publication. doi:10.1016/j.comnet.2019.106984

Barakabitze, A. A., Sun, L., Mkwawa, I.-H., & Ifeachor, E. (2019). *A Novel QoE-Aware SDN-enabled, NFV-based Management Architecture for Future Multimedia Applications on 5G Systems.* https://arxiv.org/abs/1904.09917

Barakabitze, A. A. & Walshe, R. (2022). SDN and NFV for QoE-driven multimedia services delivery: The road towards 6G and beyond networks. *Computer Networks, 214*(January 2021), 109133. doi:10.1016/j.comnet.2022.109133

Ben Azzouz, L., & Jamai, I. (2019). SDN, slicing, and NFV paradigms for a smart home: A comprehensive survey. *Transactions on Emerging Telecommunications Technologies, 30*(10), 1–13. doi:10.1002/ett.3744

Blanco, B., Fajardo, J. O., Giannoulakis, I., Kafetzakis, E., Peng, S., Pérez-Romero, J., Trajkovska, I., Khodashenas, P. S., Goratti, L., Paolino, M., Sfakianakis, E., Liberal, F., & Xilouris, G. (2017). Technology pillars in the architecture of future 5G mobile networks: NFV, MEC and SDN. *Computer Standards & Interfaces*, *54*(January), 216–228. doi:10.1016/j.csi.2016.12.007

Blenk, A., Basta, A., Reisslein, M., & Kellerer, W. (2016). Survey on network virtualization hypervisors for software defined networking. *IEEE Communications Surveys and Tutorials*, *18*(1), 655–685. doi:10.1109/COMST.2015.2489183

Celdrán, A. H., Pérez, M. G., Clemente, F. J. G., Ippoliti, F., & Pérez, G. M. (2019). Dynamic network slicing management of multimedia scenarios for future remote healthcare. *Multimedia Tools and Applications*, *78*(17), 24707–24737. doi:10.100711042-019-7283-3

Condoluci, M., & Mahmoodi, T. (2018). Softwarization and virtualization in 5G mobile networks: Benefits, trends and challenges. *Computer Networks*, *146*, 65–84. doi:10.1016/j.comnet.2018.09.005

Din, S., Paul, A., & Rehman, A. (2019). 5G-enabled Hierarchical architecture for software-defined intelligent transportation system. *Computer Networks*, *150*, 81–89. doi:10.1016/j.comnet.2018.11.035

Dong, B., Shi, Q., Yang, Y., Wen, F., Zhang, Z., & Lee, C. (2021). Technology evolution from self-powered sensors to AIoT enabled smart homes. *Nano Energy*, *79*, 105414. doi:10.1016/j.nanoen.2020.105414

El-Shorbagy, A. M. (2021). 5G Technology and the Future of Architecture. *Procedia Computer Science*, *182*, 121–131. doi:10.1016/j.procs.2021.02.017

Feng, X., Yan, F., & Liu, X. (2019). Study of Wireless Communication Technologies on Internet of Things for Precision Agriculture. *Wireless Personal Communications*, *108*(3), 1785–1802. doi:10.100711277-019-06496-7

Filali, A., Cherkaoui, S., & Kobbane, A. (2019). Prediction-based Switch Migration Scheduling for SDN Load Balancing. *ICC 2019 - 2019 IEEE International Conference on Communications (ICC)*, 1–6. 10.1109/ICC.2019.8761469

Fu, Y., Yan, Z., Li, H., Xin, X. L., & Cao, J. (2017). A secure SDN based multi-RANs architecture for future 5G networks. *Computers & Security*, *70*, 648–662. doi:10.1016/j.cose.2017.08.013

Garcia Hernando, A. B., Da Silva Farina, A., Bellido Triana, L., Ruiz Pinar, F. J., & Fernandez Cambronero, D. (2017). Virtualization of residential IoT functionality by using NFV and SDN. *2017 IEEE International Conference on Consumer Electronics, ICCE 2017*, (pp. 86–87). 10.1109/ICCE.2017.7889240

Ghafoor, U., Ali, M., Khan, H. Z., Siddiqui, A. M., & Naeem, M. (2022). NOMA and future 5G & B5G wireless networks: A paradigm. *Journal of Network and Computer Applications*, *204*(April), 103413. doi:10.1016/j.jnca.2022.103413

Gohar, A., & Nencioni, G. (2021). The role of 5g technologies in a smart city: The case for intelligent transportation system. *Sustainability (Basel)*, *13*(9), 1–24. doi:10.3390u13095188

Golkarifard, M., Chiasserini, C. F., Malandrino, F. & Movaghar, A. (2021). Dynamic VNF placement, resource allocation and traffic routing in 5G. *Computer Networks, 188*(November 2020), 107830. doi:10.1016/j.comnet.2021.107830

Gupta, A., & Jha, R. K. (2015). A Survey of 5G Network: Architecture and Emerging Technologies. *IEEE Access : Practical Innovations, Open Solutions*, *3*, 1206–1232. doi:10.1109/ACCESS.2015.2461602

Haider, U., Waqas, M., Hanif, M., Alasmary, H. & Qaisar, S. M. (2023). Network load prediction and anomaly detection using ensemble learning in 5G cellular networks. *Computer Communications, 197*(December 2021), 141–150. https://doi.org/ doi:10.1016/j.comcom...017

Hasan, K., Ahmed, K., Biswas, K., Saiful Islam, M., & Ameri Sianaki, O. (2020). Software-defined application-specific traffic management for wireless body area networks. *Future Generation Computer Systems*, *107*, 274–285. doi:10.1016/j.future.2020.01.052

Hassani, H., Heravi, S., & Zhigljavsky, A. (2013). Forecasting UK industrial production with multivariate singular spectrum analysis. *Journal of Forecasting*, *32*(5), 395–408. doi:10.1002/for.2244

Hussain, M. W., Khan, M. S., Reddy, K. H. K., & Roy, D. S. (2022). Extended indirect controller-legacy switch forwarding for link discovery in hybrid multi-controller SDN. *Computer Communications*, *189*, 148–157. doi:10.1016/j.comcom.2022.03.017

Hussain, M. W., Moulik, S., & Roy, D. S. (2021, December). A broadcast based link discovery scheme for minimizing messages in software defined networks. In *2021 IEEE Globecom Workshops (GC Wkshps)* (pp. 1-6). IEEE.

Isravel, D. P., Silas, S., & Rajsingh, E. B. (2020). Reliable Surveillance Tracking System based on Software Defined Internet of Things. In *The Cognitive Approach in Cloud Computing and Internet of Things Technologies for Surveillance Tracking Systems*. INC. doi:10.1016/B978-0-12-816385-6.00001-5

Isravel, D. P., Silas, S., & Rajsingh, E. B. (2022). Long-term traffic flow prediction using multivariate SSA forecasting in SDN based networks. *Pervasive and Mobile Computing*, *83*, 101590. doi:10.1016/j.pmcj.2022.101590

Ji, B., Zhang, X., Mumtaz, S., Han, C., Li, C., Wen, H., & Wang, D. (2020). Survey on the Internet of Vehicles: Network Architectures and Applications. *IEEE Communications Standards Magazine*, *4*(1), 34–41. doi:10.1109/MCOMSTD.001.1900053

Khan, M., Iqbal, J., Talha, M., Arshad, M., Diyan, M., & Han, K. (2018). Big Data Processing using Internet of Software Defined Things in Smart Cities. *International Journal of Parallel Programming*, 1–14. doi:10.100710766-018-0573-y

Koutlia, K., Bojovic, B., Lagén, S., Zhang, X., Wang, P. & Liu, J. (2023). System analysis of QoS schedulers for XR traffic in 5G NR. *Simulation Modelling Practice and Theory, 125*(December 2022), 102745. doi:10.1016/j.simpat.2023.102745

Latah, M. & Toker, L. (2018). *Artificial Intelligence Enabled Software Defined Networking: A Comprehensive Artificial Intelligence Enabled Software Defined Networking : A Comprehensive Overview. November*. doi:10.1049/iet-net.2018.5082

Lazaris, A., & Prasanna, V. K. (2019). Deep Learning Models For Aggregated Network Traffic Prediction. *15th International Conference on Network and Service Management (CNSM 2019)*. 10.23919/CNSM46954.2019.9012669

Lin, B.-S. P. (2020). Toward an AI-Enabled SDN-based 5G & IoT Network. *Network and Communication Technologies*, *5*(2), 7. doi:10.5539/nct.v5n2p7

Longo, F., Padovano, A., Aiello, G., Fusto, C., & Certa, A. (2021). How 5G-based industrial IoT is transforming human-centered smart factories: A Quality of Experience model for Operator 4.0 applications. *IFAC-PapersOnLine*, *54*(1), 255–262. doi:10.1016/j.ifacol.2021.08.030

Mendonça, S., Damásio, B., Charlita de Freitas, L., Oliveira, L., Cichy, M., & Nicita, A. (2022). The rise of 5G technologies and systems: A quantitative analysis of knowledge production. *Telecommunications Policy*, *46*(4), 102327. doi:10.1016/j.telpol.2022.102327

Mitra, R. N., & Agrawal, D. P. (2015). 5G mobile technology: A survey. *ICT Express*, *1*(3), 132–137. doi:10.1016/j.icte.2016.01.003

Neves, P., Calé, R., Costa, M., Gaspar, G., Alcaraz-Calero, J., Wang, Q., Nightingale, J., Bernini, G., Carrozzo, G., Valdivieso, Á., García Villalba, L. J., Barros, M., Gravas, A., Santos, J., Maia, R. & Preto, R. (2017a). Future mode of operations for 5G – The SELFNET approach enabled by SDN/NFV. *Computer Standards and Interfaces, 54*(December 2016), 229–246. doi:10.1016/j.csi.2016.12.008

Neves, P., Calé, R., Costa, M., Gaspar, G., Alcaraz-Calero, J., Wang, Q., Nightingale, J., Bernini, G., Carrozzo, G., Valdivieso, Á., García Villalba, L. J., Barros, M., Gravas, A., Santos, J., Maia, R. & Preto, R. (2017b). Future mode of operations for 5G – The SELFNET approach enabled by SDN/NFV. *Computer Standards and Interfaces, 54*(October 2016), 229–246. doi:10.1016/j.csi.2016.12.008

Özçevik, M. E., Canberk, B., & Duong, T. Q. (2017). End to end delay modeling of heterogeneous traffic flows in software defined 5G networks. *Ad Hoc Networks*, *60*, 26–39. doi:10.1016/j.adhoc.2017.02.006

Pradhan, B., Hussain, M. W., Srivastava, G., Debbarma, M. K., Barik, R. K., & Lin, J. C. W. (2022). A neuro-evolutionary approach for software defined wireless network traffic classification. *IET Communications*, cmu2.12548. doi:10.1049/cmu2.12548

Raca, D., Leahy, D., Sreenan, C. J., & Quinlan, J. J. (2020). Beyond throughput, the next generation: A 5G dataset with channel and context metrics. *MMSys 2020 - Proceedings of the 2020 Multimedia Systems Conference*, 303–308. 10.1145/3339825.3394938

Rahman, A., Islam, M. J., Band, S. S., Muhammad, G., Hasan, K., & Tiwari, P. (2022). Towards a blockchain-SDN-based secure architecture for cloud computing in smart industrial IoT. *Digital Communications and Networks*. Advance online publication. doi:10.1016/j.dcan.2022.11.003

Samrat Kumar Dey, Md. Mahbubur Rahman, M. R. U. (2018). Detection of Flow Based Anomaly in OpenFlow Controller: Machine Learning Approach in Software Defined Networking. *2018 4th International Conference on Electrical Engineering and Information & Communication Technology (iCEEiCT)*. 416-421, https://doi.org/10.1109/.8628105

Santa, J., Katsaros, K. V., Bernal-Escobedo, L., Zougari, S., Miranda, M., Castañeda, O., Dalet, B., & Amditis, A. (2022). Evaluation platform for 5G vehicular communications. *Vehicular Communications*, *38*, 100537. doi:10.1016/j.vehcom.2022.100537

Sevgican, S., Turan, M., Gokarslan, K., Yilmaz, H. B., & Tugcu, T. (2020). Intelligent network data analytics function in 5G cellular networks using machine learning. *Journal of Communications and Networks (Seoul)*, *22*(3), 269–280. doi:10.1109/JCN.2020.000019

Sharma, P., Jain, S., Gupta, S., & Chamola, V. (2021). Role of machine learning and deep learning in securing 5G-driven industrial IoT applications. *Ad Hoc Networks*, *123*(September), 102685. doi:10.1016/j.adhoc.2021.102685

Silva, R., Santos, D., Meneses, F., Corujo, D. & Aguiar, R. L. (2021). A hybrid SDN solution for mobile networks. *Computer Networks, 190*(July 2020), 107958. https://doi.org/ doi:10.1016/.comnet.2021.107958

Sodhro, A. H., Awad, A. I., van de Beek, J., & Nikolakopoulos, G. (2022). Intelligent authentication of 5G healthcare devices: A survey. *Internet of Things (Netherlands)*, *20*, 100610. doi:10.1016/j.iot.2022.100610

Tang, F., Member, S., Zhang, H., Yang, L. T., Member, S., & Chen, L. (2019). Elephant Flow Detection and Differentiated Scheduling with Efficient Sampling and Classification. *IEEE Transactions on Cloud Computing, PP*, *1*. doi:10.1109/TCC.2019.2901669

Tang, Y., Dananjayan, S., Hou, C., Guo, Q., Luo, S. & He, Y. (2021). A survey on the 5G network and its impact on agriculture: Challenges and opportunities. *Computers and Electronics in Agriculture 180* (November 2020), 1–15. https://doi.org/ doi:10.1016/.compag.2020.105895

Van Hilten, M., & Wolfert, S. (2022). 5G in agri-food - A review on current status, opportunities and challenges. *Computers and Electronics in Agriculture*, *201*(August), 107291. doi:10.1016/j.compag.2022.107291

Velasquez, K., Perez, D., Curado, M., & Monteiro, E. (2022). Resource orchestration in 5G and beyond: Challenges and opportunities. *Computer Communications*, *192*(June), 311–315. doi:10.1016/j.comcom.2022.06.019

Chapter 10
Intelligent Infrastructure of Route Scheduling for Smart Transportation Systems in Smart Cities

Shiplu Das
Brainware University, India

Buddhadeb Pradhan
University of Engineering and Management, India

Shivam Sharma
Brainware University, India

Bishwanath Jana
Brainware University, India

Gobinda Das
Brainware University, India

Prasit Chakraborty
Brainware University, India

ABSTRACT

With the increment in population, the problems of big cities regarding highly congested traffic are gaining more and more attention, with a goal of making them efficient and environmentally friendly. Most contain rich information and complex techniques that oppose ongoing optimization procedures. As security threats continue to grow, Vehicles are subject to various service attacks that can compromise security. To address these concerns, the US and European Intelligent Transportation System (ITS) standards select elliptic curve cryptography (ECC) algorithms for safe vehicle interactions. They introduced a two-layer taxonomy to Evolutionary computation for intelligent check transportation in smart cities is studied. This chapter will analyze the security architecture of the ETSI ITS standard. The results show that the existing security solution is better than the achieved level/quality of service (quality of service) and vehicular application performance regarding rising inter-arrival packet delay, packet and crypto loss, and reduced security awareness in security applications.

DOI: 10.4018/979-8-3693-0744-1.ch010

INTRODUCTION

The continued population development in large cities has resulted in hefty traffic, which has become an essential concern regarding efficiency and environmental friendliness. Smart cities have gained popularity as a means of addressing these difficulties. An intelligent city employs cutting-edge technology to improve the quality of life for its residents by fostering a more efficient and sustainable environment. It is critical to deploy an Intelligent Transportation System (ITS) capable of efficiently controlling traffic flow and enhancing the overall transportation system. However, as the use of technology grows, so does the possibility of security risks, particularly in the case of ITS. Vehicles are vulnerable to various service assaults that might jeopardize security, posing a substantial barrier to the safe running of transportation networks. To overcome these problems, ITS standards like those developed in the United States and Europe have chosen Elliptic Curve Cryptography (ECC) methods for secure vehicle interactions. Evolutionary computation has also created a two-layer taxonomy for intelligent check transportation in smart cities. Despite efforts to increase ITS security, benchmark research on continuing security requirements in real-world contexts still needs to be conducted. This article provides an intelligent route scheduling infrastructure for the smart city's innovative transportation system that uses ECC algorithms for safe vehicle interactions. The methodology that is being proposed has four main parts: intelligent metro transportation and intelligent route scheduling, intelligent car service and intelligent city communications architecture, intelligent infrastructure for electric vehicles and traffic lights, and EC for intelligent vehicle network and intelligent land transportation. Smart algorithms are used in intelligent metro transportation and route scheduling components to optimize the transportation system by determining the most effective routes for cars. This would make the transportation system more effective by reducing traffic and travel time. Modern communication technologies, intelligent car service, and smart city communications architecture enable cars to connect with the transportation network. By doing this, the transportation system would be able to acquire real-time data on vehicle movement and traffic flow, improving its ability to estimate travel times and congestion levels. Creating an infrastructure designed to assist electric cars is a part of the intelligent infrastructure for electric vehicles and traffic light components. This would include setting up charging stations and creating a smart grid system that would make it possible for cars to capture in a more effective and environmentally friendly way. The need of application of Artificial Intelligence System in Smart Cities in Table 1.

Table 1. Need of application of artificial intelligence system

	Need for Application of Artificial Intelligence System
1	Need to develop multi-modal integrated public transport system
2	Need to develop intelligent traffic control and management system to reduce congestion.
3	Need to develop smart traffic information system
4	Need to develop economical public transport system
5	Need to develop smart pavement management system
6	Need to develop of smart parking management system
7	Need to develop intelligent traffic control and management system
8	Need to development safety management and emergency system
9	Need to develop electronic pricing system
10	Need to develop user friendly & comfortable public transport system

The component would also incorporate intelligent traffic signals with timing capabilities to ensure a steady traffic flow. Elliptic curve cryptography methods are used in the EC for smart vehicle networks and intelligent land transportation components to offer secure communication between cars and the transportation system. This would ensure the safe running of the transportation system and aid in preventing cyberattacks. The findings demonstrate that, in terms of increasing inter-arrival packet latency, packet and crypto loss, and decreased security awareness in security applications, the current security solution performs better than the level/quality of service (QoS) attained and vehicle application performance. It implies a direct effect on how people perceive security. The ETSI-ITS standard and the two-tier taxonomy are the foundation for a detailed evaluation of relevant studies. In conclusion, the suggested technique offers a thorough strategy for creating a smart city's intelligent transportation system. The transportation system could function more effectively and safely if ECC algorithms were used for secure vehicle interactions combined with contemporary communication technologies and intelligent algorithms. Examining the ETSI ITS standard using the suggested technique would yield insightful findings helpful in creating safe transportation systems in smart cities. The Figure 1 describes the EC's twofold Taxonomy for Intelligent Transportation.

Figure 1. EC's twofold Taxonomy for intelligent transportation

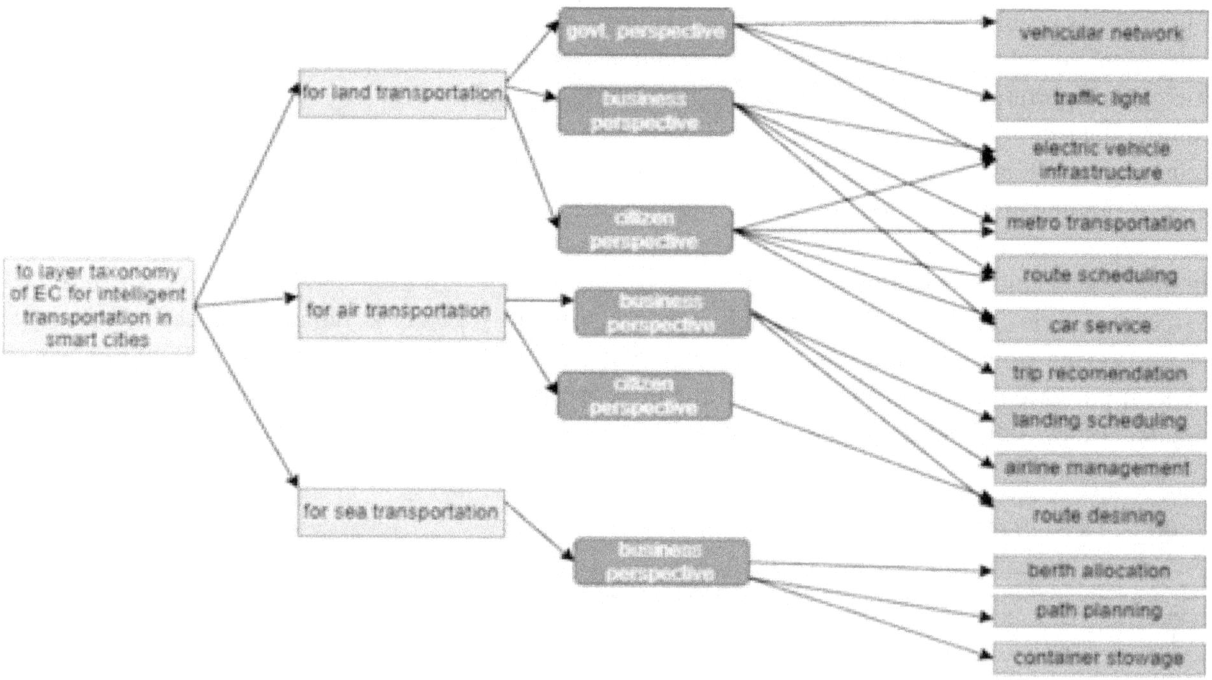

This chapter is organized as follows. In section 2, the authors have presented a review of the related works done in this area. In this section, a citation has been given regarding the way of different Infrastructures of Route Scheduling for Smart Transportation Systems. Section 3 illustrates the Intelligent Transportation System. In section 4, the authors contributed the proposed system of EC for Intelligent Vehicle Networks and Intelligent Land Transportation, Intelligent infrastructure for electric vehicles and traffic lights, and Intelligent Car Service and Smart Cities communications architecture. The next section presents a simulation of Intelligent Infrastructure of Route Scheduling for Smart Transportation Systems in a Smart City. Finally, the chapter ends with a brief conclusion.

RELATED WORKS

Constructing effective and ecologically friendly transportation systems is crucial because of the intense traffic congestion brought on by the increasing urban population expansion. Yet, since more cars are on the road, security risks have also increased. As a result, automobiles are more vulnerable to numerous service assaults that might jeopardize their security. They have also established a two-layer taxonomy for evolutionary computation to create intelligent transportation systems in smart cities. This article intends to investigate the security model of the ETSI ITS standard and assess the quality of service and performance of the current security solution for vehicles. The US and European ITS standards have chosen ECC algorithms for secure vehicle interactions. ECC has several benefits over classical cryptography, including a minor key size and quicker calculation times. ECC is a public-key cryptography method for digital signatures, critical formation, and secure communication. The drawbacks of ECC algorithms include the requirement for specialized gear and software for effective processing. Two-Layer Taxonomy for Evolutionary Computation: A two-layer taxonomy for evolutionary computation has been established to construct intelligent transportation systems in smart cities. The higher layer deals with the system's security, while the bottom layer optimizes traffic flow. This taxonomy tries to increase system security while maximizing transportation efficiency. Techniques like evolutionary algorithms and fuzzy logic are used at the bottom layer, while encryption, authentication, and access control are used in the higher layer. The ETSI ITS standard offers a thorough security architecture for vehicle communication. Security architecture includes many security services, including secure communication, authentication, authorization, and privacy protection. The critical public infrastructure (PKI), certificate revocation lists (CRL), and secure message exchange are just a few security mechanisms that are part of the security architecture. The security architecture is designed to defend against several threats, including message replay, eavesdropping, and spoofing.

Many studies have been carried out to assess the quality of service and vehicular application performance of the current security solution. Studies have demonstrated that the version of the vehicular application and obtained level/quality of service outperform the existing security solution. The research has, however, also brought to light several problems that may jeopardize the system's security. Increasing inter-arrival packet delays, packet and crypto loss, and a lack of security awareness in security applications are some of these problems. These problems raise the possibility of a security breach in the system and point to a direct influence on security perception.

For instance, the ETSI ITS standard's security and privacy protection was assessed by (Xia et al., 2021). According to the research, the security architecture offers sufficient security and privacy protection. Nevertheless, the study also identified several flaws, including the security architecture's lack of scalability and adaptability.

(Wang et al., 2020) studied the effects of packet loss on the safety of vehicle communication in another research. The study discovered that packet loss might jeopardize the system's security and offered several solutions to lessen its effects.

Several research has also assessed the effectiveness of the security architecture in-vehicle communication. For instance, (Lin et al., 2019) evaluated the ETSI ITS security architecture's performance in a vehicular network. According to the analysis, the security architecture performed satisfactorily regarding communication effectiveness and security. The research did, however, also draw attention to the need for intelligent transportation systems (ITS), which are transforming how people commute and travel by using the Internet of Things, artificial intelligence, and cloud computing. With fewer accidents, traffic jams, and pollution, these solutions make transportation more cost-effective, environmentally friendly, and safe. But, because of our growing reliance on these networks, we must now worry about their security.

Building underground networks is becoming more common in big cities since they provide a quick and convenient alternative means of transit that also relieves traffic congestion. A researcher's area of interest is intelligent metro transportation, emphasizing schedule design and speed management to reduce the cost of underground firms and improve the convenience of public mobility. To reduce waiting times for transit users, timetable planning entails figuring out the arrival and departure times of trains at each station by (R. Liu. et al., 2020). Whereas (Hassannayebi et al., 2018) employed PSO and an adaptive parameter management mechanism to increase search effectiveness, Medium (J. Zhong et al., 2013) offered a dual-population DE approach.

(Nitisiri et al. 2019) suggested a multi-target parallel GA strategy to optimize two objectives while also taking metro company running expenses into account in addition to passenger waiting time. To effectively reuse regenerative braking energy utilizing GA, energy reuse roadmaps are also being developed, such as calculating the dwell time of trains at each station (F. Lin et al., 2016).

(Liu et al.2019) suggested an artificial bee colony-based method to optimize railway travel and dwell durations for the utilization of renewable energy. (Whereas Cao et al. 2019) employed GA to maximize punctuality, passenger comfort, and energy consumption by optimizing train taxi times, (Fernandez-Rodriguez et al. 2015) developed a multi-purpose PSO strategy that reduces railway travel time and energy consumption (Hussain et al., 2020) . Vehicles are assigned to specific locations, and driving routes are planned for each car. The Vehicle Routing Problem (VRP) is a well-known route design issue, and research on it has prioritized carrier profitability and service quality (G. Kim et al. 2015). Urban logistics, which divides the delivery process into several parts, use multi-step VRP, and new VRPs are being created for smart cities (R. Cuda.et al. 2015).

(Kings et al. 2015) created a hybrid method combining PSO and GA to reduce the overall cost of multilevel logistic networks, while (Yan et al. 2020) suggested a graph-based evolutionary approach to optimize the base cost. (Poonthalir, et al. 2018) proposed a PSO-based algorithm to optimize path cost and fuel usage for lower greenhouse gas emissions as part of the Green VRP, which aims to minimize pollution. Also, using electric cars for transportation lowers automobile emissions and enhances air quality. EVs are included in VRPs. (Yang et al.2015) suggested a GA-based algorithm to reduce greenhouse gas emissions, whereas (Miao et al. 2020) discussed a carbon price. Optimizing charging fees, EV and staff payments, service quality, EV charging delays, and carbon tax expenses have all been suggested using ACO-based algorithms (Y. Li et al. 2019).

INTELLIGENT TRANSPORTATION SYSTEM

Threats to cyber security can seriously jeopardize the dependability, security, and safety of ITS. These dangers include ransomware and packet-injection attacks, denial-of-service, and man-in-the-middle assaults. Attackers may interfere with how cars and infrastructure communicate, change or manipulate traffic statistics, steal confidential information, or seize control of vehicles. Many steps may be taken to enhance ITS security to reduce these threats. One of the most important precautions is using robust encryption solutions to safeguard the integrity and confidentiality of data transmitted between cars and infrastructure. Advanced cryptographic techniques can be used, such as Elliptic Curve Cryptography (ECC), which offers high-security levels with smaller key sizes and quicker calculation times than classical encryption. Implementing secure authentication and access control techniques is another crucial step in preventing illegal access and identity theft. To achieve this, it is possible to employ critical public infrastructure (PKI) and digital certificates to confirm the reliability and legality of communication partners. In addition, installing intrusion detection and prevention systems (IDPS) can aid in the real-time detection and prevention of cyberattacks. These programs may look at network traffic, spot trends, and anomalies, and either notify the system administrators or immediately stop suspicious activity. Additionally, the dependability and resilience of ITS against cyber-attacks may be guaranteed by using secure software development techniques and thorough testing. This involves routine vulnerability assessments, security patches, and security upgrades to find and remedy any possible flaws in the system. Moreover, user education and awareness may be critical in boosting ITS security. Users must be informed about safe and secure behaviors, such as staying away from public Wi-Fi networks, updating their hardware and software, and creating strong passwords. In conclusion, ITS security is a crucial issue that needs ongoing monitoring, assessment, and development. The security of ITS may be improved by using modern encryption, authentication, access control, intrusion detection and prevention, and software development processes. Moreover, user education and awareness are essential for stopping cyberattacks and defending user security and privacy. We can ensure that intelligent transportation systems continue offering everyone safe, effective, and sustainable transportation by putting these safeguards into place. Intelligent transportation systems (ITS) are one of the most prominent developments in today's smart cities, which are continually changing. ITS is anticipated to improve mobility in metropolitan areas and address transportation issues. Unfortunately, this technology has unique difficulties, including security risks. Cyberattacks are one of the most severe security risks to ITS. Malware, ransomware, and denial-of-service assaults are just a few ways cyberattacks may be launched. These assaults have the potential to seriously disrupt transportation networks, with severe repercussions for the populace, the government, and the economy. Security experts have advised adopting several security measures to reduce the danger of cyber-attacks on ITS. The usage of intrusion detection systems is one such measure (IDS).

IDS is software that monitors network traffic for unusual activity and notifies administrators when security breaches are identified. Wide-ranging security violations, such as unauthorized access, network scanning, and other malicious behaviour, can be found with IDS. Access control system implementation is another security measure. Only authorized workers can access sensitive information and systems thanks to access control mechanisms. Passwords, smart cards, and biometric identification are just a few techniques that access control systems utilize to confirm the identity of those trying to enter restricted areas. Another essential security precaution for ITS is encryption. Data is transformed into a secret code through encryption to prevent unwanted access. To safeguard sensitive data sent between cars and the infrastructure, encryption is frequently employed in ITS. Another crucial element of ITS security firewall. Network security is provided by firewalls, hardware, or software programs that filter incoming and outgoing traffic by pre-established security criteria. Firewalls are used to stop harmful traffic from entering the network and control unauthorized access to sensitive data. The installation of security policies and procedures has been advised by ITS security specialists in addition to these security measures. Employees and system administrators can refer to security policies and procedures for guidance on managing sensitive data, access control, and security issues. Security policies and procedures ensure that everyone in the company knows their responsibilities for upholding the system's security and what to do during a security breach. Applying security measures and rules alone cannot guarantee the security of ITS. The security system must be continuously monitored and assessed to identify and respond to emerging security risks. Security professionals advise doing routine security audits to find possible system vulnerabilities and create mitigation plans.

In conclusion, the use of ITS in intelligent cities has transformed the way that transportation systems operate while simultaneously posing new security risks. Cyber-attack risk in ITS is a serious issue that might seriously disrupt transportation systems. Security experts advise reducing these threats by implementing various security solutions, such as IDS, access control systems, encryption, firewalls, and security rules and procedures. The security system must also be continuously monitored and assessed to find and address new security risks. By putting these security measures in place, intelligent cities' transportation systems will be safer and ITS will be more secure.

PROPOSED METHODOLOGY

EC for Intelligent Vehicle Network and Intelligent Land Transportation

Let's now talk about several algorithms and strategies for routing problems in wireless sensor and vehicle networks. The mobility of the nodes in these networks poses several difficulties, including the potential for unstable and transient routing pathways. Security issues may also arise, such as malicious nodes disrupting the network or broadcasting false data. Researchers have recommended using Ant Colony Optimization (ACO) techniques to overcome these issues. ACO is a metaheuristic algorithm successfully used to address discrete optimization issues, including those in network routing (Gao et al., 2021), (Nalluri et al., 2020). In wireless sensor networks, (Eiza et al. 2016) suggest utilizing an ACO-based routing algorithm that optimizes the placement of sensors and RSUs to achieve total coverage while reducing network traffic interference. They have also proposed an ACO-based routing algorithm for vehicle networks to address the issues posed by mobility and the possibility of malicious nodes. This method incorporates a plausibility check to guarantee consistency in the routing of control messages. In other research, (Safavat et al. 2021) implemented an effective way of identifying malicious nodes before using ACO to achieve low-latency, short-distance, malicious-vehicle-free routing. This research has shown how well ACO solves discrete optimization issues like routing difficulties in wireless sensor and vehicle networks. The figure 2 presents A vehicle network featuring V2I and V2V communications as an example.

Figure 2. A vehicle network featuring V2I and V2V communications as an example

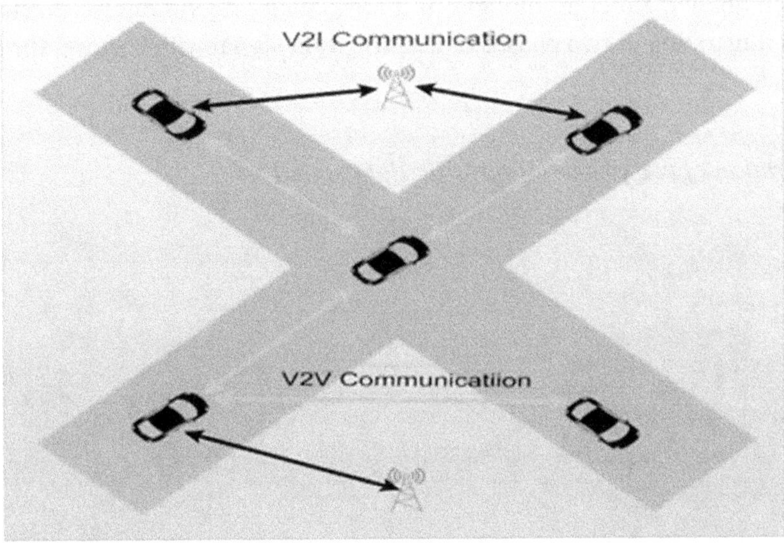

Intelligent Infrastructure for Electric Vehicles and Traffic Lights

Due to economic expansion and technological developments in the automobile industry, there is a significant demand for the transportation system and increased traffic in metropolitan areas. A realistic answer to this problem, combined with infrastructural improvements like building new highways and enlarging old ones, is traffic signal optimization. A vehicle network may be used to monitor traffic flow on roads in real time, and machine learning methods like the EC approach have been used to estimate short-term traffic patterns (X. Feng et al. 2019) (D. Chen 2017) (Pradhan et al., 2022). The traffic light patterns can then be intelligently adjusted using this information. The City Council is responsible for arranging traffic signals, and the government will consider this proposal. The sequence and duration of each signal phase are the deciding factors at a junction, and they define the length of each traffic light at the intersection. An efficient traffic network is often created by concurrently considering many corners. According to (Sanchez-Medina et al. 2010), one of the optimization goals for traffic signal design is to reduce the average travel time of vehicles to their destinations. Cellular automata technology simulates traffic flow and calculates a solution's fitness, which is the average journey time. Binary encoding is employed to encode signal phase duration. The same optimization goal and integer encoding were employed by (Li et al. 2017) while using GA. A modified traffic signal scheduling strategy was suggested by (Ferrer et al. 2019) to address traffic flow uncertainty. (Bi et al. 2014) introduced a multi-agent type 2 fuzzy logic control system to improve system parameter settings. Using GA to plan traffic signals and bus speeds, (Bid et al. 2020) studied traffic light timing for controlling bus separation. While examining signal transitions, studies often consider the vehicle and pedestrian traffic flow for optimizing the weighted sum of a pedestrian. To reduce costs and enhance service quality, the government and EV manufacturers must install charging stations for electric vehicles (EVs) in parking lots. Infrastructure for EVs must be developed and maintained by energy suppliers. Citizens want to utilize sophisticated EV infrastructure for comfortable travel, companies want to be lucrative, and governments build and administer EV infrastructure. Using GA in all three studies, (Sadeghi Barzani et al.2021) (P. Sadeghi et al.2014) modified fast-charging stations' placement and charging capacity to save construction costs and improve service quality. Ko et al. thought of a novel charging system for electric city buses. The figure 3 defines an illustration of two phases of a traffic light signal which shows the left-to-right direction signal phase.

Figure 3. An illustration of two phases of a traffic light signal

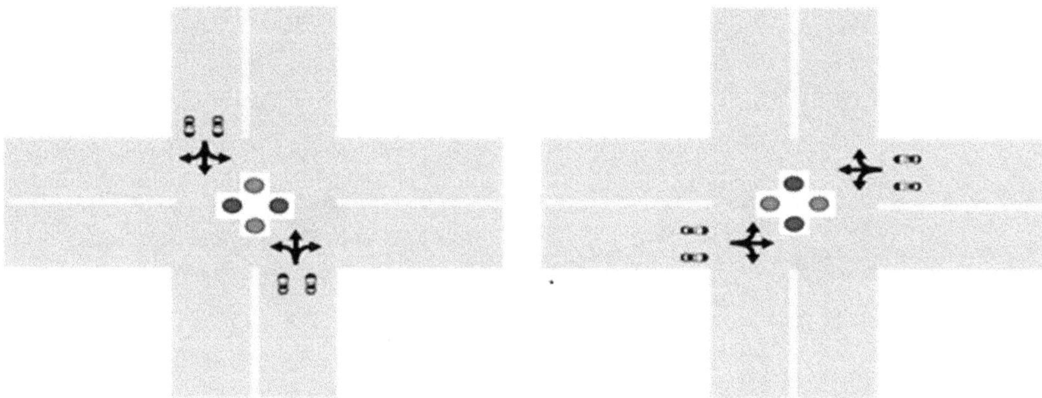

Intelligent Car Service and Smart Cities Communications Architecture

Taxi, carpooling, and parking are the three services included in intelligent city car services. Although the main objective of these services is to make money, they are also used from the point of view of the general public. Dispatching cabs to customers are a frequent difficulty in the taxi industry. Usually, taxi drivers need help finding their passengers, which causes some to have long waits and others to lose out on possibilities. Yet since the advent of taxi booking applications like Uber, the industry has transformed due to the effective matching of customers and cabs made possible by the data collected from both parties. One suggested remedy for this dispatch issue is an ACO-based algorithm that develops a taxi-passenger matching strategy to optimize revenues. With this strategy, the territory is divided into smaller areas to accommodate a high volume of travellers and taxis, and allocation is handled concurrently in each site (X. Situ et al. 2017) Taxi dispatching is another idea that considers income and service quality. According to revenue and service quality, possible taxi-passenger pairings are assessed utilizing a fuzzy logic control system in this method. Using DE (Y. Gong,2021), the membership functions and fuzzy rules are optimized. The figure 4 presents the example of carpooling system.

Figure 4. Example of carpooling

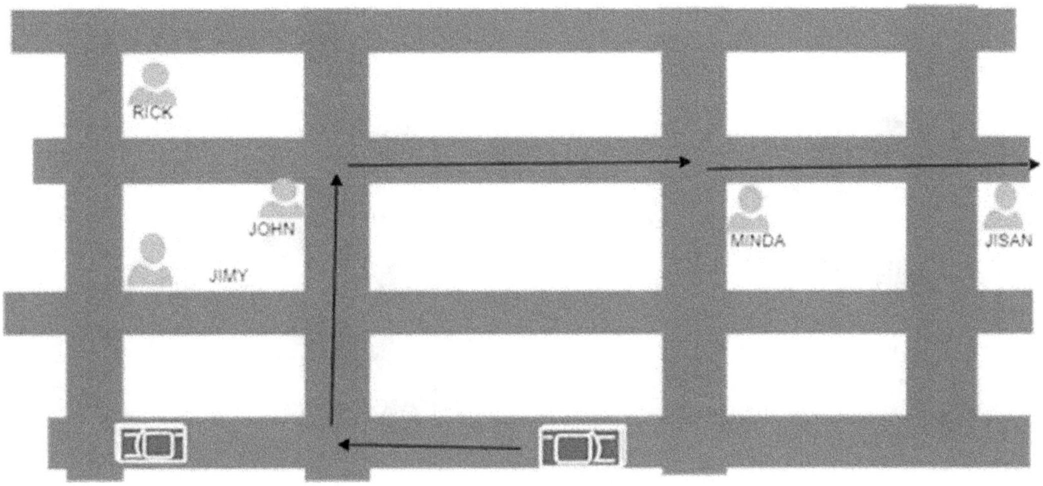

EVALUATION AND ASSESSMENT

This study utilized network and traffic simulations, and the following subsections offer specific simulation parameters and findings. The ITS communication architecture was modelled using the NS-3 network simulator. Infrastructure devices will be erected on the roadside every 500m to support V2I communication. Table 2 displays the simulation parameters. We have created two apps to simulate the ITS application for smart cities. The first application is a safety one that calls for the routine transmission of safety messages (also known as CAMs) between vehicles (v2V), and the second use is between cars and the local infrastructure (V2I)—query tools like between. The payload size for a security application was 100 bytes. When digital signatures are added to each CAM packet, the security overhead is 106 without certificates and 288 with credentials, respectively. According to the ETSI standard, the certificate is only delivered once during this period because the CAM production rate is ten packets per second. Security processing employing Intel Xeon and Intel i7 processors is referred to in this section as medium and rapid security, respectively. Due to its sluggish processing performance, the Cubie Board processor is not preferred for simulation and is inappropriate for ITS applications. The security application signing and verification intervals for medium and high-speed security. With a 200-byte packet size and additional protection, the infrastructure manages the service and returns to the vehicle (downlink). For query service applications, use the ECIES-NISTP 256-AES-CCM-128 encryption technique.

Simulations Results

Simulation results are shown in this part, separated into safety and query applications. Figure 5 depicts the ITS secure communications process. Before being sent to lower tiers, the sender signs and encrypts each ITS packet. Using the wireless channel, packets are transmitted to the receiver. At the receiver, packets are verified and decrypted. Finally, the application layer receives validated packets to assess the local dynamic map.

Figure 5. ITS secure communications process

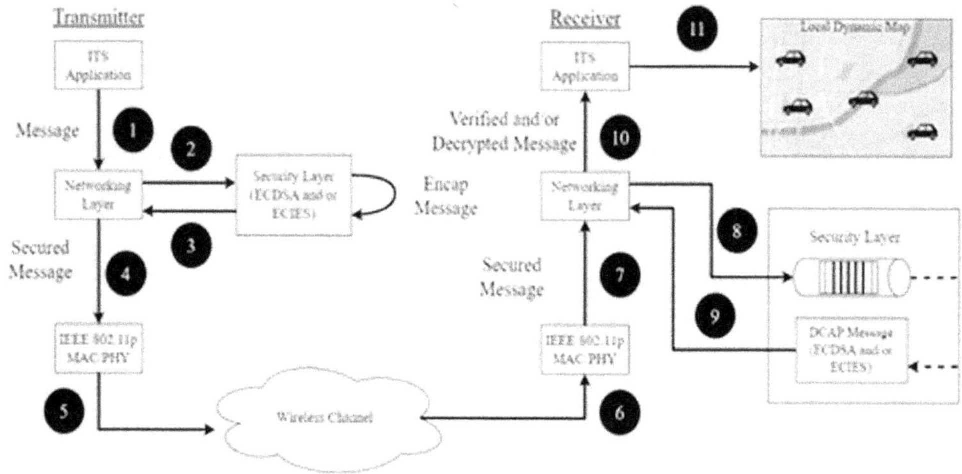

The chapter focused on the AES-CCM algorithm with a 128-bit key here. A lower-weight encryption technique is implied by using NISTP and SHA values below, which results in a shorter ENCAP delay. For NISTP values of 221, 287, and 424, respectively, the ENCAP delays needed for encryption without certificate processing and signature are 1.13, 1.5ms 4ms, and 6.12 ms for Intel Xeon processors.

Table 2. ENCAP delays for various ECDSA and ECIES schemes according to ETSI, IEEE WAVE, and NIST

Security Level	NISTP384-SHA256			NISTP384-SHA384		
	CB	Xn	i7	CB	Xn	i7
Sign w/o Certificate a	6.31	0.84	0.37	6.2	0.84	0.4
Sign with Certificate a	6.38	0.85	0.43	6.3	0.85	0.39
Encrypt w/o Certificate b	42.87	5.24	1.8	42.81	5.28	1.8
Encrypt with Certificate b	42.92	5.28	1.79	42.86	5.2	1.93
Sign w/o Certificate b	7.81	0.93	0.39	8.5	0.94	0.8
Sign with Certificate b	8.32	0.95	0.65	7.38	0.88	0.63
Encrypt w/o Certificate a	48.67	8.34	2.2	44.72	6.38	2.5
Encrypt with Certificate a	43.78	6.76	2.26	44.96	6.82	2.76

Table 2 shows that the ITS standard provides the DECAP delays for various ciphers. The Intel i7, Intel Xeon, and Cubie Board CPUs are listed from lowest to most significant in DECAP latency. On Intel Xeon processors, the DECAP latency values for validating and decrypting using the certificate technique are specifically 1.95 milliseconds, 2.69 milliseconds, and 10.99 milliseconds for NISTP values 192, 224, and 384, respectively. ECDSA is used to sign messages digitally; ECIES and A.E.S. encrypt messages. The effect of security on safety messaging. It takes longer to send a packet because security measures increase packet overhead, which increases channel occupancy time. Additionally, depending on the processor speed, validating the box takes a certain amount of time. Because of this, the safety messages must wait in line to be checked. Cryptographic loss refers to the dropping from the queue of C.A.M.s that could not be confirmed within a timeout of 100ms. The Crypto Loss Ratio (C.L.R.) is the proportion of packets arriving in the line due to validation to packets being dropped due to timeout. According to the Tx-Rx separation distance, the CAM CLR is 0.33. Safe speed is inversely related to C.L.R., according to intuition. Safety awareness level introduced in prior work to evaluate vehicle safety awareness as part of a safety application. The suggested action determines a vehicle's level of safety awareness by dividing the amount of information received by the L.D.M. by its accuracy. The resultant metric ranges from 0 to 1, representing the vehicle's application dependability or L.D.M. accuracy. The S.A. L metric according to the chosen security level. The S.A. L measure is 0.72 inside 300 meters without safety systems. The graph also displays the two CPUs' security awareness during the exercise. Within a 300m radius, medium-speed safety produces a safety awareness of 0.4; high-speed protection creates a safety awareness of 0.62. The monitoring of drivers is less about where each driver should be documented when they received training, when they completed their tasks, disciplinary measures, how frequently they violated traffic laws, etc., as it is about various other factors. Not crucial. One of the essential functions of an intelligent transportation system is driver supervision, which is useless in the case of a subpar vehicle. An operator, such as a driver, realizes the intelligent transportation system (ITS). The introduction of a smart transportation system will undoubtedly improve travel. Information services enhance passenger happiness, encourage public transportation use, and lower private automobile usage. This significantly helps reduce city traffic and protect the environment from high automobile pollution. I.T.S. ultimately has much to offer you regarding a pleasant and secure experience.

CONCLUSION

The findings from this study may help create safe transportation systems in the future. Overall, the suggested technique gives a thorough approach to tackling the difficulties faced by transportation systems in smart cities. Large cities' ongoing population development has led to congested transportation, raising questions about the effectiveness and environmental friendliness. Smart cities, which employ cutting-edge technology to provide more sustainable and effective transportation systems, have emerged as a viable remedy. However, as technology is used more often, security problems arise, especially with Intelligent Transportation Systems. (ITS). Standards like Elliptic Curve Cryptography (ECC) techniques have been created to improve the security of vehicle interactions to mitigate these threats. This study proposes a methodology for the intelligent architecture of route routing in innovative transportation systems. It includes intelligent algorithms, modern communication technologies, and ECC algorithms for safe vehicle interactions. The paper analyses the ETSI ITS standard's security architecture and demonstrates that the recommended methodology produces promising outcomes for building safer transportation systems in smart cities.

REFERENCES

Bi, Y., Srinivasan, D., Lu, X., Sun, Z., & Zeng, W. (2014). Type-2 fuzzy multi-intersection traffic signal control with differential evolution optimization. *Expert Systems with Applications, 41*(16), 7338–7349. doi:10.1016/j.eswa.2014.06.022

Bie, Y., Xiong, X., Yan, Y., & Qu, X. (2020). Dynamic headway control for high-frequency bus line based on speed guidance and intersection signal adjustment. *Computer-Aided Civil and Infrastructure Engineering, 35*(1), 4–25. doi:10.1111/mice.12446

Cao, Y., Wang, Z. C., Liu, F., Li, P., & Xie, G. (2019). Bio-inspired speed curve optimization and sliding mode tracking control for subway trains. *IEEE Transactions on Vehicular Technology, 68*(7), 6331–6342. doi:10.1109/TVT.2019.2914936

Chen, D. (2017). Research on traffic flow prediction in the big data environment based on the improved RBF neural network. *IEEE Transactions on Industrial Informatics, 13*(4), 2000–2008. doi:10.1109/TII.2017.2682855

Cuda, R., Guastaroba, G., & Speranza, M. G. (2015). A survey on two-echelon routing problems. *Computers & Operations Research, 55*, 185–199. doi:10.1016/j.cor.2014.06.008

Eiza, M. H., Owens, T., & Ni, Q. (2015). Secure and robust multi-constrained QoS aware routing algorithm for VANETs. *IEEE Transactions on Dependable and Secure Computing, 13*(1), 32–45. doi:10.1109/TDSC.2014.2382602

Feng, X., Ling, X., Zheng, H., Chen, Z., & Xu, Y. (2018). Adaptive multi-kernel SVM with spatial–temporal correlation for short-term traffic flow prediction. *IEEE Transactions on Intelligent Transportation Systems, 20*(6), 2001–2013. doi:10.1109/TITS.2018.2854913

Fernandez-Rodriguez, A., Fernández-Cardador, A., Cucala, A. P., Domínguez, M., & Gonsalves, T. (2015). Design of robust and energy-efficient ATO speed profiles of metropolitan lines considering train load variations and delays. *IEEE Transactions on Intelligent Transportation Systems, 16*(4), 2061–2071. doi:10.1109/TITS.2015.2391831

Ferrer, J., López-Ibáñez, M., & Alba, E. (2019). Reliable simulation-optimization of traffic lights in a real-world city. *Applied Soft Computing, 78*, 697–711. doi:10.1016/j.asoc.2019.03.016

Gao, X. Z., Nalluri, M. S. R., Kannan, K., & Sinharoy, D. (2021). Multi-objective optimization of feature selection using hybrid cat swarm optimization. *Science China. Technological Sciences, 64*(3), 508–520. doi:10.100711431-019-1607-7

Gong, Y. J., Liu, Y. W., Lin, Y., Chen, W. N., & Zhang, J. (2019). Real-Time Taxi–Passenger Matching Using a Differential Evolutionary Fuzzy Controller. *IEEE Transactions on Systems, Man, and Cybernetics. Systems, 51*(5), 2712–2725. doi:10.1109/TSMC.2019.2916184

Hassannayebi, E., Zegordi, S. H., Amin-Naseri, M. R., & Yaghini, M. (2018). Optimizing headways for urban rail transit services using adaptive particle swarm algorithms. *Public Transport (Berlin), 10*(1), 23–62. doi:10.100712469-016-0147-6

Hussain, M. W., Pradhan, B., Gao, X. Z., Reddy, K. H. K., & Roy, D. S. (2020). Clonal selection algorithm for energy minimization in software defined networks. *Applied Soft Computing*, *96*, 106617. doi:10.1016/j.asoc.2020.106617

Li, F., Golden, B., & Wasil, E. (2005). Solving the time dependent traveling salesman problem. In The Next Wave in Computing, Optimization, and Decision Technologies (pp. 163-182). Springer US. doi:10.1007/0-387-23529-9_12

Li, Y., Lim, M. K., Tan, Y., Lee, Y., & Tseng, M. L. (2020). Sharing economy to improve routing for urban logistics distribution using electric vehicles. *Resources, Conservation and Recycling*, *153*, 104585. doi:10.1016/j.resconrec.2019.104585

Li, Y., Soleimani, H., & Zohal, M. (2019). An improved ant colony optimization algorithm for the multi-depot green vehicle routing problem with multiple objectives. *Journal of Cleaner Production*, *227*, 1161–1172. doi:10.1016/j.jclepro.2019.03.185

Li, Z., Shahidehpour, M., Bahramirad, S., & Khodaei, A. (2016). Optimizing traffic signal settings in smart cities. *IEEE Transactions on Smart Grid*, *8*(5), 2382–2393. doi:10.1109/TSG.2016.2526032

Lin, F., Liu, S., Yang, Z., Zhao, Y., Yang, Z., & Sun, H. (2016). Multi-train energy saving for maximum usage of regenerative energy by dwell time optimization in urban rail transit using genetic algorithm. *Energies*, *9*(3), 208. doi:10.3390/en9030208

Lin, J., Zhou, K., & Zhang, Y. (2019). Performance evaluation of ETSI ITS security architecture in vehicular network. *Journal of Intelligent Transport Systems*, *23*(3), 276–285.

Liu, H., Zhou, M., Guo, X., Zhang, Z., Ning, B., & Tang, T. (2018). Timetable optimization for regenerative energy utilization in subway systems. *IEEE Transactions on Intelligent Transportation Systems*, *20*(9), 3247–3257. doi:10.1109/TITS.2018.2873145

Liu, R., Li, S., Yang, L., & Yin, J. (2018). Energy-efficient subway train scheduling design with time-dependent demand based on an approximate dynamic programming approach. *IEEE Transactions on Systems, Man, and Cybernetics. Systems*, *50*(7), 2475–2490. doi:10.1109/TSMC.2018.2818263

Nalluri, M. R., Kannan, K., Gao, X. Z., & Roy, D. S. (2020). Multiobjective hybrid monarch butterfly optimization for imbalanced disease classification problem. *International Journal of Machine Learning and Cybernetics*, *11*(7), 1423–1451. doi:10.100713042-019-01047-9

Nitisiri, K., Gen, M., & Ohwada, H. (2019). A parallel multi-objective genetic algorithm with learning based mutation for railway scheduling. *Computers & Industrial Engineering*, *130*, 381–394. doi:10.1016/j.cie.2019.02.035

Poonthalir, G., & Nadarajan, R. (2018). A fuel efficient green vehicle routing problem with varying speed constraint (F-GVRP). *Expert Systems with Applications*, *100*, 131–144. doi:10.1016/j.eswa.2018.01.052

Pradhan, B., Hussain, M. W., Srivastava, G., Debbarma, M. K., Barik, R. K., & Lin, J. C. W. (2022). A neuro-evolutionary approach for software defined wireless network traffic classification. *IET Communications*, cmu2.12548. doi:10.1049/cmu2.12548

Sadeghi-Barzani, P., Rajabi-Ghahnavieh, A., & Kazemi-Karegar, H. (2014). Optimal fast charging station placing and sizing. *Applied Energy*, *125*, 289–299. doi:10.1016/j.apenergy.2014.03.077

Safavat, S., & Rawat, D. B. (2020). On the elliptic curve cryptography for privacy-aware secure ACO-AODV routing in intent-based internet of vehicles for smart cities. *IEEE Transactions on Intelligent Transportation Systems*, *22*(8), 5050–5059. doi:10.1109/TITS.2020.3008361

Sánchez-Medina, J. J., Galán-Moreno, M. J., & Rubio-Royo, E. (2009). Traffic signal optimization in" La Almozara" district in saragossa under congestion conditions, using genetic algorithms, traffic microsimulation, and cluster computing. *IEEE Transactions on Intelligent Transportation Systems*, *11*(1), 132–141. doi:10.1109/TITS.2009.2034383

Situ, X., Chen, W. N., Gong, Y. J., Lin, Y., Yu, W. J., Yu, Z., & Zhang, J. (2017, June). A parallel ant colony system based on region decomposition for taxi-passenger matching. In *2017 IEEE congress on evolutionary computation (CEC)* (pp. 960-967). IEEE.

Wang, C., Chen, C., & Song, H. (2020). Impact of packet loss on security of vehicular communication. *IET Intelligent Transport Systems*, *14*(1), 1–8.

Wang, Y., Ma, X., Xu, M., Liu, Y., & Wang, Y. (2015). Two-echelon logistics distribution region partitioning problem based on a hybrid particle swarm optimization–genetic algorithm. *Expert Systems with Applications*, *42*(12), 5019–5031. doi:10.1016/j.eswa.2015.02.058

Xia, W., Dai, X., Li, Y., Li, W., & Wu, J. (2021). An Evaluation of the Security and Privacy Protection of ETSI ITS. *IEEE Internet of Things Journal*, *8*(2), 1002–1012.

Yan, X., Huang, H., Hao, Z., & Wang, J. (2019). A graph-based fuzzy evolutionary algorithm for solving two-echelon vehicle routing problems. *IEEE Transactions on Evolutionary Computation*, *24*(1), 129–141. doi:10.1109/TEVC.2019.2911736

Yang, H., Yang, S., Xu, Y., Cao, E., Lai, M., & Dong, Z. (2015). Electric vehicle route optimization considering time-of-use electricity price by learnable partheno-genetic algorithm. *IEEE Transactions on Smart Grid*, *6*(2), 657–666. doi:10.1109/TSG.2014.2382684

Zeng, B., Feng, J., Liu, N., & Liu, Y. (2020). Co-optimized parking lot placement and incentive design for promoting PEV integration considering decision-dependent uncertainties. *IEEE Transactions on Industrial Informatics*, *17*(3), 1863–1872. doi:10.1109/TII.2020.2993815

Zhang, Y., Gao, K., Zhang, Y., & Su, R. (2018). Traffic light scheduling for pedestrian-vehicle mixed-flow networks. *IEEE Transactions on Intelligent Transportation Systems*, *20*(4), 1468–1483. doi:10.1109/TITS.2018.2852646

Zhong, J. H., Shen, M., Zhang, J., Chung, H. S. H., Shi, Y. H., & Li, Y. (2012). A differential evolution algorithm with dual populations for solving periodic railway timetable scheduling problem. *IEEE Transactions on Evolutionary Computation*, *17*(4), 512–527. doi:10.1109/TEVC.2012.2206394

Chapter 11
An Alert and Detection System for Cyber-Attacks on IoT Devices

Arun Raj V.
Mepco Schlenk Engineering College (Autonomous), Sivakasi, India

Mohamed Arshad M.
Mepco Schlenk Engineering College (Autonomous), Sivakasi, India

F. Mathew
Mepco Schlenk Engineering College (Autonomous), Sivakasi, India

ABSTRACT

The internet of things (IoT) is still in its early stages, but it has sparked interest in a wide range of industries, including healthcare, logistics tracking, smart cities, and transportation. However, it is also vulnerable to a variety of serious network infiltration concerns. This chapter contributes to attack detection and alert system for IoT networks. This system provides alert and detection of cyber-attacks at the router level by configuring Rpi as a wireless router for IoT network. For the detection method, the authors used an anomaly-based approach that learns the packets in the network using deep learning. IoTID20 dataset is used for training the deep learning model. This model detects four kinds of attack: DoS, MITM, port scan, and scan. When the attack is detected, the user is alerted via e-mail and SMS.

INTRODUCTION

The Internet of Things has become more popular and used in a wide range of industries and the increase in IoT devices made our day-to-day life easier. Nowadays there is a huge development in developing IoT devices and innovations in the field IoT made the usage and adoption of IoT in different industries and sectors such as healthcare, agriculture, transportation and used in modern applications such as smart city, home automation and smart cars etc. Even Though IoT provides various benefits it is extremely

DOI: 10.4018/979-8-3693-0744-1.ch011

vulnerable to cyber-attacks such as data theft, Botnet attacks, DDOS attacks etc. As IoT devices are used in our day-to-day life in our homes, workplaces, and hospitals, if the IoT devices are not secured properly it can affect the user in various ways such as invading the user's privacy, user's safety and in extreme cases impact the human's health as IoT is used in healthcare. So, it is important for us to make our IoT Network secure. Much research and development is done on Securing IoT devices and networks used for commercial purposes using an Intrusion detection system in recent years, but the security of IoT devices in the home-based networks is not given importance. So, it is important to create a system which provides adequate security to these IoT Networks. Network intrusion detection system is used as a security measure to IoT networks. This system continuously monitors the packets exchanged by the devices in the IoT Network and searches for malicious activity and labels it as an attack. The goal of our project is to detect the attacks or malicious activity in the IoT network and alert the user about the attack which makes the user aware of the attack and respond to the malicious activity happening in the IoT Network.

The motivation behind the research and development of intrusion detection systems for IoT networks is the increasing popularity and usage of IoT devices in various industries and sectors. The ease of use and benefits provided by IoT devices have led to their adoption in smart cities, home automation, healthcare, and transportation, among others. However, these devices are vulnerable to cyber-attacks, which can compromise user privacy, safety, and even health. While there have been significant developments in securing commercial IoT networks, home-based networks are often overlooked. Therefore, there is a need for a system that can provide adequate security to these networks. The proposed system aims to continuously monitor the IoT network for malicious activity using a network intrusion detection system and alert the user about the attack to enable timely response and prevent damage.

The chapter begins with the section 1, which establishes the background and significance of IoT, highlighting the vulnerabilities and risks present in IoT networks. It emphasizes the importance of securing IoT networks and presents the goal of the project: to detect and alert attacks in IoT networks. The section 2 examines the advances in IoT network security, existing intrusion detection systems for IoT networks, and the datasets used for intrusion detection in IoT networks. It also identifies the limitations and gaps in current approaches, paving the way for the proposed methodology. Section 3 provides an overview of deep learning and introduces the CNN-LSTM architecture for attack detection. It also discusses the dataset used for training and testing, specifically the IoTID20 dataset. Section 4 presents the system design and architecture, hardware details of the Raspberry Pi 4 Model B, implementation of IoT nodes, packet capturing, and CSV file creation. It also covers the configuration of the Raspberry Pi as a wireless router and access point and introduces the CNN-LSTM detection model for attack classification. Section 5 brings out the further details the hardware details of the Raspberry Pi 4 Model B, implementation of IoT nodes, packet capturing, CSV file creation, and the configuration of the Raspberry Pi as a wireless router. It also explains the implementation of the CNN-LSTM detection model for attack classification. Results and Evaluation section 6 focuses on performance evaluation metrics and presents the experimental results on the IoTID20 dataset. It includes a comparative analysis with existing methods to highlight the effectiveness of the proposed approach. Finally, section 7 summarizes the contributions of the study and outlines future research directions in the field of securing IoT networks.

LITERATURE SURVEY

The field of IoT network security has witnessed significant advancements in recent years. Researchers have explored various approaches to enhance intrusion detection systems and secure IoT devices. de Almeida Florencio et al. (2018) proposed an intrusion detection system based on an MLP neural network implemented on an Arduino embedded system. They demonstrated the feasibility of using this approach for effective intrusion detection. Hyunjae et al. (2019) contributed to the field by creating a comprehensive IoT network intrusion dataset, which serves as a valuable resource for evaluating intrusion detection algorithms. Ullah and Mahmoud (2020) addressed the challenge of generating a dataset for anomalous activity detection in IoT networks. Their scheme offers insights into effectively creating datasets that capture diverse IoT network behaviors. Nagy and Coleşa (2019) proposed a router-based IoT security system using Raspberry Pi. This system not only provides affordable security but also enables the detection of malicious attacks and alerts users accordingly. Chen et al. (2020) introduced a novel network intrusion detection system based on convolutional neural networks (CNNs). Their approach leverages the capabilities of CNNs to detect and classify network intrusions accurately. Injadat, Moubayed, and Shami (2020) presented an optimized machine learning framework for detecting botnet attacks in IoT environments. Their approach demonstrates improved accuracy in identifying botnet activities. Upasani and Om (2019) contributed to real-time intrusion detection with their modified neuro-fuzzy classifier, implemented on modern GPUs. Their parallel implementation on GPUs enables efficient real-time intrusion detection. Moustafa and Slay (2015) developed the UNSW-NB15 dataset, a comprehensive dataset for network intrusion detection systems. This dataset has been widely used by researchers in the field. Hattarki, Houji, and Dhage (2021) proposed a real-time intrusion detection system specifically designed for IoT networks. Their system addresses the need for timely detection and response to intrusions in IoT environments. Babu, Karthika, and Rajan (2020) explored the use of Raspberry Pi, machine learning, and artificial intelligence techniques to develop secure IoT systems. Vinayakumar et al. (2019) introduced a deep learning approach for intelligent intrusion detection systems, which leverages the power of deep neural networks in identifying network intrusions. Al-Emadi, Al-Mohannadi, and Al-Senaid (2020) investigated the application of deep learning techniques in network intrusion detection, showcasing the potential of deep learning for improved detection accuracy. Thaseen, Poorva, and Ushasree (2020) evaluated various machine learning techniques for network intrusion detection and highlighted their effectiveness in detecting intrusions. Visoottiviseth et al. (2020) proposed a signature-based and behavior-based attack detection approach for home IoT devices, utilizing machine learning algorithms to detect and mitigate attacks effectively. Simadiputra and Surantha (2021) introduced Rasefiberry, a secure and efficient Raspberry Pi-based gateway for smarthome IoT architecture. Their system offers enhanced security measures for IoT devices in a home environment. These studies collectively contribute to the advancements in IoT network security, offering valuable insights and techniques for effective intrusion detection, dataset generation, and securing IoT devices.

The reviewed papers are tabulated as Table 1 for better comparison.

Table 1. Comparison of existing methods

Authors/Research	Proposed Method	Dataset Used	Real-Time Detection	Alert System	Accuracy
Nagy and Coleşa (2019)	Router with malicious attack detection	N/A	Yes	Yes	N/A
Hattarki, Houji, and Dhage (2021)	Machine learning model with packet capturing tool	IoT node with Arduino Uno, Node MCU, and Ultrasonic Sensor	Yes	Yes (via desktop notification)	91.18%
Thaseen, Poorva, and Ushasree (2020)	Comparison of machine learning algorithms	Wireshark captured packets with 24 different attributes and 1130 instances	N/A	N/A	99.81%
Upasani and Om (2019)	Parallel implementation of modified neuro-fuzzy classifier on GPUs	KDD dataset (not generated from IoT Network)	Yes	N/A	N/A
de Almeida Florencio et al. (2018)	IDS system using Multilayer perceptron Neural Network	NSL_KDD dataset	No	No	N/A
Injadat, Moubayed, and Shami (2020)	Optimized machine learning framework for detecting botnet attacks	Bot-IoT dataset	No (requires time-consuming feature extraction)	N/A	N/A

Survey Conclusion

Most of the research and proposed methods to detect cyber-attacks in IoT are using Intrusion Detection System and most of the Intrusion detection used datasets are not recent datasets and those datasets are not generated from IoT Networks. Some of the IDS systems use IoT specific datasets such as BoT-IoT and few create their own dataset in their IoT environment to train the model used for IDS. There is a lack of focus on alerting the user about the attack performed on IoT devices. Based on the literature survey we have performed we found that there is a lack of ways to alert the user about the detection of alert and implement the proposed intrusion detection system in Real time continuously. Continuously monitoring the IoT Network in real time and alerting the user about the detected attack happening in IoT Network should be concentrated.

DEEP LEARNING

Deep learning is the process of providing a computer model with the ability to make the computer learn and perform prediction, classification, and analysis of data from images, text, or sound. Its goal is to make the computer learn and perform like the human brain. Deep learning models use neural networks for training (Nalluri et al., 2017). In some cases, the accuracy attained by deep learning models exceeds the performance of the human. We have used Deep learning to detect the malicious activity present in the IoT Network. A cyber-attack detection system is proposed based on the CNN-LSTM architecture concept, major deep neural network architecture. CNN-LSTM is an abbreviation of CNN Long short-term memory used in the prediction of sequence data. CNN-LSTM is a hybrid model which involves convolutional neural network and LSTM where convolutional neural network is used for extracting features from the data and LSTM is used for performing predictions on sequence data.

Figure 1. Architecture of CNN_LSTM

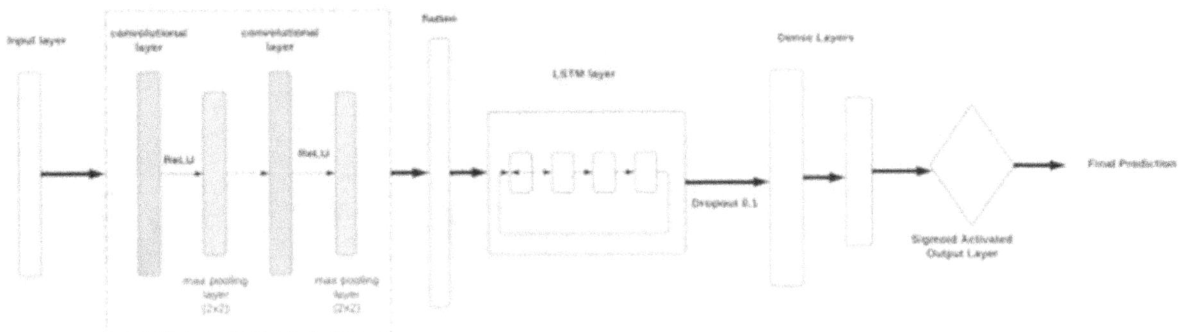

Dataset

To train the CNN_LSTM deep learning model we have used the IoTID20 Dataset. It is a well-structured dataset for Intrusion in IoT Networks. From our literature survey we can infer that most used standard and common datasets such as CICIDS2017, UNSW-NB15, NSL-KDD. These datasets are not specific for IoT Networks, so we used the IoTID20 dataset as its generated from IoT Network Intrusion dataset which consists of 42 raw packet capture files of IoT Network with normal flow and attacks such as DOS, Mirai, Scan, MITM. The IoTID20 has 83 features in which there are labels classifying it into binary, category, and subcategory the remaining 80 features can be which can be extracted from pcap files using CICflowmeter. There are 623873 instances. So this dataset is used in our model. The dataset is preprocessed and split into training and testing data. 80% of this dataset is used for training the CNN_LSTM model and 20% for testing the CNN_LSTM model.

PROPOSED METHODOLOGY

The model diagram represents the demonstration of a proposed system where the Raspberry pi is acting as an access point for the IoT Nodes and detecting the cyber attacks performed in the IoT Network. Initially the raspberry pi was configured as Wireless Router / Access Point for the IoT Network with the SSID and password protected with WPA-2 security and the bandwidth chosen is 2.4 Ghz,as the Node MCU supports 2.4 Ghz wifi band. The IoT Node 1 consists of a Node MCU interfacing with DHT11 sensor and hosts a web server to display the room temperature and humidity to the user and similarly in IoT Node 2, Node MCU is interfaced with servo motor and hosts a web server to control the servo motor remotely by the user. Now these Node MCUs are connected to the wireless Network created by raspberry pi by providing the ssid and password of Raspberry pi access point to the Node MCU and the user is also connected to the network. Thus results in the formation of the IoT Network.

Figure 2. Proposed model diagram

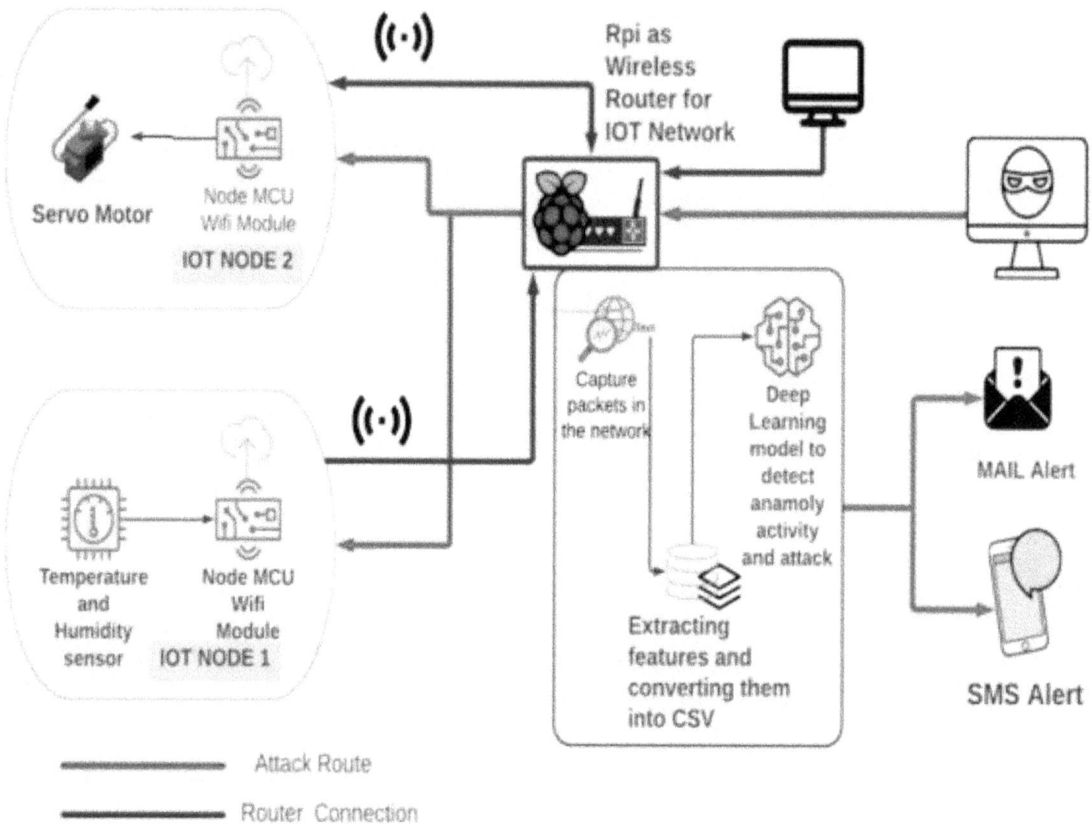

As raspberry pi entirely manages this Network, CICflowmeter tool running in the raspberry pi captures the packets transmitted in the network and extracts features from the pcap file and logs it in a CSV file. The python script running in the Raspberry preprocess the CSV file and feeds the CSV file displayed in the Figure 3 to the trained deep learning model and the deep learning model used here is CNN_LSTM, and we have used binary classification, so this model classifies the packets as Attack or Normal by giving 0 and 1 as predicted output. 0 represents the normal label and 1 represents the attack label. When a deep learning model classifies the packet as Attack then the user is alerted via Email and SMS using SMTP python library and Fast2SMS API.

Figure 3. Workflow

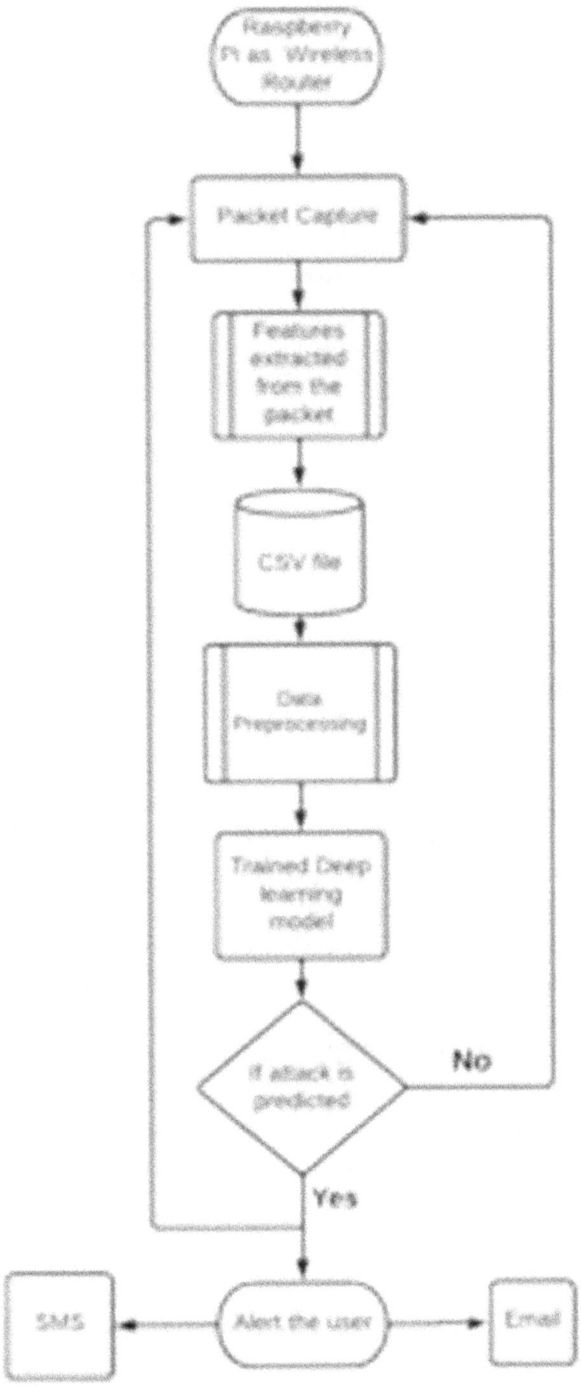

Our proposed system continuously captures the packet exchanged in the IoT Network and extracts features from the packets and analyzes the packets using a Deep learning model. If any anomaly or attack is detected then the user is alerted via Email and SMS.

SYSTEM DESIGN AND IMPLEMENTATION

Hardware Details

The main hardware we have used for this project was the Raspberry Pi 4 Model B. Raspberry pi is a credit card sized single board computer with High performance. The technical features are mentioned below:

- Rpi has Broadcom BCM2711 which is a Quad core Cortex-A72 (ARM v8) 64-bit processor with SoC @ 1.5GHz.
- Ram: 4GB LPDDR4-3200 SDRAM.
- 2.4 GHz and 5.0 GHz IEEE 802.11ac wireless.
- Bluetooth 5.0, BLE Gigabit Ethernet.

A wireless router connected to a network via Ethernet is considered in this project as a way of creating a safe subnet for devices in the Internet of Things. An attack on the IoT network is not possible from outside, as its IP address scope is local only. An attacker can only act from a compromised device if they are connected to WiFi and gaining internet access through it.

IoT Module

We have implemented two IoT Nodes.In IoT Node 1, DHT11 temperature and humidity sensor is interfaced with Node MCU. ESP8266 is uploaded with code to host a webserver which updates the temperature and humidity readings for every ten seconds. Similarly, in IoT Node 2, Servo motor SG90 is interfaced with Node MCU, and a web server is hosted by ESP8266 to control the servo motor which can be used in the application of closing and opening doors in the home environment.

Packet Capturing and Creation of CSV File

The packets in the IoT Network are captured and required features to classify the packet attack or normal is extracted using CICflowmeter (a packet capturing tool). The CICflowmeter tool is deployed in raspberry pi. Raspberry pi is programmed to run the CICflowmeter tool at the startup, the CICflowmeter tool captures the packets in the network and extracts the packet's features and logs it into a CSV file.

Figure 4. Block diagram of process performed using CICflowmeter

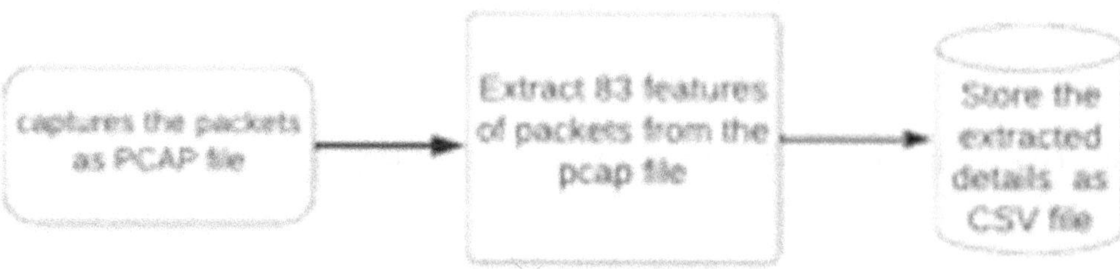

Raspberry Pi as Wireless Router

At the hardware level, we have used a Raspberry Pi. and configured it to act as a Wireless Router. A Raspberry Pi can be used as an access point with only a few requirements: the device has to be connected to an Ethernet cable, and some configurations need to be done. For configuring two software packages are required. The required software packages are Hostapd and Dnsmasq. Hostapd is used for raspberry pi as an access point and dnsmasq for network management. Hostapd is used to change the raspberry pi network interface card into access point and The DHCP server is made to run and the DNS services in the rpi by dnsmasq software installed rpi then a static IP 192.168.4.1 is assigned to the wlan0 interface of raspberry pi and configured as an access point to the IoT Network.Thus the raspberry pi is configured as the Wireless Router / Access Point for IoT Network this allows the Raspberry Pi to monitor the IoT Network.

Figure 5. Block diagram of Rpi as wireless router in the network

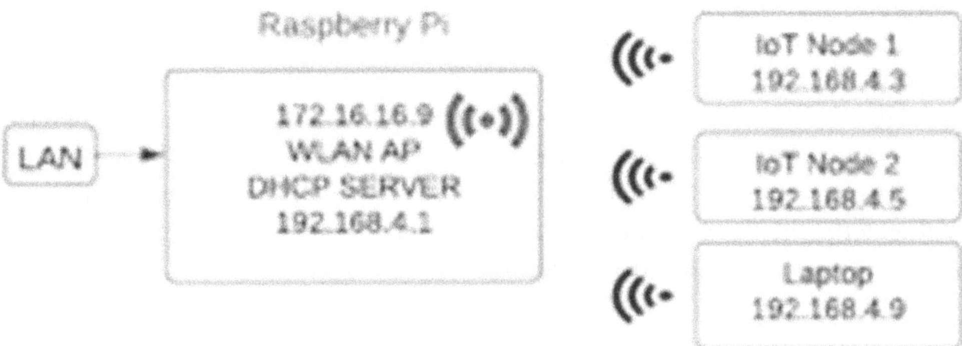

Detection Model

A deep learning model is used to detect the attack happening in the IoT Network. Here we used a hybrid deep learning model. CNN_LSTM model is used to train and test the model. IoTID20 Dataset which has 83 features and includes four types of attack. This IoTID20 dataset is used to train the CNN_LSTM model to predict the attacks in IoT Network.80 percent of the data is used for training and 20 percent of the dataset is used for testing the deep learning model. The packets in the IoT are captured by cic flow-meter a packet capturing tool which extracts 80 features of IoTid20 dataset and logs it into csv file and it is preprocessed and given as input file for the deep learning detection program, the detection program runs a trained CNN_LSTM DL model using IoTId20 dataset, so the given input logs is passed through the DL model and the classifies it as Normal or Attack.

Alert System

The end user is alerted by e-mail and sms each time an attack is detected in the network. Through this, the user knows of the attack. Since the API is faster and provides high-level security, Fast2sms api is used to send notifications via SMS. For email notification, smtplib python library is used. It can send and receive messages via email. So when the deep learning model predicts an attack the user is alerted via SMS and Email through these functions.

ATTACK PHASE

To test our proposed system and to understand how the attack is performed, we performed a few common and major attacks. Using Kali Linux OS for performing penetration testing in IoT Network, which has pre-installed network scanning tool and hacking tools such as nmap, hping3 and ettercap, this was the next step toward research of vulnerabilities.

Man In the Middle Attack

A MITM attack is a type of data eavesdropping in which attackers disguise themselves as legitimate participants in an existing communication or data transfer. Typically, a MITM attack involves two victims and an attacker. Through the communication channel, the attacker can manipulate the messages between the two endpoints. Therefore, malicious attackers may manipulate and perform theft on the data transmitted over the Nodes and Devices in the Network. Since the victims are unaware of these intruders, they believe the communication channel is protected. We have performed MITM attack using Ettercap tool for ARP Spoofing and Burpsuite for data manipulation in Kali Linux, the victim ip address is set as target 1 and router's ip address as target 2 and choosing the ARP poisoning in the MITM menu, thus we have initiated a MITM attack by ARP Spoofing

Figure 6. Performing MITM-ARP spoofing using Ettercap

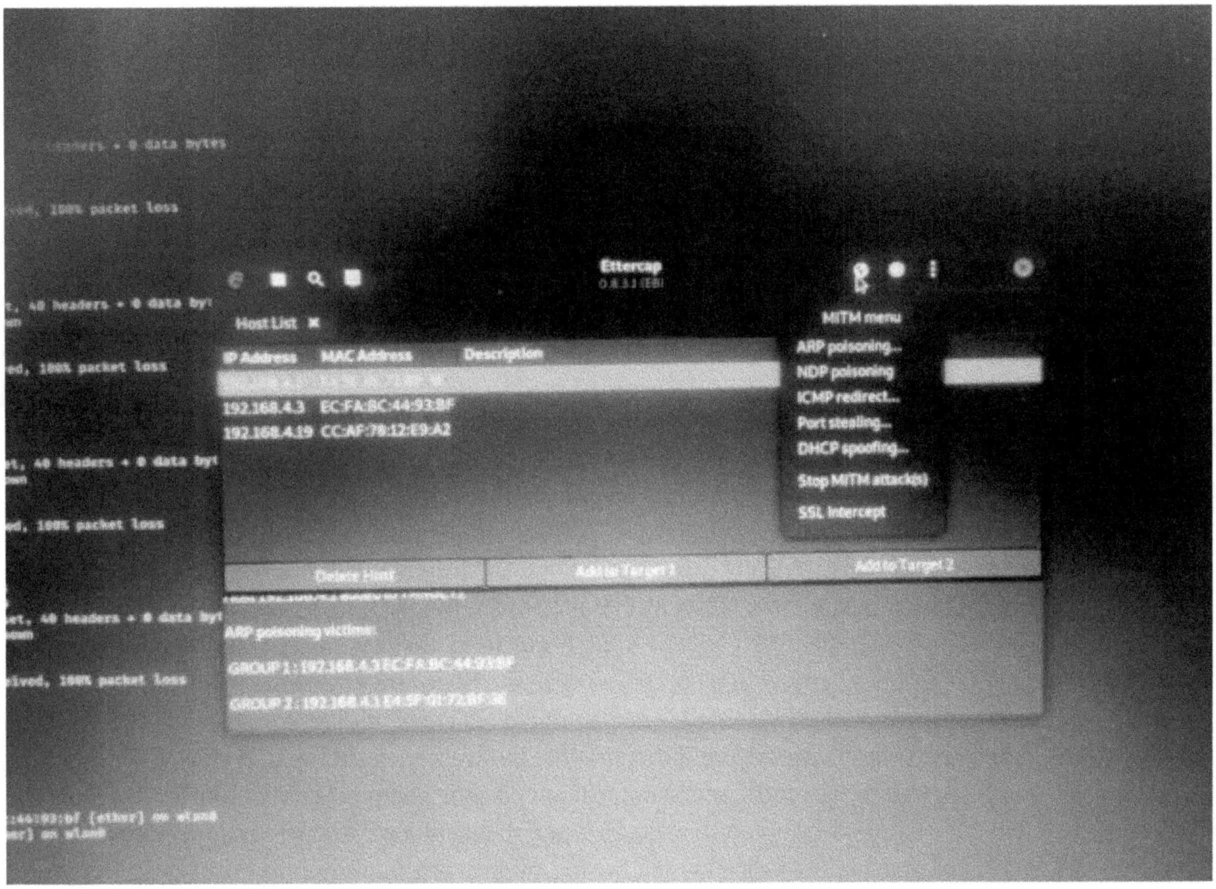

Denial of Service

An attempt is made to prevent legitimate users from accessing computer systems, networks, or services using denial-of-service attacks that exploit vulnerabilities in order to make the server unavailable to use, shut down and affect its performance. During these types of attacks, the attackers flood the victim's equipment with traffic, overloading its resources and making it impossible for anyone else to connect. Since the attacker has utilized most of the network bandwidth the target continues to function but has no ability to process legitimate network requests (Pradhan et al, 2022). Here we implemented this attack on the webserver hosted by IoT Node 1's Nodemcu.The attack is performed using Hping3 tool by SYN packets flooding to the IoT Node 1 web server by mentioning the Node MCU ip address and port number 80 as it is HTTP server in the Hping3 command.

Figure 7. Performing Dos attack to the IoT Node 1 webserver

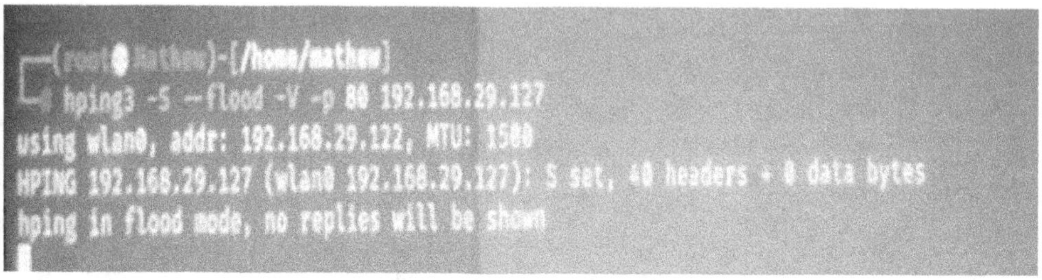

RESULTS

Python is used for programming as it has many libraries with a variety of functionalities. We used the CICflowmeter tool to capture the packets and extract the features and log it in a CSV. The CNN _LSTM model is built using Tensorflow and keras module in python and the model is trained with IoTID20 dataset. For detecting malicious behavior, the trained model is loaded in the raspberry pi and, the CSV file with features generated by CICflowmeter is given as input to the DL model and it provides the classification it Attack or Normal. This trained CNN LSTM model is tested with test data to obtain the accuracy and confusion matrix results. When the CNN_LSTM model is tested with a testing dataset. The model gives an accuracy of 99.09% which is better when compared with the literature of recent works and in Figure 8 the confusion matrix of the model is presented. The generated CSV file with features of packets captured is fed into the trained deep learning model and this model classifies each packet in the CSV file as 0 and 1 where 0 represents normal packet and 1 represents attack packet. The predicted output for each packet is logged into a text file. This text file is analyzed and when the instances of 1 is found the user is alerted via Email and SMS. For alerting the user via email using python program by importing smtplib python library and the results of alerting the user via Email are obtained and presented in Figure 9.

Figure 8. Confusion matrix

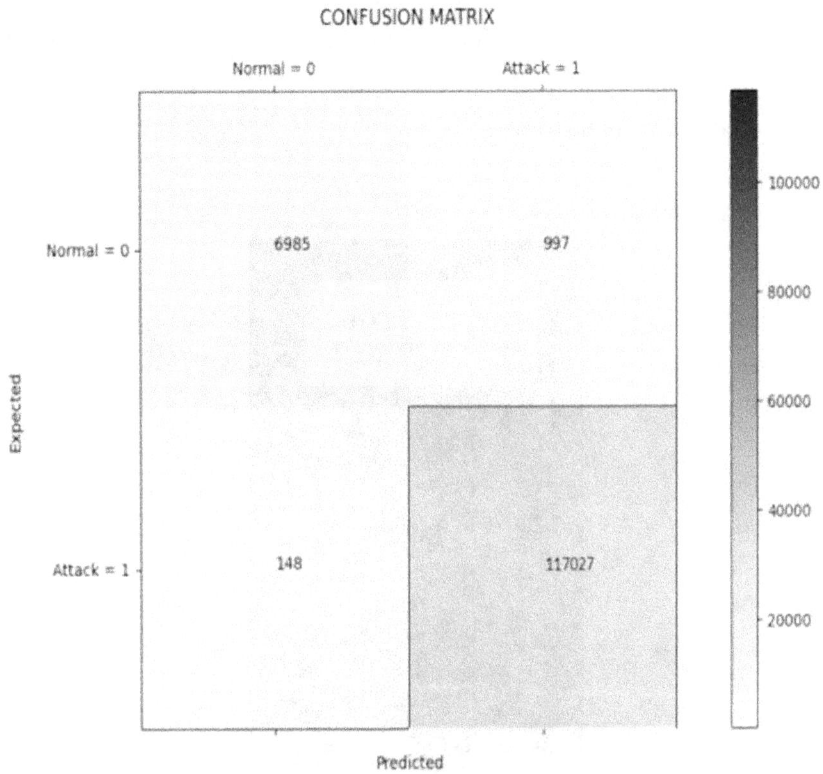

Figure 9. Email alert received by the user

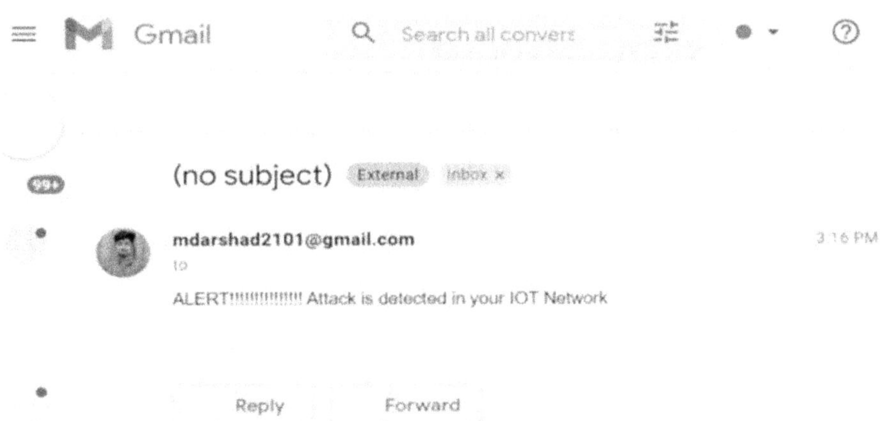

Similarly, when the attack instances are found the user is alerted via SMS using python through FasT2SMS API service. To perform this user is made to register in the Fast2SMS API and the authorization key is obtained. Using the requests module in python and including the user's authorization key, text message to be sent and the receiver's mobile number in the python program the user is alerted via SMS. The results of alerting the user via SMS are obtained and presented in Figure 10.

Figure 10. SMS alert received by the user

CONCLUSION

It was found that components of IoT systems were built without considering security schemas or responses to common vulnerability. In this work, we developed a methodology for detecting malicious network activity in a IoT environment using deep learning techniques deployed on a Raspberry Pi 4 which also act as router and by leveraging Cicflowmeter to generate logs as input, it was found that trained models can detect malicious activity with high accuracy based on the data extracted. In addition, we were able to learn which features were significant enough to identify common IoT attacks such as DOS and MITM attacks. Given these results, we can conclude that real-time detection and alerting of cyber-attack can be performed in an IoT Network using a low-cost solution, in a limited resource environment with a Raspberry Pi. Although deep learning techniques may also help improve the solution, further research is needed to develop and integrate an effective solution into the data pipeline. This is one of several areas which can be used to pursue as a future direction for this work. Some other areas include collecting data and training models for additional attacks, self-learning by introducing a feedback loop, and performing cyber-attack prevention.

FUTURE WORK

One possible future direction for this work is to collect data and train models for additional types of attacks beyond the ones identified in this study, such as botnet attacks or ransomware attacks. This would help improve the accuracy of the detection system and make it more robust against a wider range of threats. Another potential future direction is to introduce a feedback loop into the system, allowing it to self-learn and improve over time. This would enable the system to adapt to new and emerging threats and stay up to date with the latest attack techniques. Finally, there is a need to explore methods for preventing cyber-attacks from occurring in the first place. This could involve implementing stronger authentication and access control mechanisms, as well as incorporating intrusion prevention capabilities into the system. Overall, the development of more effective and robust security solutions for IoT networks will be critical in ensuring the safety and privacy of users in the future.

REFERENCES

Al-Emadi, S., Al-Mohannadi, A., & Al-Senaid, F. (2020, February). *Using deep learning techniques for network intrusion detection. In 2020 IEEE international conference on informatics, IoT, and enabling technologies (ICIoT)*. IEEE.

Babu, R. G., Karthika, P., & Rajan, V. A. (2020). Secure IoT systems using raspberry Pi machine learning artificial intelligence. In *Second International Conference on Computer Networks and Communication Technologies: ICCNCT 2019* (pp. 797-805). Springer International Publishing.

Chen, L., Kuang, X., Xu, A., Suo, S., & Yang, Y. (2020, December). A novel network intrusion detection system based on CNN. In *2020 eighth international conference on advanced cloud and big data (CBD)* (pp. 243-247). IEEE.10.1109/ROEDUNET.2019.8909551

de Almeida Florencio, F., Moreno, E. D., Macedo, H. T., de Britto Salgueiro, R. J., do Nascimento, F. B., & Santos, F. A. O. (2018, November). Intrusion detection via MLP neural network using an arduino embedded system. In *2018 VIII Brazilian Symposium on Computing Systems Engineering (SBESC)* (pp. 190-195). IEEE. 10.1109/SBESC.2018.00036

Hattarki, R., Houji, S., & Dhage, M. (2021, April). Real Time Intrusion Detection System For IoT Networks. In *2021 6th International Conference for Convergence in Technology (I2CT)* (pp. 1-5). IEEE.

HyunjaeK.AhnD. H.LeeG. M.YooJ. D.ParkK. H.KimH. K. (2019). Iot network intrusion dataset. *IEEE Dataport*. doi:10.21227/q70p-q449

Injadat, M., Moubayed, A., & Shami, A. (2020, December). Detecting botnet attacks in IoT environments: An optimized machine learning approach. In *2020 32nd International Conference on Microelectronics (ICM)* (pp. 1-4). IEEE. 10.1109/ROEDUNET.2019.8909551

Moustafa, N., & Slay, J. (2015, November). UNSW-NB15: A comprehensive data set for network intrusion detection systems (UNSW-NB15 network data set). In *2015 military communications and information systems conference (MilCIS)* (pp. 1-6). IEEE.

Nagy, L., & Coleşa, A. (2019, October). Router-based IoT Security using Raspberry Pi. In *2019 18th RoEduNet Conference: Networking in Education and Research (RoEduNet)* (pp. 1-6). IEEE.10.1109/ROEDUNET.2019.8909551

Nalluri, M. R., & Roy, D. S. (2017). Hybrid disease diagnosis using multiobjective optimization with evolutionary parameter optimization. *Journal of Healthcare Engineering*, *2017*. doi:10.1155/2017/5907264 PMID:29065626

Pradhan, B., Hussain, M. W., Srivastava, G., Debbarma, M. K., Barik, R. K., & Lin, J. C. W. (2022). A neuro-evolutionary approach for software defined wireless network traffic classification. *IET Communications*, cmu2.12548. doi:10.1049/cmu2.12548

Simadiputra, V., & Surantha, N. (2021). Rasefiberry: Secure and efficient Raspberry-Pi based gateway for smart home IoT architecture. *Bulletin of Electrical Engineering and Informatics*, *10*(2), 1035–1045. doi:10.11591/eei.v10i2.2741

Thaseen, I. S., Poorva, B., & Ushasree, P. S. (2020, February). Network intrusion detection using machine learning techniques. In *2020 International conference on emerging trends in information technology and engineering (IC-ETITE)* (pp. 1-7). IEEE.

Ullah, I., & Mahmoud, Q. H. (2020). A scheme for generating a dataset for anomalous activity detection in iot networks. In *Advances in Artificial Intelligence: 33rd Canadian Conference on Artificial Intelligence, Canadian AI 2020, Ottawa, ON, Canada, May 13–15, 2020, Proceedings 33* (pp. 508-520). Springer International Publishing. 10.1007/978-3-030-47358-7_52

Upasani, N., & Om, H. (2019). A modified neuro-fuzzy classifier and its parallel implementation on modern GPUs for real time intrusion detection. *Applied Soft Computing, 82*, 105595.

Vinayakumar, R., Alazab, M., Soman, K. P., Poornachandran, P., Al-Nemrat, A., & Venkatraman, S. (2019). Deep learning approach for intelligent intrusion detection system. *IEEE Access : Practical Innovations, Open Solutions*, *7*, 41525–41550. doi:10.1109/ACCESS.2019.2895334

Visoottiviseth, V., Sakarin, P., Thongwilai, J., & Choobanjong, T. (2020, November). Signature-based and behavior-based attack detection with machine learning for home IoT devices. In 2020 IEEE REGION 10 CONFERENCE (TENCON) (pp. 829-834). IEEE. doi:10.1109/TENCON50793.2020.9293811

Chapter 12
Blockchain-Enabled Secured Smart City Services

Vrinda Gupta
National Institute of Technology, Kurukshetra, India

Vamsi Reddy Punugoti
National Institute of Technology, Kurukshetra, India

Sanath Kalyan Veereju
National Institute of Technology, Kurukshetra, India

ABSTRACT

Smart city incorporates multiple living methods for the sustainability of resources. As the number of interconnected devices is expanding day by day, we need to secure the transmission of data. Blockchain is seen as a way to eliminate tampering and reduce the risks of malware threats with IoT devices and data. In smart cities, blockchain-based IoT applications can be used for a wide variety of services in a secure and decentralized way. This chapter introduces blockchain technology and how it secures the data and then explores the integration of blockchain technology in smart city services like healthcare, transportation, supply chain management, smart grid, and banking.

INTRODUCTION

In recent years, the rise of smart cities has gained significant attention globally, integrating advanced technologies such as Artificial Intelligence (AI), Internet of Things (IoT), Blockchain Technology (BCT), and data analytics (S. Rani et al., 2021). Smart cities aim to provide citizens with efficient and sustainable services that enhance their quality of life while reducing costs and environmental impact. Blockchain technology, in particular, has emerged as a promising tool to enable secure, transparent, and decentralized systems for innovative city services.

This chapter comprehensively studies blockchain-based secured intelligent city services in different domains. The motive behind exploring blockchain-enabled smart city services is to address the current

DOI: 10.4018/979-8-3693-0744-1.ch012

challenges traditional centralized systems face, such as data privacy, security, transparency, and accountability (C. Shen et al., 2018). By leveraging blockchain technology, cities can create tamper-proof and immutable records of transactions and data, enabling citizens to have greater trust and control over their data while reducing the risk of fraud and cyber-attacks. In traditional centralized systems, personal data is often stored in a single location, making it vulnerable to cyber-attacks and data breaches. Blockchain technology provides a decentralized solution where data is stored across a network of nodes, making it more secure and less susceptible to hacks or breaches. Blockchain-enabled smart city services can also increase transparency and accountability, as every transaction is recorded on a public ledger that authorized parties can access. This can lead to greater trust between citizens and government agencies, and different stakeholders in a smart city ecosystem.

Another key advantage of blockchain-enabled smart city services is the potential for increased efficiency and cost savings. By automating processes and improving interoperability between different systems and stakeholders, blockchain technology can help reduce administrative costs and improve service delivery. Blockchain applications include energy management, waste management, public safety, construction, transportation, traffic management, power plants, water and gas supply management, healthcare, information systems, government services, and other community services (S. Ahmed et al., 2020; Makani et al., 2022; J. Xie et al., 2019).

Overall, the integration of blockchain technology in smart city services has the potential to transfigure the way cities are designed, managed, and experienced by citizens. By addressing key challenges such as data privacy, security, transparency, and accountability, blockchain-enabled smart city services can help create more sustainable and efficient urban environments that enhance the quality of life for citizens while reducing costs and environmental impact. The emergence of blockchain technology has opened up new possibilities for smart city services. As the adoption of blockchain technology continues to grow, safer smart city services are expected to develop.

The rest of the chapter is structured as follows. The literature review is specified in Section 2. Section 3 provides an overview of the working, advantages, features, and applications of blockchain. Section 4 details the discussion of emerging smart cities along with their features and challenges of smart city development. Section 5 discusses integrating BCT with various smart city services in the health sector, transportation, smart grid, supply chain management (SCM), and banking sector. Finally, the limitations, further scope, and conclusions are discussed in Section 6.

LITERATURE REVIEW

Background

The study and evolution of smart cities have expanded quickly over the past years. A smart city, according to some experts, uses information and communication technology (ICT) to improve its infrastructure and services (S. Rani et al., 2021). Others describe it as a city that makes decisions based on data to enrich the living standards of its citizens. ICT infrastructure, sensors and data gathering equipment, data analytics platforms, and citizen interaction tools are the elements that make up a smart city. The effectiveness, sustainability, and livability of metropolitan areas, as well as public safety, transportation, and energy consumption, can all be improved through smart cities.

Numerous cities across the world are working to become smart cities. According to IMD Smart City Index 2023, Zurich (Switzerland) has taken the lead, with Oslo (Norway) in second place and Canberra (Australia) in third. Along with these cities, Singapore, London, New York, Tokyo, Dubai, Helsinki, Amsterdam, Seoul, and Barcelona are also the leading smart cities in the world. For instance, Zurich has implemented smart city technologies, Namely IoT, AI, and cloud computing to enhance the efficiency and effectiveness of urban systems. And also particularly focus on smart city services like smart streetlights, smart parking, smart waste management, smart mobility, smart water management, and open data platform.

In the literature, several research works are available which discuss the role of technology like IoT, cloud computing, blockchain, etc. The integration of blockchain technology in smart cities provides an opportunity to improve the efficiency, security, and transparency of various services and systems. It includes technical aspects, impact on different industries, and potential future developments (Majeed et al., 2021). In the technical aspect, research focuses on the underlying blockchain algorithms and their performance, security, and scalability. In terms of industry-specific applications, BCT has been studied in various domains such as healthcare, SCM, energy, and finance.

However, there are also challenges and limitations in the blockchain and its integration in smart cities (J. Xie et al., 2019; Majeed et al., 2021; J. Leng et al., 2020; J. Bernal Bernabe et al., 2019). These challenges include privacy and security concerns, data management issues, and the digital divide.

Related Work

The creation of smart cities requires a multidisciplinary and trans-disciplinary approach rather than a one-dimensional one. Numerous cutting-edge technologies, including IoT, AI, BCT, big data, and cloud computing, might contribute to the sustainable growth of various smart city functional sectors. Cyber-Physical Systems (CPS) will improve sustainable growth in smart cities (S. Rani et al., 2021; Hussain et al, 2021). Through legislative initiatives and extensive pilot programs in both the public and private sectors, several cities throughout the globe have previously begun the race for the blockchain future (C. Shen et al., 2018). Blockchain will initially require a lot of resources, even though it will reduce the cost and time of transaction processing (S. Ahmed et al., 2020; Makani et al., 2022). In terms of challenges, several studies have explored the potential challenges associated with the implementation of blockchain technology in smart cities (J. Xie et al., 2019; Majeed et al., 2021; J. Leng et al., 2020; J. Bernal Bernabe et al., 2019). Three stages, referred to as the PDI model of blockchain privacy, are used to categorize the security of the blockchain: process, data, and infrastructure level (J. Leng et al., 2020).

Blockchain technology can be applied in various areas like medical care, transportation, smart grid, SCM, finance systems, energy trading, waste management, governance, and so on (J. Xie et al., 2019). Internet of Things (IoHT) frameworks for the healthcare industry can be secured and made more effective with the help of BCT (E. M. Abou-Nassar et al., 2020). To assist cut costs and improve communication between patients and healthcare providers, more healthcare organizations have started implementing IoMT in the age of the Internet of Things. To address the cyber-terrorist issue, a trust management system based on blockchain technology is implemented to detect rogue nodes (W. Meng et al., 2020). Several systems are implemented to assist in reducing the spread of contagious diseases generally and the COVID-19 disease specifically (H. R. Hasan et al., 2020). A blockchain-based architecture for the pharmaceutical supply chain is proposed to produce shielded logs of events within the logistics (A. Musamih et al., 2021; Haleem et al., 2021).

Blockchain technology has the potential to transform transportation systems in smart cities by enabling secure, transparent, and efficient transactions. There are several issues, including communication bandwidth, energy effectiveness, centralization, privacy, security, and integrity, present difficulties for smart parking and suggested a Blockchain-enabled Secure substructure for Energy-Efficient Smart Parking in a feasible City Environment, which was inspired by AI and blockchain technologies (Singh et al., 2022). For managing EV charging in the IoE, a segregated security model known as LNSC is developed and achieved a 97.78% success rate (X. Huang et al., 2018). A blockchain-based, budgeted reverse auction mechanism-based system for traffic monitoring by providing a simple information trading architecture employing asymmetric encryption to increase the system's security and dependability (J. Guo et al., 2022).

In the context of the smart grid ecosystem, a blockchain-based method for safe demand response management is provided (A. Jindal et al., 2020). And the benefit is that since a transaction is only put to the blockchain once it has been approved by all miner nodes, even an adversary engaging in the energy transfer would not be able to tamper with it. Smart contracts are used to carry out transactions, and the network serves as a transaction verifier. The immutability of the transactions offered by the blockchain guarantees that every transaction between consumers and generators will always be carried out (Agung et al., 2022). There is a necessity for a green component in blockchain-based energy auctions before outlining some design considerations that must be taken into account when creating such auction techniques (M. U. Hassan et al., 2022).

A unique blockchain-based POMS for the supply chain is presented, which renders counterfeiters' efforts to copy real tags pointless. Customers may refuse to buy counterfeit goods even if they have a valid EPC, as long as the seller has no proof of ownership (K. Toyoda et al., 2017). A general architecture utilizing Ethereum blockchain and smart contracts are offered to monitor, track, and carry out business transactions while removing middlemen and a centralized point of processing for soybean traceability along the agricultural supply chain (K. Salah et al., 2019). The usage of blockchain-based platforms with integrated smart contracts might improve information sharing across reputable and illegitimate entities with fewer security risks (P. K. Wan et al., 2020). There are two blockchain-based scenarios, namely the financing of warehouse receipts and the financing of accounts receivable to address how the use of the blockchain changed the business model and process (M. Du et al., 2020; P. K. Sharma et al., 2019).

Blockchain technology has the potential to upgrade and reinvent banks' credit information and payment clearing systems by revolutionizing their underlying technology. The Chinese banking sector faces some issues, namely interest rate liberalization, fall in profits brought on by the interest-rate spreads, financial breakthroughs, Internet expansion, and economic change. and the government of China developed a "regulatory sandbox" immediately and created industry norms (Guo et al., 2016). Implementing a hybrid blockchain system for CBDC, which is novel on three levels: the technical framework, network design, and consensus mechanism will improve the processing speed, transaction speed, and consensus speed (J. Zhang et al., 2021).

An energy trading system for residential dwellings that are built on a secure blockchain and for the system's choice of miners and block construction, a novel proof-of-computational closeness (PoCC) consensus mechanism is suggested (Samuel O et al., 2022). The use of blockchain in a voting system for smart cities can improve the transparency and accountability of the voting process, as well as reduce fraud and manipulation risks (Rathee et al., 2021). A blockchain-based solution for secure and efficient data transferring in smart cities is proposed. The solution employs a consensus algorithm called Improved Byzantine Fault Tolerance (IBFT) to ensure efficient transaction processing and secure data storage (Li et al., 2021). A thorough analysis of blockchain's potential for data promulgation in smart cities is provided, with a particular emphasis on the elements of smart cities' healthcare, transportation, energy, education, and building sectors (Shari et al., 2022). And also Energy efficient operation for Software Defined Networks (SDN) for resource management and requirement of Quality of Service (QoS) is presented (Reddy et al., 2022; Hussain et al., 2022). Overall, the literature covers various aspects of smart cities, blockchain technology, blockchain implementation in potential smart city applications, and the challenges and opportunities associated with it.

OVERVIEW OF BLOCKCHAIN

About Blockchain

Blockchain has emerged in recent years as the cutting-edge remedy for many IT industry issues. Blockchain is one of the quickest-growing and most dynamic technologies available right now, even though it was initially created to account for the well-known cryptocurrency Bitcoin. Blockchain facilitates a Peer-to-Peer (P2P) connection to build a decentralized database. This implies that the database won't be managed by a single entity. A public register of who owns what and who transacts with whom is essentially what a blockchain is. It offers a productive technique to collaborate with multiple parties without having mutual trust. Blockchain technology, known as Distributed Ledger Technology (DLT), enables financial institutions to control data-sharing governance (S. Ahmed et al., 2020).

Additionally, blockchain's decentralized ledgers are unchangeable. Each transaction is saved by the network as history information. It supports a ledger of records that can only be appended to later be added to the chain. Therefore, sharing information between parties is made simpler and safer by keeping track of consumer information and transaction records on a decentralized network.

1. **Structure of the Blockchain:** A linear chain of blocks makes up a blockchain. A collection of transactions, as well as other crucial information, are contained in each block. Blocks are secured by cryptography and are connected linearly. The structure of the Block in a Blockchain is shown in Figure 1.

Figure 1. Structure of a blockchain
Source: Majeed et al. (2021)

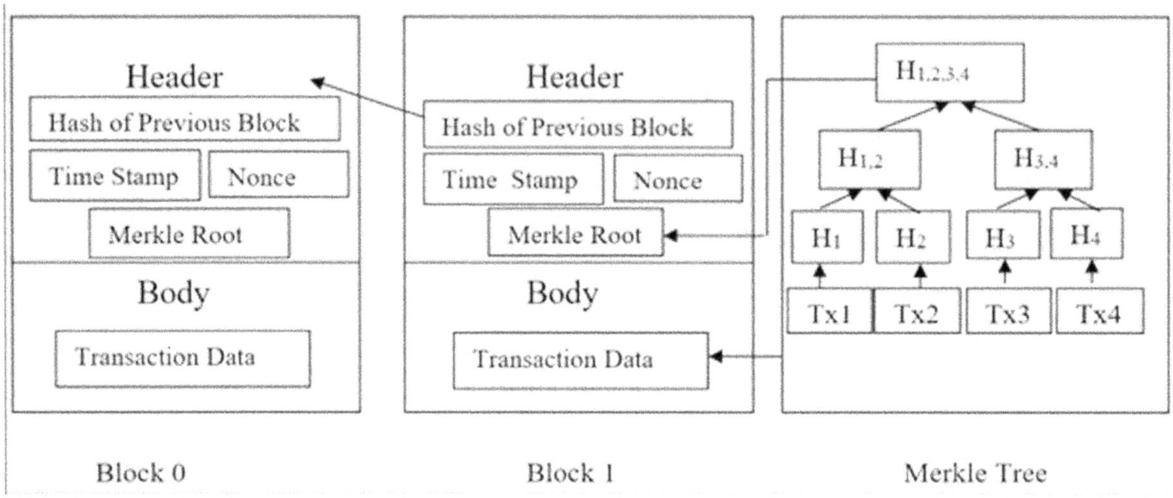

The following are the key components of a block:

a. **Block Height:** It is the block's position in the chain of blocks or its sequence number. The genesis block is Block Height: 1.
b. **Block Length:** The block size is stored in a 4-byte field that is 32 bits wide. Size is increased in bytes, for example, 216 bytes.
c. **Block Reward:** The payment given to the miner for including a block of transactions is shown in this field.
d. **Text Count:** The block's total number of transactions is indicated by the transaction counter. The field can only be as large as 9 bytes.
e. **Block Header:** The metadata information about the block is contained in the block header, an 80-byte field. The block header consists of the preceding block hash, time, version, bits, nonce & Merkle root (S. Ahmed et al., 2020).

2. **Functioning of the Blockchain:** The functioning of a blockchain is illustrated in Figure 2.

Figure 2. Functioning of blockchain technology
Source: Makani et al. (2022)

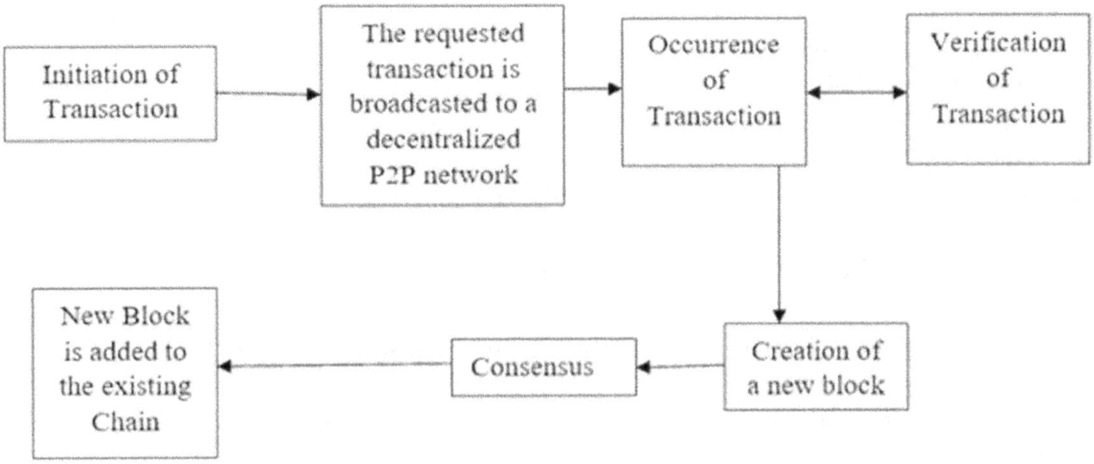

The steps for using a blockchain are as follows:

- The sender starts a transaction and signs the block using the unique key assigned to them.
- The transaction pool receives the transaction request.
- Transactions are selected by miners from the transaction pool and verified.
- The minor creates a block of chosen and validated transactions.
- The block is included in the blockchain network only after validating the user and measuring the hash value calculated from the previous blocks.
- The recorded transaction is permanently saved in the chain network and cannot be interfered with.
- In exchange for using his computing power, the miner receives the mining reward.

3. The characteristics of blockchain technology:

- Digital signature and cryptography-based advanced security.
- Immutability - Records are unchangeable.
- Permanently stores historical records.
- Accountability and transparency.
- More rapid settlement.

Types of Blockchain

Based on accessing and monitoring the network blockchain is classified into the following types:

1. **Public Blockchain:** This blockchain is like an open network. It is available to everyone, so anyone can enter the chain network and use it. Since everyone can join, the system lacks security and privacy and requires immense computational power. If blockchains are being used for business, there are a lot of crucial factors that need to be considered. Ex: Litecoin, Ethereum, Bitcoin, etc.

2. **Private Blockchain:** It is a distributed P2P network, and both private and public blockchains are similar. However, the whole network is monitored and organized by a sole firm. This firm controls the ledger's sharing. By controlling access to others, the trust and confidentiality of the chain network can increase. Ex: Ripple, Corda, Hyperledger, etc.
3. **Consortium Blockchains:** A blockchain can be maintained by several organizations. A pre-selected group of organizations determines who can review transactions or access the data in the network. The consortium blockchain is the most viable option when a business transaction requires everyone's approval to distribute possession of the blockchain.

Use Cases and Applications of Blockchain

A few key use cases of blockchain and several applications are discussed below:

1. **Cryptocurrencies:** A decentralized virtual currency called cryptocurrency is created to serve as a medium of exchange for online commerce. Payments can be sent and received by anybody, anywhere, using a P2P system. Individual cryptocurrency transactions are recorded in an online database as digital inputs, unlike traditional physical money transactions. When transferring cryptocurrency, the transactions are secured by cryptography and recorded in a public ledger using blockchain technology.
2. **Smart Contracts:** An automatically executable software with the aforementioned business logic or requirement is included in a smart contract. It comes after if-then clauses. Perform a certain action if a specific condition is true. The Ethereum Virtual Machine executes the smart contract code (EVM). As soon as the software is run, the action will be conducted automatically by the contract's specifications.
3. **Decentralized Applications (DApps):** One way to reclaim the freedom of users' data from centralized control is through decentralized applications (dApps). As a result, one's requests contact the Blockchain for information rather than a centralized server. dApps are simply apps with no centralized management.

App = Frontend + Backend, hosted on centralized network servers.

DApp = Frontend+ Backend+ Smart Contracts, hosted on Blockchain.

The rules and conditions of the decentralized application are assisted by smart contracts. It functions in tandem with the application's backend.

4. **Non-Fungible Tokens (NFTs):** A non-fungible token, often known as an NFT, is a distinct and non-transferable data unit. It is a digital ledger connected to digital media items like audio, video, and pictures. A certificate of ownership for the digital file is provided by an NFT. Utilizing blockchain technology, NFTs are produced. These will be present on that blockchain and serve as verification of the purchase's validity. The blockchain does not save the file.

Some other applications where blockchain technology can be used are Web 3.0, Metaverse, Finance and Banking, Data Retention, Real estate, Healthcare, Insurance, Voting, Identification, Transportation, and distribution. Integration of some of these applications with blockchain is discussed in upcoming sections.

Blockchain's Benefits and Drawbacks

The benefits and drawbacks of BCT are as follows:

1. Benefits:
    - Decentralized management of the network.
    - Since each node has its corresponding copy of the updated records, decentralization makes the system impenetrable to tampering.
    - Increases accuracy by reducing human involvement and increasing algorithm.
    - The system becomes synchronized and effective when consensus techniques are used for network agreement.
    - Encourages transaction traceability, security, and transparency.
2. Drawbacks:
    - Setup costs for technology infrastructure.
    - Mining challenges like putting together highly computational hardware.
    - Concern over hackers' potential use in criminal activity.
    - Regulations and awareness of blockchain must be established.

OVERVIEW OF SMART CITIES

About Smart Cities

ICT (S. Rani et al., 2021) is utilized in smart cities to partake information, enhance citizen services, and increase functional effectiveness. An ideal smart city maximizes city services and fosters profitable development while enhancing its resident's quality of life. Ultimately, it is less critical how vital technology is accessible than how it is being used. Several factors are considered when calculating a city's smartness, including

- A structure grounded in technology.
- Environmental protection enterprise.
- Efficient and essentially practical public conveyance.
- Create cities with assurance and development.
- Making use of city coffers for both work and living.

Because original governments typically do not bear the bulk of the burden in creating and upholding a data-driven society, a smart city's success depends on cooperation between the public and private sectors. To identify and correct any problems, data judges are also required to evaluate the data generated by smart cities. For example, numerous businesses can be required to provide technology and input for smart security cameras.

1. **History of Smart Cities:** The US Community Analysis Bureau collected data, disseminated resources, and published findings using databases, aerial photography, and cluster analysis for directing services, averting disasters, and reducing poverty, initially presenting the hypothesis of a smart

city during1960s and 1970s. The first smart cities were created as a result. Technology companies created the first wave of smart cities to more clearly illustrate how technology affects daily living. Second-generation smart cities seek to achieve integrated external results through the use of cutting-edge technology and other innovations. The public is directly involved and engaged in the third generation of smart cities rather than relying on technology providers or pioneers. Vienna espoused the third-generation conception with the aid of the Wien Energy company. This helped to address enterprises with gender equivalency and affordable casing while enabling locals to invest in near solar power installations. Through its 10000 citizen-created 2020 action plan, Vancouver was named the greenest city in the world.

2. **Need for Smart Cities:** A smart city should provide its residents with a high standard of living while simultaneously encouraging successful development. This includes providing inhabitants with a range of related services while spending less on the building itself. Given the anticipated population growth in urban areas, which would necessitate a more effective use of infrastructure and resources, this assumes increasing importance. These developments will be made feasible by smart city applications and services, which will improve people's quality of life. In addition to creating new revenue streams and valuable savings, smart city innovations also contribute new value to the city's existing structure, which benefits the administration and its citizens' ability to save plutocrats.
3. **Features of Smart Cities:** It is possible to do away with smart city technologies by fusing Automation, Blockchain Technology, Machine Learning, and IoT.
    - Smart parking, for example, can facilitate online payments and assist vehicles in finding parking spaces.
    - Smart traffic management is another illustration of reducing traffic by optimizing traffic signals and examiner flows.
    - A smart city infrastructure potentially controls services for sharing rides in elevators.
    - Basic energy- and environment-saving features can be added to smart cities, such as lights that power off when the roads are vacant.
    - Smart grid technology, among other things, can enhance operations, conservation, planning, and electricity inventories.
    - Smart city projects can be used to address concerns like garbage management, air pollution, and climate change by utilizing internet-connected trash pickup, lockers, and line operating systems.
    - In addition to providing amenities, smart cities make it possible to provide preventative cautions like watching over high-malfeasance areas or employing detectors to enable early notice for events like cataracts, rockfalls, squalls, or famines.
    - Other advantages that smart buildings can offer include input on the structural health of a structure and real-time space management. Although detectors may pick up on infrastructure concerns like water pipe breaks, the public can also breach this system to alert police to any difficulties, like potholes.
    - Aside from that, smart city technology can boost the effectiveness of several processes, including manufacturing, energy consumption, and community stewardship. To provide inhabitants with comprehensive results, all services can be connected in smart cities.

Smart City Services

1. **Smart City Technologies:** Smart cities utilize software, stoner interfaces, communication networks, and the IoT to provide the general public with integrated solutions (IoT). One of these that is most well-known is the IoT. The employment of various detectors, including those in buses, home appliances, and on-road technology, is possible. The information gleaned from these biases is kept on servers or in the cloud to boost public and private sector productivity, enhance citizen quality of life, and generate profit. A few of the smart city services can be seen in below Figure 3.

Figure 3. Smart city services
Source: Makani et al. (2022)

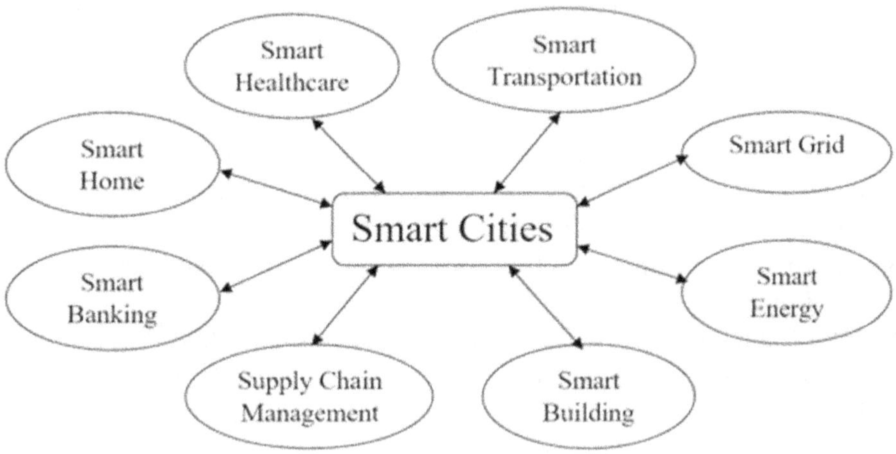

2. **Working of Smart Cities:** Four steps are taken in the deployment of a network of interconnected IoT devices and other technology in smart cities to improve living standards and promote economic growth. They are:

    a. **Real-Time Data Gathering:** Smart detectors gather information instantly.
    b. **Analysis:** The data is examined to discover more about the city's operations and services.
    c. **Information Exchange:** Decision-makers are made aware of the findings of the data analysis.
    d. **Taking Charge:** Efforts are made to improve operations, manage resources, and improve the standard of living for residents of the municipality.

To facilitate decision-making, the ICT substructure collects real-time data from connected devices, equipment, and assets. However, new opportunities for residents to interact with and engage with smart city ecosystems are provided by mobile devices, connected cars, and connected buildings. It is possible to save costs, boost feasibility, optimize processes like waste management and energy allocations, and provide better air quality and less traffic congestion by fusing devices, data, and city planning.

Issues With Smart Cities

1. **Sustainability in Smart Cities:** Sustainability is a key component of smart cities' efforts to improve citizen welfare and efficiency in urban areas. Cities have numerous advantages for the environment, such as fewer environmental remnants, but they can have drawbacks, such as using fossil fuels as a source of energy. However, these negative consequences might be lessened by smart city technologies, such as requiring an electric transportation system to lower emigration. The frequency of the electrical grid may be regulated by electric vehicles even when they are not in use. Because autonomous vehicles are expected to make owning a car less necessary for the general public, there should be fewer cars in urban areas as a result of these environmentally friendly transportation options. Such long-term effects might benefit the environment and society.
2. **Security in Smart Cities:** The benefits that smart cities offer to improve citizen safety are as follows. Intelligent highways, networked surveillance systems, and monitoring of public safety. The question is, how can the smart cities themselves be secured? The reported data must be safeguarded against hacking, cyberattacks, and data theft, and so must smart cities. To maintain the security of smart cities, physical data vaults, reliable authentication, and ID results must be implemented. The public and marketable sectors, as well as software and gadget producers, energy providers, and network service directors, must cooperate to produce integrated results that meet abecedarian security pretensions. Citizens must believe in the security of smart cities for this to happen. The following categories can be used to categorize these fundamental security concerns:
    a. **Vacuity:** To track the many aspects of smart city architecture, data has to be readily accessible and in real-time.
    b. **Integrity:** Detail accuracy must be maintained as well as fluid accessibility. Additionally, this involves taking preventive measures against external tampering.
    c. **Confidentiality:** Maintaining privacy and protecting sensitive information is crucial. The use of firewalls or anonymization of data could be examples of this.
    d. **Accountability:** Users must be responsible for their guests and their interactions with systems containing sensitive information.

To establish responsibility in the event of issues, users' logs should keep track of who accesses the data. Laws are currently being implemented in several nations to aid in the creation of basic security rules for connected devices in smart cities.

3. **Challenges in Smart Cities:** Smart cities have many advantages, but some problems need to be resolved. Public figures that promote widespread citizen participation are among them. Moreover, residents must be involved in both the public and private sectors for everyone to impact the neighborhood positively. Every enterprise in a smart city must have an open data point or mobile app that the general public can access. In this approach, residents can interact with the data and carry out private duties like bill-paying, arranging their mobility, and evaluating their home's energy efficiency. To avoid hacking or misuse, everything needs a dependable and secure method of data gathering and storage. To allay worries about sequestration, data from smart cities must likewise be anonymized. Because millions or even thousands of IoT devices may need to cooperate and communicate with one another, connectivity is possibly the biggest obstacle. This will allow for the integration of services and continuous service enhancement as demand rises. Smart cities must consider social

factors that contribute to the cultural fabric that draws residents and gives them a sense of place in addition to technology. It is essential that newly constructed cities that must draw citizens.

The main topics covered in this chapter include smart healthcare, smart transportation, smart grid, SCM, and smart finance.

INTEGRATION OF BLOCKCHAIN TECHNOLOGY IN SMART CITY SERVICES

This section explores the integration of BCT in smart city services such as healthcare, transportation, smart grid, SCM, and banking.

Smart Healthcare

Generally, a group of hospitals is monitored by a single organization, which monopolizes the data. The traditional healthcare systems cannot keep up with the rapid population increase in everyday life and limited resources. As these factors are constantly contradicting, a new efficient system is needed and can be implemented using blockchain. The usage of blockchain technology creates a smart and secure healthcare system that efficiently shares information, such as medical records, between doctors, patients, and healthcare providers like insurance and medical practitioners (E. M. Abou-Nassar et al., 2020). Everyone can access the information simultaneously.

Smart healthcare implementation can be done in several stages by responsive devices, emergency response systems, and smart ambulance responsive systems. Medical records are vital for the effective diagnosis of a patient, and instant decisions can be made by transferring data even at remote locations using blockchain. The patient can also have a quick overview of their condition. The architecture of blockchain maintains the anonymity of the patient, which is helpful for research purposes.

2. **Steps to Integrate Blockchain Technology With Healthcare:** Patient's health information is collected by IoT sensors and monitors such as blood sugar level, blood pressure, body temperature, pulse rate, respiratory rate, etc.

    ◦ The patient report is generated from the data collected by the administrators.
    ◦ Doctors analyze the report generated by the administrators and recommend an accurate diagnosis.
    ◦ For further analysis, the reports can be shared with other doctors or Healthcare centers.
    ◦ The report is shared in an encrypted format with a specific encryption key generated by the blockchain.
    ◦ Patients can access their medical records from the cloud server.
    ◦ The encrypted medical records file is only received after the validation of the patient.
    ◦ The file can be decrypted only by using the patient's private key to access their medical records.

Figure 4. Framework for smart healthcare systems
Source: Haleem et al. (2021)

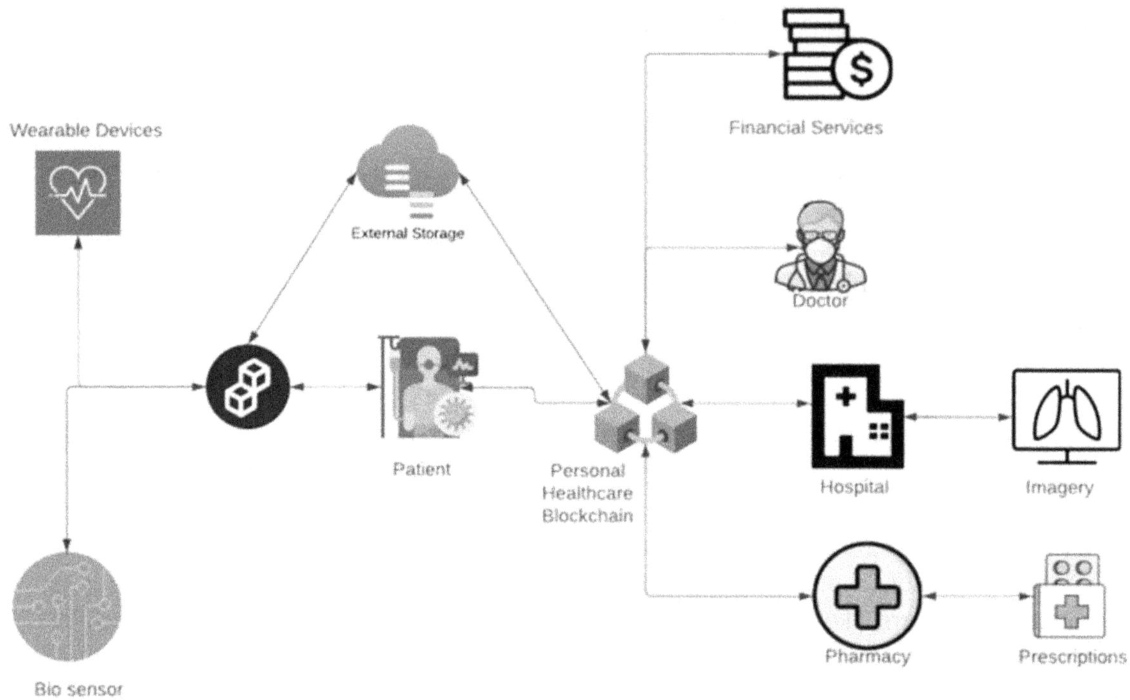

2. **IoT Module:** The IoT module collects the patient's data through the sensors present in the environment and the biosensors attached to the patient or by some wearable gadgets. If a patient is in a critical stage of diagnosis, then monitoring of the patient needs to be continuous, and data is needed to be processed quickly. So, wearable gadgets are preferred. The wearable gadgets can monitor Heart Rate, Blood glucose level, oxygen level, and sleep time by using various sensors and devices like pacemakers. By using these wearable gadgets, the data can be sensed remotely by an IOT module. If the patient is incapacitated or paralyzed, many sensors are required to monitor the patient and his/her environment.
3. **Transfer and Access of Data Using Blockchain:** The data that is recorded from observing the patient need to be organized and analyzed securely. Multiple patient data are recorded at the same time. So, management is needed to organize the data and access the information that can be implemented by blockchain technology. In this chapter, two blockchain networks are proposed Record Management Blockchain (RMB) and Personal Health Care Blockchain (PHCB).

The Record Management Blockchain is used for organizing and transferring data to doctors, Insurance organizations, and others. The RMB generally stores the data obtained from the hospitals, pharmaceutical reports, medical transaction bills, and medication required. The data that is appended to the blockchain is based upon the agreement of all the members in the blockchain on the "Proof of Stake" algorithm. In RMB, the central part of the chain consists of doctors and hospitals, as all the stakeholders are a cumulative holding of them. The RMB also allows others, such as insurance agencies, based on requests to verify the data.

The Personal Healthcare Blockchain is usually operated by the patient as it obtains the data from the patient's wearable gadgets. The access to data can be further provided to the doctors for proper recognition and diagnosis of the patient's sickness. The physiological data obtained from wearable gadgets can be stored externally in a database that is monitored by the blockchain.

Integrating blockchain into the healthcare industry to enable smart healthcare systems presents several challenges (A. Musamih et al., 2021), including:

1. **Data Privacy:** Healthcare data is highly sensitive and must be kept secure and private. While blockchain technology is inherently secure, it's important to ensure that only authorized personnel have access to the data stored on the blockchain.
2. **Interoperability:** The healthcare industry uses multiple systems and platforms, making interoperability a significant challenge. Interoperability ensures that different systems can communicate and share data effectively. Integrating blockchain technology into these systems requires a high level of standardization and compatibility.
3. **Scalability:** The blockchain is a distributed ledger that records transactions on a decentralized network. However, the blockchain's scalability is still an issue, as it can become slow and costly when handling large volumes of data.
4. **Regulatory Compliance:** Healthcare is a highly regulated industry, and integrating blockchain technology must comply with regulatory frameworks, such as HIPAA in the US. This requires a thorough understanding of the legal and regulatory requirements to ensure that the system is compliant.
5. **Adoption:** Finally, adoption is a significant challenge. While blockchain technology offers significant benefits, healthcare providers may be reluctant to adopt it due to the high cost and time required for implementation, lack of expertise, and the risk of disrupting existing systems and processes.

Overcoming these challenges requires a collaborative effort between healthcare providers, technology vendors, and regulators to ensure that the benefits of blockchain technology are maximized while addressing the challenges.

Smart Transportation

Due to the evolution of ICT, Smart vehicles are increasing now. The implementation of smart transportation is to improve vehicle road safety and enhance travel efficiency. Smart transportation is implemented by the integration of many advanced technologies like wireless sensor networks and cloud computing devices with efficient traffic management strategies. Smart transportation system involves smart parking, automatic number plate recognition, traffic signal controls according to congestion, speed detection through cameras, and ticket & toll management. These techniques can make transportation systems safe, fast, and connected.

Traffic is one of the main issues in the current civilization. Traffic congestion can be mostly avoided if most of the vehicular data on the roads are available to everyone; this can be achieved using blockchain. The government, private organizations, and individuals can easily access the available transportation data. Digital twins can be created and further used for payments such as taxes and parking (Singh et al., 2022). By using blockchain, we can improve road safety, increasing the efficiency of the current transportation system by reducing the processing time for clearances and synchronizing the required documents. Communication of automobiles with devices along the path and smartphones can be done by using the Byzantine Fault Tolerant (BFT) (Li et al., 2021) feature of blockchain. The monetary transactions can be done by the "double spending" resistance of blockchain and can avoid intermediaries. By using blockchain, we can create a shared transport system that will have peer-to-peer communication, thus reducing the monopoly of corporate transportation systems.

1. **Smart Taxis:** Smart Taxis can be implemented by sharing the ride. Blockchain already has a sharing network, and the issues can be eliminated in the current transportation system. Private car owners can also use this system by using their cars. The peer is recognized as a node in the network. The details of the owner are stored in the ledger after validation. The whole process is done in the digital layer of the architecture. All nodes are connected using a peer-to-peer network in the network layer of the architecture. Smart taxis' availability and usage are accessed by the users from the cloud, which is maintained in the application layer of the architecture. This smart taxi implementation is one of the many possibilities made by the integration of IoT with blockchain. This transportation system requires real-time data collection, transmission, and analysis of the data.
2. **Electric Vehicles:** Electric vehicles have improved a lot and are being used numerously now. Electric vehicles are battery-powered and have an inbuilt communication infrastructure that shares information with peers. Which future is going to lead to remote power charging stations everywhere and increases the payments for portable, rechargeable batteries (X. Huang et al., 2018). The vehicles need to be charged at regular intervals, and many transactions need to be done for them. Blockchains ensure the safety of these transactions using smart contracts.
3. **VANETs:** Among a few upcoming technologies, Vehicular Adhoc Networks (J. Guo et al., 2022) are present, in which the vehicles can communicate with stationary units and other vehicles to gather information. In such an environment, attacks are unavoidable. To secure the transmission of data, we utilize blockchain. Blockchain authenticates the vehicle and secures the exchange of data between the vehicles.

There are several challenges in integrating BCT for smart transportation. Here are some of them:

1. **Security:** Security is another significant challenge in integrating blockchain technology for smart transportation. The security of the system must be ensured to prevent hacking and ensure the integrity of the data. Additionally, there must be a way to recover lost or stolen data in case of a security breach.
2. **Regulation:** Blockchain technology is still a relatively new technology, and there is a lack of a regulatory framework to govern its use in the transportation sector. This creates uncertainty and makes it difficult to implement blockchain-based solutions.
3. **Privacy:** Smart transportation systems collect a lot of data about users, including their travel patterns and personal information. This data must be protected to ensure privacy and prevent misuse.

Smart Grid

Electrical grids with the intelligence to communicate and analyze data are called smart grids. These grids can be structured efficiently by these enhancements and will be able to respond quickly to changes in electrical demand. Incorporating renewable energy sources into the grid and utilizing electric vehicles as a grid source are ways to achieve more efficient use of resources. The smart grid encourages peer-to-peer transactions directly between customers and service providers (Agung et al., 2022). So, a need secure transaction network arises. Although BCT is still in its infancy, it may find use in a variety of smart grid applications, such as change management and renewable energy credit tracking for electric vehicles.

Every country tries to supply grid connectivity for each corner of their country, but due to precariousness and insufficiency, most people are not satisfied with rural grid connections. The solution to an uncertain power supply is microgrids. If the renewable energy harnessed within the microgrid is stored in a capable storage system, it is sufficient to supply reliable energy to the area under the microgrid. Since the distance is less, the power loss during transmission can be minimized. Micro-grids are efficient in diverse terrains, but macro-grids can't provide reliable supply in those terrains. The usage of both macro-grids and micro-grids produces energy efficiently. If the microgrid users use the energy efficiently and conserve it enough to supply it to the main grid, the microgrid can generate additional revenue. However, the interoperability of the macro and microgrids is an issue. Blockchain can be used to resolve this issue. The expenses to set up the microgrids can be compensated by the revenue generated from trading energy over a few years.

1. **Decentralized Energy Marketplace:** Huge dynamic loads cannot be handled by the conventional grid. Production and consumption of energy should be balanced. Due to this purpose, energy trading has increased widely. Generating revenue through energy trading by selling the energy generated by their microgrids and solar panels is another reason for the increase. Blockchain enables P2P energy trade-offs for Digital Energy Resources (DERs) owners. The smart grid infrastructure needs to be changed to distributed & decentralized from the existing centralized networking. Blockchain is transparent in nature and reliable, which helps in securing energy trading by enabling smart contracts. Practical smart contracts involve the best profit possible for seller algorithms (A. Jindal et al., 2020), making them more complex to implement.
2. **Billing Efficiency:** At places where there are high unmonitored connections, the billing is done every month. This kind of system only benefits the users with high consumption of electricity, whereas poor people who use electricity only for basic needs have to pay a high amount. Many complaints arise daily regarding the consumption of electricity and the billing amount not being in proportion. The cause may be due to the error in reading meters or using different and inaccurate billing methods, such as those stated above. Therefore connections should be established even in the most remote/rural areas and eradicate third parties involved in billing systems. So, the billing is done accurately according to the energy consumed by the household. By using blockchain technology, these transactions can be done authentically, transparently, easily & securely without any third parties involved. The payments can be made only for the energy consumed, which can also be monitored using blockchain. Blockchain-enabled smart meters can calculate the number of bills by analyzing the energy consumed. Such is the virtue of smart contracts in blockchain, as all the transactions are recorded so the users can track their daily usage and control it according to their economic standards. This type of system makes electricity affordable to everyone.

3. **Balancing of Energy Distribution:** The increase or dropdown in demand for energy can be predicted by load estimation if the prediction shows a quick rise in demand at the macro-grid for a few hours. If there are no microgrids present, the organizations that supply power have to buy them from other organizations or energy exchange markets. Suppose the microgrids are present and connected with blockchain technology. In that case, the macro-grid can alert the users from micro-grids who are consuming less amount of energy by coordinating all the micro-grids and transferring them to the macro-grids. The system that interconnects all these and the energy collectors from microgrids will play a crucial role in this. The capital allotted to the microgrids is proportional to the energy supplied to the macro grids. This will also increase the chances of adapting to blockchain-based smart grids everywhere.

There are several challenges associated with integrating blockchain technology into smart grids. Some of these challenges are:

1. **Energy Efficiency:** Blockchain technology requires a considerable amount of computational power and energy to maintain its network. Integrating blockchain technology into smart grids can lead to significant energy consumption, which may not be sustainable in the long run.
2. **Cost:** The cost of implementing blockchain technology can be significant, and it may not be economically feasible for small-scale smart grid projects.

Supply Chain Management

Many organizations are experimenting with blockchain technology to improve transparency and accountability in supply chains. Blockchain can provide all the transactions, from raw material purchasing to delivering the product, in the form of a digital ledger. This would allow transparency to all the shareholders associated with the organization and can quickly rectify the issues in the management and keep track of areas of inefficiency. As it develops, blockchain can also be used to automatically trigger the payments in the supply chain by analyzing the received data. There are still various challenges before adopting it into real-time applications, like interoperability between various divisions of various organizations (P. K. Wan et al., 2020). By adding the customers as part of a chain, they can also know about the production cycle. Blockchain can enhance SCM in the following ways.

- **Transparency Enhancement:** Tracking a product across the chain can disclose the location of the origin and destination, which helps in enhancing the trust of the product and reduces the chances of tampering with the product.
- **Scalability:** Everyone in the chain can access from anywhere; many transactions are possible in seconds.

Figure 5. SCM services
Source: M. Du et al. (2020)

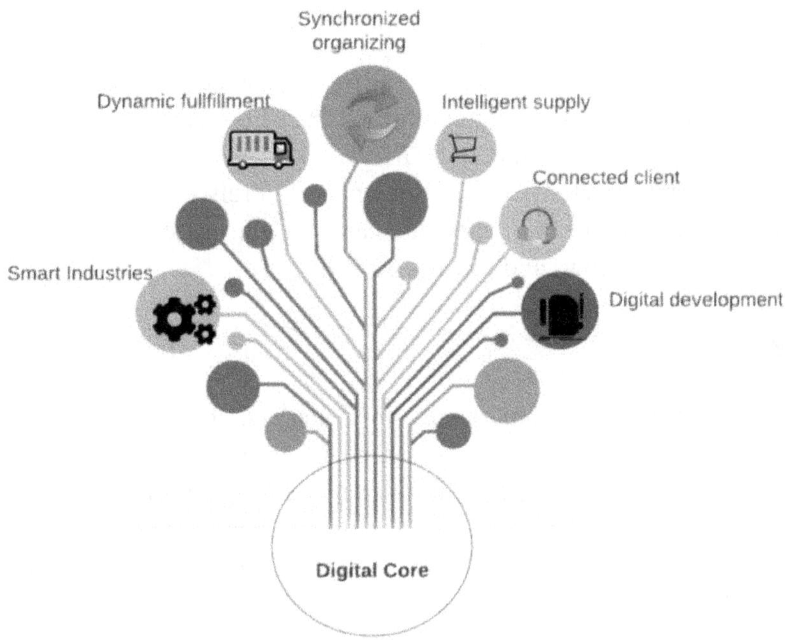

Figure 5 shows the general services of SCM provided by the logistic services. In the early stages of development, the logistics provided minimal services like transportation and warehousing (M. Du et al., 2020). However, as technology advances, the services provided by logistics have also increased, which reduces the lack of communication between the user and the service provider. The blockchain can provide the following services:

- **Transport Preference:** Depending on the product type, blockchain assists in preferring the type of transportation so that the product can be transported with no damage.
- **Distribution Plan:** Blockchain devises the distribution plan to transport the product in minimal time to different locations. So the products can reach everywhere across the area.
- **Auditing and Payments:** Blockchain increases the transaction speed for transportation bills provided by logistics. In this way, the provider can utilize their time efficiently for planning services.
- **Quick Returns:** If users need to return the commodity to the provider, blockchain makes the transactions fast to reduce the amount of time it takes to return the product, and the user can decide if they need a refund or a new commodity.
- **Dispatch Condensation:** Blockchain tracks and analyzes similar types of goods and dispatches them using the same method and transports as one to ensure quick delivery services.
- **Goods Identification:** As the blockchain recognizes each transaction and each user with a unique ID, labeling goods at the time of packaging can be skipped.
- **Path Reduction:** Blockchain identifies the package delivery locations and finds the best and most efficient route by considering the costs and delivery time.

However, several challenges need to be addressed to effectively integrate these two technologies. Some of the main challenges include:

1. **Standardization:** One of the biggest challenges is the lack of standardization in the blockchain industry. Different blockchain platforms have different protocols, which makes it difficult for supply chain stakeholders to agree on a common standard. This can lead to interoperability issues and slow down the adoption of blockchain in SCM.
2. **Integration With Legacy Systems:** SCM systems often rely on legacy systems that may not be compatible with blockchain technology. This can make it difficult to integrate blockchain into existing supply chain workflows and processes.

Smart Banking

In conventional financial systems, customers, investors, lenders, and borrowers exchange funds. Thus, maintaining the anonymity of the customer and safeguarding transaction data are a few critical challenges. Changing consumer spending patterns have led to the usage of digital banking, which raises the need to secure data and transactions. By using blockchain, we can guarantee the security of transactions and data in the financial sector. In recent years many banking-blockchain based are increasing. These include Santander, HSBC, and ING, trying to accomplish blockchain-based foreign payments and letter of credit processes. Currently, cross-border payments take multiple days to complete, with several associates needing to process and approve the transactions. Blockchain creates a record of transactions shared with everyone and is immutable. Transactions have become faster since they no longer require going through every minute legal system (J. Zhang et al., 2021). The area of trade finance can also be improved by blockchain technology. Currently, international financial trades are paper-based and can cause errors. Blockchain can eliminate these following errors and speed up the process by creating a ledger of trade transactions and can avoid any fraudulent transactions. Blockchain-based banking solutions will likely increase in the upcoming years to improve efficiency and security.

Using blockchain, IPFS (InterPlanetary File System), which is a P2P connection protocol for file sharing among devices, can be implemented in the banks to validate a client's details, such as KYC (Know Your Client). The following illustrates the implementation of smart banking through IFPS and blockchain.

Figure 6. Implementation of smart banking systems
Source: Guo et al. (2016)

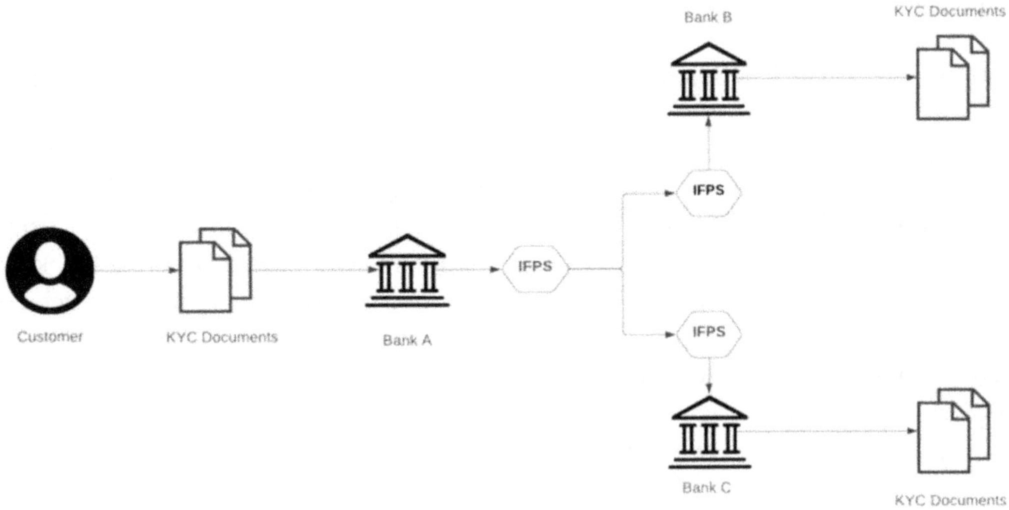

The scenario involves a client visiting two distinct banks. The client went to Bank A in the initial stage to present the bank with his KYC document for verification. After going over our suggested system design, Bank A gives the client a hash value and a proprietary decryption key. With these two keys, the client will also visit Bank B and Bank C, and each bank will swear the KYC document at a bank. The system uploaded and downloaded KYC documents from the banks' end using the IPFS network. However, it thought of encrypting the file for added protection and compressing the file size before sending out KYC documents to the IPFS network. Since anyone with knowledge of the KYC documents' hash values can access them from the IPFS network, utilizing the case of a consumer going to two conventional banks. The model considered a scenario in which a client visited Bank A to open an account in the first stage. The client provided the Bank with the account information and the KYC documents. The bank then reviewed all of the data, which, if configured properly, would be encrypted using the system's functionality, making it possible for all banks to share documents and maintain copies of original databases. Bank A would then store the encrypted file in its IPFS network. Later, the bank will upload an extremely modest in-memory hash value from IPFS to the Blockchain network.

Additionally, Bank A maintains a copy of the client's KYC and the original database. At some point, Bank A will share the client's IPFS and Blockchain hash value. Later, the client can grant access to the KYC documentation package to any other institution he intends to do business with by simply sharing the hash value. The customer can now create a new account at a different bank. The client will transfer his IPFS and Blockchain hash value to Bank B. Since the client will allow Bank B access to the document package's hash value, the Bank will have access to the Blockchain network for the required hash value. Using the hash value recovered from Blockchain, the bank will later download the encrypted KYC documents via the IPFS network. Initial KYC will be recovered by the bank with the client's private key, and a duplicate of the KYC will be kept in the bank's original database. The system attempted to use the IPFS and Blockchain networks to implement the KYC document verification and availability to a financial institution. It displayed the scenario where a customer visited a bank to open an account. The bank uploads the encrypted KYC documents to the IPFS network after validating them.

Integrating smart banking and blockchain presents several challenges, including:

1. **Regulatory and Legal Challenges:** Blockchain technology is relatively new, and there is no global regulatory framework to govern its use. Additionally, regulations surrounding the use of blockchain technology for financial services are evolving, making it challenging for financial institutions to adopt this technology while remaining compliant with applicable laws and regulations.
2. **Lack of Standardization:** There is a lack of standardization in the blockchain industry, which makes it challenging to develop interoperable smart banking systems. Different blockchain platforms have different protocols, consensus algorithms, and governance structures, which can hinder integration.
3. **Resistance to Change:** Traditional financial institutions may be resistant to adopting blockchain technology due to the perceived risk associated with new and untested technology. This can make it challenging to get buy-in from stakeholders, particularly if they are risk-averse.

CONCLUSION

This chapter discussed how blockchain technology could be integrated with smart city services to improve the quality of life and briefly explains the limitations and challenges of integrating blockchain technology with smart city services. However, blockchain is not tamper-proof. The limitation of blockchain technology is the information database. If data on 51% of the blockchain is altered, the information on the blockchain can be manipulated.

REFERENCES

Abou-Nassar, E. M., Iliyasu, A. M., El-Kafrawy, P. M., Song, O.-Y., Bashir, A. K., & El-Latif, A. A. A. (2020). DITrust Chain: Towards Blockchain-Based Trust Models for Sustainable Healthcare IoT Systems. *IEEE Access : Practical Innovations, Open Solutions*, *8*, 111223–111238. doi:10.1109/ACCESS.2020.2999468

Agung, A. A. G., & Handayani, R. (2022). Blockchain for smart grid. *Journal of King Saud University-Computer and Information Sciences*, *34*(3), 666–675. doi:10.1016/j.jksuci.2020.01.002

Ahmed, S., Shah, M. A., & Wakil, K. (2020). Blockchain as a Trust Builder in the Smart City Domain: A Systematic Literature Review. *IEEE Access : Practical Innovations, Open Solutions*, *8*, 92977–92985. doi:10.1109/ACCESS.2020.2993724

Bernal Bernabe, J., Canovas, J. L., Hernandez-Ramos, J. L., Torres Moreno, R., & Skarmeta, A. (2019). Privacy-Preserving Solutions for Blockchain: Review and Challenges. *IEEE Access : Practical Innovations, Open Solutions*, *7*, 164908–164940. doi:10.1109/ACCESS.2019.2950872

Du, M., Chen, Q., Xiao, J., Yang, H., & Ma, X. (2020). Supply Chain Finance Innovation Using Blockchain. *IEEE Transactions on Engineering Management*, *67*(4), 1045–1058. doi:10.1109/TEM.2020.2971858

Guo, J., Ding, X., & Wu, W. (2022). Reliable Traffic Monitoring Mechanisms Based on Blockchain in Vehicular Networks. *IEEE Transactions on Reliability*, *71*(3), 1219–1229. doi:10.1109/TR.2020.3046556

Guo, Ye., & Liang, C. (2016). Blockchain application and outlook in the banking industry. *Financial Innovation*, *2*(1), 1–12. doi:10.118640854-016-0034-9

Haleem, A., Javaid, M., Singh, R. P., Suman, R., & Rab, S. (2021). Blockchain technology applications in healthcare: An overview. *International Journal of Intelligent Networks*, *2*, 130–139. doi:10.1016/j.ijin.2021.09.005

Hasan, H. R., Salah, K., Jayaraman, R., Arshad, J., Yaqoob, I., Omar, M., & Ellahham, S. (2020). Blockchain-Based Solution for COVID-19 Digital Medical Passports and Immunity Certificates. *IEEE Access : Practical Innovations, Open Solutions*, *8*, 222093–222108. doi:10.1109/ACCESS.2020.3043350 PMID:34812373

Hassan, M. U., Rehmani, M. H., & Chen, J. (2022). Optimizing Blockchain Based Smart Grid Auctions: A Green Revolution. *IEEE Transactions on Green Communications and Networking*, *6*(1), 462–471. doi:10.1109/TGCN.2021.3095424

Huang, X., Xu, C., Wang, P., & Liu, H. (2018). LNSC: A Security Model for Electric Vehicle and Charging Pile Management Based on Blockchain Ecosystem. *IEEE Access : Practical Innovations, Open Solutions*, *6*, 13565–13574. doi:10.1109/ACCESS.2018.2812176

Hussain, M. W. (2021). A counter based approach for reducer placement with augmented Hadoop rackawareness. *Turkish Journal of Electrical Engineering and Computer Sciences*, *29*(1), 437–453. doi:10.3906/elk-2001-106

Hussain, M. W., Khan, M. S., Reddy, K. H. K., & Roy, D. S. (2022). Extended indirect controller-legacy switch forwarding for link discovery in hybrid multi-controller SDN. *Computer Communications*, *189*, 148–157. doi:10.1016/j.comcom.2022.03.017

Jindal, A., Aujla, G. S., Kumar, N., & Villari, M. (2020). GUARDIAN: Blockchain-Based Secure Demand Response Management in Smart Grid System. *IEEE Transactions on Services Computing*, *13*(4), 613–624. doi:10.1109/TSC.2019.2962677

Leng, J., Zhou, M., Zhao, J. L., Huang, Y., & Bian, Y. (2020). Blockchain Security: A Survey of Techniques and Research Directions. *IEEE Transactions on Services Computing*, *15*(4), 2490–2510. doi:10.1109/TSC.2020.3038641

Li, Y., Qiao, L., & Lv, Z. (2021). An optimized byzantine fault tolerance algorithm for consortium blockchain. *Peer-to-Peer Networking and Applications*, *14*(5), 2826–2839. doi:10.100712083-021-01103-8

Majeed, U., Khan, L. U., Yaqoob, I., Kazmi, S. A., Salah, K., & Hong, C. S. (2021). Blockchain for IoT-based smart cities: Recent advances, requirements, and future challenges. *Journal of Network and Computer Applications*, *181*, 103007. doi:10.1016/j.jnca.2021.103007

Makani, S., Pittala, R., Alsayed, E., Aloqaily, M., & Jararweh, Y. (2022). A survey of blockchain applications in sustainable and smart cities. *Cluster Computing*, *25*(6), 3915–3936. doi:10.100710586-022-03625-z

Meng, W., Li, W., & Zhu, L. (2020). Enhancing Medical Smartphone Networks via Blockchain-Based Trust Management Against Insider Attacks. *IEEE Transactions on Engineering Management*, *67*(4), 1377–1386. doi:10.1109/TEM.2019.2921736

Musamih, A., Salah, K., Jayaraman, R., Arshad, J., Debe, M., Al-Hammadi, Y., & Ellahham, S. (2021). A Blockchain-Based Approach for Drug Traceability in Healthcare Supply Chain. *IEEE Access : Practical Innovations, Open Solutions*, *9*, 9728–9743. doi:10.1109/ACCESS.2021.3049920

Rani, S., Mishra, R. K., Usman, M., Kataria, A., Kumar, P., Bhambri, P., & Mishra, A. K. (2021). Amalgamation of Advanced Technologies for Sustainable Development of Smart City Environment: A Review. *IEEE Access : Practical Innovations, Open Solutions*, *9*, 150060–150087. doi:10.1109/ACCESS.2021.3125527

Rathee, G., Iqbal, R., Waqar, O., & Bashir, A. K. (2021). On the design and implementation of a blockchain enabled e-voting application within iot-oriented smart cities. *IEEE Access : Practical Innovations, Open Solutions*, *9*, 34165–34176. doi:10.1109/ACCESS.2021.3061411

Reddy, K., & Hemant, K. (2022). Towards energy efficient Smart city services: A software defined resource management scheme for data centers. *Sustainable Computing: Informatics and Systems*, *35*, 100776. doi:10.1016/j.suscom.2022.100776

Salah, K., Nizamuddin, N., Jayaraman, R., & Omar, M. (2019). Blockchain-Based Soybean Traceability in Agricultural Supply Chain. *IEEE Access : Practical Innovations, Open Solutions*, *7*, 73295–73305. doi:10.1109/ACCESS.2019.2918000

Samuel, O., Javaid, N., Alghamdi, T. A., & Kumar, N. (2022). Towards sustainable smart cities: A secure and scalable trading system for residential homes using blockchain and artificial intelligence. *Sustainable Cities and Society*, *76*, 103371. doi:10.1016/j.scs.2021.103371

Shari, N. F. M., & Malip, A. (2022). State-of-the-art solutions of blockchain technology for data dissemination in smart cities: A comprehensive review. *Computer Communications*.

Sharma, P. K., Kumar, N., & Park, J. H. (2019). Blockchain-Based Distributed Framework for Automotive Industry in a Smart City. *IEEE Transactions on Industrial Informatics*, *15*(7), 4197–4205. doi:10.1109/TII.2018.2887101

Shen, C., & Pena-Mora, F. (2018). Blockchain for Cities—A Systematic Literature Review. *IEEE Access : Practical Innovations, Open Solutions*, *6*, 76787–76819. doi:10.1109/ACCESS.2018.2880744

Singh, S. K., Pan, Y., & Park, J. H. (2022). Blockchain-enabled secure framework for energy-efficient smart parking in sustainable city environment. *Sustainable Cities and Society*, *76*, 103364. doi:10.1016/j.scs.2021.103364

Toyoda, K., Mathiopoulos, P. T., Sasase, I., & Ohtsuki, T. (2017). A Novel Blockchain-Based Product Ownership Management System (POMS) for Anti-Counterfeits in the Post Supply Chain. *IEEE Access : Practical Innovations, Open Solutions*, *5*, 17465–17477. doi:10.1109/ACCESS.2017.2720760

Wan, P. K., Huang, L., & Holtskog, H. (2020). Blockchain-Enabled Information Sharing Within a Supply Chain: A Systematic Literature Review. *IEEE Access : Practical Innovations, Open Solutions*, *8*, 49645–49656. doi:10.1109/ACCESS.2020.2980142

Xie, J. (2019). A Survey of Blockchain Technology Applied to Smart Cities: Research Issues and Challenges. IEEE Communications Surveys & Tutorials, 21(3), 2794-2830. doi:10.1109/COMST.2019.2899617

Zhang, J., Tian, R., Cao, Y., Yuan, X., Yu, Z., Yan, X., & Zhang, X. (2021). A Hybrid Model for Central Bank Digital Currency Based on Blockchain. *IEEE Access : Practical Innovations, Open Solutions*, *9*, 53589–53601. doi:10.1109/ACCESS.2021.3071033

Chapter 13
Blockchain in the Healthcare Sector

Zeid Saad Hamzeh
Jinan University, Lebanon

Ghalia Nassreddine
https://orcid.org/0000-0001-9434-2914
Jinan University, Lebanon

Joumana Younis
https://orcid.org/0000-0003-0576-4264
CNAM, France

ABSTRACT

After the COVID-19 pandemic, the healthcare sector has faced many challenges as telehealth increased and the need for a secure and efficient healthcare record system became essential. Nowadays, the healthcare sector suffers from many problems, such as security, trust, availability of data, and drug traceability. Blockchain technology is a recent technology that has proven its efficiency in many sectors, such as finance, banking, bitcoin, and healthcare sectors. This chapter describes blockchain integration in the healthcare sector to cover these problems. The authors will start by introducing blockchain technology. After that, they will present the healthcare sector challenges. Then, they focus on advantages of blockchain usage to resolve existing problems in the healthcare sector, especially in the electronic health record and drug traceability.

INTRODUCTION

Health is the key to an active and happy life. Modern society has benefited from enormous technological development in improving healthcare. With each new technology, more solutions to existing health problems become feasible (Bartoletti, 2019). Indeed, some recent technologies, inclusing the Internet of things, machine learning, image processing, big data, and blockchain, allow researchers to resolve previously unreachable health problems. However, the massive data collected in healthcare may produce

DOI: 10.4018/979-8-3693-0744-1.ch013

serious problems. The enormous amount of data is circulated with limited access and cannot be easily used for computational methods. In addition, some records still need to be completed. Therefore, it is impossible to perform the complex data analysis needed to get the appropriate solutions (Tortorella, 2020). To address these fundamental challenges in the healthcare sector, researchers are focusing on the following main parts (Thapa & Camtepe, 2021):

- **Data Integrity (Pandey et al., 2020; Zarour et al., 2021):** It is a persistent challenge in today's healthcare sector. Data integrity ensures that available data is correct, and his data cannot be improperly changed. Incorrect data can pose serious health risks to patients and impose enormous responsibility on clinicians. It can lead to a variety of issues, including misconduct and poor treatment. This type of risky scenario makes handling healthcare data extremely difficult.
- **Data security and Privacy (Dasgupta et al., 2016):** The last years have witnessed an enormous appearance of stubbornly developed threats and targeted attacks against information systems. The main goal of these attacks was to export recoverable data by the attacker. Thus, data protection is considered a growing problem in the healthcare sector. This problem challenges the healthcare industry to address these various complementary and critical issues (Abouelmehdi, et al., 2017):
    - Data security governs data access during the lifecycle of data.
    - Data privacy determines who has access to data according to specific privacy policies. This data may include personal, medical or professional information. A major part of these information can be classified as confidential information.

Blockchain is a new data storage technique that makes the modification, hacking, and defrauding of data within the system very difficult or impossible. A blockchain can be considered as a set of digital transactions that have been reproduced and spread on the whole associated network of computer systems (Zheng et al., 2017). The chain contains several blocks. Each block may include several transactions. When a new transaction appears on the chain, a new block associated with this transaction will be created and added to the chain. The distributed ledger technology is used in the decentralized database operated by multiple participants (DLT). Blockchain technology belongs to distributed ledger technology. Each transaction in the blockchain has an immutable cryptographic signature called a hash (Yli-Humo et al., 2016).

Blockchain has recently been used to create valuable solutions in a variety of industries. Recently, it has been integrated into the healthcare sector in many countries. The objective of using blockchain is to maintain and share patient data between different stakeholders such as doctors, insurance companies, hospitals, clinics, and laboratories. Blockchain technology may aid in solving serious challenges in the healthcare field. As a result, it can improve the precision, safety, and transparency of health information distributed and communicated within the network associated with the healthcare system (Haleem et al., 2021).

As a result, this chapter aims to overview and analyze the role of Blockchain technology in the healthcare sector. The following is how this chapter will be organized: First, a summary of blockchain technology will be provided. The major challenges of the healthcare sector will then be addressed. Following that, the responsibility of blockchain in the healthcare domain will be discussed in terms of data integrity, privacy, and security. This chapter will conclude with a conclusion and recommendation regarding blockchain's role in the healthcare domain.

BLOCKCHAIN TECHNOLOGY

The Blockchain consists of a digital database – also known as ledger - broadcasted on nodes (see Figure 1), called blocks. These blocks "are connected by cryptography. Indeed, each block must include cryptographic hash that denotes the previous block, timestamp, and transaction data (Gorkhali et al., 2020).

Figure 1. Blockchain blocks

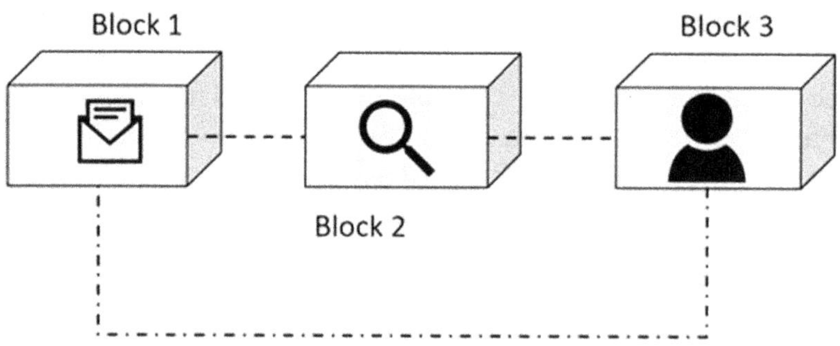

A blockchain is a separated, distributed, and general digital block that can document transactions over many computers. These records cannot be changed without modifying all other connected blocks on the same network. According to the National Institute of Standards and Technology (NIST), the blockchain can be defined as "tamper evident" and "tamper resistant" digital blocks connected in a broadcasted manner, without a primary or central depository. Thereby, there is no central authority in Blockchain technology. At the basic level, blockchain allows users to send transactions as blocks in shared nodes via the network. Therefore, without a blockchain network, no transaction can be sent or published (Xu et al., 2019).

In this section, The Blockchain technology will be presented. First, the types of blockchain will be represented. After that, the structure of the Blockchain will be described in detail.

Blockchain Types

According to the type of data accessibility, Lin and Liao (2017) classified Blockchain in:

1. **Public Blockchain:** Any user can access, read, and submit transactions on the blockchain.
2. **Private Blockchain:** Only members of a specific group of associations have access to, read, select, and execute transactions.
3. **Community/Consortium Blockchain:** Users from various organizations can access, read, and submit transaction data.
4. **Hybrid Blockchain:** This is a relatively new type of Blockchain. This type integrates the other other types of Blockchains: public, private, and community/consortium Blockchains to facilitate transactions. Hybrid Blockchain can define a Blockchain medium in multiple modes.

According to the permission required to use Blockchain, Michael et al. (2018) classified the Blockchain in:

1. **Permissionless Blockchain:** No prior permission is required of the user in this type. Any user can take part in the confirmation process and enter the Blockchain network using its computational media.
2. **Permissioned Blockchain:** Prior permission is required to access and execute block to confirm transactions in the associated network.
3. **Hybrid Blockchain:** A node in the chain can have permissionless and Permissioned Blockchain together to reduce associated communication. The Blockchain platform is configured to sustain a Permissioned or Permissionless model.

However, based on the functionality and the used intelligent contract support, Blockchain can be classified (Rauchs & Hileman, 2017) into the bellows groups:

1. **Stateless Blockchain:** Such a system concentrates only on the optimization of the transaction that can be verified using transaction by computing hashes. The transaction is separated from the smart contract logic layer in this type. Therefore, it can not be affected by the smart contract code error and defenselessness.
2. **Stateful Blockchain:** In this type, Blockchain delivers transaction computing abilities and the smart contract. In addition, this type sustains multifaceted business logic. It provides optimization and maintains logic states.

Blockchain Structure

The Blockchain (distributed ledger technology) is a decentralized data structure where the data is distributed over all nodes within the network. There is no central repository or database, and the data validity and integrity are checked by consensus protocol which controls the distributed network. Therefore, Blockchain can be considered a chain of nodes; each node represents a computer or validator in the network. Each node in the chain constitutes a set of blocks connected and linked using a cryptographic signature called a hash signature.

Once a block is mined and appended to a node, it will be synchronized with other nodes as decentralized data storage. So, it is immutable that it cannot be tampered with or altered and visible for all nodes, ensuring the data integrity and transparency of distributed networks (Zimmerman, 2020).

The block is the fundamental unit of Blockchain. It consists of mixtures of the header and the data, as illustrated in Figure 2.

Figure 2. The two parts of a block in blockchain structure

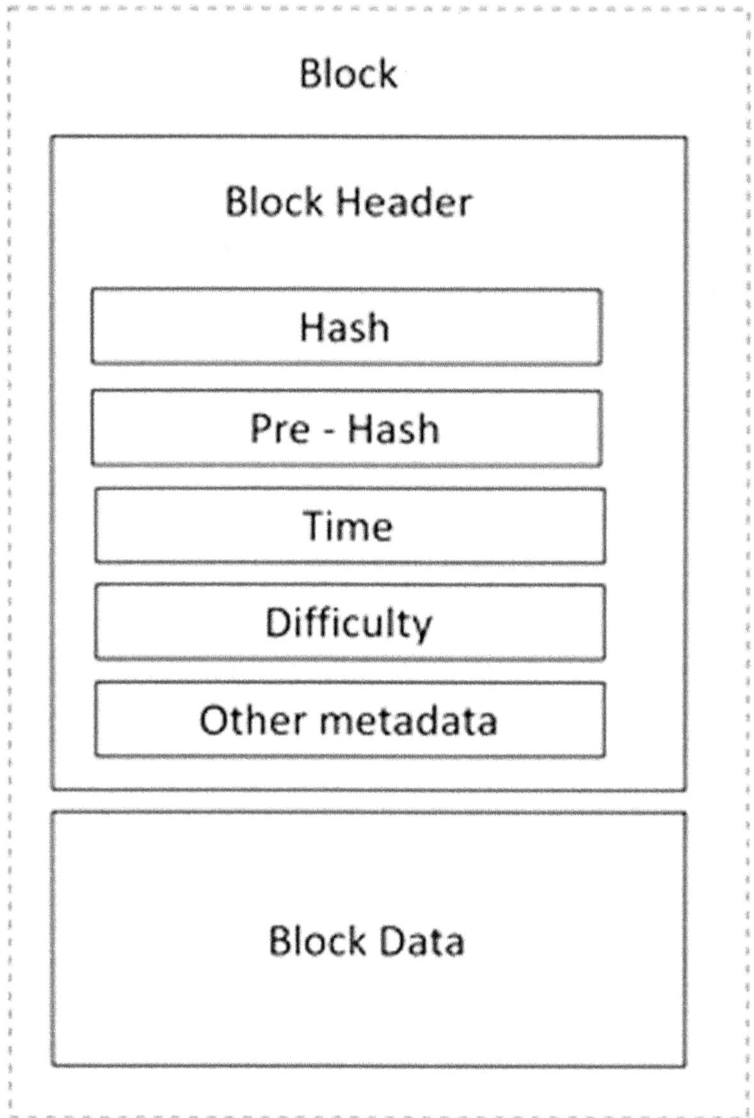

The block generally includes two different parts:

1. The block header usually contains facts like current hash, pre-hash, time, difficulty, and other metadata (Li et al., 2018).
2. The data in a block may include the total number of transactions and transaction elements such as sender address, data to be transferred, receiver address, and other elements (Shrivas & Yeboah, 2018).

The hash value in each block is generated using a cryptographic hash algorithm such as SHA-256 (binti Suhaili & Watanabe, 2017), SHA2-512, SHA-256d, SHA3-512, SHA1-160, and others (Sujatha et al., 2022). As a result, each block contains only the previous block's hash value. Each block's hash value should be unique. Thus, modifying block data after it has been registered in the Blockchain network is extremely difficult. Because Blockchain is broadcasted, any user who wishes to modify any block should change the records anywhere.

Furthermore, a change in one block may produce modification in all forward blocks. It will result in a different hash, resulting different hash values for all star blocks. To encrypt blockchain data more efficiently and securely, blockchain employs a hash tree, also known as the Merkle hash tree. A Merkle tree is a tree with both leaves and nodes that do not have leaves. A leaf node in such a tree is identified by the cryptographic hash of a data block. A non-leaf node, on the other hand, is identified by the cryptographic hash of the labels of its child nodes. The majority of hash tree implementations are binary.

Therefore, each node has only two children. A Merkle root is an easily structure for verifying the rules on a Merkle tree. It is commonly used in Blockchain to ensure that data blocks sent over a peer-to-peer network are complete, unchanged, and unaltered. It is critical in the analysis required to keep cryptocurrencies such as bitcoin and ether running (Niaz & Saake, 2015). Figure 3 shows a sample of Merkle tree (Bosamia & Patel, 2018) whereas Table 1 summarizes the advantages and disadvantages of the Merkle tree.

Figure 3. Sample of a Merkle tree, showing the node levels up to data blocks

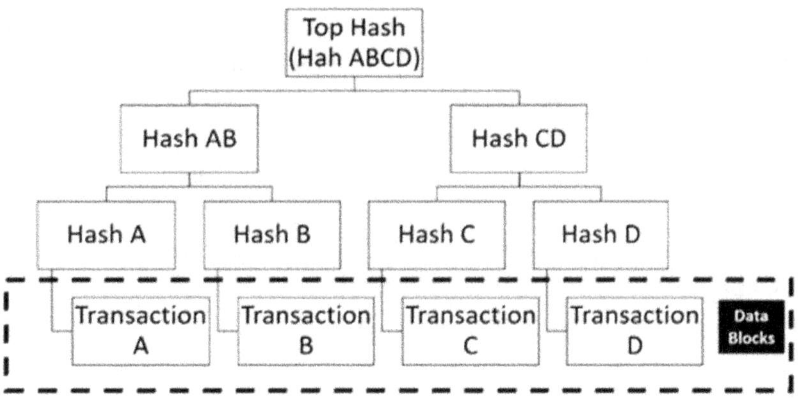

Table 1. Advantages and disadvantages of a Merkle tree

Advantages	Disadvantages
• Ensure the data's integrity • Need less disk space compared to other data structures. • Can be broken down into little pieces of data for verification on networks • Efficient Verification • Computation verification can be done in a very easy and fast way. • Include Simplified Payment Verification (SPV) for clients, • blockchain pruning, and smart pool miners. • Exclusively responsible for appending trees as the • specific system knows the number of leaves in each tree from which adding a node or tree.	• Cannot know which part of the file has been damaged. • Cannot predict the depth of the tree. • If other participants want to add a node or a tree to an existing Merkle tree, they should notify about number of leaves to perform consistency check.

Advantages and Disadvantages of Blockchain

As most of new thechnologies, Blockchain has advantages and disadvantages to be considered (Niranjanamurthy et al., 2019):

Advantages

Blockchain provides various advantages in an improving digital world (Golosova & Romanovs, 2018):

1. **High Security:** One of the primary benefits of blockchains is security. Indeed, Blockchain can provide complete data protection and security during online transactions. The digital signature component provides fraud-free transactions by making it difficult for other users to modify or change a user's data without a specific digital signature.
2. **Decentralized System:** Transactions should usually be approved by regulatory authorities such as the government or a bank before they are executed. However, using Blockchain, transactions can be completed through user agreement. It could make transactions easier, safer, and faster.
3. **Automation Capability:** When the trigger criteria are met, systematic actions, events, and payments can be executed automatically using Blockchain..

Disadvantages

Private keys are one of the drawbacks of blockchain and cryptography. The foundation of blockchain technology is the use of public and private keys. However, there is a fundamental issue with using private keys. Indeed, if a user loses their private key, they face significant difficulties, making this a major disadvantage of blockchain.

Another disadvantage is the limited scalability. The number of transactions allowed per node in a blockchain is limited. As a result, completing multiple transactions and other tasks can take a significant amount of time. Furthermore, one disadvantage is the difficulty in modifying or adding information after it has been recorded.

CHALLENGES OF HEALTHCARE SECTOR

The healthcare sector includes all businesses that provide health and medicales services like manufacture medical supplies or drugs, insurance companies, and all systems that connect healthcare providers to patients. It is one of the world's most important industries. The COVID pandemic has impacted every aspect of human life. The healthcare industry is one of the most severely impacted by the COVID pandemic. Indeed, the healthcare sector faced many challenges during the COVID pandemic, which pushed the responsibility for improving this sector by integrating new technologies and tools. The following are a summary of the challenges confronting the healthcare sector:

Cybersecurity

Even though viruses, ransomware, and other cybersecurity problems are not recent in the healthcare industry, however, the current growth of digital health industries, such as telehealth doctor visits, creates a new environment in which patient health information is compassionate. Simultaneously with the development of more online healthcare functions over the next year, it is extremely necessary to provide overall protection to ensure that information is safeguarded against outside threats (Tully et al., 2020).

Security and Integrity Challenges

Electronic Health Records (HER) have recently replaced traditional methods of storing patient records in healthcare services. It is an electronic copy of a patient's medical history that has been supported over time by the provider. It may include all key administrative and clinical data pertinent to that patient's care under a specific provider. In general, EHR records include the patient's medical history, personal information, laboratory test results, X-ray results, prescriptions, treatments, and other information. As a result, it is critical to ensure the integrity, privacy, and security of these data. Today's healthcare information systems (HIS) face numerous challenges, including a lack of privacy, drug counterfeiting, easy hacking, and so on (Shi et al., 2020).

The current healthcare system is facing vulnerability in the three pillars. The exfiltration of EHR patient records represents the confidentiality attack. Moreover, losing access to online patient records are represented an availability attack. While maliciously manipulating EHRs, causing data damage, covering up negligence, or committing fraud such as backdating to ensure insurance coverage. At the same time, the integrity challenge is much more critical because it depends on systems, processes, and operational integrity. Systems integrity is represented by the existing defender devices, antivirus software, and signature-based security controls that must be fixed. So, data breaches in healthcare institutions are regularly increasing. Simultaneously, the weakness in process integrity is the lack of interoperability caused by the exchange and transfer of data between healthcare institutions, which is expensive and takes a long time, causing harmful patient treatments. Furthermore, operational integrity is represented by Medicare fraud through improper payment, which is estimated to be worth $50 billion per year (Guardtime, 2019).

Privacy

Nowadays, most EHR systems have centralized databases and encrypted patient records. Because the patient has no access to his record, he can not control his medical record and does not know who is using his information, why, when, and for what purpose. Some privacy threats are related to illegal hacking handled by following some security procedures and enforcing laws. However, the central part of privacy challenges in the healthcare sector is related to data practices that are presently legal (Grande et al., 2020).

Invoicing and Payments

Medical coverage rules are considerably very complicated. Thus, many patients see that insurance descriptions of benefits and their parts of the bills are entirely incoherent. In addition, almost all medical bill management systems are not aligned with patients' payment preferences. Below are some suggestions to resolve this issue (Alderwick & Gottlieb, 2019):

- Align the bill format with patient expectations, beginning with simple medical bills.
- Create a user-friendly online patient system with multiple payment options.
- Make it simple to understand and devise payment plans that are not time consuming.

Big Data

The types of data generated, collected, and stored vary by industry. These data may include images, sounds, and text (Price & Cohen, 2019). Recently, the healthcare industry has generated a massive amount of data through various means, such as record keeping and regulatory requirements (Raghupathi & Raghupathi, 2014). Traditionally, this Big Data was kept on paper. However, because the healthcare sector is rapidly digitizing, another storage method should be used to handle this massive amount of data. Big Data in Healthcare refers to electronic health records that are so large and complex that they cannot be managed using traditional software or hardware (Hussain et al, 2022) . As a result, they should be managed and stored in Big Data, as represented by their volume, complexity, and variety (Pastorino et al., 2019; Hussain et al., 2021).

In comparison to other industries, healthcare may generate significantly more data, which is expected to skyrocket in the coming years. All of these data are related to patient services and health issues. Healthcare providers primarily collect, use, and store them. Doctors, hospitals and private clinics, laboratory staffs (such as x-ray technicians), and health professionals are all included in this category. A significant portion of this data is transferred to government agencies. The main characteristics of healthcare data are their volume, the speed with which they must be handled, and the special formats they contain. Images are now regarded as one of the more massive sources of Big Data, as many medical images of a single patient can be collected and stored in his EHR.

Furthermore, medical and biological data are highly heterogeneous information. Typically, data are stored using a structured format. Based on this structure, a machine can easily hold, modify, recall, analyze, and manage data. However, the healthcare sector's big data usually needs to be more structured. It may contain static-paper files, scripts, and unstructured data in general.

There exist many examples of Big Data categories in the Healthcare industry such as reports and notes of doctors, laboratory records, x-ray films, and private clinics notes. Big data and digital transformation are regarded as major revolutions in healthcare. However, one of the main challenges for healthcare stakeholders who are interetsed in maintaining the precision and trustworthiness of their patient records is data quality (Lv & Qiao, 2020).

Information Technology Healthcare Investments

Aside from the push for healthcare pricing transparency, patients want the healthcare industry to reduce wasteful spending. Indeed, 25% of health-care spending is wasteful. As a result, by removing the source of wasteful spending, the healthcare industry can significantly reduce patient bills. The healthcare sector can reduce extra spending at all levels of the healthcare world, including small private practices, by implementing information technology solutions such as EHR software. Responding to patient requests necessitates the software's ability to perform numerous critical day-to-day administration tasks, such as scheduling, care coordination, and billing (Gopal et al., 2019).

BLOCKCHAIN IN HEALTHCARE SECTOR

Recently, the healthcare sector is fronting various challenges, especially in data security, integrity, transparency, traceability, availability, and audit. In addition, a considerable part of existing healthcare methods used for controlling and storing data are centralized. This centralization can produce possible troubles of a single failure point in natural disasters (Andoni et al., 2019; Arjun et al., 2020; Dashkevich et al., 2020; Lee, 2019; Yaqoob et al., 2022). In Shahnaz et al. (2022), the authors designed blockchain technology that can be used in EHR to deliver a safe hold of electronic records by specifying fine entry restrictions for the users of the suggested framework. In addition, the proposed system examines the scalability problem fronted by the blockchain for holding the records.

Blockchain is a new decentralized technology that has proven its efficiency in a variety of industries, including bitcoin, finance, banking, and others. It is a disruptive decentralized technology that must improve, reshape, and transform the way information is handled and stored (Bodkhe et al., 2020).

This section will discuss the effects of using blockchain technology in the healthcare sector. First, the use of Blockchain in electronic health records will be described. After that, the role of Blockchain in the drug traceability problem will be presented.

Blockchain in EHR

The modern healthcare system uses an electronic health record (EHR) that contains the patient's essential critical administrative and clinical data, such as meditation, laboratory results, and other reports. The last years have witnessed serious regulation and official inefficiency that have delayed the invention of EHRs. However, after the COVID pandemic, the massive increase in telehealth doctors' visits augments the necessity of creating and adopting accurate EHRs. Recently, Blockchain technology has been used to improve EHR performance. Indeed, the healthcare industry contains many parties, such as clinics, hospitals, and insurance companies. These parties are obligated to share and manage their data. However, the standard EHR system is labeled with a decentralized design. Therefore, one party only can control the code command, database, and system results (Arun Kumar, 2022).

Azaria et al. (2016) used blockchain technology to implement MedRec, a new decentralized data management system for EHRs. This system delivers users a complete, exhaustive, unchangeable log of their medical data. It is easy to access. Using MedRec, medical information is exchanged easily between patients, providers, and treatment sites. By adopting blockchain tools, MedRec can handle data sharing, security, confidentiality, and sharing sensitive information. The users in the healthcare sector can not be confident with this decentralized system (Abunadi & Kumar, 2021).

Blockchain technology can now overcome the trust problem associated with a centralized EHR system. The patient record is stored in a chain using blockchain technology via the meta mas. The Blockchain stores all patients' EHR as separate data blocks containing encrypted data. This system can store all health information for each patient. Patients and other healthcare sector users can easily access these data on their own. EHR data are frequently encrypted using a specific algorithm to encrypt all patient data into a single line bit that is then stored in the block (Li et al., 2021).

Therefore, EHR storage using Blockchain technology is reserved suitably and symmetrically, which enables comfortable accessibility of each record through a specific application or the web. Using this technology, patients now have full access and control of developing, collecting, and thus sharing their EHRs with doctors, clinic, family, laboratory staff, and other healthcare providers (See Figure 4).

Figure 4. Access permission example applied by blockchain to potential stakeholders of EHRs
Source: Odeh et al. (2022)

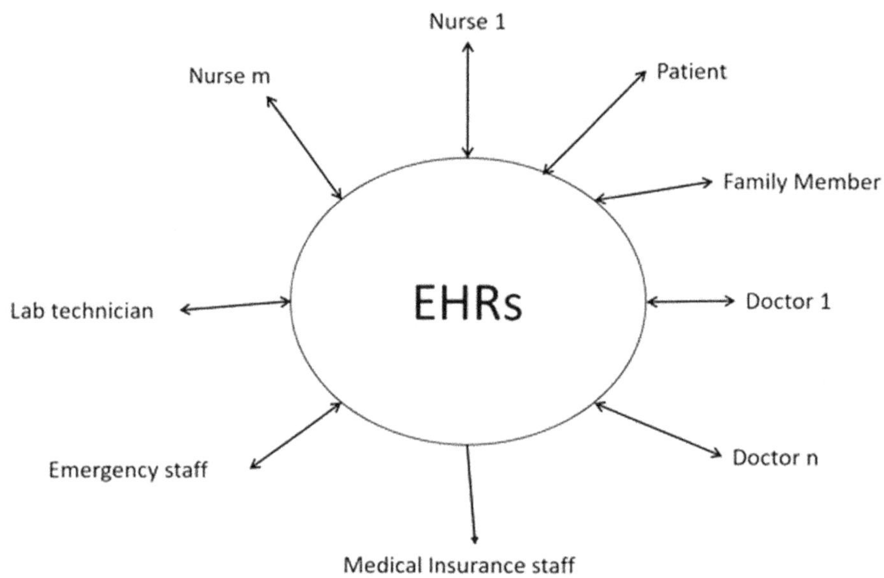

As illustrated in the figure, using blockchain protocol, distinct stakeholders will have different access permission to EHRs. Patients will have direct access to electronic health records, which will include individual patient-reported information containing significant data such as personal and demographic information. Also, they can survey data gathered from the applied instruments. However, medical records in EHRs can be updated only by specific stakeholders like nurses, doctors, and emergency staff. Some family members or healthcare providers may be granted access to read and update the patient's personal health information.

Bamakan et al. (2021) demonstrated that different stakeholders might present different EHRs contents like demographic information, laboratory results, and medicament. In addition, the laboratory result encloses different fields (Patient_ID, Patient_name, staff_ID, type_of_test, values, and other results). Each EHR in the Blockchain is associated with a specific transaction within the ledge and performed accurately. Therefore, the blockchain authorization has the following data flow diagram (DFD) (see Figure 5).

Figure 5. DFD blockchain authorization process

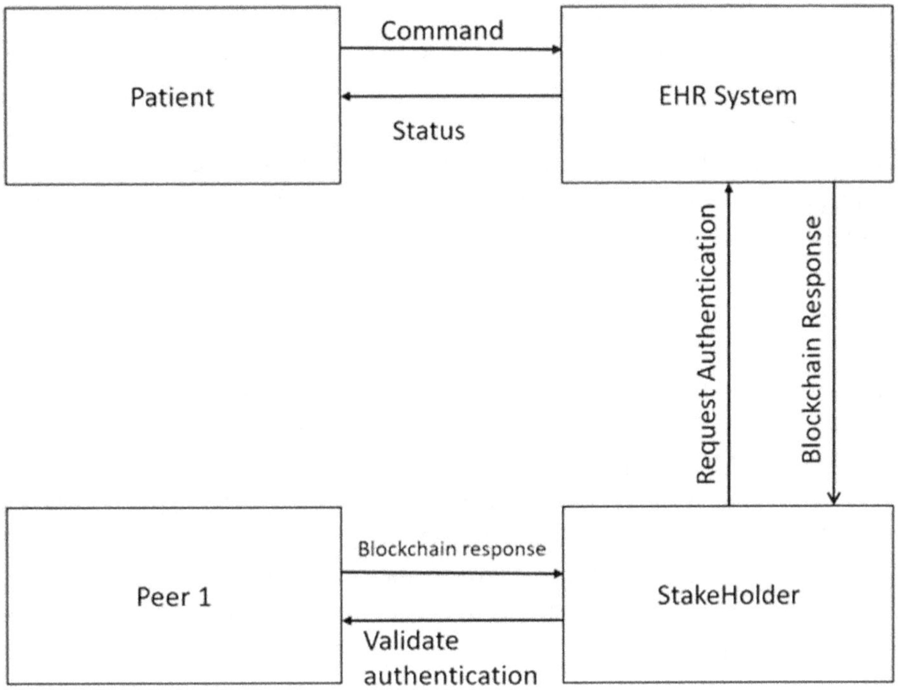

The authorization process is the focus of this data flow diagram. Before proceeding with the authorization process, the stakeholder must first be authenticated. Before attempting to use the EHR system, this model considers a stakeholder with a valid certification. The EHR system connects to the blockchain client in order to obtain the authorization hold on the network's peers. The peer system compares the stakeholder attributes contained in the certificate to the authorization regulation included in the peer system. The peer then sends the authorization response to the stakeholder (Adlam & Haskins, 2021).

According to Abunadi and Kumar (2021), the main benifit of such a system is security and confidentiality. Researchers believe that a blockchain system is more dependable and secure than other types of storage, such as paper medical records storage.

Tanwar et al. (2020) also proposed an ACP (Access Control Policy) approach for enhancing the accessibility of data among healthcare providers. This approach assists in the simulation of domains to create and share the electronic healthcare record (EHR) via the network. It employs the notion of chain code. The authors of this study use blockchain networks performance metrics such as latency, throughput, and Round Trip Time (RTT). The proposed system succeeded in enhancing the efficiency and security of data compared to others EHR systems that employ client-server architecture.

Chelladurai et al. (2021) proposed a system, containing the following:

1. Registration agreement for the creation of unchangeable patient logs.
2. Development of Digital Health Records.
3. Merkle Tree data technique for safe storage and fast access to the Health record information.
4. **Update the Permission Contract:** Access may be given in some emergencies.
5. Data sharing Permission Contract that assists in communicating medical records and information between different stakeholders like nurses, medical insurance, and doctors.
6. Viewership Permission Contract that allows the access of display health information for home care and future care.

This approach has been tested on several cases to evaluate its effectiveness. The proposed system's qualitative and quantitative metrics are calculated to estimate resource performance, transactions per second, and transaction latency.

Drug Traceability

Healthcare supply chains are complex systems that span multiple geographies and companies. They provide critical vital services to everyday human life. Furthermore, they are an important part of the healthcare sector. Because of the complexity of these systems, inaccurate information, a lack of transparency, and limited data provenance may result. Furthermore, fake and counterfeit drugs are a major issue in the healthcare industry. They have a negative impact on human health, and they also cause extreme economic failure in the healthcare industry. As a result, recent research has highlighted the critical need for a robust and traceable procedure for pharmaceutical supply chains. Existing trace systems are based on a centralized structure, which leads to issues with data safety, clarity, and authenticity in healthcare supply chains (Musamih et al., 2021).

Figure 6 depicts the relationships between the stakeholders in the pharmaceutical supply chain. Patients, ingredient suppliers, manufacturers, distributors, and pharmacies are all stakeholders in the drug supply chain. Furthermore, complex packing, unpacking, and repacking processes are required for drug distribution. This procedure makes drug tracing extremely difficult (Uddin et al., 2021).

Figure 6. Different drug supply chain stakeholders with their relationship

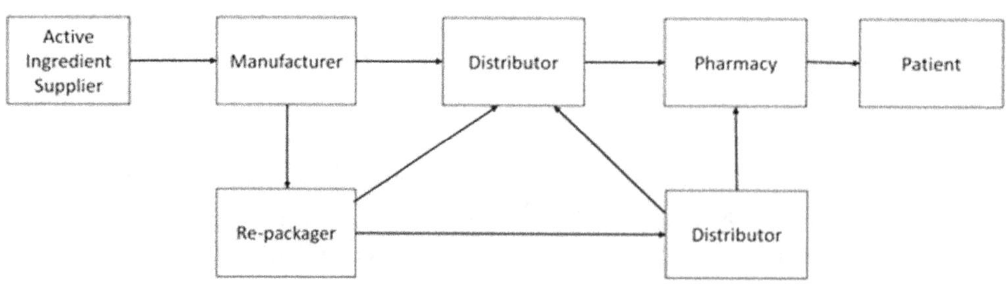

Many decentralized approaches have recently been developed to address the issue of drug traceability (Yaqoob, et al., 2022). To ensure the privacy and validity of trackable data, a blockchain model called Drugledger has been suggested. Drugledger typically uses Blockchain technology throughout the entire drug supply chain to efficiently track drugs (Konapure & Nawale, 2022). It primarily contains two distinct drug flows: information, which contains the drug ledge, and physical, which contains the actual drug.

However, the drug traceability scenario depicted in the Drugledger system appears simple in theory but is extremely complex in practice (Sohan et al., 2022). An intelligent blockchain-based system for tracking and tracing the drug supply chain has been introduced in (Liu et al., 2021). This system operates a supply chain that is transparent, secure, and integrated. It is made up of the following sections:

1. A five-layer blockchain architecture that tracks and traces drug manufacturing, logistics, sales, and usage.
2. Whether the drug data is stored on-chain or off-chain is determined by an on-chain and off-chain criterion. This section provides a useful approach for ensuring the performance of the blockchain network.

Panda and Satapathy (2021) proposed a blockchain-based drug supply chain system. Indeed, blockchain technology has the potential to solve the traditional dry chain supply efficiency problem. The proposed platform's main feature is that it stores all transfer history. To begin, a pharmaceutical company may register a medicine. The manufacturer should register each new medicine in the proposed system and upload its details to the network. Furthermore, any network exchange requires the approval of both the sender and the receiver. Any finished transaction should be saved on the network. This series of steps eliminates the possibility of third-party fraud.

According to Kamenivskyy et al. (2022), the integration of the Internet of things (IoT) with Blockchain technology makes the whole drug traceability system more secure. Many drug traceability systems have been proposed in the healthcare sector in recent years. Ratta et al. (2021) discussed the use of IoT and Blockchain in three major areas of healthcare: drug traceability, remote patient monitoring, and medical record management.

The Gcoin Blockchain model (G stands for global governance) is proposed in for the transparent flow of drugs (Tseng et al., 2018). The primary goal of this model was to improve the efficiency with which data is exchanged. It shifted the drug supply chain system from regulating to monitoring and inspecting drugs. It combines the government model with the DAO (Decentralized Autonomous Organization). Blockchain created an environment in which two parties could trust each other.

A new platform for detecting fake drugs in the supply chain system was proposed in Pandey and Litoriya (2020). The suggested system is design on the Hyperledger fabric architecture, with a computer or smart device acting as the client. However, five computers were used to place service orders. This approach was created entirely with Blockchain technology. It uses Blockchain to track drug distribution from manufacturing to local pharmaceutical distributors and hospitals/clinics, assisting in the detection of counterfeit medications. This system was eximaned in a variety of scenarios, including drug theft and unauthorized drug distribution. The proposed system performed well in many characteristics, including resistance to a single point of failure and fake medicine detection. However, the proposed system was unable to detect and eliminate the use of unauthorized medicines.

FUTURE RESEARCH DIRECTIONS

Blockchain technology plays an important role in the healthcare industry. This technology, however, has some limitations, including:

1. Interactions between different systems: Because blockchain technology lacks standards, compatibility issues between different systems can pose challenges for storing medical data.
2. Mass medical data collection may slow the exchange rate and limit its scalability.
3. A lack of knowledge about economic viability.
4. The cost of solutions is typically higher for customers.

As a result, more research should be conducted to investigate the aforementioned limitations. Furthermore, the effectiveness of using blockchain should be addressed during the pandemic.

CONCLUSION

The healthcare industry is an essential component of modern society. It is directly linked to people's social interests and lives. However, due to the covid pandemic, this sector is plagued by numerous issues, particularly with the massive amount of collected health data. Research and improvement of the healthcare sector should continue because it will improve human life quality by resolving many health problems. The huge developments in technology and the creation of new techniques can easily be seen in the Healthcare sector. By incorporating the latest computer technologies in the Healthcare field, the competence of the Healthcare and Medical Sector can be enhanced. Many new and revolutionary technologies are already being successfully integrated into other industries. These technologies include IoT, Blockchain, Artificial Intelligence, Image Processing, Natural Language Processing, and many others.

Blockchain technology has been described in this chapter. In addition, the major challenges confronting the recent healthcare sector have been presented. Blockchain integration in the healthcare sector has been investigated. The authors concentrated on the role of Blockchain technique on HER(electronic health records) and drug traceability. The authors conclude that Blockchain technology improves the safety, availability, and integrity of electronic health records. Furthermore, it plays an important role in detecting fake drugs throughout the drug supply chain. Many systems, however, have been developed to integrate blockchain technology into the healthcare sector. As a result, future comparative studies on these systems should be conducted. Furthermore, the use of Blockchain with other recent technologies, such as IoT, in the drug supply chain should be researched and debated.

FUNDING STATEMENT

This research received no specific grant from any funding agency in the public, commercial, or not-for-profit sectors.

REFERENCES

Abouelmehdi, K., Beni-Hssane, A., Khaloufi, H., & Saadi, M. (2017). Big data security and privacy in healthcare: A Review. *Procedia Computer Science*, *113*, 73–80.

Abunadi, I., & Kumar, R. L. (2021). BSF-EHR: Blockchain security framework for electronic health records of patients. *Sensors (Basel)*, *21*(8), 2865. PMID:33921738

Adlam, R., & Haskins, B. (2021). Applying Blockchain Technology to Security-Related Aspects of Electronic Healthcare Record Infrastructure. *The African Journal of Information and Communication*, *28*, 1–28.

Alderwick, H., & Gottlieb, L. M. (2019). Meanings and misunderstandings: A social determinants of health lexicon for health care systems. *The Milbank Quarterly*, *97*(2), 407. PMID:31069864

Andoni, M., Robu, V., Flynn, D., Abram, S., Geach, D., Jenkins, D., ... Peacock, A. (2019). Blockchain technology in the energy sector: A systematic review of challenges and opportunities. *Renewable & Sustainable Energy Reviews*, *100*, 143–174.

Arjun, R., & Suprabha, K. R. (2020). *Innovation and challenges of blockchain in banking: A scientometric view*. Academic Press.

Arun Kumar, B. R. (2022). Developing Business-Business Private Block-Chain Smart Contracts Using Hyper-Ledger Fabric for Security, Privacy and Transparency in Supply Chain. In *Data Management, Analytics and Innovation* (pp. 429–440). Springer.

Azaria, A., Ekblaw, A., Vieira, T., & Lippman, A. (2016, August). Medrec: Using blockchain for medical data access and permission management. In *2016 2nd international conference on open and big data (OBD)* (pp. 25-30). IEEE.

Bamakan, S. M. H., Moghaddam, S. G., & Manshadi, S. D. (2021). Blockchain-enabled pharmaceutical cold chain: Applications, key challenges, and future trends. *Journal of Cleaner Production*, *302*, 127021.

Bartoletti, I. (2019, June). AI in healthcare: Ethical and privacy challenges. In *Conference on Artificial Intelligence in Medicine in Europe* (pp. 7-10). Springer.

binti Suhaili, S., & Watanabe, T. (2017, November). Design of high-throughput SHA-256 hash function based on FPGA. In *2017 6th International Conference on Electrical Engineering and Informatics (ICEEI)* (pp. 1-6). IEEE.

Bodkhe, U., Tanwar, S., Parekh, K., Khanpara, P., Tyagi, S., Kumar, N., & Alazab, M. (2020). Blockchain for industry 4.0: A comprehensive review. *IEEE Access : Practical Innovations, Open Solutions*, *8*, 79764–79800.

Bosamia, M., & Patel, D. (2018). Current trends and future implementation possibilities of the Merkel tree. *International Journal on Computer Science and Engineering*, *6*(8), 294–301.

Chelladurai, M. U., Pandian, S., & Ramasamy, K. (2021). A blockchain-based patient-centric electronic health record storage and integrity management for e-Health systems. *Health Policy and Technology*, *10*(4), 100513.

Dasgupta, A., Maguire, E., Abdul-Rahman, A., & Chen, M. (2016). *Opportunities and challenges for privacy-preserving visualization of electronic health record data*. Academic Press.

Dashkevich, N., Counsell, S., & Destefanis, G. (2020). Blockchain application for central banks: A systematic mapping study. *IEEE Access : Practical Innovations, Open Solutions*, *8*, 139918–139952.

Golosova, J., & Romanovs, A. (2018, November). The advantages and disadvantages of the blockchain technology. In *2018 IEEE 6th workshop on advances in information, electronic and electrical engineering (AIEEE)* (pp. 1-6). IEEE. 10.1109/AIEEE.2018.8592253

Gopal, G., Suter-Crazzolara, C., Toldo, L., & Eberhardt, W. (2019). Digital transformation in healthcare–architectures of present and future information technologies. *Clinical Chemistry and Laboratory Medicine*, *57*(3), 328–335. PMID:30530878

Gorkhali, A., Li, L., & Shrestha, A. (2020). Blockchain: A literature review. *Journal of Management Analytics*, *7*(3), 321–343.

Grande, D., Marti, X. L., Feuerstein-Simon, R., Merchant, R. M., Asch, D. A., Lewson, A., & Cannuscio, C. C. (2020). Health policy and privacy challenges associated with digital technology. *JAMA Network Open*, *3*(7), e208285–e208285. PMID:32644138

Guardtime, G. (2019). *Increasing Healthcare Security with Blockchain Technology*. Academic Press.

Haleem, A., Javaid, M., Singh, R. P., Suman, R., & Rab, S. (2021). Blockchain technology applications in healthcare: An overview. *International Journal of Intelligent Networks*, *2*, 130–139.

Hussain, M. W., Reddy, K. H., & Roy, D. S. (2021). A counter based approach for reducer placement with augmented Hadoop rackawareness. *Turkish Journal of Electrical Engineering and Computer Sciences*, *29*(1), 437–453.

Hussain, M. W., & Roy, D. S. (2022). A Counter-Based Profiling Scheme for Improving Locality Through Data and Reducer Placement. In *Advances in Machine Learning for Big Data Analysis* (pp. 101–118). Springer Nature Singapore.

Kamenivskyy, Y., Palisetti, A., Hamze, L., & Saberi, S. (2022). A Blockchain-Based Solution for COVID-19 Vaccine Distribution. *IEEE Engineering Management Review*, *50*(1), 43–53.

Konapure, R. R., & Nawale, S. D. (2022, May). Smart Contract System Architecture for Pharma Supply chain. In *2022 International Conference on IoT and Blockchain Technology (ICIBT)* (pp. 1-5). IEEE.

Lee, J. Y. (2019). A decentralized token economy: How blockchain and cryptocurrency can revolutionize business. *Business Horizons*, *62*(6), 773–784.

Li, C., Hu, J., Zhou, K., Wang, Y., & Deng, H. (2018, June). Using blockchain for data auditing in cloud storage. In *International Conference on Cloud Computing and Security* (pp. 335-345). Springer.

Li, X., Wang, Z., Leung, V. C., Ji, H., Liu, Y., & Zhang, H. (2021). Blockchain-empowered data-driven networks: A survey and outlook. *ACM Computing Surveys*, *54*(3), 1–38.

Lin, I. C., & Liao, T. C. (2017). A survey of blockchain security issues and challenges. *International Journal of Network Security*, *19*(5), 653–659.

Liu, X., Barenji, A. V., Li, Z., Montreuil, B., & Huang, G. Q. (2021). Blockchain-based smart tracking and tracing platform for drug supply chain. *Computers & Industrial Engineering*, *161*, 107669.

Lv, Z., & Qiao, L. (2020). Analysis of healthcare big data. *Future Generation Computer Systems*, *109*, 103–110.

Michael, J., Cohn, A., & Butcher, J. R. (2018). BlockChain technology. *The Journal*, 34-44.

Musamih, A., Salah, K., Jayaraman, R., Arshad, J., Debe, M., Al-Hammadi, Y., & Ellahham, S. (2021). A blockchain-based approach for drug traceability in the healthcare supply chain. *IEEE Access : Practical Innovations, Open Solutions*, *9*, 9728–9743.

Niaz, M. S., & Saake, G. (2015). Merkle hash tree based techniques for data integrity of outsourced data. *GvD*, *1366*, 66–71.

Niranjanamurthy, M., Nithya, B. N., & Jagannatha, S. J. C. C. (2019). Analysis of Blockchain technology: Pros, cons and SWOT. *Cluster Computing*, *22*(6), 14743–14757.

Odeh, A., Keshta, I., & Al-Haija, Q. A. (2022). Analysis of Blockchain in the Healthcare Sector: Application and Issues. *Symmetry*, *14*(9), 1760.

Panda, S. K., & Satapathy, S. C. (2021). Drug traceability and transparency in medical supply chain using blockchain for easing the process and creating trust between stakeholders and consumers. *Personal and Ubiquitous Computing*, 1–17.

Pandey, A. K., Khan, A. I., Abushark, Y. B., Alam, M. M., Agrawal, A., Kumar, R., & Khan, R. A. (2020). Key issues in healthcare data integrity: Analysis and recommendations. *IEEE Access : Practical Innovations, Open Solutions*, *8*, 40612–40628.

Pandey, P., & Litoriya, R. (2021). Securing e-health networks from counterfeit medicine penetration using blockchain. *Wireless Personal Communications*, *117*(1), 7–25.

Pastorino, R., De Vito, C., Migliara, G., Glocker, K., Binenbaum, I., Ricciardi, W., & Boccia, S. (2019). Benefits and challenges of Big Data in healthcare: An overview of the European initiatives. *European Journal of Public Health*, *29*(Supplement_3), 23–27. PMID:31738444

Price, W. N., & Cohen, I. G. (2019). Privacy in the age of medical big data. *Nature Medicine*, *25*(1), 37–43. PMID:30617331

Raghupathi, W., & Raghupathi, V. (2014). Big data analytics in healthcare: Promise and potential. *Health Information Science and Systems*, *2*(1), 1–10. PMID:25825667

Ratta, P., Kaur, A., Sharma, S., Shabaz, M., & Dhiman, G. (2021). Application of blockchain and internet of things in healthcare and medical sector: Applications, challenges, and future perspectives. *Journal of Food Quality*.

Rauchs, M., & Hileman, G. (2010). *Global blockchain benchmarking study*. Cambridge Centre for Alternative Finance Reports.

Shi, S., He, D., Li, L. K. N., Khan, M. K., & Choo, K. K. R. (2020). Applications of blockchain in ensuring the security and privacy of electronic health record systems: A survey. *Computers & Security*, 97. PMID:32834254

Shrivas, M. K., & Yeboah, T. (2018, December). The disruptive blockchain: types, platforms and applications. *Fifth Texila World Conference for Scholars (TWCS) on Transformation: The Creative Potential of Interdisciplinary*.

Sohan, M., Al, F. A., Khan, S. R., Anannya, N. J., & Ahad, M. T. (2022). *Towards a secured smart IoT using light weight blockchain: An aim to secure Pharmacy Products*. arXiv preprint arXiv:2206.06925.

Sujatha, G., Hemavathi, D., Sornalakshmi, K., & Sindhu, S. (2022). Analysis of Cryptographic Hashing Algorithms for Image Identification in Deduplication Process. In *Mobile Computing and Sustainable Informatics* (pp. 813–823). Springer.

Tanwar, S., Parekh, K., & Evans, R. (2020). Blockchain-based electronic healthcare record system for healthcare 4.0 applications. *Journal of Information Security and Applications*, *50*, 102407.

Thapa, C., & Camtepe, S. (2021). Precision health data: Requirements, challenges and existing techniques for data security and privacy. *Computers in Biology and Medicine*, *129*, 104130. PMID:33271399

Tortorella, G. L., Fogliatto, F. S., Mac Cawley Vergara, A., Vassolo, R., & Sawhney, R. (2020). Healthcare 4.0: Trends, challenges and research directions. *Production Planning and Control*, *31*(15), 1245–1260.

Tseng, J. H., Liao, Y. C., Chong, B., & Liao, S. W. (2018). Governance on the drug supply chain via gcoin blockchain. *International Journal of Environmental Research and Public Health*, *15*(6), 1055. PMID:29882861

Tully, J., Selzer, J., Phillips, J. P., O'Connor, P., & Dameff, C. (2020). Healthcare challenges in the era of cybersecurity. *Health Security*, *18*(3), 228–231. PMID:32559153

Uddin, M., Salah, K., Jayaraman, R., Pesic, S., & Ellahham, S. (2021). Blockchain for drug traceability: Architectures and open challenges. *Health Informatics Journal*, *27*(2). PMID:33899576

Xu, M., Chen, X., & Kou, G. (2019). A systematic review of blockchain. *Financial Innovation*, *5*(1), 1–14.

Yaqoob, I., Salah, K., Jayaraman, R., & Al-Hammadi, Y. (2022). Blockchain for healthcare data management: Opportunities, challenges, and future recommendations. *Neural Computing & Applications*, *34*(14), 11475–11490.

Yli-Huumo, J., Ko, D., Choi, S., Park, S., & Smolander, K. (2016). Where is current research on blockchain technology?—A systematic review. *PLoS One*, *11*(10), e0163477. PMID:27695049

Zarour, M., Alenezi, M., Ansari, M. T. J., Pandey, A. K., Ahmad, M., Agrawal, A., ... Khan, R. A. (2021). Ensuring data integrity of healthcare information in the era of digital health. *Healthcare Technology Letters*, *8*(3), 66–77. PMID:34035927

Zheng, Z., Xie, S., Dai, H., Chen, X., & Wang, H. (2017, June). *An overview of blockchain technology: Architecture, consensus, and future trends. In 2017 IEEE international congress on big data (BigData congress)*. IEEE.

Zimmerman, P. (2020). *Blockchain structure and cryptocurrency prices.* Academic Press.

ADDITIONAL READING

Al Mamun, A., Azam, S., & Gritti, C. (2022). Blockchain-Based Electronic Health Records Management: A Comprehensive Review and Future Research Direction. *IEEE Access : Practical Innovations, Open Solutions.*

Chelladurai, U., & Pandian, S. (2022). A novel blockchain based electronic health record automation system for healthcare. *Journal of Ambient Intelligence and Humanized Computing, 13*(1), 693–703.

Huang, Y., Wu, J., & Long, C. (2018, July). Drugledger: A practical blockchain system for drug traceability and regulation. In 2018 IEEE international conference on internet of things (iThings) and IEEE green computing and communications (GreenCom) and IEEE cyber, physical and social computing (CPSCom) and IEEE smart data (SmartData) (pp. 1137-1144). IEEE. doi:10.1109/Cybermatics_2018.2018.00206

Kumar, R., & Tripathi, R. (2019, January). Traceability of counterfeit medicine supply chain through Blockchain. In *2019 11th international conference on communication systems & networks (COMSNETS)* (pp. 568-570). IEEE. 10.1109/COMSNETS.2019.8711418

Mukta, R., Paik, H. Y., Lu, Q., & Kanhere, S. S. (2022). A survey of data minimisation techniques in blockchain-based healthcare. *Computer Networks, 205*, 108766.

Panigrahi, A., Nayak, A. K., & Paul, R. (2022). HealthCare EHR: A Blockchain-Based Decentralized Application. *International Journal of Information Systems and Supply Chain Management, 15*(3), 1–15.

Shi, S., He, D., Li, L., Kumar, N., Khan, M. K., & Choo, K. K. R. (2020). Applications of blockchain in ensuring the security and privacy of electronic health record systems: A survey. *Computers & Security, 97*, 101966. PMID:32834254

KEY TERMS AND DEFINITIONS

Big Data: is a huge set of collected data. These data may contain images, sound, and text information.

Blockchain: Is a chain of blocks linked together, each block has its encrypted address using the cryptographic hash algorithm function which is not reversible, this hashed address using as a block identifier.

Cryptographic Hash Function: It is an algorithm that takes a random value as input and delivers a fixed-size output of enciphered text called a hash value, or just "hash."

Electronic Health Record (EHR): Is a set of data that store the patient health information in a digital format.

Internet of Things: Is an open and broad network of intelligent objects capable of sharing and arranging information. Then, it acts according to the current situation and status of the environment.

Merkle Tree: Called also hash tree, it is a tree in which every "leaf" (node) is marked by a cryptographic hash.

Stakeholder: It is a person or a group of person that has an interest in an activity, a system, or an organization.

Chapter 14
Co-Operation in Wireless Sensor Networks for Smart Cities

Abraham George
Alliance University, India

ABSTRACT

Sensor deployment in smart city scenarios introduce multiple challenges such as node capacity management, node management, and communication latency. As the size of the sensor network increases, there must be novel or multiple strategies to improve efficiency of the network. The goal of this chapter is to explore and highlight research strategies in this area. There has been work in this area, but there are multiple emerging challenges in this area due to explosion in number of sensor nodes and the functionalities embedded in these nodes in smart city and healthcare applications. Node co-operation or node collaboration is a method to localize large-scale sensor networks. This method has been explored in cellular networks to improve spectrum utilization. There is much interest and scope in node co-operation/ node collaboration in sensor networks as collaboration can be exploited to control the topology, minimize communication overhead, and conserve energy at the node.

INTRODUCTION

A smart city is a technologically advanced urban area that uses sensors to measure and monitor various data to improve quality of life for its citizens and streamline urban services. Large cities across the world have initiated projects to make their areas more citizen friendly in terms of transportation & utility services, waste management, energy consumption, and hospital services. There have been studies on the level of intelligence that is to be embodied in urban areas to qualify as a smart city (Halegoua, 2020). From a technological standpoint, the relevant aspect is to create a technological architecture that can scale to various levels of intelligence. Internet of Things (IoT) is the prime enabler of Smart cities that enables to acquire various kinds of data and perform an action. Urban areas around the world have created IoT deployment strategies based on the services it wants to offer to citizens and problems

DOI: 10.4018/979-8-3693-0744-1.ch014

it intends to resolve (Alablani & Alenazi, 2020). Internet of Things (IoT) is a group of inter-related or interconnected computing devices performing a mechanical, electric, or biological function. An IoT network can also be referred to as a Wireless Sensor Network (WSN). WSN can be broadly defined as embedded devices that communicate wireless in an ad-hoc or infrastructure less network (Forster, 2016). In WSN the connectivity with the public network is via a gateway node. Therefore, IoT devices can be termed as devices with direct or in direct connectivity with the public network. Many recent literatures have proposed the integration of WSNs and IoT for large scale deployments (Rani, et.al, 2020). In this article we consider WSN as a subset of IoT where all devices are connected to the public network via single hop or multi-hop.

IoT systems represent the integration of four distinct components, namely:

- Sensors/devices,
- Connectivity,
- Data processing,
- User interface.

Sensor devices perform the function of measurement or monitoring an event. Connectivity component is responsible for sharing or passing the information to a centralized location or a peer device. In the case of industrial applications, the temperature or pressure data is transmitted to a centralized processing centre that consolidates data from different locations. There are cases of distributed connectivity where there are localized master nodes to reduce the data transmission load in the system. Connectivity is realized through a wireless radio interface that can send data over the air to a peer receiving device. There are several wireless protocols for sensor devices. The distinguishing aspects of these wireless protocols are the physical layer media and media communication layer mechanism. The media layer protocols are responsible for managing the spectrum resources and conserving the energy dissipated in the device for communication. In turn this implies that the media layer is for conserving the power or energy of the wireless device. A simple analogy is a human speaker adjusting his volume to reach out to the audience he is speaking to in a room. If all the audience are in proximity, then the speaker can speak at relatively lower volumes compared to the scenario where the audience are spread out in distance or when there are unwanted sound sources. Here the human speaker has the intelligence and information to make these decisions. The media access layer has a similar role and objective of conserving the power of the transmitting device and allocating the available resources to serve the maximal number of users.

The third stated function of data processing is an important part of an IoT system where the nodes perform computations before passing on the data to the master node or perform computations on the data received from peer nodes. The early generations of WSN nodes did not perform many computations where they acquired data and relayed the data to a centralized node. Modern IoT systems have grown considerably in terms of functional complexity and size of the IoT network. The large number of nodes in the system demand or rather require novel approaches to relay and process data. Take an example of WSN network in an industrial application where there are 1000's of WSN nodes acquiring pressure, temperature, chemical concentration at various points in the system. The purpose of the WSN network in the factory is to detect anomaly in functioning and suggest/alert preventive steps in quick time to the supervisor or control centre in the factory. The conventional approach of nodes individually sending data to a central node and the centralized node computing the data to determine anomaly introduces much latency in detection of failure. Alternate or better approaches would be to localize the data within a region to detect anomaly and provide an alert to the control centre. This would imply that the WSN's have much capability and awareness to determine their localized region, perform computation and have the capability to decide. For this, the WSN nodes need to have a computing engine or a processor. This would in turn imply that the device requires power source or energy to operate the compute engine (Hussain et al., 2020). This also adds significant challenge to the WSN as WSN installations may not have direct access to a power source, where they are mostly powered by a battery. WSN installations typically have small form factor and cost of maintenance and operation needs to be low to make it a viable business proposition. In many installations, the WSN nodes are not very easily accessible which means factory personnel would want the WSN to operate with minimal intervention for a reasonably long period. The last essential component is the user interface. This is more prevalent or required in consumer sensor network devices. User Interface refers to the display of data and control interface to trigger the sensor device. In smart city and industrial application, the device is prevalently a mobile device that communicates with a cloud storage via message APIs.

This chapter specifically discusses IoT/WSN for smart city applications where large number of nodes are networked to perform a collective or assistive function. IoT network can be broadly defined as "A dynamic global network infrastructure with self-configuring capabilities". In the context of Smart cities, Internet of Things can be visualized as a group of WSN that can transmit/receive data and can execute an action. Wireless sensor nodes communicate via their radio modules. Two nodes are directly connected if they can transmit/receive data to/from each other. A sensor communication model or a transmission model is a network model that establishes connectivity between sensor nodes to create a network.

Figure 1. Typical WSN network for a smart city scenario

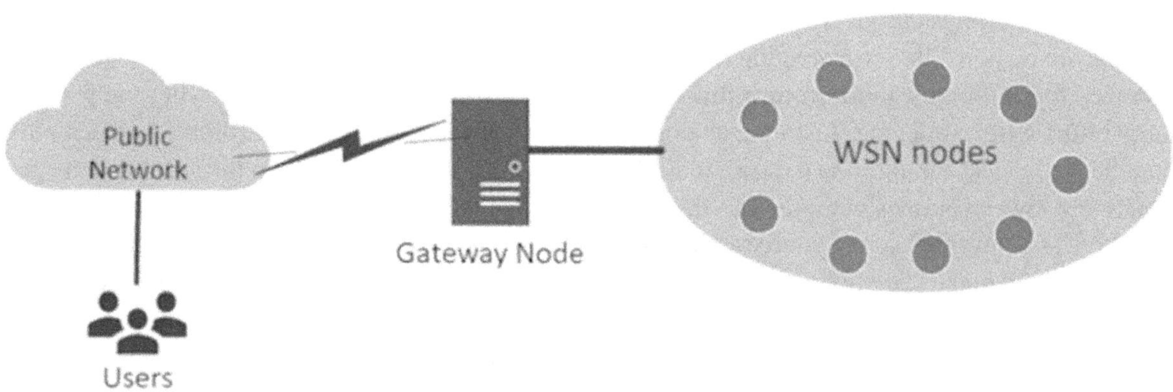

Figure 1 depicts a WSN network where a group of nodes are interconnected and their link to the external network is via a gateway node. The gateway node may be connected directly to an infrastructure network such as a cellular network. Alternately every WSN node may be directly connected to the network via a cellular link. Different connectivity models have been proposed in WSN. Much of the WSN architecture is influenced by the cellular architecture. In large smart city applications, the concept of IoT and Mobile Ad Hoc Network (MANET) is merged or integrated. MANET is an independent, decentralized, highly mobile, self-maintaining, self-repairing, self-configurable wireless network, free to move from one place to another place (Zheng & Jamalipour, 2009). These networks do not have any pre-existing infrastructure. Every node has the freedom to move randomly and change its attachment point to other nodes. Although in some literature MANETs and IoT are discussed separately, the separation between the two is narrow. In many of the commercial use cases, the IoT device is directly connected to the public network via a cellular or WLAN interface. In MANETs, node may nor may not be connected to the public network. If they are connected to the public network, it is via a gateway node that acts as an intermediary between the ad hoc network and the gateway as depicted in Figure 1. There are multiple design possibilities for a IoT application depending on the user scenario. In this chapter, the terms IoT, WSN, and MANET are used interchangeably as they are all constituents of a smart city network.

The focus of this chapter is explaining the challenges in designing an IoT network for smart city applications. Smart cities use IoT devices such as sensors, and meters to monitor, collect and analyse data. The cities then use this data to improve infrastructure, allocate services and offer new services. There have been numerous literatures on IoT systems and WSN concepts (Elhabyan, et.al, 2019) in recent years. However, the smart city scenarios introduce or impose multiple challenges in IoT system design and deployment specifically for smart city scenarios. The complexity of smart city scenarios can be primarily attributed to the volume of data generated and the localized responses to be initiated or triggered. An example of this is the surveillance scenarios where the system automatically detects anomalies and initiates an action (Anagnostopoulos, 2022). In this scenario the challenge is performing computation on the large volume of generated data to identify an anomaly in a localized region. Cloud based IoT solutions have been proposed for smart city scenarios considering the scale and variety of data (Alam, 2021). The limiting factor to cloud based processing solutions is the ability to generate accurate real time responses in a localized region. (Santi, et.al, 2019) have extensively surveyed on the deployment and management strategies for smart city deployment. Authors in here detail the various smart city application and technology layers for smart city application. Smart city deployments are in development stages, hence there are multiple challenges to be addressed at various levels namely device communication, data analysis and the response (Ismagilova et al., 2019).

Having broadly defined the IoT scenarios, and elements, the chapter sets stage to focus on an active research topic that is relevant to smart cities. This chapter narrows down to the topic of node cooperation for wireless sensor networks. Node cooperation is discussed in cellular networks to improve network performance where nodes work collectively together to improve spectrum efficiency. While spectrum availability is a challenge for WSNs as well, there exists larger challenges in node auto configuration, network communication, real time capability, network management and other areas (Javed et al., 2022). The goal of this chapter to highlight node cooperation as an effective and efficient method to address network communication, and network management challenges. The term co-operative communication implies assistance from peer or neighbouring network nodes or collective intelligence. Collective intelligence implies that a group of nodes share information with each other where the decision making is based on inputs from all the participating nodes. This is a recent paradigm in computation which will find high applications in high density sensor networks. The paradigm of co-operation can be extended beyond the lower layers of channel utilization to increase efficiency, and capacity of the system. This has implication on node deployment strategies.

BACKGROUND AND SCENARIO

A smart city IoT application is a dense deployment of WSN nodes (Halegoua, 2020). These nodes may overlap each other as several WSN networks can be deployed in each region to monitor/perform a task. For example, consider a scenario where a WSN network is deployed in a specified area in a city to monitor water pipe leaks in the distribution lines. Each node may individually measure and monitor the pressure to determine a possible leak. If a leak is suspected, it may send an alarm signal to the control centre via its network interface which may be directly connected to the public network. This is the simplistic scenario where every network operates independently and reports anomaly when detected. The shortfall of this approach is that every node is restricted to its boundary of detecting an anomaly. If the WSN density is not sufficient to cover the entire region, there will be uncovered regions. The sensors in the nodes measure the variation in water pressure and report the measurements to the central node. An alternate approach could be that a group of nodes work together to locally identify if there is a potential water leak in that region. In this case a group of nodes work together to deduce certain information. This proposition finds several applications in smart city scenarios. The specific scenarios for smart city applications can be well understood in the context of the IoT levels. The table below highlights the different IoT levels and where each IoT applications primarily reside. It is important to understand the characteristics of smart city applications to map these applications with IoT levels:

1. Large dense deployment with multiple sensor devices
2. Largely operating in the unlicensed band
3. Energy constrained devices
4. Critical applications with high reliability and low latency

IoT devices or systems can be classified into various levels based on their function, computational mode, and communication mode (Waltenegus & Poellabauer, 2010). A sensor device primarily comprises of measurement device, communication link and the application. An example of a system with these components is a temperature measurement device that reports temperature periodically to a central node. This system has a measurement recording system where the central node obtains reading from the WSN nodes. A further extension to this device is adding a controller to the system where an action such as shutting a valve is taken locally within the system and the action is initiated by a central node. The system can be further sophisticated if system is connected to several other peer devices and providing a local compute engine for localized processing. Thus, we see that the system can be extended and expanded in scope and feature richness. This level of sophistication in IoT systems is represented by the various IoT levels. The difference between each of the IoT levels is illustrated through Table 1.

Table 1. Levels of IoT

	Nodes	Data Storage	Data Volumes	Computation in the Device	Applications
Level 1	Single	Local	Small	NIL	Custom home Automation
Level 2	Single	Cloud	Small	Minimal	Standalone systems
Level 3	Single	Cloud	Large	Minimal	Factory/ standalone fault monitoring systems
Level 4	Multiple	Local/Cloud	Medium	Minimal	Industry application /Surveillance
Level 5	Multiple	Cloud	Large	Medium	Industry application /Smart Cities
Level 6	Multiple	Cloud	Large	Medium	Large Industry/ Smart Cities

The table above illustrates the different implementation template models for IoT. Simple home automation devices are at level 1 or level 2. Current large-scale deployments come under level 4 and above. As discussed above, smart city applications are characterized by large scale deployments, localized action which may be triggered internally by the observer nodes or from the external network. In dense and large-scale deployments, the question that arises is how well does a Level 6 deployment scale. (Santi, et.al, 2019) have extensively highlighted the challenges in large sensor deployments particularly highlighting the problem of placement of sensor nodes. Figure 2 illustrates a smart city scenario which will enable to evaluate if newer approaches are required for large scale IoT deployments.

Figure 2. Smart city scenario

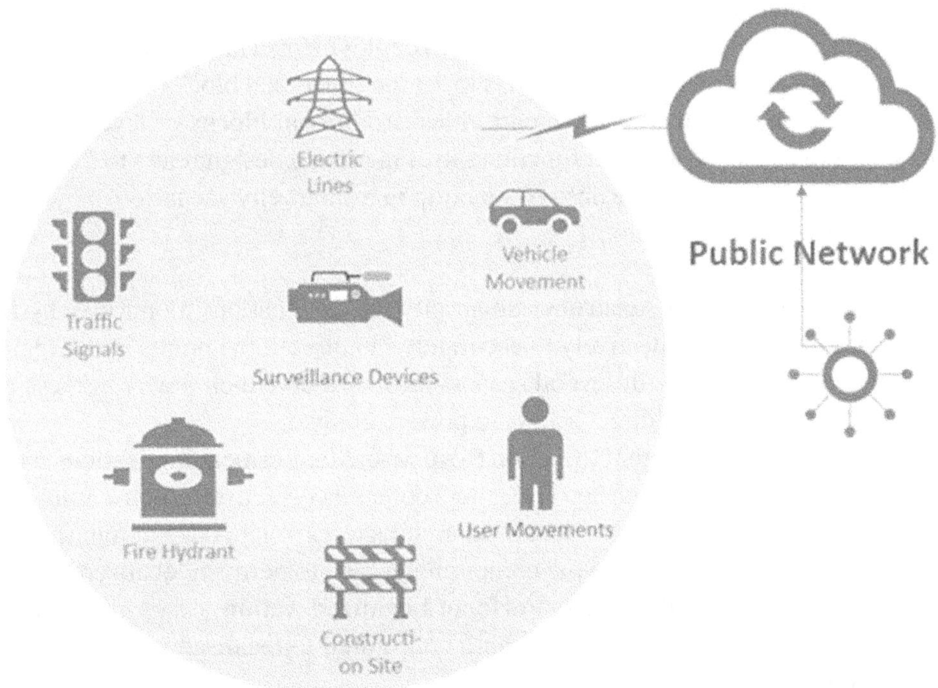

The focus of this chapter is highlighting and expanding the challenges in large scale IoT deployments in smart city scenarios. Smart city scenarios are characterised by dense deployments and it should be self-adapting and self-configuring devices. Dynamic and self-adapting refers to the ability to adapt or tune to the changing contexts or the deployment scenarios (Elhabyan et al., 2019). For example, irrigation moisture sensors switch to sleep mode during night, or a rainy day and surveillance camera may automatically change their capture mode with respect to the time of the day. Self-configuring devices refers to user devices that configure or attach themselves easily or effortlessly to the existing application. For example, take the case where public road infrastructure is fitted with vibration sensors. When the road network expands, newly added sensors should automatically configure themselves to the existing network and provide the functionality. The devices should have the ability to fetch latest software upgrades with minimal user intervention. These characteristics make IoT deployments in smart city applications complex and challenging. IoT devices operating in smart city environments have multiple sensors measurement devices which will transmit data at varying intervals. The next section outlines the functional blocks of a IoT device in smart city environment. Subsequently the chapter discusses on the co-operation aspect among devices and layers in the device that enable cooperation. Node cooperation was introduced first in cellular networks first to increase spectrum utilization. Several strategies have been proposed in literature for cellular networks (Qian et al., 2012). As mentioned earlier, the goal is of this chapter is to extend this concept to IoT networks. The need for these novel approaches arises from the challenging and constrained user scenarios in smart city deployments (Samih, 2019).

FUNCTIONAL BLOCKS OF IOT DEVICES IN A SMART CITY SCENARIO

Previous sections of this chapter sufficiently highlight the fundamental blocks of an IoT device and the capabilities of IoT devices desired in smart city scenario deployment. The levels are classified based on the deployment scenario. The goal of this section is to set the functional blocks of an IoT device in large scale deployment scenarios particularly for smart cities. Additional blocks or layers are added to the basic building blocks to provide additional functionality. Functional design refers to the building blocks of the device required to perform all the desired function in a smart city scenario.

The characteristics of this device are:

1. **Measurement Coverage and Accuracy:** Smart city IoT applications monitor and govern a large region. Devices must work collectively to accurately monitor all the points in the region.
2. **Energy Efficiency:** Devices with several sensors must conserve their power as these devices will be installed in regions without direct access to power supply.
3. **Minimal Latency in Measurement to Action Response:** Many critical applications such fire safety, water provisioning, accident avoidance and others demand corrective response immediately when an anomaly is detected. This requires localized architectures where edge computing servers have access to data in the region and have the computing engine to perform localized communication.
4. **Formation of Dynamic Sub Regions to Perform Localized Action:** Large node density and multiple applications require the devices to be auto configured to localised virtual regions or groups to execute a task.

Samih (2019) has listed various deployment and user scenarios that are a combination of these characteristics. The challenge is to create algorithms that encompass all these characteristics. This chapter specifically focusses on the last characteristic of forming sub regions to effectively trigger localized actions. There has been work done at individual layers to address challenges in large deployments primarily at the routing layer where minimizing the control overhead is a primary objective (Liu, 2015). The idea of clustering at the node level provides the benefit of minimizing communication overhead and energy spend (Shahraki, et.al, 2020). This chapter explores the concept of node cooperation within a localized region or cluster to improve efficiency and scale of deployment. Efficiency is parametrized by the control overhead, communication latency, system node capacity, node management and accuracy of response.

It is essential to understand the blocks of a device to determine the impact of clustering and node co-operation. An IoT system comprises of several functional blocks that provide the system the capabilities for identification, sensing, actuation, communication, and management. Smart City IoT Functional Blocks:

1. **Measurement Device:** An IoT device allows identification, remote sensing, actuating and remote monitoring capabilities.
2. **Communication:** Communication block enables the communication between devices via the network protocols from the physical layer to the application layer. This will encompass the wireless technology, routing schemes and the transport layer.
3. **WSN Cooperation:** This block is responsible for dynamic group formation in large IoT networks. As mentioned in earlier sections, in large IoT deployment there needs to be virtual formation of group of devices within the region to effectively perform a function. This layer is further discussed in the next section.
4. **Intelligent Services Layer:** An IoT system uses various types of IoT services such as publish/subscribe for device communication and services for device and service discovery.
5. **Computing Layer:** Devices in large scale deployments will also act as edge devices where they have computing capabilities.
6. **Management:** Management block provides various functions to govern the IoT system.
7. **Security:** Security block secures the IoT system by providing functions such as authentication, authorization, data integrity & security.
8. **Application:** IoT applications provide an interface that users engage with to control and monitor the IoT system. Applications allow users to view and analyse the captured data.

The functional block of the IoT device to execute the above functions are outlined in Figure 3.

Figure 3. Functional block of IoT smart city device

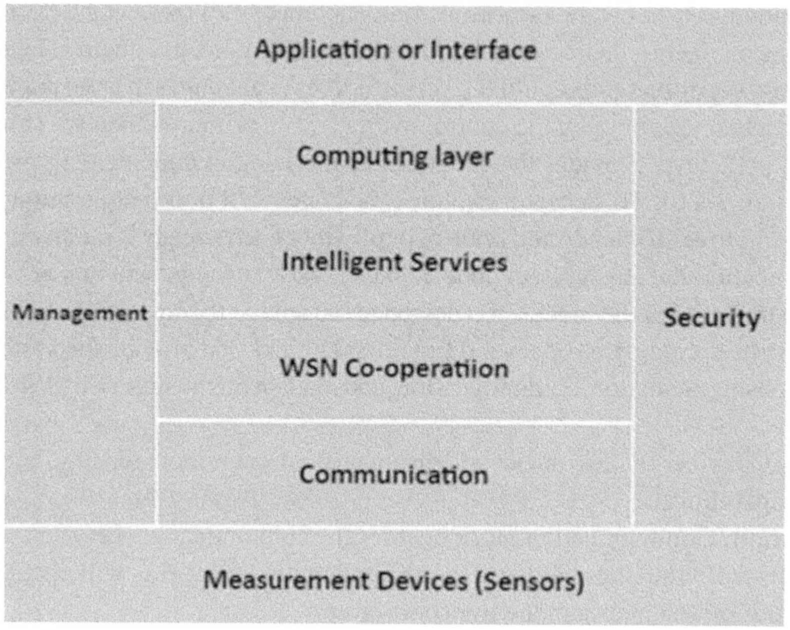

WSN COOPERATION

The central theme of this chapter is to further outline the concept of node co-operation (Silva et al., 2017) in large scale IoT deployments particularly for smart city scenarios. Prior sections sufficiently set the context and the premise to arrive at this section. The limited resources of the sensor nodes make the design of a large scale IoT application challenging (Renuka et al., 2020). Application requirements, in terms of latency, data throughput, or device lifetime, often conflict with the network capacity and energy resources. One approach for addressing these trade-offs in literature is to rely on wake-up scheduling MAC protocols, which consists in alternating the active and sleep states of sensor nodes. In the active state, all the components of a node (CPU, sensors, radio) are active, allowing the node to collect, process and communicate information. WSN nodes generate large amounts of data and this data in large WSN networks need to be routed across the nodes which considerably impact the latency and energy efficiency of the communication. There has been considerable literature to show that the performance of a WSN network can be further improved, if nodes not only synchronize, but also desynchronize with one another (Liu, 2015). Desynchronization refers to the term where nodes on different branches of the routing tree are active at different times to minimize or avoid congestion. In WSNs nodes can be logically organized in groups. In other words, the activity schedules of nodes that need to communicate with one another are synchronized to improve the message throughput. These nodes belong to a group or cohort.

The system is intelligent such that the schedules of groups of nodes which do not need to communicate are desynchronized in order to avoid congestion and packet losses. The cooperation of multiple WSNs may be able to improve the network lifetime of each WSN by load balancing all over the WSNs nodes because the energy consumption of sensor nodes is almost completely dominated by data communication rather than by sensing and processing. Hence, the whole network lifetime can be prolonged by balancing the communication load at heavily loaded nodes around a sink. There are numerous studies on load balancing using clustering approaches in large WSNs (Shahraki et al., 2020). The concept of virtual or dynamic group formation results in creating localized application at the higher network layers as well. For example, consider a scenario where sensors are deployed in a dense urban area to monitor vehicular traffic density and road vibrations. The same devices will have multiple sensors, but the granularity of the measurement is controlled or created at the service discovery and the co-operative layers.

A group a sensor will have to work cohesively to yield the required output. The optimum number of nodes required to yield desirable measurable accuracy for an application depends on spatial and temporal variation of the measurement. Measurements such as temperature will have gradual spatial variation and higher temporal variations. Hence the groups must be formed dynamically based on the application characteristics and same node may be partisan in multiple groups to yield the desirable results. The term co-operative networks for WSNs refers to the ability or capability of the WSN nodes to inherently form virtual groups to conserve the available resources such as device power, and frequency resources. Moreover, this approach also reduces the communication latency and drop rates thus improving the reliability of communication.

Figure 4 illustrates this concept or theme. This is a MANET scenario where nodes are connected to each other to reach the gateway node.

Figure 4. Sensor nodes forming regions through co-operation

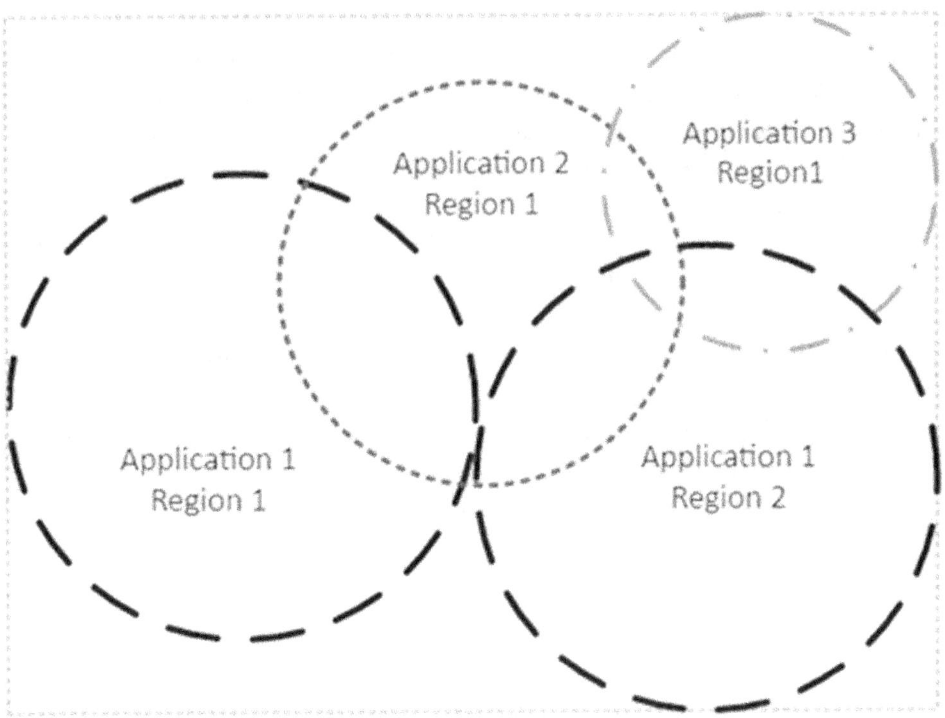

Figure 4 illustrates the theme of co-operation in large scale sensor networks where dynamic regions are formed and unformed based on node movement and application characteristics. In Figure 4, the rectangular box represents a given area. There are several co-located sensors in the region and several

IoT applications are deployed in the region. Zones are dynamically formed regions based on several parameters such as node density, measurement granularity, type of measurement, network conditions, and power source constraints. Nodes in a zone may be connected to the public network directly or via a gateway node. In Figure 4, 'Application 1 Region1' and 'Application 1 Region 2' are non-overlapping regions making the same measurement while 'Application 2' and 'Application 3'regions overlap with Application 1 and region size is not uniform. The central idea of forming localized regions is to obtain higher performance and conserve limited resources. The scheme of zoning further results in node-co-operation whereby nodes interact with few essential neighbours to perform their task and conserve their resources. There exist several literatures (Shahraki et al., 2020) where this theme is used to maximize a specific metric such as power resources, data protection, routing efficiency, application performance and others. There are multiple protocols and frameworks created for IoT scenarios (Sinche et al., 2020). The first step in the design of a smart city deployment scenario is to highlight the characteristics of the network that will subsequently enable to narrow down the protocols and frameworks at each layer. Next step is to explore strategies to fulfil the characteristics and maximize the efficiency of the network. The concept of zoning is primarily aimed at created localized regions. The larger research challenge to develop strategies that operate dynamically because many a times sensor nodes are deployed in batches and in many cases the devices are not static. Examples of non-static sensor devices are device mounted on moving vehicles and machines. Bio-inspired nature inspired algorithms such as swarm optimization algorithms are effective in dynamic group formation (Singh et al., 2021). Swarm Optimization algorithms are dynamically responsive, and the computation is distributed. An effective deployment strategy is highly dependent on the application and deployment scenario. Node co-operation is an effective strategy to build highly scalable IoT scenarios. These strategies combined with other strategies such as edge and cloud computing will enable to create large scale IoT networks (Singh & Mohan, 2019). The objective of this chapter is to highlight node co-operation as an effective strategy for smart city IoT development. It is beyond the scope of this chapter to explore algorithms and approaches on each metric. Once smaller groups are formed, several metrics can be optimized through this approach. The key open areas with respect to collaboration can be summarized as below:

1. **Node Auto Configuration:** Devices should get auto-configured to the sensor network and the localised group.
2. **Group Formation:** Dynamic formation of groups and re-balancing of groups within the sensor networks to maximize the performance.
3. **Virtual Group Formation:** Co-located or overlapping groups can exist to increase performance.
4. **Creating Sensor Networks at Scale:** Network can accommodate nodes with varying underlying protocols.

CONCLUSION

In this chapter we highlight and elucidate the concept of wireless sensor network node co-operation. This concept is highly relevant for smart city application. The early part of the chapter walks through the definitions, concepts of WSN & MANET, IoT levels leading to the functional blocks of a device. Node cooperation is the key theme of this chapter which is discussed in later sections. The goal here is to sufficiently emphasize on the concept of node cooperation and its relevance particularly in smart city

IoT deployments. This should enable technology implementers to be aware of methods to improve the efficiency of their deployments and enable new research directions specifically in smart city scenarios.

REFERENCES

Alablani, I., & Alenazi, M. (2020). EDTD-SC: An IoT Sensor Deployment Strategy for Smart Cities. *Sensors (Basel)*, *20*(24), 7191. doi:10.339020247191 PMID:33333935

Alam, T. (2021). Cloud-Based IoT Applications and Their Roles in Smart Cities. *Smart Cities*, *4*(3), 1196–1219. doi:10.3390martcities4030064

Anagnostopoulos, T. (2022). *IoT-enabled Unobtrusive Surveillance Systems for Smart Campus Safety*. John Wiley & Sons. doi:10.1002/9781119903932

Dargie, W., & Poellabauer, C. (2010). *Fundamentals of wireless sensor networks: Theory and practice*. Wiley.

Du, R., Santi, P., Xiao, M., Vasilakos, A. V., & Fischione, C. (2019). The Sensable City: A Survey on the Deployment and Management for Smart City Monitoring. *IEEE Communications Surveys and Tutorials*, *21*(2), 1533–1560. doi:10.1109/COMST.2018.2881008

Elhabyan, R., Shi, W., & St-Hilaire, M. (2019). Coverage protocols for wireless sensor networks: Review and future directions. *Journal of Communications and Networks (Seoul)*, *21*(1), 45–60. doi:10.1109/JCN.2019.000005

Forster, A. (2016). *Introduction to wireless sensor networks*. John Wiley & Sons. doi:10.1002/9781119345343

Halegoua, G. R. (2020). *Smart cities*. Mit Press. doi:10.7551/mitpress/11426.001.0001

Haque, A. K. M. B., Bhushan, B., & Dhiman, G. (2021). Conceptualizing smart city applications: Requirements, architecture, security issues, and emerging trends. *Expert Systems: International Journal of Knowledge Engineering and Neural Networks*, *39*(5). Advance online publication. doi:10.1111/exsy.12753

Hussain, M. W., Pradhan, B., Gao, X. Z., Reddy, K. H. K., & Roy, D. S. (2020). Clonal selection algorithm for energy minimization in software defined networks. *Applied Soft Computing*, *96*, 106617. doi:10.1016/j.asoc.2020.106617

Ismagilova, E., Hughes, L., Dwivedi, Y. K., & Raman, K. R. (2019). Smart cities: Advances in research—An information systems perspective. *International Journal of Information Management*, *47*, 88–100. doi:10.1016/j.ijinfomgt.2019.01.004

Javed, A. R., Shahzad, F., Rehman, S., Zikria, Y. B., Razzak, I., Jalil, Z., & Xu, G. (2022). Future smart cities requirements, emerging technologies, applications, challenges, and future aspects. *Cities (London, England)*, *129*, 103794. doi:10.1016/j.cities.2022.103794

Li, Q., Hu, R. Q., Qian, Y., & Wu, G. (2012). Cooperative communications for wireless networks: Techniques and applications in LTE-advanced systems. *IEEE Wireless Communications*, *19*(2). Advance online publication. doi:10.1109/MWC.2012.6189409

Liu, X. (2015). Atypical Hierarchical Routing Protocols for Wireless Sensor Networks: A Review. *IEEE Sensors Journal, 15*(10), 5372–5383. doi:10.1109/JSEN.2015.2445796 PMID:27761103

Quick, C., Dey, R., & Lin, X. (2021). Regression Models for Understanding COVID-19 Epidemic Dynamics With Incomplete Data. *Journal of the American Statistical Association, 116*(536), 1561–1577. doi:10.1080/01621459.2021.2001339 PMID:37206108

Renuka & Reddy. (2020b). *A Comprehensive Parameterized Resource Allocation Approach for Wireless Sensor Networks*. doi:10.1007/978-981-13-9574-1_7

Samih, H. (2019). Smart cities and internet of things. *Journal of Information Technology Case and Application Research, 21*(1), 3–12. doi:10.1080/15228053.2019.1587572

Shahraki, A., Taherkordi, A., Haugen, Ø., & Eliassen, F. (2020). Clustering objectives in wireless sensor networks: A survey and research direction analysis. *Computer Networks, 180*, 107376. doi:10.1016/j.comnet.2020.107376

Shalli Rani, Maheswar, Kanagachidambaresan, & Jayarajan. (2020). Integration of WSN and IoT for smart cities. Springer.

Sharma, P. K., & Park, J. H. (2021). Blockchain-Based Secure Mist Computing Network Architecture for Intelligent Transportation Systems. *IEEE Transactions on Intelligent Transportation Systems, 22*(8), 5168–5177. doi:10.1109/TITS.2020.3040989

Silva, B. M. C., Rodrigues, J. J. P. C., Kumar, N., & Han, G. (2017). Cooperative Strategies for Challenged Networks and Applications: A Survey. *IEEE Systems Journal, 11*(4), 2749–2760. doi:10.1109/JSYST.2015.2436927

Sinche, S., Raposo, D., Armando, N., Rodrigues, A., Boavida, F., Pereira, V., & Silva, J. S. (2020). A Survey of IoT Management Protocols and Frameworks. *IEEE Communications Surveys and Tutorials, 22*(2), 1168–1190. doi:10.1109/COMST.2019.2943087

Singh, A., Sharma, S., & Singh, J. (2021). Nature-inspired algorithms for Wireless Sensor Networks: A comprehensive survey. *Computer Science Review, 39*, 100342. doi:10.1016/j.cosrev.2020.100342

Singh, S., & Mohan Sharma, R. (2019). *Handbook of Research on the IoT, Cloud Computing, and Wireless Network Optimization*. IGI Global. doi:10.4018/978-1-5225-7335-7

Zheng, J., & Jamalipour, A. (2009). *Wireless Sensor Networks*. John Wiley & Sons.

Chapter 15
A Review on the Impact of Hybrid Renewable Energy Systems for Sustainability and Energy Management

Swetha Shekarappa G.
Alliance University, India

Manjulata Badi
Alliance University, India

Saurav Raj
Institute of Chemical Technology, Marathwada, India

Sheila Mahapatra
Alliance University, India

M. Senbagavalli
Alliance University, India

ABSTRACT

On account of continuous increase in concerns about environmental deterioration and electrical usage, sustainable energy sources are being commonly used to generate power and offer several benefits like clean energy and reduced price. To meet the fast growth in power stipulation, major renewable sources must be attained. Though renewables present a long-term solution as an alternative to fossil fuels, they are associated with uncertainty in generating power. In this chapter, to overcome the above problem, a combination of energy bases will be able to be implemented called as HRES. Due to the relatively low environmental effects, HRES have become a major choice for rural electrification. In this work, an endeavor has been made to present the outline of role of HRES. This chapter will also dispense about the power control strategies, energy assessment of a hybrid system, and battery energy storage devices in electrical networks.

DOI: 10.4018/979-8-3693-0744-1.ch015

INTRODUCTION

This section has a summary of the integration of a complete literature assessment on alternative hybrid renewable energy sources (HRES), control mechanisms, and battery energy storage systems. Due to increased global need for electricity, conventional electrical power infrastructures are undergoing a drastic transition as large-scale renewable power penetration is assimilated. The capacity to work is defined as power. In science, power cannot be created or annihilated; it can only be changed into another form. All life on the earth depends on energy and its transition, and transparency energy generation is a crucial part of that transformation.

Throughout this process, energy can be changed into a variety of diverse forms. Heterogeneous types of energy can be derived from sustainable and unsustainable energy sources. The continual growth of RES has become a crucial feature in many nations around the globe with the goal of ensuring a safe and renewable expansion as well as counteracting climate change consequences. Even though replacing fossil fuels with renewable energy bases is serious in today's world, conventional energy sources are still in use. In this situation, the usage of non-fossil fuels is still insufficient to preclude continued expansion (Dyrstad, Skonhoft, Christensen, & Ødegaard, 2019). Major key factors limiting the use of renewables to substitute fossil fuels is their variable and inconsistent nature, which makes integration into power systems difficult (Feilat, Azzam, & Al-Salaymeh, 2018). Solar and wind energy attributes may result in an overabundance of energy output that is lost if the compliance is the process and production phase do not meet. In 2013, for example, a total of 940.8 billion kWh of electrical energy was predicted to be restricted globally (Li, Shi, Cao, Wang, Kuang, Tan & Wei, 2015). Communities with few or no interconnections to the power grid, as well as those that have never been energized, are prime examples of where the installation of sources would be critical for reducing environmental loads. When it comes to rural broadband via small grids, a lack of methodology for assessing energy needs might contribute to wasteful system architecture.

HRES have attracted widespread recognition and have a significant impingement on the power grid today. They can be found in big power systems, small distribution systems, and microgrids (MG). Goals to cut carbon emissions, as well as many government subsidies to stimulate RES, have had a favorable impact on the incorporation of renewable energy technology into power grid.

However, current technological issues about the stochastic nature of RES have limited the extent of RES adoption in the incumbent power system. With RES currently accounting for < 10% of net electricity generation, significant technological progress is required to incorporate the virtually predicted 100% share of RES by 2050.

Accessibility has become a top priority in rural areas due to geographical destination, long speed and distance from the primary power network, high costs of power transmission lines, technology issues in sparsely populated locations, and concerns about electric power supply consistency due to natural calamities. RES, namely solar and wind, can be a viable option for rural power generation (Nottan, Diaf & Stoyanov, 2011; Ferrer-Marti, Garwood, Chiroque, Ramirez, Marcelo, Garfi & Velo, 2012). This structure can provide a reliable electricity supply to rural areas while also being more cost-effective than conventional electricity remedies, especially in telecoms, potentially toxic factories in remote locations, deep forests, and coastal cities, among other things.

A power system has been identified as a HRES, which comprised of one clean energy and multiple power sources. The framework shall be used in grid or stand alone, and the source can be formal, durable, or blended (Belatrache, Saifi, Harrouz & Bentouba, 2020; Girardet & Mendonca, 2009). These have been discovered that the distinct shading materials of a mixture renewable energy plant can be picked using numerous sizes variables. Additionally, many infomercial software packages are used for measurements and efficiency.

Energy management planning must be used to obtain the complete functioning of renewable energy-based hybrid approaches, as well as to guarantee supply and enhance power efficiency. A comprehensive energy management planning enables the structure to suit demand, extend device lifetimes, alleviate operating costs, maximize the utilization of renewable energy sources, drastically reduce costs amplitude, defend modules from interrupt destruction, and, as a consequence, improve the power system 's credibility, and improve power efficiency.

Solar and wind power installation potential globally totalled 903.1 GW in 2017, accounting for 41.4 percent of total renewable energy generated potential. To combat the volatility and unpredictability of a solitary renewable energy source, like solar and wind power, hybrid renewable energy methods have been designed, and more than 80% of them are off-grid installations.

Technology will continue to devour all scarce technology soon in order to satisfy the nation's ever-growing power requirements. Owing to the corona virus pandemic and complete lockdown in 2020, export growth declines by 5.9% comparison to 2019. In electric energy, the latest analysis uncovers that global financial progress substantially lowered global electricity utilization by 3.8% comparison to the starting months of 2019 in the starting months of 2020 (Ammari, Belatrache, Touhami & Makhloufi, 2022).

In the beginning months of 2020, consumption for renewable power increased by around 1.5 percent. Renewables are frequently given grid priority and are not forced to implement their output to reach requirement to protect them from the implications of lower energy demand. According to the Global Electricity Council's future energy projections, green and nuclear power will account for 25.0% of the worldwide power production in 2040. Figure 1 gives the general layout of the hybrid renewable energy structure for numerous sources of energy.

Figure 1. General hybrid renewable energy structure

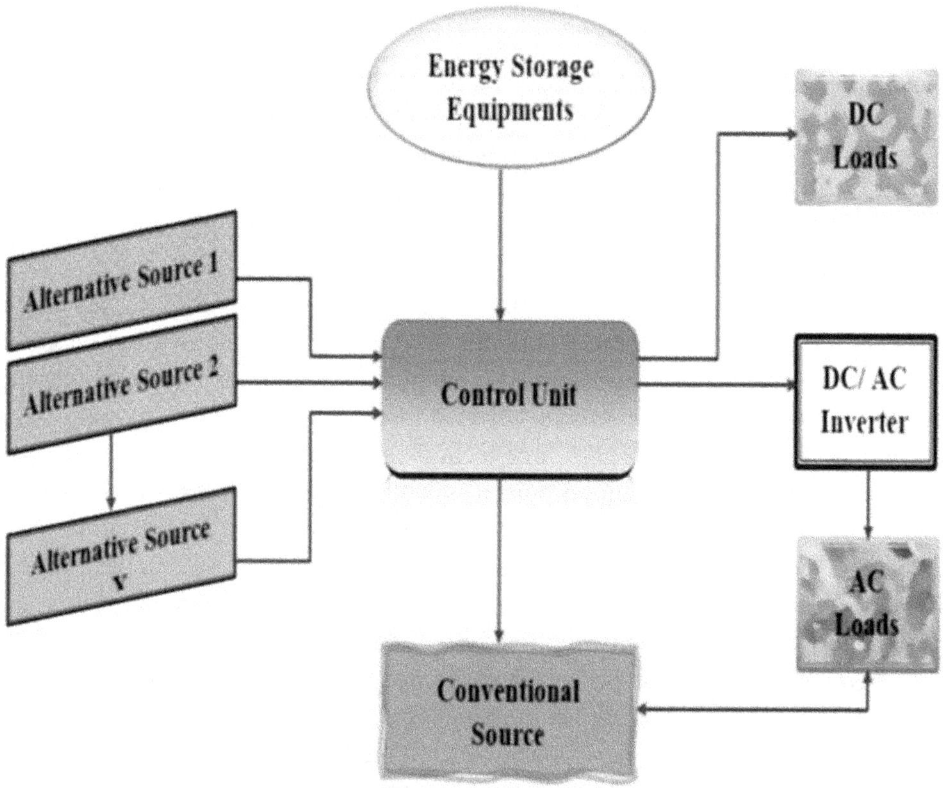

The book chapter first aims to exhibit the technology used for HRES, Power Converters used, HRES that incorporates PV modules, solar power, wind turbines, and a biogas generation. Then it focuses on presenting and analysing in depth research of the recent work published in HRES. The work proceeds to discuss about the energy storage and power control strategies in hybrid structures. An energy impetus to hybrid system that includes a photovoltaic panel, a wind turbine, and battery energy storage space device is also presented in the book chapter.

POWER CONVERTERS AND CONTROL STRATEGIES OF HRES

Power Converters

Every hybrid energy system typically has one or more power converters in order to operate efficiently. Devices that are electromechanical or electrical are used (Manwell, 2004).

Figure 2. Block diagram of the power converters

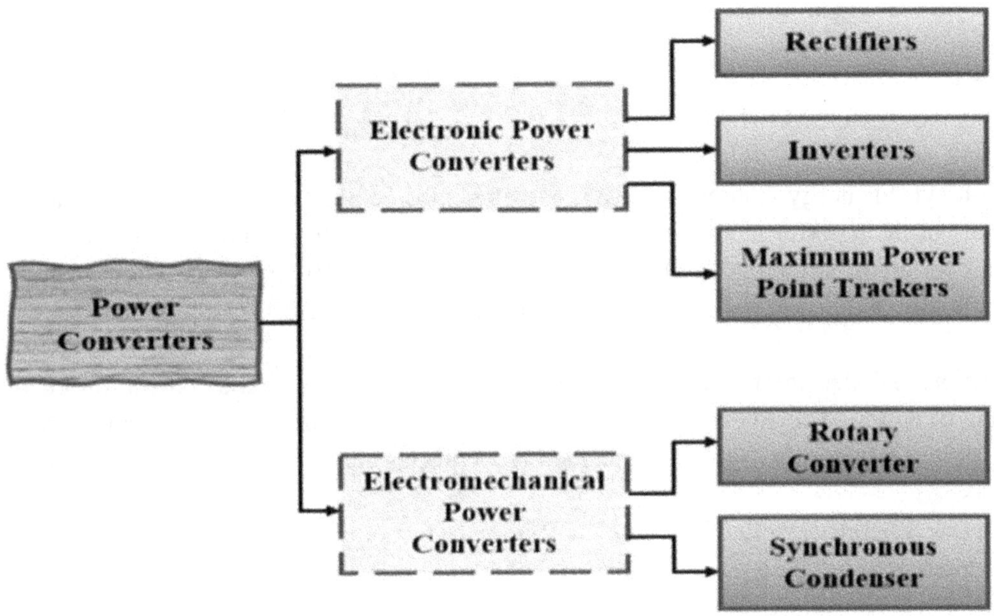

Electromechanical Power Converters

In hybrid energy systems, electromechanical converters at most 2 classes are being used. The rotatory converters and the synchronous condenser are two of them.

1. **Rotatory Converter:** An electromechanical component that transforms AC to DC or vice versa is known as a rotary converter. It is an inverter whenever it operates in the other direction. The rotary converter is made up of two revolving electrical units that are linked together. The first is a DC machine, and the second is an AC machine. Based on the target direction of power flow, one of them operates as a motor or a generator. The AC machine might either be an electromagnetic or synchronous machine. Which one is used will be determined by the system's capabilities.

Rotary converters have the benefit of being a reliable and excellently mechanism with a long history. Another downside is that they are more expensive and inefficient than digital devices that can perform the same function.

2. **Synchronous Condenser:** An alternator that is linked to an electrical community to assist sustain the system voltage is known as a synchronous condenser. In this scenario, the synchronous machine is merely a motor with no load attached. A voltage switch is attached to the alternator and performs the identical operations as formerly detailed in 224 Hybrid Energy Systems. As there are no other synchronous machines linked for at minimum portion of the period, synchronous condensers are employed in hybrid energy system. This is frequently the scenario in diesel generator systems that are designed to permit all of the diesel generators to be spurned under certain instances. A synchronous condenser, for illustration, might be utilized in a wind/diesel system with induction

generators that could generate electrical load at instances. The fuel could perhaps be shut off; however, the synchronizing machine will be essential to provide the induction generators with the requisite reactive power and sustain system voltage.

Electronic Power Converters

For usage in hybrid energy systems, a large range of electronic equipment has been invented and repurposed. Many of them perform comparable roles to the electromechanical devices discussed before, but they have a variety of strengths, including cheaper cost, higher efficiency, and more manoeuvrability. converters, loads, and power point trackers are among the most interesting equipment.

1. **Rectifiers:** Diodes are the fundamental processing information, as they only allow current to flow in one direction. The AC in a 1ϕ or 3ϕ circuit is turned to an undulating, but single- direction, electricity by using the right semiconductors. Batteries can be used to modulate the current that results.
2. **Inverter:** Silicon controlled rectifiers (SCRs) are the principal switching elements (IGBTs). They're connected in a circuit element and turned on to produce an oscillatory signal. Some inverters work in tandem with other equipment that control the frequency of the network. Line commutated is the term for them. Several inverters have the capacity to control their own frequency. Also called "self-commutated."
3. **Maximum Power Point Trackers:** The largest energy hunter is yet another electronic gadget that preserve utilized in hybrid energy systems, specifically those with photovoltaic cells. This gadget is a DC-DC converter that functions in a similar way to a DC transformer. Its job is to deliver a specific intended output to the remainder of the network during regulating the voltages at the input to enable the generator linked to it to produce the most power possible. Small wind turbines were also fitted with maximum power point trackers.

Control Strategies of HRES

The management tactics, which is linked to particular system conditions, controls the HRES power flow. The fundamental requirements for hybridised renewable energy resources are stability, protection, and energy balance. In order to accomplish various objectives, it is frequently complicated and calls for constant operation. To maximise energy efficiency and endurance, the HRES must be under optimal management. The primary objectives of controlling strategies are listed below (Zhu, Zhuo & Shi, 2013; Kollimalla & Mishra, 2014; Song, Cao, Du & Karimi, 2013; Garcia, Torreglosa, Fernandez & Jurado 2013; Wang, Tang, Ren & Li, 2015; Dash & Bajpai, 2015):

- To keep the battery from going into lateral erosion.
- Minimize the capacitors constant voltage consumption, charge/discharging cycle, and dynamical stress.
- To keep a constant DC voltage.
- Lower the probability of losing power supply (LPSP).
- To increase the system's inherent efficiency.

There are two types of manage approaches. Classical control systems such as Rule-based controllers (RBC) and Filtration-based controllers (FBC) are basic and straightforward to deploy since they do not necessitate complex processes (Brka & AL-Abdeli, 2015). They are, nevertheless, generally susceptible to characteristic changes and inflexible (Akcayol, 2004). When comparison to classical control techniques, smart control techniques like Fuzzy Logic Controller (FLC) are better stable and economical because they improve the dynamical performance of the systems without necessitating a precise description of the process (Akcayol, 2004). The Membership Functions of FLC, on the other hand, are normally calculated through trial-and-error method (Safari & Sirizi,2013).

In the research, there are numerous control strategies for wind turbines, such as using MPPT focusing on PSO (Sitharthan, Sundar & Rajasekaran 2020), based on direct power control selecting output voltages on the rotor side converter (Gil, Montoya & Garces, 2019), pitch control using rigorous sliding mode approach (Colombo, Ippoliti & Orlando, 2020). Several regulatory approaches for solar photovoltaic have been used to maximize solar array efficiency, including MPPT based in (Mirza, Ling & Mansoor, 2019), neural network based deep learning for photovoltaic power forecast, and employing MPPT in substantially shadowed conditions. Voltage, frequency, and reactive power (Mehrjerdi, Hemmati & Farrokhi, 2019) all are control strategy key study topics for diesel generators.

There are a variety of additional control techniques for HRES, involving centralized control, hybrid control, distributed control etc. Intelligent methods such as neural network, multi-objective particle swarm optimization (PSO) (Hussain, Pradhan, Gao, Reddy & Roy, 2020), fuzzy logic controllers, and adaptive neuro-fuzzy inference systems are examples of traditional methods (ANFIS).

While the style of control is utilized in a micro scale hybrid renewable energy system, it shows great efficacy, improved productivity, and flexibility in construction. Additionally, the pricing of centralize control is advantageous while in comparison with distributed control. Even then, there's a good chance they'll have to shut down the network altogether if there's an issue with the generator or production schedules.

OVERVIEW OF HRES

In today's smart grid, MG (grid-connected system, standalone mode) is the most important architecture (Mohanta, Murthy & Roy, 2016). One option for properly utilizing RES is to assure the system reliability delivery in remote places, therefore decreasing grid ambiguity. One method to promote the use of greener energy is to employ HRES in off-grid mode, which entails independent control of the major electrical grid. The MG's capacity installed can be determined by the individual use, such as for dwellings, a municipality, or a tiny village, as well as forecasted renewable energy supply, storage capacity, and load demand in that location (Jurado & Saenz, 2002). HRESs involves: (a) 1 RES and Energy Storage; (b) 2 or many RESs; or (c) 1 or many RESs. Nevertheless, runoff, sun irradiation, wind speed, and relative humidity all have an impact on the power generating properties of these resources (Khatib, Mohamed & Sopian, 2013). As a result, combining diverse energy sources can successfully tackle the difficulties of solar/wind energy's unpredictability, instability, and uncertainty (Banos, Manzano, Gil & Gomez, 2011; Iqbal, Azam, Naeem & Anpalagan, 2014).

Photovoltaic (PV): Wind Energy System

The Sun, as the fundamental source of power, offers us a plethora of options for harnessing ecological, pollution-free, and cost-free energy. Solar energy, on the other hand, is not without its downsides. Because sunlight is only accessible during the daylight and low sunshine is accessible during the wintertime, the solar radiation changes greatly with the routine global solar fluctuation over the period. The cosmic, as the primary source of energy, offers us a plethora of options for harnessing sustainable, pollution-free, and cost-free energy. Solar energy, on the other hand, is not without its downsides. As a result, the output power of either solar or wind neither ensure that the fluctuating total load will be met. Solar, on the other hand, is usually obtainable during the day, however wind is usually prevalent at night (Adarmola, 2014). In reality, this means that a hybrid power system may be built to level out the systemic issues, with photovoltaic cells supplying power throughout the day and wind supplying power at dark throughout the winter and summer seasons (Deshmukh, 2008). When it comes to the performance of renewable energy resources, solar and wind are essentially synergistic. As a result, a hybrid system that combines PV and wind renewable sources greatly enhances power quality, reduces storage space requirements, and contributes to reduced generation costs (Kaldellis, 2010). Despite the various existing RES combinations, the PV–Wind hybrid combo is far more appealing globally due to its technological advancements, cost-effective functioning, and abundant supply. Grid-connected and stand-alone hybrid solar-wind systems are the two types available. HRES usually combine different types energy to produce power. In this book chapter, HRES stands for hybrid renewable energy system, which combines PV and wind to produce power as a unit and optimize the power potential of an MG. Based on the abundance of renewable energy resources in a certain location, generation capacity, and all related expenses, such as setup, operations, and management, an HRES may have any composition of renewable energy resources. According to understanding of power conversion system in a conventional photovoltaic–wind, photovoltaic –wind–diesel, photovoltaic –wind–Battery energy storage system, and photovoltaic–wind–diesel– BESS configuration. The inconvenient aspect of Wind–PV systems can help to reduce each other's intermittent renewables, improving the hybrid system 's sustainability. In a grid- connected MG operation, however, a PV–wind combination may provide green energy to maintain the system. Only a PV–wind tandem in a standalone MG, on the other hand, can provide uninterrupted energy supply during a 24*7 period. PV and wind may be able to lessen abrupt swings, but as non dispatchable energy sources. Spinning reserve is required to sustain the system's steady-state operation and to prevent system from collapsing in the event of severe precipitation. With the PV–wind-based hybrid MG's durability in question, a diesel and storage system could be a realistic approach for ensuring the MG's performance and consistency. In terms of budget and effectiveness, as well as client convenience, the combo of RES and storage system is ideal. By retaining maximum electricity during the day, a battery system can assure that no load is dropped, particularly during peak periods of the day, lowering total energy costs. The Figures 2 and 3, represents the structure/Module of the hybrid system of wind and diesel power with energy storage.

Figure 3. Hybrid Module 1

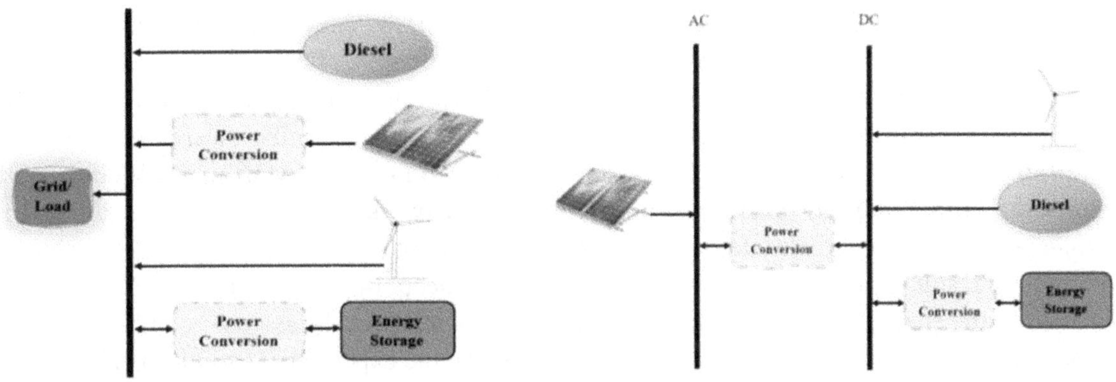

Figure 4. Hybrid Module 2

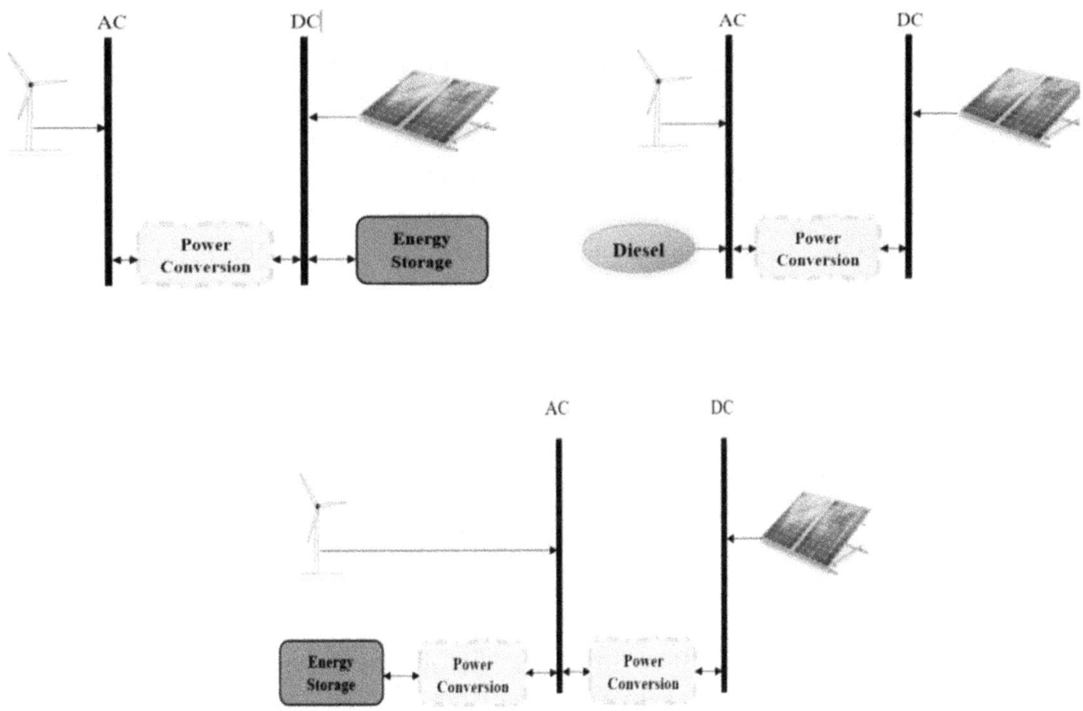

The storage device can take many different configurations, such as a cell (Fasaeenejad, Radzi & Hizam, 2014; Nandi & Ghosh, 2010) or any other storage system, depending on the storage device's price and other basic requirements. In some instances, conventional diesel (Rehman, Alam & Al-Hadhrami, 2012) or potential biodiesel (Ashnani, Johari & Hasani, 2014; Dwivedi & Sharma, 2014) is used in conjunction with the storage system to ensure that power demand is met if the store capacity is insufficient. A review was conducted by author in Habidullah, Masjuki, Rahman, and Ashraful (2015) of detection methods for a HRES, and Arul, Ramachandaramurthy, and Rajkumar (2015) conducted an evaluation of HRES optimization on wind and solar PV systems. Throughout a specific span of time, the power of one source could surpass the deficiency of another (Bhandari, Lee, Cho & Ahn, 2015; Patel, 2005; Engin, 2013). According to the results (Dalwadi, Shrinet, Mehta & Shah, 2011), the transmission size for solar and air energy was, respectively, 27.00 GW, 26.60 GW, and 11.10 GW. In Deetjan, Martin, and Webber (2018) the authors shows that multiple solar trackers in a PV-only network are comparable on seasonal and hourly time periods, and that their integration can reduce PV output variability while increasing power generation. As a result, while building hybrid systems, this concept might be addressed. Enhancing the effectiveness of the energy sources, this may enhance the efficiency of the system 's while also adding to its expenses. As a result, while developing a hybrid system, the expenditure ratio is always critical.

Photovoltaic (PV): Wind-Energy Storage System

ES is used in a PV-ES hybrid to balance out the variable nature of renewable PV production. A part of the PV energy stored by the ES system throughout the day may be exported to the electric grid or used to satisfy peak load at midnight (Erdinc, Pappi & Catalao, 2015). ES was introduced to a PV-only system in Navarra, north of Spain, to enhance financial profit of a 100 kWp roof - mounted Photovoltaic coupled to the power grid. In Yahyaoui, Atieh, Serna, and Tadea (2017) provided a scaling technique for designing a standalone PVES installation to meet the agricultural needs of a rural property in the United Arab Emirates, Tunisia's northern region. The performance characteristics of a stand-alone PV-ES system to generate energy to a social centre in Kunming, China, was explored in Li (2019). The PV-battery-fuel cell scheme with 500.00 kW PV modules, 9120.00 kWh batteries, 20.00 kW hydrogen fuel, 10.00 kW expansion valve, and 10.00 kg hydrocarbons tank were determined to be a viable approach. Significantly with the inclusion of the fuel cell system, the overall net present value (NPV) was 1.13 percent greater than that of a PV scheme.

ES stagnates the real-time variability of wind power in off-grid or matrix wind-ES systems. It also retains excess production during the nights for daylight load and/or transfers it into the electric grid (Clua, Mantz & De Battista, 2018). Luo, Shi, and Tu (2014) suggested an energy storage sizing technique for a wind-ES system to meet equilibrium state throughout grid restoration intervals of a 125 MW wind farm erected on Nan'ao island, China. With a percentage performance / energy capability of 5.5 MW and 36.4 MWh, accordingly, ES was included to maintain a regular electricity supply throughout the repair time. ES equipment were installed to a wind farm in, China, for the off wind-ES system to manage with demand and wind power changes, as well as to alleviate wind curtailing. Applying the HOMER program, Amirkhalili and Zahedi (2018) constructed a wind-fuel cell system in, Iran. The best amount of wind turbines was 3, while the best fuel cell, infrared detector, gas tank, and converters capacities were 120.0 kW, 400.0 kW, 3000.0 kg, and 400.0 kW, respectively. Furthermore, the data revealed that the fuel cell contributed 9.41%.

PV-wind-ES takes advantage of the natural substitutability of PV and wind, as well as the charge-discharge features of ES (Ahadi, Kang & Lee, 2016; Hossein Alizadeh, Amalnick & Taghipour, 2016). As a result, ES needs are lowered, and efficacy of treatment is increased. Panayiotou, Kalogirou, and Tassou (2012) provided a way for designing an alternative group that could accomplish 100% annual demand protection throughout a conventional year with minimal system cost based on residential loads for customary periods. The method was created for the city of Nice in southern France, where the summertime is dry and hot and the wintertime are moderate. PV-wind-ES has the similar ES capacity as PV-ES, according to the optimal outcomes. With 9.90 kW of PV panels, 4.80 kW of wind generators, and 108 kWh of storage, the PV-wind-ES system had a cheaper price. Sanajaoba and Fernandez (2016) used a computational formula to construct a stand-alone hybrid system for 7 un-electrified townships in India, with the goal of lowering total system expenditure. They considered seasonal variations in demand and calculated 3 different permutations: photovoltaic-ES, wind-ES, and photovoltaic -wind-ES. The simulations findings demonstrated that combining PV and wind significantly lowered battery storage demands when contrasted to PV-ES and wind-ES, with the direction of reducing size option consisting of 3 kW Photovoltaic cells, 75 kW wind generators, 20 kW converters, and 170 kWh cells. Despite conditions where the total load was completely fulfilled, the PV- wind-fuel cell was shown to be significantly economical than that of the PV- and wind-fuel cell in a review based on factual evaluation.

Photovoltaic (PV): Wind-Diesel Energy Storage System

Diesel fuel, being a typical fossil source of energy, is only employed in the PV-wind-diesel-ES system as a recovery power source while PV, wind, and ES are unable to meet the load requirement (Mandal, Das & Hoque, 2018). As a result, diesel generators improve system resilience in unusual weather situations while also increasing system efficiency. In India, 163 kW diesel generators were adjusted to off-grid hybrid system installed in a distant area with ample sunlight and intensity to high wind speeds to guarantee uninterrupted power supply (Kumar, Gupta & Bansal, 2013). With plentiful wind and solar energy on Senegal's north western coast, multi-objective GA was used to find Pareto strategies for a standalone PV-wind-diesel-ES system with various numbers of Photovoltaic cells, wind turbines, diesel engines, storage, and other components. They also discovered that loading patterns and the design of diesel generator can have an impact on the optimization ability. For a load of residential building structures in Iran, Maleki and Pourfayaz (2015) proposed the appropriate size for a standalone PV-wind-diesel-ES system that carried out the highest possible load for the whole year while concentrating on overall yearly cost reduction. They also evaluated the price of optimal size for various configurations. Further energy configurations, such as PV-wind-diesel (Bentouba & Boutouis, 2016), PV-diesel-ES (Lan, Wen, Hong & Zhang, 2015), PV-gas turbine and wind-hydrogen, have been developed by several researchers based on their specifications and attributes. Owing to the abrupt reduction in wind speed, the PV-ES system proven to be more suited than the wind-ES system, according to Askari and Ameri (2012). In another place, however, Maleki, Khajeh, and Ameri (2016) had the reverse result. Consequently, from an investment perspective, Maleki and Askarzadeh (2014) and Khare, Nema, and Bareda (2017) came to opposite results in various areas.

Hydropower/Hydro Storage-Photovoltaic (PV)-Wind Energy System

In a hydro -wind hybrid, hydro modifies its production in parameters of peak load and wind productivity to increase the incorporation of the energy, which has unique operational function than a hydro/PHS network. Because PV and wind complement each other, combining hydro/PHS-PV-wind can minimize necessary hydropower regulatory potential and PV-wind encroachments (Francois, Hingray, Borga & Creutin, 2016). Two different standalone renewable energy systems were installed in Nepal and Hong Kong to provide electricity to isolated villages and a deserted island, respectively. The Nepalese system, which consisted of a 20.0 kW hydropower generator, a 5.0 kW photovoltaic array, and a 3.0 kW wind turbine, was designed with meteorological considerations in mind. Meanwhile, the Hong Kong system used a combination of pumped hydro storage, a photovoltaic array, and a wind turbine with predicted capacities of 20.0 kW, 110.0 kW, and 10.40 kW, respectively, to meet the electrical needs of the island while accounting for the intermittency of the solar panels. Both systems demonstrated that solar and wind power can complement each other, reducing the need for energy storage. However, because of the limited capacity of micro hydropower, tiny hydroelectric power, and run-of-the-river hydropower to complement other sources of energy, alternative energy sources or energy storage may be necessary to enhance system reliability. This may lead to increased costs and/or greenhouse gas emissions, as noted (Kanase, Saini & Sharma, 2011; Menshsari, Ghiamy & Bagal, 2013). According to the research, governments all over the worldwide are steadily focusing on the merging of hydro/PHS and other renewable energies. As a result, strategists can combine conventional hydropower installations or PHS units with optimal natural resources based on topography attributes, energy resource features, budgetary variables, and unique demands to obtain the best power efficiency.

Hydrogen-Battery Energy System

Most energy storage systems suited for off-grid structures are electrochemical, chemical, or thermal. Reusable batteries with numerous scientifically competent battery composition options, such as lead-acid or Li ion, are the foundation of electrochemical energy retention technologies. These types of units are ideal for temporary storage ranging from days to months, because to their restricted capacity and self-discharge (Schmidt & Pereira, 2016). Biochemical preservation technologies, on either hand, can store vast quantities of energy electrochemically on spot and consumed as required during phases as fuel cell. Hydrogen storage of electricity, which involves turning electrical power into hydrogen, is another sort of chemical energy storage. If inexpensive power is available, the electrolyzing process, which produces hydrogen from electricity, may be carried out quickly and with the highest degree of reliability. The hydrogen must then be kept, maybe in underground tubes for extensive power storage, but Smaller-scale stockpiling can be accomplished with steel containers. Piston engines, gas turbines, and hydrogen fuel cells can all be powered by hydrogen, with the latter having the highest efficiency. Hydrogen, which may be created electrolytically from water, electrically isolated, and recycled directly to energy with a fuel cell (Jossen, Garche & Sauer, 2004), is one alternative for usage as a preservation reagent. Hydrogen has the greatest gravimetric potential density of all fuels (HHV= 39.42 kWh/kg) (Luo, Wang, Dooner & Clarke, 2015), making it an appealing storing medium. From a scientific standpoint, pressurized gas retention is arguably the most acceptable solution for housing estates (Ursua, Gandia & Sanchis, 2011). Because to safety procedures (Zheng, Liu, Xu, Liu, Zhao & Yang, 2012), the self-discharge probability from intact compressed hydrogen storage is minimal, and storage space is easy to scale, rendering it suited for precise positioning. Nevertheless, as matched to rechargeable capacitors, the round-trip effectiveness of hydrogen conversions is minimal, compelling energy storage capacity inappropriate for smaller battery durations. The third possibility, thermal storage in private buildings. In recent decades, there has been a lot of enthusiasm in HRES. Several research has looked into hybrid energy system that combine with energy sources like photovoltaics, wind, and hydro with batteries and/or hydrogen retention.

Figure 5. Types of hybrid renewable energy system

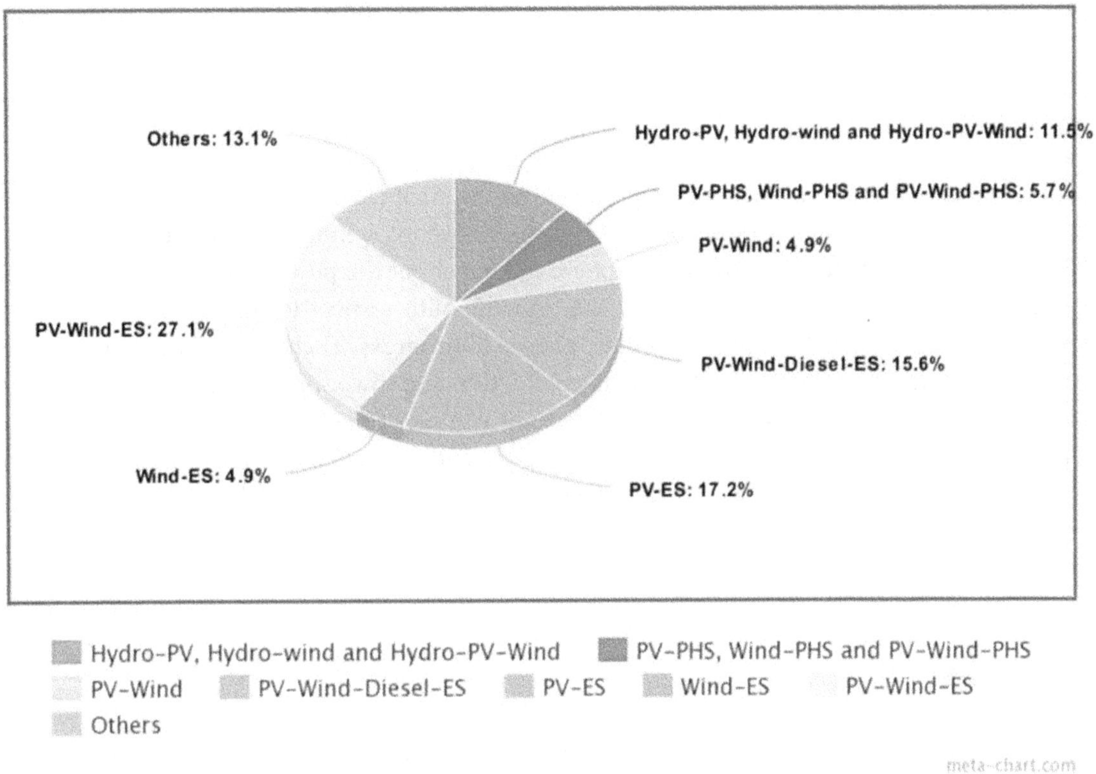

THRUST FOR HRES

There are several factors why a hybrid system could be adopted. The usage of fossil fuels is being reduced, which is one of the main reasons. Fossil fuels are expensive, specifically in inaccessible areas where the expense of delivering the fuel to the site must be factored in. Fuel oil must be kept in many isolated areas, typically for the whole winter. Warehousing expenses can be reduced by minimizing the usage of fuel used. An independent hybrid power system can be used instead of building or upgrading power lines. Hybrid power methods are generally expensive due to the large number of components they contain. Since they can be employed as a substitute to overhead wires installation, the economic benefits can help offset the hybrid system's cost. A power line may obviously operate in some circumstances, but it is not competent of transporting the required current. This could happen when a significant load is imposed. The inclusion of an existing line could facilitate hybrid system design by eliminating the requirement to establish the power line frequency and eliminating the necessity for either storage or dump loads. In several instances, distributed generation has benefits, and in some circumstances, the cumulative effect is boosted by employing a hybrid system. Combined heat and power are frequent use for dispersed generation. Waste heat from fossil fuel burning is used for ambient or industrial heating in this situation, boosting the sum of energy efficiency of the fuel use. Hybrid systems have the potential to improve local environmental conditions. Diesel generators, in general, should be used less frequently and for shorter periods of time (in isolated applications). This will diminish air pollution and noise generated locally, as well as the risks involved with fuel transportation.

CONCLUSION

This book chapter provides summary of HRES. Different attributes such as the detailed review and explanation about the various types of the HRES related to photovoltaic- Wind-hydro- diesel- hydrogen and energy storage systems. Also, the chapter explains about the power converters and the control strategy related to hybrid energy followed by the impetus with respect to the Hybrid energy system. Hybrid energy systems are yet in their immediate phases of progress. Technology is currently predicted to advance in the future, accepting for enormous application and lower prices. More consistent settings will make it simple to select the system that best fits a given set of needs. The different parts are going to communicate more frequently. Governance, monitoring, and assessment will be simpler. Furthermore, there will be an increase in the use of power electronics converters. Energy electronic devices are currently employed in a number of hybrid systems, and as pricing and performance rise, they are anticipated to be used more frequently.

REFERENCES

Adaramola, M. (Ed.). (2014). *Solar energy: Application, economics, and public perception*. CRC Press. doi:10.1201/b17731

Ahadi, A., Kang, S. K., & Lee, J. H. (2016). A novel approach for optimal combinations of wind, PV, and energy storage system in diesel-free isolated communities. *Applied Energy*, *170*, 101–115. doi:10.1016/j.apenergy.2016.02.110

Akcayol, M. A. (2004). Application of adaptive neuro-fuzzy controller for SRM. *Advances in Engineering Software*, *35*(3-4), 129–137. doi:10.1016/j.advengsoft.2004.03.005

Amirkhalili, S. A., & Zahedi, A. R. (2018). Techno-economic analysis of a stand-alone hybrid wind/fuel cell microgrid system: A case study in Kouhin region in Qazvin. *Fuel Cells (Weinheim)*, *18*(4), 551–560. doi:10.1002/fuce.201700149

Ammari, C., Belatrache, D., Touhami, B., & Makhloufi, S. (2022). Sizing, optimization, control and energy management of hybrid renewable energy system—A review. *Energy and Built Environment*, *3*(4), 399–411. doi:10.1016/j.enbenv.2021.04.002

Arul, P. G., Ramachandaramurthy, V. K., & Rajkumar, R. K. (2015). Control strategies for a hybrid renewable energy system: A review. *Renewable & Sustainable Energy Reviews*, *42*, 597–608. doi:10.1016/j.rser.2014.10.062

Ashnani, M. H. M., Johari, A., Hashim, H., & Hasani, E. (2014). A source of renewable energy in Malaysia, why biodiesel? *Renewable & Sustainable Energy Reviews*, *35*, 244–257. doi:10.1016/j.rser.2014.04.001

Askari, I. B., & Ameri, M. (2012). Techno-economic feasibility analysis of stand-alone renewable energy systems (PV/bat, Wind/bat and Hybrid PV/wind/bat) in Kerman, Iran. *Energy Sources. Part B, Economics, Planning, and Policy*, *7*(1), 45–60. doi:10.1080/15567240903330384

Banos, R., Manzano-Agugliaro, F., Montoya, F. G., Gil, C., Alcayde, A., & Gómez, J. (2011). Optimization methods applied to renewable and sustainable energy: A review. *Renewable & Sustainable Energy Reviews*, *15*(4), 1753–1766. doi:10.1016/j.rser.2010.12.008

Belatrache, D., Saifi, N., Harrouz, A., & Bentouba, S. (2020). Modelling and Numerical Investigation of the thermal properties effect on the soil temperature in Adrar region. *Algerian Journal of Renewable Energy and Sustainable Development*, *2*(2), 165–174. doi:10.46657/ajresd.2020.2.2.9

Bentouba, S., & Bourouis, M. (2016). Feasibility study of a wind–photovoltaic hybrid power generation system for a remote area in the extreme south of Algeria. *Applied Thermal Engineering*, *99*, 713–719. doi:10.1016/j.applthermaleng.2015.12.014

Bhandari, B., Lee, K. T., Lee, G. Y., Cho, Y. M., & Ahn, S. H. (2015). Optimization of hybrid renewable energy power systems: A review. *International Journal of Precision Engineering and Manufacturing-Green Technology, 2*, 99-112.

Brka, A., Kothapalli, G., & Al-Abdeli, Y. M. (2015). Predictive power management strategies for stand-alone hydrogen systems: Lab-scale validation. *International Journal of Hydrogen Energy*, *40*(32), 9907–9916. doi:10.1016/j.ijhydene.2015.06.081

Clúa, J. G. G., Mantz, R. J., & De Battista, H. (2018). Optimal sizing of a grid-assisted wind-hydrogen system. *Energy Conversion and Management*, *166*, 402–408. doi:10.1016/j.enconman.2018.04.047

Colombo, L., Corradini, M. L., Ippoliti, G., & Orlando, G. (2020). Pitch angle control of a wind turbine operating above the rated wind speed: A sliding mode control approach. *ISA Transactions*, *96*, 95–102. doi:10.1016/j.isatra.2019.07.002 PMID:31320141

Dalwadi, P., Shrinet, V., Mehta, C. R., & Shah, P. (2011, December). Optimization of solar-wind hybrid system for distributed generation. In *2011 Nirma University International Conference on Engineering* (pp. 1-4). IEEE.

Dash, V., & Bajpai, P. (2015). Power management control strategy for a stand-alone solar photovoltaic-fuel cell–battery hybrid system. *Sustainable Energy Technologies and Assessments*, *9*, 68–80. doi:10.1016/j.seta.2014.10.001

Deetjen, T. A., Martin, H., Rhodes, J. D., & Webber, M. E. (2018). Modeling the optimal mix and location of wind and solar with transmission and carbon pricing considerations. *Renewable Energy*, *120*, 35–50. doi:10.1016/j.renene.2017.12.059

Deshmukh, M. K., & Deshmukh, S. S. (2008). Modeling of hybrid renewable energy systems. *Renewable & Sustainable Energy Reviews*, *12*(1), 235–249. doi:10.1016/j.rser.2006.07.011

Dwivedi, G., & Sharma, M. P. (2014). Prospects of biodiesel from Pongamia in India. *Renewable & Sustainable Energy Reviews*, *32*, 114–122. doi:10.1016/j.rser.2014.01.009

Dyrstad, J. M., Skonhoft, A., Christensen, M. Q., & Ødegaard, E. T. (2019). Does economic growth eat up environmental improvements? Electricity production and fossil fuel emission in OECD countries 1980–2014. *Energy Policy*, *125*, 103–109. doi:10.1016/j.enpol.2018.10.051

Engin, M. (2013). Sizing and simulation of PV-wind hybrid power system. *International Journal of Photoenergy*.

Erdinc, O., Paterakis, N. G., Pappi, I. N., Bakirtzis, A. G., & Catalão, J. P. (2015). A new perspective for sizing of distributed generation and energy storage for smart households under demand response. *Applied Energy*, *143*, 26–37. doi:10.1016/j.apenergy.2015.01.025

Fadaeenejad, M., Radzi, M. A. M., AbKadir, M. Z. A., & Hizam, H. (2014). Assessment of hybrid renewable power sources for rural electrification in Malaysia. *Renewable & Sustainable Energy Reviews*, *30*, 299–305. doi:10.1016/j.rser.2013.10.003

Feilat, E. A., Azzam, S., & Al-Salaymeh, A. (2018). Impact of large PV and wind power plants on voltage and frequency stability of Jordan's national grid. *Sustainable Cities and Society*, *36*, 257–271. doi:10.1016/j.scs.2017.10.035

Ferrer-Martí, L., Garwood, A., Chiroque, J., Ramirez, B., Marcelo, O., Garfí, M., & Velo, E. (2012). Evaluating and comparing three community small-scale wind electrification projects. *Renewable & Sustainable Energy Reviews*, *16*(7), 5379–5390. doi:10.1016/j.rser.2012.04.015

François, B., Hingray, B., Raynaud, D., Borga, M., & Creutin, J. D. (2016). Increasing climate-related-energy penetration by integrating run-of-the river hydropower to wind/solar mix. *Renewable Energy*, *87*, 686–696. doi:10.1016/j.renene.2015.10.064

Garcia, P., Torreglosa, J. P., Fernandez, L. M., & Jurado, F. (2013). Optimal energy management system for stand-alone wind turbine/photovoltaic/hydrogen/battery hybrid system with supervisory control based on fuzzy logic. *International Journal of Hydrogen Energy*, *38*(33), 14146–14158. doi:10.1016/j.ijhydene.2013.08.106

Gil-Gonzalez, W., Montoya, O. D., & Garces, A. (2019). Direct power control for VSC-HVDC systems: An application of the global tracking passivity-based PI approach. *International Journal of Electrical Power & Energy Systems*, *110*, 588–597. doi:10.1016/j.ijepes.2019.03.042

Girardet, H., & Mendonça, M. (2009). *A renewable world: energy, ecology and equality. A report for the World Future Council*. Green Books & Resurgence Books.

Habibullah, M., Masjuki, H. H., Kalam, M. A., Rahman, S. A., Mofijur, M., Mobarak, H. M., & Ashraful, A. M. (2015). Potential of biodiesel as a renewable energy source in Bangladesh. *Renewable & Sustainable Energy Reviews*, *50*, 819–834. doi:10.1016/j.rser.2015.04.149

Hosseinalizadeh, R., Shakouri, H., Amalnick, M. S., & Taghipour, P. (2016). Economic sizing of a hybrid (PV–WT–FC) renewable energy system (HRES) for stand-alone usages by an optimization-simulation model: Case study of Iran. *Renewable & Sustainable Energy Reviews*, *54*, 139–150. doi:10.1016/j.rser.2015.09.046

Hussain, M. W., Pradhan, B., Gao, X. Z., Reddy, K. H. K., & Roy, D. S. (2020). Clonal selection algorithm for energy minimization in software defined networks. *Applied Soft Computing*, *96*, 106617. doi:10.1016/j.asoc.2020.106617

Iqbal, M., Azam, M., Naeem, M., Khwaja, A. S., & Anpalagan, A. (2014). Optimization classification, algorithms and tools for renewable energy: A review. *Renewable & Sustainable Energy Reviews*, *39*, 640–654. doi:10.1016/j.rser.2014.07.120

Jossen, A., Garche, J., & Sauer, D. U. (2004). Operation conditions of batteries in PV applications. *Solar Energy*, *76*(6), 759–769. doi:10.1016/j.solener.2003.12.013

Jurado, F., & Saenz, J. R. (2002). Neuro-fuzzy control for autonomous wind–diesel systems using biomass. *Renewable Energy*, *27*(1), 39–56. doi:10.1016/S0960-1481(01)00170-7

Kaldellis, J. K. (Ed.). (2010). *Stand-alone and hybrid wind energy systems: technology, energy storage and applications*. Elsevier. doi:10.1533/9781845699628

Kanase-Patil, A. B., Saini, R. P., & Sharma, M. P. (2011). Sizing of integrated renewable energy system based on load profiles and reliability index for the state of Uttarakhand in India. *Renewable Energy*, *36*(11), 2809–2821. doi:10.1016/j.renene.2011.04.022

Khare, V., Nema, S., & Baredar, P. (2017). Optimisation of the hybrid renewable energy system by HOMER, PSO and CPSO for the study area. *International Journal of Sustainable Energy*, *36*(4), 326–343. doi:10.1080/14786451.2015.1017500

Khatib, T., Mohamed, A., & Sopian, K. (2013). A review of photovoltaic systems size optimization techniques. *Renewable & Sustainable Energy Reviews*, *22*, 454–465. doi:10.1016/j.rser.2013.02.023

Kollimalla, S. K., & Mishra, M. K. (2014, April). Coordinated control and energy management of hybrid energy storage system in PV system. In *2014 International Conference on Computation of Power, Energy, Information and Communication (ICCPEIC)* (pp. 363-368). IEEE. 10.1109/ECCE-Asia.2013.6579202

Kumar, R., Gupta, R. A., & Bansal, A. K. (2013). Economic analysis and power management of a stand-alone wind/photovoltaic hybrid energy system using biogeography based optimization algorithm. *Swarm and Evolutionary Computation*, *8*, 33–43. doi:10.1016/j.swevo.2012.08.002

Lan, H., Wen, S., Hong, Y. Y., David, C. Y., & Zhang, L. (2015). Optimal sizing of hybrid PV/diesel/battery in ship power system. *Applied Energy*, *158*, 26–34. doi:10.1016/j.apenergy.2015.08.031

Li, C. (2019). Techno-economic study of off-grid hybrid photovoltaic/battery and photovoltaic/battery/fuel cell power systems in Kunming, China. *Energy Sources. Part A, Recovery, Utilization, and Environmental Effects*, *41*(13), 1588–1604. doi:10.1080/15567036.2018.1549134

Li, C., Shi, H., Cao, Y., Wang, J., Kuang, Y., Tan, Y., & Wei, J. (2015). Comprehensive review of renewable energy curtailment and avoidance: A specific example in China. *Renewable & Sustainable Energy Reviews*, *41*, 1067–1079. doi:10.1016/j.rser.2014.09.009

Logesh, R. (2017). Resources, configurations, and soft computing techniques for power management and control of PV/wind hybrid system. *Renewable & Sustainable Energy Reviews*, *69*, 129–143. doi:10.1016/j.rser.2016.11.209

Luo, X., Wang, J., Dooner, M., & Clarke, J. (2015). Overview of current development in electrical energy storage technologies and the application potential in power system operation. *Applied Energy, 137*, 511–536. doi:10.1016/j.apenergy.2014.09.081

Luo, Y., Shi, L., & Tu, G. (2014). Optimal sizing and control strategy of isolated grid with wind power and energy storage system. *Energy Conversion and Management, 80*, 407–415. doi:10.1016/j.enconman.2014.01.061

Maleki, A., & Askarzadeh, A. (2014). Optimal sizing of a PV/wind/diesel system with battery storage for electrification to an off-grid remote region: A case study of Rafsanjan, Iran. *Sustainable Energy Technologies and Assessments, 7*, 147–153. doi:10.1016/j.seta.2014.04.005

Maleki, A., Khajeh, M. G., & Ameri, M. (2016). Optimal sizing of a grid independent hybrid renewable energy system incorporating resource uncertainty, and load uncertainty. *International Journal of Electrical Power & Energy Systems, 83*, 514–524. doi:10.1016/j.ijepes.2016.04.008

Maleki, A., & Pourfayaz, F. (2015). Sizing of stand-alone photovoltaic/wind/diesel system with battery and fuel cell storage devices by harmony search algorithm. *Journal of Energy Storage, 2*, 30–42. doi:10.1016/j.est.2015.05.006

Mandal, S., Das, B. K., & Hoque, N. (2018). Optimum sizing of a stand-alone hybrid energy system for rural electrification in Bangladesh. *Journal of Cleaner Production, 200*, 12–27. doi:10.1016/j.jclepro.2018.07.257

Manwell, J. F. (2004). Hybrid energy systems. Encyclopedia of Energy, 3(2004), 215-229.

Mehrjerdi, H., Hemmati, R., & Farrokhi, E. (2019). Nonlinear stochastic modeling for optimal dispatch of distributed energy resources in active distribution grids including reactive power. *Simulation Modelling Practice and Theory, 94*, 1–13. doi:10.1016/j.simpat.2019.01.005

Menshsari, A., Ghiamy, M., Mousavi, M. M., & Bagal, H. A. (2013). Optimal design of hybrid water-wind-solar system based on hydrogen storage and evaluation of reliability index of system using ant colony algorithm. *International Research Journal of Applied and Basic Sciences, 4*(11), 3582–3600.

Mirza, A. F., Ling, Q., Javed, M. Y., & Mansoor, M. (2019). Novel MPPT techniques for photovoltaic systems under uniform irradiance and Partial shading. *Solar Energy, 184*, 628–648. doi:10.1016/j.solener.2019.04.034

Mohanta, D. K., Murthy, C., & Sinha Roy, D. (2016). A brief review of phasor measurement units as sensors for smart grid. *Electric Power Components and Systems, 44*(4), 411–425. doi:10.1080/15325008.2015.1117538

Nandi, S. K., & Ghosh, H. R. (2010). Prospect of wind–PV-battery hybrid power system as an alternative to grid extension in Bangladesh. *Energy, 35*(7), 3040–3047. doi:10.1016/j.energy.2010.03.044

Notton, G., Diaf, S., & Stoyanov, L. (2011). Hybrid photovoltaic/wind energy systems for remote locations. *Energy Procedia, 6*, 666–677. doi:10.1016/j.egypro.2011.05.076

Panayiotou, G., Kalogirou, S., & Tassou, S. (2012). Design and simulation of a PV and a PV–Wind standalone energy system to power a household application. *Renewable Energy*, *37*(1), 355–363. doi:10.1016/j.renene.2011.06.038

Patel, M. R. (2005). *Wind and solar power systems: design, analysis, and operation.* CRC Press. doi:10.1201/9781420039924

Rehman, S., Alam, M. M., Meyer, J. P., & Al-Hadhrami, L. M. (2012). Feasibility study of a wind–pv–diesel hybrid power system for a village. *Renewable Energy*, *38*(1), 258–268. doi:10.1016/j.renene.2011.06.028

Safari, S., Ardehali, M. M., & Sirizi, M. J. (2013). Particle swarm optimization based fuzzy logic controller for autonomous green power energy system with hydrogen storage. *Energy Conversion and Management*, *65*, 41–49. doi:10.1016/j.enconman.2012.08.012

Sanajaoba, S., & Fernandez, E. (2016). Maiden application of Cuckoo Search algorithm for optimal sizing of a remote hybrid renewable energy System. *Renewable Energy*, *96*, 1–10. doi:10.1016/j.renene.2016.04.069

Schmidt, J., Cancella, R., & Pereira, A. O. Jr. (2016). An optimal mix of solar PV, wind and hydro power for a low-carbon electricity supply in Brazil. *Renewable Energy*, *85*, 137–147. doi:10.1016/j.renene.2015.06.010

Sitharthan, R., Karthikeyan, M., Sundar, D. S., & Rajasekaran, S. (2020). Adaptive hybrid intelligent MPPT controller to approximate effectual wind speed and optimal rotor speed of variable speed wind turbine. *ISA Transactions*, *96*, 479–489. doi:10.1016/j.isatra.2019.05.029 PMID:31202532

Song, Y. D., Cao, Q., Du, X., & Karimi, H. R. (2013). Control strategy based on wavelet transform and neural network for hybrid power system. *Journal of Applied Mathematics*, *2013*, 2013. doi:10.1155/2013/375840

Ursua, A., Gandia, L. M., & Sanchis, P. (2011). Hydrogen production from water electrolysis: Current status and future trends. *Proceedings of the IEEE*, *100*(2), 410–426. doi:10.1109/JPROC.2011.2156750

Wang, S., Tang, Y., Shi, J., Gong, K., Liu, Y., Ren, L., & Li, J. (2015). Design and advanced control strategies of a hybrid energy storage system for the grid integration of wind power generations. *IET Renewable Power Generation*, *9*(2), 89–98. doi:10.1049/iet-rpg.2013.0340

Yahyaoui, I., Atieh, A., Serna, A., & Tadeo, F. (2017). Sensitivity analysis for photovoltaic water pumping systems: Energetic and economic studies. *Energy Conversion and Management*, *135*, 402–415. doi:10.1016/j.enconman.2016.12.096

Zheng, J., Liu, X., Xu, P., Liu, P., Zhao, Y., & Yang, J. (2012). Development of high pressure gaseous hydrogen storage technologies. *International Journal of Hydrogen Energy*, *37*(1), 1048–1057. doi:10.1016/j.ijhydene.2011.02.125

Zhu, Y., Zhuo, F., & Shi, H. (2013, June). Power management strategy research for a photovoltaic-hybrid energy storage system. In *2013 IEEE ECCE Asia Downunder* (pp. 842-848). IEEE.10.1109/ECCE-Asia.2013.6579202

Chapter 16
IoT-Based Energy Harvesting and Future Research Trends in Wireless Sensor Networks

Wasswa Shafik
https://orcid.org/0000-0002-9320-3186
School of Digital Science, Universiti Brunei Darussalam, Bandar Seri Begawan, Brunei & Dig Connectivity Research Laboratory, Kampala, Uganda

ABSTRACT

The more technology advances, the extra benefits to the public and devices that connect to the internet have increased as well, commonly known as internet of things (IoT). The battery lifespan of these devices rises with technical concerns where an alternative to traditional energy attainment is needed. As the way forward, wireless sensor networks (WSNs) and IoT are tested to be used as novel energy alternatives through energy harvesting (EH). This study identifies the availability of energy by location. Similarly, it focuses on the sensor node's architecture with EH capabilities expanding to the classification of five EH techniques. It evaluates the EH developments in search of minimal resource utilization associated with WSNs. Its extensive distribution of interconnected devices is connected via the internet and other related high-tech innovations. Finally, it discusses the feasibility of energy storage and its potential for WSNs, paving the way for future trends and motivations.

INTRODUCTION

WSNs have proved a notable multi-hop wireless network testing role, this is because of its potential application in conservation and operational systems for safety like using semi or autonomous drone for public control (Shafik, 2023), proper energy optimization. The architecture of communication protocols, localization, monitoring strategies, and power management are key in this paradigm. IoT-based hedge systems have demonstrated a positive for solar power generation. Prediction algorithms or models on edges availed a correlation coefficient of 0.917 and coefficient of determination value of 0.841 (Syu et al., 2021). WSNs were inspired by technological emphasis, for example, conserving natural resources

DOI: 10.4018/979-8-3693-0744-1.ch016

and changing them into energy. The WSN nodes usually are battery-powered. The system is considered "empty" when its power is exhausted; batteries can either be replaced or recharged in minimal applications. The replacement or recharging process tends to be slow and costly and reduces network performance, but it is inevitable (Hadas et al., 2018).

EH is defined as to the conversion ambient energy present in the ecosystem into electrical energy for both natural and artificial use. There is increased device connectivity to the internet and its associated merits like increased resource sharing, improved computation speed, and reduced latency. Regarding the IoT application in reducing energy consumption, several appropriations have been highlighted within this study as core factors that need to be addressed to proper energy utilization by the intelligent systems like situation or pandemic forecasts and the public. Identified ones include industrial condition monitoring, operation isolation setups, WSNs, wireless pressure sensors, and Pipeline Actuators. Free energy also comes at a cost and going about the entire system is critical in deciding how energy harvesting can satisfy the power needs. To affect this issue, green energy, collecting, wasted energy, self-charging, consumer (customer) electronics, and drop-in battery replacement are identified as possible ways to save energy. WSNs perform computing through sound resource management owing to their pervasive existence (Syu et al., 2021). Energy mainly entails three main chains from the supply to transformation to consumption as Figure 1 depicts; for instance, under supply, it starts from extraction and treatment, followed by primary energy supply, then import or export stock changes. At the primary energy supply, this is passed to conversion technologies, T&D system where both are transformed with some energy loss. At that point of T&D system provides final energy, to end use appliance with some energy loss to finally useful energy for consumption.

Figure 1. Energy supply chain

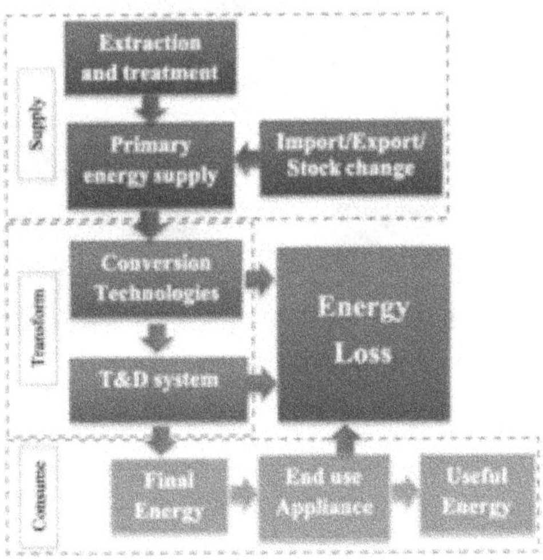

Various methods have been suggested to delay the degradation of battery capacity, including power management and the use of session-based activities. These approaches sometimes use low-current wireless transceiver techniques, the components of which can be turned off to save energy. In case the device reduces the power (similar in power efficiency) phase, the output of the device is significantly reduced versus when it is on due to the fifth-generation technology. Nevertheless, while sleeping, the device cannot relay or recognize the data packet. The task loop completes in correlation to the time; the device is on, then it rests before it finally turns off. The use of protocols running at a relatively low power level seems to be an acceptable explanation that accords with long-lasting WSNs (Yetgin et al., 2017).

Dependable IoT devices are required to generate correct data in several computations, its components are illustrated in Figure 2. The authors of this study presented an approach for characterizing IoT dependability measures. The reliability measurements are computed utilizing queuing theory. The theory explains the response time, queue length, delay time or waiting time, and busy periods, for example in recommender system, among others. To account for the reliance on items in IoT contexts, the Markov Chain traits were used, and thus better reliability measures were obtained (Zin et al., 2018).

Figure 2. Components of an IoT platform

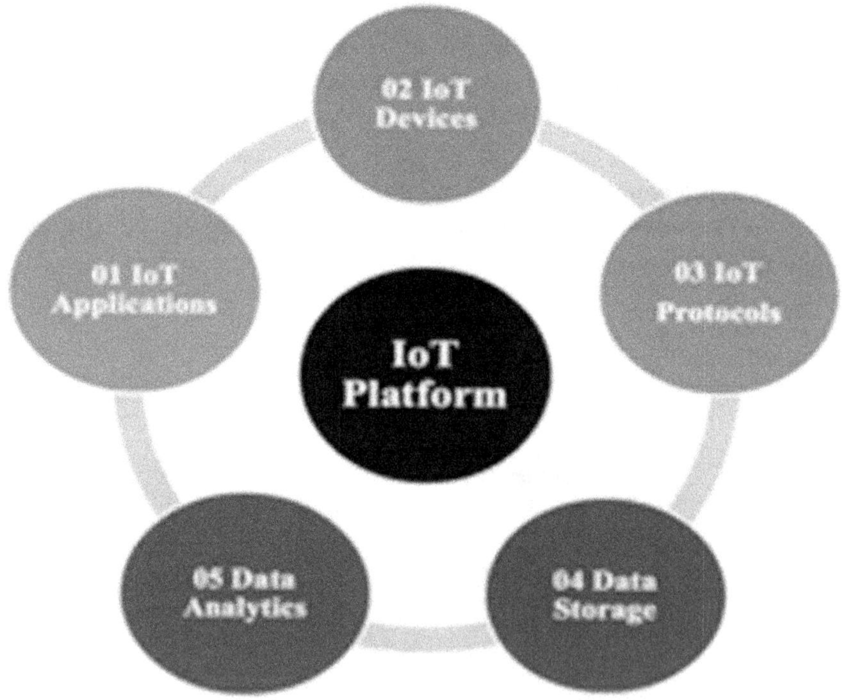

This approach leads to significant pitfalls: 1) There seems to be an apparent compromise between power consumption (reducing duty cycling) and information delay. 2) WSNs run with batteries struggling to meet the demands of many new technologies that require time-taking complex network computing. 3) Leakage depletes the batteries even though they are rarely used. Recent studies on long-lasting WSNs take a vastly different approach, suggesting “constant” WSN performance through tandem energy harvesters utilizing battery packs and superconducting materials for power storage. WSN considering EH (WSNEH), based on energy harvesting, tends to be the result of imbuing WSN entities with the ability to collect power from numerous sources.

The EH takes advantage of various power sources, such as solar energy, air, mechanical stress, temperature fluctuations, and electromagnetic waves. The EH subsystems regularly supply and process power for future use, enabling the sensor node to last forever (Adu-Manu et al., 2020). This study explores the current challenges and opportunities of the WSNEH, assessing why it is necessary to rethink the architecture of the WSNs fundamentally. The review starts with the vital definitions, followed by the WSNEH node's architecture, particularly its power system. The analysis of the different sources of energy available is also presented. Furthermore, a discussion on the classification of energy harvesting is examined.

Key Contributions of the Chapter

This chapter contributes the following:

- The study presents a survey on the current technology advancements, the public receives additional benefits, particularly through the IoT and the increasing number of connected devices.
- Highlights the technical concerns related to the battery lifespan of IoT devices and the necessity for alternative energy sources to power these devices.
- The study focuses on WSNs and IoT as potential platforms for novel energy alternatives through EH.
- The research identifies the availability of energy based on location, suggesting that different regions may offer different energy sources for EH in WSNs.
- The study examines the architecture of sensor nodes with EH capabilities, likely to investigate the integration of energy harvesting mechanisms into existing sensor networks.
- The research classifies five different EH techniques, which may include methods such as solar energy, kinetic energy, thermal energy, etc.
- The study evaluates EH developments with the objective of minimizing resource utilization associated with WSNs, aiming to optimize energy efficiency.
- The study discusses the feasibility of energy storage for WSNs, likely examining different energy storage technologies and their potential integration with EH systems.
- Finally, the research explores future trends and motivations related to EH in WSNs, potentially identifying emerging technologies and directions for further research in the field.

The Chapter Organization

The rest of the chapter contains six main sections. Section 2 presents a comprehensive overview of EH. Section 3 details the classification of EH techniques, including the EH based on radio frequency (RF), astrophysics-based EH, thermal-based EH, mechanical-based EH, and human-based EH. While the appropriation, inverse, and future directions are documented in Section 4. Regarding appropriation industrial conditions monitoring, operating isolated setups, wireless pressure sensors, and pipeline actuators are detailed. In inverse issues like alternative green energy options, collecting wasted energy, self-charging electronics, and drop-in battery replacement are demonstrated. Future research avenues are documented in the context of system integration, low power, wireless communications, smart cities, biological systems, and fluctuating prices. In section 5, some insights on EH on IoT applications which are most suitable for smart city applications are demonstrated and lastly, section 6 portrays the chapter conclusion.

ENERGY HARVESTING

Energy harvesting is widely described as converting ambient energy into electricity. We describe energy harvesting as "the on-demand, off-grid processing, and storage of ambient energy." The first concept deals with the energy transmission transducer system, which implies that energy needs to be transferred to electric power. This interpretation provides a detailed and comprehensive software-centric perspective (Hadas et al., 2018). The transmitter is part of a complete power supply network for applications for which other energy sources are inaccessible or unacceptable.

Ambient energy comes in several different forms, for example. nuclear, biological, electrical, mechanical, and many more. Either of these power sources should be available in the area to use EH. An opposite transducer must be in place to transform electricity. Power harvesting has been used for electricity generation where no external power source is available. Excavators require investment, and they are an excellent alternative when using conventional sources such as grid power or batteries become too expensive and impractical. On-demand electricity must be supplied by the energy harvester when required, not merely when it is available. Some form of power storage is usually the recommended ordering value for the requirement (Nguyen et al., 2020). In principle, there exist numerous forms of energies accessible for EH, for instance, from radiation (light, electrical, cosmic, and electromagnetic), thermal, physical (potential, mechanical, dynamic, fluid), gravitational, chemical (capacitor, battery storage, coal power, phase transition), nuclear, gravitational (magnetization, movement), and electrical.

Sound cosmic radiation, atmospheric pressure variation, and solar atomic neutrinos are readily available but have almost no related energy. When other energy fields are accessible, the harvester relies exclusively on the location and the selection of feasible forms. The options are usually limited to only one or two that are appropriate for a particular area. Sunshine is a decent energy source with a high-power density and correct consistency outdoors. Air can be suited to large facilities that are high enough to have direct air currents (Chun-Wei et al., 2020). Optimal temperature and vibration differences are challenging to detect. Such lighting systems could provide adequate indoor electricity for low-power applications, for instance, calculators. Moreover, the device waves and temperature radiation can also be employed for industrial applications such as extreme temperatures and intense oscillations occurring at a predicted behavior.

Data security and information privacy remain key challenges in such sensitive computation that has IoT and sensors. The configuration state could be attacked or updated without privacy-preserving precautions (Jun et al., 2021). This often results in security issues and sensitive data loss. An ant colony optimization approach was suggested to tackle the security aspects. This was determined by the need to preserve secret and sensitive information on sixth generation (6G) IoT networks by implementing multiple objectives and utilizing transaction deletions (Huang et al., 2020). A set of deletion operations represent each ant in the population that may be used to conceal sensitive information.

Diverse types of systems have varying requirements for electricity. A pacemaker necessitates only around five joules to operate in one day. On the other hand, a desktop PC needs about five Mega Joules. Some systems operate continuously, and regular power consumption is much like the demand for immediate electricity. Anything that is on for 1 second and then off for 9 seconds has a 'duty ratio' (electronics) of 10%. Consequently, the average requisite energy is only 10% of the total power demand. Whether or not a particular application uses EH depends on the knowledge of the energy consumption profile and its comparison with the available energy from extraction.

Sensor node energy efficiency is critical to the long-term viability of IoT networks (Renuka et al, 2018). When live nodes are many in number, the converging ratio compared to price performance is faster which implies that there are additional residual energies, the load is equally distributed, and the temperature produced by IoT nodes is lower, the energy consumption will be ideal. Within this research, we propose a hybrid whale algorithm and Moth flame optimization approach that optimizes the 500 criteria described above to find the best cluster head. In comparison with the existing algorithms, the proposed model is examined. The experiment's findings indicate that the suggested model outperforms other models. Such as load, temperature, energy, latency, cost performance, and the total number of live nodes (Maddikunta et al., 2020).

The primary goal of staying useful life estimation is to achieve maintenance at a cheap cost and resource conservation. In the field of prognostics, cutting-edge applications and the findings of the models have been outstanding. Correspondingly, the proposed approach aims to improve recurrent neural network training to make better predictions. The obtained results (Agrawal et al., 2020) show that deep learning models of short-term memory algorithms are outperformed by the improved design of long-term memory algorithms. Table 1 presents a description of the available energy for different locations. All areas in the table with "No" notation indicate that these areas remain subject to research since existing models have not explored them (Maddikunta et al., 2020). Table 2 summarizes the different sources of energy and their capacity.

Table 1. Availability of energy by location (R = radiation, AL = artificial lighting, MV = machine vibration, G = gravitational, TG = thermal gradients)

Energy by Location	R	Wind	Sunlight	AL	Human	MV	G	TG
Office or home	Yes	No	No	Yes	Yes	No	No	No
Along the street	Yes	Yes	Yes	No	No	No	No	No
Bridge	Yes	Yes	Yes	No	No	No	Yes	No
Vehicles	Yes	Yes	Yes	No	No	Yes	No	Yes
Station of the pumping	Yes	Yes	Yes	No	No	Yes	No	Yes
Petrol rig	Yes	Yes	Yes	No		Yes	No	Yes
Battlefield	Yes	Yes	Yes	No	Yes	Yes	No	
Sensing for remote locations	Yes	Yes	Yes	No	No	No	No	Yes

Throughout the study, principal component analysis (PCA)-based random forest regressions (RFR) is utilized to forecast the battery life span of an IoT network. Missing values are filled in using the attribute mean during the preprocessing stage, normalization is done using the regular scalar method, and transformation is done using the technique of one-shot encoding. The PCA algorithm is then used for feature assortment and reducing on dimensionalities. The data set's reduced dimensions are fed into RFR algorithm. The obtained results support the superiority of the presented model. It is possible to assess the suggested model. On a large-scale set of data in the future; deep neural networks can also be used to improve prediction.

Table 2. Available power sources and their vital summary

Source	Power Capacity	Vital Summary
Cosmic raying	0.1 μW(microwatt)	Negating transfer inefficiencies
EM-ray radiation	0.5 μW(microwatt)	10 x 10 cm antenna 10 m under a 10 kV(kilowatt) transmission line
The pressure of the blood	15 μW(microwatt)	The estimate of the Southampton University Hospital
The vibration of the computer	05 mW(milliwatt)	Perpetuum PP27
Lighting indoor	20 mW(microwatt)	Solar cell 5 x 5 cm
Human electricity	2 W(watt)	Winding a radio from Baygen

Sensor Node's Architecture With Harvesting Capabilities

In this subsection, an analysis of the nodes of the wireless sensor system is described. The significant components include (a) An energy harvester responsible for converting energy produced by the natural environment or a living organism into electrical power. (b) The module extracts electric power from the harvester and either saves it for immediate use or supplies it to other components, (c) Housing power for the harvester, (d) microcontroller. (e) Data-transmitting radio transceiver, (f) sensor devices, (g) A/D (analog-to-digital) converter for digitizing the audio voltage produced by the sensor and making it accessible for further transmission to the microcontroller, and (i) memory for storing sensing data, application-related data, and code (Figure 3).

Figure 3. Architectural design of a wireless node with harvesters of energy

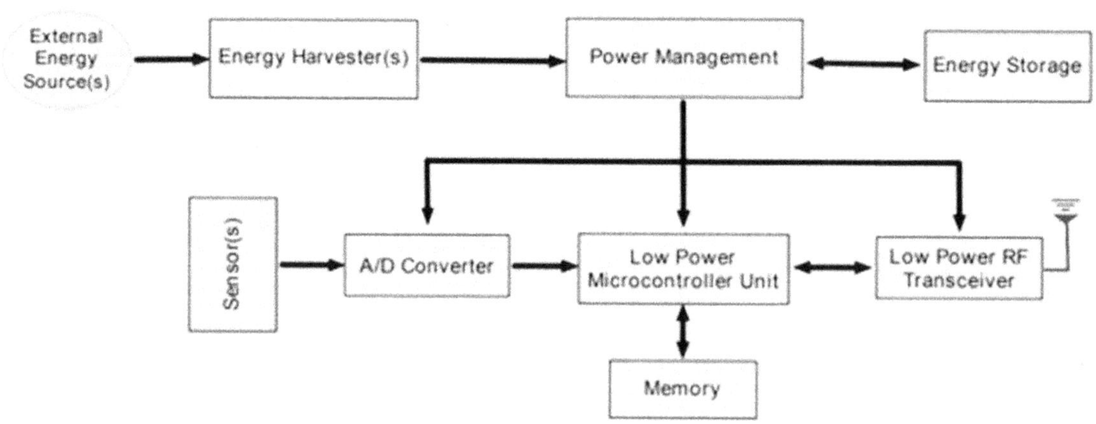

In the conversion of accessible energies from the environment to electric energy, the power system needs one or more harvesters. To transfer the energy to the node(s) or retain it for future usage is done using harvester gather. In certain applications, the sensor node may be directly powered by harvested electricity without storing energy (extract-use architecture), although it is not a viable choice (Yang et al., 2021). A relatively more rational design allows the node to use the harvested energy directly and includes a portion of the storage that acts as a power source for storing and preserving the extracted energy. When the extraction is greater than the utilization, the buffer portion can preserve the surplus energy for future consumption. Figure 4 shows the general configuration of the wireless sensor node for the power module, including the power generation functionality.

The secondary battery packs and superconducting materials (also known as ultra-capacitors) are two energy storage options. Supercapacitors are like typical condensers except those which generate exceptionally high power on a small scale. There are several advantages of powered batteries; firstly, the supercapacitors can be powered and drained almost indefinitely, while the cumulative life of electrical and chemical batteries is less than 1000 cycles. Besides, simple charging loops may power them efficiently, increasing the network's complexity and not requiring deep discharge protection circuits. Secondly, there is more charge and additional unloading flexibility than rechargeable batteries. Moreover, decreasing the environmental issues associated with the disposal of batteries is an extra benefit. Because of these characteristics, super condensers are used as energy storage by many mining systems either on their own or in conjunction with batteries (Zhang et al., 2016).

Figure 4. WSN energy subsystem design (RF = radio frequency; PV = photo voltaic)

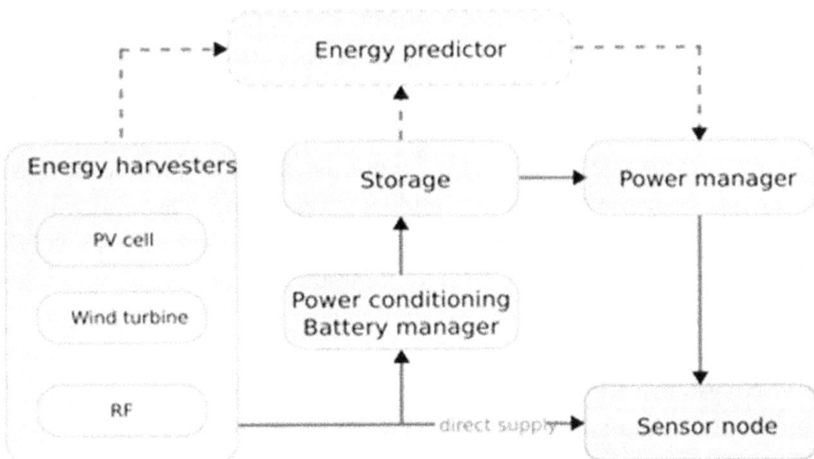

CLASSIFICATION OF TECHNIQUES OF ENERGY HARVESTING

Various sources of energy have been discovered for the EH. Whether or not a particular source can provide enough power to the sensor node is one of the critical criteria for selecting an energy source, the voltage movement dissipates the energy due to the conversions. It is crucial to guarantee that the power is generated at the required current and voltage levels for proper utilization. The energy source is an energy storage device, or a source adjusted to an optimum level of electricity. For instance, in RF, the required demand is met by increasing the source power.

A high amount of electricity is produced in the PV cell area, resulting in a greater electricity rate. Nevertheless, it is not possible to match the sources or convert energy too efficiently in some situations. Thus, the harvesting system can be extended; numerous WSNs allow a node to be compacted and be thin leading to minimized energy utilization. Researchers typically use the energy density metric to compare different strategies for extracting energy (Raja and Mookhambika, 2021). Hereafter, designers should consider this exchange after choosing a suitable EH device for a particular application. The sources of energy are divided into two broad classes, i.e., internal, and external. Biological resources are readily available in the atmosphere at almost no cost. Secondary sources are intentionally used for energy storage purposes in environments. These categories are further subdivided, as described below.

Energy Harvesting Based on Radio Frequency

After conditioning, the received radio signals are transformed into DC voltage for RF-based energy processing. Depending on the specifications of the required application (e.g., weight, output, or voltage), RF signals can be converted to DC power through various methods such as single stage versus multistage. All factors affecting the amount of electricity produced are the source of electricity, including the antennas' gain, the range between the target sources, and electrical efficiency. Usually, over an input power range of 100 m, the RF to DC exchange rate is between 50% to 75% (Sudevalayam and Kulkarni, 2010). It is superior to offer one WSN radio to reduce the complexity of the program and minimize the overall code size.

For the intentional sources of WSNs, a case point sinks to distribute energy, and the platform obligates the control to be terminated by the available power. The anticipated foundation can deliver power on a continuous, intended, or ultimatum basis, and can be used to supply power to stimulate the fully charged instrument nodes. The nodes can also predict other sensor nodes and provide the radio frequency and energy harvesting basis (Zhang et al., 2019). The intermediate nodes operate regularly or intermittently as a power source; nevertheless, the nodes cannot usually be regulated because the continuous dissemination of records may not be significant for ideal wireless and sensor networks. Radiofrequency energy harvesting improves the performance of one-to-many wireless controls involving WSNs; diffusion starting at a given node will supply power(s) to communicate or eavesdrop on the communication during such transfer (Amirinasab et al., 2020). It is vital to note that safety and health regulations restrict radiofrequency production power.

In a variety of WSN systems, RF energy storage may be used both indoors and outdoors. Their applications include environmental surveillance, smart homes, systemic safety monitoring, and supervision of locations. RF EH has greater potential for indoor usage because peripheries often need additional low-light conditions or lack of lightning, while astrophysical EH assemblies are inefficient (Khalifeh et al., 2020). Besides, temperature variations and disruptions are unlikely indoors, providing excellent conditions for wireless sensor network applications.

An Astrophysical-Based Energy Harvesting

Astrophysical energy tends to emerge as an affordable and clean source of energy due to global abundance, and it may potentially alleviate the impending issues of WSN energy. However, due to the night-time disadvantages of solar energy storage systems, engineers must achieve the best possible performance during the daytime to ensure efficiency. PV effects may be detected after specific semiconductor resources are visible to the sunshine, and cosmic rays are metamorphosed into electricity (Fu, 2019). Cosmic booth tends to be an electrical semiconductor confluence device, typically self-possessed of silicon.

As sunbeams impact an astrophysical device with adequate dynamics, the electrons are quarantined and continue to pass through an input and output regulator toward the attached charge. Cosmological harvesting employs an output stock of a consuming unit with numerous loading adoptions; these phenomenal capacitors, arrays, or a combination of both, immersed on the external surface of the astrophysical cell, yield excellent cosmological coordination that offers tremendous efficiency (Mausam et al., 2020). The astrophysical energy, overall, is generally appropriate in an outdoor environment. Indoor atmospheres, like infirmaries, grounds, and engineering construction, can also benefit; however, they usually obligate extra light than other indoor surroundings.

Thermal-Based Energy Harvesting

Transforming the temperature and corresponding energy to electrical energies require a combined container with the hot and the cold surfaces of the thermal energy generator. Several large-scale machines have been developed since the production of passionate heaters. The extreme apprehension, on a larger level, is to trigger voltage from anthropological physique malaises. A thermos-electric regenerator obligates a long service cycle, inactive parts, and stable functionality. Thermal harvesting has a low efficiency of 5% to 6%, which is a significant impediment to its widespread adoption. Recently, more than 10% of the output efficiency has been reached (Hao, 2019). The development of modern thermoelectric components and segments.

Mechanical-Based Energy Harvesting

A Mechanic-Electrical Energy Generator (MEEG) extracts energy from the atmosphere and roughness. In general, an electromagnetic harvester, for example, MEEG, uses the piezoelectric system to extract energy. Pressure variations can be rehabilitated to vigor using piezoelectrics that provide optimum and concrete impact. Vibrations are essential in processing the electromagnetic spectrum to shift a magnet around a coil and produce current. On the other hand, electrostatic converters use impulses to force the charged capacitor's plates toward the electrostatic resistance, resulting in electrical energy in arrears to the capacitance proliferation. The piezoelectric materials can generate an electric perspective transformation when stimulated by vibrations derived from electrical energy (Wang et al., 2020). The mechanical electrical energy generator, which creates generated energy reduction in the system, produces 10 mW (milliwatt) per 100 cm3 on a realistic scale.

Human-Based Energy Harvesting

The healthcare sector is of prime significance among other WSN applications due to the need to continuously track patients and ensure accurate, significant, and timely action by medical practitioners. Consequently, the wireless bodied-area networks need considerable attention; sensors are mounted on or even injected within human body in such networks to track biological constraints incessantly (Satyala et al., 2014). These systems need to be stable for long periods because of their installation by humans, preferably for their lifespan. Therefore, harvesting human energy for this purpose carries paramount importance. Table 3 depicts EH approaches, related technologies, EH methodologies, and applications.

Table 3. Energy harvesting techniques and applications (TEG = thermoelectric generator)

EH Technique	Harvesting Method	Application	Technologies	Reference
Frequency-based	High-level performing thermoelectric materials	kzrcuse3 predictions	Rectifying antenna Rectenna	(Wang et al., 2020)
Solar based	Acquaintance with dainty photovoltaic cells	Outdoor, and indoor systems	Photovoltaic (PV) cells	(Satyala et al., 2014)
Thermal based	Temperature difference, heating, or cooling pyroelectric	Wearable TEG Flex TEG, Automatic-Powered Wireless Temp Sensor	Thermoelectric and pyroelectric, TEG	(Li et al., 2016)
Flow-based	converting airflow	Outdoor	Wind turbines, Miniature wind turbines	(Zhu et al., 2020)
Mechanical based	Ambiances Power-driven stress and compression, tension from the superficial of the device	The self-powered WSN node, driving vehicles (MEEG)	Piezoelectric, electrostatic, and electromagnetic	(Elahi et al., 2018)
Human-based	Vicissitudes in extremity situations, body heat, and the blood-flows	Micro TEG	Electroactive polymers, piezoelectric, shoe-mounted rotary harvesters	(Khalid et al., 2019)

APPROPRIATION, INVERSE, AND FUTURE DIRECTIONS

EH application provides are proper energy use balance exists amongst the obtainable energies and the required energies for power storage, offer a value that cannot be accomplished with batteries or energy from the grid (Li et al., 2016). Table 4 illustrates the proposed EH models and used technology-based device applications. In this section, we outline the appropriate approach, inverse, and future motivations.

Table 4. Proposed harvesting techniques and their applications (MDGMEC = maximizing data gathering with minimum energy consumption, WPT = wireless power transfer, SDA = software-defined architecture, MPPT = novel maximum power point tracking)

Harvesting Technique	Application	Proposed Model	Tools	Pros	Cons	Reference
Frequency-based	Movement speed of a monitored asset	RF energy through WPT	Battery-free tags	Industry, Agriculture, IoT, Health	Equipment Dependency	(Zhu et al., 2020)
Solar based	Energy consumption reduction in WSN	SDA for CB communications	Collaborative beamforming (CB)	simple, cheap, efficient	Limited Solar energy supply	(Elahi et al., 2018)
Thermal based	Autonomous WSN nodes	The DA + O&SO method	MPPT	Static deployments thus outflow	Poor energy, high cost, and low output power	(Khalid et al., 2019)
Flow-based	Data collection using a mobile sink	Data gathering process	MDGMEC	Predictable energy output	Not available for commercial usage	(Rosa et al., 2020)
Mechanical based	Portable and wearable electric devices	Rectification mechanism	Bidirectional vertical oscillation	Protected and reliable	Devices deteriorate with time.	(Bao et al., 2019)
Human-based	Related electronic device	LTC3108, BQ25504 circuit	Thermoelectric energy generator	human Implantable apps	Restraint on the lifetime and reliability of biological parts	(Hou and Chen, 2020)

Appropriation

Industrial Condition Monitoring

Control and automation delve into the explosive growth in the use of WSNs in several applications over the last few years. Since wireless technology can reduce costs, increase efficiency, and make maintenance easier, it is becoming increasingly popular. Self-organization, fast deployment, versatility, and inherent intelligent processing are all advantages of industrial wireless sensor networks over conventional wired industrial monitoring and control systems. In this regard, industrial WSNs perform a significant responsibility in establishing more dependable, effective, and profitable industrial structures, thereby enhancing companies' market competitiveness (Kumar and Dash, 2020). Many parts of the vibrating machinery are usually in a large oil pumping station. Understanding the conditions of operation avoids errors and downtime, improves performance, and lowers costs. Wireless sensor networks can be expensive to install with miles of cabling and standardized battery-operated spare parts. A network of wireless-controlled independent pulsation devices offers an incredible system for delinquent data collection.

Operating Isolated Setups

EH systems can use both artificial and natural sources to generate electricity. The piezoelectric effect and the thermoelectric effect can also be used to generate electrical energy from movement. Environmental fuel, such as solar, wind, or waterpower, is an excellent outdoor source. The use of ambient heat as an energy source for remote sensors located inside a building may be beneficial. Thermoelectric devices can produce electrical energy from temperature variations through a thermocouple, while PV devices can generate electrical energy from changes in material temperature (Mi et al., 2020). A transit stop with an interactive bus information board is helpful. The technology is highly valuable in rural areas; however, due to its size, grid power is expensive to install, and single-use sequences would not continue for long. The astrophysical panels or small airstream turbines, self-propelled with a rechargeable battery and equipped with power controls, are the cheapest way to control the projector and additional electronics (Xia et al., 2020).

Wireless Sensor Networks

Due to their ubiquitous existence and broad deployment in IoT among other emerging areas, WSN technologies face a significant bottleneck due to the limited energy associated with them. The development and design reliability and high-performance EH systems for WSNs are being scrutinized to address this major limitation. Sensors seldom need much energy, meaning that flow rate, temperature, humidity, and pressure measurements can be attained with a small amount of ingathered energy (Kausar et al., 2014). The exchange rate, such as the latest readings of important wireless communication protocols, allows the use of information for saving money through the timely detection of complications and planned maintenance.

Wireless Pressure Sensors

Car manufacturers are integrating wireless communication systems into automobiles to enhance the safety and execution of the automotive transportation systems. Tire pressure monitoring systems can track real-time tire pressure in vehicles and warn drivers and passengers when a tire is in an abnormal condition, ensuring driver and passenger safety. The pressure control of tires decreases fuel consumption and enhances driving efficiency, but there is no connection from the battery to the tires by power cables (Wang et al., 2019). The Battery-powered sensors via wireless data transmission do not last long to provide ample electricity, enhancing maintenance costs for changing batteries. The processing of friction energy from everyday factors as the helm rotates is the idyllic way of undertaking the sensors explained.

Pipeline Actuators

The advancement of embedded systems and communication technology has resulted in a need in the industry to systematize duties and provide more power. Instant advances in data managing technologies, wireless networking and management have provided opportunities for change in all aspects of oil and gas processing industry practices. Because of their duration, reliable monitoring, and timely reporting to remote control rooms for the gas-carrying and the oil pipelines is still a superior challenge. There is plenty of electricity available from a natural gas tank or a steam pipe delivery system (Shaikh and Zeadally, 2016). The use of maintenance-free solid-state thermoelectric transducers can capture thermal energy. The energy can be used to open and shut down the valves without needing the actuator's cables.

The Inverse of Energy Harvesting

Free energy also comes at a cost and going about the entire system is critical in deciding how energy harvesting can satisfy the power needs. Likewise, it examines the EH reviews on the key features, proposed frameworks, and models. Specific energy source productions are focused on that WSNs use. WSNs are the assembly of spatially apart, cutting-edge sensors to monitor.

Green Energy

A fallacy that continues to spread is that energy harvesting is a moderate example of how the population can capture naturally available energy and that such systems can be industrialized and recycled in the future to power our hospices and industries (Panatik et al., 2020). The said systems are very much incompatible, except for the photovoltaic cells for capturing sunlight.

Collecting Wasted Energy

Calculations for demonstrating how much electricity is 'consumed' by a thousand people's feet are easy to do. There is little economic sense in running permitted types of machinery from passengers' pathways at subway locations. The harvesters would be costly; besides, the amount of generated energy is insignificant compared to the electricity consumed in illumination, reheating, and aeration (Iqbal et al., 2017). In case the drop in charges was the goal, it will pay off even faster to improve the operation of current construction facilities and replace old equipment.

Self-Charging Consumer Electronics

Modern palm-sized astrophysical devices can yield energy for this; however, when charging, the phone cannot be carried in a pocket (Egaji et al., 2019). The vibration energy harvesters that use movement energy usually offer sufficient power, nevertheless, merely under specific circumstances. Combine these negatives with sophisticated mobile influence conventions comparatively with mature headphones, and the alteration between the energy required and the energy obtainable is only widening.

Drop-in Battery Replacement

A battery-operated system runs wherever it is. Harvesters can only produce electricity where there is sufficient energy. Batteries are standard products that are available from a wide variety of manufacturers at a low cost (Sherazi et al., 2018). Energy harvesters are currently available from a limited range of manufacturers as new, high-cost, mostly bespoke technology solutions.

Energy Harvesting/Optimization Challenges in WSN/IoT Networks

The increasing IoT development has heightened the need of developing wireless sensors with low power consumption. Wireless sensors have now been incorporated into IoT systems to provide data in a precise and reliable way for monitoring and controlling the flow of activities in various sectors. The EH technology is a green method for extending the sensor's life and, in certain circumstances, eliminates the need for batteries. The EH also has economic and practical advantages, for instance, increased energy efficiency and cheaper grid maintenance costs. The study outlined some of the upcoming research problems that must be solved on a wide scale to fully realize the potential for EH solutions in the IoT. Even though substantial improvement in EH devices development and design are witnessed, major scientific obstacles remain before IoT device production becomes self-sustaining.

Modeling of Harvested Energies

An equilibrium concerning the quantity of energy produced and the quantity of energy used is crucial. This necessitates IoT device power profiling and customization of their functioning to the amount of gathered device. The accessibility of collected energy fluctuates with time in a non-deterministic way. As a result, prediction techniques are used to estimate the amount of energy scavenged, and to govern the power coming from the energy sources, classical power management methods (for instance, PLL (software phase locked loops) and MPPT (Maximum Power Point Tracking)) are utilized. Models for energy forecasting that have recently been offered should be improved to produce more accurate findings, and management of energy decisions must be taken to reduce energy damage. Furthermore, the power supply must offer sufficient energy for processing processes of data, activities of transmission and/or reception, and intervals of sleep (Sherazi et al., 2019). Accordingly, to lower the cost of energies during wireless data transmission, academic and industrial researchers are to expand optimum energy use algorithms (Hussain et al., 2020) and examine creative approaches to tailor wireless transmission protocols to the energy harvesting process's features.

Harvested Energy Storage

Because the technique that was employed to store the energy gathered influences the size, price, and working life of the IoT devices. This entails the advancement of rechargeable batteries and supercapacitors as acceptable storage components. Due to the cycling deterioration phenomenon, batteries with high power densities aren't ideal for IoT devices that need to last a long time. Furthermore, they are harmed by both hot and low temperatures. Although the energy density of supercapacitors is lower than that of batteries, they do not suffer from cyclic deterioration. In addition, supercapacitors experience higher current leakage, which consumes a significant portion of the energy collected. As a result (Setyawan et al., 2020), future researchers should look at new methodologies for identifying the best contender for storing collected energy, as determined by the following criteria: minimal cycle degradation, minimal energy leakage, high-density energy, and continuous functioning even at extreme temperatures.

Energy Harvesting From Multiple Sources

In certain circumstances, a single power harvesting source is inadequate to provide electricity to IoT devices. The dependability of IoT devices may be improved by integrating energy from several sources. Developed designs and methodologies for circuits for lower power administration that collect energies as of several suppliers of energy that are heterogeneous. The findings show that the suggested designs are appropriate for specified utilization. As an example, the power ring topology or the complementary usage of harvesters is the basic scheme that is acceptable when all input energy sources are not anticipated to supply a considerable amount of power at the same time. Energy is also combined from heterogeneous sources using Switched-inductor and switched capacitor converter topologies with multiple inputs (Singh et al., 2021). Developers should think about the creation of customizable matching impedance techniques for MPPT control regardless of the architecture used. Additionally, scientists must concentrate their efforts on the creation of sophisticated algorithms with the ability to pick up energy sources of information based on their accessibility, obviating the requirement for the storage of energy.

Size and Cost Efficiency

IoT device dimensions and weight are important in some cases (implantable and Wearable IoT devices, for example). However, these gadgets only create a little amount of power, which is insufficient to accomplish their primary purpose (For example, powering the gadget and any associated sensors, as well as data transfer). Micro and nanoscale harvesting systems that can power IoT devices while also supporting additional tasks (for example, monitoring patient health status and functioning as stimulators for tissue regeneration) should be created to little manufacturing costs in mind. PEHs can successfully power tiny and minuscule IoT devices, according to the scientific literature. To allow PEH mini and nanofabrication with increased versatility and output energy density, future researchers need to discover new eco-friendly materials (Cavalcanti et al., 2019). Recent breakthrough microelectronics holds a lot of promise and may be leveraged to create energy harvesters that are resilient, compact, low-cost, and low power.

Impact of Renewable Energy Sources on the Environment

Sources of renewable energy assist to reduce contamination, and as a result, they are being utilized to produce current IoT gadgets as the sector has grown significantly in recent years. In IoT devices, batteries used that do not include energy-collecting technology gradually deteriorate and are discarded after a few weeks or months. The ecology suffers if there are no battery recycling methods in place. In this scenario, the task is to design IoT devices that capture energy with a lifespan that is substantially longer than that of batteries. It's also worth mentioning that certain IoT devices that capture energy use harmful or infrequent minerals (for example, TEEHs use bismuth telluride, PEHs use lead zirconate titanate, and PVs use cadmium.). As a result, another difficulty that must be addressed is the usage of environmentally benign things, electroactive polymers, for example, and carbon nanowire semiconductors, to create electrical components for energy harvesting IoT devices (Khazaee et al., 2020).

Future Directions

The energy dispensation work has concentrated on the transducer to resolve how to extract as much energy as possible from an assumed dynamic pitch. As our knowledge progresses, the emphasis will turn to new applications recognizing the potential of energy harvesters.

System Integration and Smart Cities

The idea of smart cities is currently a reality in some nations, and it is still expanding to several counties as the technology get appreciated; connected intelligent systems as witnessed, for instance, transportation, infrastructure, and public service. Although energy harvesting can power many of the sensors that allow these applications, there is a growing demand for self-sufficient, clustered, or sensing gadgets that can also execute edge computation. The EH plug-and-play would become the standard. Some recognition of the vendors for the procurement and installation of various components of the harvester on demand. Power from these systems has been generated by portable and mechanical wireless devices, adding a great deal of useful knowledge to make travel, safety, and infrastructure changes possible.

Low Power Wireless Communications

In the last decade, rapid advances in energy harvesting have greatly improved the performance of device in transforming free energies into formally usable electric energies, allowing energy-independent system design at present. Communication protocols are being developed and are unambiguously planned to diminish the complex use of data communication.

Biological Systems and Falling Costs

Achieving an effective energy scavenging for millimeter-scale biomedical implants, the regulation of breathing or blood pressure may be operated on medical devices with ultra-low electricity. Scientists ought to build an advanced pacemaker capable of pulling a third of the required energy from the blood supply. A centralized data connectivity in a smart city perception entails mainly five key factors as demonstrated in Figure 5.

Figure 5. A centralized data connectivity in a smart city perception

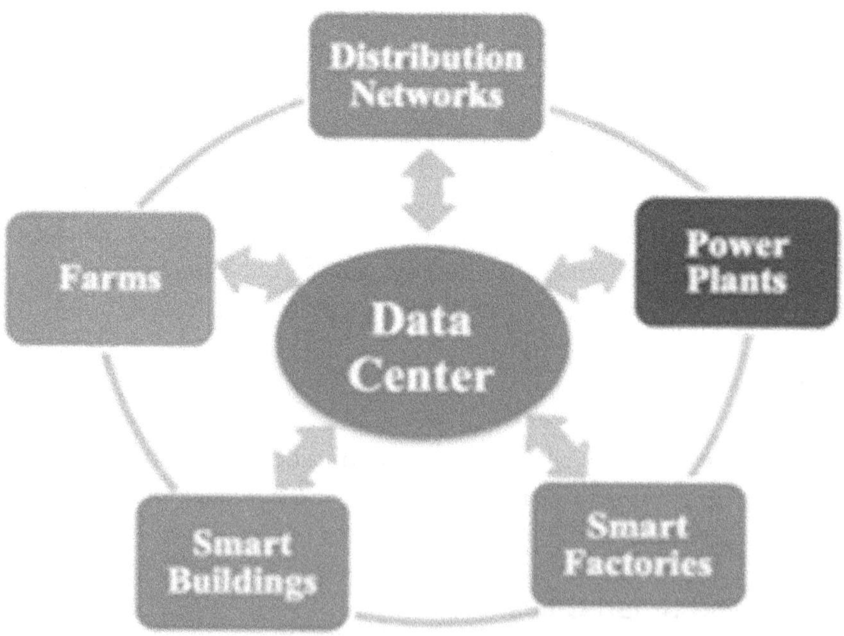

The cost of EH would reduce as it makes its way into products for global customers. Therefore, business projects should allow greater use of energy-harvesting-powered technologies supporting the developmental work, all summarized in Table 5.

Table 5. A summarized appropriation, inverse, and future directions

Harvesting Technique	Application	Proposed Model	Reference
Appropriation	Industrial condition monitoring	Pulse -centered condition monitoring	(Rosa et al., 2019)
	Operating isolated setups	Wireless power transfers	(Chamanian et al., 2019)
	Wireless Sensor Networks	Two different vibration-based harvesters: piezoelectric and electromagnetic	(Sejaan et al., 2020)
	Pipeline Actuators	Micro-electro-mechanical system using a vertical multi-junction photovoltaic cell	(Zhang and Park, 2020)
The inverse	Green Energy	Organic polymers including inorganic nanoparticle(s)	(Allam et al., 2019)
	Collecting wasted energy	Energy consumption and data delivery	(Wen et al., 2020)
	Self-charging consumer electronics	Self-operated WSNs	(Wang et al., 2019)
	Drop-in battery replacement	Two piezoelectric vibration energy harvesters via COMSOL	(Allam et al., 2019)
Future Directions	System Integrations	Nonlinear vibration absorber Integration	(Zhang et al., 2019)
	Low-power wireless communications	Secured smart home switching system	(Zungeru et al., 2019)
	Smart cities	Dependable control schemes for microgrid management	(Ha and Phung, 2019)
	Biological systems	Track and monitor of Galápagos	(Loreti et al., 2019)
	Falling costs	A self-powered human motion monitoring	(Xi et al., 2019)
	Artificial intelligence	Wearable AI-systems are examined	(Shi et al., 2019)

ENERGY HARVESTING ON IOT APPLICATIONS IN SMART CITY STANDPOINT

The process of capturing and storing energy from the environment to power IoT devices. This is particularly useful in smart city applications, where large numbers of IoT devices are deployed to collect data and provide services to citizens. Here are some of the most suitable EH technologies for smart city IoT applications:

Solar Energy Harvesting

Solar energy is a popular choice for powering IoT devices in smart cities due to its abundance and reliability. Photovoltaic (PV) panels can be installed on rooftops, streetlights, and other structures to capture sunlight and convert it into electrical energy (Zeb et al., 2023). In a smart city context, solar energy harvesting is an efficient and sustainable solution to power smart devices and infrastructure such as streetlights, traffic signals, and sensors. It reduces the reliance on grid power, lowers energy costs, and enhances the city's overall sustainability.

Vibration Energy Harvesting

Vibrations generated by traffic, pedestrian movement, and other activities in the city can be captured and converted into electrical energy using piezoelectric materials. This energy can be used to power sensors and other low-power IoT devices. Vibration energy harvesting can be applied in smart city applications by converting the mechanical vibrations from vehicles, pedestrians, and other sources into electrical energy to power devices such as wireless sensor networks, IoT devices, and structural health monitoring systems (Luo et al., 2023). This reduces the reliance on batteries and grid power, enhances sustainability, and improves the efficiency of city infrastructure.

Thermal Energy Harvesting

Thermal energy harvesting involves capturing the temperature differences between different parts of the city and converting them into electrical energy. This can be done using thermoelectric materials that generate electricity when exposed to a temperature gradient. Thermal energy harvesting can be applied in smart city applications by utilizing the temperature differences between objects to generate electrical energy. This can be used to power devices such as wireless sensors, IoT devices, and structural health monitoring systems (Liu et al., 2023). For instance, temperature differences between buildings and the surrounding environment can be harnessed to power building automation systems, reducing energy consumption and enhancing sustainability.

Radio Frequency Energy Harvesting

RF energy harvesting involves capturing and converting the energy from wireless signals, such as Wi-Fi, Bluetooth, and cellular signals, into electrical energy. This technology can be used to power low-power IoT devices such as sensors and tags. RF EH can be applied in smart city applications by utilizing the energy from ambient radio frequency waves to power devices such as wireless sensors and IoT devices (Liu et al., 2023; Zeb et al., 2023). This eliminates the need for batteries or grid power, which can be expensive and difficult to maintain. RF energy harvesting can be used to power smart city infrastructure such as streetlights, traffic signals, and environmental sensors, enhancing sustainability and reducing energy costs.

Wind Energy Harvesting (WEH)

Wind turbines can be installed on buildings and other structures to capture the kinetic energy of wind and convert it into electrical energy. This energy can be used to power IoT devices such as sensors and cameras. WEH can be applied in smart city applications by using wind turbines to generate electrical energy to power devices such as streetlights, environmental sensors, and other infrastructure. In a smart city context, wind turbines can be installed on rooftops, lampposts, and other structures to take advantage of the available wind resources. Wind energy harvesting can also be used in conjunction with solar energy harvesting to provide a reliable and sustainable source of power for smart city infrastructure (Wang et al., 2019; Yetgin et al., 2017). In totality, WEH is a promising technology that can contribute to a more sustainable and energy-efficient smart city infrastructure while reducing the reliance on grid power and lowering energy costs.

CONCLUSION

This chapter presented a clear trend of EH strategies in fulfilling the energy demands for prospective wireless sensor network installations. The WSNs sojourn attracted much interest from different shareholders due to their design and implementation. This study investigated the energy harvesting node architecture, EH hardware configurations, harvested amount of energy harvested together with the output. Moreover, the prestige, potential, and anticipated essential uses in the future were discussed. Furthermore, some open research issues that would need to be tackled have also been explored. Overall, EH, IoTs and WSNs have depicted increased interest in academia and industrialization paradigms in the recent past. These approaches can find numerous innovative applications and offer novel solutions to the problems identified, and thus deserve significant attention.

REFERENCES

Adu-Manu, K. S., Adam, N., Tapparello, C., Ayatollahi, H., & Heinzelman, W. (2020). Energy-harvesting wireless sensor networks: A review. *ACM Transactions on Sensor Networks*, *14*(2), 1–5. doi:10.1145/3183338

Agrawal, S., Sarkar, S., Srivastava, G., Maddikunta, P. K., & Gadekallu, T. R. (2021). Genetically optimized prediction of the remaining useful life. *Sustainable Computing: Informatics and Systems*, *31*, 100565. doi:10.1016/j.suscom.2021.100565

Allam, A. H., Taha, M., & Zayed, H. H. (2019). Enhanced zone-based energy aware data collection protocol for Wsns. *Journal of King Saud University-Computer and Information Sciences*, *31*(4), 415–560.

Amirinasab, M., Shamshirband, S., Chronopoulos, A. T., Mosavi, A., & Nabipour, N. (2020). Energy-efficient method for wireless sensor networks low-power radio operation in Internet of things. *Electronics (Basel)*, *9*(2), 3–20. doi:10.3390/electronics9020320

Bao, X., Liang, H., Liu, Y., & Zhang, F. (2019). A stochastic game approach for collaborative beam forming in sdn-based energy harvesting wireless sensor networks. *IEEE Internet of Things Journal, 6*(6), 9583–9595. doi:10.1109/JIOT.2019.2930073

Cavalcanti, D., Perez-Ramirez, J., Rashid, M. M., Fang, J., Galeev, M., & Stanton, K. B. (2019). Extending accurate time distribution and timeliness capabilities over the air to enable future wireless industrial automation systems. *Proceedings of the IEEE, 107*(6), 1132–1152. doi:10.1109/JPROC.2019.2903414

Chamanian, S., Baghaee, S., Uluşan, H., Zorlu, Ö., Uysal-Biyikoglu, E., & Kulah, H. (2019). Implementation of energy-neutral operation on vibration energy harvesting WSN. *IEEE Sensors Journal, 19*(8), 3092–3099. doi:10.1109/JSEN.2019.2890902

Chun-Wei, J. L., Srivastava, G., Zhang, Y., Djenouri, Y., & Aloqaily, M. (2020). Privacy-preserving multiobjective sanitization model in 6G IoT environments. *IEEE Internet of Things Journal, 8*(7), 5340–5349.

Egaji, O. A., Chakhar, S., & Brown, D. (2019). An innovative decision rule approach to tyre pressure monitoring. *Expert Systems with Applications, 124*, 252–270. doi:10.1016/j.eswa.2019.01.051

Elahi, H., Eugeni, M., & Gaudenzi, P. (2018). A review on mechanisms for piezoelectric-based energy harvesters. *Energies, 11*(7), 18–50. doi:10.3390/en11071850

Ferg, E. E., Schuldt, F., & Schmidt, J. (2019). The challenges of li-ion starter lighting and ignition battery: A review from Cradle to Grave. *Journal of Power Sources, 423*, 380–403. doi:10.1016/j.jpowsour.2019.03.063

Fu, B., Zhang, J., Chen, H., Guo, H., Song, C., Shang, W., Tao, P., & Deng, T. (2019). Optical nano fluids for direct absorption-based solar thermal energy harvesting at medium-to-high temperatures. *Current Opinion in Chemical Engineering, 25*, 51–56. doi:10.1016/j.coche.2019.07.002

Ha, Q., & Phung, M. D. (2019). Iot-enabled dependable control for solar energy harvesting in smart buildings. *IET Smart Cities, 1*(2), 61–70. doi:10.1049/iet-smc.2019.0052

Hadas, Z., Janak, L., & Smilek, J. (2018). Virtual prototypes of energy harvesting systems for industrial applications. *Mechanical Systems and Signal Processing, 110*, 152–164. doi:10.1016/j.ymssp.2018.03.036

Hao, S., Ward, L., Luo, Z., Ozolins, V., Dravid, V. P., Kanatzidis, M. G., & Wolverton, C. (2019). Design strategy for high-performance thermoelectric materials: The prediction of electron-doped kzrcuse3. *Chemistry of Materials, 31*(8), 3018–3024. doi:10.1021/acs.chemmater.9b00840

Hou, L., & Chen, W. (2020). A novel mppt method for autonomous wireless sensor network node with thermal energy harvesting. *Engineering Research Express, 2*(1), 1001–1005. doi:10.1088/2631-8695/ab638d

Huang, J., Zhou, Y., Ning, Z., & Gharavi, H. (2019). Wireless power transfer and energy harvesting: Current status and prospects. *IEEE Wireless Communications, 26*(4), 163–169. doi:10.1109/MWC.2019.1800378 PMID:32165868

Hussain, M. W., Pradhan, B., Gao, X. Z., Reddy, K. H. K., & Roy, D. S. (2020). Clonal selection algorithm for energy minimization in software defined networks. *Applied Soft Computing, 96*, 106617. doi:10.1016/j.asoc.2020.106617

Iqbal, A., Kim, Y., Ahn, J., & Lee, T. (2017). Energy level-based efficient wireless power and information transfer in sensor networks. *Proc. 11th International Conference on Ubiquitous Information Management and Communication*, 1-5. 10.1145/3022227.3022315

Jun, Y., Craig, A., Shafik, W., & Sharif, L. (2021). Artificial intelligence application in cybersecurity and cyberdefense. *Wireless Communications and Mobile Computing*, *2021*, 1–10. doi:10.1155/2021/3329581

Kausar, A. Z., Reza, A. W., Saleh, M. U., & Ramiah, H. (2014). Energizing wireless sensor networks by energy harvesting systems: Scopes, challenges, and approaches. *Renewable & Sustainable Energy Reviews*, *38*(2), 973–989. doi:10.1016/j.rser.2014.07.035

Khalid, S., Raouf, I., Khan, A., Kim, N., & Kim, H. S. (2019). A review of human-powered energy harvesting for smart electronics: Recent progress and challenges. *International Journal of Precise Engineering Manufacture Green Technology*, *6*(4), 821–851. doi:10.100740684-019-00144-y

Khalifeh, A., Saadeh, M., Darabkh, K. A., & Nagaradjane, P. (2019). Radio-frequency based energy charging- an experimental study. *2nd IEEE Middle East and North Africa Communications Conference*, 1-4. 10.1109/MENACOMM46666.2019.8988585

Khazaee, M., Rezaniakolaie, A., Moosavian, A., & Rosendahl, L. (2020). A novel method for autonomous remote condition monitoring of rotating machines using piezoelectric energy harvesting approach. *Sensors and Actuators. A, Physical*, *295*, 37–50. doi:10.1016/j.sna.2019.05.016

Kumar, N., & Dash, D. (2020). Flow based efficient data gathering in wireless sensor network using path-constrained mobile sink. *Journal of Ambient Intelligence and Humanized Computing*, *11*(3), 1163–1175. doi:10.100712652-019-01245-x

Li, D., Wu, Y., Da Ronch, A., & Xiang, J. (2016). Energy harvesting by means of flow-Induced vibrations on aerospace vehicles. *Progress in Aerospace Sciences*, *86*, 28–62. doi:10.1016/j.paerosci.2016.08.001

Liu, Y., Riba, J. R., & Moreno-Eguilaz, M. (2023). Energy Balance of Wireless Sensor Nodes Based on Bluetooth Low Energy and Thermoelectric Energy Harvesting. *Sensors (Basel)*, *23*(3), 1480. doi:10.339023031480 PMID:36772518

Loreti, P., Catini, A., Luca, M. D., Bracciale, L., & Gentile, G. (2019). The design of an energy harvesting wireless sensor node for tracking pink guanas. *Sensors (Basel)*, *19*(5), 9–85. doi:10.339019050985 PMID:30813516

Luo, A., Xu, W., Sun, J., Xi, K., Tang, S., Guo, X., Lee, C., & Wang, F. (2023). Vibration energy harvester with double frequency-up conversion mechanism for self-powered sensing system in smart city. *Nano Energy*, *105*, 108030. doi:10.1016/j.nanoen.2022.108030

Maddikunta, P. K., Gadekallu, T. R., Kaluri, R., Srivastava, G., Parizi, R. M., & Khan, M. S. (2020). Green communication in IoT networks using a hybrid optimization algorithm. *Computer Communications*, *159*, 97–107. doi:10.1016/j.comcom.2020.05.020

Mausam, K., Kumar, S., Kumar Ghosh, S., Kumar Tiwari, A., & Sehgal, M. (2020). Solicitation of nanoparticles/fluids in solar thermal energy harvesting: A review. *Materials Today: Proceedings*, *26*(2), 2289–2295. doi:10.1016/j.matpr.2020.02.495

Mi, J., Li, Q., Liu, M., Li, X., & Zuo, L. (2020). Design, modelling, and testing of a vibration energy harvester using a novel half-wave mechanical rectification. *Applied Energy*, *279*, 115–726. doi:10.1016/j.apenergy.2020.115726

Nguyen, C. V., Quyen, T. V., Le, A. M., Truong, L. H., & Nguyen, M. T. (2020). Advanced hybrid energy harvesting systems for unmanned ariel vehicles. Advances in Science. *Technology and Engineering Systems Journal*, *5*(1), 34–39.

Panatik, K. Z., Kamardin, K., Shariff, S. A., Yuhaniz, S. S., & Ahmad, N. A. (2020). Energy harvesting in wireless sensor networks: survey. *IEEE 3rd International Symposium on Telecommunication Technologies*, 1041-1054.

Raja, J., & Mookhambika, N. (2021). A novel energy harvesting with middle-order weighted probability (EHMoWP) for performance improvement in wireless sensor network (WSN). *Journal of Ambient Intelligence and Humanized Computing*, 1–12.

Renuka, K., Das, S. N., & Reddy, K. H. (2018). An Efficient Context Management Approach for IoT. *IUP Journal of Information Technology*, *14*(2).

Rosa, R. L., Dehollain, C., Pellitteri, F., Miceli, R., & Livreri, P. (2020). A battery-free asset monitoring system based on rf wireless power transfer. *IEEE 20th Mediterranean Electrotechnical Conference,* 181-186. 10.1109/MELECON48756.2020.9140484

Rosa, R. L., Livreri, P., Trigona, C., Donato, L. D., & Sorbello, G. (n.d.). Strategies and techniques for powering wireless sensor nodes through energy harvesting and wireless power transfer. *Sensors (Basel)*, *19*(12), 26–60.

Satyala, N., Norouzzadeh, P., Vashaee, D., Wang, X., & Wang, Z. M. (2014). Nano bulk thermoelectric: concepts, techniques, and modeling. Nanoscale, Thermo Electrics, 16, 141-183. doi:10.1007/978-3-319-02012-9_4

Sejaan, G. A., Lamarque, F., Hajj, N. E., Assad, J. A., & Hajjar, H. A. (2020). Optical energy harvesting in a smart material-based micro-actuator using a vertical multijunction PV cell. *Energy Harvesting and Storage Materials, Devices, and Applications X*, *11387*, 113–870.

Setyawan, E., Kurniawan, A., Rahmadianto, F., Napitupulu, R. A. M., & Siagian, P. (2020). Flat plate type solar collector performance using double thermal insulation. Jakarta, IOP Conference Service. *Materials Science and Engineering*, *852*, 1244.

Shafik, W. (2023). Cyber Security Perspectives in Public Spaces: Drone Case Study. In *Handbook of Research on Cybersecurity Risk in Contemporary Business Systems* (pp. 79–97). IGI Global. doi:10.4018/978-1-6684-7207-1.ch004

Shaikh, F. K., & Zeadally, S. (2016). Energy harvesting in wireless sensor networks: A comprehensive review. *Renewable & Sustainable Energy Reviews*, *55*, 1041–1054. doi:10.1016/j.rser.2015.11.010

Sherazi, H. H. R., Grieco, L. A., & Boggia, G. (2018). A comprehensive review on energy harvesting MAC protocols in WSNs: Challenges and tradeoffs. *Ad Hoc Networks*, *71*, 117–134. doi:10.1016/j.adhoc.2018.01.004

Shi, Q., Dong, B., He, T., Sun, Z., Zhu, J., Zhang, Z., & Lee, C. (2020). Progress in wearable electronics/photonics moving toward the era of artificial intelligence and Internet of things. *InfoMat*, *2*(6), 1131–1162. doi:10.1002/inf2.12122

Singh, J., Kaur, R., & Singh, D. (2021). Energy harvesting in wireless sensor networks: A taxonomic survey. *International Journal of Energy Research*, *45*(1), 118–140. doi:10.1002/er.5816

Sudevalayam, S., & Kulkarni, P. (2010). Energy harvesting sensor nodes: Survey and implications. *IEEE Communications Surveys and Tutorials*, *13*(3), 443–461. doi:10.1109/SURV.2011.060710.00094

Syu, J. H., Wu, M. E., Srivastava, G., Chao, C. F., & Lin, J. C. (2021). An Iot-based hedge system for solar power generation. *IEEE Internet of Things Journal*, *5*(13), 156–162. doi:10.1109/JIOT.2021.3064384

Tan, R. R., Aviso, K. B., & Ng, D. K. S. (2019). Optimization model for financing innovations in green energy technologies. *Renewable & Sustainable Energy Reviews*, *113*, 109–258. doi:10.1016/j.rser.2019.109258

Wang, G., Nixon, M., & Boudreaux, M. (2019). Toward cloud-assisted industrial Iot platform for large-scale continuous condition monitoring. *Proceedings of the IEEE*, *107*(6), 1193–1205. doi:10.1109/JPROC.2019.2914021

Wang, J., Liu, Q., Li, D., Chen, C., Chen, Z., Song, P., Hao, J., Li, Y., Fakhrhoseini, S., Naebe, M., Wang, X., & Lei, W. (2020). Lightweight, superplastic yet thermo conductive boron nitride nan composite aerogel for thermal energy regulation. *ACS Nano*, *13*(7), 7860–7870. doi:10.1021/acsnano.9b02182 PMID:31194502

Wang, L., Luo, G., Jiang, Z., Zhang, F., Zhao, L., Yang, P., Lin, Q., & Maeda, R. (2019). Broadband vibration energy harvesting for wireless sensor node power supply in train container. *The Review of Scientific Instruments*, *90*(12), 12–50. doi:10.1063/1.5127243 PMID:31893793

Wen, F., Wang, H., He, T., Shi, Q., Sun, Z., Zhu, M., Zhang, Z., Cao, Z., Dai, Y., Zhang, T., & Lee, C. (2020). Battery-free short-range self- powered wireless sensor network (SS-WSN) using TENG based direct sensory transmission mechanism. *Nano Energy*, *67*, 104–266. doi:10.1016/j.nanoen.2019.104266

Xi, Y., Hua, J., & Shi, Y. (2019). Noncontact triboelectric nanogenerator for human motion monitoring and energy harvesting. *Nano Energy*, *69*, 104–390.

Xia, C., Zhang, D., Pedrycz, W., Fan, K., & Guo, Y. (2020). Human body heat-based thermoelectric harvester with ultra-low input power management system for wireless sensor powering. *Energies*, *12*(20), 39–42.

Yang, Z., Jianjun, L., Faqiri, H., Shafik, W., Talal Abdulrahman, A., Yusuf, M., & Sharawy, A. M. (2021). Green internet of things and big data applications in smart city development. *Complexity*, *2021*, 1–15. doi:10.1155/2021/4922697

Yang, Z., Yang, Y., Liu, F., Wang, Z., Li, Y., Qiu, J., Xiao, X., Li, Z., Lu, Y., Ji, L., Wang, Z. L., & Cheng, J. (2021). Power backpack for energy harvesting and reduced load impact. *ACS Nano*, *15*(2), 2611–26123. doi:10.1021/acsnano.0c07498 PMID:33533242

Yetgin, H., Cheung, K. T. K., El-Hajjar, M., & Hanzo, L. H. (2017). A survey of network lifetime maximization techniques in wireless sensor networks. *IEEE Communications Surveys and Tutorials*, *19*(2), 828–854. doi:10.1109/COMST.2017.2650979

Zeb, H., Gohar, M., Ali, M., Ahmad, W., Ghani, A., Choi, J. G., & Koh, S. J. (2023). Zero Energy IoT Devices in Smart Cities Using RF Energy Harvesting. *Electronics (Basel)*, *12*(1), 148. doi:10.3390/electronics12010148

Zhang, D., Chen, Z., Zhou, H., Chen, L., & Shen, X. S. (2016). Energy-balanced cooperative transmission based on relay selection and power control in energy harvesting wireless sensor network. *Computer Networks*, *104*, 189–197. doi:10.1016/j.comnet.2016.05.013

Zhang, J., Bai, X., Han, W., Zhao, B., Xu, L., & Wei, J. (2019). The design of radio frequency energy harvesting and radio frequency-based wireless power transfer system for battery-less self-sustaining applications. *International Journal of RF and Microwave Computer-Aided Engineering*, *29*(1), 777–780. doi:10.1002/mmce.21658

Zhang, Y., & Park, S. J. (2019). Flexible organic thermoelectric materials and devices for wearable green energy harvesting. *Polymers*, *11*(5), 9–19. doi:10.3390/polym11050909 PMID:31137541

Zhang, Y. W., Wang, S., Ni, Z. Y., Fang, Z. W., Zang, J., & Fang, B. (2019). Integration of a nonlinear vibration absorber and levitation magnetoelectric energy harvester for whole-spacecraft systems. *Acta Mechanica Solida Sinica*, *32*(3), 298–309. doi:10.100710338-019-00081-y

Zhu, Z., Xu, L., Abdelkareem, M. A. A., Zou, J., & Mi, J. (2020). Design and simulation analysis of vibration energy harvesting system based on Adams. *International Design Engineering Technical Conferences and Computers and Information in Engineering Conference, 8*, 297-273.

Zin, T. T., Tin, P., & Hama, H. (2018). Characterizing reliability measures for Internet of things by Markov queue. *Data Science and Pattern Recognition*, *2*(2), 1–10.

Zungeru, A. M., Gaboitaolelwe, J., Diarra, B., Chuma, J. M., & Ang, L. M. (2019). A secured smart home switching system based on wireless communications and self-energy harvesting. *IEEE Access : Practical Innovations, Open Solutions*, *7*, 25063–25085. doi:10.1109/ACCESS.2019.2900305

Chapter 17
Future Indian Smart Cities' Renewable Energy Scenarios

Manjulata Badi
https://orcid.org/0000-0003-3196-8383
Alliance University, India

Sheila Mahapatra
Alliance University, India

Saurav Raj
https://orcid.org/0000-0002-1875-3903
Institute of Chemical Technology, India

Swetha Shekarappa G.
Alliance University, India

ABSTRACT

Due to the growing energy shortage and rising global temperatures, sustainable development has become more of a necessity than ever before. While renewable energy, sustainable energy resources, and a focus on low carbon emissions in the power system all contribute to sustainable development, these concepts must be coordinated if they are to have a lasting impact. These complications present a new set of challenges in the process of integrating renewables to the existing grid structure, including intermittency, system utilization efficiency, and others. The rest of this chapter deals with the topic of sustainable development and explores the various options for shifting power generation from traditional fossil fuel-powered sources to renewable energy. As renewable energy is employed, additional clean energy such as solar energy, wind energy, and photovoltaic systems will be added to the existing grid. There is another benefit to the net metering program.

DOI: 10.4018/979-8-3693-0744-1.ch017

INTRODUCTION AND BACKGROUND

To comprehend the connection between smart city concepts and environmental sustainability, analyses scientific research that are both focused on these topics. This chapter provides a thorough survey of the literature on smart governance, which is defined as the use of technology to enable local governments and citizens to work together to achieve sustainable development. In today's data-rich economy, it helps with policy creation and city planning. relating to smart sustainable cities, sustainable development, and sustainability. The difficulties that must be resolved in order to advance towards future cities and sustainable potential for smart cities. At this rate, the overall greenhouse gas emissions and fuel costs will climb rapidly, necessitating rapid efforts to adopt renewable energy such as natural gas or electricity. While renewable energy has numerous advantages, there are also significant drawbacks, such as the lack of continuous supply, and as such, must be designed, planned, and controlled to achieve continuity.

Literature Review

The global economy has developed rapidly in the last decade, especially in emerging economies, and this has resulted in a dramatic increase in energy requirements. Johnsson, Kjärstad, and Rootzén (2019) describe the fossil fuel resources diminish, environmental protection and energy conservation are more appealing. To reduce our dependency on fossil resources, we must decrease our consumption of energy by implementing energy-saving programs that are applied in both industrial and domestic sectors. An additional way to accomplish this goal is to use green energy, for stand-alone systems. Abujarad, Mustafa, and Jamian (2017) elaborate one of the major drawbacks of renewable energy technologies is their intermittent nature and green energy sources have some disadvantages, such as having a low-capacity factor and requiring active storage systems. In addition, renewable energy sources eliminate the dangers associated with atomic power, so socially speaking, it is seen as more advantageous to utilize renewable energy power plants (Pradhan, Reddy, Roy, & Mohanta, 2011). Decisions made by governments and businesses include deciding whether to put in place green energy. We discovered that wind power is the most fuel-efficient power source, uses the least water, has fewer environmental impacts, and offers numerous advantages to society, has a significantly higher capital cost. In the study of Cantarero (2020), three major technological changes that include demand-side energy savings, green energy were factored into a sustainable development of renewable energy. As assessed the effects of RE systems on various areas of energy, the economy, and the environment include. By making advances in renewable energy technologies, sustainable development can be accomplished while resolving several environmental problems caused by energy issues. It is worth noting that when we use optimization algorithms to help with the optimization of renewable energy systems, we're getting results that are favourable (Hussain et al., 2020).

According to forecasts, India's energy demand will triple in just over two decades in Arent et al. (2021). Additionally, existing traditional sources are responsible for both climate conditions and being unlimited in capacity. Because of this, a different method of generation will be needed that is cleaner and limitless. As of July 2019, total power generating capacity had been installed using renewable energy. India, a country rich in natural resources, has the potential to use renewable energy to generate electricity on a massive scale. Kasdan, Kuhl, and Kurukulasuriya (2021) presents today's technology has made it possible to use these renewable resources more efficiently for electricity generation. India has a competitive advantage in renewable energy production because of its plentiful natural resources.

There are a wide variety of renewable energy resources available in India, including wind, solar, small-hydro, biomass, tidal, and geothermal energy, and of those, wind and solar are the most popular. There are many possible reasons for India's focus on renewable energy, including its importance to the country. A significant increase in renewable energy generation in India has been witnessed in the past decade. From Tsung-Han, Bin, Shih-Ming, and Yen-Chiang (2020) and Reynolds, Boulding, Pollock, Sweet, Ruiz, and Draeger de Teran (2020) shown in Figure 1, the nation's total capacity of RE has increased. The Indian government founded the of MNRE to help generate and deploy alternate energy sources, to help meet the country's energy needs. The firm has initiated a number of projects since its formation to boost electricity generation from renewable energy. Also, it is less expensive to create resources over time using renewable sources, in comparison to non-renewable ones. Kim, Park, and Lee (2021) presents in India's renewable energy potential is about 900 GW, split evenly between wind and solar with 12% of wind power and 83% of solar power. Bioenergy sources contribute 3%, while small hydro makes up 2.2%. India has promised to help reduce environmental harm and has committed to increase the use of renewable energy by 2030, when 40 percent of its energy generation will come from renewable sources. India could be one of the world's biggest producers of renewable energy if this ambitious goal is met. As illustrated in Alemzero, Acheampong, and Huaping (2021) and Sawhney (2021), Figure 2, RES capacity factor by type of RE sources is listed. India has vast land areas that can be used for solar energy generation. India's sun exposure, moreover, is widespread.

- Many areas with strong wind speeds exist, and they could lead to increased wind energy generation.
- The decent annual biomass energy yield.
- And the nation's numerous rivers and waterways, which can generate hydroelectric power on a small scale.

With population growth limiting economic and industrial growth, the fact that the per-capita consumption rate is rising rapidly is a major concern in Vaka, Walvekar, Rasheed, and Khalid (2020). The Karnataka, Tamil Nadu, and Gujarat states make up most of India's 86.76 GW of renewable energy capacity as of February 2020. Andhra Pradesh, Maharashtra, and Rajasthan are some of the other top states. Despite the fact that it has vast potential, only a few states have succeeded in generating enough energy from renewable sources because of a lack of plans, policies, and regulations to promote their use in Oehler-Şincai (2021). On several occasions, these power plants were set up on farmlands, which was of benefit. Raising RE manufacturing with cropland may help generate a notable increase.

GLOBAL ASPECTS OF RENEWABLE ENERGY

The UN SDGs form a framework for governments to follow as they work to realize the objectives with sustainability and environmental protection. Mukherjee and Chakrabarti (2004) describes the SDGs have set the timetable for every nation to accomplish their potential by 2030, and the UN has interfered to ensure that significant hurdles are resolved. The principle of "doing more and better with less" (Goal 12 of the SDGs) is focused on improving energy efficiency, sustainable infrastructure, consumption, and production. While Goal 7 emphasizes affordable and clean energy for all, nations around the world are struggling to make this a reality. More work is required, and additional private and public funds should be allocated. Additionally, new models and regulatory frameworks must be implemented to meet this goal. Almost 24% of the total energy consumed was generated by renewable sources, with the rest coming from conventional sources. Fossil fuels make up a significant portion of energy production, so global warming, climate change, and Environmental impacts are all triggered in a domino effect. The Paris agreement's primary goal is to prevent a global temperature increase of less than 2 degrees Celsius. The mission also targets aiding nations in addressing global climate change. In Sim and Mills (2021) in contrast to the many existing accords, the Paris Agreement implemented a bottom-up approach with the national contributions of the signatories, in order to reach a target of 40% of its electricity from renewable resources by2030, India has agreed.

Some countries have yet to ratify the treaty despite its being signed by 185 countries. The United States has announced its plans to disengage from the agreement by 2020, whereas China had met its 2020 target and European countries such as Sweden, Portugal, and France have achieved the most progress with 77%, 66%, and 65% respectively in Kazi, Short, Isafiade, and Biegler (2021). To satisfy the demands and limit the effect of global warming, it is necessary to increase the share of renewables in global energy production. Countries have developed a number of measures to enhance the penetration of renewable energy into the energy mix. In the last decade, a lot of new policies in the world in support of renewable energy have been adopted in the power sector, such as FIT introduction in 61 countries and green certificate (Das, Shah, & Suyal, 2020). In 2017, 121 countries had renewable energy policies in place. Renewable energy production is growing by the day and in 2018, the global energy mix includes 171 GW of new renewable energy with a growth rate of 7.9% due to the incorporation of solar and wind energy. The global share of installed RE capacity is seen in Figure 4, where Asia is the leading continent with 44% of the total. The three leading Asian renewable energy producers are China, India, and Japan. According to Figure 5, the total installed capacity of some of the leading Asian countries can be seen in the following Table 1. In Figure 4, China is shown to have huge potential in solar and hydroelectric/wind power, renewable energy-producing countries. According to the country's Energy Information Administration, as of 2018, India's installed renewable energy capacity is 695.86 GW, six times the total capacity in (Priyadarshini 2021). To meet the target of sourcing 680 GW of power from renewable sources, China's 13th Five-Year Plan for Renewable Energy established a goal of obtaining 200 GW of hydropower capacity and 580 GW of other types of renewable energy. As shown in Figure 1, Indian aspects of total capacity are represented. By 2020, the capacity of renewable energy sources will be around 210 GW, with wind energy contributing about half of that amount. Even though renewable energy capacity rose 12 percent in 2017, China's total installed capacity was still 728 GW in 2018, up from 693 GW in 2017. Various incentives are being provided to Chinese companies in order to lessen the country's reliance on foreign countries. In recent years, biomass capacity has soared, with 17.8 GW of total installed capacity. Additionally, China's self-defence energy policy seeks to extend its facilities across the nation and promote the advancement of renewable energy technologies. Figure 7 demonstrates the region's renewable energy growth from 2010 to 2018. The regional RE generation from a variety of sources in 2018 is displayed in Figure 7 (Andrew, 2020). North America's renewable energy leaders include the United States, Canada, and Mexico, where the USA boasts an installed renewable energy capacity of approximately 245.24 GW as of 2018 in Gupta and Bonds (2020). Although the USA only accounts for 14.6% of the gobal carbon emissions, it is the number one producer of renewable energy, just behind China. The U.S. has a massive wind energy capacity of 314 GW. According to Majid (2020), the government is expected to allocate resources to expand the wind energy capacity even further. There has been a notable increase in the number of households that are going solar recently, including SolarCity Corporation, in increasing the amount of solar energy that is used in American homes. According to forecasts, solar PV production will increase to 48 percent of total renewable energy production by 2050, while wind is projected to amount to 28 percent and hydroelectric at 18 percent. Since additional structures are unlikely, the hydropower has been limited. Renewable energy is projected to be the world's most plentiful energy source by 2030, accounting for half of the world's energy supply. Renewable energy production in Europe is led by Germany, France, Portugal, Sweden, Finland, and Denmark. In Irfan, Zhao, Ikram, Gilal, Li, and Rehman (2020), with more than half of Sweden's energy supply coming from renewable sources, the country of zero emission. According to IRENA, an agency which promotes renewable energy, it has an installed capacity of about approx. 30 GW. Since 1974, the country has been a member of the International Energy Agency (IEA) and today's lowest CO2 emissions are at one-quarter of the United States. This has been possible because the country has promote nuclear power over the last 30 years, as the country became less dependent on fossil fuels for energy production. While the country's energy supply is composed of over 68.6 TWh (Terawatt hours) of nuclear and conventional sources, hydropower produces nearly 30% of the total. It has significant water resources, but despite this, hydropower development is still limited as a means of preserving the big rivers. Even though the country had already attained a 50 percent total energy production RE by 2012, it now aims to reach 100 percent RE by 2040. The global aspects of total capacity of the countries in Africa in 2018 is illustrated in Figure 8. In the last year of 2018, Africa's renewable energy capacity was 46,269 MW. African countries with the most renewable energy production include Ethiopia, Egypt, Morocco, and South Africa. The charts in Figure 8 demonstrate that the installed capacities in several African countries have been boosted by RE. South Africa leads African countries in renewable energy output, and the National Development Plan's goal is to heavily invest in renewable energy capacity and generation by 2030. The necessity of a mixed energy generation mix in the country, i.e., hybrid energy. A significant leap in renewable energy capacity was noted between 2010 and 2015, during which the installed capacity of zero was raised to 7.3 GW. SADOE in South Africa has focused on growing solar panel use and ignoring the construction of new nuclear power reactors. Nearly 20,000 MW of new power generation capacity was obtained via 27 renewable energy projects which is estimated to reach over 1.5 million people. South Africa has an average of about 2,500 hours of sunshine every year. The country's average solar radiation is 4.5 and 6.5 kWh/m2. At present, approximately 250 MW of solar PV capacity has been installed on rooftops. Although some wind farms, such as Metrowin Van Stadens (27 MW), Jeffreys Bay (138 MW), and Kouga, are not operational, they all hold the potential to generate wind energy. It is also able to produce an estimated 2,500 MW of power. The government has set an ambitious goal of building 21.5 GW of renewable energy capacity by 2030, and it's working to increase the use of renewables, with plans to ultimately decrease coal consumption.

Table 1. Global increase in renewable energy sources from 2007-2035

Region	2007	2015	2020	2025	2030	2035	Estimated Capital %, 2007–2035
Hydro Energy (HE)	2999	3689	4166	4591	5034	5418	2.1
Wind Energy (WE)	165	682	902	1115	1234	1355	7.8
Geothermal Energy (GE)	57	98	108	119	142	160	3.7
Solar Energy (SE)	6	95	126	140	153	165	12.7
Other	235	394	515	653	773	874	4.8
Total	3462	4958	5817	6618	7336	7972	3.0

Figure 1. Global generation of renewable energy sources in billion kWh from 2007-2035

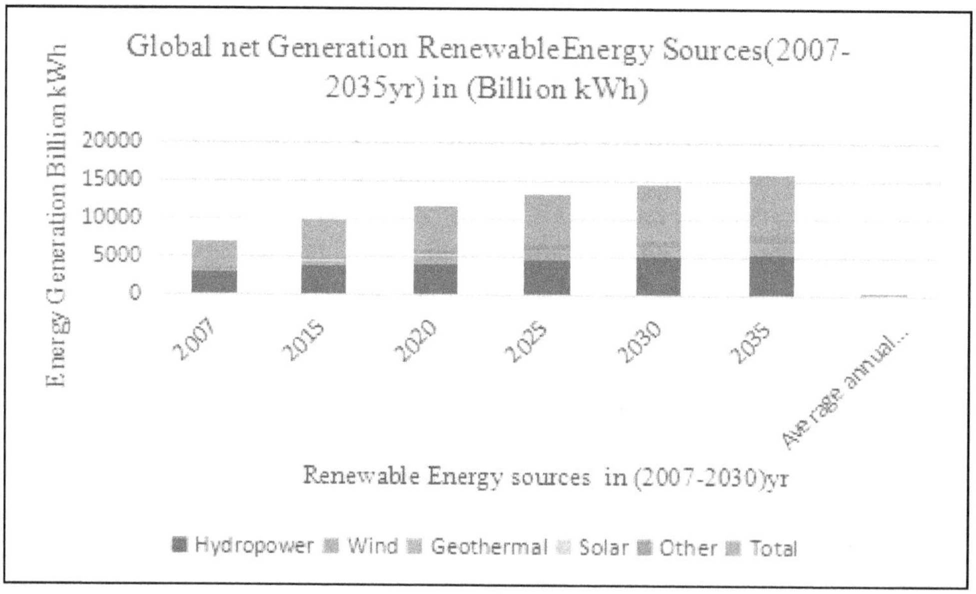

INDIAN ASPECTS OF RENEWABLE ENERGY

India makes steady progress while regularly setting targets to promote the use of renewable energy, which aids in reducing carbon dioxide emissions and aids in slowing global warming and improving air quality. The traditional vehicles and replacing them with electric vehicles by 2025. Though these initiatives have been adopted throughout India, renewable energy generation isn't being distributed uniformly. International Energy Agency (IEA). The future need for 90000 MW of electrical power will be met to meet the basic requirements in 2035, as forecasted by the results of load forecasting. Early in the development process, photovoltaic (PV) cells are more expensive and less efficient than other source of energy.

Switching to PV resources for electricity generation is encouraged by a decline in PV costs of around 80%. Many Indian states have implemented regulations that invite the private sector to boost RE generation and enable wheeling, banking, and reverse supply of electricity. Private firms are offered the benefits to encourage them to join the deal. Because of the third party's control of the network, buyers and sellers can transmit power using the third party's network. A form of renewable energy trading referred to as "Bay back" exists. In certain states, generation capacity is far greater than in most other states. RE capacity in India, as demonstrated in Figure 8, totals up to this presentation's information is derived from the MNRE report, which was published on February 29, 2020. It is shown that only 10 states in India generate more than 1,000 MW of renewable energy. Solar and wind energy generation had a larger percentage of India's total renewable energy generation. All 29 states in the country are generated by the table. States in India are divided into those in the north, south, east, west, and central and into the northeast or southern region, depending on where each state is located. The analysis of the table shows that the north-eastern states have a deficient generation of 0 MW. The north-eastern states of India have a very small amount of renewable energy sources (RES) generation, being provided by a small-scale hydroelectric power industry. Their poor production is primarily due to the weather and geographical features. Due to the country's cold climate and wet summers, the generation of energy through solar and wind is limited.

Because of this, the wind (WE) and solar (SE) exposure necessary to produce economically unfeasible. According to 54° C, these states can reach a maximum temperature of 30 degrees Celsius. Nevertheless, the greatest amount of precipitation occurs in the northeast of India, with an annual average of 11,418 mm. Because of an annual deluge and a wealth of river water, it is possible to get a generation of smaller hydropower in these states. Goa's smallest RE generation state. It is difficult to build anything there because it is the tiniest state. As a coastal state, it has the option of harnessing wave and tidal power. The problem has not been solved, owing of a lack of resources and the state's policies.

Table 1 reveals that SE source and WE source generation is the greatest in southern states. The massive generation is a result of the states' climatic conditions and the government's policies. There are several different state-level organizations that are responsible for promoting and maintaining the green energy by introducing new policies and promoting general awareness. From Table 1, we can see that most of the states in which wind power is generated have a low MW. Even though India has plenty of wind, the lack of instruments, money, and industry expertise has made things difficult. Problems with gaining grid connection and construction approvals, as well as with R&D and the transmission infrastructure also plague the situation. Due to these barriers, poor wind energy generation exists. Several states, including (AP), (KA), (TN), (GU), (RA), and (MR), are overcoming electricity generation issues, but Maharashtra leads the way with wind farm capacity of over 4000 MW. The quick winds in those regions have led to a massive increase in offshore wind capacity, and new policies, such as offshore wind energy policies and wind bidding schemes, have helped. As of month of Feb of 2020, the total green energy capacity in India was 86.76 GW. Despite an increase in the potential for off-grid renewable power, the on-grid renewable power capacity has decreased. The top Indian states for renewable energy production are KA, TN, and GU. The installed renewable energy capacity in KA, TN, and GU the three most populous states in India is, respectively, 15,232 MW, 14,335 MW, and 10,511 MW. The progress of solar and wind energy installation, as well as the current capacity of renewable energy resources. This meant that these three states of India which were previously analysed and explained in detail became the context for the choice we are currently discussing. It was determined how much progress had been made in each state as well as which plants were involved in each renewable energy sector and what sorts of policies were in place.

Hydro Power Source

The power produced by hydropower accounts can potentially supply up to 870 GW, or 17 percent of the total power produced in the world. The remaining 10 percent of this power is produced through large hydroelectric dams; by small plants with the run-of-river method, the remaining 10 percent is produced. The long-term limitations of large hydro due to the fact that many large rivers have already been dammed cannot be avoided.

Wind Power Source

Wind power technology, among all other technologies reviewed in this report, has the second-highest rate of growth, at 34 percent annually. The technology is fully mature and straightforward, and extensive experience is available in a few countries. Despite being limited to land, wind turbines have been successful due to their large economies of scale. These have led to wind farms being deployed offshore. However, the wind energy industry is still very competitive. In total, wind power currently provides 120 GW of installed capacity, or about 1.5 percent of the world's total generation of electricity, with an average capacity factor of 25 percent. The fastest-growing technology in the field is photovoltaic, with annual growth rates of 40 percent. As one of the largest markets, the former place of prominence was held by remote power supplies, but recently the developed countries have pursued the residential-roof deployment programs, changing the scenario. It is difficult to know the global capacity of photovoltaic modules because they are installed in small quantities. The current estimate is that 9 GW of them are in use. Generation globally is 12 TWh if the average capacity factor is 15 percent.

Thermal Solar Power

Thermal solar power, also known as concentrating solar power, has attracted renewed interest in recent years. The world's existing 1.5 GW of solar power is produced by a combination of trough, dish, and Fresnel systems in large-scale plants. Solar-power plants work well with standard thermal plants because they can be used as energy-saving fuel alternatives. Capacity factors typically sit at 20 percent but can exceed 40 percent when high-capacity heat transfer fluids are used for storage on an hourly basis.

Geothermal Power

Since 1920, geothermal power has been used for energy production. Some countries draw a high percentage of their electricity from geothermal reservoirs, though they only make up 10 GW globally. The performance of a geothermal plant is dependent on the quality of the resource. For the sake of using steam turbines, low-temperature resources must go through one or two flashing processes. Although the global electricity generation rose by only 4 percent annually and was around 60 TWh in 2013, average capacity factors of 70 percent are within reach, with 90 percent being possible. Despite its great technical potential, geothermal power is hobbled by two major hurdles: the question of whether it can be economically used, and the very high cost of drilling. It takes only a short while before new oil wells are dug in.

Biomass Power

Biomass power is not a primary application of biomass, but it is still used in a handful of industries, including pulp and sugar manufacturing. The interest in alternative energy sources was spurred described the 1980 reintroduction of biodiesel as an alternative energy source. Biomass is the leading alternative power source option in use today. In the last 30 years, extensive research has been conducted on the use of biomass to produce transportation fuels in researched the various methods of making bioethanol, as well as the fuel's global production trends. Biomass-based transportation fuels of the modern era designed mathematical models for the generation.

Energy Mixed With Renewable Resources

Energy from renewable sources is produced by harnessing natural phenomena. Energy sources for these technologies include solar radiation, wind, water flow, biomass, gravitational forces, and geothermal heat. These resources are extremely powerful, though, due to their dispersion and the difficulties in accessing them, they are hard to tap. Most of them are intermittent, and they also differ by region. The most progress over the last few years has been the increase in efficiency.

Sustainable Development

It evolved at a faster rate than ever before over the past decades. New technologies, new climate knowledge and new political and economic configurations make global energy systems assessments outdated faster than before. As the industrial revolution started, many new and intensive systems, especially in the low-power sector, began to develop quickly in the world. As evolution accelerated, humans began to greatly increase their power output with the aid of technology. To reach various objectives, such as generating electricity, heating enclosed spaces, or moving transportation vehicles, energy systems typically combine different types of energy: thermal, mechanical, and electrical. A system-based approach to problem solving can be used because of the nature of energy systems. The decision makers of energy systems often must consider multiple local, regional or global objectives (physical, financial or environmental). In Chabhadiya, Srivastava, and Pathak (2021), sustainable development is an excellent idea today, which involves pursuing a variety of objectives, including energy management, in various economic activities. The transition to a sustainable path for the global energy system has been identified as a priority policy objective. The deregulation of the electricity market requires efficient, safe operation and a simplified energy system that can respond quickly to changing circumstances. In addition, it is necessary to coordinate different utility decisions affecting the same market. The issues of energy system engineering, particularly at decision and planning stages. The authors are stated this additional in-depth analysis and decision-making capability enables.

Figure 2. Electricity generation technology costs in United States in 2020-2050

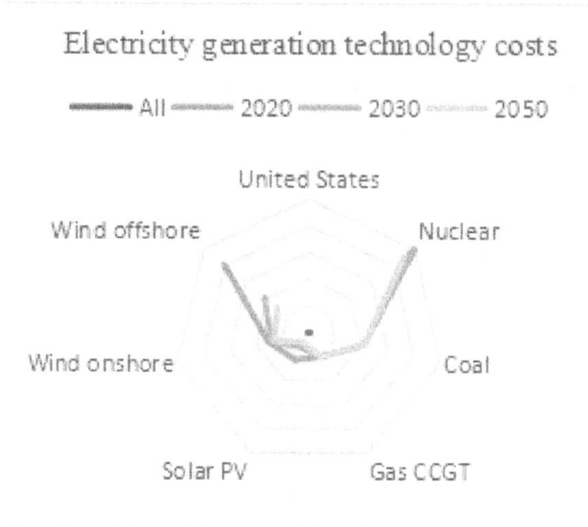

Figure 3. Electricity generation technology costs in European Union in 2020-2050

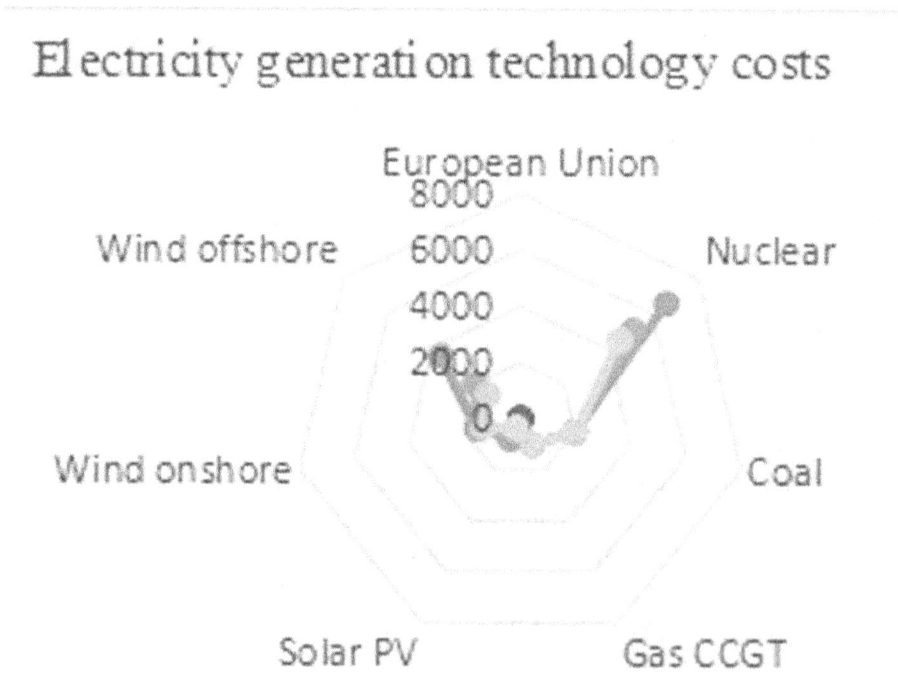

Figure 4. Electricity generation technology costs of China in 2020-2050

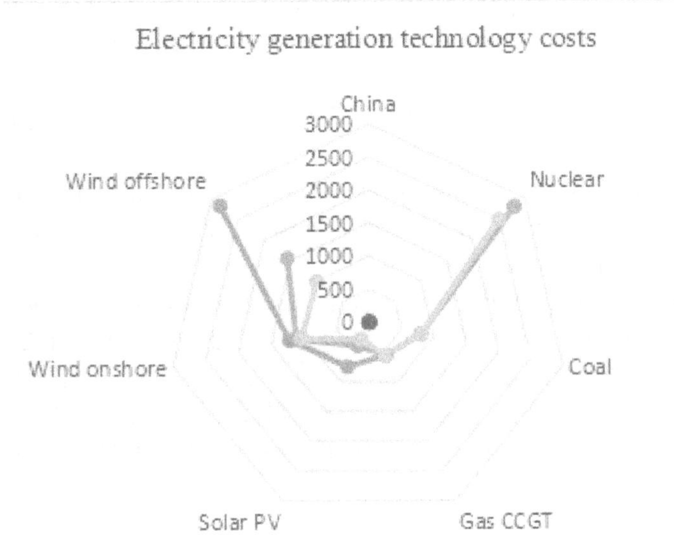

Figure 5. Electricity generation technology costs of India in 2020-2050

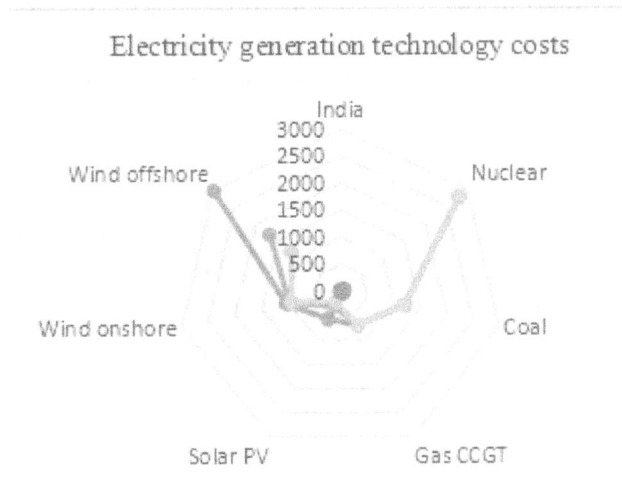

INDIA'S RENEWABLE ENERGY SECTOR ARE

- In Thiruselvi, Kumar, Kumar, Lay, Aathika, Mani, and Show (2021), Indian Renewable Energy Development Agency Ltd. (IREDA) has called for bids from solar module manufacturers to set up solar manufacturing(SM) at the cost Rs. 4,500 crore (US$ 616.76 million) (PLI) scheme, which offers incentives for setting up new solar manufacturing units.

- The Competition Commission of India (CCI) approved Renewal Power's existing shareholders' swap of their equity in the company with shares of Renewal Global in June 2021. This move was supported by the CCI, who additionally approved a reverse triangular merger of Renewal Global's subsidiary with RMG II.
- The India Renewables Dashboard was launched by CEA and CEEW-CEF in April 2021 to provide details about India's RE projects.
- In 2021, inviting stakeholders, including information received from energy transmission companies, the Indian Reserve Bank, the HDFC Bank, ICICI Bank, the industrial, solar and wind industry and government associations.
- A Memorandum of Understanding on cooperation between India and the Franco-Republic in the field of renewable energy was approved by the Union Cabinet in March 2021.
- A 40-percent subsidy plan for a 3 KW solar system in residences was initiated in March 2021 by Haryana in accordance with the guidelines of the Ministry of New and Renewable Energy for the promotion of solar energy in the country. The installation of 4-10 KW solar systems by designated companies is subject to a 20% subsidy.
- In March 2021, Gram Ojala, India's most ambitious project to provide rural poor Rs. 10 LED bulbs (USD 0.14), helping the country to advance its climate change and self-reliance policies, came into effect.
- Besides giving the Solar Energy Corporation of India (SECI) a capital infusion of Rs. 1 000 crores (US$ 137.04 million), the Indian Government granted an Indian Renewable Energy Development Agency Rs. 1.500 crores (US$ 205.57 million).
- Taxes on solar inverters(SI) increased from 5 to 20 percent to support domestic manufacturing, while tariffs on solar lanterns increased from 5 to 15 percent.
- The 1,5-megawatt solar energy project in November 2020 Ladakh received at the Leh Indian Air Force Station under the Make in India Center Government initiative.
- A $1.07 billion Production-Linked Incentive (PLI) scheme for five years to produce high efficiency solar photovoltaic modules are set.
- On 17 November a memorandum of understanding with the Government of Goa was signed between the Minister and venture RE Department (DNRE) energy efficiency services limited (EESL), which discusses the launch of the first Indian Convergence Project in the state.

Figure 6. Total emission of India in 2011-2016

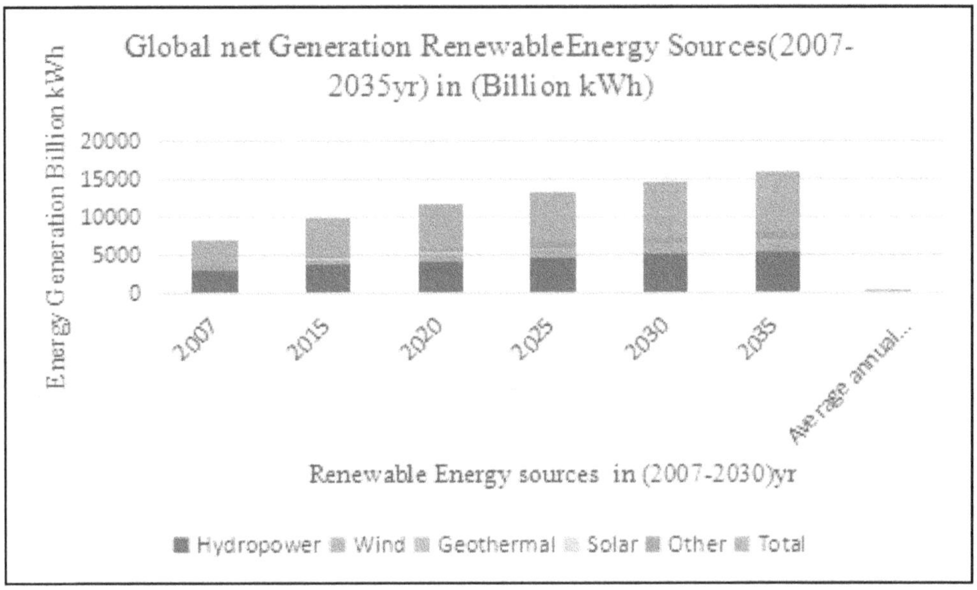

Figure 7. Sustainable development 2019-2050

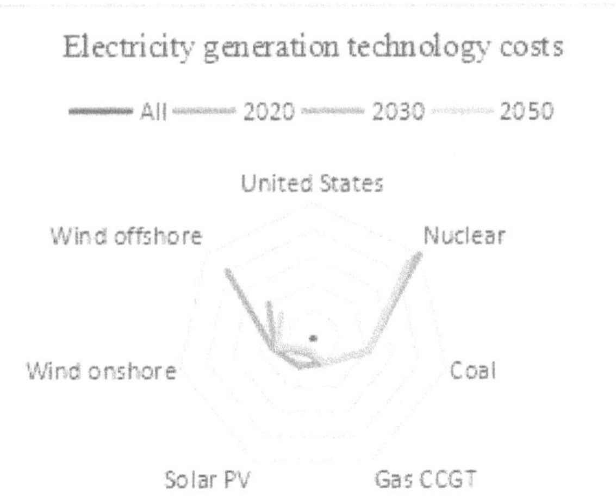

The government announced in October 2020 that an inter-ministerial committee, Aayog would lead energy modelling research and studies in the west, India plans to generate 30 GW in Rajasthan and Gujarat. The Delhi government decides to turn the thermal power plant Rajghat into a solar park of 5,000 KW. The Indian government proposes to spend $238 million for a national mission to advance ultra-supercritical coal-cleaning technologies. In Badi (2012) and Shiva, Badi, Shekarappa, Babu, Mahapatra,Vedik, and Rangarajan (2022), the Indian Railways is introducing an energy efficiency plan to reduce emissions by 33% by 2030.

Figure 8. Electrical generation capacity in GW from 2019-2016

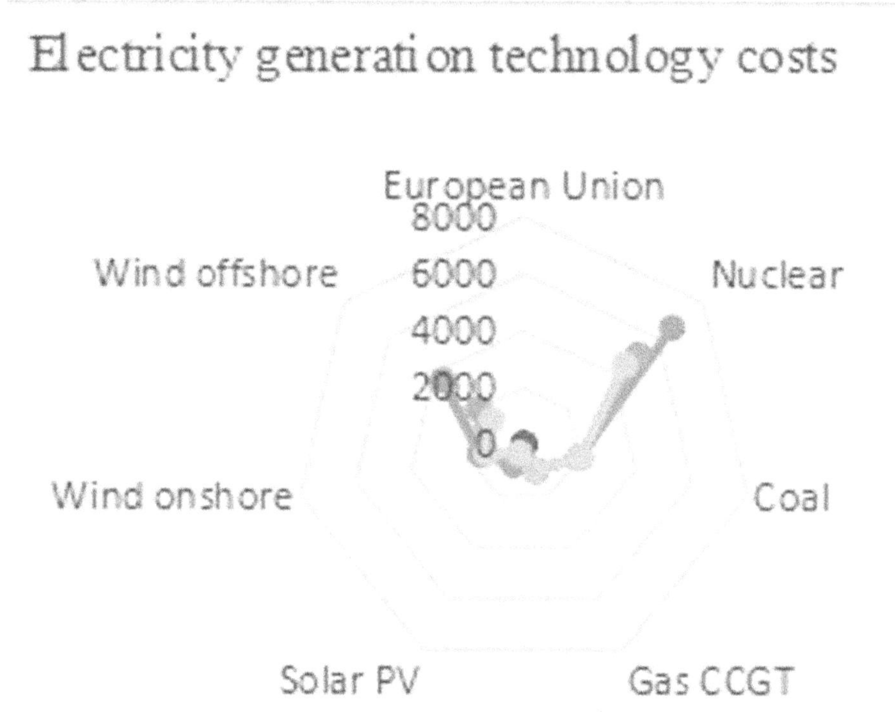

FUTURE SCOPE

The development of renewable or sustainable energy systems depends greatly on energy policy. Policy-makers need to build policies about the diverse options and thorough evaluations of numerous scenarios.

CONCLUSION

Nobody thought that until the 1960s there was a better way to generate power. Their highly integrated nature makes them vulnerable to supply chain disruption. The paradigm of electricity delivery, in particular, falls short. Although these decentralized small systems are still in infancy, they have become a viable alternative to the traditional centralized energy supply, which is more dependent on a single source of energy. The scientists expected to decentralize the energy supply, which they believed would be particularly beneficial to the environment. Due to the multiplication of technological options, decentralized power planning is becoming more complicated and difficult to decide.

REFERENCES

Abujarad, S. Y., Mustafa, M. W., & Jamian, J. J. (2017). Recent approaches of unit commitment in the presence of intermittent renewable energy resources: A review. *Renewable & Sustainable Energy Reviews*, *70*, 215–223. doi:10.1016/j.rser.2016.11.246

Alemzero, D., Acheampong, T., & Huaping, S. (2021). Prospects of wind energy deployment in Africa: Technical and economic analysis. *Renewable Energy*, *179*, 652–666. doi:10.1016/j.renene.2021.07.021

Andrew, R. M. (2020). Timely estimates of India's annual and monthly fossil CO< sub> 2</sub> emissions. *Earth System Science Data*, *12*(4), 2411–2421.

Arent, D. J., Bragg-Sitton, S. M., Miller, D. C., Tarka, T. J., Engel-Cox, J. A., Boardman, R. D., Balash, P. C., Ruth, M. F., Cox, J., & Garfield, D. J. (2021). Multi-input, multi-output hybrid energy systems. *Joule*, *5*(1), 47–58. doi:10.1016/j.joule.2020.11.004

Badi, M. (2012). *Power Quality Improvement using passive shunt filter, TCR and TSC combination* [Doctoral dissertation].

Cantarero, M. M. V. (2020). Of renewable energy, energy democracy, and sustainable development: A roadmap to accelerate the energy transition in developing countries. *Energy Research & Social Science*, *70*, 101716. doi:10.1016/j.erss.2020.101716

Chabhadiya, K., Srivastava, R. R., & Pathak, P. (2021). Growth projections against set-target of renewable energy and resultant impact on emissions reduction in India. *Environmental Engineering Research*, *26*(2).

Das, S. P. K., Shah, S. C. N., & Suyal, S. S. (2020). Indian Renewable Energy Development Agency Limited (A Government of India Enterprise) Board of Directors. *Water and Energy International*, *63*(8), 35–36.

Gupta, A. R., & Bonds, G. (2020). Financing India's renewable energy vision. *ORF Issue Brief, 336*.

Hussain, M. W., Pradhan, B., Gao, X. Z., Reddy, K. H. K., & Roy, D. S. (2020). Clonal selection algorithm for energy minimization in software defined networks. *Applied Soft Computing, 96*, 106617.

Irfan, M., Zhao, Z. Y., Ikram, M., Gilal, N. G., Li, H., & Rehman, A. (2020). Assessment of India's energy dynamics: Prospects of solar energy. *Journal of Renewable and Sustainable Energy*, *12*(5), 053701.

Johnsson, F., Kjärstad, J., & Rootzén, J. (2019). The threat to climate change mitigation posed by the abundance of fossil fuels. *Climate Policy*, *19*(2), 258–274. doi:10.1080/14693062.2018.1483885

Kasdan, M., Kuhl, L., & Kurukulasuriya, P. (2021). The evolution of transformational change in multilateral funds dedicated to financing adaptation to climate change. *Climate and Development*, *13*(5), 427–442. doi:10.1080/17565529.2020.1790333

Kazi, S. R., Short, M., Isafiade, A. J., & Biegler, L. T. (2021). Heat exchanger network synthesis with detailed exchanger designs—2. Hybrid optimization strategy for synthesis of heat exchanger networks. *AIChE Journal. American Institute of Chemical Engineers*, *67*(1), e17057.

Kim, H., Park, S., & Lee, J. (2021). Is renewable energy acceptable with power grid expansion? A quantitative study of South Korea's renewable energy acceptance. *Renewable & Sustainable Energy Reviews, 139*, 110584.

Majid, M. A. (2020). Renewable energy for sustainable development in India: Current status, future prospects, challenges, employment, and investment opportunities. *Energy, Sustainability and Society, 10*(1), 1–36.

Mukherjee, D., & Chakrabarti, S. (2004). *Fundamentals of renewable energy systems*. New Age International.

Oehler-Şincai, I. M. (2021). Dominant Contribution of the Developing Countries to the Renewable Energy Sector 1. *Global Economic Observer, 9*(1), 195–202.

Pradhan, B., Reddy, K. H., Roy, D. S., & Mohanta, D. K. (2011, December). Intentional islanding of electric power systems in a grid computing framework: a graph-theoretic approach. In *2011 International Conference on Recent Trends in Information Systems* (pp. 156-160). IEEE. 10.1109/ReTIS.2011.6146859

Priyadarshini, M. (2021). *Status of renewable energy in India and a case of financing viability of wind energy project* [Doctoral dissertation]. Delhi Technological University.

Reynolds, C., Boulding, A., Pollock, H., Sweet, N., Ruiz, J., & Draeger de Teran, T. (2020). *Halving Food Loss and Waste in the EU by 2030: The major steps needed to accelerate progress*. Academic Press.

Sawhney, A. (2021). Striving towards a circular economy: Climate policy and renewable energy in India. *Clean Technologies and Environmental Policy, 23*(2), 491–499. doi:10.100710098-020-01935-7

Shiva, C. K., Badi, M., Shekarappa, G. S., Babu, R., Mahapatra, S., Vedik, B., & Rangarajan, S. S. (2022, May). Solution for reactive power planning problem using salp swarm algorithm. In AIP Conference Proceedings: Vol. 2418. *No. 1* (p. 040001). AIP Publishing LLC.

Sim, L. C., & Mills, R. (2021). Low Carbon Energy in the Middle East and North Africa: Panacea or Placebo? *Low Carbon Energy in the Middle East and North Africa*, 1-17.

Thiruselvi, D., Kumar, P. S., Kumar, M. A., Lay, C. H., Aathika, S., Mani, Y., ... Show, P. L. (2021). A critical review on global trends in biogas scenario with its up-gradation techniques for fuel cell and future perspectives. *International Journal of Hydrogen Energy, 46*(31), 16734–16750.

Tsung-Han, T., Bin, X., Shih-Ming, K., & Yen-Chiang, C. (2020). China's Diplomatic Strategy towards Climate Change Negotiations in the Post-Paris Agreement Era. *China. International Journal, 18*(2), 186–203.

Vaka, M., Walvekar, R., Rasheed, A. K., & Khalid, M. (2020). A review on Malaysia's solar energy pathway towards carbon-neutral Malaysia beyond Covid'19 pandemic. *Journal of Cleaner Production, 273*, 122834. doi:10.1016/j.jclepro.2020.122834 PMID:32834565

Chapter 18
Smart Cities:
Operational Concepts for an Elusive Framework

Nelson deMatos
https://orcid.org/0000-0002-6263-5007
ESGHT and CinTurs, Universidade do Algarve, Portugal

Célia M. Q. Ramos
https://orcid.org/0000-0002-3413-4897
ESGHT and CinTurs, Universidade do Algarve, Portugal

ABSTRACT

Human and technological development allowed cities to be built upon structures to increase the quality of life of their citizens. But evolution also brought challenges like high consumption patterns and reduced natural resources. The chapter aims to provide common ground among the main concepts of smart cities and shed light on the often-elusive framework of the "smart city," highlighting the need to incorporate a more holistic approach and integrate sustainable quality of life. A conceptual model was proposed and discussed, framing the dimensions: nature, infrastructure, technology, services, sustainability, and social. The influence of technology to better manage was also taken into account, without neglecting the importance of efficiency and innovation in a holistic system. The conclusions reinforce the composite nature, the need for more consistency, measurement scales, and the interconnectivity between management and its citizens, which is needed for better population well-being.

INTRODUCTION

Since pre-historic times, the human species have had to adapt to environmental and life circumstances, and the natural answer to those always-changing circumstances has been the creation and development of place to live, habitations and cities (Schuurman, Baccarne, De Marez, & Mechant, 2012). Thus, nowadays, like in the past, similar decisions are made by citizens striving for a large concentration of resources and

DOI: 10.4018/979-8-3693-0744-1.ch018

facilities (Perera, Zaslavsky, Christen, & Georgakopoulos, 2014) with the cooperation and incentive of governments, organizations, and agencies around the world, particularly in the western countries.

However, challenges arise since, according to the United Nations (2015) projections, the world population (7.3 billion by mid-2015) show a tendency to grow. Consequently, local and national authorities and organizations (private and public) will, like all citizens worldwide, be pressured constantly in every aspect of their daily routine in the cities to keep their life quality. The pressuring dilemma lies in the metabolism of cities, in which societal consumption transforms the input of goods and resources into the output of waste (Albino, Berardi, & Dangelico, 2015) and pollution.

This predicament led since the late 90s some scholars, such as Graham and Marvin (2004), to address the potential of technology to create better management systems and platforms to reduce consumption and intensify sustainability potential. The Internet of Things (IoT) (Perera et al., 2014; Vlacheas et al., 2013; Zanella, Bui, Castellani, Vangelista, & Zorzi, 2014) aims to "connect billions of sensors to the Internet and expects to use them for efficient and effective resource management in Smart Cities" (Perera et al., 2014, p. 1) presents itself as an opportunity to attain this objective, i.e., sustainability. Furthermore, environmental concerns have dictated new trends in the citizens' behaviour and caused changes in how organizations, governments and agencies act to reduce those costs and consumption. Sustainability is key, either through the promotion of natural capital and resources (Albino et al., 2015) or by the reduction of consumption (Caird, 2018).

In this environment characterized by rapid and complex societal changes, Smart Cities (SC) managers and stakeholders are required to define strategies rapidly and incisively to improve performance, engagement, and connection with its citizens in the urban setting. It also requires information and communication technologies (ICTs) (McFarlane, & Söderström, 2017; Schuurman et al., 2012; Toppeta, 2010) to be addressed, including problems related to management productivity through the different organizations (Chourabi et al., 2012). However, despite societal and technological developments, a better understanding and balance between these two parties, and how it contributes to a better management of SC is lacking.

The reason lies in the highly complex nature of SC, which consists of "a collection of elements that act independently of one another but nevertheless manage to act in concert" (Mora, Bolici & Deakin, 2017, p. 3). Thus, the relationships between the various elements (e.g. ICTs, IoT) must be assessed with more profundity, without neglecting the social perspective. As Turcu (2013) notes, a more anthropocentric approach should be taken for cities to be able to respond to their citizens' needs, which means SC should provide sustainable solutions as inputs towards better and improved social and economic outputs (e.g., live conditions). One such example can be found in Venezia or Florence in Italy, which strives to keep the balance between the tourism economic and social development with the assistance of technology to build and create a smarter city (Papa, Gargiulo, & Galderisi, 2013), to improve its conservation (Lazzeretti, Capone, & Cinti, 2011), to improve human conditions (and quality of life) (Kummitha, & Crutzen, 2017) and to contribute to environmental sustainability (Ahvenniemi, Huovila, Pinto-Seppä, & Airaksinen, 2017).

This chapter seeks to provide a common ground among the main concepts of SC, regarding its definition, dimensions and influential factors, that considers the influential variables and the relation between them. The study will be based on a review of the literature from 1997 to 2017. First, the origin and development of SC will be introduced in section 2, followed by the various definitions and dimensions. Next, the influential variables of SC are highlighted. Afterwards, a conceptual model is described in section 3, encompassing the different perspectives reviewed under the literature review will be presented and discussed in section 4. In the end in section 5, some conclusions and implications to the academia will be shown.

SMART CITY (SC) CONCEPT

Origin and Development of the Concept

The origin of the SC concept was initially used in 1994 (Dameri & Cocchia, 2013) to respond to a need to frame the new understandings about urban and cities technological development (Anthopoulos, 2017). As the author claims "smart city was not the initial term that scholars used" (Anthopoulos, 2017, p. 13). Only at the 1990s, did the scholars started using terms similar to SC, such as virtual city (see e.g., Graham & Aurigi, 1997) in their search for new definitions regarding the new period or era, in which (among other) the technological progress, social and economic developments (e.g., globalization), environmental concerns, were the main global topics. These challenges awoke the attention and support of political forces, public and private organizations (e.g., IBM) and institutions (e.g., European Union) to the SC "endeavor" (Zygiaris, 2013; Reddy et al, 2023). As seen in Figure 1, from the initial practices in 1994 (e.g. first digital practice Amsterdam), and 1999 at Dubai, to the primary SC attempts in creating rankings by the European Smart city group in 2007 (e.g. Giffinger, Fertner, Kramar, Meijers, Pichler-Milanovic, 2007) indicators (Urban indicators, UN-Habitat, 1996) and standards (ISO, 2014), overall more than two decades passed.

Figure 1. Smart City evolution timeline
Source: Adapted from Anthopoulos (2017, p. 14)

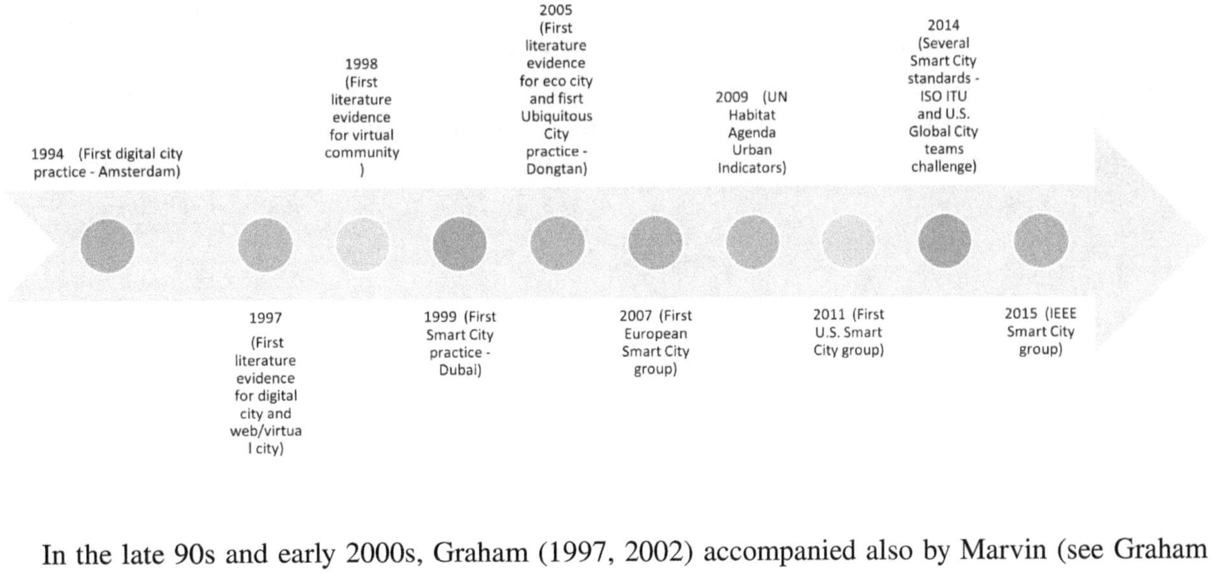

In the late 90s and early 2000s, Graham (1997, 2002) accompanied also by Marvin (see Graham & Marvin, 1999, 2004), brought forth several seminal books and papers addressing: a) the integration of telecommunications b) the development of network infrastructures and the technological mobilities (within the urban planning scope), with the purpose of offering a comprehensive theoretical and practical understanding on the cities at that time, but also about the future, i.e., cybercities. Hence, the continuous efforts from scholars and several organizations (e.g. United Nations) permitted the development of a more robust and sounder theoretical framework.

On the other hand, it also led to the first conflicts with grey literature technicians and researchers, i.e., research and technical documents produced by governments, agencies or organizations external to the mainstream and traditional academic and/or commercial channels. As point by Mora et al. (2017) in their literature review of 1067 documents, which included academic and grey literature, SC research was found to be fragmented and to lack cohesion. Moreover, two distinct developments were found by the authors, one supporting a holistic perspective on SC, originating from peer-reviewed publications produced by European universities, and the other relating to a technocentric view of the construct, by American business communities within the grey literature. Nevertheless, despite the conflicts arising from different perspectives, the theoretical body of knowledge continued to evolve, and new trends became evident. According to Chourabi et al. (2012) these trends focused on the conjugation of three different perspectives: (i) digital city – which argues that the Internet-of-Things and all the technology has an ubiquos communication (Khan, Khan, Zaheer, & Khan, 2012; Perera et al., 2014; Schaffers, Komninos, Pallot, Trousse, Nilsson, & Oliveira, 2011), (ii) green city – which seeks the integration of environmental and sustainability concerns (Kramers, Höjer, Lövehagen, & Wangel, 2014) and (iii) knowledge city - where the knowledge, skills, information, efficiency, planning associated with cities organizations' management are central elements (Kramers et al., 2014).

Defining Smart City (SC)

The SC concept remains, after three decades (Hanley, 2017) a relevant, popular and fast-growing topic (Mora et al., 2017). In Table 1 it is possible to see the evolution of the definitions presented overtime regarding SC. Consequently, Albino et al. (2016, p. 4) opinion is that SC is a fuzzy concept to the degree that "the range of conceptual variants is often obtained by replacing "smart" with alternative adjectives", such as intelligent or even digital. Another critic offered, is the repetitive reference (direct or indirect) to cities' performance, as one of the main goals for cities to be "smarter" (Castelnovo, Misuraca, & Savoldelli, 2016). In spite of these diverging positions, other authors such as Chourabi et al., (2012, p. 2289) argue that "One way to conceptualize a smart city is as an icon of a sustainable and liveable city".

Table 1. Definitions of a smart city

Construct Definition	Literature Source
A city well performing in a forward-looking way in these six characteristics [smart economy, smart people, smart governance, smart mobility, smart environment, and smart living], built on the smart combination of endowments and activities of self-decisive, independent and aware citizens.	Giffinger, Fertner, Kramar, Kalasek, Pichler-Milanović, and Meijers (2007, p. 11).
A city "connecting the physical infrastructure, the IT infrastructure, the social infrastructure, and the business infrastructure to leverage the collective intelligence of the city".	Harrison, Eckman, Hamilton, Hartswick, Kalagnanam, Paraszczak, and Williams (2010, p. 2)
"The use of Smart Computing technologies to make the critical infrastructure components and services of a city—which include city administration, education, healthcare, public safety, real estate, transportation, and utilities—more intelligent, interconnected, and efficient".	Washburn, Sindhu, Balaouras, Dines, Hayes and Nelson (2010, p. 2).
"A smart city infuses information into its physical infrastructure to improve conveniences, facilitate mobility, add efficiencies, conserve energy, improve the quality of air and water, identify problems and fix them quickly, recover rapidly from disasters, collect data to make better decisions, deploy resources effectively, and share data to enable collaboration across entities and domains."	Nam and Pardo (2011, p. 284).
"Smart city as a high-tech intensive and advanced city that connects people, information and city elements using new technologies in order to create a sustainable, greener city, competitive and innovative commerce, and an increased life quality with a straightforward administration and a good maintenance system".	Bakıcı, Almirall, and Wareham (2012, p. 139).
"Being a smart city means using all available technology and resources in an intelligent and coordinated manner to develop urban centers that are at once integrated, habitable, and sustainable."	Barrionuevo, Berrone, and Ricart (2012, p. 50).
"A smart city is understood as a certain intellectual ability that addresses several innovative socio-technical and socio-economic aspects of growth. These aspects lead to smart city conceptions as "green" referring to urban infrastructure for environment protection and reduction of CO2 emission, "interconnected" related to revolution of broadband economy, "intelligent" declaring the capacity to produce added value information from the processing of city's real-time data from sensors and activators, whereas the terms "innovating", "knowledge" cities interchangeably refer to the city's ability to raise innovation based on knowledgeable and creative human capital."	Zygiaris (2013, p. 218).
"Smart Cities initiatives try to improve urban performance by using data, information and information technologies (IT) to provide more efficient services to citizens, to monitor and optimize existing infrastructure, to increase collaboration among different economic actors, and to encourage innovative business models in both the private and public sectors."	Marsal-Llacuna Colomer-Llinàs, and Meléndez-Frigola (2014, p. 618).

Source: Author's elaboration.

Each definition listed in Table 1, presents a perspective which not always is congruent, therefore, based on the previous authors' definitions in Table 1, a word cloud generator was used to retrieve the most common, frequent, words authors employed, which can be seen in the Figure 2, where it is possible to distinguish three main words: City, Smart and Information. Topics central to SC and the information era. However, in a second level of less frequent words, words such as: innovative, data, intelligent, improve and urban can be seen. All these words, can be useful words to understand the concept of SC.

Figure 2. Words employed to define SC
Source: Author's elaboration using word cloud generator.

Nevertheless, another approach could be attempted, one, which proposes a definition in which, based on the theoretical framework and the previous words found, a new definition can be presented:

A smart city uses tangible and intangible capital, to design critical infrastructures and implement activities with the use of ICT, in an innovative, intelligent and optimized way, so that citizens may be more informed and their quality of life improved in a more sustainable urban environment.

The author's proposed definition, which will be used in the present paper, denotes the importance of comprehending the tangible (e.g., waste, water, electricity systems, housing) and intangible (e.g., security, skills, well-being) capital, but it also highlights the need to design and plan infrastructures and activities (both at the core of the SC concept). Moreover, it reinforces the role of innovation and technology, to provide more efficient, sustainable and liveable cities for its residents, and at the same time with environmental concerns and quality lifestyles.

Smart City Multi-Dimensions

The SC dimensions are a topic for intense debate among scholars with several assuming different positions. Among these, Giffinger et al. (2007) presented six categories of SC: governance, economy, mobility, people, environment and living. Later, Mandelson and Bradshaw (2009) added four more dimensions, to a total of 10 dimensions SC needed to consider: education, innovative services, health, ICT literacy, effective use of resources, public administration, regional economics, public safety, culture and recreation.

Contrasting to these positions, Nam and Pardo (2011) only suggested three dimensions: technology, people and institutions. Their model established a direct relationship between the people and the technology dimensions, as the drivers of change in the economy, environment, and community of SC. Lee, Hancock, and Hu (2014) on the other hand, developed an enlarged conceptual framework with five dimensions: urban openness, service innovation, partnership formation, urban proactiveness, smart city infrastructure integration, and smart city governance. For the latter, they suggested five more subdimensions: smart city strategy, a dedicated organization for promoting the smart city, smart city development and management processes, smart city principles, performance measurements.

Calzada and Cobo (2015) decided to explore and debate a cross-disciplinary research agenda about the hyper-connected societies and their digital natives. The authors suggested unplugging to be an advantage, and provide a conceptual framework with ten dimensions (who, how, systems, governance, information, what, space, design, socio-political processes, political economy) "…comprised a complex interdependent corpus driven by human-interaction meta-factors" (Calzada & Cobo, 2015, p. 37). Overall, the scholars' descriptions and arguments extend from the number of dimensions and Helixes (see e.g., Lombardi, Giordano, Farouh, & Yousef, 2012), since other comprehensive dimensions, such as the sustainable economy, governance, and ICT, among other, could be suggested (Tachizawa, Alvarez-Gil, & Montes-Sancho, 2015).

However, drawing on the definitions presented earlier and on the author's different perspectives, it is argued that SC dimensions could be grouped into six main clusters: a) Nature, b) Infrastructure, c) Technology, d) Services, e) Sustainability, f) Social. As seen in Figure 3, management is a central element influencing all the six dimensions, since managers will influence the degree of resources' consumption, processes used, technologies and services employed, and the level of sustainability that can be reached to attain better social quality of life. However, the dimensions in the figure still miss an order regarding their ranking and interrelationship.

Figure 3. Six dimensions of a smart city
Source: Author's elaboration.

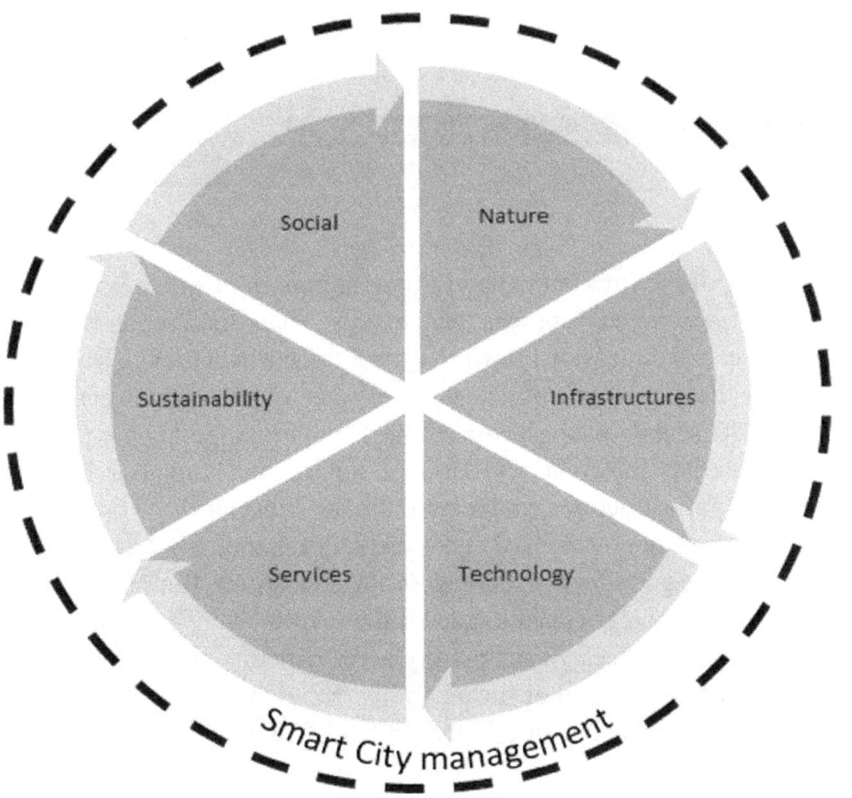

Therefore, as shown in Figure 4, SC development could be regarded as a flow in which a process composed of several steps (six), with each step representing an element of a whole organic entity (i.e., SC). To reach the end of the process, it would be necessary throughout all the steps to increase the innovation effort (as the arrow at the bottom shows), the level of efficiency would also increase (as the arrow on top shows). At the same time, the organic entity (SC) needs to perform several actions (e.g. from input data to output indicators) to improve the city development and its management throughout all the six dimensions.

Figure 4. Six dimensions flow of a smart city
Source: Author's elaboration.

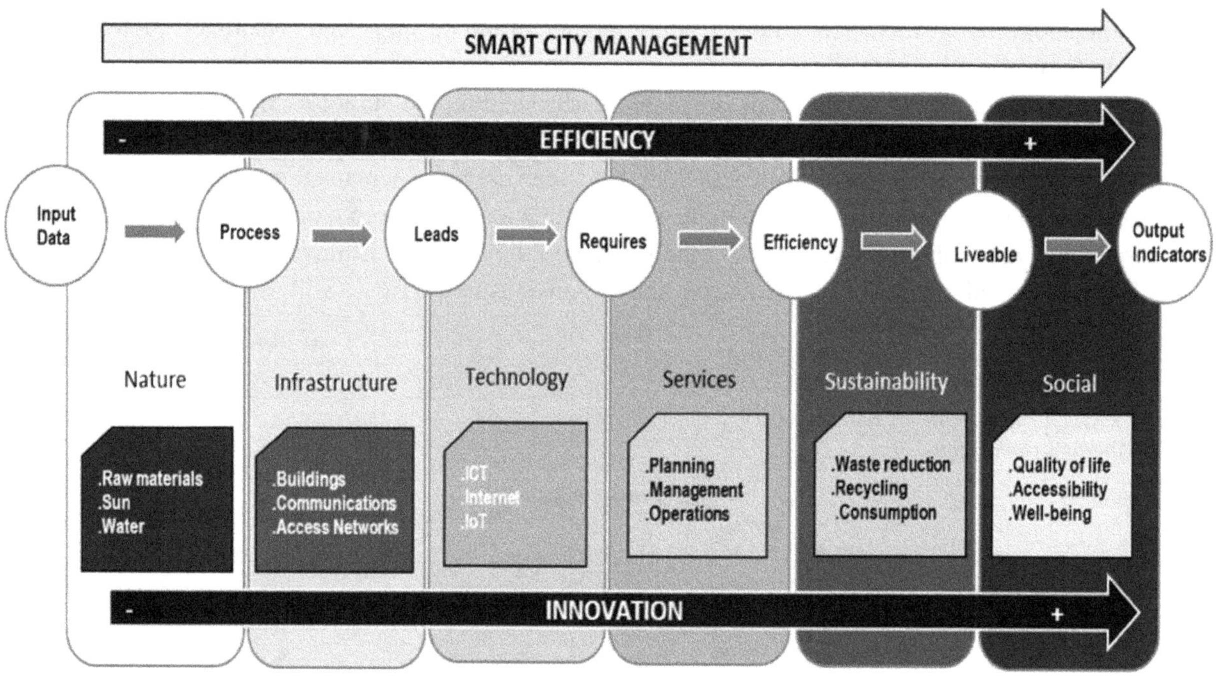

Thus, at the beginning of the flow is the nature-based dimension, which is composed of the nature elements (e.g., water, sun, wind) and resources (e.g., energy, water, food) upon which society and cities rely on the survive. The second dimension is infrastructure, upon which society trusts to accomplish their daily tasks and everyday life (e.g., roads, ports, airports, water, electricity power). The third dimension, technology (e.g., ICT, IoT, Mobile phones, cars, planes) supported the human progress, helped in the transformation of raw materials into goods and services. It permitted humans to have higher mobility or assisted in the building of infrastructures, an increase the life expectancy.

The fourth is services (economy) since SC and society, in general, rely on planners, managers, technicians to get the job done (e.g., human resources, skills, education). But particularly, economies and societies (including human resources education and training) which are constantly changing and being dominated more and more by services. Sustainability is the fifth dimension since one of the main concerns SCs have is to attain a higher level of sustainability due to the scarcity of resources and overflow of waste, pollution. The sixth, social dimension, the goal of SC and their citizens is to attain good living conditions and potentially people well-being. This dimension is at the top of the flow because it is the cities' fundamental or ultimate goal.

CONCEPTUAL MODEL

Drawing on a range of theoretical and a wide body of knowledge approaches (Albino et al., 2015; Calzada & Cobo, 2015; Hollands, 2015), it is argued in the following conceptual model (see Figure 5) the positive relationships (e.g., technology effects positively infrastructures) between the diverse dimensions that compose the SC concept, i.e., six dimensions (nature, infrastructure, technology, services, sustainability, social).

Figure 5. Six dimensions smart city conceptual model
Source: Author's elaboration

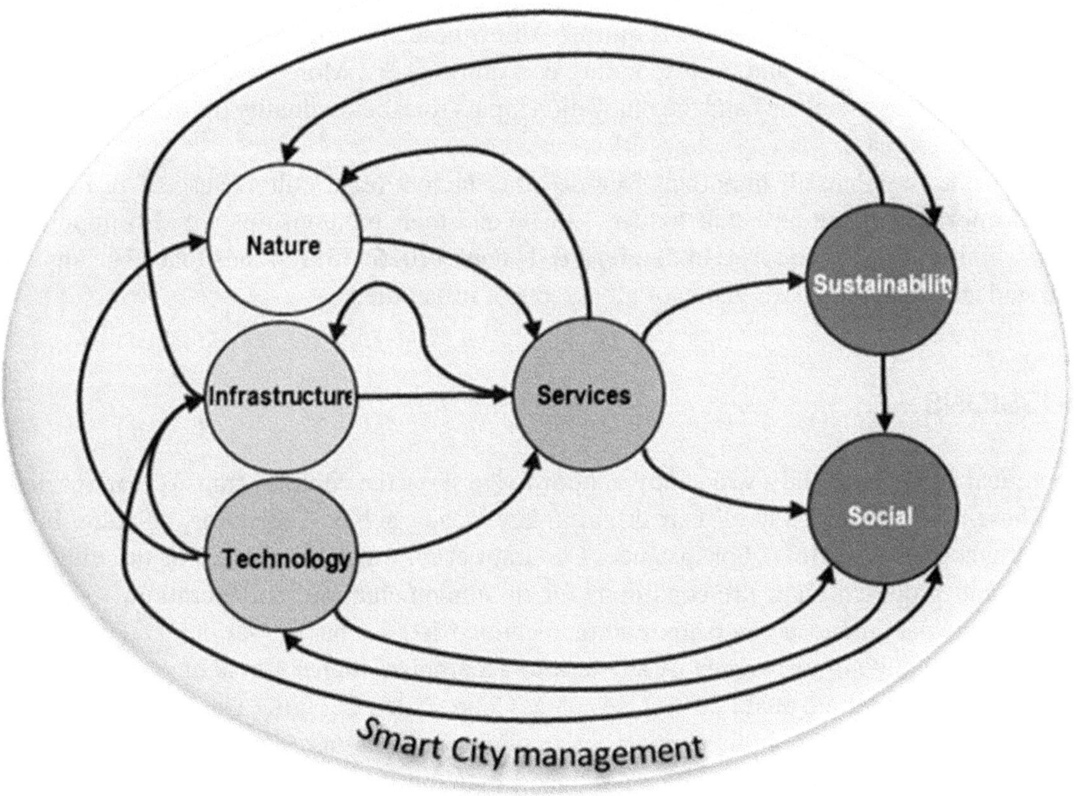

Nature dimension is one of the foundations upon infrastructures are created, and technology operates. In effect, raw materials, roads, habitations, cities, to name a few, are built and developed after the transformation of natural resources. These natural resources are transformed using technology to create the infrastructures to support the human life, and humans' desire and need to construct and live in large cities. Technology influences not only the capacity of cities dealing with the citizens demands (Harrison et al., 2010; Perera et al., 2014; Vlacheas et al. 2013; Zanella et al., 2014), particularly ICT (Ebrahim & Irani, 2005; Mandelson & Bradshaw, 2009), which functions as a key driver of SCs (Hollands, 2008).

The infrastructure dimension consists of a housing, building, roads, ports (i.e., man-made) structures indispensable for day-to-day tasks. The technology is considered to support services, infrastructure, nature and social, as a way to increase human well-being. (Chourabi et al., 2012; Gil-Garcia, & Pardo, 2005; Scholl, Barzilai-Nahon, Ahn, Olga & Barbara, 2009). The services, in which governance policies are defined to increase the economy growth, efficiency (i.e., education, skills, and training), together with leadership and better decision-making, are critical aspects for the success of any SC, contributing to the development of sustainability and at the same time to the social conditions of the population. These two dimensions infrastructure and services affect directly sustainability.

After SC reach satisfactory levels of sustainability, better living conditions can be provided for its citizens – social dimension (Giffinger et al., 2007; Turcu, 2013). This dimension impact on citizen's quality of life, but also, on their community participation and on governance actions. In this regard, Chourabi et al. (2012, p. 2292) affirm that "Addressing the topic of people and communities as part of smart cities is critical, and traditionally has been neglected on the expense of understanding more technological and policy aspects of smart cities." All of these six dimensions need to be managed by the organic Smart City entity and corresponding decision-makers. Moreover, all parties need to work together to increase the efficiency and the innovation inputs for a better quality of life of the SC residents and visitors (e.g. tourists).

In sum, while these are all important factors, other factors (e.g., culture, use of ICT, the role of formal and informal institutions, stakeholders' goals) and their relationships are also important, thus more opportunities for debate arise. In this regard, Hajduk (2016: 36) reminds that "The smart city is an integrated and comprehensive vision of all aspects of urban life."

DISCUSSIONS

The theoretical approaches and a wide body of knowledge show the complex transformations underway in SCs. These transformations have their origin in key areas, such as Technology, Nature, Infrastructure, Governance, ICTs or IoTs. For instance, Chourabi et al. (2012) reminded of the importance of governance and proposed eight pre-conditions for its implementation, collaboration, leadership and champion, participation and partnership, communication, data-exchange, service and application integration, accountability, transparency. A key task to accomplish higher levels of governance is using ICT. Several authors (Albino et al., 2015; Calzada & Cobo, 2015; Caragliu, Del Bo & Nijkamp, 2011; Hollands, 2015) have addressed this element, particularly Graham and Marvin seminal book in 1996, "Telecommunications and the City" which provided the first critical and state-of-the-art review of the relations between telecommunications and all aspects of city development and management. Another important element is the IoT, which theorizes people and things must be connected (using any network or service) at any moment or place.

This ideology faces a new and emergent challenge, the need for better and more reliable infrastructures since most of those platforms are now based on cloud technologies (Perera et al., 2014). On the other hand, it also requires ICT programs to improve the skills of employees and technicians. Ebrahim and Irani (2005) suggested in this regard, that challenges can be grouped in IT skills (education and training for employees) and organization dimension (more cooperation, coordination). Gil-Garcia and Pardo (2005) call for managerial and organization success relying on the theoretical framework.

However other debates need to be addressed, in particular, certain areas are fertile grounds for the SC development, such as Nature's preservation, and safekeeping of fauna and flora, efficient use of land and water. Infrastructures affect transportation (by land, sea and air), everyday life routines, water, and food access, infrastructure's capacity or availability. Technology, needs to assimilate more integrated systems, for instance, the use of sensors related with pollution indicators, security, weather, quality of the air, traffic flows, residents (Rao et al., 2022). (e.g., sensors, Wi-Fi, network).

Services, adoption of best practices for planning, managing and operating, establishing comparable indicators and standards, improvement of human resources. Sustainability, reduction of consumption patterns, more and better regulation for environmental protection and preservation, waste policies, pollution surveillance, fair trade policies. Social, quality of life, equality, education, safety-related to health, terrorism, hackers, privacy threats.

Other implications were found from the literature review, such as:

1. SC concept is difficult to frame, since SC is composite (amalgamated of other disciplines, areas, like for example, engineering, ITC, Social Sciences) by nature, complex, and multifaceted. In addition, more global views taking a holistic approach are missing;
2. Consistency and standards are lacking among the body of knowledge – due to grey literature bringing different and contradictory arguments and perspectives conflicting with the academic view;
3. The measurement of SC (e.g., indicators, indexes, standards) are complex, reflected on the difficulty scholars and practitioners have to measure it, on one hand, due to the singularity of each SC, and on the other hand, due to the goals, visions, values, each SC wishes to attain;
4. More interconnection and linking between SC and its citizens are needed, this can be supported by ICT and IoT, for the citizens to be more informed and knowledgeable.
5. Scholars and practitioners need to take into consideration several elements, dimensions when addressing the smartness of their city. They also need to monitor the inputs and outputs of their policies on the citizen's liveable conditions.

Cities and their citizens will always be consumers of resources (Albino et al., 2015), which increases the challenge to make cities more sustainable. As Chourabi et al., (2011, p. 2289), notes "Making a city "smart" is emerging as a strategy to mitigate the problems generated by the urban population growth and rapid urbanization", but it also demands the development of a more livable city for its citizens.

CONCLUSION

This paper attempted to clarify the meaning of the concept SC. Despite its youth when compared to other traditional constructs (e.g., economics), its relevance and importance are evident within the new social, technologic, economic, and environmental scenario, i.e., high-population density, climate change, scarcity of natural resources, economic crisis, starvation, energy efficiency, pollution. The goal of this paper was to provide a common ground among the main concepts of SC. Thus, an all-inclusive definition was proposed, including not only the tangible and intangible elements of a city but also the planning, managing, and control that every SC should have, including the relevant role of innovation and technology. The multi-dimensional perspectives from the different scholars were also explored, and a similar all-inclusive suggestion of six dimensions (Nature, Technology, Infrastructure, Services, Sustainability, Social) was made, without disregarding other sub-dimension (innovation and efficiency). It was also highlighted, that several dynamic elements (i.e., always changing) must be accompanied continuously, due to their nature and influence on SC success and competitiveness.

In effect, it is essential to have an adequate SC management to transform the physical space and engage all the dimensions into a holistic system, to preserve the nature and to contribute to changes in the human quality of life.

The study's limitations are bound by the nature of the paper, conceptual, confining the implications presented. Also, governance and legal dimensions are not explored with depth. The cities to become smarter, i.e., SC, also need in the future to identify and anticipate their citizen's behaviour, taking in consideration their emotion and soul states, especially regarding how information is sought, perceived. It is also important to assess, how the available information impacts on the citizen's expectations, and afterwards their city experience, with the aim to predict their mood at the moment or the next day. In other words, cities are dynamic places in which different organisms, need to interact and relate with intelligence and knowledge. They also need, better and more tools to measure the SC inputs and outputs. As a future work, an empirical study should be developed with all performance indicators considered pertinent, to assess and monitor all the six dimensions, variables, indicators considered to investigate the satisfaction level of the population with the SC system as a whole. In the end, each specific dimension considered in this study can be evaluated and monitored to measure more effectively the SC as a holistic system.

ACKNOWLEDGMENT

This chapter is financed by National Funds provided by FCT - Foundation for Science and Technology through project CinTurs (UIDB/04020/2020).

REFERENCES

Ahvenniemi, H., Huovila, A., Pinto-Seppä, I., & Airaksinen, M. (2017). What are the differences between sustainable and smart cities? *Cities (London, England)*, *60*, 234–245. doi:10.1016/j.cities.2016.09.009

Albino, V., Berardi, U., & Dangelico, R. M. (2015). Smart Cities: Definitions, Dimensions, Performance, and Initiatives. *Journal of Urban Technology*, *22*(1), 3–21. doi:10.1080/10630732.2014.942092

Anthopoulos, L. G. (2017). Understanding Smart Cities: A Tool for Smart Government or an Industrial Trick? In *Public Administration and Information Technology*. Springer International Publishing AG. doi:10.1007/978-3-319-57015-0

Bakıcı, T., Almirall, E., & Wareham, J. (2012). A Smart City Initiative: The Case of Barcelona. *Journal of the Knowledge Economy*, *2*(1), 1–14.

Barrionuevo, J. M., Berrone, P., & Ricart, J. E. (2012). Smart Cities, Sustainable Progress. *IESE Insight*, *14*(14), 50–57. doi:10.15581/002.ART-2152

Caird, S. (2018). City approaches to smart city evaluation and reporting: Case studies in the United Kingdom. *Urban Research & Practice*, *11*(2), 159–179. doi:10.1080/17535069.2017.1317828

Calzada, I., & Cobo, C. (2015). Unplugging: Deconstructing the Smart City. *Journal of Urban Technology*, *22*(1), 23–43. doi:10.1080/10630732.2014.971535

Caragliu, A., Del Bo, C., & Nijkamp, P. (2011). Smart Cities in Europe. *Journal of Urban Technology*, *18*(2), 65–82. doi:10.1080/10630732.2011.601117

Castelnovo, W., Misuraca, G., & Savoldelli, A. (2016). Smart Cities Governance: The Need for a Holistic Approach to Assessing Urban Participatory Policy Making. *Social Science Computer Review*, *34*(6), 724–739. doi:10.1177/0894439315611103

Chourabi, H., Nam, T., Walker, S., Gil-Garcia, J. R., Mellouli, S., Nahon, K., Pardo, T. A., & Scholl, H. J. (2012). Understanding smart cities: An integrative framework. *Proceedings of the Annual Hawaii International Conference on System Sciences*, 2289–2297. 10.1109/HICSS.2012.615

Dameri, R. P., & Cocchia, A. (2013). Smart city and digital city: twenty years of terminology evolution. *ItAIS2013, X Conference of the Italian Chapter of AIS*.

Ebrahim, Z., & Irani, Z. (2005). E-government adoption: Architecture and barriers. *Business Process Management Journal*, *11*(5), 589–611. doi:10.1108/14637150510619902

Giffinger, R., Fertner, C., Kramar, H., Meijers, E., & Pichler-Milanovic, N. (2007). *Smart cities: Ranking of European medium-sized cities. Rapport technique*. Center of Regional Science, Vienna University of Technology.

Gil-García, J. R., & Pardo, T. A. (2005). E-government success factors: Mapping practical tools to theoretical foundations. *Government Information Quarterly*, *22*(2), 187–216. doi:10.1016/j.giq.2005.02.001

Graham, S. (1997). Telecommunications and the Future of Cities: Debunking the Myths. *Cities (London, England)*, *14*(1), 21–29. doi:10.1016/S0264-2751(37)00037-8

Graham, S. (2002). Bridging Urban Digital Divides? Urban Polarisation and Information and Communications Technologies (ICTs). *Urban Studies (Edinburgh, Scotland)*, *39*(1), 33–56. doi:10.1080/00420980220099050

Graham, S., & Aurigi, A. (1997). Urbanizing cyberspace? *City (London, England)*, *2*(7), 18–39. doi:10.1080/13604819708900051

Graham, S., & Marvin, S. (1996). *Telecommunications and the city*. Routledge.

Graham, S., & Marvin, S. (1999). Planning Cybercities: Integrating Telecommunications Into Urban Planning. *The Town Planning Review*, *70*(1), 89–114. doi:10.3828/tpr.70.1.w34454x3475g2858

Graham, S., & Marvin, S. (2004). Planning Cyber-cities? Integrating Telecommunications into Urban Planning. In S. Graham (Ed.), *The Cybercities Reader*. Routledge.

Hajduk, S. (2016). The Concept of a Smart City In Urban Management. *Business. Management in Education*, *14*(1), 34–49.

Hanley, R. E. (2017). From the Editor. *Journal of Urban Technology*, *24*(1), 1–2. doi:10.1080/10630732.2017.1307629 PMID:28083903

Harrison, C., Eckman, B., Hamilton, R., Hartswick, P., Kalagnanam, J., Paraszczak, J., & Williams, P. (2010). Foundations for Smarter Cities. *IBM Journal of Research and Development*, *54*(4), 1–16. doi:10.1147/JRD.2010.2048257

Hollands, R. G. (2008). Will the real smart city please stand up? *City (London, England)*, *12*(3), 303–320. doi:10.1080/13604810802479126

Hollands, R. G. (2015). Critical Interventions into the Corporate Smart City. *Cambridge Journal of Regions, Economy and Society*, *8*(1), 61–77. doi:10.1093/cjres/rsu011

ISO. (2014). *Smart cities Preliminary Report 2014*. International Standards Organization. Retrieved May 2016 from https://www.iso.org/iso/smart_cities_report-jtc1.pdf

Khan, R., Khan, S. U., Zaheer, R., & Khan, S. (2012, December). Future internet: the internet of things architecture, possible applications and key challenges. In *Frontiers of Information Technology (FIT), 2012 10th International Conference on* (pp. 257-260). IEEE. 10.1109/FIT.2012.53

Kramers, A., Höjer, M., Lövehagen, N., & Wangel, J. (2014). Smart sustainable cities–Exploring ICT solutions for reduced energy use in cities. *Environmental Modelling & Software*, *56*, 52–62. doi:10.1016/j.envsoft.2013.12.019

Kummitha, R. K. R., & Crutzen, N. (2017). How do we understand smart cities? An evolutionary perspective. *Cities (London, England)*, *67*, 43–52. doi:10.1016/j.cities.2017.04.010

Lazzeretti, L., Capone, F., & Cinti, T. (2011). Open innovation in city of art: The case of laser technologies for conservation in Florence. *City. Cultura e Scuola*, *2*(3), 159–168. doi:10.1016/j.ccs.2011.09.001

Lee, J. H., Hancock, M. G., & Hu, M. C. (2014). Towards an effective framework for building smart cities: Lessons from Seoul and San Francisco. *Technological Forecasting and Social Change*, *89*, 80–99. doi:10.1016/j.techfore.2013.08.033

Lombardi, P., Giordano, S., Farouh, H., & Yousef, W. (2012). Modelling the smart city performance. *Innovation (Abingdon)*, *25*(2), 137–149. doi:10.1080/13511610.2012.660325

Mandelson, H. L., & Bradshaw, H. B. (2009). Digital Britain. Department of Culture, Media and Sport and Department of Business, Innovation and Skills.

Marsal-Llacuna, M. L., Colomer-Llinàs, J., & Meléndez-Frigola, J. (2014). Lessons in urban monitoring taken from sustainable and livable cities to better address the Smart Cities initiative. *Technological Forecasting and Social Change*, *90*, 611–622. doi:10.1016/j.techfore.2014.01.012

McFarlane, C., & Söderström, O. (2017). On alternative smart cities: From a technology-intensive to a knowledge-intensive smart urbanism. *City (London, England)*, *21*(3-4), 312–328. doi:10.1080/13604813.2017.1327166

Mora, L., Bolici, R., & Deakin, M. (2017). The First Two Decades of Smart-City Research: A Bibliometric Analysis. *Journal of Urban Technology*, *24*(1), 3–27. doi:10.1080/10630732.2017.1285123

Nam, T., & Pardo, T. A. (2011). Conceptualizing Smart City with Dimensions of Technology, People, and Institutions. *Proc. 12th Conference on Digital Government Research,* 282-291. 10.1145/2037556.2037602

Papa, R., Gargiulo, C., & Galderisi, A. (2013). Towards an Urban Planners' Perspective on Smart City. *Journal of Land Use, Mobility and Environment*, *6*(1), 6–17. doi:10.6092/1970-9870/1536

Perera, C., Zaslavsky, A., Christen, P., & Georgakopoulos, D. (2014). Sensing as a service model for smart cities supported by internet of things. *Transactions on Emerging Telecommunications Technologies*, *25*(1), 81–93. doi:10.1002/ett.2704

Rao, M. G., Pawar, S., Priyanka, H., & Reddy, K. H. K. (2022, December). Amalgamation Biometric Deep Features in Smart City-ITS Authentication. In *2022 6th International Conference on Computation System and Information Technology for Sustainable Solutions (CSITSS)* (pp. 1-6). IEEE. 10.1109/CSITSS57437.2022.10026408

Reddy, K. H. K., Goswami, R. S., & Roy, D. S. (2023). An Artificial Intelligence Approach to Enabled Smart Service Towards Futuristic Smart Cities. In Handbook of Research on Applications of AI, Digital Twin, and Internet of Things for Sustainable Development (pp. 12-29). IGI Global. doi:10.4018/978-1-6684-6821-0.ch002

Schaffers, H., Komninos, N., Pallot, M., Trousse, B., Nilsson, M., & Oliveira, A. (2011, May). Smart cities and the future internet: Towards cooperation frameworks for open innovation. In *The future internet assembly* (pp. 431–446). Springer. doi:10.1007/978-3-642-20898-0_31

Scholl, H. J., Barzilai-Nahon, K., Ahn, J.-H., Olga, P., & Barbara, R. (2009). E-commerce and e-government: How do they compare? What can they learn from each other? *Proceedings of the 42nd Hawaiian International Conference on System Sciences.*

Schuurman, D., Baccarne, B., De Marez, L., & Mechant, P. (2012). Smart ideas for smart cities: Investigating crowdsourcing for generating and selecting ideas for ICT innovation in a city context. *Journal of Theoretical and Applied Electronic Commerce Research*, *7*(3), 49–62. doi:10.4067/S0718-18762012000300006

Tachizawa, E. M., Alvarez-Gil, M. J., & Montes-Sancho, M. J. (2015). How "smart cities" change supply chain management. *Supply Chain Management*, *20*(3), 237–248. doi:10.1108/SCM-03-2014-0108

Toppeta, D. (2010). The smart city vision: How innovation and ICT can build smart,"livable", sustainable cities. *The Innovation Knowledge Foundation*, *5*, 1–9.

Turcu, C. (2013). Re-thinking Sustainability Indicators: Local Perspectives of Urban Sustainability. *Journal of Environmental Planning and Management*, *56*(5), 695–719. doi:10.1080/09640568.2012.698984

UN-Habitat. (1996 June). *Second United Nations Conference on Human Settlements. United Nations Habitat.* Author.

United Nations. (2015). *World Population Prospects: The 2015 Revision, Key Findings and Advance Tables.* United Nations Department of Economic and Social Affairs and Population Division. Working Paper, No. ESA/P/WP. 241.

Vlacheas, P., Giaffreda, R., Stavroulaki, V., Kelaidonis, D., Foteinos, V., Poulios, G., Demestichas¸, P., Somov, A., Biswas, A., & Moessner, K. (2013). Enabling smart cities through a cognitive management framework for the internet of things. *IEEE Communications Magazine*, *51*(6), 102–111. doi:10.1109/MCOM.2013.6525602

Washburn, D., Sindhu, U., Balaouras, S., Dines, R. A., Hayes, N. M., & Nelson, L. E. (2010). *Helping CIOs Understand "Smart City" Initiatives: Defining the Smart City, Its Drivers, and the Role of the CIO*. Forrester Research, Inc. Available at http://public.dhe.ibm.com/partnerworld/pub/smb/smarterpla net/forr_help_cios_und_smart_city_initiatives.pdf

Zanella, A., Bui, N., Castellani, A., Vangelista, L., & Zorzi, M. (2014). Internet of things for smart cities. *IEEE Internet of Things Journal*, *1*(1), 22–32. doi:10.1109/JIOT.2014.2306328

Zygiaris, S. (2013). Smart city reference model: Assisting planners to conceptualize the building of smart city innovation ecosystems. *Journal of the Knowledge Economy*, *4*(2), 217–231. doi:10.100713132-012-0089-4

Chapter 19
Artificial Intelligence and Machine Learning Approaches in Smart City Services

Mona Bakri Hassan Dahab
Sudan University of Science and Technology, Sudan

Elmustafa Sayed Ali Ahmed
Red Sea University, Sudan

Rania A. Mokhtar
Taif University, Saudi Arabia

Rashid A. Saeed
Taif University, Saudi Arabia

ABSTRACT

Recently, the concept of smart cities has been linked to artificial intelligence (AI) technologies, which greatly help in improving the efficiency of various applications related to smart cities and the green environment. Machine learning (ML) and deep learning (DL) techniques play an important role in upgrading the design of control and management systems at various levels in many smart city applications such as transportation, public safety, smart energy, and building automation. This chapter introduces the concept of artificial intelligence technologies and their uses in smart cities and their methods in many related applications, in addition to challenges and future directions for using artificial intelligence to provide smart city services.

DOI: 10.4018/979-8-3693-0744-1.ch019

INTRODUCTION

Artificial intelligence (AI) approaches such as machine learning (ML), deep learning (DL), are embrace a much of promises for handling activities and automation in smart cities. The aim of the smart cities is to offer efficient services to the public by implementing modern data analytics and technologies (Ullah et al., 2020). There are several benefits of smart cities such as enhance city planning and development, E-government services delivered faster and at a lower operating to citizens, enhance safety and security, manage waste for energy and fuel, manage waste water to be treated, smart meters, smart grid and many more (Pradeep et al., 2019).

By 2030, AI is predicted to allow over 50% of smart cities services, amongst which urban solutions for mobility, significantly contributing to sustainability, vitality, resilience, and social welfare of urban life. Using AI and ML in smart cities will improve the personalize services delivery, help makes expectation and forthcoming services predictions. Also, simulate the utilization of different strategies beforehand applied (Pradeep et al., 2019). Moreover, it will enhance the city's finance management via predict target and expenditure management. ML and DL in smart city would completely influence the environment through waste, traffic, and energy management. Furthermore, it would increase production of employees with the assistance of effective services and products which will increase the economic capital growing of the city's (Elmustafa et al., 2021).

Figure 1. Classification of AI technologies in a smart city

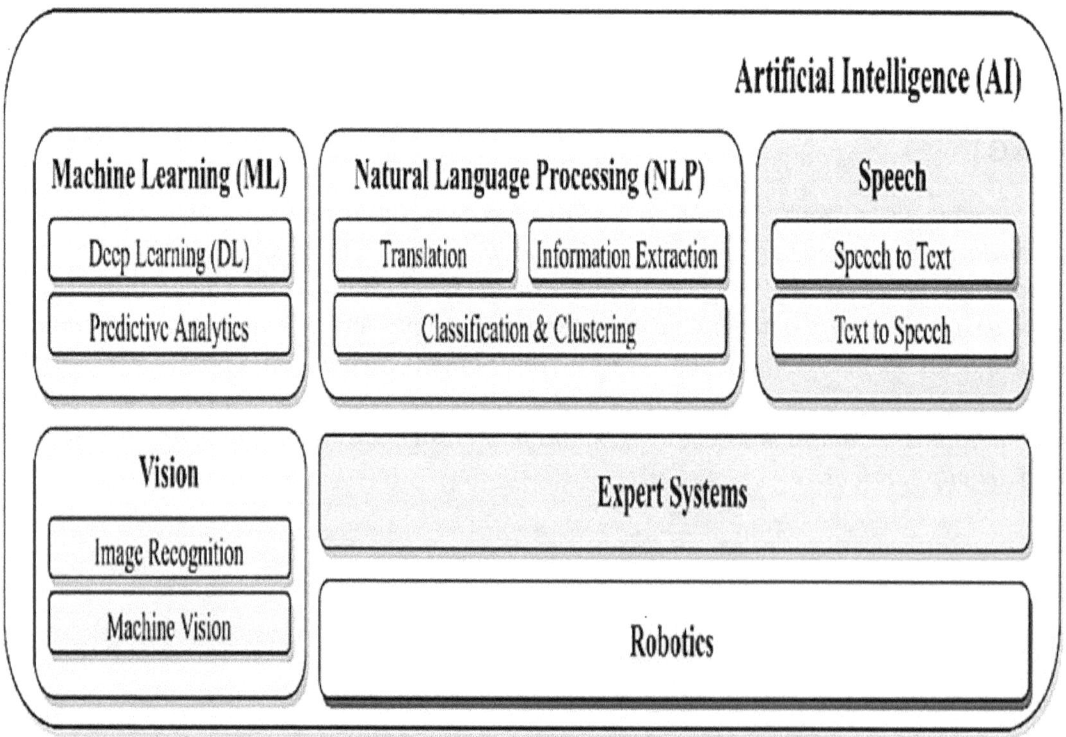

AI allowing smart cities solutions including noise and traffic congestion, more efficient energy, water and waste management, reduced pollution. It is the science of simulating intelligence in machines and program them to emulate human actions. As shown in Figure 1, AI technologies in smart cities could be classified into AI/ML, natural speech, expert system, expert systems, robotics and language processing (Elmustafa et al., 2021). The major goals of AI are learning, reasoning and perception. The different growing field of AI used in many fields including medical, robot control, finance, remote sensing, semantic web, computer vision, virtual reality, game theory and more fields. AI is predicted to support sustainable development of future smart cities (Ullah et al., 2020). AI approaches such as ML and DL enable to provide many intelligent services in smart cities which could be classified in to seven categories as follows:

- For governance including tailored funding provisioning, urban planning, disaster management, and prevention (Mansour, 2021).
- For live ability, healthcare, safety, and security including smart monitoring, noise management, personalized healthcare, and enhanced cyber security (Mansour, 2021).
- For education and citizen participation including actionable and validated knowledge support for making decisions (Nada, 2022).
- For economy including resources efficiency and enhanced affordability through, customers tailored solutions, effective supply chain and sharing services (Aswathy, 2022).
- For mobility and logistics including smart routing and parking assistance, supply chain resiliency and traffic management, autonomous and sustainable mobility (Nada, 2022).
- For infrastructure including optimized infrastructure deployment, use and maintenance as well as transportation, energy grids, waste and water management, and urban lighting (Aswathy, 2022).
- For the environment including air quality management, biodiversity preservation and urban farming (Nada, 2022).

Due to the great improvement that ML/DL algorithms can achieve in developing many smart city applications and services. It is important to highlight some important roles and methods of integrating AI into smart city applications. Accordingly, concepts about these roles and methods are presented with the review of some applications and their challenges as well as future directions, as they are presented according to the following organization, Section 2 provides a background and some related works to the AI in smart cities. The roles of using AI techniques in smart cities services are reviewed in Section 3. The use of ML and DL approaches in addition to their integration to smart cities are discussed in Sections 4 and 5 respectively. Section 6 introduces the ML and DL services in some important smart city applications. The challenges of using AI in smart cities and future directions are reviewed in Section 7. Finally, the chapter is concluded in Section 8.

BACKGROUND AND RELATED WORKS

Recently, AI/ML have been utilized extensively in smart cities projects and research. AI encourages effectively and enhance the life quality for the cities of the future by illustrating huge resources pools and merging modern robotics, machine vision, ML, neural language processing (NLP) and other technologies (Reham et al., 2022). Smart cities initiative in many countries are currently focus on DL and ML services. Conferring to the statistics in Washington DC, by 2030, the ML/AI industry would be grow up to $200 billion. In 2023, the global investment in AI and cognitive systems would grow up to $60 billion, with AI/ML being adopted in up to 75% of the city applications (Ali, 2021).

While China has the highest smart cities number in the globe, that govern cities and public places by using cameras, embedded sensors, metering equipment, and many others monitor techniques in addition to AI/ ML-based data analytics technologies (Reham et al., 2022). The forthcoming paragraph will be discussing the related work that AI and ML used in smart cities.

In study by Zaib Ullah et al. (2020), authors present the smart cities concept and the implementation realization for modern big data analytics methodologies. Also, they explore the role of AI, ML, and Deep Reinforcement Learning techniques in different applications in smart cities. Moreover, they present deeply the services of the prior methods in smart grid energy-efficient utilizations, intelligent transportation system (ITS), cybersecurity, effective use of unmanned aerial vehicles (UAVs) to guarantee the best utilization of 5G and beyond (B5G) network, and Intelligent healthcare systems for a smart cities (Nada et al., 2022). Finally, they determine different research challenges and future research directions trends for implementing the prior techniques in smart city.

Pramathi and Vindhya (2018) represent all the main areas of AI/ML. Also, it determines deeply in various ways of applying smart cities challenges and its probable solutions. With the technologies implementations including recognize images, big data analytics, patterns recognition, DL/ANN, many issues relating to traffics management, waste and water management, parking, industrial and education sectors which could be determined proficiently (Alatabani, 2021; Pradhan et al., 2022).

Trevor et al. (2018) have shown a brief review to discover different significant and essential issues of smart cities. Some of the challenges have been discussed to ensure data security and privacy, networks protection against probable attack, encouraging responsible and mature data share philosophy, and implement of AI/ML/DRL methods for that.

Badri and Prangya (2019) present a survey for ML applications in smart city, ML algorithm that provides services in smart city. Selecting appropriate algorithm could give a great results for some of the crucial issues. Big data is required for ML algorithm accuracy. ML has a challenge due to variety, velocity and volume of big data management to attain suitable and good decision for various algorithms to have appropriate results (Ashu et al., 2021).

Daniel Luckey et al. (2020) identifies objectives of smart monitoring, serving as a basis to categorize Artificial Intelligence algorithms or Machine Learning algorithms for smart monitoring. Also, an overview of Machine Learning algorithms used for smart monitoring is presented, providing an overview of using Machine Learning algorithms in smart monitoring that may be modified to achieve Artificial Intelligence in civil engineering.

Nosratabadi et al. (2019) present an overview and describe the benefits of using DL and ML algorithms in smart city. Also, they present new applications of using ML and DL in urban sustainability and smart cities. From study, it approved that five DL and ML methods is the most applied to address the different aspects of smart cities they are support vector machines decision trees, ensembles, Bayesians, hybrids, neuron fuzzy, artificial neural networks (ANN), and deep learning as well as it discover that DL and ML methods contributed to solve the problems in the main domains of smart cities such as health, energy and public transport (Nalluri et al., 2019).

M. Batty (2018) explained relationship between AI and smart cities and proposed ML techniques for real-time city applications. In study by Ebenezer et al. (2018), authors determine the benefits and challenges of smart cities. Also, they discusses future production of smart cities and characteristics of smart city. Sweta et al. (2020) proposed a survey on usage of Deep Learning in Smart City data as well as several future research directions on deep learning on smart city applications are suggested.

ROLES OF AI IN SMART CITY

A smart city is a smart physical, civil and economic infrastructure that provides innovative technology for a number of applications related to utilities and transportation. This promotes improved quality of life, ease of living, economic growth, and sustainable development (Shahab et al., 2022). The general roles of implementing smart cities is related to building three layers, namely:

- A technical database of smartphones and sensors that produce data and are connected to high-speed networks.
- Fast computing and data processing systems to process raw data and give alerts.
- Technology platforms for people to interact with various smart applications that help make better decisions and change behavior.

The above mentioned roles are strongly related to AI technology, because its enables an intelligent way and decisions related to different smart cities application such as, traffic management, environment conservation, public transport, healthcare, waste management, and security. For traffic management, AI algorithms help solve congestion in intelligent traffic management systems by informing drivers of roadblocks and delays. The use of machine learning can also predict and reduce traffic (Othman et al., 2022). Deep learning can work on building systems capable of significantly reducing road accidents by using systems for detecting traffic violations, cameras, and analysing the information collected through these devices. It also enables live updates about public transportation, improving timeliness and customer satisfaction.

For the roles of environment conservation, AI can be used to analyse citizens' energy usage data and determine where to use renewable energy sources with the aim of reducing energy waste. It also helps in analysing and predicting pollution levels, which will help the authorities to make the most appropriate decisions for the environment (Othman et al., 2022; Mamoon et al., 2022). The roles of AI in healthcare section, its enable the patient monitoring systems to detect chronic conditions in advance and help prevent them. In addition, ML and DL enable to provide health reports of citizens by analyse the medical report and provides consultations.

In the security field, cameras that support artificial intelligence detect criminal behaviour and report it to the authorities immediately. It also enables the recognition of human faces and compares them with a database to track their identity and authenticate the entry of a person into the city or restricted areas. Smart cities based on AI roles can play a pivotal role in transforming urban areas to increase the standard of living and build economic growth (Othman et al., 2022).

ML AND DL APPROACHES IN SMART CITIES

Recently, DL and DL methods are contributed to the advancement of models in the different aspects of prediction, planning, designing and analysis of smart cities. ML is a subset of AI which provides system the ability of learning automatically by accessing the data provided and implementing it to learn for themselves and to enhance performance without being programmed (Ebenezer et al., 2018).

Machine learning is one of the technologies that is coming to contribute in deploying the smart cities in all phases. Application domains include the main aspects of the smart cities such as healthcare, energy, education, homes, transportation and pollution as shown in Figure 2. Also, it is contributing techniques to improve society and useful to identify malicious in cyber world (Ebenezer et al., 2018). The diagnosis is a critical phase which comes to ensure the achievement of a project in reality of the city diagnosed, also, this step requires an important financial commitment.

ML methods are divided into four categories including supervised, unsupervised, Reinforcement Learning and Deep Learning. It already gained the attention of the researchers involved in smart city with other advanced technologies like Internet of Things, big data, cloud computing, or analytics. Deep Learning (DL) is a ML technology which is used to extract insights from data, thus helping in better decision making (Elmustafa et al., 2021).

Figure 2. Applications of machine learning

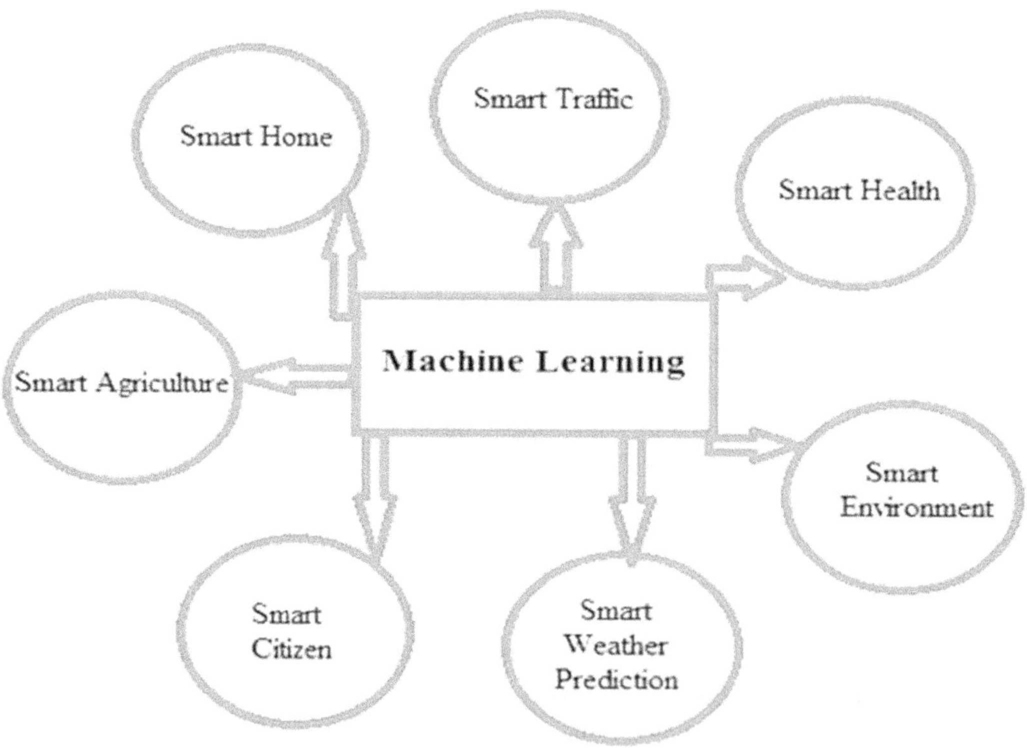

BENEFITS OF INTEGRATING ML IN SMART CITIES

Using ML in smart cities has multiple advantages to human interaction. From an eco-friendly environment to sustainable environment, using ML comes with various types of benefits.

A. Environmental Impact

One of the key disadvantages of industrial cities environment the CO2 emission which would be the main motivation behind the fast growing of sustainable and smart cities.

B. Optimized Energy and Water Management

The smart and grid water management are foremost influences that support to produce energy with low pollution. Also, it benefits of getting clean healthy water for drink.

C. Transportation Systems

Efficient and clean transportation of people, services and goods are crucial for the smart cities. In the optimism of improving mobility, several cities were utilizing AI technologies to less traffic congestions and afford customers with real-time updates.

D. Advanced Security and Public Safety

The safety of the people is at highest priority in the smart cities. The ML-enabled environment of smart cities are tolerating municipalities for better citizen's monitor thanks to CCTV cameras with image recognition (Othman et al., 2022).

ML/DL SERVICES IN SMART CITIES

Using ML/DL in smart cities will improve the life, if we implement in the right way. There are many applications in cities or in urban zones where ML and DL could be implemented to enhance the efficiency and performance of the eco-system (Ullah et al., 2020; Mamoon et al., 2022). In general, cities purpose are becoming smart and sustainable, which have to become more sustainable, attractive, balanced and inclusive for the public. Figure 3 shows categorization of AI services and applications for smart cities. As it becomes an agenda of several governments all around the world. The citizen's satisfaction is one of the main demands in terms of effective services, security, decent and comfort transportation, etc.

Figure 3. AI smart cities applications

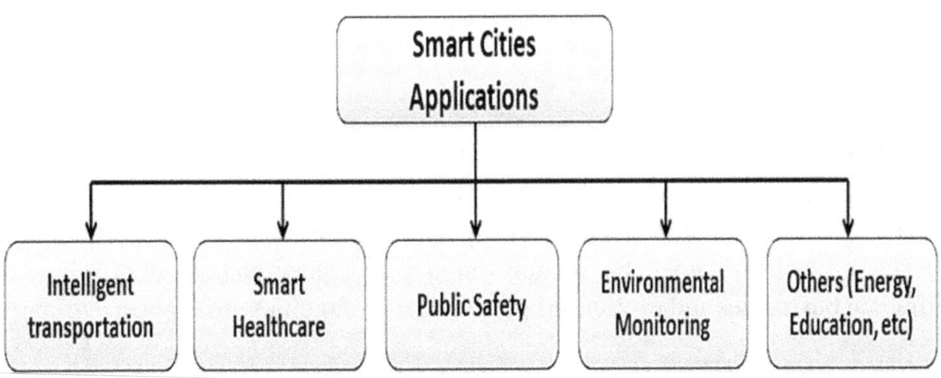

Intelligent Traffic Management Control System

Transportation plays an important role in smart city planning. It will be used for better city transport services for public, automatic vehicles positioning systems, and gathering over-the-air data and information, which to be utilized and shared over screens and displays at bus stops, in the bus as well as website and mobile. Also, it can solve the city congestion problems by updating the drivers with roads situations and latency (Adnane et al., 2021). It could estimate and decrease traffic by utilizing DL algorithms, which can assist to lower emissions of carbon. Also, it can reduce the accidents in the highways by configuring AI-enabled surveillance systems, radars, sensors, and traffic and weather information along the road.

Figure 4. AI for intelligent traffic management system (traffic monitoring example)

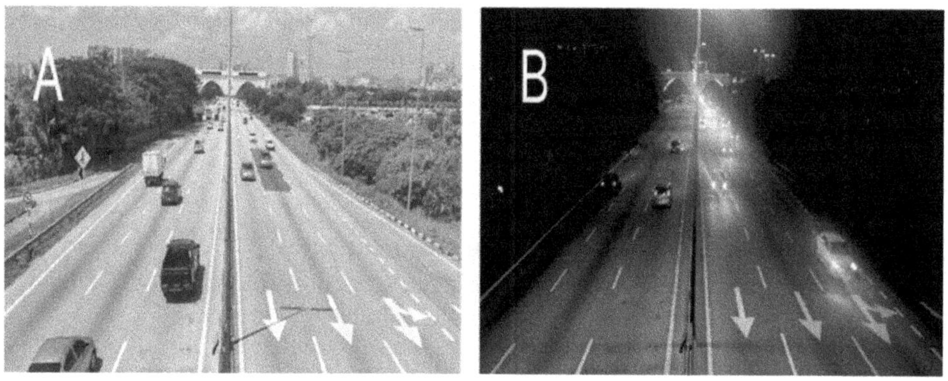

Vehicles detection in ITS is a crucial aspect in guaranteeing safety of the roads as it is essential for vehicles flow monitoring, illegal vehicles type detections, incidents detection and vehicles speed prediction. Despite the grow and popularity in smart cities research, there are still several challenges and problems that need be resolved. The usage of Convolutional Neural Networks (CNNs) could be utilized for the vehicle's detection from roadway cameras output to implement video signal processing methods for features extraction (Lina et al., 2022). Such DL approaches provide solutions that have recently been utilized for vehicles detection such as radars and supersonic suffer a serious limitations in its capability to measure significant factors in traffic monitoring which are needed to precisely evaluate traffic environments (Shahab et al., 2022). For example, a traffic camera can be placed directly across the bidirectional highway enabling monitor of the traffic both day and night to monitoring traffic as shown in Figure 4. Deep learning can process image data to build a model that can rate vehicle detection by analysing standardized vehicle detection image datasets.

Security and Public Safety

Security and public safety in cities have been basically enhanced by utilizing CCTV camera with image and face recognition feature. An AI-enabled surveillance systems recognize the pattern and forecast potential criminal activities and implements security and safety measure (Shahab et al., 2022). The application of AI-based security camera has demonstrated to be a game-changer in offering fast responses at the threat times at businesses and institutions premises. A smart cities are supposed to support reliable, safe, and secure connected relays, sensors, and actuators to collect, manipulate and transmit information to confirm efficient and trusted digital applications. This interconnectivity of different nodes has unlocked up cyber-security challenges that require to be addressed and improved (Trevor et al., 2018). Most of the information and data are produced by cloud-based IoT nodes that accomplish a crucial role in various services in smart cities.

For public safety and security, human behaviour recognition applications are one of the most important issues. AI techniques enable to recognition of the motion patterns of persons in video surveillance captured from several types of sensors. It also works on adaptive information merging to combine features and action recognition of sensors for optimizing video sampling and joint recognition of the adaptive weight of each action recognition sensor (Nosratabadi et al., 2019). In addition, these technologies help in the retrieval and viewing of data for long video clips. ML algorithms enable to detection of the motion of long video by optimizing the detection of Spatio-temporal points of interest. Figure 5 shows intelligent human behaviour recognition as an example for AI-based Public Safety and Security applications.

Figure 5. DL approach for intelligent human behavior recognition

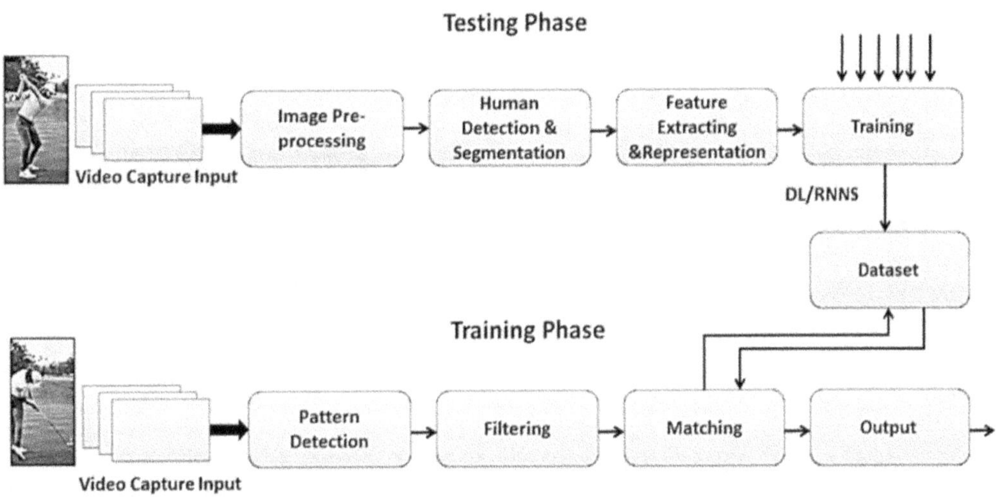

DL methodologies assist to simplify state-of-the-art solutions to deal with the problematic issues of smart services in dense urban and which are related to the transportation, security, people, and environment. These methodologies assist to enhance data manipulation and convert it into suitable information and implement cognitive intelligences for a sustainable city (Khalifa et al., 2022). Lately, the mixture of ML and DL methods have become more common as an unsupervised learning techniques to recognise objects and patterns through video footages in various Services, giving high recognition capabilities with a precision of more than 85%. Deep learning techniques analyse integrated and aggregated big data associated to cloud computing, sensors, videos, images, and resources management method to develop several smart operations related to prediction and detection.

Smart Energy Metering

Using ML in smart grids will improve the safety of power grids and enhance performance management. Smart grids could make intelligent meter measures for large data amounts to predict and assess requirement responses and cluster loading. Forecast models could be setup on the grid platform to predict the requirement and price of energy for specific time zone (Rania et al., 2021). The internet of energy (IoE) is one of the modern technologies to provide smart solutions for the two-way flow of energy and information in the Internet style, and it is considered an extension of the smart grid. Figure 6 shows an example of IoE based energy management system.

Figure 6. IoE-based energy management system

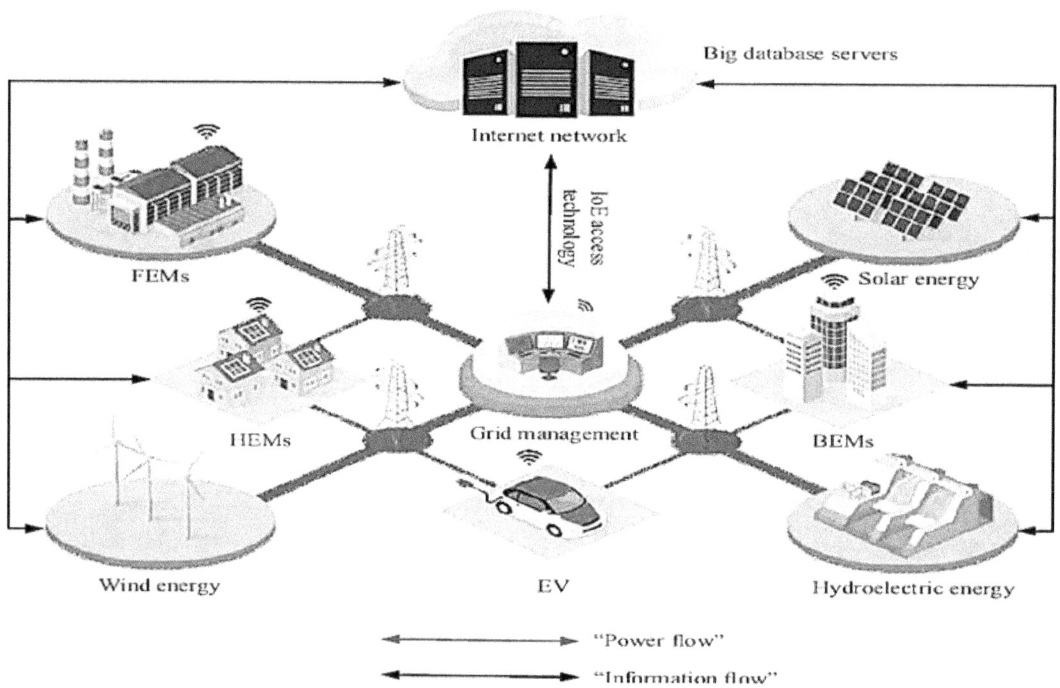

Smart metering technology plays a sufficient role in IoE in that it enables the automation of smart consumption metering and energy sensing systems with electronic or electromechanical components, helping consumers manage and optimize energy resources in both different commercial and residential applications.

Building Automation Systems

The goal of a smart building is to achieve better energy management reduce costs and carbon emissions, helping organizations achieve cost and sustainability goals. Also, create more enjoyable and comfortable management working environments. Moreover, better systems optimization results in better uptime and productivity for systems and users (Shahab et al., 2022; Rania et al., 2021). For instance, retailers and stores owners' can utilize sensors for tracking peak time when individuals come across the stores, as well as near areas of the public gravitate. Through utilize of ML and DL, the data is produced can assist to generate reliable forecasts and track annually, weekly, and daily differences (Rania et al., 2021).

Water Management Plan

An intelligent water management systems are an efficient in enhancing water quality in a city without exposing water distribution and pressure. Many cities have on-began to apply the smart meters to avoid possible leakages across underground water cylinders. Water supplies and protection are crucial part for dense urban cities sustainable living (Shahab et al., 2022). The action of installing a water management systems such as smart meters is useful to track-down the water consumptions as well as enterprises, households, and industries average consumption, which can be assessed by using ML techniques. Also, forthcoming consumption statistics could be assessed through ML algorithms implemented into historical data.

CHALLENGES AND FUTURE RESEARCH DIRECTIONS

There are several challenges of using ML, and DL in smart cities such as, hardware installation and maintenance costs, physical damage to AI equipment, and automation,

Hardware Installation and Costs of Maintenance

Generally, AI and ML technologies work via surveillance camera and sensor. This high-tech equipment required an expensive cost, particularly in public services. This equipment is regularly maintained which will lead to recurring costs. It is important to have a plane for implementation to analyse future costs (Zhou et al., 2021). Although of this high cost, in due course, AI techniques improve the procedures of smart city efficiency and this will lead to an increase the revenues.

Physical Damage or Stealing of AI Equipment

Physical damage such as natural disasters can destroy AI equipment due to setup in the risk areas. Also, these equipment are an exhibition to theft on some time, based on location and accessibility (Freire et al., 2021). It is necessary to plan the proper setup locations and keep in mind the weather effect.

AI Automation in Smart City

AI automaton is a complete stack of AI companies that provide the capability to adopt AI and ML. It provides end-to-end services like Data Labelling, Model Deployment, and Application Development. Also, it could carry AI technical and software real-world solutions use in Smart cities accessibility (Freire et al., 2021; Zhang et al., 2019). AI techniques are being applied to implement applications in smart cities to reduce the local wealth and resources drain and improve applications. Lately, the educational system is modernized with e-learning systems that allow humans to learn everywhere over the internet. Transportation and mobility platforms have also developed, and engineers are still conducting various studies to manage traffic in cities. AI/DL is inflowing the security sectors to publics protection to improve several IoT-based platform. With the start of IoT-based systems, intelligent systems for cyber-security were developed very quickly (Zhang et al., 2019). All countries have faced a health pandemic since the outbreak began, rising complex economic, ethical, and social challenges.

CONCLUSION

AI and ML techniques are currently an important part for cities and industries. There are many types of research are focused on this field around the wide world. Using AI, ML, and DL in smart cities creates a positive impact on the environment, and cyber-physical space that includes traffic management, monitor health, road safety, industrial control systems, water resource management, e-mobility, public safety, and law enforcement, newer automation system, reduce the accident and monitor the traffic in the urban cities. It participates in various fields of smart city such as traffic management, public safety and security as well as smart building and other applications.

REFERENCES

Abdalla, R. S. (2021). IoE Design Principles and Architecture, In book: Internet of Energy for Smart Cities: Machine Learning Models and Techniques. CRC Group, Taylor & Francis Group.

Alatabani, L. E., Ali, E. S., & Saeed, R. A. (2021). Deep Learning Approaches for IoV Applications and Services. In N. Magaia, G. Mastorakis, C. Mavromoustakis, E. Pallis, & E. K. Markakis (Eds.), *Intelligent Technologies for Internet of Vehicles. Internet of Things (Technology, Communications, and Computing)*. Springer. doi:10.1007/978-3-030-76493-7_8

Ali. (2022). Blockchain for IoT-Based Cyber-Physical Systems (CPS): Applications and Challenges. Blockchain based Internet of Things. Lecture Notes on Data Engineering and Communications Technologies, 112.

Ali, E. S., Hasan, M. K., Hassan, R., Saeed, R. A., Hassan, M. B., Islam, S., Nafi, N. S., & Bevinakoppa, S. (2021). Machine Learning Technologies for Secure Vehicular Communication in Internet of Vehicles: Recent Advances and Applications. *Security and Communication Networks, 2021*, 8868355. doi:10.1155/2021/8868355

Ali, E. S., Hassan, M. B., & Saeed, R. A. (2021). Machine Learning Technologies on Internet of Vehicles. In N. Magaia, G. Mastorakis, C. Mavromoustakis, E. Pallis, & E. K. Markakis (Eds.), *Intelligent Technologies for Internet of Vehicles. Internet of Things (Technology, Communications, and Computing)*. Springer. doi:10.1007/978-3-030-76493-7_7

Ashu, A., Hussain, M. W., Sinha Roy, D., & Reddy, H. K. (2021). Intelligent data compression policy for Hadoop performance optimization. In *Proceedings of the 11th International Conference on Soft Computing and Pattern Recognition (SoCPaR 2019) 11* (pp. 80-89). Springer International Publishing. 10.1007/978-3-030-49345-5_9

Aswathy, R. H., Suresh, P., Sikkandar, M. Y., Abdel-Khalek, S., & Alhumyani, H. (2022). Optimized Tuned Deep Learning Model for Chronic Kidney Disease Classification. CMC-Computers. *Materials & Continua*, *70*(2), 2097–2111. doi:10.32604/cmc.2022.019790

Badri, M., & Prangya, P. (2019). Machine learning applications to smart city. *ACCENTS Transactions on Image Processing and Computer Vision*, *5*(14), 2019.

Bhattacharya, S. (2020). A Review on Deep Learning for Future Smart Cities. *Internet Technology Letters*, *5*(1), 2020.

Ebenezer, O. (2018). Smart cities survey. *IEEE 20th International Conference on High Performance Computing and Communications*.

Elfatih, N. M., Hasan, M. K., Kamal, Z., Gupta, D., Saeed, R. A., Ali, E. S., & Hosain, M. S. (2022). Internet of vehicle's resource management in 5G networks using AI technologies: Current status and trends. *IET Communications*, *16*(5), 400–420. doi:10.1049/cmu2.12315

Founoun. (2021). Machine Learning to Support Smart City Initiatives. *Journal of Tianjin University Science and Technology*.

Freire, C. A. R., Ferreira, F. A. F., Carayannis, E. G., & Ferreira, J. J. M. (2021). Artificial Intelligence and Smart Cities: A DEMATEL Approach to Adaptation Challenges and Initiative. *IEEE Transactions on Engineering Management*. Advance online publication. doi:10.1109/TEM.2021.3098665

Khalifa, O. O., Roubleh, A., Esgiar, A., Abdelhaq, M., Alsaqour, R., Abdalla, A., Ali, E. S., & Saeed, R. (2022). An IoT-Platform-Based Deep Learning System for Human Behavior Recognition in Smart City Monitoring Using the Berkeley MHAD Datasets. *Systems.*, *10*(5), 177. doi:10.3390ystems10050177

Khalifa, O. O., Roubleh, A., Esgiar, A., Abdelhaq, M., Alsaqour, R., Abdalla, A., Ali, E. S., & Saeed, R. (2022). An IoT-Platform-Based Deep Learning System for Human Behavior Recognition in Smart City Monitoring Using the Berkeley MHAD Datasets. *Systems*, *10*(5), 177. doi:10.3390ystems10050177

Khalifa, O. O., Wajdi, M. H., Saeed, R. A., Hashim, A. H. A., Ahmed, M. Z., & Ali, E. S. (2022). Vehicle Detection for Vision-Based Intelligent Transportation Systems Using Convolutional Neural Network Algorithm. *Journal of Advanced Transportation*, *2022*, 9189600. doi:10.1155/2022/9189600

Lina, E. A., Elmustafa, S. A., Rania, A. M., Rashid, A. S., Hesham, A., & Mohammad, K. H. (2022). Deep and Reinforcement Learning Technologies on Internet of Vehicle (IoV) Applications: Current Issues and Future Trends. *Journal of Advanced Transportation*, *2022*, 1947886.

Luckey. (2020). Artificial intelligence techniques for smart city applications. *The International ICCCBE and CIB W78 Joint Conference on Computing in Civil and Building Engineering*.

Mansour, R. F., Alfar, N. M., Abdel-Khalek, S., Abdelhaq, M., Saeed, R. A., & Alsaqour, R. (2022). Optimal deep learning based fusion model for biomedical image classification. *Expert Systems: International Journal of Knowledge Engineering and Neural Networks*, *39*(3), e12764. doi:10.1111/exsy.12764

Nalluri, M. S. R., Kannan, K., Gao, X. Z., & Roy, D. S. (2019). An efficient hybrid meta-heuristic approach for cell formation problem. *Soft Computing*, *23*(19), 9189–9213. doi:10.100700500-019-03798-7

Nosratabadi, S. (2019). State of the art survey of deep learning and machine learning models for smart cities and urban sustainability. *in Proc. Int. Conf. Global. Research in Education, 2019*, 228–238.

Pradeep, P. T. (2019). Smart City Services - Challenges and Approach. *International Conference on Machine Learning, Big Data, Cloud and Parallel Computing.*

Pradhan, B., Hussain, M. W., Srivastava, G., Debbarma, M. K., Barik, R. K., & Lin, J. C. W. (2022). A neuro-evolutionary approach for software defined wireless network traffic classification. *IET Communications*, cmu2.12548. doi:10.1049/cmu2.12548

Pramathi, J. N., & Vindhya, P. M. (2018). Artificial Intelligence in Smart City Analysis. *International Conference on Smart Systems and Inventive Technology (ICSSIT).*

Saeed, M. M., Saeed, R. A., Mokhtar, R. A., Alhumyani, H., & Ali, E. S. (2022). A Novel Variable Pseudonym Scheme for Preserving Privacy User Location in 5G Networks. *Security and Communication Networks*, *2022*, 7487600. doi:10.1155/2022/7487600

Shahab, S. (2022). When Smart Cities Get Smarter via Machine Learning: An In-Depth Literature Review. *IEEE Access : Practical Innovations, Open Solutions*, *10*, 2022.

Trevor, B. (2018, May). Security and Privacy Challenges in Smart Cities. *Sustainable Cities and Society*, *39*, 499–507. doi:10.1016/j.scs.2018.02.039

Ullah, Z., Al-Turjman, F., Mostarda, L., & Gagliardi, R. (2020). (. Applications of Artificial Intelligence and Machine learning in smart cities. *Computer Communications*, *154*, 313–323. doi:10.1016/j.comcom.2020.02.069

Zhang, L., Wu, J., Mumtaz, S., Li, J., Gacanin, H., & Rodrigues, J. J. P. C. (2019). Edge-to-Edge Cooperative Artificial Intelligence in Smart Cities with On-Demand Learning Offloading. *2019 IEEE Global Communications Conference (GLOBECOM),* 1-6. 10.1109/GLOBECOM38437.2019.9013878

Zhou, Y., & Kankanhalli, A. (2021). AI Regulation for Smart Cities: Challenges and Principles. In E. Estevez, T. A. Pardo, & H. J. Scholl (Eds.), *Smart Cities and Smart Governance. Public Administration and Information Technology* (Vol. 37). Springer. doi:10.1007/978-3-030-61033-3_5

Compilation of References

Abate, F., Carratù, M., Liguori, C., & Paciello, V. (2019). A low cost smart power meter for IoT. *Measurement*, *136*, 59–66. doi:10.1016/j.measurement.2018.12.069

Abdalla, R. S. (2021). IoE Design Principles and Architecture, In book: Internet of Energy for Smart Cities: Machine Learning Models and Techniques. CRC Group, Taylor & Francis Group.

Abouelmehdi, K., Beni-Hssane, A., Khaloufi, H., & Saadi, M. (2017). Big data security and privacy in healthcare: A Review. *Procedia Computer Science*, *113*, 73–80.

Abou-Nassar, E. M., Iliyasu, A. M., El-Kafrawy, P. M., Song, O., Bashir, A. K., & El-Latif, A. A. (2020). DITrust chain: Towards Blockchain-based trust models for sustainable healthcare IoT systems. *IEEE Access : Practical Innovations, Open Solutions*, *8*, 111223–111238. doi:10.1109/ACCESS.2020.2999468

Abujarad, S. Y., Mustafa, M. W., & Jamian, J. J. (2017). Recent approaches of unit commitment in the presence of intermittent renewable energy resources: A review. *Renewable & Sustainable Energy Reviews*, *70*, 215–223. doi:10.1016/j.rser.2016.11.246

Abunadi, I., & Kumar, R. L. (2021). BSF-EHR: Blockchain security framework for electronic health records of patients. *Sensors (Basel)*, *21*(8), 2865. PMID:33921738

Adaramola, M. (Ed.). (2014). *Solar energy: Application, economics, and public perception*. CRC Press. doi:10.1201/b17731

Adedeji, K.B., Ponnle, A.A., Abu-Mahfouz, A.M., & Kurien, A.M. (2022). Towards Digitalization of Water Supply Systems for Sustainable Smart City Development—Water 4.0. *Applied Sciences (Switzerland)*, *12*(18).

Adlam, R., & Haskins, B. (2021). Applying Blockchain Technology to Security-Related Aspects of Electronic Healthcare Record Infrastructure. *The African Journal of Information and Communication*, *28*, 1–28.

Adu-Manu, K. S., Adam, N., Tapparello, C., Ayatollahi, H., & Heinzelman, W. (2020). Energy-harvesting wireless sensor networks: A review. *ACM Transactions on Sensor Networks*, *14*(2), 1–5. doi:10.1145/3183338

Aggarwal, S., Kumar, N., Tanwar, S., & Alazab, M. (2021). A Survey on Energy Trading in the Smart Grid: Taxonomy, Research Challenges and Solutions. *IEEE Access : Practical Innovations, Open Solutions*, *9*, 116231–116253. doi:10.1109/ACCESS.2021.3104354

Agrawal, S., Sarkar, S., Srivastava, G., Maddikunta, P. K., & Gadekallu, T. R. (2021). Genetically optimized prediction of the remaining useful life. *Sustainable Computing: Informatics and Systems*, *31*, 100565. doi:10.1016/j.suscom.2021.100565

Agung, A. A. G., & Handayani, R. (2022). Blockchain for smart grid. *Journal of King Saud University-Computer and Information Sciences*, *34*(3), 666–675. doi:10.1016/j.jksuci.2020.01.002

Ahad, A., Tahir, M., & Yau, K. A. (2019). 5G-based smart healthcare network: Architecture, taxonomy, challenges, and future research directions. *IEEE Access : Practical Innovations, Open Solutions*, *7*, 100747–100762. doi:10.1109/ACCESS.2019.2930628

Ahadi, A., Kang, S. K., & Lee, J. H. (2016). A novel approach for optimal combinations of wind, PV, and energy storage system in diesel-free isolated communities. *Applied Energy*, *170*, 101–115. doi:10.1016/j.apenergy.2016.02.110

Ahmad, M., Zaman, N., & Al-Amin, M. (2017). An experimental research in health informatics for enhancing ovarian cancer identification in ovarian imaging analysis using fuzzy histogram equalization. *Journal of Medical Imaging and Health Informatics*, *7*(6), 1385–1390. doi:10.1166/jmihi.2017.2218

Ahmad, T., Madonski, R., Zhang, D., Huang, C., & Mujeeb, A. (2022). Data-driven probabilistic machine learning in sustainable smart energy/smart energy systems: Key developments, challenges, and future research opportunities in the context of the smart grid paradigm. *Renewable & Sustainable Energy Reviews*, *160*, 112128. doi:10.1016/j.rser.2022.112128

Ahmed, S., Shah, M. A., & Wakil, K. (2020). Blockchain as a Trust Builder in the Smart City Domain: A Systematic Literature Review. *IEEE Access : Practical Innovations, Open Solutions*, *8*, 92977–92985. doi:10.1109/ACCESS.2020.2993724

Ahmed, U., Srivastava, G., Yun, U., & Lin, J. C. W. (2022). EANDC: An explainable attention network based deep adaptive clustering model for mental health treatment. *Future Generation Computer Systems*, *130*, 106–113. doi:10.1016/j.future.2021.12.008

Ahsan, M.M. Gupta, K.D. Islam, M.M. Sen, S. Rahman, M.L. & Hossain, M. S. (2020). *Study of Different Deep Learning Approach With Explainable AI for Screening Patients With Covid-19 Symptoms: Using CT Scan and Chest X-ray Image Dataset*". arXiv.

Ahvenniemi, H., Huovila, A., Pinto-Seppä, I., & Airaksinen, M. (2017). What are the differences between sustainable and smart cities? *Cities (London, England)*, *60*, 234–245. doi:10.1016/j.cities.2016.09.009

Aidya S. & Nandi C.(2020). Green Energy Generation Using Renewable Energy Technologies. In *Advances in Greener Energy Technologies* (pp. 259-276). Springer. Singapore.

Airbus (2023). Available online: https://www.airbus.com/

Akcayol, M. A. (2004). Application of adaptive neuro-fuzzy controller for SRM. *Advances in Engineering Software*, *35*(3-4), 129–137. doi:10.1016/j.advengsoft.2004.03.005

Akyildiz, I. F., Lin, S. C., & Wang, P. (2015). Wireless software-defined networks (W-SDNs) and network function virtualization (NFV) for 5G cellular systems: An overview and qualitative evaluation. *Computer Networks*, *93*, 66–79. doi:10.1016/j.comnet.2015.10.013

Alablani, I., & Alenazi, M. (2020). EDTD-SC: An IoT Sensor Deployment Strategy for Smart Cities. *Sensors (Basel)*, *20*(24), 7191. doi:10.339020247191 PMID:33333935

Alam, T. (2021). Cloud-based IoT applications and their roles in smart cities. *Smart Cities*, *4*(3), 1196–1219. doi:10.3390martcities4030064

Alam, T., Tajammul, M., & Gupta, R. (2022). Towards the Sustainable Development of Smart Cities Through Cloud Computing. *Studies in Computational Intelligence*, *1002*, 199–222. doi:10.1007/978-981-16-7498-3_13

Alatabani, L. E., Ali, E. S., & Saeed, R. A. (2021). Deep Learning Approaches for IoV Applications and Services. In N. Magaia, G. Mastorakis, C. Mavromoustakis, E. Pallis, & E. K. Markakis (Eds.), *Intelligent Technologies for Internet of Vehicles. Internet of Things (Technology, Communications, and Computing)*. Springer. doi:10.1007/978-3-030-76493-7_8

Albino, V., Berardi, U., & Dangelico, R. M. (2015). Smart Cities: Definitions, Dimensions, Performance, and Initiatives. *Journal of Urban Technology*, *22*(1), 3–21. doi:10.1080/10630732.2014.942092

Alderwick, H., & Gottlieb, L. M. (2019). Meanings and misunderstandings: A social determinants of health lexicon for health care systems. *The Milbank Quarterly*, *97*(2), 407. PMID:31069864

Al-Emadi, S., Al-Mohannadi, A., & Al-Senaid, F. (2020, February). *Using deep learning techniques for network intrusion detection. In 2020 IEEE international conference on informatics, IoT, and enabling technologies (ICIoT)*. IEEE.

Alemzero, D., Acheampong, T., & Huaping, S. (2021). Prospects of wind energy deployment in Africa: Technical and economic analysis. *Renewable Energy*, *179*, 652–666. doi:10.1016/j.renene.2021.07.021

Ali. (2022). Blockchain for IoT-Based Cyber-Physical Systems (CPS): Applications and Challenges. Blockchain based Internet of Things. Lecture Notes on Data Engineering and Communications Technologies, 112.

Ali, E. S., Hasan, M. K., Hassan, R., Saeed, R. A., Hassan, M. B., Islam, S., Nafi, N. S., & Bevinakoppa, S. (2021). Machine Learning Technologies for Secure Vehicular Communication in Internet of Vehicles: Recent Advances and Applications. *Security and Communication Networks*, *2021*, 8868355. doi:10.1155/2021/8868355

Ali, E. S., Hassan, M. B., & Saeed, R. A. (2021). Machine Learning Technologies on Internet of Vehicles. In N. Magaia, G. Mastorakis, C. Mavromoustakis, E. Pallis, & E. K. Markakis (Eds.), *Intelligent Technologies for Internet of Vehicles. Internet of Things (Technology, Communications, and Computing)*. Springer. doi:10.1007/978-3-030-76493-7_7

Ali, F., El-Sappagh, S., Islam, S. R., Kwak, D., Ali, A., Imran, M., & Kwak, K. (2020). A smart healthcare monitoring system for heart disease prediction based on ensemble deep learning and feature fusion. *Information Fusion*, *63*, 208–222. doi:10.1016/j.inffus.2020.06.008

Allam, A. H., Taha, M., & Zayed, H. H. (2019). Enhanced zone-based energy aware data collection protocol for Wsns. *Journal of King Saud University-Computer and Information Sciences*, *31*(4), 415–560.

Al-Marridi, A. Z., Mohamed, A., Erbad, A., Al-Ali, A., & Guizani, M. (2019). Efficient EEG mobile edge computing and optimal resource allocation for smart health applications. 15th international wireless communications & mobile computing conference (IWCMC). IEEE; June 2019. p. 1261e6.

Al-Marridi, A., Mohamed., A., & Erbad. A. (2020). AI-based techniques on edge devices to optimize energy efficiency in m-Health applications. *AI-based techniques on edge devices.*. doi:10.1016/B978-0-12-819045-6.00001-7

Al-Turjman, F., Zahmatkesh, H., & Shahroze, R. (2022). An overview of security and privacy in smart cities' IoT communications. *Transactions on Emerging Telecommunications Technologies*, *33*(3), e3677. doi:10.1002/ett.3677

Alzubi, J. A., Movassagh, A. A., Gheisari, M., Najafabadi, H. E., Abbasi, A. A., Liu, Y., Pingmei, Z., Izadpanahkakhk, M., & Najafabadi, A. H. P. (2022). A Dynamic SDN-based Privacy-Preserving Approach for Smart City Using Trust Technique. *2022 9th Iranian Joint Congress on Fuzzy and Intelligent Systems,* CFIS 2022.

Amann, J., Blasimme, A., Vayena, E., Frey, D., & Madai, V. I. (2020). Explainability for artificial intelligence in healthcare: A multidisciplinary perspective. *BMC Medical Informatics and Decision Making*, *20*(1), 310. doi:10.118612911-020-01332-6 PMID:33256715

Amazon. (n.d.). *What is Digital Technology?* Amazon. https://aws.amazon.com/what-is/digital-twin/

Amirinasab, M., Shamshirband, S., Chronopoulos, A. T., Mosavi, A., & Nabipour, N. (2020). Energy-efficient method for wireless sensor networks low-power radio operation in Internet of things. *Electronics (Basel)*, *9*(2), 3–20. doi:10.3390/electronics9020320

Amirkhalili, S. A., & Zahedi, A. R. (2018). Techno-economic analysis of a stand-alone hybrid wind/fuel cell microgrid system: A case study in Kouhin region in Qazvin. *Fuel Cells (Weinheim)*, *18*(4), 551–560. doi:10.1002/fuce.201700149

Ammari, C., Belatrache, D., Touhami, B., & Makhloufi, S. (2022). Sizing, optimization, control and energy management of hybrid renewable energy system—A review. *Energy and Built Environment*, *3*(4), 399–411. doi:10.1016/j.enbenv.2021.04.002

Amsterdam Smart City. (n.d.). *Amsterdam Smart City*. ASC. https://amsterdamsmartcity.com/

Anagnostopoulos, T. (2022). *IoT-enabled Unobtrusive Surveillance Systems for Smart Campus Safety*. John Wiley & Sons. doi:10.1002/9781119903932

Andoni, M., Robu, V., Flynn, D., Abram, S., Geach, D., Jenkins, D., ... Peacock, A. (2019). Blockchain technology in the energy sector: A systematic review of challenges and opportunities. *Renewable & Sustainable Energy Reviews*, *100*, 143–174.

Andrew, R. M. (2020). Timely estimates of India's annual and monthly fossil CO< sub> 2</sub> emissions. *Earth System Science Data*, *12*(4), 2411–2421.

Angelidou, M. (2017).. . *The Role of Smart City Characteristics in the Plans of Fifteen Cities.*, *24*(4), 3–28.

Anitha, M., & Senbagavalli, M. (2023). Dynamic Mobile Cloud Eco System Security - A Review, *International Journal of Data Informatics and Intelligent Computing*, *2*(1), 62–69. https://doi.org/10.59461/ijdiic.v2i1.44

Anthopoulos, L. G. (2017). Understanding Smart Cities: A Tool for Smart Government or an Industrial Trick? In *Public Administration and Information Technology*. Springer International Publishing AG. doi:10.1007/978-3-319-57015-0

Arent, D. J., Bragg-Sitton, S. M., Miller, D. C., Tarka, T. J., Engel-Cox, J. A., Boardman, R. D., Balash, P. C., Ruth, M. F., Cox, J., & Garfield, D. J. (2021). Multi-input, multi-output hybrid energy systems. *Joule*, *5*(1), 47–58. doi:10.1016/j.joule.2020.11.004

Arjun, R., & Suprabha, K. R. (2020). *Innovation and challenges of blockchain in banking: A scientometric view*. Academic Press.

Arul, P. G., Ramachandaramurthy, V. K., & Rajkumar, R. K. (2015). Control strategies for a hybrid renewable energy system: A review. *Renewable & Sustainable Energy Reviews*, *42*, 597–608. doi:10.1016/j.rser.2014.10.062

Arun Kumar, B. R. (2022). Developing Business-Business Private Block-Chain Smart Contracts Using Hyper-Ledger Fabric for Security, Privacy and Transparency in Supply Chain. In *Data Management, Analytics and Innovation* (pp. 429–440). Springer.

Ashnani, M. H. M., Johari, A., Hashim, H., & Hasani, E. (2014). A source of renewable energy in Malaysia, why biodiesel? *Renewable & Sustainable Energy Reviews*, *35*, 244–257. doi:10.1016/j.rser.2014.04.001

Ashu, A., Hussain, M. W., Sinha Roy, D., & Reddy, H. K. (2021). Intelligent data compression policy for Hadoop performance optimization. In *Proceedings of the 11th International Conference on Soft Computing and Pattern Recognition (SoCPaR 2019)* (pp. 80-89). Springer International Publishing. 10.1007/978-3-030-49345-5_9

Asiri, S. A. (2022). Smart solutions for monitoring, control, and safety of swimming pools using a savvy boat. *Measurement and Control*, *55*(Jul), 603–615. doi:10.1177/00202940221113593

Askari, I. B., & Ameri, M. (2012). Techno-economic feasibility analysis of stand-alone renewable energy systems (PV/bat, Wind/bat and Hybrid PV/wind/bat) in Kerman, Iran. *Energy Sources. Part B, Economics, Planning, and Policy*, *7*(1), 45–60. doi:10.1080/15567240903330384

Aswathy, R. H., Suresh, P., Sikkandar, M. Y., Abdel-Khalek, S., & Alhumyani, H. (2022). Optimized Tuned Deep Learning Model for Chronic Kidney Disease Classification. CMC-Computers. *Materials & Continua*, *70*(2), 2097–2111. doi:10.32604/cmc.2022.019790

Azaria, A., Ekblaw, A., Vieira, T., & Lippman, A. (2016, August). Medrec: Using blockchain for medical data access and permission management. In *2016 2nd international conference on open and big data (OBD)* (pp. 25-30). IEEE.

Babu, R. G., Karthika, P., & Rajan, V. A. (2020). Secure IoT systems using raspberry Pi machine learning artificial intelligence. In *Second International Conference on Computer Networks and Communication Technologies: ICCNCT 2019* (pp. 797-805). Springer International Publishing.

Badi, M. (2012). *Power Quality Improvement using passive shunt filter, TCR and TSC combination* [Doctoral dissertation].

Badii, C., Bellini, P., Difino, A., & Nesi, P. (2020). *Smart City IoT Platform Respecting GDPR Privacy and Security Aspects*. IEEE.

Badii, C., Bellini, P., Difino, A., & Nesi, P. (2018). Sii-mobility: An IoT/IoE architecture to enhance smart city mobility and transportation services. *Sensors (Basel)*, *19*(1), 1. doi:10.339019010001 PMID:30577434

Badri, M., & Prangya, P. (2019). Machine learning applications to smart city. *ACCENTS Transactions on Image Processing and Computer Vision*, *5*(14), 2019.

Baker, M., Carpenter, B., & Shafi, A. (2006). MPJ Express: Towards thread safe Java HPC, *IEEE International Conference on Cluster Computing*, (pp. 1-10). IEEE. 10.1109/CLUSTR.2006.311890

Bakıcı, T., Almirall, E., & Wareham, J. (2012). A Smart City Initiative: The Case of Barcelona. *Journal of the Knowledge Economy*, *2*(1), 1–14.

Bamakan, S. M. H., Moghaddam, S. G., & Manshadi, S. D. (2021). Blockchain-enabled pharmaceutical cold chain: Applications, key challenges, and future trends. *Journal of Cleaner Production*, *302*, 127021.

Banos, R., Manzano-Agugliaro, F., Montoya, F. G., Gil, C., Alcayde, A., & Gómez, J. (2011). Optimization methods applied to renewable and sustainable energy: A review. *Renewable & Sustainable Energy Reviews*, *15*(4), 1753–1766. doi:10.1016/j.rser.2010.12.008

Bao, X., Liang, H., Liu, Y., & Zhang, F. (2019). A stochastic game approach for collaborative beam forming in sdn-based energy harvesting wireless sensor networks. *IEEE Internet of Things Journal*, *6*(6), 9583–9595. doi:10.1109/JIOT.2019.2930073

Barakabitze, A. A. & Walshe, R. (2022). SDN and NFV for QoE-driven multimedia services delivery: The road towards 6G and beyond networks. *Computer Networks, 214*(January 2021), 109133. doi:10.1016/j.comnet.2022.109133

Barakabitze, A. A., Ahmad, A., Mijumbi, R., & Hines, A. (2020). 5G network slicing using SDN and NFV: A survey of taxonomy, architectures and future challenges. *Computer Networks*, *167*, 106984. Advance online publication. doi:10.1016/j.comnet.2019.106984

Barakabitze, A. A., Sun, L., Mkwawa, I.-H., & Ifeachor, E. (2019). *A Novel QoE-Aware SDN-enabled, NFV-based Management Architecture for Future Multimedia Applications on 5G Systems.* https://arxiv.org/abs/1904.09917

Barcevicius, E.; Cibaite, G.; Codagnone, G.; Gineikyte, V.; Klimaviciute, L.; Liva, G.; Matulevic, L.; Misuraca, G.; Vanini, I. (2019). *Exploring Digital Government transformation in the EU*. Publications Office of the European Union: Luxembourg.

Barricelli, B. R., Casiraghi, E., & Fogli, D. (2019). A survey on digital twin: Definitions, characteristics, applications, and design implications. In I. E. E. E. Access (Ed.), *Institute of Electrical and Electronics Engineers Inc* (Vol. 7). doi:10.1109/ACCESS.2019.2953499

Barrionuevo, J. M., Berrone, P., & Ricart, J. E. (2012). Smart Cities, Sustainable Progress. *IESE Insight, 14*(14), 50–57. doi:10.15581/002.ART-2152

Barro-Torres, S., Fernández-Caramés, T. M., Pérez-Iglesias, H. J., & Escudero, C. J. (2012). Real-time personal protective equipment monitoring system. *Computer Communications, 36*(1), 42–50. doi:10.1016/j.comcom.2012.01.005

Bartoletti, I. (2019, June). AI in healthcare: Ethical and privacy challenges. In *Conference on Artificial Intelligence in Medicine in Europe* (pp. 7-10). Springer.

Bauer, M., Sanchez, L., & Song, J. (2021). IoT-Enabled Smart Cities: Evolution and Outlook. *Sensors, 21*(13), 4511.

Bauer, M., Sanchez, L., & Song, J. S. (2021). IoT-enabled smart cities: Evolution and outlook. *Sensors (Basel), 21*(13), 4511. doi:10.339021134511 PMID:34209436

Belatrache, D., Saifi, N., Harrouz, A., & Bentouba, S. (2020). Modelling and Numerical Investigation of the thermal properties effect on the soil temperature in Adrar region. *Algerian Journal of Renewable Energy and Sustainable Development, 2*(2), 165–174. doi:10.46657/ajresd.2020.2.2.9

Bellini, P., Nesi, P., & Pantaleo, G. (2022). IoT-enabled smart cities: A review of concepts, frameworks and key technologies. *Applied Sciences (Basel, Switzerland), 12*(3), 1607. doi:10.3390/app12031607

Ben Azzouz, L., & Jamai, I. (2019). SDN, slicing, and NFV paradigms for a smart home: A comprehensive survey. *Transactions on Emerging Telecommunications Technologies, 30*(10), 1–13. doi:10.1002/ett.3744

Bentouba, S., & Bourouis, M. (2016). Feasibility study of a wind–photovoltaic hybrid power generation system for a remote area in the extreme south of Algeria. *Applied Thermal Engineering, 99*, 713–719. doi:10.1016/j.applthermaleng.2015.12.014

Bermeo-Ayerbe, M. A., Ocampo-Martinez, C., & Diaz-Rozo, J. (2022, January). CarlosOcampo., JavierDiaz-Rozo. (2021). Data-driven energy prediction modeling for both energy efficiency and maintenance in smart manufacturing systems. *Energy, 238*, 121691. doi:10.1016/j.energy.2021.121691

Bernal Bernabe, J., Canovas, J. L., Hernandez-Ramos, J. L., Torres Moreno, R., & Skarmeta, A. (2019). Privacy-Preserving Solutions for Blockchain: Review and Challenges. *IEEE Access : Practical Innovations, Open Solutions, 7*, 164908–164940. doi:10.1109/ACCESS.2019.2950872

Bhandari, B., Lee, K. T., Lee, G. Y., Cho, Y. M., & Ahn, S. H. (2015). Optimization of hybrid renewable energy power systems: A review. *International Journal of Precision Engineering and Manufacturing-Green Technology, 2*, 99-112.

Bhattacharya, S. (2020). A Review on Deep Learning for Future Smart Cities. *Internet Technology Letters, 5*(1), 2020.

Bhatti, G., Mohan, H., & Raja Singh, R. (2021). Towards the future of smart electric vehicles: Digital twin technology. In *Renewable and Sustainable Energy Reviews* (Vol. 141). Elsevier Ltd. doi:10.1016/j.rser.2021.110801

Bhoi, S. K., Panda, S. K., Jena, K. K., Sahoo, K. S., Jhanjhi, N. Z., Masud, M., & Aljahdali, S. (2022). IoT-EMS: An Internet of Things Based Environment Monitoring System in Volunteer Computing Environment. *Intelligent Automation & Soft Computing, 32*(3).

Bie, Y., Xiong, X., Yan, Y., & Qu, X. (2020). Dynamic headway control for high-frequency bus line based on speed guidance and intersection signal adjustment. *Computer-Aided Civil and Infrastructure Engineering*, *35*(1), 4–25. doi:10.1111/mice.12446

Bilberg, A., & Malik, A. A. (2019). Digital twin driven human–robot collaborative assembly. *CIRP Annals*, *68*(1), 499–502. doi:10.1016/j.cirp.2019.04.011

binti Suhaili, S., & Watanabe, T. (2017, November). Design of high-throughput SHA-256 hash function based on FPGA. In *2017 6th International Conference on Electrical Engineering and Informatics (ICEEI)* (pp. 1-6). IEEE.

Bi, Y., Srinivasan, D., Lu, X., Sun, Z., & Zeng, W. (2014). Type-2 fuzzy multi-intersection traffic signal control with differential evolution optimization. *Expert Systems with Applications*, *41*(16), 7338–7349. doi:10.1016/j.eswa.2014.06.022

Blanco, B., Fajardo, J. O., Giannoulakis, I., Kafetzakis, E., Peng, S., Pérez-Romero, J., Trajkovska, I., Khodashenas, P. S., Goratti, L., Paolino, M., Sfakianakis, E., Liberal, F., & Xilouris, G. (2017). Technology pillars in the architecture of future 5G mobile networks: NFV, MEC and SDN. *Computer Standards & Interfaces*, *54*(January), 216–228. doi:10.1016/j.csi.2016.12.007

Blasi, S., Ganzaroli, A., & De Noni, I. (2022). Smartening sustainable development in cities: Strengthening the theoretical linkage between smart cities and SDGs. *Sustainable Cities and Society*, *80*, 103793. doi:10.1016/j.scs.2022.103793

Blenk, A., Basta, A., Reisslein, M., & Kellerer, W. (2016). Survey on network virtualization hypervisors for software defined networking. *IEEE Communications Surveys and Tutorials*, *18*(1), 655–685. doi:10.1109/COMST.2015.2489183

Bodkhe, U., Tanwar, S., Parekh, K., Khanpara, P., Tyagi, S., Kumar, N., & Alazab, M. (2020). Blockchain for industry 4.0: A comprehensive review. *IEEE Access : Practical Innovations, Open Solutions*, *8*, 79764–79800.

Bonner, C., Bell, K., Jansen, J., Glasziou, P., Irwig, L., Doust, J., & McCaffery, K. (2018). Should heart age calculators be used alongside absolute cardiovascular disease risk assessment? *BMC Cardiovascular Disorders*, *18*(1), 18–19. doi:10.118612872-018-0760-1 PMID:29409444

Bosamia, M., & Patel, D. (2018). Current trends and future implementation possibilities of the Merkel tree. *International Journal on Computer Science and Engineering*, *6*(8), 294–301.

Botín-Sanabria, D. M., Mihaita, S., Peimbert-García, R. E., Ramírez-Moreno, M. A., Ramírez-Mendoza, R. A., & Lozoya-Santos, J. de J. (2022). Digital Twin Technology Challenges and Applications: A Comprehensive Review. In Remote Sensing, 14(6). MDPI. doi:10.3390/rs14061335

Boukerche, A., & Coutinho, R. W. (2019). Crowd management: The overlooked component of smart transportation systems. *IEEE Communications Magazine*, *57*(4), 48–53. doi:10.1109/MCOM.2019.1800641

Bouras, C., Kapoulas, V., Kokkinos, V., Leonardos, D., Pipilas, C., & Papachristos, N. (2018). Extension to Middleware for IoT Devices, with Applications in Smart Cities. In Cloud Infrastructures, Services, and IoT Systems for Smart Cities. Springer, Cham. doi:10.1007/978-3-319-67636-4_13

Bracco, S., Rosales-Asensio, E., González-Martínez, A., Rosen, M. A., & Badidi, E. (2022). Edge AI and Blockchain for Smart Sustainable Cities: Promise and Potential. *Sustainability*, *14*(13), 7609. doi:10.3390/su14137609

British Standards Institute. (2014). *Smart city framework – Guide to establishing strategies for smart cities and communities*. BSI.

Brka, A., Kothapalli, G., & Al-Abdeli, Y. M. (2015). Predictive power management strategies for stand-alone hydrogen systems: Lab-scale validation. *International Journal of Hydrogen Energy*, *40*(32), 9907–9916. doi:10.1016/j.ijhydene.2015.06.081

Burhanuddin, M. A., Mohammed, A. A. J., Ismail, R., & Basiron, H. (2017). Internet of things architecture: Current challenges and future direction of research. *International Journal of Applied Engineering Research: IJAER*, *12*(21), 11055–11061.

Byk, C., Abareshi, A., Paz, A., Ruiz, R. A., Battarra, R., Rogers, C. D., & Lizarraga, C. (2021). *Smart Mobility Adoption: A Review of the Literature*. University of Birmingham.

Caird, S. (2018). City approaches to smart city evaluation and reporting: Case studies in the United Kingdom. *Urban Research & Practice*, *11*(2), 159–179. doi:10.1080/17535069.2017.1317828

Calzada, I., & Cobo, C. (2015). Unplugging: Deconstructing the Smart City. *Journal of Urban Technology*, *22*(1), 23–43. doi:10.1080/10630732.2014.971535

Cantarero, M. M. V. (2020). Of renewable energy, energy democracy, and sustainable development: A roadmap to accelerate the energy transition in developing countries. *Energy Research & Social Science*, *70*, 101716. doi:10.1016/j.erss.2020.101716

Cao, Y., Wang, Z. C., Liu, F., Li, P., & Xie, G. (2019). Bio-inspired speed curve optimization and sliding mode tracking control for subway trains. *IEEE Transactions on Vehicular Technology*, *68*(7), 6331–6342. doi:10.1109/TVT.2019.2914936

Caragliu, A., Del Bo, C., & Nijkamp, P. (2011). Smart Cities in Europe. *Journal of Urban Technology*, *18*(2), 65–82. doi:10.1080/10630732.2011.601117

Caromel, D., di Costanzo, A., & Mathieu, C. (2007, May). Peer-to-peer for computational grids: Mixing clusters and desktop machines. *Parallel Computing*, *33*(4-5), 275–288. doi:10.1016/j.parco.2007.02.011

Castelnovo, W., Misuraca, G., & Savoldelli, A. (2016). Smart Cities Governance: The Need for a Holistic Approach to Assessing Urban Participatory Policy Making. *Social Science Computer Review*, *34*(6), 724–739. doi:10.1177/0894439315611103

Cavalcanti, D., Perez-Ramirez, J., Rashid, M. M., Fang, J., Galeev, M., & Stanton, K. B. (2019). Extending accurate time distribution and timeliness capabilities over the air to enable future wireless industrial automation systems. *Proceedings of the IEEE*, *107*(6), 1132–1152. doi:10.1109/JPROC.2019.2903414

Celdrán, A. H., Pérez, M. G., Clemente, F. J. G., Ippoliti, F., & Pérez, G. M. (2019). Dynamic network slicing management of multimedia scenarios for future remote healthcare. *Multimedia Tools and Applications*, *78*(17), 24707–24737. doi:10.100711042-019-7283-3

Chabhadiya, K., Srivastava, R. R., & Pathak, P. (2021). Growth projections against set-target of renewable energy and resultant impact on emissions reduction in India. *Environmental Engineering Research*, *26*(2).

Cha, J., Singh, S. K., Kim, T. W., & Park, J. H. (2021). Blockchain-empowered cloud architecture based on secret sharing for smart city. *Journal of Information Security and Applications*, *57*, 102686. doi:10.1016/j.jisa.2020.102686

Chamanian, S., Baghaee, S., Uluşan, H., Zorlu, Ö., Uysal-Biyikoglu, E., & Kulah, H. (2019). Implementation of energy-neutral operation on vibration energy harvesting WSN. *IEEE Sensors Journal*, *19*(8), 3092–3099. doi:10.1109/JSEN.2019.2890902

Chang, F., & Das, D. (2020). Smart Nation Singapore: Developing Policies for a Citizen-Oriented Smart City Initiative. *Developing National Urban Policies*, 425–440.

Chaves, R., Motta, C., Correia, A., Paredes, H., Caetano, B., De Souza, J. M., & Schneider, D. (2022, May). Crowd and Urban Storytelling: Evaluating a Collective Intelligence Model to Support Discussions about the City. In 2022, *IEEE 25th International Conference on Computer Supported Cooperative Work in Design (CSCWD) (pp. 1473-1479), Hangzhou, China*. IEEE.

Chelladurai, M. U., Pandian, S., & Ramasamy, K. (2021). A blockchain-based patient-centric electronic health record storage and integrity management for e-Health systems. *Health Policy and Technology*, *10*(4), 100513.

Chen, L., Kuang, X., Xu, A., Suo, S., & Yang, Y. (2020, December). A novel network intrusion detection system based on CNN. In *2020 eighth international conference on advanced cloud and big data (CBD)* (pp. 243-247). IEEE.10.1109/ROEDUNET.2019.8909551

Chen, X., Kang, E., Shiraishi, S., Preciado, V. M., & Jiang, Z. (2018). Digital behavioral twins for safe connected cars. In *Proceedings of the 21st ACM/IEEE Int. Conf. Model Driven Eng. Lang. Syst. Models* (pp. 144–153). IEEE. 10.1145/3239372.3239401

Chen, C., Hu, Y., Karuppiah, M., & Kumar, P. M. (2021, October). Artificial intelligence on economic evaluation of energy efficiency and renewable energy technologies. *Sustainable Energy Technologies and Assessments*, *47*, 101358. doi:10.1016/j.seta.2021.101358

Chen, D. (2017). Research on traffic flow prediction in the big data environment based on the improved RBF neural network. *IEEE Transactions on Industrial Informatics*, *13*(4), 2000–2008. doi:10.1109/TII.2017.2682855

Chen, M., Ma, Y., Li, Y., Wu, D., Zhang, Y., & Youn, C. H. (2017). Wearable 2.0: Enabling human-cloud integration in next generation healthcare systems. *IEEE Communications Magazine*, *55*(1), 54–61. doi:10.1109/MCOM.2017.1600410CM

Chen, Q., Wang, W., Wu, F., De, S., Wang, R., Zhang, B., & Huang, X. (2019). A survey of an emerging area: Deep learning for smart city data. *IEEE Transactions on Emerging Topics in Computational Intelligence*, *3*(5), 392–410. doi:10.1109/TETCI.2019.2907718

Chourabi, H., Nam, T., Walker, S., Gil-Garcia, J. R., Mellouli, S., Nahon, K., Pardo, T. A., & Scholl, H. J. (2012). Understanding smart cities: An integrative framework. *Proceedings of the Annual Hawaii International Conference on System Sciences*, 2289–2297. 10.1109/HICSS.2012.615

Chui, K., Alhalabi, W., Pang, S., Pablos, P., Liu, R., & Zhao, M. (2017). Disease diagnosis in smart healthcare: Innovation technologies and applications. *Sustainability (Basel)*, *9*(12), 2309. doi:10.3390u9122309

Chun-Wei, J. L., Srivastava, G., Zhang, Y., Djenouri, Y., & Aloqaily, M. (2020). Privacy-preserving multiobjective sanitization model in 6G IoT environments. *IEEE Internet of Things Journal*, *8*(7), 5340–5349.

Clúa, J. G. G., Mantz, R. J., & De Battista, H. (2018). Optimal sizing of a grid-assisted wind-hydrogen system. *Energy Conversion and Management*, *166*, 402–408. doi:10.1016/j.enconman.2018.04.047

Colombo, L., Corradini, M. L., Ippoliti, G., & Orlando, G. (2020). Pitch angle control of a wind turbine operating above the rated wind speed: A sliding mode control approach. *ISA Transactions*, *96*, 95–102. doi:10.1016/j.isatra.2019.07.002 PMID:31320141

Condoluci, M., & Mahmoodi, T. (2018). Softwarization and virtualization in 5G mobile networks: Benefits, trends and challenges. *Computer Networks*, *146*, 65–84. doi:10.1016/j.comnet.2018.09.005

Conti, M., Das, S. K., Bisdikian, C., Kumar, M., Ni, L. M., Passarella, A., Roussos, G., Tröster, G., Tsudik, G., & Zambonelli, F. (2012). Looking ahead in pervasive computing: Challenges and opportunities in the era of cyber–physical convergence. *Pervasive and Mobile Computing*, *8*(1), 2–21. doi:10.1016/j.pmcj.2011.10.001

Cuda, R., Guastaroba, G., & Speranza, M. G. (2015). A survey on two-echelon routing problems. *Computers & Operations Research*, *55*, 185–199. doi:10.1016/j.cor.2014.06.008

Curzon, J., Almehmadi, A., & El-Khatib, K. (2019). A survey of privacy enhancing technologies for smart cities. *Pervasive and Mobile Computing*, *55*, 76–95. doi:10.1016/j.pmcj.2019.03.001

Dalamagkas, C., Sarigiannidis, P., Ioannidis, D., Iturbe, E., Nikolis, O., Ramos, F., Rios, E., Sarigiannidis, A., & Tzovaras, D. (2019). A Survey On Honeypots, Honeynets And Their Applications On Smart Grid. *2019 IEEE Conference on Network Softwarization (NetSoft),* (pp. 93–100). IEEE. 10.1109/NETSOFT.2019.8806693

Dalwadi, P., Shrinet, V., Mehta, C. R., & Shah, P. (2011, December). Optimization of solar-wind hybrid system for distributed generation. In *2011 Nirma University International Conference on Engineering* (pp. 1-4). IEEE.

Dameri, R. P., & Cocchia, A. (2013). Smart city and digital city: twenty years of terminology evolution. *ItAIS2013, X Conference of the Italian Chapter of AIS.*

Dargie, W., & Poellabauer, C. (2010). *Fundamentals of wireless sensor networks: Theory and practice.* Wiley.

Dasgupta, A., Maguire, E., Abdul-Rahman, A., & Chen, M. (2016). *Opportunities and challenges for privacy-preserving visualization of electronic health record data.* Academic Press.

Dashkevich, N., Counsell, S., & Destefanis, G. (2020). Blockchain application for central banks: A systematic mapping study. *IEEE Access : Practical Innovations, Open Solutions, 8,* 139918–139952.

Dash, V., & Bajpai, P. (2015). Power management control strategy for a stand-alone solar photovoltaic-fuel cell–battery hybrid system. *Sustainable Energy Technologies and Assessments, 9,* 68–80. doi:10.1016/j.seta.2014.10.001

Das, S. P. K., Shah, S. C. N., & Suyal, S. S. (2020). Indian Renewable Energy Development Agency Limited (A Government of India Enterprise) Board of Directors. *Water and Energy International, 63*(8), 35–36.

de Almeida Florencio, F., Moreno, E. D., Macedo, H. T., de Britto Salgueiro, R. J., do Nascimento, F. B., & Santos, F. A. O. (2018, November). Intrusion detection via MLP neural network using an arduino embedded system. In *2018 VIII Brazilian Symposium on Computing Systems Engineering (SBESC)* (pp. 190-195). IEEE. 10.1109/SBESC.2018.00036

Deetjen, T. A., Martin, H., Rhodes, J. D., & Webber, M. E. (2018). Modeling the optimal mix and location of wind and solar with transmission and carbon pricing considerations. *Renewable Energy, 120,* 35–50. doi:10.1016/j.renene.2017.12.059

Deloitte. (n.d.). *Smart Cities Funding and Financing Strategies.* Deloitte. https://www.deloitte.com/global/en/Industries/government-public/perspectives/smart-cities-funding-and-financing-strategies.html

Demirel, D. (2021). *How the smart governance model shapes cities? Cases from Europe.* J. Enterprising Communities.

Deren, L., Wenbo, Y., & Zhenfeng, S. (2021). Smart city based on digital twins. *Computational Urban Science, 1*(1), 1–11. doi:10.100743762-021-00005-y

Deshmukh, M. K., & Deshmukh, S. S. (2008). Modeling of hybrid renewable energy systems. *Renewable & Sustainable Energy Reviews, 12*(1), 235–249. doi:10.1016/j.rser.2006.07.011

Dey, N., Ashour, A. S., & Bhatt, C. (2017). Internet of things driven connected healthcare. In *Internet of things and big data technologies for next generation healthcare* (pp. 3–12). Springer. doi:10.1007/978-3-319-49736-5_1

Dhungana, D., Engelbrecht, G., Parreira, J. X., Schuster, A., & Valerio, D. (2015). Aspern smart ICT: Data analytics and privacy challenges in a smart city. *2015 IEEE 2nd World Forum on Internet of Things (WF-IoT),* (pp. 447–452). IEEE.

Din, S., Rathore, M. M., Ahmad, A., Paul, A., & Khan, M. (2017, October). Sdiot: Software defined internet of thing to analyze big data in smart cities. In *2017 IEEE 42nd Conference on Local Computer Networks Workshops (LCN Workshops)* (pp. 175-182). IEEE.

Din, S., Paul, A., & Rehman, A. (2019). 5G-enabled Hierarchical architecture for software-defined intelligent transportation system. *Computer Networks, 150,* 81–89. doi:10.1016/j.comnet.2018.11.035

Diogo, A. C. (2020, November). Application of machine learning tools for energy efficiency in industry: A review. *Energy Reports*, *6*, 1181–1199. doi:10.1016/j.egyr.2020.04.035

Dong, B., Shi, Q., Yang, Y., Wen, F., Zhang, Z., & Lee, C. (2021). Technology evolution from self-powered sensors to AIoT enabled smart homes. *Nano Energy*, *79*, 105414. doi:10.1016/j.nanoen.2020.105414

Doshi-Velez, F., & Kim, B. (2017). *Towards A Rigorous Science of Interpretable Machine Learning*. Ml.

Drost, N., van Nieuwpoort, R. V., & Bal, H. (2006). Simple locality-aware co-allocation in peer-to-peer supercomputing. In *Sixth IEEE International Symposium on Cluster Computing and the Grid Workshops (CCGRID'06)*, (pp. 14–21). IEEE.

Duda. O., Kunanets. N., Matsiuk. O & Pasichnyk. V. (2022). Cloud-based IT Infrastructure for "Smart City" Projects. *InDependable IoT for Human and Industry,* 389-409 River Publishers.

Du, M., Chen, Q., Xiao, J., Yang, H., & Ma, X. (2020). Supply Chain Finance Innovation Using Blockchain. *IEEE Transactions on Engineering Management*, *67*(4), 1045–1058. doi:10.1109/TEM.2020.2971858

Du, R., Santi, P., Xiao, M., Vasilakos, A. V., & Fischione, C. (2019). Sensable city: A Survey on the deployment and management of smart city monitoring. *IEEE Communications Surveys and Tutorials*, *21*(2), 1533–1560. doi:10.1109/COMST.2018.2881008

Dwivedi, G., & Sharma, M. P. (2014). Prospects of biodiesel from Pongamia in India. *Renewable & Sustainable Energy Reviews*, *32*, 114–122. doi:10.1016/j.rser.2014.01.009

Dyrstad, J. M., Skonhoft, A., Christensen, M. Q., & Ødegaard, E. T. (2019). Does economic growth eat up environmental improvements? Electricity production and fossil fuel emission in OECD countries 1980–2014. *Energy Policy*, *125*, 103–109. doi:10.1016/j.enpol.2018.10.051

Ebenezer, O. (2018). Smart cities survey. *IEEE 20th International Conference on High Performance Computing and Communications*.

Ebrahim, Z., & Irani, Z. (2005). E-government adoption: Architecture and barriers. *Business Process Management Journal*, *11*(5), 589–611. doi:10.1108/14637150510619902

Egaji, O. A., Chakhar, S., & Brown, D. (2019). An innovative decision rule approach to tyre pressure monitoring. *Expert Systems with Applications*, *124*, 252–270. doi:10.1016/j.eswa.2019.01.051

Eiza, M. H., Owens, T., & Ni, Q. (2015). Secure and robust multi-constrained QoS aware routing algorithm for VANETs. *IEEE Transactions on Dependable and Secure Computing*, *13*(1), 32–45. doi:10.1109/TDSC.2014.2382602

Ejaz, W., & Anpalagan, A. (2019). *Internet of Things for Smart Cities: Technologies, Big Data, and Security*. Springer. doi:10.1007/978-3-319-95037-2

el Jaouhari, S. (2022). Toward a Secure Firmware OTA Update for constrained IoT devices. *2022 IEEE International Smart Cities Conference (ISC2),* (pp. 1–6). IEEE. 10.1109/ISC255366.2022.9922087

Elahi, H., Eugeni, M., & Gaudenzi, P. (2018). A review on mechanisms for piezoelectric-based energy harvesters. *Energies*, *11*(7), 18–50. doi:10.3390/en11071850

Elfatih, N. M., Hasan, M. K., Kamal, Z., Gupta, D., Saeed, R. A., Ali, E. S., & Hosain, M. S. (2022). Internet of vehicle's resource management in 5G networks using AI technologies: Current status and trends. *IET Communications*, *16*(5), 400–420. doi:10.1049/cmu2.12315

Elhabyan, R., Shi, W., & St-Hilaire, M. (2019). Coverage protocols for wireless sensor networks: Review and future directions. *Journal of Communications and Networks (Seoul)*, *21*(1), 45–60. doi:10.1109/JCN.2019.000005

Elhoseny, M., Ramírez-González, G., Abu-Elnasr, O. M., Shawkat, S. A., Arunkumar, N., & Farouk, A. (2018). Secure medical data transmission model for IoT-based healthcare systems. *IEEE Access : Practical Innovations, Open Solutions*, *2018*(6), 20596–20608. doi:10.1109/ACCESS.2018.2817615

Elrawy, M. F., Awad, A. I., & Hamed, H. F. (2018). Intrusion detection systems for IoT-based smart environments: A survey. *Journal of Cloud Computing (Heidelberg, Germany)*, *7*(1), 1–20. doi:10.118613677-018-0123-6

El-Shorbagy, A. M. (2021). 5G Technology and the Future of Architecture. *Procedia Computer Science*, *182*, 121–131. doi:10.1016/j.procs.2021.02.017

Enders, M. R., & Hoßbach, N. (2019). *Dimensions of digital twin applications-a literature review.*

Engin, M. (2013). Sizing and simulation of PV-wind hybrid power system. *International Journal of Photoenergy.*

Erdinc, O., Paterakis, N. G., Pappi, I. N., Bakirtzis, A. G., & Catalão, J. P. (2015). A new perspective for sizing of distributed generation and energy storage for smart households under demand response. *Applied Energy*, *143*, 26–37. doi:10.1016/j.apenergy.2015.01.025

Fadaeenejad, M., Radzi, M. A. M., AbKadir, M. Z. A., & Hizam, H. (2014). Assessment of hybrid renewable power sources for rural electrification in Malaysia. *Renewable & Sustainable Energy Reviews*, *30*, 299–305. doi:10.1016/j.rser.2013.10.003

Falconer, G., & Mitchell, S. (2012). *Smart City Framework A Systematic Process for Enabling Smart Connected Communities*. CISCO. https://www.cisco.com/web/about/ac79/docs/ps/motm/Smart-City-Framework.pdf

Fatos, X. Parallel Programming, Models and Applications in Grid and P2P Systems, (pp.118–147). IOS Press.

Feilat, E. A., Azzam, S., & Al-Salaymeh, A. (2018). Impact of large PV and wind power plants on voltage and frequency stability of Jordan's national grid. *Sustainable Cities and Society*, *36*, 257–271. doi:10.1016/j.scs.2017.10.035

Feng, X., Ling, X., Zheng, H., Chen, Z., & Xu, Y. (2018). Adaptive multi-kernel SVM with spatial–temporal correlation for short-term traffic flow prediction. *IEEE Transactions on Intelligent Transportation Systems*, *20*(6), 2001–2013. doi:10.1109/TITS.2018.2854913

Feng, X., Yan, F., & Liu, X. (2019). Study of Wireless Communication Technologies on Internet of Things for Precision Agriculture. *Wireless Personal Communications*, *108*(3), 1785–1802. doi:10.100711277-019-06496-7

Ferg, E. E., Schuldt, F., & Schmidt, J. (2019). The challenges of li-ion starter lighting and ignition battery: A review from Cradle to Grave. *Journal of Power Sources*, *423*, 380–403. doi:10.1016/j.jpowsour.2019.03.063

Fernandez-Rodriguez, A., Fernández-Cardador, A., Cucala, A. P., Domínguez, M., & Gonsalves, T. (2015). Design of robust and energy-efficient ATO speed profiles of metropolitan lines considering train load variations and delays. *IEEE Transactions on Intelligent Transportation Systems*, *16*(4), 2061–2071. doi:10.1109/TITS.2015.2391831

Ferrer, A. J., Hernández, F., Tordsson, J., Elmroth, E., Ali-Eldin, A., Zsigri, C., Sirvent, R., Guitart, J., Badia, R. M., Djemame, K., Ziegler, W., Dimitrakos, T., Nair, S. K., Kousiouris, G., Konstanteli, K., Varvarigou, T., Hudzia, B., Kipp, A., Wesner, S., & Sheridan, C. (2012). OPTIMIS: A holistic approach to cloud service provisioning. *Future Generation Computer Systems*, *28*(1), 66–77. doi:10.1016/j.future.2011.05.022

Ferrer, J., López-Ibáñez, M., & Alba, E. (2019). Reliable simulation-optimization of traffic lights in a real-world city. *Applied Soft Computing*, *78*, 697–711. doi:10.1016/j.asoc.2019.03.016

Ferrer-Martí, L., Garwood, A., Chiroque, J., Ramirez, B., Marcelo, O., Garfí, M., & Velo, E. (2012). Evaluating and comparing three community small-scale wind electrification projects. *Renewable & Sustainable Energy Reviews*, *16*(7), 5379–5390. doi:10.1016/j.rser.2012.04.015

Filali, A., Cherkaoui, S., & Kobbane, A. (2019). Prediction-based Switch Migration Scheduling for SDN Load Balancing. *ICC 2019 - 2019 IEEE International Conference on Communications (ICC)*, 1–6. 10.1109/ICC.2019.8761469

Filali, F. Z., & Yagoubi, B. (2015). Global trust: A trust model for cloud service selection. *International Journal of Computer Network and Information Security*, *7*(5), 41–50. doi:10.5815/ijcnis.2015.05.06

Fizza, K., Banerjee, A., Mitra, K., Jayaraman, P. P., Ranjan, R., Patel, P., & Georgakopoulos, D. (2021). QoE in IoT: A vision, survey and future directions. *Discov. Internet Things*, *1*(1), 4. doi:10.100743926-021-00006-7

Forster, A. (2016). *Introduction to wireless sensor networks*. John Wiley & Sons. doi:10.1002/9781119345343

Founoun. (2021). Machine Learning to Support Smart City Initiatives. *Journal of Tianjin University Science and Technology*.

Francisco, A., Mohammadi, N., & Taylor, J. (2020). Smart city digital twin–enabled energy management: Toward real-time urban building energy benchmarking. *Journal of Management in Engineering, 36*(2).

François, B., Hingray, B., Raynaud, D., Borga, M., & Creutin, J. D. (2016). Increasing climate-related-energy penetration by integrating run-of-the river hydropower to wind/solar mix. *Renewable Energy*, *87*, 686–696. doi:10.1016/j.renene.2015.10.064

Freire, C. A. R., Ferreira, F. A. F., Carayannis, E. G., & Ferreira, J. J. M. (2021). Artificial Intelligence and Smart Cities: A DEMATEL Approach to Adaptation Challenges and Initiative. *IEEE Transactions on Engineering Management*. Advance online publication. doi:10.1109/TEM.2021.3098665

Fu, B., Zhang, J., Chen, H., Guo, H., Song, C., Shang, W., Tao, P., & Deng, T. (2019). Optical nano fluids for direct absorption-based solar thermal energy harvesting at medium-to-high temperatures. *Current Opinion in Chemical Engineering*, *25*, 51–56. doi:10.1016/j.coche.2019.07.002

Fuller, A., Zhong, F., Day, C., & Barlow, C. (2020). IDigital twin: Enabling technologies, challenges and open Research. *IEEE Access, 8*, 108952–108971

Fu, Y., Yan, Z., Li, H., Xin, X. L., & Cao, J. (2017). A secure SDN based multi-RANs architecture for future 5G networks. *Computers & Security*, *70*, 648–662. doi:10.1016/j.cose.2017.08.013

Gahlot, S., Reddy, S. R. N., & Kumar, D. (2019, April). Review of smart health monitoring approaches with survey analysis and proposed framework. *IEEE Internet of Things Journal*, *6*(2), 2116–2127. doi:10.1109/JIOT.2018.2872389

Gai, K., Wu, Y., Zhu, L., Qiu, M., & Shen, M. (2019). Privacy-preserving energy trading using consortium Blockchain in smart grid. *IEEE Transactions on Industrial Informatics*, *15*(6), 3548–3558. doi:10.1109/TII.2019.2893433

Gai, K., Wu, Y., Zhu, L., Xu, L., & Zhang, Y. (2019). Permissioned blockchain and edge computing empowered privacy-preserving smart grid networks. *IEEE Internet of Things Journal*, *6*(5), 7992–8004. doi:10.1109/JIOT.2019.2904303

Galache, J. A., Santana, J. R., Gutiérrez, V., Sánchez, L., Sotres, P., & Muñoz, L. (2012). Towards experimentation service duality within a Smart City scenario. *2012 9th Annual Conference on Wireless On-Demand Network Systems and Services, WONS* 2012, 175–181.

Gao, X. Z., Nalluri, M. S. R., Kannan, K., & Sinharoy, D. (2021). Multi-objective optimization of feature selection using hybrid cat swarm optimization. *Science China. Technological Sciences*, *64*(3), 508–520. doi:10.100711431-019-1607-7

Garcerá, G. (2017). A Novel Locality Algorithm and Peer-to-Peer Communication Infrastructure for Optimizing Network Performance in Smart Microgrids. *Special Issue Control and Communication in Distributed Generation Systems, 10*(9).

Garcia Hernando, A. B., Da Silva Farina, A., Bellido Triana, L., Ruiz Pinar, F. J., & Fernandez Cambronero, D. (2017). Virtualization of residential IoT functionality by using NFV and SDN. *2017 IEEE International Conference on Consumer Electronics, ICCE 2017*, (pp. 86–87). 10.1109/ICCE.2017.7889240

Garcia, P., Torreglosa, J. P., Fernandez, L. M., & Jurado, F. (2013). Optimal energy management system for stand-alone wind turbine/photovoltaic/hydrogen/battery hybrid system with supervisory control based on fuzzy logic. *International Journal of Hydrogen Energy, 38*(33), 14146–14158. doi:10.1016/j.ijhydene.2013.08.106

Gartner Top Strategic Technology Trends. (2023). *Detailed Guide (eBook).* Gartner. https://www.gartner.com/en/information-technology/insights/top-technology-trends

Ge, M., Bangui, H., & Buhnova, B. (2018). Big data for internet of things: A survey. *Future Generation Computer Systems, 87*, 601–614. doi:10.1016/j.future.2018.04.053

Genaud, S., & Rattanapoka, C. (2007). P2P-MPI: A Peer-to-Peer Framework for Robust Execution of Message Passing Parallel Programs on Grids. *Journal of Grid Computing, 5*(1), 27–42. doi:10.100710723-006-9056-2

Genaud, S., & Rattanapoka, C. (2009). *A Peer-to-Peer Framework for Message Passing Parallel Programs.* 10.1145/775152.775242

Gerlings, J., Jensen, M. S., & Shollo, A. (2022). Explainable AI, But Explainable to Whom? An Exploratory Case Study of xAI in Healthcare. In C. P. Lim, Y. W. Chen, A. Vaidya, C. Mahorkar, & L. C. Jain (Eds.), *Handbook of Artificial Intelligence in Healthcare. Intelligent Systems Reference Library* (Vol. 212). Springer. doi:10.1007/978-3-030-83620-7_7

Ghafoor, U., Ali, M., Khan, H. Z., Siddiqui, A. M., & Naeem, M. (2022). NOMA and future 5G & B5G wireless networks: A paradigm. *Journal of Network and Computer Applications, 204*(April), 103413. doi:10.1016/j.jnca.2022.103413

Gharaibeh, A., Salahuddin, M. A., Hussini, S. J., Khreishah, A., Khalil, I., Guizani, M., & Al-Fuqaha, A. (2017). Smart cities: A survey on data management, security, and enabling technologies. *IEEE Communications Surveys and Tutorials, 19*(4), 2456–2501. doi:10.1109/COMST.2017.2736886

Ghassemi, M., Oakden-Rayner, L., & Beam, A. L. (2021). The false hope of current approaches to explainable artificial intelligence in health care. *The Lancet. Digital Health, 3*(11), E745–E750. doi:10.1016/S2589-7500(21)00208-9 PMID:34711379

Gheisari, M., Najafabadi, H. E., Alzubi, J. A., Gao, J., Wang, G., Abbasi, A. A., & Castiglione, A. (2021). OBPP: An ontology-based framework for privacy-preserving in IoT-based smart cities. *Future Generation Computer Systems, 123*, 1–13. doi:10.1016/j.future.2021.01.028

Giang, N. K., Leung, V. C., & Lea, R. (2016). On developing smart transportation applications in the fog computing paradigm. *Proceedings of the 6th ACM Symposium on Development and Analysis of Intelligent Vehicular Networks and Applications - DIVANet '16.* ACM. 10.1145/2989275.2989286

Giffinger, R., Fertner, C., Kramar, H., Meijers, E., & Pichler-Milanovic, N. (2007). *Smart cities: Ranking of European medium-sized cities. Rapport technique.* Center of Regional Science, Vienna University of Technology.

Gil-García, J. R., & Pardo, T. A. (2005). E-government success factors: Mapping practical tools to theoretical foundations. *Government Information Quarterly, 22*(2), 187–216. doi:10.1016/j.giq.2005.02.001

Gil-Gonzalez, W., Montoya, O. D., & Garces, A. (2019). Direct power control for VSC-HVDC systems: An application of the global tracking passivity-based PI approach. *International Journal of Electrical Power & Energy Systems, 110*, 588–597. doi:10.1016/j.ijepes.2019.03.042

Gill, S. S., Arya, R. C., Wander, G. S., & Buyya, R. (2018). Fog-based smart healthcare as a big data and cloud service for heart patients using IoT. In *International Conference on Intelligent Data Communication Technologies and Internet of Things* (pp. 1376-1383). Springer, Cham.

Girardet, H., & Mendonça, M. (2009). *A renewable world: energy, ecology and equality. A report for the World Future Council*. Green Books & Resurgence Books.

Gohar, A., & Nencioni, G. (2021). The role of 5g technologies in a smart city: The case for intelligent transportation system. *Sustainability (Basel), 13*(9), 1–24. doi:10.3390u13095188

Golkarifard, M., Chiasserini, C. F., Malandrino, F. & Movaghar, A. (2021). Dynamic VNF placement, resource allocation and traffic routing in 5G. *Computer Networks, 188*(November 2020), 107830. doi:10.1016/j.comnet.2021.107830

Golosova, J., & Romanovs, A. (2018, November). The advantages and disadvantages of the blockchain technology. In *2018 IEEE 6th workshop on advances in information, electronic and electrical engineering (AIEEE)* (pp. 1-6). IEEE. 10.1109/AIEEE.2018.8592253

Gong, Y. J., Liu, Y. W., Lin, Y., Chen, W. N., & Zhang, J. (2019). Real-Time Taxi–Passenger Matching Using a Differential Evolutionary Fuzzy Controller. *IEEE Transactions on Systems, Man, and Cybernetics. Systems, 51*(5), 2712–2725. doi:10.1109/TSMC.2019.2916184

Gopal, G., Suter-Crazzolara, C., Toldo, L., & Eberhardt, W. (2019). Digital transformation in healthcare–architectures of present and future information technologies. *Clinical Chemistry and Laboratory Medicine, 57*(3), 328–335. PMID:30530878

Gorkhali, A., Li, L., & Shrestha, A. (2020). Blockchain: A literature review. *Journal of Management Analytics, 7*(3), 321–343.

Graham, S. (1997). Telecommunications and the Future of Cities: Debunking the Myths. *Cities (London, England), 14*(1), 21–29. doi:10.1016/S0264-2751(37)00037-8

Graham, S. (2002). Bridging Urban Digital Divides? Urban Polarisation and Information and Communications Technologies (ICTs). *Urban Studies (Edinburgh, Scotland), 39*(1), 33–56. doi:10.1080/00420980220099050

Graham, S., & Aurigi, A. (1997). Urbanizing cyberspace? *City (London, England), 2*(7), 18–39. doi:10.1080/13604819708900051

Graham, S., & Marvin, S. (1996). *Telecommunications and the city*. Routledge.

Graham, S., & Marvin, S. (1999). Planning Cybercities: Integrating Telecommunications Into Urban Planning. *The Town Planning Review, 70*(1), 89–114. doi:10.3828/tpr.70.1.w34454x3475g2858

Graham, S., & Marvin, S. (2004). Planning Cyber-cities? Integrating Telecommunications into Urban Planning. In S. Graham (Ed.), *The Cybercities Reader*. Routledge.

Grande, D., Marti, X. L., Feuerstein-Simon, R., Merchant, R. M., Asch, D. A., Lewson, A., & Cannuscio, C. C. (2020). Health policy and privacy challenges associated with digital technology. *JAMA Network Open, 3*(7), e208285–e208285. PMID:32644138

Gropp, W., Lusk, E., & Skjellum, A. (1999). Using MPI, Portable Parallel Programming with the Message-Passing Interface. Scientific and Engineering Computation Series. MIT Press, 2nd edition edition.

Guardtime, G. (2019). *Increasing Healthcare Security with Blockchain Technology*. Academic Press.

Guo, J., Ding, X., & Wu, W. (2022). Reliable Traffic Monitoring Mechanisms Based on Blockchain in Vehicular Networks. *IEEE Transactions on Reliability*, *71*(3), 1219–1229. doi:10.1109/TR.2020.3046556

Guo, Ye., & Liang, C. (2016). Blockchain application and outlook in the banking industry. *Financial Innovation*, *2*(1), 1–12. doi:10.118640854-016-0034-9

Gupta, A. R., & Bonds, G. (2020). Financing India's renewable energy vision. *ORF Issue Brief, 336*.

Gupta, A., & Jha, R. K. (2015). A Survey of 5G Network: Architecture and Emerging Technologies. *IEEE Access : Practical Innovations, Open Solutions*, *3*, 1206–1232. doi:10.1109/ACCESS.2015.2461602

Haar, C., & Buchmann, E. (2019). *Fane: A Firewall Appliance for The Smart Home,* 449–458. Annals of Computer Science and Information Systems.

Habibullah, M., Masjuki, H. H., Kalam, M. A., Rahman, S. A., Mofijur, M., Mobarak, H. M., & Ashraful, A. M. (2015). Potential of biodiesel as a renewable energy source in Bangladesh. *Renewable & Sustainable Energy Reviews*, *50*, 819–834. doi:10.1016/j.rser.2015.04.149

Hadas, Z., Janak, L., & Smilek, J. (2018). Virtual prototypes of energy harvesting systems for industrial applications. *Mechanical Systems and Signal Processing*, *110*, 152–164. doi:10.1016/j.ymssp.2018.03.036

Haider, U., Waqas, M., Hanif, M., Alasmary, H. & Qaisar, S. M. (2023). Network load prediction and anomaly detection using ensemble learning in 5G cellular networks. *Computer Communications, 197*(December 2021), 141–150. https://doi.org/ doi:10.1016/j.comcom...017

Hajduk, S. (2016). The Concept of a Smart City In Urban Management. *Business. Management in Education*, *14*(1), 34–49.

Haleem, A., Javaid, M., Singh, R. P., Suman, R., & Rab, S. (2021). Blockchain technology applications in healthcare: An overview. *International Journal of Intelligent Networks*, *2*, 130–139. doi:10.1016/j.ijin.2021.09.005

Halegoua, G. R. (2020). *Smart cities*. Mit Press. doi:10.7551/mitpress/11426.001.0001

Hamid, K., Sajjad, U., Yang, K. S., Wu, S.-K., & Wang, C.-C. (2022, January). Assessment of an energy efficient closed loop heat pump dryer for high moisture contents materials: An experimental investigation and AI based modelling. *Energy*, *238*, 121819. doi:10.1016/j.energy.2021.121819

Hanley, R. E. (2017). From the Editor. *Journal of Urban Technology*, *24*(1), 1–2. doi:10.1080/10630732.2017.1307629 PMID:28083903

Hao, S., Ward, L., Luo, Z., Ozolins, V., Dravid, V. P., Kanatzidis, M. G., & Wolverton, C. (2019). Design strategy for high-performance thermoelectric materials: The prediction of electron-doped kzrcuse3. *Chemistry of Materials*, *31*(8), 3018–3024. doi:10.1021/acs.chemmater.9b00840

Ha, Q., & Phung, M. D. (2019). Iot-enabled dependable control for solar energy harvesting in smart buildings. *IET Smart Cities*, *1*(2), 61–70. doi:10.1049/iet-smc.2019.0052

Haque, A. K. M. B., Bhushan, B., & Dhiman, G. (2021). Conceptualizing smart city applications: Requirements, architecture, security issues, and emerging trends. *Expert Systems: International Journal of Knowledge Engineering and Neural Networks*, *39*(5). Advance online publication. doi:10.1111/exsy.12753

Harrison, C., Eckman, B., Hamilton, R., Hartswick, P., Kalagnanam, J., Paraszczak, J., & Williams, P. (2010). Foundations for Smarter Cities. *IBM Journal of Research and Development*, *54*(4), 1–16. doi:10.1147/JRD.2010.2048257

Hasan, H. R., Salah, K., Jayaraman, R., Arshad, J., Yaqoob, I., Omar, M., & Ellahham, S. (2020). Blockchain-Based Solution for COVID-19 Digital Medical Passports and Immunity Certificates. *IEEE Access : Practical Innovations, Open Solutions*, *8*, 222093–222108. doi:10.1109/ACCESS.2020.3043350 PMID:34812373

Hasan, K., Ahmed, K., Biswas, K., Saiful Islam, M., & Ameri Sianaki, O. (2020). Software-defined application-specific traffic management for wireless body area networks. *Future Generation Computer Systems*, *107*, 274–285. doi:10.1016/j.future.2020.01.052

Hassani, H., Heravi, S., & Zhigljavsky, A. (2013). Forecasting UK industrial production with multivariate singular spectrum analysis. *Journal of Forecasting*, *32*(5), 395–408. doi:10.1002/for.2244

Hassan, M. U., Rehmani, M. H., & Chen, J. (2022). Optimizing Blockchain Based Smart Grid Auctions: A Green Revolution. *IEEE Transactions on Green Communications and Networking*, *6*(1), 462–471. doi:10.1109/TGCN.2021.3095424

Hassannayebi, E., Zegordi, S. H., Amin-Naseri, M. R., & Yaghini, M. (2018). Optimizing headways for urban rail transit services using adaptive particle swarm algorithms. *Public Transport (Berlin)*, *10*(1), 23–62. doi:10.100712469-016-0147-6

Hassija, V., Chamola, V., Saxena, V., Jain, D., Goyal, P., & Sikdar, B. (2019). A survey on IoT security: Application areas, security threats, and solution architectures. *IEEE Access : Practical Innovations, Open Solutions*, *7*, 82721–82743. doi:10.1109/ACCESS.2019.2924045

Hattarki, R., Houji, S., & Dhage, M. (2021, April). Real Time Intrusion Detection System For IoT Networks. In *2021 6th International Conference for Convergence in Technology (I2CT)* (pp. 1-5). IEEE.

Haupt, S. E., McCandless, T. C., Dettling, S., Alessandrini, S., Lee, J. A., Linden, S., Petzke, W., Brummet, T., Nguyen, N., Kosović, B., Wiener, G., Hussain, T., & Al-Rasheedi, M. (2020). Combining artificial intelligence with physics-based methods for probabilistic renewable energy forecasting. *Energies*, *13*(8), 1979. doi:10.3390/en13081979

Hauser, K., Kurz, A., Haggenmüller, S., Maron, R. C., von Kalle, C., Utikal, J. S., Meier, F., Hobelsberger, S., Gellrich, F. F., Sergon, M., Hauschild, A., French, L. E., Heinzerling, L., Schlager, J. G., Ghoreschi, K., Schlaak, M., Hilke, F. J., Poch, G., Kutzner, H., & Brinker, T. J. (2022). Explainable artificial intelligence in skin cancer recognition: A systematic review. *European Journal of Cancer*, *167*, 54–69. doi:10.1016/j.ejca.2022.02.025 PMID:35390650

Heba Kurdi, H., Alshayban, B., Altoaimy, L., & Alsalamah, S. (2018). *TrustyFeer: A Subjective Logic Trust Model for Smart City Peer-to-Peer Federated Clouds.* Wireless Communications and Mobile Computing. https://doi.org/. doi:10.1155/2018/1073216

Himeur, Y., Alsalemi, A., Al-Kababji, A., Bensaali, F., Amira, A., Sardianos, C., Dimitrakopoulos, G., & Varlamis, I. (2021, August). A survey of recommender systems for energy efficiency in buildings: Principles, challenges and prospects. *Information Fusion*, *72*, 1–21. doi:10.1016/j.inffus.2021.02.002

Hollands, R. G. (2008). Will the real smart city please stand up? *City (London, England)*, *12*(3), 303–320. doi:10.1080/13604810802479126

Hollands, R. G. (2015). Critical Interventions into the Corporate Smart City. *Cambridge Journal of Regions, Economy and Society*, *8*(1), 61–77. doi:10.1093/cjres/rsu011

Holzinger, A., Biemann, C., Pattichis, C. S., & Kell, D. B. (2017). *What do we need to build explainable AI systems for the medical domain?* M1.

Hossain, M. S., & Muhammad, G. (2017). Emotion-aware connected healthcare big data towards 5G. *IEEE Internet of Things Journal*, *5*(4), 2399–2406. doi:10.1109/JIOT.2017.2772959

Hosseinalizadeh, R., Shakouri, H., Amalnick, M. S., & Taghipour, P. (2016). Economic sizing of a hybrid (PV–WT–FC) renewable energy system (HRES) for stand-alone usages by an optimization-simulation model: Case study of Iran. *Renewable & Sustainable Energy Reviews*, *54*, 139–150. doi:10.1016/j.rser.2015.09.046

Hou, L., & Chen, W. (2020). A novel mppt method for autonomous wireless sensor network node with thermal energy harvesting. *Engineering Research Express*, *2*(1), 1001–1005. doi:10.1088/2631-8695/ab638d

Hu, W., Zhang, T., Deng, X., Liu, Z., & Tan, J. (2021). Digital twin: A state-of-the-art review of its enabling technologies, applications and challenges. *Journal of Intelligent Manufacturing and Special Equipment, 2*(1), 1-34.

Huaiqing, L., Xuezhi, W., & Haitao, L. (August 2009). Hierarchical fuzzy trust management for peer-to-peer network. In *Proceedings of the 2009 Second ISECS International Colloquium on Computing, Communication, Control, and Management, CCCM 2009*, China.

Huang, J., Zhou, Y., Ning, Z., & Gharavi, H. (2019). Wireless power transfer and energy harvesting: Current status and prospects. *IEEE Wireless Communications*, *26*(4), 163–169. doi:10.1109/MWC.2019.1800378 PMID:32165868

Huang, X., Xu, C., Wang, P., & Liu, H. (2018). LNSC: A Security Model for Electric Vehicle and Charging Pile Management Based on Blockchain Ecosystem. *IEEE Access : Practical Innovations, Open Solutions*, *6*, 13565–13574. doi:10.1109/ACCESS.2018.2812176

Humayun, M. (2020). Role of emerging IoT big data and cloud computing for real time application. *International Journal of Advanced Computer Science and Applications*, *11*(4). doi:10.14569/IJACSA.2020.0110466

Hussain, M. W., & Roy, D. S. (2023). Performance Optimization Strategies for Big Data Applications in Distributed Framework. In: Dash, S.R., Das, H., Li, KC., Tello, E.V. (eds) Intelligent Technologies: Concepts, Applications, and Future Directions. Springer, Singapore. doi:10.1007/978-981-99-1482-1_10

Hussain, M. W., Moulik, S., & Roy, D. S. (2021, December). A broadcast based link discovery scheme for minimizing messages in software defined networks. In *2021 IEEE Globecom Workshops (GC Wkshps)* (pp. 1-6). IEEE.

Hussain, M. W., Pradhan, B., Gao, X. Z., Reddy, K. H. K., & Roy, D. S. (2020). Clonal selection algorithm for energy minimization in software defined networks. *Applied Soft Computing, 96*, 106617.

Hussain, M. W. (2021). A counter based approach for reducer placement with augmented Hadoop rackawareness. *Turkish Journal of Electrical Engineering and Computer Sciences*, *29*(1), 437–453. doi:10.3906/elk-2001-106

Hussain, M. W., Khan, M. S., Reddy, K. H. K., & Roy, D. S. (2022). Extended indirect controller-legacy switch forwarding for link discovery in hybrid multi-controller SDN. *Computer Communications*, *189*, 148–157. doi:10.1016/j.comcom.2022.03.017

Hussain, M. W., Pradhan, B., Gao, X. Z., Reddy, K. H. K., & Roy, D. S. (2020). Clonal selection algorithm for energy minimization in software defined networks. *Applied Soft Computing*, *96*, 106617. doi:10.1016/j.asoc.2020.106617

Hussain, M. W., Reddy, K. H. K., Rodrigues, J. J., & Roy, D. S. (2020). An indirect controller-legacy switch forwarding scheme for link discovery in hybrid SDN. *IEEE Systems Journal*, *15*(2), 3142–3149. doi:10.1109/JSYST.2020.3011902

Hussain, M. W., & Roy, D. S. (2022). A Counter-Based Profiling Scheme for Improving Locality Through Data and Reducer Placement. In *Advances in Machine Learning for Big Data Analysis* (pp. 101–118). Springer Nature Singapore.

Hussain, S., Mahmood, K., Khan, M. K., Chen, C. M., Alzahrani, B. A., & Chaudhry, S. A. (2022). Designing secure and lightweight user access to drones for smart city surveillance. *Computer Standards & Interfaces*, *80*, 103566. doi:10.1016/j.csi.2021.103566

HyunjaeK.AhnD. H.LeeG. M.YooJ. D.ParkK. H.KimH. K. (2019). Iot network intrusion dataset. *IEEE Dataport*. doi:10.21227/q70p-q449

Ibrahim, T. S., Saleh, A. I., Elgaml, N., & Abdelsalam, M. M. (2020). A fog-based recommendation system for promoting the performance of E-learning environments. *Computers & Electrical Engineering*, *87*, 106791. doi:10.1016/j.compeleceng.2020.106791

Iqbal, A., Kim, Y., Ahn, J., & Lee, T. (2017). Energy level-based efficient wireless power and information transfer in sensor networks. *Proc. 11th International Conference on Ubiquitous Information Management and Communication*, 1-5. 10.1145/3022227.3022315

Iqbal, M., Azam, M., Naeem, M., Khwaja, A. S., & Anpalagan, A. (2014). Optimization classification, algorithms and tools for renewable energy: A review. *Renewable & Sustainable Energy Reviews*, *39*, 640–654. doi:10.1016/j.rser.2014.07.120

Irfan, M., Zhao, Z. Y., Ikram, M., Gilal, N. G., Li, H., & Rehman, A. (2020). Assessment of India's energy dynamics: Prospects of solar energy. *Journal of Renewable and Sustainable Energy*, *12*(5), 053701.

Ismagilova, E., Hughes, L., Rana, N. P., & Dwivedi, Y. K. (2020). Security, Privacy and Risks Within Smart Cities: Literature Review and Development of a Smart City Interaction Framework. *Information Systems Frontiers*, *24*(2), 393–414.

Ismagilova, E., Hughes, L., Dwivedi, Y. K., & Raman, K. R. (2019). Smart cities: Advances in research—An information systems perspective. *International Journal of Information Management*, *47*, 88–100. doi:10.1016/j.ijinfomgt.2019.01.004

Ismail, L., Materwala, H., & Zeadally, S. (2019). Lightweight Blockchain for healthcare. *IEEE Access : Practical Innovations, Open Solutions*, *7*, 149935–149951. doi:10.1109/ACCESS.2019.2947613

ISO. (2014). *Smart cities Preliminary Report 2014*. International Standards Organization. Retrieved May 2016 from https://www.iso.org/iso/smart_cities_report-jtc1.pdf

Isravel, D. P., Silas, S., & Rajsingh, E. B. (2020). Reliable Surveillance Tracking System based on Software Defined Internet of Things. In *The Cognitive Approach in Cloud Computing and Internet of Things Technologies for Surveillance Tracking Systems*. INC. doi:10.1016/B978-0-12-816385-6.00001-5

Isravel, D. P., Silas, S., & Rajsingh, E. B. (2022). Long-term traffic flow prediction using multivariate SSA forecasting in SDN based networks. *Pervasive and Mobile Computing*, *83*, 101590. doi:10.1016/j.pmcj.2022.101590

Jagadeeswari, V., Subramaniyaswamy, V., Logesh, R., & Vijayakumar, V. (2018). A study on medical Internet of Things and Big Data in personalized healthcare system. *Health Information Science and Systems*, *6*(1), 1–20. doi:10.100713755-018-0049-x PMID:30279984

Jain, D., Krishna, P. V., & Saritha, V. (2012). A study on Internet of Things based applications. *arXiv preprint arXiv:1206.3891*.

Jameer, B., Malathi, M., Balaganes, S., & Maheshwari, R. (2018). Patient Tracking Using IoT and Big Data. In *Proceedings of First International Conference on Smart System, Innovations and Computing* (pp. 613-621). Springer, Singapore. 10.1007/978-981-10-5828-8_59

Jamwal, R., Jarman, H. K., Roseingrave, E., Douglas, J., & Winkler, D. (2022). Smart home and communication technology for people with disabilities: A scoping review. *Disability and Rehabilitation. Assistive Technology*, *17*(6), 624–644. doi:10.1080/17483107.2020.1818138 PMID:32924660

Janani, R. P., Renuka, K., Aruna, A., & Lakshmi Narayanan, K. (2021). IoT in smart cities: A contemporary survey. *Global Transitions Proceedings*, *2*(2), 187–193. doi:10.1016/j.gltp.2021.08.069

Javed, A. R., Shahzad, F., Rehman, S., Zikria, Y. B., Razzak, I., Jalil, Z., & Xu, G. (2022). Future smart cities requirements, emerging technologies, applications, challenges, and future aspects. *Cities (London, England), 129*, 103794. doi:10.1016/j.cities.2022.103794

Jiang, F., Ma, L., Broyd, T., & Chen, K. (2021). Digital twin and its implementations in the civil engineering sector. *Automation in Construction, 130*, 103838. doi:10.1016/j.autcon.2021.103838

Jiang, Z., Guo, Y., & Wang, Z. (2021). Digital twin to improve the virtual-real integration of industrial IoT. *Journal of Industrial Information Integration, 22*, 100196. doi:10.1016/j.jii.2020.100196

Ji, B., Zhang, X., Mumtaz, S., Han, C., Li, C., Wen, H., & Wang, D. (2020). Survey on the Internet of Vehicles: Network Architectures and Applications. *IEEE Communications Standards Magazine*, *4*(1), 34–41. doi:10.1109/MCOMSTD.001.1900053

Jincheng, S. (2022). Research on Digital Twin for Building Structure Health Monitoring. In *Business Intelligence and Information Technology: Proceedings of the International Conference on Business Intelligence and Information Technology BIIT 2021* (pp. 754-760). Springer International Publishing 10.1007/978-3-030-92632-8_71

Jindal, A., Aujla, G. S., Kumar, N., & Villari, M. (2020). GUARDIAN: Blockchain-Based Secure Demand Response Management in Smart Grid System. *IEEE Transactions on Services Computing*, *13*(4), 613–624. doi:10.1109/TSC.2019.2962677

Johnsson, F., Kjärstad, J., & Rootzén, J. (2019). The threat to climate change mitigation posed by the abundance of fossil fuels. *Climate Policy*, *19*(2), 258–274. doi:10.1080/14693062.2018.1483885

Joordens, M., & Jamshidi, M. (2018). On the development of robot fish swarms in virtual reality with digital twins. In Proc. *13th Annu. Conf. Syst. Syst. Eng. (SoSE)* (pp. 411–416). IEEE. 10.1109/SYSOSE.2018.8428748

Jossen, A., Garche, J., & Sauer, D. U. (2004). Operation conditions of batteries in PV applications. *Solar Energy*, *76*(6), 759–769. doi:10.1016/j.solener.2003.12.013

Jun, Y., Craig, A., Shafik, W., & Sharif, L. (2021). Artificial intelligence application in cybersecurity and cyberdefense. *Wireless Communications and Mobile Computing, 2021*, 1–10. doi:10.1155/2021/3329581

Jurado, F., & Saenz, J. R. (2002). Neuro-fuzzy control for autonomous wind–diesel systems using biomass. *Renewable Energy*, *27*(1), 39–56. doi:10.1016/S0960-1481(01)00170-7

Kaldellis, J. K. (Ed.). (2010). *Stand-alone and hybrid wind energy systems: technology, energy storage and applications*. Elsevier. doi:10.1533/9781845699628

Kalinaki, K., Thilakarathne, N. N., Mubarak, H. R., Malik, O. A., & Abdullatif, M. (2023). Cybersafe Capabilities and Utilities for Smart Cities. In *Cybersecurity for Smart Cities* (pp. 71–86). Springer. doi:10.1007/978-3-031-24946-4_6

Kamenivskyy, Y., Palisetti, A., Hamze, L., & Saberi, S. (2022). A Blockchain-Based Solution for COVID-19 Vaccine Distribution. *IEEE Engineering Management Review*, *50*(1), 43–53.

Kanase-Patil, A. B., Saini, R. P., & Sharma, M. P. (2011). Sizing of integrated renewable energy system based on load profiles and reliability index for the state of Uttarakhand in India. *Renewable Energy*, *36*(11), 2809–2821. doi:10.1016/j.renene.2011.04.022

Kasaeian A., Razmjoo A., Shirmohammadi R., Pourfayaz F., Sumper A. (2020). Deployment of a stand-alone hybrid renewable energy system in coastal areas as a reliable energy source. *Environ Prog Sustainable Energy, 39*(3). https://doi.org/. v39.310.1002/ep.13354. doi:10.1002/ep

Kasdan, M., Kuhl, L., & Kurukulasuriya, P. (2021). The evolution of transformational change in multilateral funds dedicated to financing adaptation to climate change. *Climate and Development*, *13*(5), 427–442. doi:10.1080/17565529.2020.1790333

Kausar, A. Z., Reza, A. W., Saleh, M. U., & Ramiah, H. (2014). Energizing wireless sensor networks by energy harvesting systems: Scopes, challenges, and approaches. *Renewable & Sustainable Energy Reviews*, *38*(2), 973–989. doi:10.1016/j.rser.2014.07.035

Kazi, S. R., Short, M., Isafiade, A. J., & Biegler, L. T. (2021). Heat exchanger network synthesis with detailed exchanger designs—2. Hybrid optimization strategy for synthesis of heat exchanger networks. *AIChE Journal. American Institute of Chemical Engineers*, *67*(1), e17057.

Kelley, S. B., Lane, B. W., Stanley, B. W., Kane, K., Nielsen, E., & Strachan, S. (2019). Smart transportation for all? A typology of recent U.S. smart transportation projects in midsized cities. *Annals of the American Association of Geographers*, *110*(2), 547–558. doi:10.1080/24694452.2019.1643702

Kezai, P. K., Fischer, S., & Lados, M. (2020). Smart economy and startup enterprises in the Visegrád Countries—A comparative analysis based on the Crunchbase Database. *Smart Cities*, *3*(4), 70. doi:10.3390martcities3040070

Khadidos, A. O., Shitharth, S., Manoharan, H., Yafoz, A., Khadidos, A. O., & Alyoubi, K. H. (2022). An Intelligent Security Framework Based on Collaborative Mutual Authentication Model for Smart City Networks. *IEEE Access : Practical Innovations, Open Solutions*, *10*, 85289–85304. doi:10.1109/ACCESS.2022.3197672

Khalid, S., Raouf, I., Khan, A., Kim, N., & Kim, H. S. (2019). A review of human-powered energy harvesting for smart electronics: Recent progress and challenges. *International Journal of Precise Engineering Manufacture Green Technology*, *6*(4), 821–851. doi:10.100740684-019-00144-y

Khalifa, O. O., & Japar, D. F. bin, Rahman, F. D. A., & Nasir, H. (2022). Authentication of IoT in Smart City Applications. *2022 IEEE 8th International Conference on Smart Instrumentation, Measurement and Applications (ICSIMA)*, (pp. 58–63). IEEE.

Khalifa, O. O., Roubleh, A., Esgiar, A., Abdelhaq, M., Alsaqour, R., Abdalla, A., Ali, E. S., & Saeed, R. (2022). An IoT-Platform-Based Deep Learning System for Human Behavior Recognition in Smart City Monitoring Using the Berkeley MHAD Datasets. *Systems.*, *10*(5), 177. doi:10.3390ystems10050177

Khalifa, O. O., Wajdi, M. H., Saeed, R. A., Hashim, A. H. A., Ahmed, M. Z., & Ali, E. S. (2022). Vehicle Detection for Vision-Based Intelligent Transportation Systems Using Convolutional Neural Network Algorithm. *Journal of Advanced Transportation*, *2022*, 9189600. doi:10.1155/2022/9189600

Khalifeh, A., Saadeh, M., Darabkh, K. A., & Nagaradjane, P. (2019). Radio-frequency based energy charging- an experimental study. *2nd IEEE Middle East and North Africa Communications Conference,* 1-4. 10.1109/MENACOMM46666.2019.8988585

Khan, R., Khan, S. U., Zaheer, R., & Khan, S. (2012). Future internet: the internet of things architecture, possible applications and key challenges. In *2012 10th international conference on frontiers of information technology*(pp. 257-260). IEEE. 10.1109/FIT.2012.53

Khan, Z., & Kiani, S. L. (2012). A cloud-based architecture for citizen services in smart cities. In *2012 IEEE Fifth international conference on utility and cloud computing* (pp. 315-320). IEEE. 10.1109/UCC.2012.43

Khan, Z., Pervez, Z., & Ghafoor, A. (2014). Towards cloud based smart cities data security and privacy management. In *2014 IEEE/ACM 7th International Conference on Utility and Cloud Computing* (pp. 806-811). IEEE. 10.1109/UCC.2014.131

Khan, M., Iqbal, J., Talha, M., Arshad, M., Diyan, M., & Han, K. (2018). Big Data Processing using Internet of Software Defined Things in Smart Cities. *International Journal of Parallel Programming*, 1–14. doi:10.100710766-018-0573-y

Khare, V., Nema, S., & Baredar, P. (2017). Optimisation of the hybrid renewable energy system by HOMER, PSO and CPSO for the study area. *International Journal of Sustainable Energy*, *36*(4), 326–343. doi:10.1080/14786451.2015.1017500

Khatib, T., Mohamed, A., & Sopian, K. (2013). A review of photovoltaic systems size optimization techniques. *Renewable & Sustainable Energy Reviews*, *22*, 454–465. doi:10.1016/j.rser.2013.02.023

Khazaee, M., Rezaniakolaie, A., Moosavian, A., & Rosendahl, L. (2020). A novel method for autonomous remote condition monitoring of rotating machines using piezoelectric energy harvesting approach. *Sensors and Actuators. A, Physical*, *295*, 37–50. doi:10.1016/j.sna.2019.05.016

Khazaei. H., Zareian. S. Veleda. R & Litoiu. M. (2016). Sipresk: A big data analytic platform for smart transportation. *Smart City 360 Lecture Notes of the Institute for Computer Sciences, Social Informatics and Telecommunications Engineering*, 419–430.

Khedkar, S., Subramanian, V., Shinde, G., & Gandhi, P. (2019) "*Explainable AI in Healthcare*", SSRN Electronic Journal. doi:10.2139/ssrn.3367686

Kim, H., Park, S., & Lee, J. (2021). Is renewable energy acceptable with power grid expansion? A quantitative study of South Korea's renewable energy acceptance. *Renewable & Sustainable Energy Reviews*, *139*, 110584.

Kim, S., & Lim, H. (2018). Reinforcement learning based energy management algorithm for smart energy buildings. *Energies*, *11*(8), 2010. doi:10.3390/en11082010

Kirimtat, A., Krejcar, O., Kertesz, A., & Tasgetiren, M. F. (2020). Future trends and current state of smart city concepts: A survey. *IEEE Access : Practical Innovations, Open Solutions*, *8*, 86448–86467. doi:10.1109/ACCESS.2020.2992441

Kollimalla, S. K., & Mishra, M. K. (2014, April). Coordinated control and energy management of hybrid energy storage system in PV system. In *2014 International Conference on Computation of Power, Energy, Information and Communication (ICCPEIC)* (pp. 363-368). IEEE. 10.1109/ECCE-Asia.2013.6579202

Konapure, R. R., & Nawale, S. D. (2022, May). Smart Contract System Architecture for Pharma Supply chain. In *2022 International Conference on IoT and Blockchain Technology (ICIBT)* (pp. 1-5). IEEE.

Koshy, A. S., Fatima, N., Agarwal, P., & Rodrigues, J. J. P. C. (2022). Security and Privacy Threats in IoT-Enabled Smart Cities. *Internet of Things*, 277–300.

Koutlia, K., Bojovic, B., Lagén, S., Zhang, X., Wang, P. & Liu, J. (2023). System analysis of QoS schedulers for XR traffic in 5G NR. *Simulation Modelling Practice and Theory*, *125*(December 2022), 102745. doi:10.1016/j.simpat.2023.102745

Kramers, A., Höjer, M., Lövehagen, N., & Wangel, J. (2014). Smart sustainable cities–Exploring ICT solutions for reduced energy use in cities. *Environmental Modelling & Software*, *56*, 52–62. doi:10.1016/j.envsoft.2013.12.019

Kreutz, D., Ramos, F. M., & Verissimo, P. (2013, August). Towards secure and dependable software-defined networks. In *Proceedings of the second ACM SIGCOMM workshop on Hot topics in software defined networking* (pp. 55-60). ACM. 10.1145/2491185.2491199

Kritzinger, W., Karner, M., Traar, G., Henjes, J., & Sihn, W. (2018). Digital Twin in manufacturing: A categorical literature review and classification. *IFAC-PapersOnLine*, *51*(11), 1016–1022. doi:10.1016/j.ifacol.2018.08.474

Ktari, J., Frikha, T., Hamdi, M., Elmannai, H., & Hmam, H. (2022). Lightweight AI framework for industry 4.0 case study: Water meter recognition. *Big Data and Cognitive Computing*, *6*(3), 72. doi:10.3390/bdcc6030072

Kumaria., A., Guptaa., R., Tanwara., S., & Kumar, N. (2020). Blockchain and AI Amalgamation for Energy Cloud Management: Challenges, Solutions, and Future Directions. *Journal of Parallel and Distributed Computing*. . doi:10.1016/j.jpdc.2020.05.004

Kumar, N., & Dash, D. (2020). Flow based efficient data gathering in wireless sensor network using path-constrained mobile sink. *Journal of Ambient Intelligence and Humanized Computing*, *11*(3), 1163–1175. doi:10.100712652-019-01245-x

Kumar, R., Gupta, R. A., & Bansal, A. K. (2013). Economic analysis and power management of a stand-alone wind/photovoltaic hybrid energy system using biogeography based optimization algorithm. *Swarm and Evolutionary Computation*, *8*, 33–43. doi:10.1016/j.swevo.2012.08.002

Kumar, S., Tiwari, P., & Zymbler, M. (2019). Internet of Things is a revolutionary approach for future technology enhancement: A review. *Journal of Big Data*, *6*(1), 1–21. doi:10.118640537-019-0268-2

Kumar, T. M. V. (2017). *Smart Economy in Smart Cities: International Collaborative Research.* Springer

Kumar, T. V. (Ed.). (2018). *Smart Economy in Smart Cities: International Collaborative Research: Ottawa, St. Louis, Stuttgart, Bologna, Cape Town, Nairobi, Dakar, Lagos, New Delhi, Varanasi, Vijayawada*. Springer Singapore.

Kumar, V., & Ray, S. (2022). *Continuous Behavioral Authentication System for IoT Enabled Applications*. Lecture Notes in Networks and Systems. doi:10.1007/978-981-19-3182-6_5

Kummitha, R. K. R., & Crutzen, N. (2017). How do we understand smart cities? An evolutionary perspective. *Cities (London, England)*, *67*, 43–52. doi:10.1016/j.cities.2017.04.010

Kylili, A., & Fokaides, P. A. (2015). European smart cities: The role of zero energy buildings. *Sustainable Cities and Society*, *15*, 86–95. doi:10.1016/j.scs.2014.12.003

Lakkaraju, H., Bach, S. H., & Leskovec, J. (2016). *Interpretable decision sets: A joint framework for description and prediction.* Proceedings of the ACM SIGKDD International Conference on Knowledge Discovery and Data Mining, (pp. 1675-1684). ACM. 10.1145/2939672.2939874

Land, Millman (2020). The Future Of Telecommunications: What Is Millimeter Wave Technology? | Millman National Land Services. *Millman Land, millmanland.com.*

Lan, H., Wen, S., Hong, Y. Y., David, C. Y., & Zhang, L. (2015). Optimal sizing of hybrid PV/diesel/battery in ship power system. *Applied Energy*, *158*, 26–34. doi:10.1016/j.apenergy.2015.08.031

Latah, M. & Toker, L. (2018). *Artificial Intelligence Enabled Software Defined Networking: A Comprehensive Artificial Intelligence Enabled Software Defined Networking : A Comprehensive Overview. November.* doi:10.1049/iet-net.2018.5082

Lau, B. P. L., Marakkalage, S. H., Zhou, Y., Hassan, N. U., Yuen, C., Zhang, M., & Tan, U. X. (2019). A survey of data fusion in smart city applications. *Information Fusion*, *52*, 357–374. doi:10.1016/j.inffus.2019.05.004

Laufs, J., Borrion, H., & Bradford, B. (2020). Security and smart city: A systematic review. *Sustainable Cities and Society*, *55*, 102023. doi:10.1016/j.scs.2020.102023

Lazaris, A., & Prasanna, V. K. (2019). Deep Learning Models For Aggregated Network Traffic Prediction. *15th International Conference on Network and Service Management (CNSM 2019).* 10.23919/CNSM46954.2019.9012669

Lazzeretti, L., Capone, F., & Cinti, T. (2011). Open innovation in city of art: The case of laser technologies for conservation in Florence. *City. Cultura e Scuola*, *2*(3), 159–168. doi:10.1016/j.ccs.2011.09.001

Lee, J. (2011). Smart health: concepts and status of ubiquitous health with smartphone. In: ICTC2011. IEEE; (pp. 388e9). IEEE. doi:10.1109/ICTC.2011.6082623

Lee, J. H., Hancock, M. G., & Hu, M. C. (2014). Towards an effective framework for building smart cities: Lessons from Seoul and San Francisco. *Technological Forecasting and Social Change*, *89*, 80–99. doi:10.1016/j.techfore.2013.08.033

Lee, J. Y. (2019). A decentralized token economy: How blockchain and cryptocurrency can revolutionize business. *Business Horizons*, *62*(6), 773–784.

Lehner, H., & Dorffner, L. (2020). *Towards a digital twin city as Geodata Hub*. Digital geo Twin Vienna.

Leng, J., Zhou, M., Zhao, J. L., Huang, Y., & Bian, Y. (2020). Blockchain Security: A Survey of Techniques and Research Directions. *IEEE Transactions on Services Computing*, *15*(4), 2490–2510. doi:10.1109/TSC.2020.3038641

Li, F., Golden, B., & Wasil, E. (2005). Solving the time dependent traveling salesman problem. In The Next Wave in Computing, Optimization, and Decision Technologies (pp. 163-182). Springer US. doi:10.1007/0-387-23529-9_12

Li, Q., Hu, W.-Y., Li, J.-Y., Liu, Y., & Li, M.-X. (2022). A survey of person re-identification based on deep learning. Chinese Journal of Engineering, 8(3), 920-932.

Li, C. (2019). Techno-economic study of off-grid hybrid photovoltaic/battery and photovoltaic/battery/fuel cell power systems in Kunming, China. *Energy Sources. Part A, Recovery, Utilization, and Environmental Effects*, *41*(13), 1588–1604. doi:10.1080/15567036.2018.1549134

Li, C., Hu, J., Zhou, K., Wang, Y., & Deng, H. (2018, June). Using blockchain for data auditing in cloud storage. In *International Conference on Cloud Computing and Security* (pp. 335-345). Springer.

Li, C., Shi, H., Cao, Y., Wang, J., Kuang, Y., Tan, Y., & Wei, J. (2015). Comprehensive review of renewable energy curtailment and avoidance: A specific example in China. *Renewable & Sustainable Energy Reviews*, *41*, 1067–1079. doi:10.1016/j.rser.2014.09.009

Li, D., Deng, L., Cai, Z., & Souri, A. (2022). Blockchain as service model in the Internet of Things management: Systematic review. *Transactions on Emerging Telecommunications Technologies*, *33*(4), e4139. doi:10.1002/ett.4139

Li, D., Wu, Y., Da Ronch, A., & Xiang, J. (2016). Energy harvesting by means of flow-Induced vibrations on aerospace vehicles. *Progress in Aerospace Sciences*, *86*, 28–62. doi:10.1016/j.paerosci.2016.08.001

Lina, E. A., Elmustafa, S. A., Rania, A. M., Rashid, A. S., Hesham, A., & Mohammad, K. H. (2022). Deep and Reinforcement Learning Technologies on Internet of Vehicle (IoV) Applications: Current Issues and Future Trends. *Journal of Advanced Transportation*, *2022*, 1947886.

Lin, B.-S. P. (2020). Toward an AI-Enabled SDN-based 5G & IoT Network. *Network and Communication Technologies*, *5*(2), 7. doi:10.5539/nct.v5n2p7

Lin, F., Liu, S., Yang, Z., Zhao, Y., Yang, Z., & Sun, H. (2016). Multi-train energy saving for maximum usage of regenerative energy by dwell time optimization in urban rail transit using genetic algorithm. *Energies*, *9*(3), 208. doi:10.3390/en9030208

Lin, I. C., & Liao, T. C. (2017). A survey of blockchain security issues and challenges. *International Journal of Network Security*, *19*(5), 653–659.

Lin, J., Niu, J., Li, H., & Atiquzzaman, M. (2019). A secure and efficient location-based service scheme for smart transportation. *Future Generation Computer Systems*, *92*, 694–704. doi:10.1016/j.future.2017.11.030

Lin, J., Zhou, K., & Zhang, Y. (2019). Performance evaluation of ETSI ITS security architecture in vehicular network. *Journal of Intelligent Transport Systems*, *23*(3), 276–285.

Li, Q., Hu, R. Q., Qian, Y., & Wu, G. (2012). Cooperative communications for wireless networks: Techniques and applications in LTE-advanced systems. *IEEE Wireless Communications*, *19*(2). Advance online publication. doi:10.1109/MWC.2012.6189409

Li, S., Xu, L. D., & Zhao, S. (2015). The internet of things: A survey. *Information Systems Frontiers*, *17*(2), 243–259. doi:10.100710796-014-9492-7

Liu, Y. Y., Hung, M. H., Lin, Y. C., Chen, C. C., Gao, W. L., & Cheng, F. T. (2018). A Cloud-based pluggable manufacturing service scheme for smart factory. In *Proceedings of the 14th IEEE International Conference on Automation Science and Engineering (CASE)*. IEEE. 10.1109/COASE.2018.8560401

Liu, H., Zhou, M., Guo, X., Zhang, Z., Ning, B., & Tang, T. (2018). Timetable optimization for regenerative energy utilization in subway systems. *IEEE Transactions on Intelligent Transportation Systems*, *20*(9), 3247–3257. doi:10.1109/TITS.2018.2873145

Liu, L., Guo, X., & Lee, C. (2021). Promoting smart cities into the 5G era with multi-field Internet of Things (IoT) applications powered with advanced mechanical energy harvesters. *Nano Energy*, *88*, 106304. doi:10.1016/j.nanoen.2021.106304

Liu, R., Li, S., Yang, L., & Yin, J. (2018). Energy-efficient subway train scheduling design with time-dependent demand based on an approximate dynamic programming approach. *IEEE Transactions on Systems, Man, and Cybernetics. Systems*, *50*(7), 2475–2490. doi:10.1109/TSMC.2018.2818263

Liu, X. (2015). Atypical Hierarchical Routing Protocols for Wireless Sensor Networks: A Review. *IEEE Sensors Journal*, *15*(10), 5372–5383. doi:10.1109/JSEN.2015.2445796 PMID:27761103

Liu, X., Barenji, A. V., Li, Z., Montreuil, B., & Huang, G. Q. (2021). Blockchain-based smart tracking and tracing platform for drug supply chain. *Computers & Industrial Engineering*, *161*, 107669.

Liu, Y., Riba, J. R., & Moreno-Eguilaz, M. (2023). Energy Balance of Wireless Sensor Nodes Based on Bluetooth Low Energy and Thermoelectric Energy Harvesting. *Sensors (Basel)*, *23*(3), 1480. doi:10.339023031480 PMID:36772518

Liu, Y., Zhang, L., Yang, Y., Zhou, L., Ren, L., Wang, F., & Deen, M. J. (2019). A novel cloud-based framework for the elderly healthcare services using digital twin. *IEEE Access : Practical Innovations, Open Solutions*, *7*, 49088–49101. doi:10.1109/ACCESS.2019.2909828

Li, X., Wang, Z., Leung, V. C., Ji, H., Liu, Y., & Zhang, H. (2021). Blockchain-empowered data-driven networks: A survey and outlook. *ACM Computing Surveys*, *54*(3), 1–38.

Li, Y., Lim, M. K., Tan, Y., Lee, Y., & Tseng, M. L. (2020). Sharing economy to improve routing for urban logistics distribution using electric vehicles. *Resources, Conservation and Recycling*, *153*, 104585. doi:10.1016/j.resconrec.2019.104585

Li, Y., Qiao, L., & Lv, Z. (2021). An optimized byzantine fault tolerance algorithm for consortium blockchain. *Peer-to-Peer Networking and Applications*, *14*(5), 2826–2839. doi:10.100712083-021-01103-8

Li, Y., Soleimani, H., & Zohal, M. (2019). An improved ant colony optimization algorithm for the multi-depot green vehicle routing problem with multiple objectives. *Journal of Cleaner Production*, *227*, 1161–1172. doi:10.1016/j.jclepro.2019.03.185

Li, Z., Shahidehpour, M., Bahramirad, S., & Khodaei, A. (2016). Optimizing traffic signal settings in smart cities. *IEEE Transactions on Smart Grid*, *8*(5), 2382–2393. doi:10.1109/TSG.2016.2526032

Logesh, R. (2017). Resources, configurations, and soft computing techniques for power management and control of PV/ wind hybrid system. *Renewable & Sustainable Energy Reviews, 69*, 129–143. doi:10.1016/j.rser.2016.11.209

Loh, H. W., Ooi, C. P., Seoni, S., Barua, P. D., Molinari, F., & Acharya, U. R. (2022). Application of explainable artificial intelligence for healthcare: A systematic review of the last decade (2011–2022). *Computer Methods and Programs in Biomedicine, 226*, 107161. doi:10.1016/j.cmpb.2022.107161 PMID:36228495

Lombardi, M., Pascale, F., & Santaniello, D. (2021). Internet of Things: A general overview between architectures, protocols and applications. *Information (Basel), 12*(2), 87. doi:10.3390/info12020087

Lombardi, P., Giordano, S., Farouh, H., & Yousef, W. (2012). Modelling the smart city performance. *Innovation (Abingdon), 25*(2), 137–149. doi:10.1080/13511610.2012.660325

Longo, F., Padovano, A., Aiello, G., Fusto, C., & Certa, A. (2021). How 5G-based industrial IoT is transforming human-centered smart factories: A Quality of Experience model for Operator 4.0 applications. *IFAC-PapersOnLine, 54*(1), 255–262. doi:10.1016/j.ifacol.2021.08.030

Lopes, S. F., Pereira, R. M., Lopes, S. O., Coutinho, M., Malheiro, A., & Fonte, V. (2020). Yet a smarter irrigation system. *Lect. Notes Inst. Comput. Sci. Soc. Inform. Telecommun. Eng. LNICST, 323*, 337–346.

Loreti, P., Catini, A., Luca, M. D., Bracciale, L., & Gentile, G. (2019). The design of an energy harvesting wireless sensor node for tracking pink guanas. *Sensors (Basel), 19*(5), 9–85. doi:10.339019050985 PMID:30813516

Luckey. (2020). Artificial intelligence techniques for smart city applications. *The International ICCCBE and CIB W78 Joint Conference on Computing in Civil and Building Engineering.*

Lundberg, S. M., & Lee, S.-I. (2017). A unified approach to interpreting model predictions. *Advances in Neural Information Processing Systems*, 4765–4774.

Luo, A., Xu, W., Sun, J., Xi, K., Tang, S., Guo, X., Lee, C., & Wang, F. (2023). Vibration energy harvester with double frequency-up conversion mechanism for self-powered sensing system in smart city. *Nano Energy, 105*, 108030. doi:10.1016/j.nanoen.2022.108030

Luo, X., Wang, J., Dooner, M., & Clarke, J. (2015). Overview of current development in electrical energy storage technologies and the application potential in power system operation. *Applied Energy, 137*, 511–536. doi:10.1016/j.apenergy.2014.09.081

Luo, Y., Shi, L., & Tu, G. (2014). Optimal sizing and control strategy of isolated grid with wind power and energy storage system. *Energy Conversion and Management, 80*, 407–415. doi:10.1016/j.enconman.2014.01.061

Lv, Z., & Qiao, L. (2020). Analysis of healthcare big data. *Future Generation Computer Systems, 109*, 103–110.

Maddikunta, P. K., Gadekallu, T. R., Kaluri, R., Srivastava, G., Parizi, R. M., & Khan, M. S. (2020). Green communication in IoT networks using a hybrid optimization algorithm. *Computer Communications, 159*, 97–107. doi:10.1016/j.comcom.2020.05.020

Mahmoud, M. M., Rodrigues, J. J., Ahmed, S. H., Shah, S. C., Al-Muhtadi, J. F., Korotaev, V. V., & De Albuquerque, V. H. C. (2018). Enabling technologies on the cloud of things for smart healthcare. *IEEE Access : Practical Innovations, Open Solutions, 6*, 31950–31967. doi:10.1109/ACCESS.2018.2845399

Majeed, U., Khan, L. U., Yaqoob, I., Kazmi, S. M. A., Salah, K., & Hong, C. S. (2021). Blockchain for IoT-based smart cities: Recent advances, requirements, and future challenges. *Journal of Network and Computer Applications, 181*, 103007. doi:10.1016/j.jnca.2021.103007

Majid, M. A. (2020). Renewable energy for sustainable development in India: Current status, future prospects, challenges, employment, and investment opportunities. *Energy, Sustainability and Society*, *10*(1), 1–36.

Makani, S., Pittala, R., Alsayed, E., Aloqaily, M., & Jararweh, Y. (2022). A survey of blockchain applications in sustainable and smart cities. *Cluster Computing*, *25*(6), 3915–3936. doi:10.100710586-022-03625-z

Maleki, A., & Askarzadeh, A. (2014). Optimal sizing of a PV/wind/diesel system with battery storage for electrification to an off-grid remote region: A case study of Rafsanjan, Iran. *Sustainable Energy Technologies and Assessments*, *7*, 147–153. doi:10.1016/j.seta.2014.04.005

Maleki, A., Khajeh, M. G., & Ameri, M. (2016). Optimal sizing of a grid independent hybrid renewable energy system incorporating resource uncertainty, and load uncertainty. *International Journal of Electrical Power & Energy Systems*, *83*, 514–524. doi:10.1016/j.ijepes.2016.04.008

Maleki, A., & Pourfayaz, F. (2015). Sizing of stand-alone photovoltaic/wind/diesel system with battery and fuel cell storage devices by harmony search algorithm. *Journal of Energy Storage*, *2*, 30–42. doi:10.1016/j.est.2015.05.006

Malik, V., & Singh, S. (2019). Cloud, big data & IoT: risk management. In *2019 International Conference on Machine Learning, Big Data, Cloud and Parallel Computing (COMITCon)* (pp. 258-262). IEEE.

Mandal, S., Das, B. K., & Hoque, N. (2018). Optimum sizing of a stand-alone hybrid energy system for rural electrification in Bangladesh. *Journal of Cleaner Production*, *200*, 12–27. doi:10.1016/j.jclepro.2018.07.257

Mandelson, H. L., & Bradshaw, H. B. (2009). Digital Britain. Department of Culture, Media and Sport and Department of Business, Innovation and Skills.

Manju bargavi S. K. & Senbagavalli, M. (2022). Artificial Intelligence and Medical Information Modeling. In Handbook of Research on Mathematical Modeling for Smart Healthcare Systems. (pp. 1-11). IGI Global. 10.4018/978-1-6684-4580-8.ch001

Mankad, U., & Arolkar, H. (2022). Smart Water Metering Implementation. *Lecture Notes in Networks and Systems, 6th International Conference on Smart Trends in Computing and Communications, SmartCom*, (*Vol 396*, pp. 721-731). IEEE.

Manogaran, G., Lopez, D., Thota, C., Abbas, K. M., Pyne, S., & Sundarasekar, R. (2017). Big data analytics in healthcare Internet of Things. In *Innovative healthcare systems for the 21st century* (pp. 263–284). Springer. doi:10.1007/978-3-319-55774-8_10

Manogaran, G., Thota, C., Lopez, D., & Sundarasekar, R. (2017). Big data security intelligence for healthcare industry 4.0. In *Cybersecurity for industry 4.0* (pp. 103–126). Springer. doi:10.1007/978-3-319-50660-9_5

Manogaran, G., Varatharajan, R., Lopez, D., Kumar, P. M., Sundarasekar, R., & Thota, C. (2018). A new architecture of Internet of Things and big data ecosystem for secured smart healthcare monitoring and alerting system. *Future Generation Computer Systems*, *82*, 375–387. doi:10.1016/j.future.2017.10.045

Mansour, R. F., Alfar, N. M., Abdel-Khalek, S., Abdelhaq, M., Saeed, R. A., & Alsaqour, R. (2022). Optimal deep learning based fusion model for biomedical image classification. *Expert Systems: International Journal of Knowledge Engineering and Neural Networks*, *39*(3), e12764. doi:10.1111/exsy.12764

Manwell, J. F. (2004). Hybrid energy systems. Encyclopedia of Energy, 3(2004), 215-229.

Marinakis, V., Doukas, H., Tsapelas, J., Mouzakitis, S., Sicilia, A., Madrazo, L., & Sgouridis, S. (2018). From big data to smart energy services: An application for intelligent energy management. *Future Generation Computer Systems*, *110*, 572–586. doi:10.1016/j.future.2018.04.062

Marr, B. (2017). *IoT and big data at Caterpillar: How predictive maintenance saves millions of dollars.*

Marsal-Llacuna, M. L., Colomer-Llinàs, J., & Meléndez-Frigola, J. (2014). Lessons in urban monitoring taken from sustainable and livable cities to better address the Smart Cities initiative. *Technological Forecasting and Social Change*, *90*, 611–622. doi:10.1016/j.techfore.2014.01.012

Mathur, P., & Nishchal, N. (2010). Cloud computing: New challenge to the entire computer industry. In *2010 First International Conference On Parallel, Distributed and Grid Computing (PDGC 2010)* (pp. 223-228). IEEE. 10.1109/PDGC.2010.5679897

Mausam, K., Kumar, S., Kumar Ghosh, S., Kumar Tiwari, A., & Sehgal, M. (2020). Solicitation of nanoparticles/fluids in solar thermal energy harvesting: A review. *Materials Today: Proceedings*, *26*(2), 2289–2295. doi:10.1016/j.matpr.2020.02.495

McFarlane, C., & Söderström, O. (2017). On alternative smart cities: From a technology-intensive to a knowledge-intensive smart urbanism. *City (London, England)*, *21*(3-4), 312–328. doi:10.1080/13604813.2017.1327166

Mehmood, M. U., Chun, D., Zeeshan, Han, H., Jeon, G., & Chen, K. (2019). Review of the applications of artificial intelligence and big data to buildings for energy-efficiency and a comfortable indoor living environment. *Energy and Building*, *202*, 109383. doi:10.1016/j.enbuild.2019.109383

Mehrjerdi, H., Hemmati, R., & Farrokhi, E. (2019). Nonlinear stochastic modeling for optimal dispatch of distributed energy resources in active distribution grids including reactive power. *Simulation Modelling Practice and Theory*, *94*, 1–13. doi:10.1016/j.simpat.2019.01.005

Mendonça, S., Damásio, B., Charlita de Freitas, L., Oliveira, L., Cichy, M., & Nicita, A. (2022). The rise of 5G technologies and systems: A quantitative analysis of knowledge production. *Telecommunications Policy*, *46*(4), 102327. doi:10.1016/j.telpol.2022.102327

Mengelkamp, E., Notheisen, B., Beer, C., Dauer, D., & Weinhardt, C. (2018). A blockchain-based smart grid: Towards sustainable local energy markets. *Computer Science -. Research for Development*, *33*, 207–214.

Meng, W., Li, W., & Zhu, L. (2020). Enhancing Medical Smartphone Networks via Blockchain-Based Trust Management Against Insider Attacks. *IEEE Transactions on Engineering Management*, *67*(4), 1377–1386. doi:10.1109/TEM.2019.2921736

Menshsari, A., Ghiamy, M., Mousavi, M. M., & Bagal, H. A. (2013). Optimal design of hybrid water-wind-solar system based on hydrogen storage and evaluation of reliability index of system using ant colony algorithm. *International Research Journal of Applied and Basic Sciences*, *4*(11), 3582–3600.

Merabeta, G. H. (2021, July). Intelligent building control systems for thermal comfort and energy-efficiency: A systematic review of artificial intelligence-assisted techniques. *Renewable & Sustainable Energy Reviews*, *144*, 110969. doi:10.1016/j.rser.2021.110969

Michael, J., Cohn, A., & Butcher, J. R. (2018). BlockChain technology. *The Journal*, 34-44.

Mi, J., Li, Q., Liu, M., Li, X., & Zuo, L. (2020). Design, modelling, and testing of a vibration energy harvester using a novel half-wave mechanical rectification. *Applied Energy*, *279*, 115–726. doi:10.1016/j.apenergy.2020.115726

Milidonis, K., Blanco, M. J., Grigoriev, V., Panagiotou, C. F., Bonanos, A. M., Constantinou, M., Pye, J., & Asselineau, C.-A. (2021, August). Review of application of AI techniques to Solar Tower Systems. *Solar Energy*, *224*, 500–515. doi:10.1016/j.solener.2021.06.009

Minoli, D., & Occhiogrosso, B. (2019). Practical aspects for the integration of 5G networks and IoT applications in smart cities environments. *Wireless Communications and Mobile Computing*, *2019*, 2019. doi:10.1155/2019/5710834

Mirza, A. F., Ling, Q., Javed, M. Y., & Mansoor, M. (2019). Novel MPPT techniques for photovoltaic systems under uniform irradiance and Partial shading. *Solar Energy*, *184*, 628–648. doi:10.1016/j.solener.2019.04.034

Mishra, T. K., Sahoo, K. S., Bilal, M., Shah, S. C., & Mishra, M. K. (2023). Adaptive Congestion Control Mechanism to Enhance TCP Performance in Cooperative IoV. *IEEE Access : Practical Innovations, Open Solutions*, *11*, 9000–9013. doi:10.1109/ACCESS.2023.3239302

Mishra, T. K., & Tripathi, S. (2019). Minimizing End-to-End Delay on Real-Time Applications. *Wireless Personal Communications*, *107*(1), 41–55. doi:10.100711277-019-06239-8

Mitra, R. N., & Agrawal, D. P. (2015). 5G mobile technology: A survey. *ICT Express*, *1*(3), 132–137. doi:10.1016/j.icte.2016.01.003

Mohammadi, N., & Taylor, J. E. (2017). Smart city digital twins. In *Proc. IEEE Symp. Ser. Computational Intelligence (SSCI),* (pp. 1–5). IEEE. 10.1109/SSCI.2017.8285439

Mohanta, D. K., Murthy, C., & Sinha Roy, D. (2016). A brief review of phasor measurement units as sensors for smart grid. *Electric Power Components and Systems*, *44*(4), 411–425. doi:10.1080/15325008.2015.1117538

Mora, L., Bolici, R., & Deakin, M. (2017). The First Two Decades of Smart-City Research: A Bibliometric Analysis. *Journal of Urban Technology*, *24*(1), 3–27. doi:10.1080/10630732.2017.1285123

Morley, J., Machado, C. C. V., Burr, C., Cowls, J., Joshi, I., Taddeo, M., & Floridi, L. (2020). The ethics of AI in health care: A mapping review. *Social Science & Medicine, 260.*

Moustafa, N. (2021). A Systemic IoT–Fog–Cloud Architecture for Big-Data Analytics and Cyber Security Systems: A Review of Fog Computing. *Secure Edge Computing*, 41-50.

Moustafa, N., & Slay, J. (2015, November). UNSW-NB15: A comprehensive data set for network intrusion detection systems (UNSW-NB15 network data set). In *2015 military communications and information systems conference (MilCIS)* (pp. 1-6). IEEE.

Moyle, B. D., Weaver, D. B., Gössling, S., McLennan, C. L., & Hadinejad, A. (2022). Are water-centric themes in sustainable tourism research congruent with the UN Sustainable Development Goals? *Journal of Sustainable Tourism*, *30*(8), 1821–1836. doi:10.1080/09669582.2021.1993233

Mukherjee, D., & Chakrabarti, S. (2004). *Fundamentals of renewable energy systems*. New Age International.

Musamih, A., Salah, K., Jayaraman, R., Arshad, J., Debe, M., Al-Hammadi, Y., & Ellahham, S. (2021). A Blockchain-Based Approach for Drug Traceability in Healthcare Supply Chain. *IEEE Access : Practical Innovations, Open Solutions*, *9*, 9728–9743. doi:10.1109/ACCESS.2021.3049920

Musamih, A., Salah, K., Jayaraman, R., Arshad, J., Debe, M., Al-Hammadi, Y., & Ellahham, S. (2021). A blockchain-based approach for drug traceability in the healthcare supply chain. *IEEE Access : Practical Innovations, Open Solutions*, *9*, 9728–9743.

Musleh, A. S., Yao, G., & Muyeen, S. M. (2019). Blockchain Applications in Smart Grid-Review and Frameworks. *IEEE Access : Practical Innovations, Open Solutions*, *7*, 86746–86757. doi:10.1109/ACCESS.2019.2920682

Nagarajan, S. M., Deverajan, G. G., Chatterjee, P., Alnumay, W., & Muthukumaran, V. (2022). Integration of IoT based routing process for food supply chain management in sustainable smart cities. *Sustainable Cities and Society*, *76*, 103448. doi:10.1016/j.scs.2021.103448

Nalluri, M. R., Kannan, K., Gao, X. Z., & Roy, D. S. (2020). Multiobjective hybrid monarch butterfly optimization for imbalanced disease classification problem. *International Journal of Machine Learning and Cybernetics*, *11*(7), 1423–1451. doi:10.100713042-019-01047-9

Nalluri, M. R., & Roy, D. S. (2017). Hybrid disease diagnosis using multiobjective optimization with evolutionary parameter optimization. *Journal of Healthcare Engineering*. doi:10.1155/2017/5907264 PMID:29065626

Nalluri, M. S. R., Kannan, K., Gao, X. Z., & Roy, D. S. (2019). An efficient hybrid meta-heuristic approach for cell formation problem. *Soft Computing*, *23*(19), 9189–9213. doi:10.100700500-019-03798-7

Nam, K. J., Heo, S. K., Rhee, G. H., Kim, M. J., & Yoo, C. K. (2021, May). Dual-objective optimization for energy-saving and fouling mitigation in MBR plants using AI-based influent prediction and an integrated biological-physical model. *Journal of Membrane Science*, *626*, 119208. doi:10.1016/j.memsci.2021.119208

Nam, T., & Pardo, T. A. (2011). Conceptualizing a smart city with dimensions of technology, people, and institutions. *Proceedings of the 12th Annual International Digital Government Research Conference on Digital Government Innovation in Challenging Times,* (pp. 282-291). ACM. 10.1145/2037556.2037602

Nandi, S. K., & Ghosh, H. R. (2010). Prospect of wind–PV-battery hybrid power system as an alternative to grid extension in Bangladesh. *Energy*, *35*(7), 3040–3047. doi:10.1016/j.energy.2010.03.044

Nath, N. R., & v Nath, H. (2022). Critical analysis of layered and systematic approaches for understanding IoT security threats and challenges. *Computers & Electrical Engineering*, *100*, 107997. doi:10.1016/j.compeleceng.2022.107997

Neves, P., Calé, R., Costa, M., Gaspar, G., Alcaraz-Calero, J., Wang, Q., Nightingale, J., Bernini, G., Carrozzo, G., Valdivieso, Á., García Villalba, L. J., Barros, M., Gravas, A., Santos, J., Maia, R. & Preto, R. (2017a). Future mode of operations for 5G – The SELFNET approach enabled by SDN/NFV. *Computer Standards and Interfaces, 54*(December 2016), 229–246. doi:10.1016/j.csi.2016.12.008

Nguyen, C. V., Quyen, T. V., Le, A. M., Truong, L. H., & Nguyen, M. T. (2020). Advanced hybrid energy harvesting systems for unmanned ariel vehicles. Advances in Science. *Technology and Engineering Systems Journal*, *5*(1), 34–39.

Niaz, M. S., & Saake, G. (2015). Merkle hash tree based techniques for data integrity of outsourced data. *GvD*, *1366*, 66–71.

Nicholson Price, W. II. (2019). *Artificial intelligence in the medical system: four roles for potential transformation.* Yale Journal of Health Poly L. & Ethics.

Niranjanamurthy, M., Nithya, B. N., & Jagannatha, S. J. C. C. (2019). Analysis of Blockchain technology: Pros, cons and SWOT. *Cluster Computing*, *22*(6), 14743–14757.

Nitisiri, K., Gen, M., & Ohwada, H. (2019). A parallel multi-objective genetic algorithm with learning based mutation for railway scheduling. *Computers & Industrial Engineering*, *130*, 381–394. doi:10.1016/j.cie.2019.02.035

Noseworthy, P. A., Kaufman, E. S., Chen, L. Y., Chung, M. K., Elkind Mitchell, S. V., & Joglar, J. A. (2019). Subclinical and device-detected atrial fibrillation: pondering the knowledge gap: a scientific statement from the American Heart Association. *Circulation*, *2019*(140), e944–e963. doi:10.1161/CIR.0000000000000740 PMID:31694402

Nosratabadi, S. (2019). State of the art survey of deep learning and machine learning models for smart cities and urban sustainability. *in Proc. Int. Conf. Global. Research in Education, 2019*, 228–238.

Notton, G., Diaf, S., & Stoyanov, L. (2011). Hybrid photovoltaic/wind energy systems for remote locations. *Energy Procedia*, *6*, 666–677. doi:10.1016/j.egypro.2011.05.076

Noura, H., Couturier, R., Pham, C., & Chehab, A. (2019). Lightweight Stream Cipher Scheme for Resource-Constrained IoT Devices. *International Conference on Wireless and Mobile Computing, Networking and Communications*. IEEE. 10.1109/WiMOB.2019.8923144

Obaidat, M. A. (2022). Threats and vulnerabilities of wireless sensor networks in smart cities. *The Rise of Smart Cities: Advanced Structural Sensing and Monitoring Systems*, 463–491.

Odeh, A., Keshta, I., & Al-Haija, Q. A. (2022). Analysis of Blockchain in the Healthcare Sector: Application and Issues. *Symmetry*, *14*(9), 1760.

Oehler-Şincai, I. M. (2021). Dominant Contribution of the Developing Countries to the Renewable Energy Sector 1. *Global Economic Observer*, *9*(1), 195–202.

Okai, E., Feng, X., & Sant, P. (2018). Smart cities survey. In *Proceedings of the IEEE 20th International Conference on High Performance Computing and Communications and IEEE 16th International Conference on Smart City*. IEEE.

Olabi, A. G. (2017). *Renewable energy and energy storage systems*. Elsevier. doi:10.1016/j.energy.2017.07.054

Oueida, S., Aloqaily, M., & Ionescu, S. (2018). A smart healthcare reward model for resource allocation in smart city. *Multimedia Tools and Applications*, *78*(17), 24573–24594. doi:10.100711042-018-6647-4

Özçevik, M. E., Canberk, B., & Duong, T. Q. (2017). End to end delay modeling of heterogeneous traffic flows in software defined 5G networks. *Ad Hoc Networks*, *60*, 26–39. doi:10.1016/j.adhoc.2017.02.006

Oztemel, E., & Gursev, S. (2020). Literature review of Industry 4.0 and related technologies. *Journal of Intelligent Manufacturing*, *31*(1), 127–182. doi:10.100710845-018-1433-8

Paiva, S., Ahad, M. A., Tripathi, G., Feroz, N., & Casalino, G. (2021). Enabling technologies for urban smart mobility: Recent trends, opportunities and challenges. *Sensors (Basel)*, *21*(6), 2143. doi:10.339021062143 PMID:33803903

Panatik, K. Z., Kamardin, K., Shariff, S. A., Yuhaniz, S. S., & Ahmad, N. A. (2020). Energy harvesting in wireless sensor networks: survey. *IEEE 3rd International Symposium on Telecommunication Technologies*, 1041-1054.

Panayiotou, G., Kalogirou, S., & Tassou, S. (2012). Design and simulation of a PV and a PV–Wind standalone energy system to power a household application. *Renewable Energy*, *37*(1), 355–363. doi:10.1016/j.renene.2011.06.038

Panda, S. K., & Satapathy, S. C. (2021). Drug traceability and transparency in medical supply chain using blockchain for easing the process and creating trust between stakeholders and consumers. *Personal and Ubiquitous Computing*, 1–17.

Pandey, A. K., Khan, A. I., Abushark, Y. B., Alam, M. M., Agrawal, A., Kumar, R., & Khan, R. A. (2020). Key issues in healthcare data integrity: Analysis and recommendations. *IEEE Access : Practical Innovations, Open Solutions*, *8*, 40612–40628.

Pandey, P., & Litoriya, R. (2021). Securing e-health networks from counterfeit medicine penetration using blockchain. *Wireless Personal Communications*, *117*(1), 7–25.

Papa, R., Gargiulo, C., & Galderisi, A. (2013). Towards an Urban Planners' Perspective on Smart City. *Journal of Land Use, Mobility and Environment*, *6*(1), 6–17. doi:10.6092/1970-9870/1536

Papyshev, G., & Yarime, M. (2021). Exploring city digital twins as policy tools: A task-based approach to generating synthetic data on urban mobility. *Data & Policy*, *3*, e16. doi:10.1017/dap.2021.17

Pargmann, H., Euhausen, D., & Faber, R. (2018). Intelligent big data processing for wind farm monitoring and analysis based on cloud-technologies and digital twins: A quantitative approach. In *Proc. IEEE 3rd Int. Conf. Cloud Comput. Big Data Anal. (ICCCBDA)* (pp. 233–237). IEEE. 10.1109/ICCCBDA.2018.8386518

Park, S. M., Ju, S., & Lee, J. (2014). Efficient routing for traffic offloading in Software-defined Network. *Procedia Computer Science*, *34*, 674–679. doi:10.1016/j.procs.2014.07.096

Pastorino, R., De Vito, C., Migliara, G., Glocker, K., Binenbaum, I., Ricciardi, W., & Boccia, S. (2019). Benefits and challenges of Big Data in healthcare: An overview of the European initiatives. *European Journal of Public Health*, *29*(Supplement_3), 23–27. PMID:31738444

Patel, M. R. (2005). *Wind and solar power systems: design, analysis, and operation*. CRC Press. doi:10.1201/9781420039924

Perera, C., Zaslavsky, A., Christen, P., & Georgakopoulos, D. (2014). Sensing as a service model for smart cities supported by internet of things. *Transactions on Emerging Telecommunications Technologies*, *25*(1), 81–93. doi:10.1002/ett.2704

Petch, J., Di, S., & Nelson, W. (2022). Opening the black box: The promise and limitations of explainable machine learning in cardiology. *The Canadian Journal of Cardiology*, *38*(2), 204–213. doi:10.1016/j.cjca.2021.09.004 PMID:34534619

Philip, M. S., & Singh, P. (2022). An energy efficient algorithm for sustainable monitoring of water quality in smart cities. *Sustainable Computing: Informatics and Systems*, *35*, 721–731. doi:10.1016/j.suscom.2022.100768

Piyushji(2022).Communication Models in IoT (Internet of Things - GeeksforGeeks, https://www.geeksforgeeks.org/communication-models-in-iot-internet-of-things, Retrieved on 20/10/2022

Piyushji. (2022). Peer to Peer P2P communications for IoT. IOT. https://iot.onesimcard.com/Peer-to-Peer-communications-for-IoT

Poonthalir, G., & Nadarajan, R. (2018). A fuel efficient green vehicle routing problem with varying speed constraint (F-GVRP). *Expert Systems with Applications*, *100*, 131–144. doi:10.1016/j.eswa.2018.01.052

Porter, M., & Heppelman, J. (2015, October). How smart, connected products are transforming companies. *Harvard Business Review*, *93*, 96–114.

Pradeep, P. T. (2019). Smart City Services - Challenges and Approach. *International Conference on Machine Learning, Big Data, Cloud and Parallel Computing*.

Pradhan, B., Hussain, M. W., Srivastava, G., Debbarma, M. K., Barik, R. K., & Lin, J. C. W. (2022). A neuro-evolutionary approach for software defined wireless network traffic classification. *IET Communications*, cmu2.12548. doi:10.1049/cmu2.12548

Pradhan, B., Reddy, K. H., Roy, D. S., & Mohanta, D. K. (2011, December). Intentional islanding of electric power systems in a grid computing framework: a graph-theoretic approach. In *2011 International Conference on Recent Trends in Information Systems* (pp. 156-160). IEEE. 10.1109/ReTIS.2011.6146859

Pramathi, J. N., & Vindhya, P. M. (2018). Artificial Intelligence in Smart City Analysis. *International Conference on Smart Systems and Inventive Technology (ICSSIT)*.

Price, W. N., & Cohen, I. G. (2019). Privacy in the age of medical big data. *Nature Medicine*, *25*(1), 37–43. PMID:30617331

Prince, & Hati, A. S. (2021, August). A comprehensive review of energy-efficiency of ventilation system using Artificial Intelligence. *Renewable & Sustainable Energy Reviews*, *146*, 111153. doi:10.1016/j.rser.2021.111153

Priyadarshini, M. (2021). *Status of renewable energy in India and a case of financing viability of wind energy project* [Doctoral dissertation]. Delhi Technological University.

Qayyum, A., Ijaz, A., Usama, M., Iqbal, W., Qadir, J., Elkhatib, Y., & Al-Fuqaha, A. (2020). Securing Machine Learning in the Cloud: A Systematic Review of Cloud Machine Learning Security. *Frontiers in Big Data*, *3*, 43. doi:10.3389/fdata.2020.587139 PMID:33693420

Quick, C., Dey, R., & Lin, X. (2021). Regression Models for Understanding COVID-19 Epidemic Dynamics With Incomplete Data. *Journal of the American Statistical Association*, *116*(536), 1561–1577. doi:10.1080/01621459.2021.2001339 PMID:37206108

Raca, D., Leahy, D., Sreenan, C. J., & Quinlan, J. J. (2020). Beyond throughput, the next generation: A 5G dataset with channel and context metrics. *MMSys 2020 - Proceedings of the 2020 Multimedia Systems Conference*, 303–308. 10.1145/3339825.3394938

Radó, N., Girasek, E., Békási, S., & Győrffy, Z. (2022). Digital Technology Access and Health-Related Internet Use Among People Experiencing Homelessness in Hungary: Quantitative Survey. *Journal of Medical Internet Research*, *24*(10), e38729. doi:10.2196/38729 PMID:36260379

Raghupathi, W., & Raghupathi, V. (2014). Big data analytics in healthcare: Promise and potential. *Health Information Science and Systems*, *2*(1), 1–10. PMID:25825667

Rahman, A., Islam, M. J., Band, S. S., Muhammad, G., Hasan, K., & Tiwari, P. (2022). Towards a blockchain-SDN-based secure architecture for cloud computing in smart industrial IoT. *Digital Communications and Networks*. Advance online publication. doi:10.1016/j.dcan.2022.11.003

Rajab, H., & Cinkelr, T. (2018). IoT based Smart Cities. *2018 International Symposium on Networks, Computers and Communications (ISNCC)*, (pp. 1-4). IEEE. 10.1109/ISNCC.2018.8530997

Raja, J., & Mookhambika, N. (2021). A novel energy harvesting with middle-order weighted probability (EHMoWP) for performance improvement in wireless sensor network (WSN). *Journal of Ambient Intelligence and Humanized Computing*, 1–12.

Rajpurkar, P., Chen, E., Banerjee, O., & Topol, E. J. (2022). AI in health and medicine. *Nature Medicine*, *28*(1), 31–38. doi:10.103841591-021-01614-0 PMID:35058619

Rani, S., Mishra, R. K., Usman, M., Kataria, A., Kumar, P., Bhambri, P., & Mishra, A. K. (2021). Amalgamation of Advanced Technologies for Sustainable Development of Smart City Environment: A Review. *IEEE Access : Practical Innovations, Open Solutions*, *9*, 150060–150087. doi:10.1109/ACCESS.2021.3125527

Rao, M. G., Pawar, S. H. P., & Reddy, H. K. (2023). Minimize the Energy Consumption for Communication Protocol in IoT. In R. Gatti, C. Singh, S. P., & S. Bhat (Eds.), Energy Systems Design for Low-Power Computing (pp. 214-234). IGI Global. doi:10.4018/978-1-6684-4974-5.ch011

Rao, M. G., Pawar, S., Priyanka, H., & Reddy, K. H. K. (2022, December). Amalgamation Biometric Deep Features in Smart City-ITS Authentication. In *2022 6th International Conference on Computation System and Information Technology for Sustainable Solutions (CSITSS)* (pp. 1-6). IEEE. 10.1109/CSITSS57437.2022.10026408

Rao, P. M., & Deebak, B. D. (2022). Security and privacy issues in smart cities/industries: Technologies, applications, and challenges. *Journal of Ambient Intelligence and Humanized Computing*, *2022*, 1–37. doi:10.100712652-022-03707-1

Rath, M. (2020). Big data and iot-allied challenges associated with healthcare applications in smart and automated systems. In data analytics in medicine: Concepts, methodologies, tools, and applications (pp. 1401-1414). IGI Global. doi:10.4018/978-1-7998-1204-3.ch070

Rathee, G., Iqbal, R., Waqar, O., & Bashir, A. K. (2021). On the design and implementation of a blockchain enabled e-voting application within iot-oriented smart cities. *IEEE Access : Practical Innovations, Open Solutions*, *9*, 34165–34176. doi:10.1109/ACCESS.2021.3061411

Rathore, M. M. U., Shah, S. A., Shukla, D., Bentafat, E., & Bakiras, S. (2021, February). The role of AI, machine learning, and big data in digital twinning: A systematic literature review, challenges, and opportunities. *IEEE Access : Practical Innovations, Open Solutions*, *99*, 1–1. doi:10.1109/ACCESS.2021.3060863

Ratta, P., Kaur, A., Sharma, S., Shabaz, M., & Dhiman, G. (2021). Application of blockchain and internet of things in healthcare and medical sector: Applications, challenges, and future perspectives. *Journal of Food Quality*.

Rauchs, M., & Hileman, G. (2010). *Global blockchain benchmarking study*. Cambridge Centre for Alternative Finance Reports.

Ravi, G., & Kashwan, K. R. (2015, November). A new routing protocol for energy efficient mobile applications for ad hoc networks. *Computers & Electrical Engineering*, *48*, 77–85. doi:10.1016/j.compeleceng.2015.03.023

Reddy, K. H. K., Goswami, R. S., & Roy, D. S. (2023). An Artificial Intelligence Approach to Enabled Smart Service Towards Futuristic Smart Cities. In Handbook of Research on Applications of AI, Digital Twin, and Internet of Things for Sustainable Development (pp. 12-29). IGI Global. doi:10.4018/978-1-6684-6821-0.ch002

Reddy, K. H. K., Luhach, A. K., Kumar, V. V., Pratihar, S., Kumar, D., & Roy, D. S. (2022). Towards energy efficient Smart city services: A software defined resource management scheme for data centers. *Sustainable Computing: Informatics and Systems*, *35*, 100776. doi:10.1016/j.suscom.2022.100776

Reddy, S., Allan, S., Coghlan, S., & Cooper, P. (2020, March). A governance model for the application of AI in health care. *Journal of the American Medical Informatics Association : JAMIA*, *27*(3), 491–497. doi:10.1093/jamia/ocz192 PMID:31682262

Rehman, S., Alam, M. M., Meyer, J. P., & Al-Hadhrami, L. M. (2012). Feasibility study of a wind–pv–diesel hybrid power system for a village. *Renewable Energy*, *38*(1), 258–268. doi:10.1016/j.renene.2011.06.028

Rejeb, A., Karim, S, Simske, J., Keogh, J. G., Rejeb, K., Simske, S. J., & Org, J. (2021). Blockchain technology in the smart city: a bibliometric review. *Quality & Quantity, 56*(5), 2875–2906. doi:10.1007/s11135-021-01251-2

Renuka & Reddy. (2020b). *A Comprehensive Parameterized Resource Allocation Approach for Wireless Sensor Networks*. doi:10.1007/978-981-13-9574-1_7

Renuka, K., Das, S. N., & Reddy, K. H. (2018). An Efficient Context Management Approach for IoT. *IUP Journal of Information Technology, 14*(2).

Renuka, K., Das, S. N., & Reddy, K. H. (2018). An Efficient Context Management Approach for IoT. *IUP Journal of Information Technology*, *14*(2).

Renuka, K., Roy, D. S., & Reddy, K. H. K. (2021). An SDN empowered location aware routing for energy efficient next generation vehicular networks. *IET Intelligent Transport Systems*, *15*(2), 308–319. doi:10.1049/itr2.12026

Reynolds, C., Boulding, A., Pollock, H., Sweet, N., Ruiz, J., & Draeger de Teran, T. (2020). *Halving Food Loss and Waste in the EU by 2030: The major steps needed to accelerate progress*. Academic Press.

Reynvoet, M., Gheibi, O., Quin, F., & Weyns, D. (2022). Detecting and Mitigating Jamming Attacks in IoT Networks Using Self-Adaptation. *2022 IEEE International Conference on Autonomic Computing and Self-Organizing Systems Companion (ACSOS-C),* (pp. 7–12). IEEE. 10.1109/ACSOSC56246.2022.00019

Ribeiro, M. T., & Guestrin, C. (2016). *Why Should I Trust You?* Explaining the Predictions of Any Classifier. doi:10.1145/2939672.2939778

Rivera, W., & Rodriguez-Martinez, M. (2016). *Towards cloud services in smart power grid. 2016 IEEE innovative smart grid technologies - Asia.* ISGT-Asia.

Rodriguez, J. (2022). *Building an IOT Platform: Centralized vs. Decentralized Models.* LinkedIn. https://www.linkedin.com/pulse/building-iot-platform-centralized-vs-decentralized-models-rodriguez

Rong, G., Mendez, A., Assi, E., Zhao, B., & Sawan, M. (2020). Artificial Intelligence in Healthcare: Review and Prediction Case Studies. *Engineering, 6*(3), 291-301.

Rosa, R. L., Dehollain, C., Pellitteri, F., Miceli, R., & Livreri, P. (2020). A battery-free asset monitoring system based on rf wireless power transfer. *IEEE 20th Mediterranean Electrotechnical Conference,* 181-186. 10.1109/MELECON48756.2020.9140484

Rosa, R. L., Livreri, P., Trigona, C., Donato, L. D., & Sorbello, G. (n.d.). Strategies and techniques for powering wireless sensor nodes through energy harvesting and wireless power transfer. *Sensors (Basel), 19*(12), 26–60.

Ruohomäki, T., Airaksinen, E., Huuska, P., Kesäniemi, O., Martikka, M., & Suomisto, J. (2018, September). Smart city platform enabling digital twin. In *2018 International Conference on Intelligent Systems (IS)* (pp. 155-161). IEEE 10.1109/IS.2018.8710517

Sadeghi-Barzani, P., Rajabi-Ghahnavieh, A., & Kazemi-Karegar, H. (2014). Optimal fast charging station placing and sizing. *Applied Energy, 125*, 289–299. doi:10.1016/j.apenergy.2014.03.077

Saeed, M. M., Saeed, R. A., Mokhtar, R. A., Alhumyani, H., & Ali, E. S. (2022). A Novel Variable Pseudonym Scheme for Preserving Privacy User Location in 5G Networks. *Security and Communication Networks, 2022*, 7487600. doi:10.1155/2022/7487600

Safari, S., Ardehali, M. M., & Sirizi, M. J. (2013). Particle swarm optimization based fuzzy logic controller for autonomous green power energy system with hydrogen storage. *Energy Conversion and Management, 65*, 41–49. doi:10.1016/j.enconman.2012.08.012

Safavat, S., & Rawat, D. B. (2020). On the elliptic curve cryptography for privacy-aware secure ACO-AODV routing in intent-based internet of vehicles for smart cities. *IEEE Transactions on Intelligent Transportation Systems, 22*(8), 5050–5059. doi:10.1109/TITS.2020.3008361

Salah, K., Nizamuddin, N., Jayaraman, R., & Omar, M. (2019). Blockchain-Based Soybean Traceability in Agricultural Supply Chain. *IEEE Access : Practical Innovations, Open Solutions, 7*, 73295–73305. doi:10.1109/ACCESS.2019.2918000

Samih, H. (2019). Smart cities and internet of things. *Journal of Information Technology Case and Application Research, 21*(1), 3–12. doi:10.1080/15228053.2019.1587572

Samrat Kumar Dey, Md. Mahbubur Rahman, M. R. U. (2018). Detection of Flow Based Anomaly in OpenFlow Controller: Machine Learning Approach in Software Defined Networking. *2018 4th International Conference on Electrical Engineering and Information & Communication Technology (iCEEiCT).* 416-421, https://doi.org/10.1109/.8628105

Samuel, O., Javaid, N., Alghamdi, T. A., & Kumar, N. (2022). Towards sustainable smart cities: A secure and scalable trading system for residential homes using blockchain and artificial intelligence. *Sustainable Cities and Society, 76*, 103371. doi:10.1016/j.scs.2021.103371

Sanajaoba, S., & Fernandez, E. (2016). Maiden application of Cuckoo Search algorithm for optimal sizing of a remote hybrid renewable energy System. *Renewable Energy, 96*, 1–10. doi:10.1016/j.renene.2016.04.069

Sánchez-Medina, J. J., Galán-Moreno, M. J., & Rubio-Royo, E. (2009). Traffic signal optimization in" La Almozara" district in saragossa under congestion conditions, using genetic algorithms, traffic microsimulation, and cluster computing. *IEEE Transactions on Intelligent Transportation Systems*, *11*(1), 132–141. doi:10.1109/TITS.2009.2034383

Sankaran, V., & Chopra, A. (2020). Creating global sustainable smart cities (a case study of Masdar City). *Journal of Physics: Conference Series*, *1706*(1), 012141. doi:10.1088/1742-6596/1706/1/012141

Santa, J., Katsaros, K. V., Bernal-Escobedo, L., Zougari, S., Miranda, M., Castañeda, O., Dalet, B., & Amditis, A. (2022). Evaluation platform for 5G vehicular communications. *Vehicular Communications*, *38*, 100537. doi:10.1016/j.vehcom.2022.100537

Saraswat, D., Bhattacharya, P., Verma, A., Prasad, V. K., Tanwar, S., Sharma, G., Bokoro, P. N., & Sharma, R. (2022). Explainable AI for Healthcare 5.0: Opportunities and Challenges. *IEEE Access : Practical Innovations, Open Solutions*, *10*, 84486–84517. doi:10.1109/ACCESS.2022.3197671

Satyala, N., Norouzzadeh, P., Vashaee, D., Wang, X., & Wang, Z. M. (2014). Nano bulk thermoelectric: concepts, techniques, and modeling. Nanoscale, Thermo Electrics, 16, 141-183. doi:10.1007/978-3-319-02012-9_4

Sawhney, A. (2021). Striving towards a circular economy: Climate policy and renewable energy in India. *Clean Technologies and Environmental Policy*, *23*(2), 491–499. doi:10.100710098-020-01935-7

Schaffers, H., Komninos, N., Pallot, M., Trousse, B., Nilsson, M., & Oliveira, A. (2011, May). Smart cities and the future internet: Towards cooperation frameworks for open innovation. In *The future internet assembly* (pp. 431–446). Springer. doi:10.1007/978-3-642-20898-0_31

Schmidt, J., Cancella, R., & Pereira, A. O. Jr. (2016). An optimal mix of solar PV, wind and hydro power for a low-carbon electricity supply in Brazil. *Renewable Energy*, *85*, 137–147. doi:10.1016/j.renene.2015.06.010

Scholl, H. J., Barzilai-Nahon, K., Ahn, J.-H., Olga, P., & Barbara, R. (2009). E-commerce and e-government: How do they compare? What can they learn from each other? *Proceedings of the 42nd Hawaiian International Conference on System Sciences.*

Schrotter, G., & Hürzeler, C. (2020). The digital twin of the city of Zurich for urban planning. PFG–Journal of Photogrammetry. *Remote Sensing and Geoinformation Science*, *88*(1), 99–112.

Schuurman, D., Baccarne, B., De Marez, L., & Mechant, P. (2012). Smart ideas for smart cities: Investigating crowdsourcing for generating and selecting ideas for ICT innovation in a city context. *Journal of Theoretical and Applied Electronic Commerce Research*, *7*(3), 49–62. doi:10.4067/S0718-18762012000300006

Sehrawat, D., & Gill, N. S. (2019, April). Smart sensors: Analysis of different types of IoT sensors. In *2019 3rd International Conference on Trends in Electronics and Informatics (ICOEI)* (pp. 523-528). IEEE.

Sejaan, G. A., Lamarque, F., Hajj, N. E., Assad, J. A., & Hajjar, H. A. (2020). Optical energy harvesting in a smart material-based micro-actuator using a vertical multijunction PV cell. *Energy Harvesting and Storage Materials, Devices, and Applications X*, *11387*, 113–870.

Senbagavalli, M., & Tholkappia Arasu, G. (2016). Opinion Mining for Cardiovascular Disease using Decision Tree based Feature Selection. *Asian Journal of Research in Social Sciences and Humanities*, *6*(8), 891–897. doi:10.5958/2249-7315.2016.00658.4

Sethi, P., & Sarangi, S. R. (2017). Internet of Things: Architectures, protocols, and applications. *Journal of Electrical and Computer Engineering*, *2017*, 9324035. doi:10.1155/2017/9324035

Setyawan, E., Kurniawan, A., Rahmadianto, F., Napitupulu, R. A. M., & Siagian, P. (2020). Flat plate type solar collector performance using double thermal insulation. Jakarta, IOP Conference Service. *Materials Science and Engineering*, *852*, 1244.

Sevgican, S., Turan, M., Gokarslan, K., Yilmaz, H. B., & Tugcu, T. (2020). Intelligent network data analytics function in 5G cellular networks using machine learning. *Journal of Communications and Networks (Seoul)*, *22*(3), 269–280. doi:10.1109/JCN.2020.000019

Shafik, W. (2023). Cyber Security Perspectives in Public Spaces: Drone Case Study. In *Handbook of Research on Cybersecurity Risk in Contemporary Business Systems* (pp. 79–97). IGI Global. doi:10.4018/978-1-6684-7207-1.ch004

Shafiq, M., Tian, Z., Bashir, A. K., Du, X., & Guizani, M. (2020). IoT malicious traffic identification using wrapper-based feature selection mechanisms. *Computers & Security*, *94*, 101863. doi:10.1016/j.cose.2020.101863

Shahab, S. (2022). When Smart Cities Get Smarter via Machine Learning: An In-Depth Literature Review. *IEEE Access : Practical Innovations, Open Solutions*, *10*, 2022.

Shahraki, A., Taherkordi, A., Haugen, Ø., & Eliassen, F. (2020). Clustering objectives in wireless sensor networks: A survey and research direction analysis. *Computer Networks*, *180*, 107376. doi:10.1016/j.comnet.2020.107376

Shaikh, F. K., & Zeadally, S. (2016). Energy harvesting in wireless sensor networks: A comprehensive review. *Renewable & Sustainable Energy Reviews*, *55*, 1041–1054. doi:10.1016/j.rser.2015.11.010

Shalli Rani, Maheswar, Kanagachidambaresan, & Jayarajan. (2020). Integration of WSN and IoT for smart cities. Springer.

Shari, N. F. M., & Malip, A. (2022). State-of-the-art solutions of blockchain technology for data dissemination in smart cities: A comprehensive review. *Computer Communications*.

Sharma, A., & Roy, S. (2010). Cloud computing 21st Century Paradigm for Internet. *Proceeding of national seminar on Advancement in Cloud Computing & Green IT Technology.* Springer.

Sharma, P. K., Kumar, N., & Park, J. H. (2019). Blockchain-Based Distributed Framework for Automotive Industry in a Smart City. *IEEE Transactions on Industrial Informatics*, *15*(7), 4197–4205. doi:10.1109/TII.2018.2887101

Sharma, P. K., & Park, J. H. (2021). Blockchain-Based Secure Mist Computing Network Architecture for Intelligent Transportation Systems. *IEEE Transactions on Intelligent Transportation Systems*, *22*(8), 5168–5177. doi:10.1109/TITS.2020.3040989

Sharma, P., Jain, S., Gupta, S., & Chamola, V. (2021). Role of machine learning and deep learning in securing 5G-driven industrial IoT applications. *Ad Hoc Networks*, *123*(September), 102685. doi:10.1016/j.adhoc.2021.102685

Sharma, S., Chen, K., & Sheth, A. (2018). Toward practical privacy-preserving analytics for IoT and cloud-based healthcare systems. *IEEE Internet Computing*, *22*(2), 42–51. doi:10.1109/MIC.2018.112102519

Shen, C., & Pena-Mora, F. (2018). Blockchain for Cities—A Systematic Literature Review. *IEEE Access : Practical Innovations, Open Solutions*, *6*, 76787–76819. doi:10.1109/ACCESS.2018.2880744

Sherazi, H. H. R., Grieco, L. A., & Boggia, G. (2018). A comprehensive review on energy harvesting MAC protocols in WSNs: Challenges and tradeoffs. *Ad Hoc Networks*, *71*, 117–134. doi:10.1016/j.adhoc.2018.01.004

Shina, W. (2021, April). AI-assistance for predictive maintenance of renewable energy systems. *Energy*, *221*, 119775. doi:10.1016/j.energy.2021.119775

Shi, Q., Dong, B., He, T., Sun, Z., Zhu, J., Zhang, Z., & Lee, C. (2020). Progress in wearable electronics/photonics moving toward the era of artificial intelligence and Internet of things. *InfoMat*, *2*(6), 1131–1162. doi:10.1002/inf2.12122

Shi, Q., Zhang, Z., He, T., Sun, Z., Wang, B., Feng, Y., Shan, X., Salam, B., & Lee, C. (2020). Deep learning enabled smart mats as a scalable floor monitoring system. *Nature Communications*, *11*(1), 4609. doi:10.103841467-020-18471-z PMID:32929087

Shirazi, E., & Jadid, S. (2019). Autonomous self-healing in smart distribution grids using multi agent systems. *IEEE Transactions on Industrial Informatics*, *15*(12), 6291–6301. doi:10.1109/TII.2018.2889741

Shi, S., He, D., Li, L. K. N., Khan, M. K., & Choo, K. K. R. (2020). Applications of blockchain in ensuring the security and privacy of electronic health record systems: A survey. *Computers & Security*, 97. PMID:32834254

Shiva, C. K., Badi, M., Shekarappa, G. S., Babu, R., Mahapatra, S., Vedik, B., & Rangarajan, S. S. (2022, May). Solution for reactive power planning problem using salp swarm algorithm. In AIP Conference Proceedings: Vol. 2418. *No. 1* (p. 040001). AIP Publishing LLC.

Shrivas, M. K., & Yeboah, T. (2018, December). The disruptive blockchain: types, platforms and applications. *Fifth Texila World Conference for Scholars (TWCS) on Transformation: The Creative Potential of Interdisciplinary.*

Shukla, S., Balachandran, K., & Sumitha, V. S. (2016). A framework for smart transportation using big data. *International Conference on ICT in Business Industry & Government (ICTBIG)*, Indore, India.

Siddiqui, B. (June 2018). *JXTA-A Messaging System for Wireless Java.* Developer.com. https://www.developer.com/mobile/java-mobile/jxta-a-messaging-system-for-wireless-java/

Silva, R., Santos, D., Meneses, F., Corujo, D. & Aguiar, R. L. (2021). A hybrid SDN solution for mobile networks. *Computer Networks, 190*(July 2020), 107958. https://doi.org/ doi:10.1016/.comnet.2021.107958

Silva, B. M. C., Rodrigues, J. J. P. C., Kumar, N., & Han, G. (2017). Cooperative Strategies for Challenged Networks and Applications: A Survey. *IEEE Systems Journal*, *11*(4), 2749–2760. doi:10.1109/JSYST.2015.2436927

Silva, B. N., Khan, M., & Han, K. (2018). Towards sustainable smart cities: A review of trends, architectures, components, and open challenges in smart cities. *Sustainable Cities and Society*, *38*, 697–713. doi:10.1016/j.scs.2018.01.053

Sim, L. C., & Mills, R. (2021). Low Carbon Energy in the Middle East and North Africa: Panacea or Placebo? *Low Carbon Energy in the Middle East and North Africa*, 1-17.

Simadiputra, V., & Surantha, N. (2021). Rasefiberry: Secure and efficient Raspberry-Pi based gateway for smart home IoT architecture. *Bulletin of Electrical Engineering and Informatics*, *10*(2), 1035–1045. doi:10.11591/eei.v10i2.2741

Sinche, S., Raposo, D., Armando, N., Rodrigues, A., Boavida, F., Pereira, V., & Silva, J. S. (2020). A Survey of IoT Management Protocols and Frameworks. *IEEE Communications Surveys and Tutorials*, *22*(2), 1168–1190. doi:10.1109/COMST.2019.2943087

Singh, J., Sajid, M., Gupta, S. K., & Haidri, R. A. (2022). Artificial Intelligence and Blockchain Technologies for Smart City. *Intelligent Green Technologies for Sustainable Smart Cities,* 317-330.

Singh, A., Sharma, S., & Singh, J. (2021). Nature-inspired algorithms for Wireless Sensor Networks: A comprehensive survey. *Computer Science Review*, *39*, 100342. doi:10.1016/j.cosrev.2020.100342

Singh, D., Pati, B., Panigrahi, C. R., & Swagatika, S. (2020). *Security Issues in IoT and their Countermeasures in Smart City Applications*. doi:10.1007/978-981-15-1483-8_26

Singh, J., Kaur, R., & Singh, D. (2021). Energy harvesting in wireless sensor networks: A taxonomic survey. *International Journal of Energy Research*, *45*(1), 118–140. doi:10.1002/er.5816

Singh, S. K., Pan, Y., & Park, J. H. (2022). Blockchain-enabled secure framework for energy-efficient smart parking in sustainable city environment. *Sustainable Cities and Society*, *76*, 103364. doi:10.1016/j.scs.2021.103364

Singh, S., & Mohan Sharma, R. (2019). *Handbook of Research on the IoT, Cloud Computing, and Wireless Network Optimization*. IGI Global. doi:10.4018/978-1-5225-7335-7

Sitharthan, R., Karthikeyan, M., Sundar, D. S., & Rajasekaran, S. (2020). Adaptive hybrid intelligent MPPT controller to approximate effectual wind speed and optimal rotor speed of variable speed wind turbine. *ISA Transactions*, *96*, 479–489. doi:10.1016/j.isatra.2019.05.029 PMID:31202532

Situ, X., Chen, W. N., Gong, Y. J., Lin, Y., Yu, W. J., Yu, Z., & Zhang, J. (2017, June). A parallel ant colony system based on region decomposition for taxi-passenger matching. In *2017 IEEE congress on evolutionary computation (CEC)* (pp. 960-967). IEEE.

Sivalingam, K., Sepulveda, M., Spring, M., & Davies, P. (2018). A review and methodology development for remaining useful life prediction of offshore fixed and floating wind turbine power converter with digital twin technol- ogy perspective. *In Proceedings of the 2nd Int. Conf. Green Energy Appl. (ICGEA)* (pp. 197–204). IEEE. 10.1109/ICGEA.2018.8356292

Skaržauskienė, A. (2022). Monitoring collective intelligence in Lithuania's online community. *In Proceedings of the 55th Hawaii International Conference on System Sciences* (pp. 357-365). University of Hawai'i at Manoa. 10.24251/HICSS.2022.043

Smart Industry. (2022). *Six Real World Examples of Digital Transformation*. Smart Identity. https://www.smartindustry.com/blog/smart-industry-connect/six-real-world-examples-of-digital-transformation/ (accessed on 17 January 2022).

Snir, M., Otto, S. W., Walker, D. W., Dongarra, J., & Huss-Lederman, S. (1995). *MPI: The Complete Reference*. MIT Press.

Sodhro, A. H., Awad, A. I., van de Beek, J., & Nikolakopoulos, G. (2022). Intelligent authentication of 5G healthcare devices: A survey. *Internet of Things (Netherlands)*, *20*, 100610. doi:10.1016/j.iot.2022.100610

Sohan, M., Al, F. A., Khan, S. R., Anannya, N. J., & Ahad, M. T. (2022). *Towards a secured smart IoT using light weight blockchain: An aim to secure Pharmacy Products*. arXiv preprint arXiv:2206.06925.

Solaimuthu, C., Ganesan, V., Senthilkumar, D., & Ramasamy, K. K. (2015). Emission reductions studies of a biodiesel engine using EGR and SCR for agriculture operations in developing countries. *Applied Energy*, *138*, 91–98. doi:10.1016/j.apenergy.2014.04.023

Sonam, J. R., & Johari, R. (2023). Crypto-Economic Model for Data Security in IoT Network. *Lecture Notes in Networks and Systems*, *492*, 427–434. doi:10.1007/978-981-19-3679-1_34

Song, Y. D., Cao, Q., Du, X., & Karimi, H. R. (2013). Control strategy based on wavelet transform and neural network for hybrid power system. *Journal of Applied Mathematics*, *2013*, 2013. doi:10.1155/2013/375840

Sookhak, M., Tang, H., He, Y., & Yu, F. R. (2019). Security and privacy of smart cities: Survey research issues and challenges. *IEEE Communications Surveys and Tutorials*, *21*(2), 1718–1743. doi:10.1109/COMST.2018.2867288

Soward, E., & Li, J. (2021). ArcGIS Urban: An application for plan assessment. *Computational Urban Science*, *1*(1), 1–10. doi:10.100743762-021-00016-9

Srinivasu, P., Sandhya, N., Jhaveri, R., & Raut, R. (2022). From Blackbox to Explainable AI in Healthcare: Existing Tools and Case Studies. Mobile Information Systems.

Suciu, G., Vulpe, A., Halunga, S., Fratu, O., Todoran, G., & Suciu, V. (2013, May). Smart cities built on resilient cloud computing and secure internet of things. In *2013 19th international conference on control systems and computer science* (pp. 513-518). IEEE. 10.1109/CSCS.2013.58

Sudevalayam, S., & Kulkarni, P. (2010). Energy harvesting sensor nodes: Survey and implications. *IEEE Communications Surveys and Tutorials*, *13*(3), 443–461. doi:10.1109/SURV.2011.060710.00094

Suhail, S., Zeadally, S., Jurdak, R., Hussain, R., Matulevičius, R., & Svetinovic, D. (2022). *Security attacks and solutions for digital twins.* arXiv preprint arXiv:2202.12501

Sujatha, G., Hemavathi, D., Sornalakshmi, K., & Sindhu, S. (2022). Analysis of Cryptographic Hashing Algorithms for Image Identification in Deduplication Process. In *Mobile Computing and Sustainable Informatics* (pp. 813–823). Springer.

Sunshine Smart City. (n.d.). *Smart Cities.* Sunshine Coast. https://www.sunshinecoast.qld.gov.au/smartcities

Su, Z., Liu, L., Li, M., Fan, X., & Zhou, Y. (2015). Reliable and resilient trust management in distributed service provision networks [TWEB]. *ACM Transactions on the Web*, *9*(3), 14. doi:10.1145/2754934

Syed, A. S., Sierra-Sosa, D., Kumar, A., & Elmaghraby, A. (2021). IoT in smart cities: A survey of technologies, practices, and challenges. *Smart Cities*, *4*(2), 429–475. doi:10.3390martcities4020024

Syed, A. S., Sierra-Sosa, D., Kumar, A., & Elmaghraby, A. (2022). Making Cities Smarter—Optimization Problems for the IoT Enabled Smart City Development: A Mapping of Applications, Objectives, Constraints. *Sensors (Basel)*, *22*(12), 4380. doi:10.339022124380 PMID:35746161

Syu, J. H., Wu, M. E., Srivastava, G., Chao, C. F., & Lin, J. C. (2021). An Iot-based hedge system for solar power generation. *IEEE Internet of Things Journal*, *5*(13), 156–162. doi:10.1109/JIOT.2021.3064384

Tachizawa, E. M., Alvarez-Gil, M. J., & Montes-Sancho, M. J. (2015). How "smart cities" change supply chain management. *Supply Chain Management*, *20*(3), 237–248. doi:10.1108/SCM-03-2014-0108

Tadros, C. N., Rizk, M. R., & Mokhtar, B. M. (2020). Software defined network-based management for enhanced 5G network services. *IEEE Access : Practical Innovations, Open Solutions*, *8*, 53997–54008. doi:10.1109/ACCESS.2020.2980392

Tang, Y., Dananjayan, S., Hou, C., Guo, Q., Luo, S. & He, Y. (2021). A survey on the 5G network and its impact on agriculture: Challenges and opportunities. *Computers and Electronics in Agriculture 180* (November 2020), 1–15. https://doi.org/ doi:10.1016/.compag.2020.105895

Tang, F., Member, S., Zhang, H., Yang, L. T., Member, S., & Chen, L. (2019). Elephant Flow Detection and Differentiated Scheduling with Efficient Sampling and Classification. *IEEE Transactions on Cloud Computing, PP, 1.* doi:10.1109/TCC.2019.2901669

Tang, S., Shelden, D. R., Eastman, C. M., Pishdad-Bozorghi, P., & Gao, X. (2019). A review of building information modeling (BIM) and the internet of things (IoT) devices integration: Present status and future trends. *Automation in Construction*, *10*, 127–139. doi:10.1016/j.autcon.2019.01.020

Tan, H., & Chung, I. (2020). Secure authentication and key management of Blockchain in vanets. *IEEE Access : Practical Innovations, Open Solutions*, *8*, 2482–2498. doi:10.1109/ACCESS.2019.2962387

Tan, R. R., Aviso, K. B., & Ng, D. K. S. (2019). Optimization model for financing innovations in green energy technologies. *Renewable & Sustainable Energy Reviews*, *113*, 109–258. doi:10.1016/j.rser.2019.109258

Tanwar, S., Parekh, K., & Evans, R. (2020). Blockchain-based electronic healthcare record system for healthcare 4.0 applications. *Journal of Information Security and Applications*, *50*, 102407. doi:10.1016/j.jisa.2019.102407

Tariq, N., Asim, M., Al-Obeidat, F., Zubair Farooqi, M., Baker, T., Hammoudeh, M., & Ghafir, I. (2019). The security of big data in fog-enabled IoT applications including blockchain: A survey. *Sensors (Basel)*, *19*(8), 1788. doi:10.339019081788 PMID:31013993

Teacy, W. T., Luck, M., Rogers, A., & Jennings, N. R. (2012). An efficient and versatile approach to trust and reputation using hierarchical Bayesian modelling. *Artificial Intelligence*, *193*, 149–185. doi:10.1016/j.artint.2012.09.001

Thapa, C., & Camtepe, S. (2021). Precision health data: Requirements, challenges and existing techniques for data security and privacy. *Computers in Biology and Medicine*, *129*, 104130. PMID:33271399

Thaseen, I. S., Poorva, B., & Ushasree, P. S. (2020, February). Network intrusion detection using machine learning techniques. In *2020 International conference on emerging trends in information technology and engineering (IC-ETITE)* (pp. 1-7). IEEE.

Thilakarathne, N. N., & Madhuka Priyashan, W. D. (2022). *An Overview of Security and Privacy in Smart Cities*. doi:10.1007/978-3-030-82715-1_2

Thiruselvi, D., Kumar, P. S., Kumar, M. A., Lay, C. H., Aathika, S., Mani, Y., ... Show, P. L. (2021). A critical review on global trends in biogas scenario with its up-gradation techniques for fuel cell and future perspectives. *International Journal of Hydrogen Energy*, *46*(31), 16734–16750.

Tian, S., Yang, W., Le Grange, J. M., Wang, P., Huang, W., & Ye, Z. (2019). Smart healthcare: Making medical care more intelligent. *Global Health Journal (Amsterdam, Netherlands)*, *3*(3), 62–65. doi:10.1016/j.glohj.2019.07.001

Tilson, D., Lyytinen, K., & Sørensen, C. (2010). Digital Infrastructures: The Missing IS Research Agenda (PDF). *Information Systems Research, 21* (4), 748–759. . JSTOR 23015642 doi:10.1287/isre.1100.0318

Tomašev, N., Glorot, X., Rae, J. W., Zielinski, M., Askham, H., Saraiva, A., Mottram, A., Meyer, C., Ravuri, S., Protsyuk, I., Connell, A., Hughes, C. O., Karthikesalingam, A., Cornebise, J., Montgomery, H., Rees, G., Laing, C., Baker, C. R., Peterson, K., & Mohamed, S. (2019). A clinically applicable approach to continuous prediction of future acute kidney injury. *Nature*, *572*(7767), 116–119. doi:10.103841586-019-1390-1 PMID:31367026

Toppeta, D. (2010). The smart city vision: How innovation and ICT can build smart,"livable", sustainable cities. *The Innovation Knowledge Foundation*, *5*, 1–9.

Tortorella, G. L., Fogliatto, F. S., Mac Cawley Vergara, A., Vassolo, R., & Sawhney, R. (2020). Healthcare 4.0: Trends, challenges and research directions. *Production Planning and Control*, *31*(15), 1245–1260.

Toyoda, K., Mathiopoulos, P. T., Sasase, I., & Ohtsuki, T. (2017). A Novel Blockchain-Based Product Ownership Management System (POMS) for Anti-Counterfeits in the Post Supply Chain. *IEEE Access : Practical Innovations, Open Solutions*, *5*, 17465–17477. doi:10.1109/ACCESS.2017.2720760

Trevor, B. (2018, May). Security and Privacy Challenges in Smart Cities. *Sustainable Cities and Society*, *39*, 499–507. doi:10.1016/j.scs.2018.02.039

Triantafilou, J. T. (2021, August 27). The role of digital twins in smart cities. https://resources.esri.ca/news-and-updates/the-role-digital-twins-in-smart-cities. https://resources.esri.ca/news-and-updates/the-role-digital-twins-in-smart-cities

Tripathi, G., Ahad, M. A., & Paiva, S. (2020). S2HS- A Blockchain based approach for smart healthcare systems. *Health Care*, *8*(1), 100391. PMID:31753750

Tseng, J. H., Liao, Y. C., Chong, B., & Liao, S. W. (2018). Governance on the drug supply chain via gcoin blockchain. *International Journal of Environmental Research and Public Health*, *15*(6), 1055. PMID:29882861

Tsung-Han, T., Bin, X., Shih-Ming, K., & Yen-Chiang, C. (2020). China's Diplomatic Strategy towards Climate Change Negotiations in the Post-Paris Agreement Era. *China. International Journal, 18*(2), 186–203.

Tully, J., Selzer, J., Phillips, J. P., O'Connor, P., & Dameff, C. (2020). Healthcare challenges in the era of cybersecurity. *Health Security, 18*(3), 228–231. PMID:32559153

Turcu, C. (2013). Re-thinking Sustainability Indicators: Local Perspectives of Urban Sustainability. *Journal of Environmental Planning and Management, 56*(5), 695–719. doi:10.1080/09640568.2012.698984

Uddin, M., Salah, K., Jayaraman, R., Pesic, S., & Ellahham, S. (2021). Blockchain for drug traceability: Architectures and open challenges. *Health Informatics Journal, 27*(2). PMID:33899576

Ullah, I., & Mahmoud, Q. H. (2020). A scheme for generating a dataset for anomalous activity detection in iot networks. In *Advances in Artificial Intelligence: 33rd Canadian Conference on Artificial Intelligence, Canadian AI 2020, Ottawa, ON, Canada, May 13–15, 2020, Proceedings 33* (pp. 508-520). Springer International Publishing. 10.1007/978-3-030-47358-7_52

Ullah, Z., Al-Turjman, F., Mostarda, L., & Gagliardi, R. (2020). (. Applications of Artificial Intelligence and Machine learning in smart cities. *Computer Communications, 154*, 313–323. doi:10.1016/j.comcom.2020.02.069

UN-Habitat. (1996 June). *Second United Nations Conference on Human Settlements. United Nations Habitat.* Author.

United Nations. (2015). *World Population Prospects: The 2015 Revision, Key Findings and Advance Tables.* United Nations Department of Economic and Social Affairs and Population Division. Working Paper, No. ESA/P/WP. 241.

Upasani, N., & Om, H. (2019). A modified neuro-fuzzy classifier and its parallel implementation on modern GPUs for real time intrusion detection. *Applied Soft Computing, 82*, 105595.

Ursua, A., Gandia, L. M., & Sanchis, P. (2011). Hydrogen production from water electrolysis: Current status and future trends. *Proceedings of the IEEE, 100*(2), 410–426. doi:10.1109/JPROC.2011.2156750

Vaka, M., Walvekar, R., Rasheed, A. K., & Khalid, M. (2020). A review on Malaysia's solar energy pathway towards carbon-neutral Malaysia beyond Covid'19 pandemic. *Journal of Cleaner Production, 273*, 122834. doi:10.1016/j.jclepro.2020.122834 PMID:32834565

Valli, M. S., & Arasu, G. T. (2016). *An Efficient Feature Selection Technique of Unsupervised Learning Approach for Analyzing Web Opinions*, 221-224. . NISCAIR-CSIR, India. https://nopr.niscpr.res.in/handle/123456789/34053

Van Bastelaer, B. (1998). *Digital cities and transferability of results.* In European digital cities: 4th conference: changing patterns of urban life, Salzburg, Austria. https://www.info.fundp.ac.be/~cita/publications/4thEDC.pdf

Van Hilten, M., & Wolfert, S. (2022). 5G in agri-food - A review on current status, opportunities and challenges. *Computers and Electronics in Agriculture, 201*(August), 107291. doi:10.1016/j.compag.2022.107291

Vander Valk, H., Haße, H., Möller, F., Arbter, M., Henning, J. L., & Otto, B. (2020, August). A Taxonomy of Digital Twins. In AMCIS.

Velasquez, K., Perez, D., Curado, M., & Monteiro, E. (2022). Resource orchestration in 5G and beyond: Challenges and opportunities. *Computer Communications, 192*(June), 311–315. doi:10.1016/j.comcom.2022.06.019

Venkatesan, V. (2022). *Bamboo by Vignesh Venkatesan.* ArchDaily. https://my.archdaily.com/us/@vignesh-venkatesan-1/folders/bamboo,

Vinayakumar, R., Alazab, M., Soman, K. P., Poornachandran, P., Al-Nemrat, A., & Venkatraman, S. (2019). Deep learning approach for intelligent intrusion detection system. *IEEE Access : Practical Innovations, Open Solutions*, *7*, 41525–41550. doi:10.1109/ACCESS.2019.2895334

Visoottiviseth, V., Sakarin, P., Thongwilai, J., & Choobanjong, T. (2020, November). Signature-based and behavior-based attack detection with machine learning for home IoT devices. In 2020 IEEE REGION 10 CONFERENCE (TENCON) (pp. 829-834). IEEE. doi:10.1109/TENCON50793.2020.9293811

Vlacheas, P., Giaffreda, R., Stavroulaki, V., Kelaidonis, D., Foteinos, V., Poulios, G., Demestichas, P., Somov, A., Biswas, A., & Moessner, K. (2013). Enabling smart cities through a cognitive management framework for the internet of things. *IEEE Communications Magazine*, *51*(6), 102–111. doi:10.1109/MCOM.2013.6525602

Wang, D., Yang, Q., Abdul, A., & Lim, B. Y. (2019). Designing Theory-Driven User-Centric Explainable AI. *Proceedings of the 2019 CHI Conference on Human Factors in Computing Systems - CHI '19*, (pp. 1-15). ACM. 10.1145/3290605.3300831

Wang, C., Chen, C., & Song, H. (2020). Impact of packet loss on security of vehicular communication. *IET Intelligent Transport Systems*, *14*(1), 1–8.

Wang, G., Nixon, M., & Boudreaux, M. (2019). Toward cloud-assisted industrial Iot platform for large-scale continuous condition monitoring. *Proceedings of the IEEE*, *107*(6), 1193–1205. doi:10.1109/JPROC.2019.2914021

Wang, J., & Liu, J. (2016). The comparison of distributed P2P trust models based on quantitative parameters in the file downloading scenarios. *Journal of Electrical and Computer Engineering*, *2016*, 4361719. doi:10.1155/2016/4361719

Wang, J., Liu, Q., Li, D., Chen, C., Chen, Z., Song, P., Hao, J., Li, Y., Fakhrhoseini, S., Naebe, M., Wang, X., & Lei, W. (2020). Lightweight, superplastic yet thermo conductive boron nitride nan composite aerogel for thermal energy regulation. *ACS Nano*, *13*(7), 7860–7870. doi:10.1021/acsnano.9b02182 PMID:31194502

Wang, L., Luo, G., Jiang, Z., Zhang, F., Zhao, L., Yang, P., Lin, Q., & Maeda, R. (2019). Broadband vibration energy harvesting for wireless sensor node power supply in train container. *The Review of Scientific Instruments*, *90*(12), 12–50. doi:10.1063/1.5127243 PMID:31893793

Wang, S., Cao, H., Wang, D., & Li, A. (2022). Security of Intelligent Sensors and Their Collaborative Roles in Human Resource Management in the Development of Smart Cities. *Wireless Communications and Mobile Computing*, *2022*, 2022. doi:10.1155/2022/6285777

Wang, S., Liu, X., Liu, S., Muhammad, K., Heidari, A. A., Ser, J. D., & De Albuquerque, V. H. C. (2022). Human Short Long-Term Cognitive Memory Mechanism for Visual Monitoring in IoT-Assisted Smart Cities. *IEEE Internet of Things Journal*, *9*(10), 7128–7139. doi:10.1109/JIOT.2021.3077600

Wang, S., Tang, Y., Shi, J., Gong, K., Liu, Y., Ren, L., & Li, J. (2015). Design and advanced control strategies of a hybrid energy storage system for the grid integration of wind power generations. *IET Renewable Power Generation*, *9*(2), 89–98. doi:10.1049/iet-rpg.2013.0340

Wang, Y., Ma, X., Xu, M., Liu, Y., & Wang, Y. (2015). Two-echelon logistics distribution region partitioning problem based on a hybrid particle swarm optimization–genetic algorithm. *Expert Systems with Applications*, *42*(12), 5019–5031. doi:10.1016/j.eswa.2015.02.058

Wan, P. K., Huang, L., & Holtskog, H. (2020). Blockchain-Enabled Information Sharing Within a Supply Chain: A Systematic Literature Review. *IEEE Access : Practical Innovations, Open Solutions*, *8*, 49645–49656. doi:10.1109/ACCESS.2020.2980142

Washburn, D., Sindhu, U., Balaouras, S., Dines, R. A., Hayes, N. M., & Nelson, L. E. (2010). *Helping CIOs Understand "Smart City" Initiatives: Defining the Smart City, Its Drivers, and the Role of the CIO*. Forrester Research, Inc. Available at http://public.dhe.ibm.com/partnerworld/pub/smb/smarterpla net/forr_help_cios_und_smart_city_initiatives.pdf

Wehbe, R. M. (2020). Deep COVID-XR: An artificial intelligence algorithm to detect COVID-19 on chest radiographs trained and tested on a large US clinical dataset. *Radiology*, 203511. PMID:33231531

Wen, F., Wang, H., He, T., Shi, Q., Sun, Z., Zhu, M., Zhang, Z., Cao, Z., Dai, Y., Zhang, T., & Lee, C. (2020). Battery-free short-range self- powered wireless sensor network (SS-WSN) using TENG based direct sensory transmission mechanism. *Nano Energy*, *67*, 104–266. doi:10.1016/j.nanoen.2019.104266

White, G., Zink, A., Codecá, L., & Clarke, S. (2021). A digital twin smart city for citizen feedback. *Cities (London, England)*, *110*, 103064. doi:10.1016/j.cities.2020.103064

Whitmore, A., Agarwal, A., & Da Xu, L. (2015). The Internet of Things—A survey of topics and trends. *Information Systems Frontiers*, *17*(2), 261–274. doi:10.100710796-014-9489-2

Willems, J., van den Bergh, J., & Viaene, S. (2017). Smart city projects and citizen participation: the case of London. *Public Sector Management in a Globalized World*, 249–266.

Xia, C., Zhang, D., Pedrycz, W., Fan, K., & Guo, Y. (2020). Human body heat-based thermoelectric harvester with ultra-low input power management system for wireless sensor powering. *Energies*, *12*(20), 39–42.

Xia, W., Dai, X., Li, Y., Li, W., & Wu, J. (2021). An Evaluation of the Security and Privacy Protection of ETSI ITS. *IEEE Internet of Things Journal*, *8*(2), 1002–1012.

Xie, J. (2019). A Survey of Blockchain Technology Applied to Smart Cities: Research Issues and Challenges. IEEE Communications Surveys & Tutorials, 21(3), 2794-2830. doi:10.1109/COMST.2019.2899617

Xie, Y., Gao, G., & Chen, X. A. (2019). Outlining the design space of explainable intelligent systems for medical diagnosis. *arXiv preprint arXiv:1902.06019.*

Xi, Y., Hua, J., & Shi, Y. (2019). Noncontact triboelectric nanogenerator for human motion monitoring and energy harvesting. *Nano Energy*, *69*, 104–390.

Xu, M., Chen, X., & Kou, G. (2019). A systematic review of blockchain. *Financial Innovation*, *5*(1), 1–14.

Xu, X., Liu, Q., Luo, Y., Peng, K., Zhang, X., Meng, S., & Qi, L. (2019). A computation offloading method over big data for IoT-enabled cloud-edge computing. *Future Generation Computer Systems*, *95*, 522–533. doi:10.1016/j.future.2018.12.055

Yaacoub, J.-P. A., Noura, M., Noura, H. N., Salman, O., Yaacoub, E., Couturier, R., & Chehab, A. (2020). Securing Internet of medical things systems: Limitations, issues, and recommendations. *Future Generation Computer Systems*, *105*, 581–606. doi:10.1016/j.future.2019.12.028

Yahyaoui, I., Atieh, A., Serna, A., & Tadeo, F. (2017). Sensitivity analysis for photovoltaic water pumping systems: Energetic and economic studies. *Energy Conversion and Management*, *135*, 402–415. doi:10.1016/j.enconman.2016.12.096

Yang, H., Yang, S., Xu, Y., Cao, E., Lai, M., & Dong, Z. (2015). Electric vehicle route optimization considering time-of-use electricity price by learnable partheno-genetic algorithm. *IEEE Transactions on Smart Grid*, *6*(2), 657–666. doi:10.1109/TSG.2014.2382684

Yang, X., Shu, L., Liu, Y., Hancke, G. P., Ferrag, M. A., & Huang, K. (2022). Physical security and safety of IoT equipment: A survey of recent advances and opportunities. *IEEE Transactions on Industrial Informatics*, *18*(7), 4319–4330. doi:10.1109/TII.2022.3141408

Yang, Z., Hu, S., Dongliang, Z. (2021). AI-based composition model for energy utilization efficiency optimization of gas hydrate recovery by combined method of depressurization and thermal stimulation. *Journal of Natural Gas Science and Engineering*. doi:10.1016/j.jngse

Yang, Z., Jianjun, L., Faqiri, H., Shafik, W., Talal Abdulrahman, A., Yusuf, M., & Sharawy, A. M. (2021). Green internet of things and big data applications in smart city development. *Complexity*, *2021*, 1–15. doi:10.1155/2021/4922697

Yang, Z., Yang, Y., Liu, F., Wang, Z., Li, Y., Qiu, J., Xiao, X., Li, Z., Lu, Y., Ji, L., Wang, Z. L., & Cheng, J. (2021). Power backpack for energy harvesting and reduced load impact. *ACS Nano*, *15*(2), 2611–26123. doi:10.1021/acsnano.0c07498 PMID:33533242

Yan, J., Liu, J., & Tseng, F. (2020). An evaluation system based on the self-organizing system framework of smart cities: A case study of smart transportation systems in China. *Technological Forecasting and Social Change*, *153*, 119371. doi:10.1016/j.techfore.2018.07.009

Yan, X., Huang, H., Hao, Z., & Wang, J. (2019). A graph-based fuzzy evolutionary algorithm for solving two-echelon vehicle routing problems. *IEEE Transactions on Evolutionary Computation*, *24*(1), 129–141. doi:10.1109/TEVC.2019.2911736

Yaqoob, I., Ahmed, E., Hashem, I. A. T., Ahmed, A. I. A., Gani, A., Imran, M., & Guizani, M. (2017). Internet of Things Architecture: Recent Advances, Taxonomy, Requirements, and Open Challenges. *IEEE Wireless Communications*, *24*(3), 10–16. doi:10.1109/MWC.2017.1600421

Yaqoob, I., Salah, K., Jayaraman, R., & Al-Hammadi, Y. (2022). Blockchain for healthcare data management: Opportunities, challenges, and future recommendations. *Neural Computing & Applications*, *34*(14), 11475–11490.

Yassine, A., Singh, S., Hossain, M. S., & Muhammad, G. (2019). IoT big data analytics for smart homes with fog and cloud computing. *Future Generation Computer Systems*, *91*, 563–573. doi:10.1016/j.future.2018.08.040

Ye, C., Butler, L., Calka, B., Iangurazov, M., Lu, Q., Gregory, A., Girolami, M., & Middleton, C. (2019). *A Digital Twin of Bridges for Structural Health Monitoring*. Conference: Proceedings of the 12th International Workshop on Structural Health Monitoring 2019, Stanford, California, USA.10.12783hm2019/32287

Yereseme, A. K., Surendra, H. J., & Kuntoji, G. (2022). Sustainable integrated urban flood management strategies for planning of smart cities: A review. *Sustainable Water Resources Management*, *8*(3), 603–615. doi:10.100740899-022-00666-5

Yetgin, H., Cheung, K. T. K., El-Hajjar, M., & Hanzo, L. H. (2017). A survey of network lifetime maximization techniques in wireless sensor networks. *IEEE Communications Surveys and Tutorials*, *19*(2), 828–854. doi:10.1109/COMST.2017.2650979

Yilmaz, T., Gokkoca, G., & Akan, O. B. (2016). Millimetre wave communication for 5G IoT applications. In *Internet of Things (IoT) in 5G Mobile Technologies* (pp. 37–53). Springer International Publishing. doi:10.1007/978-3-319-30913-2_3

Yli-Huumo, J., Ko, D., Choi, S., Park, S., & Smolander, K. (2016). Where is current research on blockchain technology?—A systematic review. *PLoS One*, *11*(10), e0163477. PMID:27695049

Zaman, N., Seliaman, M. E., Hassan, M. F., & Márquez, F. P. G. (Eds.). (2015). *Handbook of research on trends and future directions in big data and web intelligence*. Information Science. doi:10.4018/978-1-4666-8505-5

Zanella, A., Bui, N., Castellani, A., Vangelista, N., & Zorzi, M. (2014). Internet of Things for smart cities. *IEEE Internet of Things Journal*, *1*(1), 22–32. doi:10.1109/JIOT.2014.2306328

Zantalis, F., Koulouras, G., Karabetsos, S., & Kandris, D. (2019). A review of machine learning and IoT in smart transportation. *Future Internet*, *11*(4), 94. doi:10.3390/fi11040094

Zaragoza, M. G., Kim, H. K., & Lee, R. Y. (2017, May). Big data and IoT for u-healthcare security. In *International Conference on Computer and Information Science* (pp. 1-11). Springer, Cham.

Zarour, M., Alenezi, M., Ansari, M. T. J., Pandey, A. K., Ahmad, M., Agrawal, A., ... Khan, R. A. (2021). Ensuring data integrity of healthcare information in the era of digital health. *Healthcare Technology Letters*, *8*(3), 66–77. PMID:34035927

Zeb, H., Gohar, M., Ali, M., Ahmad, W., Ghani, A., Choi, J. G., & Koh, S. J. (2023). Zero Energy IoT Devices in Smart Cities Using RF Energy Harvesting. *Electronics (Basel)*, *12*(1), 148. doi:10.3390/electronics12010148

Zeng, B., Feng, J., Liu, N., & Liu, Y. (2020). Co-optimized parking lot placement and incentive design for promoting PEV integration considering decision-dependent uncertainties. *IEEE Transactions on Industrial Informatics*, *17*(3), 1863–1872. doi:10.1109/TII.2020.2993815

Zhang, C., Duan, X., Liu, F., Li, X., & Liu, S. (2022). Three-way naive Bayesian collaborative filtering recommendation model for smart city. *Sustainable Cities and Society*, *76*, 103373. doi:10.1016/j.scs.2021.103373

Zhang, D., Chen, Z., Zhou, H., Chen, L., & Shen, X. S. (2016). Energy-balanced cooperative transmission based on relay selection and power control in energy harvesting wireless sensor network. *Computer Networks*, *104*, 189–197. doi:10.1016/j.comnet.2016.05.013

Zhang, H., Babar, M., Tariq, M. U., Jan, M. A., Menon, V. G., & Li, X. (2020). SafeCity: Toward safe and secured data management design for IoT-enabled Smart City planning. *IEEE Access : Practical Innovations, Open Solutions*, *8*, 145256–145267. doi:10.1109/ACCESS.2020.3014622

Zhang, J., Bai, X., Han, W., Zhao, B., Xu, L., & Wei, J. (2019). The design of radio frequency energy harvesting and radio frequency-based wireless power transfer system for battery-less self-sustaining applications. *International Journal of RF and Microwave Computer-Aided Engineering*, *29*(1), 777–780. doi:10.1002/mmce.21658

Zhang, J., Tian, R., Cao, Y., Yuan, X., Yu, Z., Yan, X., & Zhang, X. (2021). A Hybrid Model for Central Bank Digital Currency Based on Blockchain. *IEEE Access : Practical Innovations, Open Solutions*, *9*, 53589–53601. doi:10.1109/ACCESS.2021.3071033

Zhang, L., Wu, J., Mumtaz, S., Li, J., Gacanin, H., & Rodrigues, J. J. P. C. (2019). Edge-to-Edge Cooperative Artificial Intelligence in Smart Cities with On-Demand Learning Offloading. *2019 IEEE Global Communications Conference (GLOBECOM)*, 1-6. 10.1109/GLOBECOM38437.2019.9013878

Zhang, Y. W., Wang, S., Ni, Z. Y., Fang, Z. W., Zang, J., & Fang, B. (2019). Integration of a nonlinear vibration absorber and levitation magnetoelectric energy harvester for whole-spacecraft systems. *Acta Mechanica Solida Sinica*, *32*(3), 298–309. doi:10.100710338-019-00081-y

Zhang, Y., Gao, K., Zhang, Y., & Su, R. (2018). Traffic light scheduling for pedestrian-vehicle mixed-flow networks. *IEEE Transactions on Intelligent Transportation Systems*, *20*(4), 1468–1483. doi:10.1109/TITS.2018.2852646

Zhang, Y., & Park, S. J. (2019). Flexible organic thermoelectric materials and devices for wearable green energy harvesting. *Polymers*, *11*(5), 9–19. doi:10.3390/polym11050909 PMID:31137541

Zheng, J., & Jamalipour, A. (2009). *Wireless Sensor Networks*. John Wiley & Sons.

Zheng, J., Liu, X., Xu, P., Liu, P., Zhao, Y., & Yang, J. (2012). Development of high pressure gaseous hydrogen storage technologies. *International Journal of Hydrogen Energy*, *37*(1), 1048–1057. doi:10.1016/j.ijhydene.2011.02.125

Zheng, Y., Yang, S., & Cheng, H. (2019). An application framework of digital twin and its case study. *Journal of Ambient Intelligence and Humanized Computing*, *10*(3), 1141–1153. doi:10.100712652-018-0911-3

Zheng, Z., Xie, S., Dai, H., Chen, X., & Wang, H. (2017, June). *An overview of blockchain technology: Architecture, consensus, and future trends. In 2017 IEEE international congress on big data (BigData congress)*. IEEE.

Zhong, J. H., Shen, M., Zhang, J., Chung, H. S. H., Shi, Y. H., & Li, Y. (2012). A differential evolution algorithm with dual populations for solving periodic railway timetable scheduling problem. *IEEE Transactions on Evolutionary Computation*, *17*(4), 512–527. doi:10.1109/TEVC.2012.2206394

Zhou. R., Canady. S., Bao, A. Gokhale.(2020). Cost-effective hardware accelerator recommendation for edge computing, in: 3rd{USENIX}Workshop on HotTopics in Edge Computing (HotEdge 20).

Zhou, K., Fu, C., & Yang, S. (2016). Big data driven smart energy management: From big data to big insights. *Renewable & Sustainable Energy Reviews*, *56*, 215–225. doi:10.1016/j.rser.2015.11.050

Zhou, Y., & Kankanhalli, A. (2021). AI Regulation for Smart Cities: Challenges and Principles. In E. Estevez, T. A. Pardo, & H. J. Scholl (Eds.), *Smart Cities and Smart Governance. Public Administration and Information Technology* (Vol. 37). Springer. doi:10.1007/978-3-030-61033-3_5

Zhu, W., Yan, R., & Song, Y. (2022). Analysing the impact of smart city service quality on citizen engagement in a public emergency. *Cities (London, England)*, *120*, 103439. doi:10.1016/j.cities.2021.103439 PMID:34539020

Zhu, Z., Xu, L., Abdelkareem, M. A. A., Zou, J., & Mi, J. (2020). Design and simulation analysis of vibration energy harvesting system based on Adams. *International Design Engineering Technical Conferences and Computers and Information in Engineering Conference*, *8*, 297-273.

Zimmerman, P. (2020). *Blockchain structure and cryptocurrency prices*. Academic Press.

Zin, T. T., Tin, P., & Hama, H. (2018). Characterizing reliability measures for Internet of things by Markov queue. *Data Science and Pattern Recognition*, *2*(2), 1–10.

Zungeru, A. M., Gaboitaolelwe, J., Diarra, B., Chuma, J. M., & Ang, L. M. (2019). A secured smart home switching system based on wireless communications and self-energy harvesting. *IEEE Access : Practical Innovations, Open Solutions*, *7*, 25063–25085. doi:10.1109/ACCESS.2019.2900305

Zygiaris, S. (2013). Smart city reference model: Assisting planners to conceptualize the building of smart city innovation ecosystems. *Journal of the Knowledge Economy*, *4*(2), 217–231. doi:10.100713132-012-0089-4

About the Contributors

Hemant Kumar Reddy received his M.Tech and PhD. and from Berhampur University, BhanjaVihar, India. He is currently with the VIT AP University Andhra Pradesh, India, as an Associate Professor Grade-II. Currently serving as an Associate Editor, Journal of Intelligent Fuzzy System (JIFS). He has published several papers in High-Quality SCI/SCIE/ESCI Impact Factor Journals cum Scopus/ESCI indexed Journals, 25+ Papers in International Conferences indexed with ACM, Springer, IEEE Xplore. His current research interests include distributed and cloud computing, fog computing, IoT, Edge, Fog computing, and service-oriented architectures.

Diptendu Sinha Roy was born in India. He received his B. Tech from Kalyani University in 2003 and subsequently his M. Tech and Ph.D from Birla Institute of Technology, Mesra, India in 2005 and 2010 respectively. He is currently with the National Institute of Technology, Meghalaya, India Dr. Sinha Roy's research interests include distributed, grid computing, Cloud computing, Fog computing, software reliability and optimization in engineering. He also works towards design and analysis of distributed infrastructure of power systems.

Tapas Mishra completed his Ph.D. in the year 2017 from Indian Institute of Technology, Dhanbad, India. Now he is working as an assistant professor at SRM University, Andhra Pradesh, India. His research area includes quality of service in Ad hoc and sensor networks, localization of sensor nodes, recommended system, Robot navigation using artificial intelligence, Internet of things. He has more than 20 international journals and conference publication in his name.

Mir Wajahat Hussain was born in Jammu & Kashmir, India. He received the B.Tech. degree from University of Kashmir, India in 2014, and the master's degree and Ph.D. from the National Institute of Technology Arunachal Pradesh and National Institute of Technology Meghalaya, India in 2017 and 2021. He is currently with the Alliance University, India, as an Assistant Professor. His research interests include software-defined networks and big data.

* * *

Rania Abdelhameed Mokhtar (Member, IEEE) received the B.Sc. degree in electronics engineering (computer engineering) from the Sudan University of Science & Technology (SUST), Khartoum, Sudan, in 2001, the master's (Diploma) degree in information technology (advanced networking and telecommunications) from the International Institute of Information Technology (I2IT), Pune, India, in 2003, and the M.Sc. and Ph.D. degrees from University Putra Malaysia (UPM), Kuala Lumpur, Malaysia, in 2005 and 2010, respectively. In May 2009, she earned the IEEE Wireless Communication Professional (IEEE WCP) certificate in the Wireless Communication Engineering Technology (WCET) Exam. Currently, she is an Associate Professor at Department of Computer Engineering, College of Computers and Information Technology, Taif University. She has published over 30 scientific papers and two books. She was awarded the Elsevier Foundation Award for Women in Engineering, in 2017

Manjulata Badi has done her B.E. in Electrical Engineering from Biju Pattnayak University of Technology, Rourkela, Odisha, India in 2005. Thereafter she has completed her M.Tech in Control and Automation specialization from National Institute of Technology, Rourkela in 2012. Currently she is pursuing PhD and working as a Assistant Professor in Electrical and Electronics Engineering Department of Alliance University, Bangalore. She is a life time member of ISTE and IAENG professional bodies including her research areas are Power System Optimization, Evolutionary Computing Techniques.

Mona Bakri Hassan received her M.Sc. in electronics engineering and telecommunication in 2021 and B.Sc. (Honors) in electronics engineering and telecommunication in 2013. She has completed Cisco Certified Network Professional (CCNP) routing and switching course and passed the Cisco Certified Network Administrator (CCNA) routing and switching. She has gained experience in network operations center as a network engineer in back officece department in Sudan Telecom Company (Sudatel) and in vision valley as well. She has also worked as a teacher assistant in Sudan University of Science and Technology, which has given her a great opportunity to gain teaching experience. She published book chapters, and papers on wireless communications and networking in peer- reviewed academic international journals. Her areas of research interest include cellular LPWAN, IoT and wireless communication.

Elijah Blessing Rajsingh is the Registrar of Karunya Institute of Technology and Sciences and Professor in the Department of Computer Science and Engineering. He received his Ph.D. degree in Information and Communication Engineering from the College of Engineering, Anna University, India in 2005. His research areas include network security, mobile computing, wireless and ad hoc networks, grid computing and pervasive computing. He is an Associate Editor for International Journal of Computers and Applications, Taylor and Francis and a member of the editorial review board for many peer-reviewed journals. He is a member of IEEE, ISTE and has served as an International advisory board member for various International conferences.

Prasit Chakraborty is associated with Brainware University.

Niranjan Chiplunkar is currently Principal of NMAM Institute of Technology, Nitte and Professor in Computer Science and Engineering in NMAM Institute of Technology. His research areas include algorithm design for VLSI CAD, multicore architecture, program optimization, Ad-Hoc networks, Wireless Sensor Networks, E-learning and Advanced microprocessors. Dr. Niranjan has published "VLSI CAD" (PHI Learning Publications,2011) and "CAD for VLSI" (2007). Dr.Chiplunkar has achieved "Excellent Achievement Award" by Center for International Corporation on Computerization (CICC), Govt. of Japan, in 2002.

Gobinda Das is associated with Brainware University.

Shiplu Das is an Assistant Professor in the Department of Computer Science and Engineering.

Nelson deMatos is an Assistant Professor at ESGHT, where he teaches several curricular units in Marketing and Tourism. He holds a doctoral degree in Tourism from UAlg and is a member of CinTurs. He has held various marketing management roles in the hospitality and services industry and has participated in various business projects as a marketing consultant and trainer. His main research interests are in the areas of Marketing (namely brands and consumer behaviour), tourism (namely smart cities and tourism experience), and neuromarketing. He is the author of publications in scientific books and journals.

Mathew F. is an undergraduate student from Mepco Schlenk Engineering College.

Swetha Shekarappa G. received her B.E. Eng. Degree in Electrical and Electronics Engineering from Visvesvaraya Technological University, Belagavi, India in 2010. She received her M. Tech in 2012 from Visvesvaraya Technological University, Belagavi, India. She is pursuing PhD in Alliance University, Bangalore, India. Her area of interest includes power system optimization, FACTS devices, renewable energy, distributed generation, Swarm and evolutionary optimization techniques.

Abraham George is Professor and Head of the Department of Computer Science and Information Technology at Alliance University, Bangalore. Dr. Abraham George earned his Doctorate degree in Computer Science from University of Louisville, USA and Master's degree in Computer Science from Ball State University, USA. Dr. George has over a decade and half of industry experience in multinational companies such as Kyocera and National Instruments. Primary areas of interest of Dr. George include wireless networks, distributed computing, and Machine Learning. His work has been published in reputed journals such as Elsevier and IJPCC. He has several publications in top rated IEEE conferences.

Vrinda Gupta received her Bachelor's degree in Electronics Engineering from Nagpur University and a Master's and a Ph.D. degree in Electronics and Communication Engineering from Kurukshetra University and National Institute of Technology Kurukshetra, respectively. Dr. Vrinda Gupta has worked as an Engineering Teacher for over 27 years. Dr. Vrinda is currently heading the Department of Electronics and Communication Engineering at the National Institute of Technology Kurukshetra and is an Associate Professor. She previously worked as a Lecturer at Banasthali Vidyapith (1988-1990). She has teaching and research interest in the field of Communications Networks and the Internet of Things. Dr. Vrinda has authored more than 65 publications. She is a Reviewers' Committee member of some SCI/Scopus-indexed Journals. She has chaired the Electronics and Telecommunication Engineering Division sessions at National and International Conferences. She is a member of professional societies, viz. IEEE, IETE, IAENG, and Fellow of IE(I).

Deva Priya Isravel is currently working as an Assistant Professor in the Department of Computer Science and Engineering, Karunya Institute of Technology and Sciences. She is presently pursuing her Ph.D. in Computer Science and Engineering in KITS. She received her Bachelor of Engineering degree from Anna University in 2005. She received her Master of Engineering from Karunya University in 2008. Her areas of interest include computer networks, wireless sensor networks and software defined networks.

Rajashree Jain is a veteran academician with more than 20 years of experience. She is associated with Symbiosis Institute of Computer Studies and Research for more than 17 years. Her expertise is in the areas of electronics, Entrepreneurship, Logic Development. She also has essayed various roles at IEEE Pune Section for ore than 10 Years.

Bishwanath Jana is associated with Brainware University.

Kassim Kalinaki is a technology enthusiast, researcher and lecturer with more than 5 years teaching experience and currently pursuing his PhD in Computer Science at Universiti Brunei Darussalam (UBD). He completed both his bachelor's and master's degrees in Computer Science and engineering with technical education at the Islamic University of Technology (IUT) in Dhaka, Bangladesh. Prior to embarking on his PhD career, he served as the HOD computer science at Islamic University in Uganda (IUIU l. His research interests include: Cybersecurity, IoT, computer vision, Machine learning and deep learning, Remote sensing, digital image processing and data analytics.

Senbagavalli M. received doctoral degree in Computer Science Engineering (Opinion Mining of Health Data for Cardiovascular Disease Diagnosis Using Unsupervised Feature Selection Algorithm) from Anna University. She also holds an M.E. degree in Computer Science and Engineering from Anna University and a B.E. degree in Information Technology from Periyar University. Dr. Senbagavalli has close to two decades of teaching experience in subjects likes computer networks, object oriented programming (C++ and Java), object oriented analysis and design, visual programming, career development program - aptitude, reasoning and technical, C# and .Net, software testing, software engineering and quality assurance, design and analysis of algorithms, computer organization and architecture, data modelling and optimization, operating system, problem solving using C, fundamentals of data modelling. Her research area includes data mining, big data analytics, machine learning, deep learning, and IoT. Dr. Senbagavalli has presented and published papers in national and international conferences and reputed journals focusing on data mining, big data analytics, cloud computing, and opinion mining.

Sheila Mahapatra received her B.E degree in Electrical Engineering from Utkal University, Orissa, India in 2002. She received her Master's degree in Power System & Automation from GITAM, Andhra University, Vizag, India in 2008. She received her PhD from The North Cap University, Gurgaon, Haryana. Currently, she is working as an Associate Professor and Head Department of Electrical and Electronics Engineering, in Alliance University, Bangalore. She is a lifetime member of IET. Her area of interest includes power system optimization, stability and control, evolutionary computing. (IEEE TPEC).

Ghalia Nassreddine is an Associate Professor at the Jinan University, Lebanon. She is a Ph.D holder in information technology and systems from University of Technology of Compiegne, France since 2009. Currently, she is serving as a chairperson in Business Computing School in Jinan University of Lebanon. She is currently doing a lot of research in Machine Learning, education and Dempster Shafer theory.

Sumathi Pawar did her PhD in NMAMIT, Nitte under the guidance of Dr. Niranjan N. Chiplunkar. She completed her M-Tech in NITK Suratkal. Dr Sumathi has got research experience of 15 years and teaching experience of 22 years. She has published 25 research papers published in various journals and conferences.

Samaya Pillai Iyengar is a full-time faculty in Symbiosis Institute of Digital and Telecom Management, Symbiosis International University, Pune (India). She holds MCA, MCM and MPhil degree under the Faculty of Management. She is Perusing her PhD with (Savitribai Phule Pune University) SPPU, Pune University under Computer-Management. She has 18 years of teaching experience with specialisation in databases. Her research interests focus around computer sciences and big data domains. She has taught subjects in programming -Java, Python, C. Databases –Oracle, MySQL, MongoDB, Operating Systems, MIS, Basic Statistics, and Networking etc. She has 8 publications in Scopus. 10 Papers in Conference proceedings.

Buddhadeb Pradhan is Associate Professor in the Department of Computer Science and Engineering.

Vamsi Punugoti received his B.Tech degree in and Electronics and Communications Engineering from Lakireddy Balireddy College of Engineering, Mylavaram, Andhra Pradesh, India in 2022. Currently he is pursuing his Master Degree in Communication Systems from National Institute of Technology Kurukshetra.

Pradnya Purandare is an assistant professor at Symbiosis Centre for Information Technology, Symbiosis International (Deemed University), Pune, India. She has about two decades academic and research experience in information technology area. Her major research area publications are in IT Project Risk Management. She has published several research papers in international journals and participated in IEEE and other conferences.

Rajagopal R. completed his Ph.D. degree at Anna University, Chennai. He has received his post-graduation and bachelors from the Computer Science and Engineering also from Anna University, Chennai. He served as a reviewer for Inder Science and other prestigious Scopus-indexed journals. He serves on the editorial board of the International Journal of Mathematical Sciences, Engineering, and Sciences Publication. Dr. Rajagopal has published in more than 50 international journals and presented in many international conferences. His research interests include cloud computing, high performance computing, big data analytics, and algorithms.

Saurav Raj has done his B.Sc. Engg. in Electrical and Electronics Engineering from R.P. Sharma Institute of Technology, Patna, India in 2012. Thereafter he completed his Ph.D. degree in the Department of Electrical Engineering at IIT(ISM) Dhanbad, India in 2018. Currently, he is working as Assistant Professor in the Institute of Chemical Technology Mumbai, Marathwada Campus, Jalna, India. His areas of interest include power system optimization, reactive power planning, Swarm and evolutionary optimization techniques and FACTS devices.

Célia M. Q. Ramos graduated in Computer Engineering from the University of Coimbra, obtained her Master in Electrical and Computers Engineering from the Higher Technical Institute, Lisbon University, and the PhD in Econometrics from the University of the Algarve (UALG), Faculty of Economics, Portugal. She is Coordinator Professor at School for Management, Hospitality and Tourism, also in the UALG, where she lectures computer science. Areas of research and special interest include the conception and development of information systems, tourism information systems, big data, etourism, econometric modelling and panel-data models. Célia Ramos has published in the fields of information systems and tourism, namely, she has authored a book, six book chapters, conference papers and journal articles. At the level of applied research, she has participated in several funded projects.

Manjula Rao has did her PhD in RV College of Engineering. She completed her M-Tech in NMAMIT, Nitte. Dr Manjula has got research experience of 10 years and teaching experience of 20 years. She has published more than 25 research papers published in various journals and conferences.

Aashrit S. is working on IoT. He is currently a student at SRM AP.

Rashid A. Saeed received his Ph.D. in Communications Network Engineering, Universiti Putra Malaysia (UPM). Currently, he is a professor in Computer Engineering Department, Taif University. He is also working in the Electronics Department, Sudan University of Science and Technology (SUST). He was a senior researcher in Telekom Malaysia™ Research and Development (TMRND) and MIMOS. Rashid published more than 200 research papers, books, and book chapters on wireless communications and networking in peer-reviewed academic venues. His areas of research interest are around wireless communication network. He is successfully awarded 13 WO, EP, CN, MY patents in these areas. He supervised more than 50 MSc/Ph.D. students. Rashid is a Senior Member of IEEE, a Member in IEM (I.E.M), SigmaXi, and SEC. Rashid co-founder and Technical Committee Chair (TPC) of International Conference on Computing, Electrical and Electronics Engineering (ICCEEE) in Sudan. ·He is an editorial board member in the journal of advances in computer sciences, and editor in Scientific African (SCIAF) journal. He is a guest editor in many journals.

Elmustafa Sayed Ali received his M.Sc degree in electronics and communication engineering from Sudan University of Science & Technology, in 2012. He worked as a senior engineer at Sudan sea ports corporation (SPC) for five years as a team leader to plan and execute a new projects in wireless networks (Tetra System, Wi-Fi, WI-Max, and CCTV). He has also worked as a senior lecturer, and a head of Electrical and Electronic Engineering dept., Faculty of Engineering, Red Sea University. He has published more than 45 research articles and book chapters on wireless communications systems and networking in peer-reviewed academic international journals. His research interests include routing protocols, computer and wireless networks, the IoT applications, underwater communications, and artificial intelligence (AI) in wireless networks. He is a member of IEEE Communication Society (ComSoc), International Association of Engineers (IAENG), Six Sigma Yellow Belt (SSYB), Scrum Fundamentals Certified (SFC), and Sudanese Engineering Council (SEC).

Wasswa Shafik, IEEE member, P.Eng, received a bachelor of science in Information Technology Engineering with a minor in Mathematics in 2016 from Ndejje University, Kampala, Uganda, a master of engineering in Information Technology Engineering (MIT) in 2020, from the Computer Engineering Department, Yazd University, Islamic Republic of Iran. He is an associate researcher at the Computer Science department, Network Interconnectivity Lab at Yazd University, Islamic Republic of Iran, and at Information Sciences, Prince Sultan University, Saudi Arabia. He is the author and co-author of more than 80 papers in IEEE/ACM/IET/CRC press/IGI-Global/Wiley/Springer/Elsevier journals, conference papers, books and book chapters. His areas of interest are Anomaly Detection, Drones (UAVs), Machine/Deep Learning, AI-enabled IoT/IoMTs, IoT/IIoT/OT Security, Cyber Security and Privacy. Shafik is the chair/co-chair/program chair of some Scopus/EI conferences. Also, academic editor/ associate editor for set of indexed journals (Scopus journals' quartile ranking). He is the founder and lead investigator of Dig Connectivity Research Laboratory (DCRLab) and the Managing Executive director of Asmaah Charity Organisation (ACO).

Archana Sharma, PhD (Computer Science) in Mobile Database, is distinguished Academician with overall 27+ years of experience of different hierarchy levels in Institutes/Organizations and having successfully covered various work areas in academics and excelling in each with commendations as Star Performer and Distinguished Academician & Researcher Award. Her area of expertise includes Database, IoT, Cloud and Blockchain. Further, She has authored Text Book for UG/PG Students and published/presented more than 50 research papers and several Book Chapters in reputed Journals indexed in Scopus. She has participated and successfully completed various FDPs conducted by ATAL (AICTE Training and Learning Academic). Her research focus towards the various dimensions of IoT implementations like Industrial IoT for digital transformation of Industry, Role of IoT and Cloud to build up the Smart City, Cloud of Things and Blockchain revolution.

Shivam Sharma is associated with Brainware University.

Salaja Silas is currently working as a Professor in the Department of Computer Science and Engineering, Karunya Institute of Technology and Sciences. She received her Bachelor of Engineering Degree in computer science and engineering with Distinction from the University of Madras, India in 2000. She received her Master of Engineering Degree with Distinction from Madurai Kamaraj University, India in 2002. She completed her Ph.D. in computer science and engineering in 2012. Her research interests include computer networks, pervasive computing, cloud computing and data analytics. She has a good number of publications in peer-reviewed journals and is a reviewer in the Journal of supercomputing and Journal of Cluster Computing, Springer publications.

Arun Raj V. is currently working as an Assistant Professor/ECE, Mepco Schlenk Engineering College (Autonomous), Sivakasi.

Sanath Kalyan Veereju received his B.Tech degree in and Electronics and Communications Engineering from Gayatri Vidya Parishad College for Degree and PG Courses (A), Visakhapatnam, Andhra Pradesh, India in 2020. Currently he is pursuing his Master Degree in Embedded Systems Design from National Institute of Technology Kurukshetra.

Joumana Younis received her PhD degree in Information and Communication Technology, Managerial Innovation from the CNAM University France; Doctorate in Business Administration (DBA) in Human Resources at ASMP University - France. Executive Doctorate in Business Administration (EDBA) in Entrepreneurship at Montpellier University - France. Former Dean of the Faculty of Sciences at Jinan University. Actually she is the Dean of Business Administration at Jinan University for undergraduate, graduate, and post-graduate degrees, in addition to the DBA program in partnership with ASMP.

Index

Q

R

S

T

V

W

www.ingramcontent.com/pod-product-compliance
Lightning Source LLC
LaVergne TN
LVHW062112300926
849161LV00010B/2441
* 9 7 9 8 3 6 9 3 0 7 4 4 1 *